Sport Management

Principles, Applications, Skill Development

Robert N. Lussier, Ph.D.
Springfield College

David Kimball, Ph.D.
Elms College

THOMSON
—✦—™
SOUTH-WESTERN

Australia · Canada · Mexico · Singapore · Spain · United Kingdom · United States

THOMSON

SOUTH-WESTERN

Sport Management: Principles, Applications, Skill Development

Robert N. Lussier and David Kimball

Editor-in-Chief:
Jack W. Calhoun

Vice President/Team Leader:
Michael P. Roche

Executive Editor:
John Szilagyi

Senior Developmental Editor:
Judith O'Neill

Senior Marketing Manager:
Rob Bloom

Production Editor:
Emily S. Gross

Manufacturing Coordinator:
Rhonda Utley

Compositor:
Lachina Publishing Services

Printer:
West Group
Eagan, MN

Design Project Manager:
Bethany Casey

Internal Designer:
Patti Hudepohl

Cover Designer:
Bethany Casey

Cover Photographer:
Jon Bradley/Getty Images, Inc.

Chapter Opener Photographs:
PhotoDisc, Inc.

To my wife, Marie, and our six children:
Jesse, Justin, Danielle, Nicole, Brian, and Renee.
      – RNL

To my wife, Amy, and our two children:
Carly and Jacob.
      – DCK

Brief Contents

Contents

Chapter 4

Strategic and Operational Planning

Chapter 5

Facility and Event Planning

PART 3 ORGANIZING SKILLS

Chapter 6

Organizing and Delegating Work

Chapter 7

Managing Change: Sport Culture, Innovation, and Diversity

Chapter 8

Human Resources Management

PART 4 LEADING SKILLS

Chapter 9

Behavior in Organizations: Power, Politics, Conflict, and Stress

Chapter 10

Team Development

Chapter 11

Communicating for Results

Chapter 12

Motivating to Win

Preface

The growth in the field of sport management parallels an increased interest both in sports and in managing well. This growth is apparent in the new outlets in cable television and on the Internet that allow sport businesses and organizations to increase the flow of goods and services and reach more specific market segments. But, as every good manager knows, pursuing new opportunities always comes at a price. Efforts to control costs, reduce waste, increase market presence, and stay competitive require that managers act wisely and decisively, make better decisions, and build better teams of employees. Yet producing higher-quality outputs, more championships, and better customer service isn't easy, and it would be misleading to suggest otherwise.

OUR APPROACH

We wrote *Sport Management: Principles, Applications, Skill Development* to be a fully integrated textbook that constructively applies the principles of business management to sport industry specifics. We provide a meticulous and comprehensive overview of fundamental management topics, putting a continual in-depth focus on how to manage sport organizations. The addition of a variety of applications and skill-development exercises makes this text a logical alternative for any professor who seeks thorough coverage of the principles of management combined with robust applications, exercises, and cases that reinforce student understanding.

We use specific examples and applications so that the four functions of management—planning, organizing, leading, and controlling—are grounded in sport contexts. We also rely on the principles of the North American Society for Sport Management (NASSM), using its mission statement to guide our choices.

- *Management Competencies.* We not only stress the four functions of management, we also strive to build the management competencies necessary for productive careers. Applications and skill-building exercises specifically designed to develop management competencies appear throughout the book, ensuring that practical considerations are never treated as afterthoughts.

- *Leadership.* Leading, as noted earlier, is a core management function. We devote five chapters (Chapters 9 through 13) to this important topic, looking at leadership from a variety of angles and tying it closely to our examination of motivating, communicating, team building, and power.

- *Organizational Structure.* Part 3 of this book (Chapters 6 through 8) is devoted to organization.

- *Personnel Management, and Sport and the Law.* Chapter 8, "Human Resources Management," covers these topics.

- *Sport Marketing.* We discuss the marketing function in Chapters 4, 6, and 14.

- *Facilities Management.* Chapter 5 on facility and event planning and Chapter 14 on control systems cover this topic.

- *Future Directions in Management.* Future trends receive special attention in Chapter 2, "The Sport Industry Environment: Globalization, Ethics, and Social Responsibility."

- *Conflict Resolution.* In Chapter 9, "Behavior in Organizations: Power, Politics, Conflict, and Stress," we present tools for diagnosing conflict and working toward resolutions.

- *Employment Perspectives.* Our discussion of careers begins with our definition of sport management on page 5 and continues throughout the text—one notable example being the career opportunities found in the cases at the beginning and end of each chapter. Appendix A, " Careers in Sport Management," sums up the many opportunities this growing field has to offer.

SPECIAL FEATURES

The concepts of sport management are developed throughout each chapter using the following special features.

- *Learning Outcomes.* At the beginning of every chapter, we highlight several conceptual priorities. To ensure that students stay connected to these core concepts, we repeat them at specific points within the chapter as each learning outcome is fulfilled.

1 LEARNING OUTCOME
Describe career opportunities in sport management.

sport management
A multidisciplinary field that integrates the sport industry and management.

- *Key Terms.* **Key terms** are listed at the outset of each chapter as the last learning outcome for that chapter. We focus on building students' business vocabularies within a sport context. Within each chapter, terms are defined as they are encountered via a running marginal glossary. At the end of the chapter, a fill-in-the-blanks vocabulary review tests student recall and understanding. The key terms and definitions are also collected at the back of the book in the Glossary of Key Terms

- *"Reviewing Their Game Plan" Opening Cases.* High-interest opening cases, all featuring real-world sport organizations such as Adidas-Salomon and the Seattle Mariners, serve to get students into chapter material quickly. Featured organizations are frequently referred to throughout the body of the chapter to push students toward a deeper understanding of that organization's operations and strategies. These "flashbacks" to chapter-opening cases are designated with **BOLDFACE** type. Cases close with an annotated list of *Internet Resources.*

REVIEWING THEIR GAME PLAN

Ichiro Suzuki and Pat Gillick of the Seattle Mariners

Think of one single figure who personifies the globalization of sports, and **SEATTLE MARINERS'** outfielder Ichiro Suzuki immediately springs to mind. After years of falling short of the World Series, the Seattle Mariners and their fans watched helplessly as their three star players threw in the proverbial towel and made a beeline for the exit. Randy Johnson, Ken Griffey, Jr., Alex Rodriguez—all hailed as some the game's greatest-ever players, and all gone within the space of three short years. Fans and sportswriters alike predicted doom and gloom and, at a minimum, a screeching halt to the young team's ascendancy.

Only someone forgot to mention this to the Mariners' management. No matter, they wouldn't have heeded the dire predictions anyway because they were too busy scanning the environment for solutions. And in November 2000, they found one. His numbers with Orix of the Japanese Pacific League were good (averaged per 162 games)—a batting average of .353, with 36 doubles, 20 home runs, 90 RBI, and 34 steals thrown in for good measure—and all this packaged in a quiet, unassuming (real) team player from Japan named Ichiro Suzuki.

. . .

- *"Developing Your Skills" Skill-Development Insets.* Immediately following the opening cases, students are directed to begin to observe the managerial behaviors of those around them and actively practice the successful behaviors they take note of. Every experience can be profitable as students embark on their management career paths. We provide the guidance that students need to take full advantage of their opportunities.

- *Pop-Up Questions.* **Question marks pop up in the margins of chapters whenever a problem-oriented task of practicing managers is discussed.** Building managerial competencies requires that students think reflexively about management how-tos. We include these questions to jump-start this process.

- *"Timeout."* A unique self-study tool, these short applications ask students to take a quick inventory of their experiences and relate it to managerial roles, resources, functions, and decisions. Students can be directed to submit their answers to these questions to their instructors via e-mail, a function supported on the text's companion web site at http://lussier.swlearning.com.

- *In-Text Self Assessments.* At least one Self Assessment, such as the one pictured below, appears in most chapters. Student centered and practice oriented, these assessments are designed to apprise instructor and student alike of growing skills and insights.

- *"Applying the Concept" Boxes.* Several short, multiple-choice exercises appear in each chapter to gauge student understanding of key concepts. For a preview of one of these self-tests, turn the page.

- *Chapter Summary.* A brief review of important chapter content organized by learning outcomes concludes each chapter. Each summary includes a fill-in-the-blank exercise for reviewing chapter vocabulary.

- *Review and Discussion.* A selection of questions for review and discussion accompanies each chapter.

- *Cases.* A short, real-world case is included in every chapter. A range of application questions—multiple choice, true/false, short essay—concludes each case.

- *Video Cases.* Selected chapters include a short video case, featuring Ping Golf, Burton Snowboards, Cannondale, World Gym, and Sunshine Cleaning (a janitorial services

TIMEOUT

Think about a coach and a manager you know and explain what makes them a good manager or a poor one. In what ways are they alike? In what ways do they differ? Give examples to support your conclusions.

_____

_____

_____

_____

_____

_____

SELF ASSESSMENT   *Which Acquired Need Drives You?*

For the following 15 statements, rate how similar each one is to you on a scale of 1 (not like me) to 5 (very much like me).

_____ 1. I enjoy working hard.

_____ 2. I like to compete, and I like to win.

_____ 3. I take good care of my friends.

_____ 4. I don't shrink from difficult challenges.

_____ 5. I usually end up deciding which movie or restaurant we'll go to.

_____ 6. I want other people to really like me.

_____ 7. I check on how I'm progressing as I complete tasks.

_____ 8. I confront people who do things I disagree with.

_____ 9. I love parties.

_____ 10. I go to great lengths to set and achieve realistic goals.

_____ 11. I try to influence other people to get my way.

_____ 12. I belong to lots of groups/organizations.

_____ 13. The satisfaction of completing a difficult task is as good as life gets.

_____ 14. I take charge when a group I'm in is floundering.

_____ 15. I prefer to work with others rather than alone.

Enter your scores from above here and total each column. The column with the highest score is your dominant or primary need.

Achievement	Power	Affiliation
___ 1.	___ 2.	___ 3.
___ 4.	___ 5.	___ 6.
___ 7.	___ 8.	___ 9.
___ 10.	___ 11.	___ 12.
___ 13.	___ 14.	___ 15.
___	___	___ Totals

It is a common experience among recent graduates to assess themselves strictly in terms of their knowledge of management rather than in terms of their management attitudes and skills. If you've never systematically considered your attitudes about acquired needs, this assessment will reveal them.

APPLYING
THE CONCEPT   *Selecting Conflict Management Styles*

Identify the most appropriate conflict management style for each situation:

a. avoidance   **c.** forcing   **e.** collaboration

b. accommodation   **d.** negotiation

_____ 11.   While serving on a committee that allocates athletic funds for building a new football stadium, you make a recommendation that another member opposes quite aggressively. Your interest in what the committee does is low. You can see quite clearly that yours is the better idea.

_____ 12.   The task force you've been assigned to has to select new fitness equipment. The four alternatives will all do the job. Members disagree on their brand, price, and service.

_____ 13.   You manage golf cart sales for the Hole In One stores. Beth, who makes a lot of the sales, is in the midst of closing the season's biggest sale, and you and she disagree on which strategy to use.

_____ 14.   You're late and on your way to an important meeting. As you leave your office, at the other end of the work area you see Chris, one of your employees, goofing off instead of working.

_____ 15.   You're over budget for labor this month. It's slow, so you ask Kent, a part-time employee, to leave work early. Kent tells you he doesn't want to because he needs the money.

Time is money. The more time you spend doing a task, the more expensive you will be to your eventual employer. Our "Applying the Concept" boxes force you to identify and focus on practical skills and insights needed for career advancement.

provider for sport facilities such as the Florida Citrus Bowl and Orlando Arena). Each case includes a short introduction to the video, points to consider while viewing the segment, and questions.

■ *Exercises.* Two types of end-of-chapter exercises are included in every chapter: a "Skill-Builder" and an "Internet Skills" exercise. Taking a true drill-and-practice approach, the exercises are very hands-on and geared toward developing practical management skills. Students work through the exercises on their own, but options are provided for in-class debriefing and, where appropriate, for implementing as group exercises.

ANCILLARY SUPPORT

A comprehensive set of ancillaries is available to instructors who adopt *Sport Management: Principles, Applications, Skill Development.*

■ *Instructor's Manual with Test Bank; ISBN 0-324-17597-3.* Prepared by the text authors, Lussier and Kimball, the combined Instructor's Manual with Test Bank provides faculty with comprehensive and integrated teaching support. Each chapter includes detailed outlines for lecture enhancement and answers for Applying the Concept questions, Review and Discussion questions, and Case and Video Case questions. Instructions and tips for using the text's Self Assessments, exercises, videos, and Timeout applications are also included. The Test Bank provides a range of true/false, multiple-choice, and short-essay questions, which test understanding of each chapter's learning outcomes. All questions are ranked by difficulty level, among other measures, and include cross-references to the student text chapters in which answers can be found.

- *Video; ISBN 0-324-17598-1.* Over sixty minutes of video support is available to instructors on VHS cassette to accompany six in-text cases. Featured organizations include Burton Snowboards, Cannondale, World Gym, Ping Golf, and Sunshine Cleaning.

- *PowerPoint.* A set of PowerPoint slides accompanies every chapter, providing instructors with a complete set of basic notes for lectures, and students with a helpful set of review materials.

- *Web Site.* Broad online support is provided on the text's dedicated web site, including chapter links, downloadable ancillaries, news summaries on topics of interest to future managers arranged by topic, and more. Both students and instructors are invited to visit http://lussier.swlearning.com.

ACKNOWLEDGMENTS

Although confidentiality prohibits us from recognizing everyone who contributed reviews of our manuscript, we gratefully acknowledge the help of the following sport management faculty, who read drafts of our work and provided many helpful suggestions. Our thanks go to:

Carol A. Barr
University of Massachusetts, Amherst

Colleen Colles
Nichols College

Corrine Daprano
University of Dayton

Yong Jae Ko
Washington State University

Mark McDonald
University of Massachusetts, Amherst

Jeffrey Meyer
Wayne State College

Gordon M. Nesbit
Millersville University

Andrea Pent
Albany State University

Lynn Ridinger
Old Dominion University

Roy Schneider
Bowling Green State University

Ellen J. Staurowsky
Ithaca College

About the Authors

Robert N. Lussier is professor of management at Springfield College (SC). SC enjoys an international reputation as The Birthplace of Basketball and offers physical education study through the doctorate degree. It has one of the highest, if not the highest, percentages of student athletes in the country with approximately one-third of its undergraduate students participating in 35 intercollegiate athletic teams (26 varsity and 9 subvarsity). Dr. Lussier has taught NASSM-approved undergraduate sport management majors at SC for more than 15 years. He has also supervised students during sport internships and has served as adviser for master's research projects in sport management.

Dr. Lussier plays a variety of sports and works out daily. He was an MVP intercollegiate athlete in cross country and track and field, setting course and track records. He has coached high school cross country and indoor and outdoor track and field, intercollegiate cross country, and youth baseball teams.

Dr. Lussier is also a practicing manager as director of Israel Programs at SC. He is a prolific writer with more than 200 publications to his credit, including four other textbooks, refereed journal articles, and proceedings in the management field. He has also consulted with profit and non-profit organizations, including YMCAs.

Dr. Lussier holds a bachelor of science in business administration from Salem State College, two master's degrees in business and education from Suffolk University, and a doctorate in management from the University of New Haven.

David C. Kimball is an associate professor of management at Elms College. He is the director of the Sports Management program at Elms College. He has successfully advised students in the fields of both management and sports. His students and advisees are often soccer players, softball players, golfers, field hockey players, and swimmers. His students integrate their love of sports with a solid management education. Students are required to complete an internship in their field to complete their program.

Dr. Kimball has taught undergraduate- and graduate-level management courses for the last 12 years. His students regularly study sport firms such as Nike, Reebok, Ryka, and Spalding.

Dr. Kimball also has many connections in the sport arena. He is a member of the North American Society for Sport Management (NASSM). He has the ability to network with sport agents, collegiate coaches, fitness directors, sporting event organizers, athletes, owners, and other sport professionals. These connections are incorporated into the cases at the beginning and end of each chapter.

Dr. Kimball holds a bachelor of science in marketing and a master's degree in management from Western New England College and a doctorate in management from the University of New Haven.

Sport Management

Principles, Applications, Skill Development

1 Managing Sports

Learning Outcomes

After studying this chapter, you should be able to:

1. Describe career opportunities in sport management.
2. Describe a sport manager's responsibilities.
3. Define the five management skills.
4. Define the four management functions.
5. Explain the interpersonal, informational, and decisional roles of management.
6. Diagram the hierarchy of management levels.
7. Describe general, functional, and project managers.
8. Explain how skills and functions differ by management level.
9. Define the following key terms (in order of appearance in the chapter):

- sport management
- sport manager
- manager's resources
- performance
- management skills
- technical skills
- people skills
- communication skills
- conceptual skills
- decision-making skills
- management functions
- planning
- organizing
- leading
- controlling
- management roles
- levels of management
- types of managers

Dick's Sporting Goods

About a half century ago (1948 to be exact), a young man with a passion for fishing with an entry-level job at an Army and Navy store in Binghamton, New York, approached his boss with an idea (and a business plan to boot) for expanding their offerings to include fishing gear. For whatever reason, the owner rudely rejected the young man's idea out of hand. Too bad for the boss!

Why? Because the young man had a vision—and maybe a visionary grandmother, who lent him $300 from her proverbial cookie jar, and told her grandson to follow his dream.

The rest of the story is, well, history. The young man was Dick Stack, and in 1958 the "fishing tackle and bait shop" became **DICK'S SPORTING GOODS,** when at the urging of his loyal customers, Mr. Stack expanded his offerings and became one of the first "one-stop" destinations for sporting enthusiasts. Dick's is now 100 stores strong (in 21 states), and growing. The moral of this story is, you never know where a good idea might take you, and you won't find out if you don't pursue it.

Dick's Sporting Goods chain is famous for its mission—"to redefine sports and fitness specialty retailing for all athletes and outdoor enthusiasts"—and successful because of it. How does it go about fulfilling this mission? "Through quality brands, information, technology and superior service." This doesn't sound particularly revolutionary today, since this is what our consumer economy has grown to expect and enjoy, but you have to remember sport retailing wasn't always like this.

Dick's is now being run by Dick's son, Ed. Ed Stack owns about 37 percent of Dick's; investment firm Vulcan Ventures owns about 12 percent. Dick's filed to go public in July 2002. Dick's continues to offer the finest-quality products at competitive prices, backed by the best service anywhere. Dick's has a real passion for sports and is now excited to bring this enthusiasm and experience to the online community.

If you love sports and want to be part of a winning team for a rapidly growing company, retailers like Dick's Sporting Goods, REI, and the Sports Authority may be your ticket to the career you want.[1] For current information on Dick's, visit http://www.dickssportinggoods.com. (For ideas on using the Internet, see Appendix B.)

INTERNET RESOURCES

http://www.nassm.com *The sport management literature is growing to accommodate the corresponding growth in the field. The North American Society for Sport Management (NASSM) is a leading professional organization that has helped—and continues to help—the field to develop. NASSM produces* The Journal of Sport Management, *which offers many informative and influential articles.*

http://www.streetandsmiths.com Street & Smith's *is one of the leading annuals to distribute information about the business of sport. They provide statistics and schedules, profiles of teams and players, and incisive commentary—and their previews and predictions are renowned for their accuracy.*

http://www.espn.com *and* **http://www.sportsline.com** *These two sites offer access to sports information 24 hours a day. Use them to find up-to-the-minute news and scores.*

DEVELOPING YOUR SKILLS   Effective managers use their skills to conceptualize solutions and business strategies all the time—after all, this is what managers *do*. They also adjust their management style to fit the needs of the situation. To do this, you need to practice being observant (what works well in situations you and others around you come up against) and objective (how to extract your subjective feelings and get to the heart of the issue). You also need to take the plunge and take on leadership roles in your classes, in your job, in your team—practice *does* make perfect.

THE SPORT INDUSTRY

Sports are a *big* part of the U.S. economy. Just how big may surprise you. One estimate states that the sport industry is a $350- to $400-billion-a-year industry.[2] So, what does this mean in terms of jobs? Well, for one thing it means *lots* of them—from coaches for children's swimming and soccer teams to accountants at retail chains to athletic directors at schools and universities to managers at whitewater rafting companies. And jobs mean opportunities in management. Why? Because successful sport programs have found that good managers are crucial if they are to retain and motivate the kind of employees that will make their program thrive.[3]

Think about jobs that made you love going to work and jobs that made you dread the end of the weekend. Did management figure in your answer? Very likely it did. Why? Because managers set the tone at work, create the culture of the organization, and literally have the power to make or break it. You are interested in a career in management, or you wouldn't be taking this course. This means you *already* have energy, ambition, a desire to make a difference, people skills, and probably some leadership skills. Now it's time to put your energy and ambition to work. This book will help you hone the skills you have, and develop ones that you don't yet have. You will find that the skills you develop through this course will stand you well in both your personal life and your professional life. So let's get going.

WHAT IS SPORT MANAGEMENT?

1 LEARNING OUTCOME
Describe career opportunities in sport management.

There are many different careers in the sport industry. The following is a list of examples:

- Athletic directors (ADs) and their assistants hold excellent administrative jobs in the field of college sport management. Remember that every college needs an athletic director. Another collegiate position is that of a sport information director. They are responsible for managing and distributing information about their college teams. This textbook will frequently refer to the position of an athletic director as an example of managing sports.

- Stadiums and arenas need general managers, business managers, operations managers, box office managers, and event managers to run their organizations. These jobs are exciting if you like to help produce live sporting events.

- Sport marketing agencies manage corporate-sponsored events. Sports like golfing and NASCAR rely heavily on sport sponsorships and need managers to make sure their products gain attention at sponsored events.

- Sport marketing agencies and independent agents represent athletes, handling the business side of affairs for the athlete.

- The field of sport broadcasting includes careers in daily sport news programs, all-sports radio, and live game broadcasts.[4] All-sports radio stations have become very popular and are an excellent place to find an internship. The Internet has opened up positions managing web sites and providing statistical data for sport teams.

■ *Recreation management* is a broad term for careers such as athletic directors at YMCAs and JCCs, directors of public parks and recreation, workers in leisure fields such as fitness centers, and directors of activities at resorts.

■ Sporting goods manufacturers such as And 1 and Wilson need employees in sales, operations, human resources, and finance. Sporting goods stores such as the Sports Authority also need employees to be purchasing agents and accountants, and to staff the human resources (HR) department at their headquarters. Managers are also needed to operate each store.

■ The more obvious career path is working in professional leagues. Major League Baseball (MLB), the National Football League (NFL), the National Basketball Association (NBA), and the National Hockey League (NHL) are professional leagues that sport management students often dream about when planning their careers. An internship with these professional teams is a good way to get started. However, in almost all situations you will be required to start at the bottom of the organization and work your way up the ladder. Newer professional leagues such as the WUSA (women's soccer) and AFL and AFL2 (arena football) offer additional opportunities to work for professional teams.

Sport management is a multidisciplinary field that integrates the sport industry and management. Sport management programs train people for management positions in such areas as college athletics, professional teams, fitness centers, recreational centers, coaching, officiating, marketing, youth organizations, and sporting goods manufacturing and retailing.

sport management
A multidisciplinary field that integrates the sport industry and management.

An Interview with a Sport Manager

Cheryl Condon, Athletic Director for Elms College (Chicopee, Massachusetts), started as an admissions counselor at Elms. She has always loved and lived sports, and she pursued her passion by coaching Elms's women's softball team. Her successes as coach and her management skills did not go unnoticed, and she was eventually made athletic director.

QUESTION: Although opportunities to play sports have never been greater for women, opportunities in management are still few and far between. How did you prepare for the job of being an athletic director (AD) of a small college?

ANSWER: I think with my background in coaching, and being around sports for so many years that I have the experience to be able to do it professionally and properly. I've been around sports all my life.

QUESTION: Before you were an AD you were an admissions counselor. How did your career path evolve?

ANSWER: The previous AD left for a similar position at another college. I interviewed for the position and was fortunate enough to be selected by the search committee. I was very fortunate to be able to move from a career in recruiting student athletes into an administrative sport position. I feel the key reason I was able to get the position was the extra effort I put into coaching the women's softball team. Coaching was not one of my required job responsibilities, and the college realized my commitment to sports by my extra efforts to make the team a success.

QUESTION: What responsibilities do you have as an AD?

ANSWER: Many, many responsibilities. Hiring coaches, scheduling gymnasiums and fields for teams to practice and play regular season games, arranging for van and bus transportation to away games, printing tickets and game programs, acquiring advertisers for the game programs, fund-raising, and watching many games. When I watch the games, I appreciate all the work that my staff and the students have put into making the event a success.

QUESTION: Now you are about to take on different responsibilities as director of intramural sports. Why make the change?

ANSWER: The number of teams at my college is increasing, and the new AD will be responsible for managing even more budgets, teams, coaches, and game logistics. However, my college has never had any intramural sports. I want to get the whole student body more involved in sports on a daily basis, and I think an intramural program is the way to bring this about.

QUESTION: What do you think is the most important issue for sport managers?

ANSWER: Ethics. Sport managers need to live by a high moral code. They need to make sure the physical environment is safe for all athletes and fans. They need to conduct themselves in a professional managerial role whether they are on or off the athletic field. Conducting oneself in an ethical manner is something *every* manager should do.

Source: Interview with Cheryl Condon reprinted with permission.

The Sport Manager's Responsibilities

sport manager
The person responsible for achieving the sport organization's objectives through efficient and effective utilization of resources.

manager's resources
These include human, financial, physical, and informational resources.

A **sport manager** is responsible for achieving the sport organization's objectives through efficient and effective utilization of resources. So that we start with a good perspective on what sport managers are all about, let's take a closer look at a couple of these terms. *Efficient* means getting the maximum out of your available resources. *Effective* means doing the right thing (following the proper strategy) in order to attain your objective; it also describes how well you achieve the objectives. The **manager's resources** include human, financial, physical, and informational resources.

2   LEARNING OUTCOME
Describe a sport manager's responsibilities.

HUMAN RESOURCES. As you no doubt know, human resources are people. People are a manager's most valuable resource. As a manager, you will endeavor to recruit and/or hire the best people available. These athletes and/or employees must then be trained to use the organization's other resources to maximize productivity. Whether you are managing a team of players or a team of employees, they will not be productive if they cannot work well together. Throughout this book we will focus on how you as a manager can work with employees to accomplish your organization's objectives.

FINANCIAL RESOURCES. Most managers have budgets. Their budgets state how much it should cost to operate their department/store/team for a set period of time. In other words, a budget tells you what financial resources you have available to achieve your objectives. As a manager, you will be responsible for seeing that your department does not waste resources. You will see flush financial times and lean ones. When times are flush, budgets expand, but you must still watch them carefully to make sure resources are not squandered. When times are lean, you may need to find new avenues to finance your team or department, and you may have to cut budgets.[5] Cheryl Condon disperses her budget very creatively to make sure that each sport at Elms has a chance to have a successful season.

PHYSICAL RESOURCES. Getting the job done requires effective and efficient use of physical resources. For a retailer like **DICK'S SPORTING GOODS,** physical resources include store buildings (there are over 100 of them), the merchandise they sell, the fixtures that display the merchandise, and the computers they use to record sales and inventory. Dick's physical resources also include supplies such as price tags, hangers, and charge slips. **What kinds of resources would a Little League baseball team be able to tap into? What kind of resources would Cheryl Condon have at her disposal?** Managers are responsible for keeping equipment in working condition and for making sure that materials and supplies are readily available. Current sales and future business can be lost if Dick's physical resources are neither available when needed nor used and maintained properly.

INFORMATIONAL RESOURCES. Managers need all kinds of information. **DICK'S** needs to know how its sales in Huntsville, Alabama, and in Green Bay, Wisconsin, compare. They need to know which suppliers will get them golf balls fastest and most cheaply. They need to track healthcare insurance costs for all their employees. Computers store and retrieve information like this for all of Dick's stores, and for their home office in Pittsburgh. When managers at Dick's check their voice mail, give employees directions on setting up displays, and attend the district meeting with store walk-through, they are using informational resources. **Name some informational resources that your team or organization uses.** Increasing the speed at which information is disseminated through organizations is crucial today as a means of getting products to consumers faster (and hopefully ahead of the competition) and as a way to compete in the global economy. This means taking advantage of new technologies, and this means that you as a manager must stay abreast of new information technologies.[6]

Performance is a measure of how well managers achieve organizational objectives. Managers are responsible for meeting these objectives, and they are evaluated on how well they meet them. This means they must marshal their available resources effectively, efficiently, and creatively.

performance
A measure of how well managers achieve organizational objectives.

WHAT DOES IT TAKE TO BE A SUCCESSFUL MANAGER?

We don't have a short, simple answer for you. Over the years, numerous researchers have devoted many hours and much funding to answering this question. What follows are some of their findings.

The Good Managers and the Poor Ones

In a Gallup survey conducted for the *Wall Street Journal,* 782 top executives in 282 large corporations were asked, "What are the most important traits for success as a supervisor?"[7] Before you read their answers, complete the Self Assessment on page 8 to find out if *you* have what *they* think it takes.

The executives in the Gallup poll listed integrity, industriousness, and the ability to get along with people as the three most important traits of successful managers. Other traits of managers who succeed as managers included business knowledge, intelligence, leadership ability, education, sound judgment, ability to communicate, flexibility, and ability to plan and set objectives. According to these executives, managers who fail as managers have a limited viewpoint, are unable to understand others, do not work well with others, are indecisive, lack initiative, do not assume responsibility, and lack integrity. They also lack the ability to change, are reluctant to think independently, cannot solve problems, and have too strong a desire to be popular (which prevents them from making the tough decisions).

TIMEOUT
Categorize the resources used by one of your present or past coaches or managers.

_____

_____

_____

_____

_____

TIMEOUT
Think about a coach and a manager you know and explain what makes them a good manager or a poor one. In what ways are they alike? In what ways do they differ? Give examples to support your conclusions.

_____

_____

_____

_____

_____

_____

_____

Exhibit 1–1
Management Skills

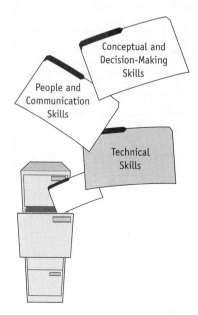

Building Strong Management Skills

People with strong management skills are in demand today (hence this book's focus on skill building!). Experience in the workplace and completing courses similar to this one will help you develop these skills. As with all endeavors worth pursuing, the key to success is perseverance. If you persevere, you *can* develop and hone strong management skills. And don't leave your newly acquired skills at the classroom door—use them in your daily life.

Almost 30 years ago Robert Katz conducted a study that is still widely used today. Katz found that effective administrators have strong technical skills, strong people skills, and strong conceptual skills.[8] Over the years other researchers have added administrative, communication, political, and problem-solving and decision-making skills. For our purposes then, we will paraphrase Katz and define **management skills** to include (1) technical skills, (2) people skills, (3) communication skills, (4) conceptual skills, and (5) decision-making skills. (See Exhibit 1–1.)

management skills
Management skills include
(1) technical skills,
(2) people skills,
(3) communication skills,
(4) conceptual skills, and
(5) decision-making skills.

In the exhibit image: Conceptual and Decision-Making Skills; People and Communication Skills; Technical Skills

SELF ASSESSMENT

Getting to Know Yourself

Objective:

To practice assessing yourself objectively.

Preparation:

The following questions relate to key qualities that successful managers have. Rate yourself on each item by placing the number 1–4 that best describes your behavior for each item.

4—The statement is not very descriptive of me.

3—The statement is somewhat descriptive of me.

2—The statement is descriptive of me.

1—The statement is very descriptive of me.

_____ 1. I enjoy working with people. I prefer to work with others rather than work alone.

_____ 2. I can motivate others. I can get people to do things they may not want to do.

_____ 3. I am well liked. People enjoy working with me.

_____ 4. I am cooperative. I strive to help the team do well, rather than to be the star.

_____ 5. I am a leader. I enjoy teaching, coaching, and instructing people.

_____ 6. I want to be successful. I do things to the best of my ability to be successful.

_____ 7. I am a self-starter. I get things done without having to be told to do them.

_____ 8. I am a problem-solver. If things aren't going the way I want them to, I take corrective action to meet my objectives.

_____ 9. I am self-reliant. I don't need the help of others.

_____ 10. I am hardworking. I enjoy working and getting the job done.

_____ 11. I am trustworthy. If I say I will do something by a set time, I do it.

_____ 12. I am loyal. I do not do or say things to intentionally hurt my friends, relatives, or coworkers.

_____ 13. I can take criticism. If people tell me negative things about myself, I give them serious thought and change when appropriate.

_____ 14. I am honest. I do not lie, steal, or cheat.

_____ 15. I am fair. I treat people equally. I don't take advantage of others.

(Add up your total score.)

The *lower* your score, the better your chances of succeeding in management. If you are interested in being a manager someday, look closely at your scores on integrity (items 11–15), industriousness (items 6–10), and ability to get along with people (items 1–5) both in this course and in your personal life. As a start, review the traits listed in the text, and work to improve them. Which are your strongest and weakest traits? Think about how you can improve in the weaker areas, or preferably, write out a plan.

IN-CLASS APPLICATION

Complete the skill-building preparation noted above before class.

Choose one (10–30 minutes):

■ Break into groups of three to five and choose a well-known coach of a pro sports team you are all familiar with. As a group, try to guess how he or she would answer the above questions. As a group, present your speculations to the class.

■ Informal, whole-class discussion of students' personal responses to the questionnaire.

Wrap-up:

Take a few minutes and write down your answers to the following questions:

■ What did I learn from this experience?

_____

_____

_____

_____

_____

■ How will I use this knowledge in the future?

_____

_____

_____

_____

_____

As a class, discuss student responses.

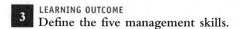

3 LEARNING OUTCOME
Define the five management skills.

Technical skills are the ability to use methods and techniques to perform a task. When managers work on budgets, they use spreadsheet software, so they need computer skills; they also need some knowledge of accounting (a great deal of accounting has to do with budgets and finances). **DICK'S** managers need computer skills just to *open* the store, and of course they also need them when they record transfers and sales. **What sort of technical skills do you currently possess?** Most people get promoted to their first management position primarily because of their technical skills. Because technical skills vary widely from job to job, developing these skills is not the primary focus of this book. However, in our discussion of planning (Chapters 5 and 14) we give you a brief overview of the financial and budgetary tools you will use as a manager.

technical skills
The ability to use methods and techniques to perform a task.

People skills are the ability to work well with people. Your people skills are what will make athletes, parents, employees, and other coaches want to work with you and for you. **Communication skills** are the ability to get your ideas across clearly and effectively. Without communication skills, you cannot be an effective team member or manager. Today, not only do employees *want* to participate in management,[9] management encourages group decision making in all manner of business endeavors (see Chapter 3). With this increased use of teams comes the need for good people skills to help groups stay on task, and stay motivated.[10] Another key area of people skills is political savvy—"street smarts" help you manage teams, develop a power base and political skills, manage conflict, and improve employee performance. How well you get along with employees will affect how well you can manage them. Throughout this book, in the Skill-Builders and other exercises you will learn to work with a diversity of people, hone your people skills, improve your communication skills, and learn how to motivate and lead others. As director of the athletic department at Elms, Cheryl Condon has many *stakeholders* (see Chapter 2) to satisfy—she wouldn't last a minute if she didn't have great people skills and great communication skills.

people skills
The ability to work well with people.

communication skills
The ability to get your ideas across clearly and effectively.

Conceptual skills are the ability to understand abstract ideas. Another term for conceptual skills is *systems thinking,* or the ability to understand an organization/department as a whole and the relationships among its parts. As businesses compete in the global marketplace, creative analysis and judgment—critical thinking—are needed to resolve conflict and solve problems.[11] **Decision-making skills** are the ability to select alternatives to solve problems. An important part of Cheryl's job is to decide what facilities to use, which marketing strategies will work, which coaches fit with Elms's objectives, and which student athletes she should recruit.

conceptual skills
The ability to understand abstract ideas.

decision-making skills
The ability to select alternatives to solve problems.

The Ghiselli Study

In his classic 1971 study, Professor Edwin Ghiselli identified six traits as important for managers, although not all are necessary to succeed as a manager.[12] They are, in reverse order of importance, (6) initiative, (5) self-assurance, (4) decisiveness, (3) intelligence, (2) need for occupational achievement, and (1) supervisory ability. The number-one trait, supervisory ability, requires skills in planning, organizing, leading, and controlling. Ghiselli's four areas of supervisory ability are more commonly referred to as the *management functions;* we discuss them in the next section.

TIME OUT
Think about a coach and a manager you know and list the management skills they use on the job. Be specific and try to identify each of the five skills identified above.

_____

_____

_____

_____

_____

WHAT DO SPORT MANAGERS DO?

Lots of things, as you can well imagine.

Management Functions

Managers get the job done through others. They also plan, organize, lead, and control to achieve organizational objectives—these are the four **management functions.**[13]

4 LEARNING OUTCOME
Define the four management functions.

management functions
The activities all managers perform, such as planning, organizing, leading, and controlling.

This book is organized around the four management functions. Each function serves as a title for a part of the book, and three to five chapters are devoted to developing skills in each function. Here, and in later chapters, we examine each function separately. However, always keep in mind that the four functions *together* comprise a system; they are interrelated and are often performed simultaneously.

PLANNING. Planning is typically the starting point in the management process. To succeed, organizations need a great deal of planning. The people who work for organizations, from the CEO to the summer intern, need goals and objectives and plans by which they will achieve them. **Planning** is the process of setting objectives and determining in advance exactly how the objectives will be met. Managers schedule the work employees perform and also develop budgets. At **DICK'S,** managers schedule employees' work rotations so that high-volume times in stores are well covered, and they also select the merchandise that Dick's will sell. **What planning functions does your team or organization perform? Which managers are responsible for different aspects of planning?** Performing the planning function well requires strong conceptual and decision-making skills.

ORGANIZING. Successful managers put a great deal of effort into the organizing function. They also design and develop systems to implement plans.[14] **Organizing** is the process of delegating and coordinating tasks and resources to achieve objectives. Managers allocate and arrange resources. An important part of allocating human resources is assigning people to various jobs and tasks. Cheryl Condon plans for regular-season games, holiday tournaments, and post-season games. To do this, she has to organize the athletic department employees (including janitors, coaches, assistants, team doctors, equipment people, and ticket takers) so that they cover each and every game. An important part of organizing, sometimes listed as a separate function, is staffing. *Staffing* is the process of selecting, training, and evaluating employees; Cheryl is responsible for staffing her teams. Effective organizing requires both conceptual and decision-making skills as well as people skills and communication skills.

LEADING. In addition to planning and organizing, managers work with employees on a daily basis as they perform their tasks. **Leading** is the process of influencing employees to work toward achieving objectives. Managers must not only communicate the objectives to employees, they must also motivate them to achieve the objectives.[15] An important part of Cheryl's job is to communicate objectives, and then motivate and lead individuals and teams. Cheryl coaches her employees as they perform their jobs. Effective leaders have strong people skills and strong communication skills.

CONTROLLING. Only three out of ten people do the things they say they will do.[16] Therefore, objectives will not be met without follow-through. **Controlling** is the process of establishing and implementing mechanisms to ensure that objectives are achieved. An important part of controlling is measuring progress and taking corrective action when nec-

planning
The process of setting objectives and determining in advance exactly how the objectives will be met.

organizing
The process of delegating and coordinating tasks and resources to achieve objectives.

leading
The process of influencing employees to work toward achieving objectives.

controlling
The process of establishing and implementing mechanisms to ensure that objectives are achieved.

APPLYING THE CONCEPT   *Management Functions*

Identify which function fits the situation described.

a. planning   **c.** leading   **e.** nonmanagement

b. organizing   **d.** controlling

_____ 6. Coach Sally shows Kelly how to kick a ball.

_____ 7. Coach Tom determines how many players were hurt during the first half of the game.

_____ 8. Ace forward Jason has missed practice several times. Coach Dave is discussing the situation with Jason to get him to understand that he cannot continue to miss practice.

_____ 9. Coach Sheryl is interviewing applicants for the position of physical therapist.

_____ 10. Coach Terry is fixing a broken Nautilus machine.

essary. Cheryl controls throughout each sporting season. She monitors, along with coaches, the progress of each team and makes adjustments in the team rosters. Effective controlling requires technical skills (you have to use appropriate measures), as well as conceptual and decision-making skills.

Nonmanagement Functions

All managers perform the four functions of management as they and their team get the work done. However, many managers perform nonmanagement, or employee, functions as well. If Cheryl makes a photocopy of the athletic department budget she is working on, she is performing a nonmanagement function. Many—indeed, most—managers are called "working managers" because they perform both management and employee functions.

Management Functions Work as a System

Management functions do not work in a linear fashion. Managers do not plan, *then* organize, *then* lead, and *then* control. The functions are both separate and interrelated. Managers often perform these functions simultaneously. In addition, each function depends on the others. For example, if you start with a poor plan, your objective will not be met even though things are well organized, well led, and well controlled. Also, if you start with a great plan, but are poorly organized, or poorly led, you will probably not meet your objective. Plans without controls are rarely implemented effectively. Exhibit 1–2 illustrates this process. Remember, management functions are based on setting (planning) and achieving (organizing, leading, and controlling) objectives.

 5 LEARNING OUTCOME
Explain the interpersonal, informational, and decisional roles of management.

> **TIMEOUT**
> Using the coach and manager you've been analyzing in previous Timeouts, give examples of how they perform each of the four management functions.
>
> _____
> _____
> _____
> _____

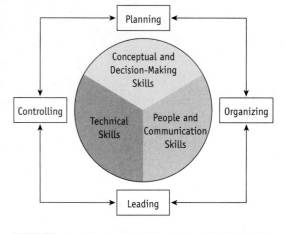

Exhibit 1–2   Management Skills and Functions

Management Roles

Henry Mintzberg identifies ten roles that managers undertake to accomplish their planning, organizing, leading, and controlling functions. A *role* is a set of expectations of how one will

management roles
The roles managers undertake to accomplish the management function, including interpersonal, informational, and decisional.

behave in a given situation. Several studies support Mintzberg's management role theory.[17] Mintzberg categorizes the ten **management roles** as shown in Exhibit 1–3.[18]

INTERPERSONAL ROLES. Interpersonal roles include figurehead, leader, and liaison. When managers play interpersonal roles, they use their people skills and their communication skills. Managers are *figureheads* when they represent the organization or department in ceremonial and symbolic activities. Cheryl Condon played the figurehead role when she granted an interview to the author. Managers are *leaders* when they motivate, train, communicate with, and influence others. Throughout the day, Cheryl functions as a leader when she directs players to prepare for the upcoming game. Managers are *liaisons* when they interact with people outside their unit to gain information and favors. Cheryl plays liaison when she solicits local businesses to place advertisements in game programs.

INFORMATIONAL ROLES. Informational roles include monitor, disseminator, and spokesperson. When managers play informational roles, they use their people skills and communication skills. Managers are *monitors* when they read and talk to others to gather information. Cheryl continually monitors her situation by following the performance of other local colleges and other Division III teams in her league. Managers are *disseminators* when they send information to others. They are *spokespersons* when they provide information to people outside the organization. Cheryl is both disseminator and spokesperson when she gives interviews to the local newspaper.

Exhibit 1–3   Ten Roles Managers Play

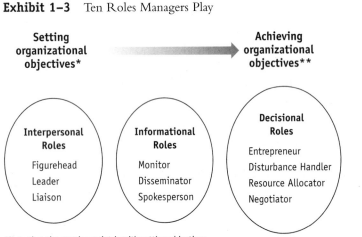

*Note that the starting point is with setting objectives.
**Managers play the necessary role while performing management functions to achieve objectives.

DECISIONAL ROLES. Decisional roles include entrepreneur, disturbance handler, resource allocator, and negotiator. When managers play decisional roles, they use their conceptual and decision-making skills. Managers are *entrepreneurs* when they innovate and when they improve products, systems, or services. Cheryl demonstrates an entrepreneurial spirit in her desire to start an intramural sport program. Managers are *disturbance handlers* when they take corrective action to diffuse disputes or crises. Cheryl is a disturbance handler when she negotiates a settlement between a coach and his or her players. Managers are *resource allocators* when they schedule, request authorization, and perform budgeting and programming activities. Cheryl is a resource allocator when she authorizes departmental budgets and purchases made against these budgets. Managers are *negotiators* when they represent their department or organization during nonroutine transactions to gain agreement and commitment. After Elms went coeducational in 1999, Cheryl played a major role as a negotiator when she helped the college add teams for male students.

As sport businesses compete in the global economy, both the business environment and technology affect management's interpersonal, informational, and decisional roles.

TIMEOUT
Using the coach and manager you've been analyzing in previous Timeouts, give examples of how they perform their management roles.

_____

_____

_____

_____

_____

HOW MANAGERS DIFFER

At various levels of management, different management skills are needed, different management functions are performed, and different roles are played. Managers who work for large organizations typically have very different jobs than those who work for small organizations; this also holds true for managers who work for for-profit and nonprofit organizations.

The Three Levels of Management

levels of management
Top, middle, and first-line.

The three **levels of management** (also called strategic, tactical, and operational management) are top, middle, and first-line management. (See Exhibit 1–4.)

APPLYING THE CONCEPT   *Management Roles*

Identify the role played by management in each situation.

a. interpersonal   **c.** decisional

b. informational

_____ 11. Baseball Commissioner Bud Selig discusses the players' contract with union representatives.

_____ 12. An Adidas HR manager shows a new hire how to fill out a form.

_____ 13. Seattle Mariners' Pat Gillick reads *Street & Smith's* with his cup of coffee first thing in the morning.

_____ 14. Cheryl Condon develops new total quality management techniques.

_____ 15. Oakland Raiders' sales and ticket managers discuss a complaint with a customer.

6   LEARNING OUTCOME
Diagram the hierarchy of management levels.

TOP MANAGERS. These executive positions have titles such as chairman of the board, chief executive officer (CEO), president, or vice president. Top managers manage the entire organization or major parts of it. They develop and fine-tune the organization's mission, objectives, strategies, and long-term plans. They report to other executives or the board of directors and supervise the activities of middle managers. The president of Elms College is a top manager. Most organizations have relatively few top management positions.

MIDDLE MANAGERS. People holding these positions have titles such as general manager, athletic director, sales manager, branch manager, and department head. Middle managers implement top management's strategies by developing short-term operating plans. They generally report to executives and supervise the work of first-line managers. Cheryl Condon is a middle manager at Elms College.

Exhibit 1–4   Management Levels and Functional Areas

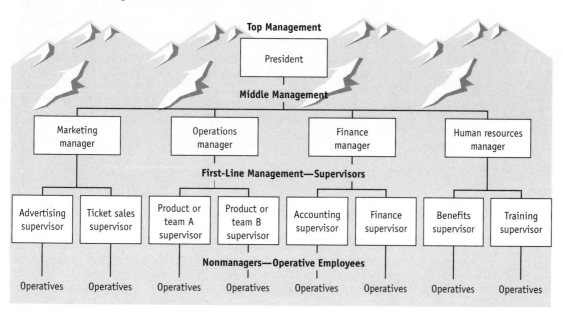

FIRST-LINE MANAGERS. Examples of the titles at this level include coach, assistant coach, academic advising coordinator, ticket manager, event manager, supervisor, head nurse, and office manager. These managers implement middle managers' operational plans. They generally report to middle managers. Unlike those at the other two levels of management, first-line managers do not supervise other managers; they supervise operative employees.

OPERATIVES. The workers that comprise the teams that managers lead do not hold management positions. Operatives, as we use the term here, are the people who report to first-line managers. They work in the concessions, take tickets, make the products, wait on customers, perform repairs, and so on.

Types of Managers

7 LEARNING OUTCOME
Describe general, functional, and project managers.

types of managers
General, functional, and project.

The three **types of managers** are general, functional, and project managers. Top-level and some middle managers are *general managers* because they supervise the activities of several departments. Middle and first-line managers are often *functional managers* who supervise the activities of related tasks. The four most common functional management areas are marketing, operations/production, finance/accounting, and human resources. Marketing managers are responsible for selling and advertising products and services. Production managers are responsible for making products such as Spalding basketballs, whereas operations managers are responsible for providing a service. However, both product and service organizations now use the broader term *operations*. Accounting managers are responsible for tracking sales and expenses (accounts receivable and payable) and for determining profitability, whereas financial managers are responsible for obtaining funding and for investing. The term *finance*, as commonly used, includes both accounting and financing activities. Human resources managers are responsible for forecasting future employee needs and recruiting, selecting, evaluating, and compensating employees. They also ensure that employees follow legal guidelines and regulations.

Management Skills

8 LEARNING OUTCOME
Explain how skills and functions differ by management level.

All managers need technical skills, people and communication skills, and conceptual and decision-making skills. However, the need for these skills varies by level of management. Various studies have endeavored to determine the skill needs at each level of management, and it is generally agreed that the need for people skills and communication skills is fairly constant across all three levels. Top-level managers have a greater need for conceptual and decision-making skills; first-line managers need better technical skills. This is logical—as managers move up the corporate ladder, they are less concerned with the daily details of conducting business and more concerned with the Big Picture. And Big Picture thinking requires conceptualizing and strategizing. First-line managers focus on the detail—the day-to-day creation of the product or service. Middle managers typically need a balance of all three skills, but this of course varies from organization to organization.

Management Functions

As noted earlier, every manager plans, organizes, leads, and controls. However, the time spent on each function varies by level of management. Studies of the amount of time managers spend on each function are inconclusive. However, it is generally agreed that first-line managers spend more time leading and controlling, middle-level managers spend equal time on all four functions, and top managers spend more time planning and organizing. Exhibit 1–5 summarizes the differences by management levels.

TIMEOUT
Think about a sport organization you are personally familiar with and identify the levels of management in the organization by level and title. Does this organization utilize all three levels? If so, why? If not, why not?

_____

_____

_____

_____

_____

_____

_____

TIMEOUT
Which type of manager have you worked under? Write a job description for this person, and categorize the tasks he/she performs by function.

_____

_____

_____

_____

_____

APPLYING THE CONCEPT   *Differences between Management Levels*

Identify the level of management in each situation.

a. top   **c.** first-line

b. middle

_____ 16. Coaches the players

_____ 17. The team owner

_____ 18. Spends more time motivating and developing skills

_____ 19. Athletic director reporting to the president

_____ 20. Has a more balanced need for the management skills and functions

---

Exhibit 1–5   Skills and Functions Performed by Management Level

MANAGEMENT LEVEL	PRIMARY MANAGEMENT SKILLS NEEDED	PRIMARY MANAGEMENT FUNCTIONS PERFORMED
Top	Conceptual and people skills	Planning and organizing
Middle	Balance of all skills	Balance of all four
First-line	Technical and people skills	Leading and controlling

Managing Large Businesses and Small Businesses

Exhibit 1–6 lists the major differences between large and small businesses. Note, however, that these are general statements and many large and small businesses share certain characteristics. "Small business" can be defined in numerous ways. The Small Business Administration (SBA) definition will suffice for our purposes: A *small business* is independently owned and operated, is not dominant in its field, and has fewer than 500 employees. Cheryl Condon works for a small business.

Exhibit 1–6   The Functions and Roles in Large and Small Businesses

FUNCTIONS AND ROLES	LARGE BUSINESS	SMALL BUSINESS
Planning	Commonly have formal written objectives and plans with a global business focus.	Commonly have informal objectives and plans that are not written with a global focus.
Organizing	Tend to have formal organization structures with clear policies and procedures, with three levels of management. Jobs tend to be specialized.	Tend to have informal structures without clear policies and procedures, with fewer than three levels of management. Jobs tend to be more general.
Leading	Managers tend to be more participative, giving employees more say in how they do their work and allowing them to make more decisions.	Entrepreneurs tend to be more autocratic and want things done their way, often wanting to make decisions.
Controlling	Tend to have more sophisticated computerized control systems.	Tend to use less sophisticated control systems and to rely more on direct observation.
Important management roles	Resource allocator.	Entrepreneur and spokesperson.

Managing For-Profits and Nonprofits

Are managers' jobs the same in nonprofit and for-profit organizations? In a word, yes. Whether you work for your local Little League team (nonprofit) or for the Brazilian World Cup champions (for profit), you will still need the same management skills, you will perform the same management functions, and you will play the same roles.

That said, the two types of organizations do exhibit key differences. These mainly occur in how they measure performance and how they staff their organizations. The primary measure of performance in for-profit organizations is, well, profit. In addition, organizations in business to make money must pay their workers. Nonprofit organizations measure performance differently—for example, by whether they can pay for the team's swimming pool rental fees, whether team membership is increasing, whether they are reaching their stakeholders (such as inner-city kids), and so forth. Typically a lot of the staff of nonprofits are unpaid volunteers. Many athletic associations, such as the NCAA, are organized as nonprofits.

CHAPTER SUMMARY

1. Describe career opportunities in sport management.

Sport management is a multidisciplinary field that integrates sport and management. Sport management programs train interested people for management positions in such areas as college athletics, professional teams, fitness centers, recreation centers, coaching, officiating, marketing, youth organizations, and sporting goods manufacturing and retailing.

2. Describe a sport manager's responsibilities.

Sport managers are responsible for achieving organizational objectives through efficient and effective use of resources. Sport managers utilize their organization's human, financial, physical, and informational resources to achieve the objectives.

3. Define the five management skills.

The five management skills are technical skills, people and communication skills, and conceptual and decision-making skills. *Technical skills* are the ability to use methods and techniques to perform a task. *People skills* are the ability to work well with people. *Communication skills* are the ability to get your ideas across clearly and effectively. *Conceptual skills* are the ability to understand abstract ideas, and *decision-making skills* are the ability to select alternatives to solve problems.

4. Define the four management functions.

The four management functions are planning, organizing, leading, and controlling. *Planning* is the process of setting objectives and determining in advance exactly how the objectives will be met. *Organizing* is the process of delegating and coordinating tasks and resources to achieve objectives. *Leading* is about influencing employees to work toward achieving objectives. *Controlling* is the process of establishing and implementing mechanisms to ensure that the organization achieves its objectives.

5. Explain the interpersonal, informational, and decisional roles of management.

Managers play the interpersonal role when they act as figureheads, leaders, and liaisons. Managers play the informational role when they act as monitors, disseminators, and spokespersons. Managers play the decisional role when they act as entrepreneurs, disturbance handlers, resource allocators, and negotiators.

6. Diagram the hierarchy of management levels.

The three levels are top, middle, and first-line management.

7. Describe general, functional, and project managers.

General managers supervise the activities of several departments or units. *Functional managers* supervise related activities such as marketing, operations, finance, and human resources management. *Project managers* coordinate employees and other resources across several functional departments to accomplish a specific task.

8. Explain how skills and functions differ by management level.

Top managers have a greater need for conceptual and decision-making skills. Middle managers need a balance of all five skills. First-line managers need better technical skills.

9. Define the key terms discussed in the text.

Fill in the missing key terms from memory, or match the key terms from the list in the margin with their definitions below.

_____ is a multidisciplinary field of study that integrates the sport industry and management.

A _____ is the person responsible for achieving the sport organization's objectives through efficient and effective utilization of resources.

The _____ include human, financial, physical, and informational.

_____ is a measure of how well managers achieve organizational objectives.

_____ include (1) technical, (2) people, (3) communication, (4) conceptual, and (5) decision-making skills.

_____ are the ability to use methods and techniques to perform a task.

_____ are the ability to work well with people.

_____ are the ability to get your ideas across clearly and effectively.

_____ are the ability to understand abstract ideas.

_____ are the ability to select alternatives to solve problems.

_____ are the activities all managers perform, such as planning, organizing, leading, and controlling.

_____ is the process of setting objectives and determining in advance exactly how the objectives will be met.

_____ is the process of delegating and coordinating tasks and resources to achieve objectives.

_____ is the process of influencing employees to work toward achieving objectives.

_____ is the process of establishing and implementing mechanisms to ensure that objectives are achieved.

Key Terms

communication skills
conceptual skills
controlling
decision-making skills
leading
levels of management
management functions
management roles
management skills
manager's resources
organizing
people skills
performance
planning
sport management
sport manager
technical skills
types of managers

_____ are the roles managers undertake to accomplish the management function, including interpersonal, informational, and decisional.

There are three _____: top, middle, and first-line.

There are three _____: general, functional, and project.

REVIEW AND DISCUSSION

1. What is sport management? Name some possible career opportunities available to sport management majors.

2. What are the five management skills? Do all sport managers need these skills?

3. What are the four functions of management? Do all sport managers perform all four functions?

4. What are the three management roles? Do all sport managers perform all three roles?

5. What are the three types of managers? How do they differ?

6. Is it more important for a sport manager to be efficient or effective? Can you be both?

7. Should a sport management course focus on teaching students about sports or management? Explain your answer.

8. Can college students really develop their management skills through a college course? Why or why not?

9. Do you believe that sport management theory is or should be as precise as physics or chemistry? Explain your answer.

10. What are three career paths in sport management that you find interesting?

11. There were four information resources listed at the beginning of this chapter for exploring the field of sport management. Can you find four more?

CASE

Nike, Inc.

Nike founder Phil Knight learned a *lot* from his running coach Bill Bowerman. Together Knight and Bowerman started the Nike Corporation. Sports *are* Nike, innovative redefiner of what the fleetest athletes and the slowest couch potatoes put on their feet. Nike has played hard on the retail courts around the world to earn the right to wear this mantle.

As a kid, Knight played hoops and ran track and got good enough to earn a place on the University of Oregon track team coached by Bill Bowerman. Coach Bowerman taught Knight that reaching for personal excellence and for lightning-fast running require the same stern stuff. And from their trademark mix of raw confidence (Knight started the company selling shoes out of his car at University of Oregon track meets), bold dreams (Bowerman has been known to take a waffle iron to running shoes, looking for the perfect tread), and hard work, Knight and Bowerman built a multimillion-dollar business, and in the process changed forever what Americans wear on their feet.[19]

But, nearly forty years later, Nike can no longer "Just do it." After decades of stellar growth, Nike finds itself the uncomfortable symbol for a stinging controversy—sweatshop conditions in Asian and Mexican factories in which it has been alleged that children and women work 12-hour days 6 days a week for pennies an hour in unhealthy conditions while star athletes rake in millions endorsing products made by these workers. This is no small charge, given that Nike (directly and indirectly) employs some 500,000 workers around the world.

The million-dollar question has been whether—and how—Phil Knight and his management team would address these problems. In May 1998, Mr. Knight announced a series of initiatives to improve working conditions in factories in developing countries that he hoped would set new benchmark standards for the industry.

Three years later, Nike continues to tackle its labor issues, although the stigma has lingered. The company has worked hard to address troubling working conditions and low wages in its foreign factories. Along with such high-profile names as Reebok, Adidas, and Patagonia, Nike is helping fund the FLA's (Fair Labor Association) efforts to reform labor practices in the developing world. "The FLA is very important to us because it is going to replace anecdote with fact and set the record straight once and for all," says Vada Manager, Nike's director of global issues management.[20] Nike has devoted large portions of its web site to update consumers on the policies it has installed to correct factory problems.

Meanwhile, in the Battle of the Superstar Endorsers, Nike faces stiffer competition with Reebok and Adidas figuring out that star endorsers mean Sales with a capital S, and with their signing of LA Lakers' Kobe Bryant and Philadelphia 76ers' Allen Iverson. Nike's answer is a new superstar spokesperson, golfer Tiger Woods. And Nike scored big recently with Brazil's flamboyant journey to become World Cup champions.

For current information on Nike, use the Internet to conduct a name search for Nike and visit its web site at http://www.nike.com.

CASE QUESTIONS

1. As CEO, Phil Knight needs technical skills more than he needs conceptual skills.
   a. true   b. false

2. Phil Knight is a general manager.
   a. true   b. false

3. Which resources play the most important role in Nike's success?
   a. human   c. financial
   b. physical   d. informational

4. Which management skills does Nike call into play for the various situations discussed above?
   a. technical skills
   b. people and communication skills
   c. conceptual and decision-making skills

5. Which management function(s) are Nike managers performing in the situations discussed above?
   a. planning
   b. organizing
   c. leading
   d. controlling
   e. all of the above

6. Which management role did Phil Knight primarily play in Nike's journey to success?
   a. interpersonal—leader
   b. informational—monitor
   c. decisional—negotiator

7. As CEO, Phil Knight spends more of his time
   a. planning and organizing
   b. leading and controlling
   c. balancing the above

8. Who is responsible for the poor working conditions in Asian factories?
   a. Asian employees
   b. Asian factory managers
   c. Phil Knight
   d. Nike's Board of Directors
   e. all of the above

9. Which area of sport management is Nike's primary focus?
   a. sport broadcasting
   b. stadium and arena management
   c. recreation management
   d. sporting goods manufacturing

10. Nike manufactures their own athletic footwear.

    a. true   b. false

11. Use the Internet to determine for yourself whether Phil Knight has properly addressed Nike's labor problems.

12. Is Phil Knight the type of manager who would be successful in other sport organizations?

EXERCISES

Skill-Builder: Getting to Know You

Objectives:

- To get acquainted with your classmates and instructor.
- To get a feel for what this course is all about.

Activities:

1. Break into groups of five or six, preferably with people you don't know. State your name and tell two or three significant things about yourself. After everyone has finished, ask each other questions about themselves. (5–8 minutes)

2. (a) Can anyone in your group call the others by name? If so, they should do so. If not, have every member repeat their names. Take turns calling each other by name. Do this until everyone knows each other's first name. (1–2 minutes)

   (b) Brainstorm ways you can improve your ability to remember names. (4–8 minutes)

   _____

   _____

   _____

   _____

3. Elect a spokesperson or recorder for your group. Look over the following categories and develop several statements or questions you would like to ask the instructor, then hand in your list. (5–10 minutes)

   (a) _Expectations._ What do you hope to learn from this course?

   _____

   _____

   _____

   _____

   (b) _Doubts or concerns._ Is there anything about the course that you don't understand? Express any doubts or concerns that you may have or ask questions for clarification.

   _____

   _____

   _____

   _____

(c) *Getting to know your instructor.* Make a list of questions about your instructor's background, experience, or expectations that you would like to know.

_____

_____

_____

4. Instructor's responses to class questions (10–20 minutes).

In-Class Application

Complete the skill-building activities noted above during class.

Choose one (10–30 minutes):
- Break into *different* groups of three to five members, and discuss your experiences in the activities.
- Informal, whole-class discussion of student experiences.

Wrap-up:
Take a few minutes and write down your answers to the following questions:

- What did I learn from this experience?

_____

_____

_____

_____

- How will I use this knowledge in the future?

_____

_____

_____

_____

As a class, discuss student responses.

Internet Skills: Getting to Know the Internet

Objective:
- To get comfortable doing Internet searches.

Preparation (15–20 minutes):
Visit http://www.nassm.com, review the major hyperlinks, and answer the following questions.

1. What year was the North American Society of Sport Management started?

_____

2. What journal does the North American Society of Sport Management publish?

_____

3. How does the NASSM web site describe sport management?

_____

_____

_____

4. What details are available on the next NASSM conference?

_____

_____

_____

5. Summarize what you find at the following NASSM hyperlinks:

(a) *About NASSM*

_____

_____

_____

(b) *Publications*

_____

_____

_____

_____

_____

(c) *Membership*

_____

_____

_____

_____

_____

6. Review the *About NASSM* hyperlink and determine what associations the following acronyms stand for:

(a) SMAANZ

_____

(b) EASM

_____

(c) NASPE

_____

(d) AAHPERD

_____

Wrap-up:
Take a few minutes and write down your answers to the following questions:

■ What did I learn from this experience?

_____

_____

_____

_____

■ How will I use this knowledge in the future?

_____

_____

_____

_____

As a class, discuss student responses.

2

The Sport Industry Environment: Globalization, Ethics, and Social Responsibility

Learning Outcomes

After studying this chapter, you should be able to:

1. Describe the five components of the internal environment.

2. Explain the two primary principles of total quality management.

3. Explain how factors in the external environment affect the internal business environment.

4. State the differences between domestic, international, and multinational businesses.

5. List the lowest- and highest-risk ways to take a business global.

6. Explain the stakeholders' approach to ethics.

7. Discuss the four levels of social responsibility in business.

8. Explain how downsizing and reengineering differ.

9. Define the following key terms (in order of appearance in the chapter):

- internal environment
- mission
- stakeholders
- systems process
- structure
- quality
- customer value
- total quality management (TQM)
- external environment
- international business
- multinational corporation (MNC)
- global sourcing
- joint venture
- direct investment
- ethics
- stakeholders' approach to ethics
- social responsibility
- downsizing
- reengineering

REVIEWING THEIR GAME PLAN

Ichiro Suzuki and Pat Gillick of the Seattle Mariners

Think of one single figure who personifies the globalization of sports, and **SEATTLE MARINERS'** outfielder Ichiro Suzuki immediately springs to mind. After years of falling short of the World Series, the Seattle Mariners and their fans watched helplessly as their three star players threw in the proverbial towel and made a beeline for the exit. Randy Johnson, Ken Griffey, Jr., Alex Rodriguez—all hailed as some the game's greatest-ever players, and all gone within the space of three short years. Fans and sportswriters alike predicted doom and gloom and, at a minimum, a screeching halt to the young team's ascendancy.

Only someone forgot to mention this to the Mariners' management. No matter, they wouldn't have heeded the dire predictions anyway because they were too busy scanning the environment for solutions. And in November 2000, they found one. His numbers with Orix of the Japanese Pacific League were good (averaged per 162 games)—a batting average of .353, with 36 doubles, 20 home runs, 90 RBI, and 34 steals thrown in for good measure—and all this packaged in a quiet, unassuming (real) team player from Japan named Ichiro Suzuki.

Mariners' management (and Suzuki himself) expected a period of adjustment as he brought his game to America and to the major leagues. But he hit the ground running (and hitting, and stealing), all the while being modest and self-effacing and working tirelessly to better his skills. The Mariners became first and foremost a team of team players, and the City of Seattle, and maybe a whole sport, fell in love with a quiet young man from Japan.

In 2001, Ichiro broke the record for most hits by a rookie (240) and was the first player since Jackie Robinson (1949) to lead the league in hits and steals.[1] He was named AL Rookie of the Year and Most Valuable Player. Ichiro's popularity has redefined the Mariners in surprising and endearing ways. He has been credited with raising the visibility of Japanese-made cars around Seattle, and Safeco Field may be the only ballpark in America where fans enjoy teriyaki, sushi, and sake. The area's "bottom line" has also profited from the influx of Japanese tourists/baseball fans and journalists.[2]

So, what is the secret to the Mariners' success? Two things: (1) the team's internal environment, and (2) its ability to adapt to the external environment. Management recognized their internal weakness—star players leaving—and addressed it creatively. They looked globally. General Manager Pat Gillick (who won the 1992 and 1993 World Series with the Toronto Blue Jays) has built an organization around Ichiro's speedy and slashing style. The millions Gillick spent to buy out Ichiro's Japanese contract and sign him to a multiyear contract are paying off handsomely.

Environmental scanning, a management tool used to search and organize external data, helped Gillick find the turnaround player his team needed. If success can be measured by how much your competition imitates you, the Mariners have started an industrywide trend. In the last year, several MLB (Major League Baseball) teams have signed Japanese baseball players, albeit not with Ichiro's skill and experience. It may have been inevitable that the team would sign Ichiro, since the Japanese-based Nintendo Corporation owns the Mariners, but the point is, they had the vision to do so.

In the 2001 season, the Seattle Mariners won more games than any team in 95 years, and Pat Gillick was named MLB Executive of the Year. Gillick succeeded because he thinks outside the box. He didn't replace superstars with superstars. Instead, he assembled a team of team players whose whole was greater than the sum of their individual strengths.[3] Houston Astros' president Tal Smith (who gave Gillick his start in 1963) said, "What makes

[Gillick] special are two things: First is his extraordinary commitment, dedication, and work ethic. He is as tireless as anyone I've ever seen. The second thing is his great reliance on his staff. He has an ability to treat people in such an extraordinary fashion they all make the same kind of commitment."[4]

For current information on the Seattle Mariners and Ichiro Suzuki, go to http://www.sportingnews.com or http://www.mlb.com.

INTERNET RESOURCES

http://www.nd.edu/~cscc *and* **http://www.ets.uidaho.edu/center_for_ethics** *The University of Notre Dame's Mendelson Center for Sport, Character, and Culture and the University of Idaho's Center for Ethics are two great places to find a wealth of information on ethics and social responsibility in the sporting world. On Notre Dame's site, click the* Resources *link for a list of web sites devoted to the importance of character in sports, including Athletes for a Better World and Citizenship Through Sports Alliance. On the University of Idaho's site, click the* Research Fact Sheet *link for thought-provoking study results concerning student athletes' ethical thought processes and the* Measurement Tool *link for information regarding the Hahm-Beller Values Choice Inventory (HBVCI), which was created to evaluate moral reasoning in sports.*
http://www.coach.ca/member/ethics_e.htm *Here you will find the Coaching Code of Ethics developed by the Canadian Professional Coaches Association. The four main principles include a list of ethical standards that illustrate how the principles apply to coaching activities. Topics covered: respecting team members; coaching responsibly through training and self knowledge; maintaining integrity in relationships; and honoring sport by instilling values.*
http://www.theglobalist.com *Under the* Globalization and . . . *heading, click the* Sports *link to read articles covering the latest topics in sports and its importance to cultures around the world. This site is also a great source for learning about globalization's effect on a wide variety of other issues, including the environment, finance, health, and technology.*

DEVELOPING YOUR SKILLS Top-level managers routinely analyze their company's environment and management practices and those of their competitors. Analyze the company you work for in terms of its internal and external environments. What is its market strategy? What is its style of management? Who are its competitors? What strengths would you like to see your company play to? What weaknesses would you like to improve on?

THE INTERNAL ENVIRONMENT

1 **LEARNING OUTCOME**
Describe the five components of the internal environment.

Profit and nonprofit organizations are created to produce products and services for customers. The organization's **internal environment** includes the factors within its boundaries that affect its performance. They are called internal factors because the organization has control over them, as opposed to external factors, which are outside its control. The five internal environment factors that you will learn about in this section are management, mission, resources, the systems process, and structure. (See Exhibit 2–1.)

internal environment
Factors that affect an organization's performance from within its boundaries.

Exhibit 2–1 The Internal Environment

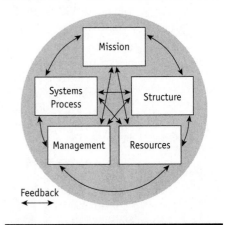

Management

Managers are responsible for their organization's performance. They plan, they organize, they lead, and they control. The leadership style they use and the decisions they make affect the performance of the entire organization. Effective managers imbue their organization's internal environment with a culture of success and constantly scan the external environment for business opportunities. Clearly, the **SEATTLE MARINERS** would not be the hot team they are today if Pat Gillick didn't continually scrutinize both environments. **Which environmental factors are important to a general manager like Pat Gillick?**

Mission

The organization's **mission** is its purpose or reason for being. Developing the mission is the responsibility of top management. Carefully crafted missions identify both present and future products. The term *product* is commonly used to mean both goods and services. The major reason businesses fail is that management doesn't look ahead. The organization produces the wrong product—one with no market or too small a market.[5] Managers with vision change their organization's mission by offering products that are in demand. Missions should clearly state the organization's objectives. The YMCA's mission statement is both clear and straightforward. (See Exhibit 2–2.) Note its objective to satisfy each customer.

Russell Ackoff, consultant and professor emeritus of the Wharton School of Business, stated that missions should include objectives that enable performance to be measured and evaluated. Missions should also state how the organization differs from its competitors—that is, What unique product/service/expertise does our organization offer customers?[6] Missions should be relevant to all stakeholders. **Stakeholders** are people whose interests are affected by organizational behavior. Stakeholders include employees, alumni, fans, shareholders, customers, suppliers, and the government, among others (more about stakeholders later in this chapter).

A mission can also be defined as the *ends* the organization strives to attain. The other internal environmental factors—management, resource, systems process, and structure—are the *means* the organization uses to achieve its ends. (See Exhibit 2–3.) Note that managers develop the mission statement and set objectives, but they are also one of the means to the ends. As a manager, you may not write the mission statement, but you will definitely be responsible for helping to achieve it.

Resources

Organizations need resources to accomplish their mission.[7] As stated in Chapter 1, organizational resources include human, financial, physical, and informational resources. *Human resources*—the organization's workforce—are responsible for achieving the organization's mission and objectives. According to the YMCA's people-service-nonprofit philosophy, when the company puts its people first, it is building a healthy spirit, mind, and body for all.

mission
An organization's purpose or reason for being.

stakeholders
People whose interests are affected by organizational behavior.

TIMEOUT

Note: For each Timeout in this chapter use a different sport organization or several different ones.

State the mission of a sport organization. Does it differ in any way from the missions of other types of organizations?

_____
_____
_____
_____
_____

Exhibit 2–2   The YMCA's Mission Statement

YMCA Mission: To put Christian principles into practice through programs that build healthy spirit, mind and body for all.

ABOUT THE YMCA

Together, nearly 2,500 American YMCAs comprise the nation's largest not-for-profit community service organization and largest provider of child care, working to meet the health and social service needs of 18.3 million men, women and children in 10,000 communities. Ys are for people of all faiths, races, ages, incomes and abilities. No one is turned away for inability to pay. YMCA's strength is in the people they bring together.

Because all communities have different needs, all YMCAs are different. A YMCA in your community may offer child care or teen leadership clubs. A Y in the next town may have swimming lessons or drawing classes. Every Y makes its own decisions on what programs to offer and how to operate.

YMCAs stretch beyond the United States. YMCAs are at work in more than 120 countries around the world, serving more than 30 million people. About 275 U.S. YMCAs maintain relationships with Ys in other countries. So the YMCA really does build strong kids, strong families and strong communities—worldwide.

Source: http://ymca.net.

The Y's *physical resources* include fitness centers, swimming pools, gymnasiums, and inexpensive temporary housing. The Y's *financial resources* are used to purchase and maintain its physical resources and to pay employees. *Informational resources* include a YMCA directory and local YMCA web sites. As a manager, you will use these four resources to achieve your organization's mission.

The Systems Process

systems process
The method used to transform inputs into outputs.

The **systems process** is the method used to transform inputs into outputs. As shown in Exhibit 2–4, the systems process has four components:

1. *Inputs.* Inputs provide the organization with operating necessities. They are the organization's resources (human, financial, physical, and informational). At the YMCA, the primary input is the labor of thousands of employees who provide services to Y members.

2. *Transformation.* Inputs must be transformed into outputs. At the YMCA, employees work (input) to provide services (transformation) such as fitness instruction, after-school sport programs, and database management to members.

3. *Outputs.* Outputs are the different levels of satisfaction experienced by each member. At the Y, the desired output is that members be better off in spirit, mind, and body.

4. *Feedback.* Feedback ensures that the inputs and transformation process produce the desired results (outputs). Y members are asked to complete satisfaction surveys on the services they receive.

Exhibit 2–3   Internal Environment Means and Ends

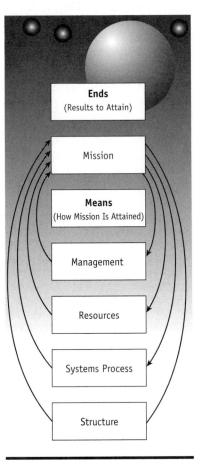

Managers with a systems perspective view their organization as a process, and they focus on how these four components fit together, complement one another, and play to the organization's strengths.

Structure

structure
The way in which an organization groups its resources to accomplish its mission.

As noted in Chapter 1, every organization is a system. As such, it has a structure. An organization's **structure** is the way in which it groups its resources to accomplish its mission. The structure may be organized as departments—finance, marketing, production, personnel, and so on. Each department affects the organization as a whole, and each department affects

---

TIMEOUT

Describe the systems process for an organization you have worked for or a team you have played on.

_____

_____

_____

_____

_____

Exhibit 2–4   The Systems Process

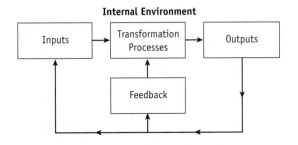

APPLYING THE CONCEPT   *The Internal Environment*

Match each statement with the internal environmental factor it pertains to.

a. management   **d.** systems process

b. mission   **e.** structure

c. resources

_____ 1. We take these chemicals and make them into a liquid, which then goes into these molds. When it's hard, we've got golf balls.

_____ 2. We deliver pizza and buffalo wings to the basketball tournament.

_____ 3. It's the people here who make this team what it is.

_____ 4. As we grew, we added a new department for human resources services.

_____ 5. Management does not trust us. All the major decisions around here are made by top-level managers.

---

every other department. Organizations strive mightily to structure their resources effectively so that they can achieve their main objective—to transform inputs into outstanding outputs.[8] As a manager you will be responsible for some part of the organization's structure—perhaps a department or a team within the department. You will learn more about organizational structure in Chapters 6–8.

A WORD ABOUT QUALITY—THE CORNERSTONE OF SUCCESSFUL SPORT ORGANIZATIONS

2   **LEARNING OUTCOME**
Explain the two primary principles of total quality management.

In today's intensely competitive business environment, quality is a crucial issue for every organization. Quality is an internal factor because organizations can control the quality of their products and services. Proponents of total quality management (TQM) believe that customers (fans in the case of many sport organizations) assess the **quality** of the organization's outputs by comparing what they require (or want) from the product to their actual use of, or experience with, the product or service. Accordingly, **customer value** is the benefit(s) that customers obtain if they buy a product or service. From the viewpoint of TQM, customers aren't buying only the product or service itself. They are also buying the benefit (value) they expect to derive from it. Value therefore motivates us to buy products or services. When the authors bought tickets to a recent Washington Wizards/Boston Celtics game, we did so because we expected to watch a high-quality game, and because star player Michael Jordan would be playing with the Wizards.[9] Effective sport organizations pay close attention to quality and value because they are what attracts—and retains—fans and customers.

Total quality management is a management philosophy that stresses quality within the organization. **Total quality management (TQM)** is the process through which everyone in the organization focuses on the customer in order to continually improve product value. TQM uses a systems perspective because it views quality as the responsibility of *everyone* in the organization—not simply that of a single, self-contained department (*the* Quality Control Department). The two primary principles of TQM are (1) to deliver customer value, and (2) to continually improve the system and its processes.[10] (We will examine quality and TQM in greater detail in Chapter 7.)

quality
Comparing actual use to requirements to determine value.

customer value
The purchasing benefits used by customers to determine whether or not to buy a product.

total quality management (TQM)
The process that involves everyone in the organization focusing on the customer to continually improve product value.

THE EXTERNAL ENVIRONMENT

3 LEARNING OUTCOME
Explain how factors in the external environment affect the internal business environment.

external environment
The factors that affect an organization's performance from outside its boundaries.

The organization's **external environment** includes factors outside its boundaries that affect its performance. Although managers can control the organization's internal environment, their influence over what happens outside the organization is limited. The nine factors in the external environment are the customers, the competition, suppliers, the workforce, shareholders, society, technology, the economy, and governments.

The Customers

As you have no doubt discerned, customers have a major effect on the performance of organizations. After all, they are the ones who purchase its products and services. Without customers, organizations cannot exist. This goes without saying, but we say it anyway to stress how important this concept is today. Effective managers structure their organizations so they can offer products that customers value. Continually improving a product's value to customers is often the difference between success and failure in business. Customer value changes over time, and if sport products and teams don't change with the times, companies lose customers and fans to the competition.

Here's an example from outside the sport industry that capitalized on a key aspect of professional sports—the star athlete. When changing tastes dented Campbell's canned-soup sales, Campbell's changed its tune.[11] For the past five years, the company has aired a very successful ad campaign using star athletes—and their mothers. NHL player and owner of the Pittsburgh Penguins Mario Lemieux recently joined NFL quarterbacks Kurt Warner and Donovan McNabb in happily slurping up Campbell's Chunky brand soups to the amusement of fans everywhere and to the delight of the people who pay attention to Campbell's market share.[12]

The Competition

TIMEOUT
Give an example of how one sport firm's competitors have affected the firm's performance.

_____

_____

_____

_____

_____

Organizations must compete with their competitors for customers. Competitors' strategic moves can therefore affect the performance of the organization.[13] The YMCA, for example, competes with many organizations—fitness centers, community centers, daycare centers, and health clubs. The race to satisfy mind, body, and spirit through exercise is much more competitive today than when the YMCA was one of the few organizations in the industry.

Another important aspect of the competition is pricing. When a competitor lowers prices, firms often have to match them to keep customers. For example, to provide services that Y members expect (or can get elsewhere), the YMCA must continually update its fitness machines using such companies such as Cybex and Precor. This adds significantly to expenses, yet membership fees also need to stay competitive. Members remain loyal only as long as they perceive they receive good value for their money. Effective managers derive business strategies from their mission statements in order to gain key advantages over the competition.[14]

Suppliers

The resources of organizations often come from outside the firm. Organizations buy land, buildings, machines, equipment, natural resources, and component parts from suppliers. Reebok recently won out over Nike to be sole supplier of athletic uniforms for all NFL and NBA teams. This was a major coup, and the leagues will expect Reebok to be a reliable, high-quality supplier.[15] Effective managers recognize that suppliers are a key factor in their success and develop close working relationships with them. (As you will find out in Chapter 7, this is an important cornerstone of TQM.)

The Workforce

An organization's employees have a direct impact on its performance. Management recruits its workforce from the available labor pool, which of course is outside its boundaries and is therefore an external factor. How capable employees are is determined partially by the quality of the available labor pool (how many Ichiro Suzukis are there?), and partially by internal factors (how can the **MARINERS'** physical therapists help Ichiro prevent injuries?). **How are the skills needed by Seattle Mariners' employees similar to those needed by YMCA employees, and how are they different?**

Unions are a key source of employees for many organizations. They are also considered an external factor because they become a third party when they negotiate with organizations for wages and benefit packages. Mariners' players are members of the Major League Players Association, whereas YMCA employees don't belong to a major union. Unions have the power to strike, and strikes mean lost revenues, lost wages, and lost goodwill. The 1994 baseball strike ended the baseball season without the World Series being played.[16] Eight years later, labor issues remained a thorny issue for pro sports as rumblings of another baseball strike grew louder but were settled at the last minute.

Shareholders

Shareholders are the owners of corporations because they have purchased a "share" (stock) in the corporation. They can have a significant influence on management, but it is not often through their individual votes. Although they do vote for the corporation's board of directors, shareholders must hold vast quantities of stock to influence the choice of directors. Their most significant influence is in whether they choose to hold or sell their stock. When *many* shareholders want to sell stock in a company, that stock is likely to fall in price, and this elicits keen interest from the board of directors, who have the power to hire and fire top management. The board can then respond by calling the CEO (Chief Executive Officer) and CFO (Chief Financial Officer) on the carpet.

The Disney Corporation owns both the Anaheim Mighty Ducks (NHL) and the Anaheim Angels (MLB). Consequently, the shareholders of Disney receive reports on the rising and falling fortunes of those teams. Although Disney shareholders certainly don't run the teams on a daily basis, they will most assuredly take an interest if the teams are not successful or profitable. Unfortunately, because of September 11, Disney finds itself in difficult financial straits as tourists make significantly fewer visits to destinations such as Disney World. However, Disney denies it is selling its MLB team, the Anaheim Angels, to concentrate on its core businesses.[17]

Society

Society also exerts pressure on organizations.[18] Individuals and groups lobby businesses for change, and they get it. People who live near factories don't want them to pollute the environment and have forced tougher pollution requirements. Society expects business to be socially responsible and ethical, and in that context has become increasingly concerned with player salaries. The Texas Rangers will pay shortstop Alex Rodriguez approximately $22 million a year for the next ten years.[19] The $22 million questions may well be, Will fans continue to pay higher and higher ticket prices to foot the bill for player salaries that have shot into the stratosphere? Will families be priced out of the all-American pastime? Are athletes proper role models for our children? Why do people long for the days of baseball legends like Ted Williams, and why have young stars, who make more in one season than the legends made in their whole careers, not captured the hearts of fans, who complain that they are remote and greedy? We will return to ethics and social responsibility later in this chapter.

Technology

The rate of technological change will continue to increase. Few organizations operate today as they did even a decade ago. Products not envisioned a few years ago are now fixtures in

TIMEOUT

Give an example of how technology has affected several different sport organizations.

_____

_____

_____

_____

_____

our lives. The computer has changed the way sport organizations conduct and transact business. Today computers are a major part of every firm's systems process.

The Internet has revolutionized how we do business. Sports by their very nature are interactive, and fans (by their very nature) want to be part of the action. The web feeds that desire with message boards and fantasy leagues.[20] The Internet is also creating global opportunities for many organizations. Companies that have been slow to embrace it find themselves losing business to competitors. New technology creates new opportunities for some companies and new threats for others.

RaceLineDirect.com is an Internet-based company that sells NASCAR-related items. The owners of the site used the Internet to grow their business beyond what their normal catalog sales would bring in. Recently, the untimely death of Dale Earnhardt—the "Terminator"—rapidly expanded demand for NASCAR items. RaceLine's Internet operations enabled them to quickly respond to the uptick in sales.[21] To keep your management career on track, keep up with the latest technology in your field, and be the first to volunteer to learn new things.

The Economy

Organizations have no control over economic growth, inflation, interest rates, or foreign exchange rates, yet these factors have a direct impact on performance. In general, as measured by gross domestic product (GDP), businesses do better when the economy is growing than during times of decreased GDP, or recession. When business activity is slow, fewer fans attend games live at the stadium.

During periods of inflation, businesses experience increased costs, which cannot always be passed along to consumers. This results in decreased profits. When interest rates are high, it costs more to borrow money, which can affect profits. Foreign exchange rates affect businesses both at home and abroad. When the dollar is weak, foreign goods are more expensive in the United States, and vice versa. A weak dollar creates business opportunities for the United States because our goods and services sell for less. An understanding of economics, and more importantly global economics, can help you to advance to top-level management.

The 1990s were particularly good times for the sport industry, exceeding even the highly optimistic predictions made at the beginning of the decade. However, looking forward ten years, Mahony and Howard predict a general decline in the U.S. economy, which will almost certainly impact the sport industry. Because of the problems facing sports—including increased competition, heavy debt, and poor relations with consumers—sport industry professionals will need creative strategies to continue to thrive.[22]

Governments

Foreign, federal, state, and local governments all set laws and regulations that businesses must obey. These laws remain pretty much intact through generations of political turnover, even though their interpretations, guidelines, and enforcement depend heavily on the government officials of the time. The governmental environment is sometimes referred to as the political and legal environment.

State and local governments both create business opportunities and take them away. The difference between the door opening to opportunity and the door closing on it is often determined by the support of local government. Let's say fans are calling for a new stadium to be built in your city. Will your mayor support a new minor league baseball team? Does the city council want to find the requisite financing? Will the state government float bonds to fund the stadium? Will people other than fans vote for it? **SAFECO FIELD** in Seattle offers a good example of the role of local politics in building a new ballpark. The first attempt to build a park was on September 19, 1995. This proposal hoped to gain public financing by increasing the sales tax by .01 percent in King County to pay for construction. The proposal was narrowly defeated by voters. However, on October 14, 1995, a special session of the state legislature authorized a different funding package that included a credit against the state sales tax, sale of special stadium license plates, lottery funds, food and beverage tax, and ballpark admissions tax. This package was approved and also established the Washington State Major League Baseball Public Facilities District to build and own the ballpark.[23]

APPLYING THE CONCEPT   *The External Environment*

Identify each statement by its external environmental factor.

a. customers   **d.** workforce   **g.** technology

b. competition   **e.** shareholders   **h.** governments

c. suppliers   **f.** society   **i.** economy

_____   6. Some critics blame the media for the escalating salaries of major league baseball players.

_____   7. At one time Nike was the coolest sneaker company, but then others have come along and taken some of its market share.

_____   8. I applied for a loan to start my own dance company, but I might not get it because money is tight these days, and the bank may not provide a loan.

_____   9. Team owners have threatened to fire the general manager if the team doesn't improve this year.

_____   10. Management was going to sell our team to Disney, but the feds said that would be in violation of antitrust laws.

Chaos in the External Environment and Interactive Management

In many industries the external environment changes at an incredibly fast pace and is often chaotic. *Chaos theory* (as used in business) refers to the need for managers to adapt quickly to a constantly changing environment. Today's managers must be able to thrive on chaos.[24] And they should also be interactive in their management style.

According to Russell Ackoff, unlike *reactive* managers (who make changes only when forced to by external factors) and *responsive* managers (who prepare for change that they predict will come about), *interactive* managers *design* a desirable future and then invent ways of bringing it about.[25] They believe they can create a significant part of their future and thereby control how it will affect their organization. They try to prevent—not merely prepare for—threats and to create—not merely exploit—opportunities. Interactive managers thus make things happen for their own benefit and for that of their stakeholders.

To those who dismiss interactive management as a fancy consultant's pipe dream, look again. Few people would have predicted the **MARINERS'** meteoric rise to the top in the gloom-and-doom times that followed the loss of their best three players. The Mariners, however, dreamed of an even better team and set about making their dream a reality—now some are calling them the best team in the history of baseball. Against the odds they forged their own future, and may in the process have started the redefining of modern baseball. Team cohesiveness—a team of team players—has proven more effective than relying on a few star players. **It's your turn to think outside the box. Dream up a future you think you can make come true, and then draw up a plan that will help you get there.**

CONDUCTING SPORT BUSINESS IN A GLOBAL ENVIRONMENT

As businesses grow, the complexity of their internal and external environments increases. One major factor in this increased complexity is the globalization of markets. (For a review of the organizational environment, see Exhibit 2–5.) So you're thinking, "Well, this sure doesn't affect the YMCA!" Think again. YMCAs do business worldwide. This means finding out about (not a small task by itself) and then complying with the rules and regulations of

Exhibit 2–5   The Business Environment

Global
Multiple Sets of Factors for Various Countries

External
Customers

Internal

Competition

Suppliers

Mission

Economy

Systems
Process

Structure

Labor
Force

Management

Resources

Governments

Shareholders

Technology

Society

Feedback

countries with vastly different economies, workforces, and cultures. An immense undertaking even for a business that's been around as long as the Y.

4 LEARNING OUTCOME
State the differences between domestic, international, and multinational businesses.

Competing in the global environment is necessary for any company's survival.[26] Even most small local businesses do, or will, compete with global companies at home. Not surprisingly then, managers, particularly in large companies, are embracing global management systems. Rapidly transforming economies, instant communication, interconnected business alliances, close relationships with suppliers, and rapidly changing technology characterize the global environment.[27] The question is no longer, Should our business go global? It's, How do we go global and how fast?[28]

The primary reason for conducting business globally is to increase sales and profits. If you start a domestic business (business conducted in only one country) in the United States, your potential customer base is about 268 million people. If you expand to transact business (buy and sell some inputs and outputs) in Canada and Mexico—North American Free Trade Agreement (NAFTA) countries—your potential customer base increases to around 375 million. At this point, you would have an international business. An **international business** is primarily based in one country but transacts business in other countries. If you expand to the European Union (EU) by setting up operations in one of those 15 countries and transact business throughout the EU, you have 350 million more potential customers, for a total of around 725 million. Set up shop in China and India and your market climbs to around 3 billion people.[29]

international business
A business primarily based in one country that transacts business in other countries.

China is a great example for the sport industry in particular. The Chinese economy, politics, culture, and education system have greatly changed since China opened its doors to the global economy in 1978. Its attitudes about sports have also changed. Professional sports and commercial sports, which had previously been prohibited, have since become a key part of the lives of the Chinese people, who have embraced "fandom" with great enthusiasm. Industry watchers believe that the Chinese sport industry is making global development a primary objective. It is very important that businesses that are currently investing or planning to invest in the Chinese sports market understand the changes in its sport system.[30]

At the point when your firm has significant operations (an established place of conducting business at home and in at least one other country and sales outside your home country of 25 percent or more), you can consider yourself a multinational or global business.[31] A **multinational corporation (MNC)** has significant operations in more than one country. Larger MNCs with established places of conducting business in many countries include Nike, Reebok, and Adidas. You may never start your own global business, but you may become an international manager. An international manager manages across a number of countries and cultures simultaneously.

multinational corporation (MNC)
A business with significant operations in more than one country.

5 LEARNING OUTCOME
List the lowest- and highest-risk ways to take a business global.

Taking a Sport Business Global

Some would argue that the globalization of the sport industry should be termed the "Americanization of sports." Why? Because as industries go global, they typically follow the dominant market player, and for the time being in sports that is America. Indeed, U.S. corporate sports currently appear to have a dominant position. The NFL owns American football teams that play in Europe, regular-season NBA games are played in Japan, and the NHL draws a large percentage of its players from Europe.[32]

Even though America is a leader in the sport industry, it is important to note that multinational corporations and transnational organizations (for example, Federation Internationale de Football Association, FIFA, and the International Olympic Committee, IOC) are also playing important roles in the growth of sports worldwide. Because local and regional cultural patterns greatly affect the popularity of certain sports, local factors (culture, modes of organization, economics, and politics) need to be fully understood if a sport is to expand successfully into a new country. For example, every corporation that endeavors to build another golf course in Japan faces environmental activists and advocates for the poor who oppose the diverting of waters from rice paddies to golf courses or the increased use of grass fertilizers.[33] Organizations should make sure they are culturally aware to avoid faux pas like the time Nike used a design on the soles of its shoes that meant *Allah* in Arabic, which caused a recall and not a little embarrassment.

Domestic sport businesses go global six ways—by global sourcing, by importing and exporting, by licensing, by contracting, in joint ventures, and through direct investment. In Exhibit 2–6 these six approaches are mapped by cost/risk and by whether they tend to be the strategy of international businesses or that of multinational corporations.

GLOBAL SOURCING. **Global sourcing** (also called outsourcing) is the use of worldwide resources for inputs and transformation.[34] The difference between domestic managers and global managers is where they look for the best deal on inputs and where they think inputs can be most advantageously transformed into outputs. A major barrier to passing NAFTA was the potential loss of jobs to Mexican maquiladoras. (*Maquiladoras* are light-industrial assembly plants built in Mexico, near the U.S. border, to take advantage of low-cost labor.) Both international corporations and MNCs use global sourcing.[35] **PAT GILLICK** used global sources to find Ichiro Suzuki. **What sorts of inputs and transformations do you think are good candidates for global sourcing?**

global sourcing
The use of worldwide resources for inputs and transformation.

IMPORTING AND EXPORTING. With importing, domestic firms buy products from foreign firms and sell them at home. U.S. retailers must thus import Adidas sneakers (Adidas is based in Germany) in order to sell them. With exporting, domestic firms sell their products to

Exhibit 2-6   Taking Your Business Global

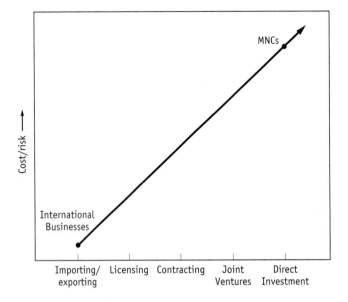

Note: Global sourcing can be used alone (at low cost/risk), but is commonly used with the other approaches.

foreign buyers. Companies like Spalding export their products to almost every country in the world.

LICENSING. Under a *licensing* agreement, one company allows another to use its intellectual assets, such as brand name, trademarks, technology, patents, or copyrights. For a fee, Walt Disney allows companies around the world to make all kinds of products using the ESPN brand.

CONTRACTING. With *contract manufacturing,* a company has a foreign firm manufacture the goods but it retains the marketing process. Nike uses this approach in Vietnam. Contract manufacturers make products with Nike's name on them, and Nike sells them in retail stores.

joint venture
Created when firms share ownership (partnership) of a new enterprise.

JOINT VENTURE. A **joint venture** is created when firms share ownership (partnership) of a new enterprise. In February 2001, Manchester United (a soccer team based in the United Kingdom) and the New York Yankees announced a partnership that makes them the biggest sport marketing force in the world. With the partnership, the two clubs will share marketing and sponsorship, and also sport training knowledge. The company that owns the Yankees, YankeeNets, also controls the NBA's New Jersey Nets and the NHL's New Jersey Devils. YankeeNets hopes to use United's network in Europe and the Far East, and United will have direct access to the American market.[36]

direct investment
Occurs when a company builds or purchases operating facilities (subsidiaries) in a foreign country.

DIRECT INVESTMENT. **Direct investment** occurs when a company builds or purchases operating facilities (subsidiaries) in a foreign country. In 1991, the NFL developed the NFL Europe subsidiary. The league is starting to produce players, such as quarterback Jon Kitna, for the NFL. Joe Bailey, the World League's Chief Operating Officer, has noted "Decisions which were made during that time period will have a significant impact on the future of the league. We were making history, breaking new ground in the globalization of American football."[37]

Risks in Global Sport Management

Even as the number of globally watched sporting events grew by leaps and bounds in the 1990s, the threat of injury to athletes at international competitions was never a major concern. Although terrorism tragically disrupted the 1972 Olympic Games in Munich, other sports never seriously thought the shadow of terrorism would come to haunt them. However, September 11 has sharply and forever changed this thinking. Football in the

United States was postponed for a weekend. The Ryder Cup of Golf (which attracts the top professional golfers from America and Europe) was postponed for a year. The Australian Rugby Union encouraged players to consider security concerns but make their own decisions about whether they participate in the Wallaby Tour of Europe.[38] The aftereffects of September 11 are felt at every sporting event. All arenas and stadiums have an increased awareness of security. Fans have been willing to accept these increased security measures because they know they are for their own protection.

ETHICS IN SPORT MANAGEMENT

Unfortunately, there is no shortage of unethical behavior in sports. Some of the behavior can be attributed to the players themselves and a lack of judgment. For instance, a charge against NBA player Allen Iverson of terrorist threats against his wife is pending at the time of writing. Even more disturbing is the pending trial of former NBA star Jayson Williams, who is charged with killing a man at his mansion in the New Jersey area. Do athletes such as Iverson and Williams believe they are above the law because they are celebrities and are wealthy, and therefore deserve special treatment? In the case of Iverson, the more severe charges were thrown out of court. The list of athletes who have had trouble with the law is lengthy. It is not important to list all the names and cases. However, athletes need to be made to realize that the youth of America look up to them as role models.

On the other hand, sometimes sport managers might be to blame for unethical behavior. On July 31, 2001, Kory Stringer of the NFL's Minnesota Vikings collapsed of heatstroke during training camp and died 15 hours later.[39] A legal suit filed by his wife against the Vikings is pending. Is the Vikings management to blame? Were the conditioning drills too difficult considering the hot weather? Should the NFL (and all sport teams) have a system in place for training in extremely hot weather? These questions are still being investigated.

One of the touchier ethical issues in sports involves the use of steroids. NFL players are regularly tested for the use of steroids. However, MLB does not test for the use of steroids because of a lack of agreement between the owners and the players association. Recently, former players Ken Caminitti and Jose Canseco have been quoted as saying that many current ballplayers use steroids to enhance performance. Should management make sure steroids are banned from baseball in the next collective bargaining agreement? Or is it the responsibility of individual players not to use steroids (which can cause permanent damage)?

Yes, Ethical Behavior Does Pay

As stated, recent years have seen an increased awareness of ethics, or the lack of it, in the sport industry. Not many days go by without the media reporting on some scandal involving unethical behavior. **Ethics** are the standards of right and wrong that influence behavior. What, you say? Don't we have laws and regulations to govern business behavior? Yes, we do, but ethics go beyond legal requirements. Unfortunately, it is not always easy to distinguish between ethical and unethical behavior. A gift in one country is a bribe in another. Coaches and athletes who are faced with not winning because they followed the rules and with winning because they didn't follow the rules are frequently willing to pay the (often very small) cost. This section makes the case that ethical behavior does pay and presents simple guidelines that will help you make ethical decisions and guide the behavior of others.

ethics
Standards of right and wrong that influence behavior.

Simple Guidelines to Ethical Behavior

Every day in your personal and professional life you face decisions in which you can make ethical or unethical choices. You make your choices based on your past learning experiences with parents, teachers, friends, coaches, managers, and coworkers. Your life history shapes your conscience, which helps you choose right and wrong in a given situation. Following are some guidelines that can help you make the right decisions.

THE FOUR-WAY TEST. Rotary International developed the four-way test to frame our thinking and business actions in an ethical manner. So, when you are faced with an ethical dilemma, ask yourself the following: (1) Is it the truth? (2) Is it fair to all concerned? (3) Will it build goodwill and better friendship? (4) Will it be beneficial to all concerned? If you can answer yes to these questions, you are probably making an ethical choice.

For example, a former coach of the women's basketball team at Howard University was found to be in violation of rules governing recruitment inducements. The coach had improperly paid for an airline ticket for a prospective student-athlete to visit the university, even though the coach knew that the prospect did not have appropriate test scores and transcripts on file, which were required before a visit could occur. The coach then approached the players on her team, requesting that they provide false information about the visit.[40] Did this coach pass the Rotary International test? Did she tell the truth? Was her behavior fair to all concerned? Did it build more goodwill and better friendships? Was it beneficial to all concerned? The NCAA ruled that the coach did not pass this test. It believed the coach was trying to hide the truth. Her own team would no longer be able to trust her as a coach. The penalty to the university for this infraction was to limit the coach's athletic responsibilities.

6 LEARNING OUTCOME
Explain the stakeholders' approach to ethics.

stakeholders' approach to ethics
Creating a win-win situation for all stakeholders so that everyone benefits from the decision.

STAKEHOLDERS' APPROACH TO ETHICS. Under the **stakeholders' approach to ethics**, when making decisions, you try to create a win-win situation for all relevant stakeholders so that everyone benefits from the decision. (Of course, this is not always possible—we'll deal with that in a moment.) The higher up in management you go, the more stakeholders you have to deal with. So, in muddy situations, ask yourself one simple question: Am I proud to tell my stakeholders of my decision?

If you are proud, then your decision is probably ethical. If you are not proud or you keep rationalizing your decision, it may not be ethical. If you are still unsure whether a decision you are considering is ethical, talk to your boss, higher-level managers, ethics committee members, or other people whose ethics you trust. A reluctance to ask others for advice may be a signal that your choice is unethical.

Unfortunately, sometimes decisions must be made that do not benefit all stakeholders— layoffs for one. Yet even layoffs can—and should—be done ethically. Companies can, for example, offer severance pay and outplacement services to help the employees get jobs with other organizations. **What stakeholders did the MARINERS disappoint when they lost their three big stars? What stakeholders did they satisfy when they successfully rebuilt their team?**

Managing Ethics

Simply put, an organization's ethics are the collective behavior of its employees. If each employee acts ethically, the actions of the organization will be ethical too. The starting place for ethics, therefore, is *you*. Are you an ethical person? It's an important question, and one that you should devote some thought to because managers develop their organization's guidelines for ethical behavior, set the example, and enforce the rules they want to play by. The Self Assessment exercise will help you answer this question.

CODES OF ETHICS. Codes of ethics (also called codes of conduct) underscore the importance of conducting business in an ethical manner and provide guidelines for ethical behavior.[41] Most large businesses and sport organizations have written codes of ethics. Exhibit 2–7 presents the code of conduct for the National Association of Sports Officials (NASO).

THE SUPPORT OF TOP MANAGEMENT. It is the responsibility of management from the top down to develop codes of ethics, to ensure that employees are trained and instructed on what is and is not considered ethical behavior, and to enforce the company's code of ethics.[42] However, their primary responsibility is to lead by example. Employees look to managers, especially top managers, to set the standard. Managers who set the bar high help ensure that they will be leading ethical employees.

ENFORCING ETHICAL BEHAVIOR. If employees are rewarded for unethical behavior, they will continue to pursue questionable business practices. To solve this ongoing problem, many organizations create ethics committees. Such committees act as judge and jury to determine whether unethical behavior has in fact occurred and what the punishment should be for

TIMEOUT
Examine a recent scandal in the sport industry, preferably a local one, and identify which decisions led to unethical behavior, and why.

_____

_____

_____

_____

_____

_____

SELF ASSESSMENT
The Ethics of Whistle-Blowing

Objective:

To practice thinking ethically.

Preparation:

Respond to the same set of statements twice. In your first responses, focus on your own behavior and the frequency with which you use it. In the first column, place the number 1–5 that represents how often you did, do, or would do the behavior if you had the chance. These numbers will allow you to determine your level of ethics. Be honest—sharing ethics scores is *not* part of this exercise.

In your second responses, focus on current or past coworkers. Place an "O" on the line after the number if you observed someone doing this behavior. Also place a "W" on it if you blew the whistle on this behavior within the organization or externally.

Column 1: Frequently .... Never

             1   2   3   4   5

Column 2: O (observed)   W (reported)

COLLEGE

_____ 1. _____ Cheating on homework assignments.

_____ 2. _____ Turning in papers completed by someone else, as your own work.

_____ 3. _____ Cheating on exams.

TEAM

_____ 4. _____ Coming to practice late.

_____ 5. _____ Leaving practices early.

_____ 6. _____ Taking longer breaks than allowed.

_____ 7. _____ Calling in sick to skip practice, when not sick.

_____ 8. _____ Socializing or goofing off during practice rather than working diligently.

_____ 9. _____ Socializing or goofing off during games.

_____ 10. _____ Using the team phone to make personal calls.

_____ 11. _____ Using the team copier for personal use.

_____ 12. _____ Mailing personal things through the team mail.

_____ 13. _____ Taking home team supplies and keeping them.

_____ 14. _____ Taking home team equipment without permission for personal use and returning it.

_____ 15. _____ Giving team merchandise to friends or allowing them to take them without saying anything.

_____ 16. _____ Falsifying reimbursement paperwork for meals and travel or other expenses.

_____ 17. _____ Drinking alcohol before games.

_____ 18. _____ Taking spouse/friends out to eat and charging it to the team expense account.

_____ 19. _____ Taking a spouse/friend on business trips and charging the expense to the team.

_____ 20. _____ Taking illegal drugs before games.

To determine your ethics score, add up your numbers. Your total will be between 20 and 100. Place your score here _____ and on the continuum below that represents your score.

Unethical   Ethical

20—30—40—50—60—70—80—90—100

DISCUSSION QUESTIONS

1. For the college items 1–3, who is harmed by and who benefits from these unethical behaviors?

_____

_____

2. For team items 4–20, select the three (circle their numbers) you consider the most severe unethical behaviors. Who is harmed by and who benefits from these unethical behaviors?

_____

_____

3. If you observed unethical behavior but didn't report it, why did you not do so? If you did blow the whistle, why did you do so? What was the result?

_____

_____

_____

4. As a manager it is your responsibility to hold your team to high standards of behavior. If you know employees are behaving unethically, will you take action to enforce compliance with your organization's code of ethics?

(continued)

SELF ASSESSMENT (*continued*)

IN-CLASS APPLICATION

Complete the Self Assessment on the previous page. Then take a class tally, by item, of how many students personally observed behaviors 1–20 in coworkers or team members, and also of how many students reported each behavior.

Choose one:

- Break into groups of three to five, share your answers to the above questions, and try to come to a consensus. Select a spokesperson and present your findings to the class.

- Whole-class discussion of student responses to the four ethics questions.

Wrap-up:

Take a few minutes and write down your answers to the following questions:

- What did I learn from this exercise?

  _____

  _____

  _____

- How will I use this knowledge in the future?

  _____

  _____

  _____

As a class, share your responses.

---

violating company policy. A recent trend is the establishment of ethics offices, in which a director or vice president reports directly to the CEO, establishes ethics policies, listens to employees' complaints, conducts training, and investigates abuses such as sexual harassment. For example, one of the corrective actions that can be taken when a university is in violation of an NCAA rule is to add an assistant director position in the compliance office to increase the understanding of NCAA rules on campus.

As a means of enforcing ethical behavior, employees should be encouraged to "blow the whistle" on questionable behavior.[43] *Whistle-blowing* occurs when employees expose what they believe to be unethical behavior by fellow employees. Historically, this has been a dangerous and dicey action to take. Whistle-blowers have often ended up losing their jobs.

Exhibit 2–7   NASO's Code of Conduct for Sports Officials

1. **Officials shall** bear a great responsibility for engendering public confidence in sports.

2. **Officials shall** be free of obligation to any interest other than the impartial and fair judging of sports competitions.

3. **Officials shall** hold and maintain the basic tenets of officiating, which include history, integrity, neutrality, respect, sensitivity, professionalism, discretion, and tactfulness.

4. **Officials shall** master both rules of the game and mechanics necessary to enforce the rules, and shall exercise authority in an impartial, firm, and controlled manner.

5. **Officials shall** uphold the honor and dignity of the profession in all interactions with student-athletes, coaches, school administrators, colleagues, and the public.

6. **Officials shall** display and execute superior communication skills, both verbal and non-verbal.

7. **Officials shall** recognize that anything that may lead to a conflict of interest, either real or apparent, must be avoided. Gifts, favors, special treatment, privileges, employment or a personal relationship with a school or team that can compromise the perceived impartiality of officiating must be avoided.

8. **Officials shall** prepare themselves both physically and mentally, shall dress neatly and appropriately, and shall comport themselves in a manner consistent with the high standards of the profession.

9. **Officials shall** not be party to actions designed to unfairly limit or restrain access to officiating, officiating assignments or to association membership. This includes selection for positions of leadership based upon economic factors, race, creed, color, age, sex, physical handicap, country or national origin.

10. **Officials shall** be punctual and professional in the fulfillment of all contractual obligations.

11. **Officials shall** work with each other and their governing bodies in a constructive and cooperative manner.

12. **Officials shall** resist every temptation and outside pressure to use one's position as an official to benefit oneself.

13. **Officials shall** never participate in any form of illegal gambling on sports contests, may never gamble on any sporting event in which they have either a direct or indirect involvement, and may never gamble on events involving high school athletics.

14. **Officials shall** not make false or misleading statements regarding their qualifications, rating, credentials, experience, training, or competence.

15. **Officials shall** accept responsibility for all actions taken.

Source: © National Association of Sports Officials. Reprinted with permission.

APPLYING THE CONCEPT *Stakeholders*

Identify each statement by its stakeholder.

a. employees   **c.** society   **e.** suppliers

b. customers   **d.** competitors   **f.** government

_____ 11. We're going to fight this—we do NOT want a baseball stadium in downtown!

_____ 12. I bought an ice-level seat for the hockey game. The glass shattered in my face when a player was checked into the boards, causing me injury.

_____ 13. The town board is very political, so you have to play games if you want to get a liquor license for home games.

_____ 14. I'm sorry to hear your retail sales are down at your sporting goods stores, because that means we'll have to cut back production on team T-shirts.

_____ 15. I bid on the job, but PIP's got the contract to print the programs for home games.

However, companies are coming round (albeit reluctantly) to the idea that listening to whistle-blowers is in their best interest. How do you feel about reporting unethical behavior to your managers? What if *they* are the ones engaging in the behavior—would you go outside the organization to report them? It's not easy to say, is it? Especially without a specific situation, but also because we have a deeply embedded cultural reluctance to "tattle." It would behoove you to give this some thought, however, because you may someday be faced with just such a dilemma.

SOCIAL RESPONSIBILITY

Ethics and social responsibility are two peas from the same pod. **Social responsibility** is the conscious effort to operate in a manner that creates a win-win situation for all stakeholders. Ethical behavior is often socially responsible and vice versa.

social responsibility
The conscious effort to operate in a manner that creates a win-win situation for all stakeholders.

Being a Good Corporate Citizen

Socially responsible companies step up to society's "plate" and see in what ways they can marshal resources and make a difference. For *customers and fans,* such companies endeavor to provide safe products and services with customer value. For *society,* responsible companies work to improve the quality of life—this can be as varied as working with kids in the inner-city ghetto near a ballpark or improving working conditions for factory workers in an Indonesian athletic shoe factory. Ethical companies compete fairly with *competitors.* They use *technology* such as team web sites to develop new ways to increase customer value and the quality of life. They work with *suppliers* such as food vendors in a cooperative manner. Ethical companies abide by the laws and regulations of *government.* Socially responsible companies strive to provide equal-employment opportunities for the *workforce.* These companies remain financially responsible with their eye on the *economy* in good times and bad, and they provide *shareholders* with reasonable profits. Socially responsible companies go to great lengths to provide *employees* with safe working conditions with adequate pay and benefits.[44]

Does It Pay to Be Socially Responsible?

Although research does not show a clear link between social responsibility and the bottom line, many companies would answer with a resounding yes! The value of the goodwill engendered by being a good corporate citizen is difficult to assign numbers to in the financial statements, but company stakeholders benefit, and that is a win-win situation for the company. Take, for example, the Boston Red Sox, where top-level managers and star players work closely with the Dana Farber Cancer Institute to help children.[45] The **SEATTLE MARINERS'** wives produce a cookbook featuring favorite recipes of the players and coaches on the team. The cookbook serves as a fundraiser for youth-oriented programs and cancer research in the Puget Sound area. **Can you name all the stakeholders that benefit from this partnership?**

Levels of Corporate Social Responsibility

7 LEARNING OUTCOME
Discuss the four levels of social responsibility in business.

Capitalism as we know and understand it today owes much to economist Adam Smith's ideas. Smith theorized that in the long run public interests are served by individuals and businesses that pursue their own self-interest, and that government should play a limited role. Milton Friedman, economist and Nobel laureate, agrees with Smith; when a business makes a profit, it *is* being socially responsible. Social responsibility is about serving the public interest. Friedman also postulates that a corporation has no responsibility to society beyond that of obeying the law and maximizing profits for shareholders.[46] Other economists believe that because corporations are part of the greater society and often represent immense concentrations of wealth and power, they too have a responsibility to work for the greater good by shouldering some of the burden. Most views fall between these two extremes. In Exhibit 2–8 the four levels of social responsibility are shown in the continuum from lowest level to highest one.

SOCIAL OBSTRUCTION. At this level, managers deliberately perform, or request employees to perform, unethical or illegal business practices. For example, on July 2, 2002, the University of Minnesota was found guilty of violations in their women's basketball program. The violations, which occurred primarily in 1998 and 1999, involved giving extra benefits, unethical recruiting and conduct, and lack of institutional control. Worse, these violations followed infractions involving the men's basketball program, which means the University of Minnesota will be on probation until 2006.[47]

SOCIAL OBLIGATION. At this level managers meet only the minimum legal requirements. Compliance is an approach in which firms rely on easy solutions and resist voluntarily initiating socially responsible programs.

SOCIAL REACTION. Here, managers respond to appropriate societal requests. The most common type of social reaction takes place when civic groups ask companies for donations for the arts, college scholarships, or anti-drug programs; sponsorship of sports teams; or the use of company facilities for meetings or sport team use.

SOCIAL INVOLVEMENT. At this level, managers voluntarily initiate socially responsible acts. The NFL is an active participant with the United Way, for example, and has for the past few decades aired many commercials showing players working with children at United Way–supported agencies.[48] In reality, it would be very difficult to find any professional team that is not involved in helping with some worthwhile cause.

Coaches and physical education teachers hold a special responsibility when it comes to "walking the talk of good sportsmanship." Paul "Bear" Bryant, former football coach at the University of Alabama, once stated, "We have the opportunity to teach intangible lessons to our players that will be priceless to them in future years. We are in a position to teach these young [people] intrinsic values that cannot be learned at home, school, or any place outside of the athletic field."[49]

SOCIAL AUDIT. A *social audit* measures corporate citizenship. Businesses often set social objectives and then measure whether they have met their objectives. Many corporations include a social audit in their annual reports. Note that although certain organizations maintain their social responsibilities at a given, consistent level, others score at different levels for different issues.

TIMEOUT
Select a sport organization and identify its level of social responsibility for a current issue.

_____

_____

_____

_____

_____

Exhibit 2–8 Four Levels of Social Responsibility

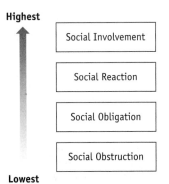

Highest

Social Involvement

Social Reaction

Social Obligation

Social Obstruction

Lowest

APPLYING THE CONCEPT   *Social Responsibility*

Identify each statement by its level of social responsibility.

a. social obstruction   **c.** social reaction

b. social obligation   **d.** social involvement

_____ 16. I agree—a Boys and Girls Club downtown would be helpful in developing new sport programs in our city. We'll give you $1,000 to get the ball rolling.

_____ 17. I'm disappointed with the reading levels of players coming from our local high school. Betty, I want you to contact the principal and see if you can work together to develop a program to improve reading skills.

_____ 18. Bill, the auditor will be here next week, so we'd better make sure that the hockey equipment we took from inventory does not show up as missing.

_____ 19. We reviewed factory workers' hourly labor rates in Vietnam because of the bad press we were receiving. Now we pay higher than the minimum wages in Vietnam, which is more expensive for our company.

_____ 20. As of June 1 the new regulations go into effect. We will have to cut the amount of waste we dump into the river by half. Get the lowest bidder to pick up the other half and dispose of it.

Are Downsizing and Reengineering Socially Responsible?

8 LEARNING OUTCOME
Explain how downsizing and reengineering differ.

To increase *productivity,* many firms are downsizing. In **downsizing**, the organization's resources are cut, and more is done with less in an effort to increase productivity. Typically, the primary area on the block is human resources. In today's highly competitive environment, organizations often slash jobs by the thousands as they struggle to cut costs and maintain profitability. In 1998, Nike eliminated 450 full-time U.S.-based employees, or 3.5 percent of its total U.S. workforce. This was in response to the Asian economic crisis and the slowdown in U.S. footwear sales.[50] Companies like Nike must do more with less, but simply cutting jobs and requiring the remaining employees to do the jobs of two or three people does not work in the long run. An alternative to downsizing is reengineering, which involves downsizing in a systematic manner.

In **reengineering** job tasks are redesigned (fragmented tasks are combined into streamlined processes) to save time and money (time-based competition). Reengineering endeavors to "think outside the box" by wondering, What would happen if we could start from scratch using what we know now? It therefore starts out by assuming there are no current jobs and strives to design a more efficient work process and the jobs that go with it. In the new design, *teams* work together using *participative management* all the way through the process, from acquiring inputs to transforming them into outputs. Reengineered work usually requires fewer workers and far fewer managers. With reengineering, teams work on a whole process from start to finish and have a real sense of ownership because they make the decisions—"*We* made that happen." Reengineered jobs tend to be much more rewarding than traditional jobs.[51] However, the employees who lose their jobs because of reengineering do not benefit. According to Hammer, co-author of the book that coined the term *reengineering,* "The biggest lie told by most corporations, and they tell it proudly, is that people are

downsizing
The process of cutting organizational resources to get more done with less as a means of increasing productivity.

reengineering
The radical redesign of work to combine fragmented tasks into streamlined processes that save time and money.

our most important assets. Total fabrication. They treat people like raw materials. If you're serious about treating people as an asset, we're looking at a dramatic increase in investment in them."[52] "I tell companies they need to quintuple their investment in education. Training is about skills; education is about understanding broad knowledge. Everybody who works in a company needs to understand the business." Therefore, *everyone in the company* needs to understand the company mission, its objectives, and its business strategy.[53]

CHAPTER SUMMARY

1. Describe the five components of the internal environment.

Management refers to the people responsible for an organization's performance. *Mission* is the organization's purpose or reason for being. The organization uses human, physical, financial, and informational *resources* to accomplish its mission. The *systems process* is the organization's method of transforming inputs into outputs. *Structure* refers to the way in which the organization groups its resources to accomplish its mission.

2. Explain the two primary principles of total quality management.

The two primary principles of total quality management are (1) focus on delivering customer value, and (2) continually improve the system and its processes. To be successful, businesses must continually offer value to attract and retain customers. Without customers you don't have a business.

3. Explain how factors in the external environment affect the internal business environment.

Customers should decide what products the business offers, for without customer value there are no customers or business. *Competitors'* business practices, such as features and prices, often have to be duplicated in order to maintain customer value. Poor-quality inputs from *suppliers* result in poor-quality outputs without customer value. Without a qualified *workforce,* products and services will have little or no customer value. *Shareholders,* through an elected board of directors, hire top managers and provide directives for the organization. *Society* pressures business to perform or not perform certain activities, such as pollution control. The business must develop new *technologies,* or at least keep up with them, to provide customer value. *Economic* activity affects the organization's ability to provide customer value. For example, inflated prices lead to lower customer value. *Governments* set the rules and regulations that business must adhere to.

4. State the differences between domestic, international, and multinational businesses.

Domestic firms do business in only one country. International firms are primarily based in one country but transact business with other countries. Multinational corporations have significant operations in more than one country.

5. List the lowest- and highest-risk ways to take a business global.

Importing and exporting are the lowest-risk strategy, and direct investment is the highest-risk strategy. Global sourcing can be part of either method.

6. Explain the stakeholders' approach to ethics.

In this approach to ethics, organizations create a win-win situation for the relevant parties affected by the decision. If as a manager you are proud to tell relevant stakeholders of your decision, it is probably ethical. If you are not proud, or keep rationalizing your decision, it may not be ethical.

7. Discuss the four levels of social responsibility in business.

Social responsibility can be broken into four levels, which range from low to high. At the low end, *social obstruction,* managers behave unethically and illegally. At the next level, *social obligation,* managers meet only the minimum legal requirements. With *social reaction,* managers respond to societal requests. At the highest level, *social involvement,* managers voluntarily initiate socially responsible acts.

8. Explain how downsizing and reengineering differ.

In downsizing, an organization's resources are cut to get more done with less in order to increase productivity. Reengineering involves the radical redesigning of work (fragmented tasks are combined into streamlined processes) to save time and money. Downsizing focuses on cutting resources, whereas reengineering focuses on developing new jobs that are "smarter" than the old ones.

9. Define the key terms discussed in the text.

Fill in the missing key terms from memory, or match the key terms from the list in the margin with their definitions below.

The _____ is the factors that affect an organization's performance within its boundaries.

The _____ is an organization's purpose or reason for being.

_____ are people whose interests are affected by organizational behavior.

The _____ is the method used to transform inputs into outputs.

_____ is the way in which an organization groups its resources to accomplish its mission.

_____ involves comparing actual use to requirements to determine value.

_____ is the purchasing benefit(s) used by customers to determine whether or not to buy a product.

_____ is a process that involves everyone in the organization focusing on the customer to continually improve product value.

The _____ is the factors that affect an organization's performance from outside its boundaries.

An _____ is primarily based in one country but transacts business in other countries.

A _____ is a business with significant operations in more than one country.

_____ is the use of worldwide resources for inputs and transformation.

A _____ is created when firms share ownership (partnership) of a new enterprise.

_____ occurs when a company builds or purchases operating facilities (subsidiaries) in a foreign country.

_____ are the standards of right and wrong that influence behavior.

The _____ involves creating a win-win situation for all stakeholders so that everyone benefits from the decision.

_____ is the conscious effort to operate in a manner that creates a win-win situation for all stakeholders.

Key Terms

customer value
direct investment
downsizing
ethics
external environment
global sourcing
internal environment
international business
joint venture
mission
multinational
   corporation (MNC)
quality
reengineering
social responsibility
stakeholders
stakeholders' approach
   to ethics
structure
systems process
total quality
   management (TQM)

_____ is the process of cutting organizational resources to get more done with less as a means of increasing productivity.

_____ is the radical redesign of work to combine fragmented tasks into streamlined processes that save time and money.

REVIEW AND DISCUSSION

1. In your opinion, do most sport organizations really focus on creating customer value? Use specific examples to defend your position.

2. Do you think that all sport organizations should use TQM? If so, why? If not, why not?

3. Describe the relationship between management and an organization's mission, resources, the systems process, and structure. Which of these internal factors are ends and which are means?

4. What technological breakthrough has had the greatest impact on the quality of your life, and why?

5. Should government regulation of sports and business be increased, decreased, or remain the same? Defend your position.

6. Categorize a few sport companies you are familiar with as international or multinational.

7. For the companies you listed in question 6, identify their method(s) of going global.

8. Do you believe that ethical behavior pays off in the long run? If so, why? If not, why not?

9. What guides your behavior now? Will you use one of the ethical guides from the text? If yes, which one and why?

10. Can ethics be taught and learned? Defend your position.

11. How do companies benefit from being socially responsible? Give some examples.

12. As a CEO, what level of social responsibility would you aspire to? How might you go about attaining it?

13. Has Alex Rodriguez demonstrated that he is worth 22 million dollars a year? Does his ethical behavior on and off the field have anything to do with this?

14. Research what socially responsible activities Alex Rodriguez is involved with off the playing field.

CASE

Ethics and the Salt Lake City Olympics 2002

The scandals associated with the Salt Lake City Olympics (the bribery involved in the site location process and the judging practices used to award the figure skating medals, among others) have forced the International Olympic Committee (IOC) to reevaluate their practices. The IOC faces two problems that have been difficult to manage. First, there is the long-standing problem of illegal doping by athletes. Second, the committee looking to bring the Olympics to Salt Lake City in 2002 was found guilty of offering bribes to IOC members.

The last years of Juan Antonio Samaranch's 21-year presidency were dominated by the Salt Lake bribery scandal, which led to sweeping reforms and the expulsion of ten IOC members for breaking rules on accepting gifts from Salt Lake City officials when they were bidding on hosting the 2002 Winter Games. Looking back on the incidents, Samaranch, whose reign ended with the election of a new president, Belgium's Jacques Rogge, said that the reforms implemented in the wake of the 1999 Salt Lake City bribes-for-votes scandal have strengthened the organization by widening its committee base (which originally included only national VIPs) to include heads of major international sport federations and athletes. Samaranch stated, "We have transformed the IOC from being just part of the Olympic movement to being THE Olympic movement."

On the challenges ahead, he noted that much remains to be done in the fight against doping: "You can win many battles but the war is more difficult. You find ways to discover drugs but there are new drugs coming." He hails the collaboration between the World Anti-Doping Agency and governments, which "have means we don't have like customs and police investigations." However, he also notes that "the end of this fight is very far from now. The war is very difficult. But with the new World Anti-Doping Agency, there is a very good collaboration now between the world of sport and governments. For the last few years, governments have become very interested in this fight."[54] While the battle against doping in sports rages on, Samaranch declared the fight against corruption within IOC ranks over.

Looking back on the biggest crisis in the Olympic movement's history, Samaranch said he believes the IOC acted swiftly and decisively, putting in place reforms to prevent such things from happening again. The most important among those reforms was the banning of visits by IOC members to bidding cities. "I maintain that visits of members of the IOC to bidding cities have stopped," said Samaranch. "This is not a decision of the president, it is a decision of the session and I believe they will be wise enough to maintain this policy."

"I think we solved the corruption because we acted very quickly. Three or four months after the scandal of Salt Lake City we had a special session in Lausanne and expelled some members. We faced these difficulties because of visits of IOC members to bidding cities."[55] Samaranch is confident the reforms he drove through will remain in place with the election of Rogge.

For more information about the planning, the implementing, and the results of the Salt Lake City Olympics, visit the official web site at http://www.ci.slc.ut.us. Details about the appointment of Jacques Rogge and other IOC information can be found at http://www.ft.com.

CASE QUESTIONS

1. The Olympics provide a quality product with customer value.
   a. true   b. false

2. The Olympics have shareholders.
   a. true   b. false

3. Technology has had a major effect on the Olympics.
   a. true   b. false

4. The Olympics have been accused of unethical practices.
   a. true   b. false

5. Salt Lake City Olympics managers appeared to strongly enforce ethical behavior.
   a. true   b. false

6. Which of the following external factors is the primary pressure facing the Olympics?
   a. customers and competition
   b. society and governments
   c. suppliers and labor
   d. economy and competition
   e. stakeholders and technology

7. Are the Olympics a domestic, international, or multinational sport organization?

8. What level of social responsibility did the IOC utilize?
   a. social obstruction
   b. social obligation
   c. social reaction
   d. social involvement

9. What management procedures could President Samaranch have implemented before the Salt Lake City bribes took place that would have prevented the scandal?

10. Using the web sites provided, find out who was originally scheduled to become the new president of the IOC. Why was his appointment withdrawn?

11. Have the changes in monitoring procedures stopped the doping problems of Olympic athletes?

12. Using the web sites provided, describe what management role Mitt Romney played in the effort to get the Salt Lake Olympic games back on track.

EXERCISES

Skill-Builder: Analyzing Organizational Environment and Management Practices

Objective:
- To develop your ability to analyze an organization's business and management practices.

Preparation:
Select a sport organization, preferably one that you work for or have played for, and answer the following questions. You may need to contact people in the organization to answer certain questions.

The Internal Environment
1. Identify the organization's top managers and briefly discuss their leadership style.

   _____

   _____

   _____

2. State the organization's mission.

   _____

   _____

   _____

3. Identify some of its major resources.

   _____

4. Explain its systems process. Discuss how it maintains quality and customer value.

   _____

   _____

   _____

5. Identify the organization's structure by listing its major departments.

   _____

The External Environment

Note: State how each external factor affects the organization.

6. Identify the organization's target customers.

_____

7. Identify its major competitors.

_____

8. Identify its major suppliers.

_____

9. Which labor pool does the organization recruit most of its workforce from?

_____

10. Is the organization publicly held? If yes, which stock exchanges is it listed on? If not, state who owns it.

_____

11. Describe the ways in which the organization affects society (at the local, state, and national levels), and also the ways in which society affects it.

_____

_____

_____

12. Describe some technologies that the organization and its industry niche have used in the past, use now, and may use in the future. Is the organization a technology leader?

_____

_____

_____

13. Identify which governments affect the organization, and list some major laws and regulations that it must abide by.

_____

_____

_____

14. Explain how the economy affects the organization.

_____

_____

_____

Globalization

15. Is the organization a domestic, an international, or a multinational company? If it falls in one of the two latter categories, list and briefly describe (a) some of its global activities (import/export, etc.), and (b) some of its business practices (management style, strategy, etc.)

_____

_____

_____

Ethics

16. Does the organization have a formal code of ethics? If yes, describe the code and how it is used and disseminated to employees. If no, how does it manage ethical issues?

_____

_____

_____

17. Does management lead by example? How are ethical behaviors encouraged? How are the rules enforced?

_____

_____

_____

Social Responsibility

18. Overall, on which level of social responsibility does the organization operate? Identify some of the things it does to be a good corporate citizen.

_____

_____

_____

In-Class Application

Complete the skill-building preparation noted above before class.

Choose one (10–30 minutes):

- Break into groups of three to five members, and present your findings to the above questions. Select one student's example and as a group present it to the entire class.
- Informal, whole-class discussion of student findings.

Wrap-up:

Take a few minutes and write down your answers to the following questions:

- What did I learn from this experience?

_____

_____

- How will I use this knowledge in the future?

_____

_____

As a class, discuss student responses.

Internet Skills: Learning about Safety Issues in Sport Management

Objectives:

- To understand that safety issues are an extremely important part of a sport manager's responsibilities.
- To experience the http://www.worldstadiums.com web site and find articles related to stadium safety. Unfortunately, the tragic events of September 11, 2001, have made issues of global security more important than ever.

Preparation (20 minutes):

Visit http://www.worldstadiums.com, review the various links to gain information about stadiums where European football (soccer) is played, and answer the following questions.

1. Explore the *Latest Stadium News* link. Why is stadium security determined to be a priority?

   _____

   _____

   _____

2. Check out the *Violence and Disaster News* link and read about all the tragic events that have occurred at stadiums. What happened in Ghana on May 10, 2001?

   _____

   _____

   _____

3. Click on the *North America* link. How many stadiums are there in your state?

   _____

4. Click on the *Construction News* link. Give a brief summary of the attempt to build a new Wembley stadium.

   _____

   _____

   _____

5. Using the *Construction News* link, determine why former New York City mayor Giuliani promised to build new stadiums for the New York Yankees and New York Mets.

   _____

   _____

   _____

   _____

In-Class Application

Complete the questionnaire above.

Choose one:

- Break into groups of three to five, share your answers to the above questions, and try to come to a consensus. Select a spokesperson and present your findings to the class.
- Whole-class discussion of student responses to the four ethics questions.

Wrap-up:

Take a few minutes and answer the following questions:

- What did I learn from this experience?

   _____

   _____

- How will I use this experience in the future?

   _____

   _____

   _____

As a whole class, share your thoughts and answers.

3 Creative Problem Solving and Decision Making

Learning Outcomes

After studying this chapter, you should be able to:

1. Describe how meeting objectives, solving problems, and making decisions are connected.

2. Explain how management functions, decision making, and problem solving relate.

3. Describe the six steps in the decision process.

4. Identify programmed and nonprogrammed decisions and recognize certain, uncertain, and risky business conditions.

5. Know when to use different decision models and when to make decisions as a group or as an individual.

6. State the difference between an objective and "must" and "want" criteria.

7. Explain how creativity and innovation differ.

8. Describe the three stages in the creative process.

9. Explain how quantitative techniques and cost-benefit analysis facilitate selecting alternatives.

10. Define the following key terms (in order of appearance in the chapter):

- problem
- problem solving
- decision making
- reflexive decision style
- reflective decision style
- consistent decision style
- programmed decisions
- nonprogrammed decisions
- decision-making conditions
- criteria
- innovation
- creativity
- creative process
- devil's advocate
- brainstorming
- synectics
- nominal grouping
- consensus mapping

REVIEWING THEIR GAME PLAN

Adidas-Salomon Is Cool Again

For the past eighty years legendary soccer players trotted around playing fields all over the world, from Seoul to Manchester to Sao Paulo to Kabul, sporting the three-swoosh **ADIDAS** logo on their footwear. Yet, caught in the downdraft that swept through the athletic footwear industry in the 1990s, Adidas—the original sport brand—somehow lost its firm footing on the bottom line. By 1993 Adidas was losing roughly $100 million per year. Company management realized "the original authentic sport brand" was looking a wee bit tired and, well, dowdy. Dowdy doesn't make it in the sport brand market, so Adidas set about putting the buzz back in its products, status and personality back in its advertising (witness its blanket coverage in the World Cup and its quirky presence in the surprise hit movie *The Royal Tenenbaums*), and good business practices back in its distribution systems. It also moved boldly into new industries. Adidas merged with Salomon, purchased TaylorMade Golf, and strode confidently into the ski, golf, and bike markets. Maybe too boldly—by 1999 with U.S. sales off 7.5 percent, the company struggled under its heavy debt burden.[1]

Enter CEO Herbert Hainer, whose mandate was to grow Adidas sales to a healthier market share. Hainer defends the company's 1997 purchase of Salomon saying, "Yes, I would say we paid too much for Salomon, but it fit with our strategy. There isn't another sporting goods company with as wide an assortment of premium brands."[2] Optimism aside, Adidas has some difficult obstacles to overcome if it is to move within striking distance of Nike, whose market share is holding steady at 42.6 percent.[3]

That's where Ross McMullin figures in Hainer's strategy. Hired in May 2000, McMullin, previously a European division president at Gillette, is now ensconced in Portland, Oregon, as Adidas America's turnaround president, just across town from arch rival Nike. McMullin believes the American operations have been "leaderless," and cites the 30 percent employee turnover as proof.[4] He believes Adidas America's young workforce (average age: 27) will work in its favor once he strengthens communication and gets this youthful enthusiasm and energy behind company goals and objectives.[5] He has also snagged long-term all-sport, all-school contracts with Notre Dame, UCLA, Nebraska, and Tennessee, with an eye on shifting teen perceptions of Adidas back to "cool."

Adidas managers have ambitious goals—nothing less than capturing 20 percent of the American footwear market (they currently have 11.3 percent)[6] and trimming product-to-market time from a company high of 70 weeks to 36 weeks by 2003—and know all too well that their footwork will have to be deft and skillful to make these goals a reality.[7] The buzz surrounding first the Kobe, named for Los Angeles Lakers star forward Kobe Bryant—and now Clima Cool, A3, and KobeTwo—has been strong. Adidas didn't stop with the basketball shoe market, but has coaxed tennis star Anna Kournikova, track star Ato Boldon, and Spanish golf sensation Sergio Garcia into its stable of star athletes promoting its wares. The company is now turning its attention to its internal environment; top management knows if it can't get its new products to teenage-savvy outlets *fast,* it won't matter how sexy and cool they are.

Adidas is endeavoring to cut purchasing costs, reduce its product range, and grow sales of Salomon ski equipment and TaylorMade golf brands. Adidas executives have a passion for sports and for business, and this means they will not be settling for second place.[8] For current information on Adidas, visit http://www.adidas.com. (For ideas on using the Internet, see Appendix B.)

INTERNET RESOURCES

http://www.bbhighway.com/Talk/Coaching_Box/Clinics/ALambert/decision.asp
The Basketball Highway's web site offers a great article called "Teaching Decision Making in Team Offense." Even the most naturally gifted athletes will perform below their abilities if they have not learned how to make quick, informed judgments in game situations. Although this article is specific to basketball, its principles can be easily adapted and applied to any team sport.
http://www.vta.spcomm.uiuc.edu *The University of Illinois at Urbana-Champaign offers a web site called Teamworks, the Virtual Team Assistant. Click the* Team Problem-Solving *link to find four lessons that will help you identify problems and then apply one of three group problem-solving models: reflective, conflict-based, and creative. You will also find several problem-solving activities geared toward figuring out how your team makes decisions so that you can learn to work together more effectively.*
http://www.decisionsciences.org *The Decision Sciences Institute publishes the* Decision Sciences *journal and the* Decision Line *news publication. The Institute's goal is to share research and foster communication relating to decision processes on an international basis. Members can keep up to date on the latest developments in decision sciences through discounted fees to attend the annual meeting and its numerous programs and workshops.*
http://DSSResources.com *Decision Support Systems Resources is a web-based compendium of resources, papers, and tutorials geared toward professionals interested in using information technology and software to enhance their decision making.*

DEVELOPING YOUR SKILLS **Problem solving and decision making are crucial skills of effective managers. Choose two managers, one whom you admire and one whom you don't, and assess their abilities in these two crucial areas. In what ways do they differ? In what ways are they alike? In what ways do you think the ineffective manager could improve in these two areas?**

SOLVING PROBLEMS AND MAKING DECISIONS— AN OVERVIEW

Innovative problem solving and decisiveness are two abilities employers value highly. And of course problem solving and decision making are what managers do. Bad decisions not only destroy careers, they also destroy companies, as we know all too well from watching repercussions ripple through our economy because of the disastrous decisions at Worldcom, Enron, Xerox, and perhaps others. The sport industry is not immune to bad decisions—witness the Starter Corporation, for example. Starter was the leading licensed sport apparel provider in the 1980s and 1990s. However, Starter failed to expand its merchandise line from licensed sport apparel to a branded apparel line. Nike decided to take a branded approach and emphasized its name instead of its licenses with professional leagues. Fans who were turned off by labor problems in the MLB, NHL, and NBA turned to athletic brands such as Nike and Fila as well as fashion designer brands such as Tommy Hilfiger, Nautica, and the Gap.[9] Needless to say, it takes good decisions to make companies superstars in their industry.

Some researchers claim that managers typically make about 80 decisions daily, or one every 5 or 6 minutes; others claim that daily decisions number in the hundreds.[10] The good news is—as with all management skills—you can hone your problem-solving and decision-making abilities to levels you might not now believe you would ever be able to "play at."

In its simplest form, managing is about one thing—making decisions. But what does it take to make a "good" decision? Is it about going by the book (facts and percentages)—or about following your gut? **ADIDAS's** CEO, Herbert Hainer, is famous for trusting his gut.[11] **Do you think most CEOs follow their gut, or do they go for facts and figures? Why?**

Does time (the ivory tower, feet on the desk, let's ruminate about this context) produce better decisions, or does pressure (on the front lines under fire) bring the clarity that makes for wiser decisions? And, is decision making something that you can learn?[12]

Objectives, Problem Solving, and Decision Making

 LEARNING OUTCOME
1 Describe how meeting objectives, solving problems, and making decisions are connected.

As a manager, you and your boss will sometimes set objectives together, and your boss will sometimes assign objectives for you and your team to achieve. These will not always be easy tasks—you will find your mettle tested, sometimes seriously—and you will grow as a manager through both your successes *and* your failures. Meeting objectives is about solving problems. To solve problems, you must make decisions. The better you can develop plans that prevent problems before they occur, the fewer problems you will encounter and the more you will be able to take advantage of opportunities that continuously increase customer value. Effective managers give the same consideration to seeking opportunities as they give to solving problems.

A **problem** exists whenever company or team objectives are not being met. In other words, you have a problem whenever a difference exists between what is happening and what you and your team want to happen. If your objective is to make the playoffs but your team finishes last, you have a problem. The key thing to remember here is that the system causes 85 percent of the problems in organizations, not the people. **Problem solving** is the process of taking corrective action to meet objectives. **Decision making** is the process of selecting a course of action that will solve a problem.

When you are faced with a problem, you also face decisions—it's that simple. Your first decision concerns whether or not to take corrective action. Some problems cannot be solved, and others do not deserve the time and effort it would take to solve them. Therefore, your organization will sometimes perform "triage," and not make solving such problems an organizational objective. At other times, your bosses will "beard the lion," think outside the box, and end up solving the seemingly "unsolvable" problem. Such results will jump them to the front of the race. However, most of the time your organization and you will set objectives that are definitely doable, although not always obviously doable. It is your job to figure out how.

Management Functions, Decision Making, and Problem Solving

 LEARNING OUTCOME
2 Explain how management functions, decision making, and problem solving relate.

In Chapter 2 we noted that all managers perform the same four functions—they plan, they organize, they lead, and they control. To perform these functions, managers must make decisions. Keep in mind that every action is preceded by a decision. As planners, managers decide on the objectives they want to pursue and when, where, and how the objectives will be met. As organizers, managers decide what to delegate and how to coordinate the department's resources, including whom to hire and how to train and evaluate them. As leaders, managers must decide how best to influence employees. As controllers, managers assess whether—and how well—objectives are being met. When managers laser in on their four functions with skilled decision making, they minimize the problems they need to solve and maximize "their opportunities to seek opportunity."

ADIDAS saw opportunity in new markets. Its objective? Provide a broader selection of sporting goods than their competitors. Its decision? Enter the skiing, golf, and cycling markets. However, Adidas's decision to diversify has not been without problems. Adidas has not yet been able to capitalize on efficiencies within its divisions, and one of Ross McMullin's primary objectives is to build bridges between Adidas's European and American operations. His

problem
Exists whenever objectives are not being met.

problem solving
The process of taking corrective action to meet objectives.

decision making
The process of selecting an alternative course of action that will solve a problem.

TIMEOUT
Give an example of an objective from your manager or coach that was not met. Identify the problem created and the decision that prevented the objective from being met.

_____

_____

_____

_____

_____

vision? "[A] new corporate culture that works together as one team across the globe . . . and a company that people love to work for again."[13] Adidas thus faces important decisions—how best to share skills, abilities, and resources. What pitfalls await Adidas as it endeavors to grow market share? How might the company sidestep them?

Making Decisions

3 LEARNING OUTCOME
Describe the six steps in the decision process.

Effective decision making consists of six steps (see Model 3–1). You will find that in the real world you will not proceed in the conveniently tidy manner implied in Model 3–1. At *any* step in the process you may find yourself returning to a prior step to make changes. Let's say you have gotten to implementation, but it isn't going well. Perhaps this time you simply need to tweak the implementation plan, but other times you will need to backtrack and select a new alternative or even change your original objective. A problematic implementation may reveal that you haven't defined the problem precisely enough, and you may have to return to square one.

Following the steps laid out in Model 3–1 will not guarantee your making good decisions. However, using these steps increases your chances of success.[14] Consciously use these six steps in your daily life, and you will improve your ability to make effective decisions. The remainder of this chapter delves into the details of each step to help you develop and hone this all-important skill. But first, find out what your decision-making style is—take the Self Assessment.

So, you may well be asking, what *exactly* is a reflexive or reflective decision style? Read on. . . .

reflexive decision style
Making snap decisions without taking time to get all the information needed and without considering alternatives.

THE REFLEXIVE DECISION STYLE. Reflexive decision makers "shoot from the hip"—that is, they make snap decisions without taking the time to get all the information they need and without considering alternatives. On the positive side, reflexive decision makers *are* decisive—they do not procrastinate. On the negative side, making a quick decision doesn't necessarily mean making the best possible decision. Hasty decisions, without adequate information, are a dangerous form of "business roulette"—you may get lucky and make some great decisions, but most often you will stumble badly. If you use a reflexive style for important decisions, you may want to slow down and spend more time gathering information and analyzing alternatives.

reflective decision style
Taking plenty of time to decide, gathering considerable information, and analyzing numerous alternatives.

THE REFLECTIVE DECISION STYLE. Reflective decision makers take plenty of time to decide, gathering considerable information and analyzing numerous alternatives. On the positive side, they certainly don't make hasty decisions. On the negative side, they waste valuable time and other resources because they are overwhelmed by the details. Too much information can lead to paralysis—if you can't see the forest (the big picture) because you are looking at the twigs on the ground, you will be viewed as wishy-washy and

Model 3–1
Making a Decision

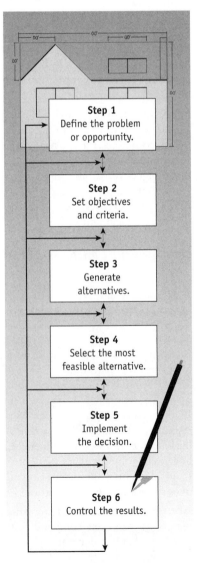

SELF ASSESSMENT   *Your Decision Style*

We all differ in the way we approach decisions. To determine whether your decision-making style is reflexive, reflective, or consistent, select a number from 1 to 5 on the continuum below that best describes your behavior in each statement.

A common behavior			An uncommon behavior	
1	2	3	4	5

OVERALL

_____ 1. I make decisions quickly.

WHEN MAKING DECISIONS

_____ 2. I go with my first thought or hunch.

_____ 3. I don't bother to recheck my work.

_____ 4. I gather little or no information.

_____ 5. I consider very few alternatives.

_____ 6. I usually make it well before the deadline.

_____ 7. I don't ask others for advice.

AFTERWARD

_____ 8. I don't look for other alternatives or wish I had waited longer.

_____ Total score

To determine your style, add up your answers. Your total score will be between 8 and 40. Place an X on the continuum that represents your score.

Reflexive	Consistent		Reflective
8	20	30	40

indecisive. If you use a reflective style, remind yourself to step back and look at the "forest." To paraphrase Andrew Jackson: Take time to deliberate—absolutely—*but* when the time for action comes, stop thinking and get moving.

THE CONSISTENT DECISION STYLE. Consistent decision makers don't rush and they don't waste time. They know when they need more information and when it's time to stop analyzing and get moving. Consistent decision makers also boast the best decision-making record. Not surprisingly, they typically follow the steps outlined in Model 3–1.

In his referee days, Jerry Seeman, now Senior Director of Officiating for the National Football League, personified consistent decision making. Seeman notes that the pressures were the same whether he officiated a preseason game or a Super Bowl. "Being on the field was like being in a fishbowl: Everyone—players, coaches, fans, the media—is waiting for

consistent decision style Taking time but not wasting time; knowing when more information is needed and when enough analysis has been done.

APPLYING THE CONCEPT   *Making Decisions*

Identify which step in the decision process each statement represents.

a. step 1   **d.** step 4

b. step 2   **e.** step 5

c. step 3   **f.** step 6

_____ 1. We brainstorm to solve problems.

_____ 2. Betty, is the machine making baseball caps still jumping out of sequence, or has it stopped?

_____ 3. I don't understand what the new owners are trying to accomplish.

_____ 4. What symptoms have you observed that indicate the team has a problem?

_____ 5. Break-even analysis should help us in this situation.

your decision. A successful call depended on three things: You must be in position, you must have a deep knowledge of the game, and you must have intense concentration. No matter what the reaction to your decision may be, you answer to only one thing: your conscience. Above all, when making a decision, you have to keep your cool."[15] (Not the worst advice for *any* decision maker!) Seeman continues, "One of the biggest errors that officials fall into is making calls too quickly. Each decision has two phases: You read and analyze the play, and then you make the call. But when things happen in a split second, it can be tempting to throw a penalty flag before you know what happened. That's why officials need to work in cruise control. The fans may go crazy, the players and coaches may get excited, but there should be seven people on the field who work every game the same way from beginning to end—and who exude a quiet confidence."[16] (Also not the worst definition of an effective manager!)

As you may already have noted in your team and work experiences, groups also develop definite decision-making styles, based on group dynamics, among other things. (More about group decision making later in this chapter.)

Now that you've got an idea of the various decision styles, it's time to look more closely at the six steps of effective decision making.

STEP 1: DEFINE THE PROBLEM OR OPPORTUNITY

In the first step in your decision process, you set about defining the problem you want to solve or the opportunity you want to capitalize on. This step requires that you classify the problem, select an appropriate level of employee participation, and distinguish the cause of the problem from its symptoms.

Classify the Problem

4 | **LEARNING OUTCOME**
Identify programmed and nonprogrammed decisions and recognize certain, risky, and uncertain business conditions.

Problems can be classified in terms of how the decision is structured, the conditions in which decisions are made, and the decision model used.

HOW DECISIONS ARE STRUCTURED. Decisions can be categorized as programmed or nonprogrammed. With **programmed decisions** (recurring or routine situations) decision makers use "decision rules," or organizational policies and procedures, to make the decision. Here is a typical decision rule: Order X number of golf balls every time stock reaches level Y. With **nonprogrammed decisions** (significant and nonrecurring and nonroutine situations) decision makers use the six-step decision process. To qualify as significant, a decision must be expensive (purchasing major assets) and/or have major consequences (a new product or reduction of employees). **ADIDAS** made a nonprogrammed decision when it purchased Salomon and TaylorMade. **Name a recent programmed decision and a nonprogrammed decision made by your firm or team.** Nonprogrammed decisions obviously take longer to make than programmed decisions. Note also that decisions fall along a continuum from totally programmable to numerous combinations of the two types to totally nonprogrammable (see Exhibit 3–1).

You must be able to differentiate between the two types of decisions, because they alert you to the time and effort you should be spending. Upper-level managers typically make more nonprogrammed decisions than do lower-level managers, who tend to make programmed decisions.

DECISION-MAKING CONDITIONS. Decisions are made in an environment of certainty, risk, and uncertainty. When managers make decisions in a *certain* environment, they know the outcome of each alternative in advance. When they make decisions in a *risky* environment, managers don't know each outcome in advance but can assign probabilities of occurrence to each one. In an *uncertain* environment, lack of information or knowledge makes the

programmed decisions
With recurring or routine situations, the decision maker should use decision rules or organizational policies and procedures to make the decision.

nonprogrammed decisions
With significant and nonrecurring and nonroutine situations, the decision maker should use the decision-making model.

decision-making conditions
Certainty, risk, and uncertainty.

Exhibit 3–1   The Continuum of Decision Structure

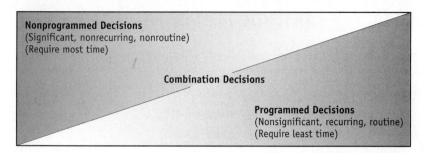

Nonprogrammed Decisions
(Significant, nonrecurring, nonroutine)
(Require most time)

Combination Decisions

Programmed Decisions
(Nonsignificant, recurring, routine)
(Require least time)

outcomes unpredictable so that probabilities cannot be assigned easily. **ADIDAS'S** purchase of Salomon was made in risky conditions. For instance, Adidas entered the skiing market, with which it had little management experience. This moved the company into building and selling skiing equipment, which was quite different from selling footwear and apparel. Decisions made in risky conditions are the purview of upper-level management. When decisions are made in uncertain conditions, it is difficult to determine which resources will solve the problem, or create or capitalize on an opportunity. Although risk and uncertainty can never be eliminated, they *can* be reduced. In the real world, only rarely can conditions be neatly categorized as certain, *or* risky, *or* uncertain. Instead, decisions get made in a blend of the three conditions, as shown in Exhibit 3–2.

5 **LEARNING OUTCOME**
Know when to use the different decision models and when to make decisions as a group or as an individual.

DECISION MODELS. The two primary decision models are the rational model and the bounded rationality model. The rational model uses "optimizing"—that is, it endeavors to select the best possible alternative. The bounded rationality model, a subset of the rational model, uses "satisficing"—it selects the first alternative that meets certain specified minimal criteria. Model 3–1 presents the rational model. With satisficing, only parts, or none, of the model would be used.

Savvy managers know which conditions dictate the use of each model. The more unstructured the decision and the higher the risk and uncertainty, the greater the need to conduct the research required in the rational model. Thus, you want to optimize (go for the best possible alternative) when you make nonprogrammed decisions in uncertain or high-risk conditions (the rational model), and you should satisfice (go with the first alternative that meets your minimum criteria) when you make programmed decisions in low-risk or highly certain conditions (the bounded rationality model).

Select an Appropriate Level of Employee Participation

When a problem arises, managers must choose the best people to solve it. As a rule of thumb, only key people who are directly involved with the problem should participate in the solution process. Because current trends favor increased employee participation, the

TIMEOUT
Analyze a recent decision of your organization, and decide which decision model your managers used. Be sure to identify the environmental conditions and the type of decision (programmed or nonprogrammed).

_____

_____

_____

_____

_____

Exhibit 3–2   The Continuum of the Decision-Making Environment

Uncertainty	Risk	Certainty
←——————————————————————————→		
(Outcome of alternatives unpredictable)		(Outcome of alternatives predictable)

APPLYING THE CONCEPT   *Classify the Problem*

Classify the following problems according to the type of decision and the environmental conditions in which the decision is being made.

   a. programmed, certain   **d.** nonprogrammed, certain

   b. programmed, uncertain   **e.** nonprogrammed, uncertain

   c. programmed, risky   **f.** nonprogrammed, risky

_____ 6. When I graduate from college, I will buy an existing fitness center rather than work for someone else.

_____ 7. Sondra, a small business owner of a health center, has experienced a turnaround in her business; it's now profitable. She wants to be able to keep her excess cash accessible in case she needs it to cover shortfalls. How should she invest it?

_____ 8. Every six months, a purchasing agent selects new materials for the soccer balls his company makes.

_____ 9. In the early 1970s, investors decide to start the World Football League.

_____ 10. A manager in a department with high turnover hires a new employee.

question is not whether managers should encourage employees to problem-solve and make decisions, but when and how they should participate in the process.[17] To begin, let's examine individual and group decision making. Note, however, that even though today the trend is toward group decision making, some people are comfortable with this idea, but others are not.[18]

The key to successful group decisions is to avoid the pitfalls and capitalize on the strengths of the group process (see Exhibit 3–3).

THE UPSIDE OF GROUP DECISION MAKING. When group members participate in the decision process, six advantages often accrue:

1. *Better-quality decisions.* The saying "two heads are better than one" can be an important strength of group decision making. Groups often do a better job of solving complex

Exhibit 3–3   Strengths and Pitfalls in Group Decision Making

Strengths	Pitfalls
1. Better-quality decisions	1. Wasted time and slower decision making
2. More information, more alternatives, heightened creativity, and innovation	2. Satisficing
3. Better understanding of the problem and the decision	3. Domination by subgroup or individual and goal displacement
4. Greater commitment to the decision	4. Conformity and groupthink
5. Improved morale and motivation	
6. Good training	

problems than the best individual in the group going solo. Thus, groups do well with nonprogrammed decisions in risky or uncertain conditions.

2. *More information, more alternatives, heightened creativity and innovation.* Groups typically bring more information to the table than do individuals. Group members bring different points of view to bear on the problem and are thus able to generate more alternatives. And creative, innovative ideas (and products) emerge from the synergy of members building on each other's ideas.

3. *Better understanding of the problem and the decision.* When people participate in the decision process, they gain a fuller understanding of the alternatives and why the final selection was made. This makes implementation easier.

4. *Greater commitment to the decision.* People involved in a decision are more committed to making the implementation succeed.

5. *Improved morale and motivation.* "Ownership" of the process, the decision, and the results improves morale and motivates people. Why? Because participation in the process is rewarding and personally satisfying. Encouraging group participation says, "We value your input."

6. *Good training.* Participation in decision making trains people to work in groups by developing group-process skills.[19] Group participation helps employees better understand problems faced by the organization, and this results in greater productivity.[20]

THE DOWNSIDE OF GROUP DECISION MAKING. Careful leadership is required to avoid the following pitfalls of group decision making:

1. *Wasted time and slower decision making.* It takes longer for groups to reach consensus. Employees who are solving problems and making decisions are not on the job producing. Because group involvement costs the organization time and money, for programmed decisions in certain or low-risk business conditions, individual decision making is generally more cost effective.

2. *Satisficing.* Groups are more likely to satisfice than individuals, especially when groups are not run effectively. Members may take the attitude, "Let's be done with this." Part of the reason groups satisfice is that members in poorly run groups don't feel responsible for the outcome. Individuals stand alone—and stand out—when they and they alone must make the decision. In groups no one person gets the blame—or the credit—for the decision, so attendance and commitment can be lower.

3. *Domination by subgroup or individual and goal displacement.* Group dynamics can be destructive if not managed properly. Cliques can develop, and destructive conflict can be the result. Also, cliques (or an individual member) can dominate the process and nullify the decision. *Goal displacement* occurs when an individual or clique tries to get their decision accepted, or dominates for personal reasons, rather than endeavoring to find the best solution.

4. *Conformity and groupthink.* Members may feel pressured to go along with the group's decision without raising reasonable criticisms because they fear rejection or they don't want to cause conflict. *Groupthink* occurs when members withhold differing views in order to appear to be in agreement. This nullifies one of the strong points of effective groups—their diversity. Conformity is especially problematic in highly cohesive groups because members can put getting along ahead of finding the best solution. Conformity is less problematic in groups that value diversity because members seek out and embrace differing viewpoints.

> **TIMEOUT**
> Give an example of a group decision and an individual one from your organization or team. Describe the strengths and weaknesses encountered in each process.
> _____
> _____
> _____
> _____
> _____

In general, group decision making works well with nonprogrammed decisions made in conditions of high risk or uncertainty. Individual decision making works well with programmed decisions in low-risk or certain conditions.

To succeed at decision making, you need (1) to categorize the decision (problem or opportunity) as programmable or nonprogrammable, and (2) to determine the appropriate level

Exhibit 3–4   Four Continuums in Classifying the Decision

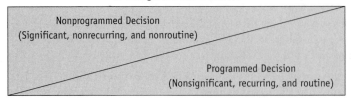

1. Categorize the Decision

Nonprogrammed Decision
(Significant, nonrecurring, and nonroutine)

Programmed Decision
(Nonsignificant, recurring, and routine)

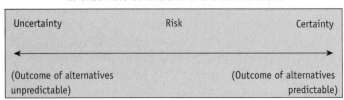

2. Check the Conditions in the Environment

Uncertainty	Risk	Certainty

(Outcome of alternatives unpredictable)   (Outcome of alternatives predictable)

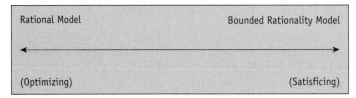

3. Choose the Decision Model

Rational Model	Bounded Rationality Model

(Optimizing)   (Satisficing)

4. Choose the Level of Participation

Group Decisions	Individual Decisions

| **TIME OUT** |
Define a problem your organization or team is facing or an opportunity they would like to capitalize on. Be sure to clearly distinguish the problem symptoms from the problem cause(s).

of participation in the decision process (see the Skill-Builder at the end of the chapter). Use Exhibit 3–4 to help you classify decisions.

Distinguish Symptoms from the Cause of the Problem

To do this, first observe the situation, then describe in simple terms (do this purposefully—simplicity will clarify your thinking) recent occurrences. This will help you determine the cause of the problem. For example, Sam, your star first baseman of six years, has been sick or late more times in the last month than in the past two years. So what is the problem? If your answer is "absenteeism" or "tardiness," you are confusing symptoms with the cause. Symptoms only indicate that there is a problem, they don't tell you what is causing the problem. If the causes of problems are not found out and addressed directly, problem symptoms often reappear.

At **ADIDAS** the problem symptom was lost market share. The causes (notice there are several, as defined by Adidas, were lack of sizzle in its products, not enough variety in its offerings, and inability to get the product to market fast enough. **Name some other possible causes of lost market share. Do any of these causes fit the situation at Adidas?** However, it might have behooved the company to pay more attention to the price it paid for Salomon, and the timing of that purchase. Remember that defining the problem is the key to successful solutions and strategies. When making nonprogrammed decisions in high-risk or uncertain conditions, take your time and clearly distinguish symptoms from causes.

STEP 2: SET OBJECTIVES AND CRITERIA

6 LEARNING OUTCOME
State the difference between an objective and "must" and "want" criteria.

With programmed decisions, the objective and criteria are typically already set, and you can skip steps 2–4 in the decision process. However, with nonprogrammed decisions, it is important to complete all six steps.

Set Objectives

Setting objectives helps managers make better decisions. Groups take longer than individuals to set objectives and criteria, but groups that set their own objectives perform better than those that do not.[21] Objectives state what the individual, group, or organization intends to accomplish. Objectives can address a problem of long or short standing, or they can address opportunities in the marketplace. One goal of **ADIDAS** is to reduce purchasing costs.[22] This will help them accomplish their objective of reducing overall production costs. **Go to a recent Adidas annual report and find a company objective that addresses an opportunity in the marketplace.**

Set Criteria

You should also specify the criteria for achieving the objective. **Criteria** are the standards that must be met to accomplish the objective.[23] It is a good idea to distinguish between "must" and "want" criteria. "Must" criteria *have* to be met in order to achieve the objective, whereas "want" criteria are desirable but not absolutely necessary. Thus, every acceptable alternative (and there may be several that are acceptable in the initial stages of the decision process) have to meet the "must" criteria; thereafter, you must decide which alternative meets the most "want" criteria. With satisficing, you select the first acceptable alternative; with optimizing, you endeavor to select the best possible option, one that meets as many "want" criteria as possible.

Suppose your team manager has quit and you must hire a new one. Your objective is to hire a manager by June 30. Your "must" criteria include, among other things, five years' experience as a team manager. Your "want" criterion is that the new manager be from a minority group. That is, you want to hire a minority employee but will not hire someone with less than five years' experience. In addition, if a significantly more qualified nonminority person applies for the job, he or she will be offered the job. In this situation you would optimize the decision rather than satisfice. We will discuss criteria again later in this chapter.

criteria
The standards that must be met to accomplish an objective.

TIME**OUT**
List the qualifications for a job at an organization that you are familiar with, and distinguish between "must" and "want" criteria.

STEP 3: GENERATE ALTERNATIVES

After you and your team have defined the problem and set objectives and criteria, it is time to generate alternatives. You will often find that there are many ways to solve a problem. Note also that with a programmed decision, this step can be skipped because the alternative has already been selected. However, with nonprogrammed decisions, the time and effort invested in generating alternatives pay off handsomely. In this section we examine innovation and creativity, using information and technology to generate alternatives, and group methods for generating creative alternatives.

Innovation and Creativity

7 LEARNING OUTCOME
Explain how creativity and innovation differ.

INNOVATION. An **innovation** alters what is established by introducing something new. Product innovations are changes in outputs (goods or service) to increase consumer value,

innovation
The implementation of a new idea.

or new outputs. Modern exercise equipment, such as an EFX fitness machine, are product innovations in the field of fitness. *Process innovations* are changes in the transformation of inputs into outputs. Innovation comes about when people solve problems creatively.

creativity
A way of thinking that generates new ideas.

CREATIVITY. Creativity is a way of thinking that generates new solutions to problems and new ways to approach opportunities. Creative people think outside the box. Let's be fair to **ADIDAS**. It took a risk in purchasing Salomon and TaylorMade Golf at a premium price. Adidas entered the equipment business even though its experience was in footwear and apparel. However, it was creative in its thinking and tried a different approach. Not even Nike or Reebok (Adidas's main competitors in footwear and apparel) have an equipment business on the same scale. And Adidas's creativity appears to be paying off. TaylorMade Golf is the number two club maker after Callaway Golf. Adidas-Salomon has returned to consistent profitability with a total net income of $184 million in 2001. Even better—Adidas is the number-two maker of sporting goods worldwide (behind only Nike).

In contrast, Mike Ditka thought outside the box and it didn't quite work out. When he was the coach of the New Orleans Saints, he traded his remaining draft picks for the right to select number 5, Ricky Williams, in the draft.[24] Although Williams was a solid performer for the Saints, he was never able to lift the Saints up to championship status. Ditka lost his job as coach while Williams was traded to the Miami Dolphins. Sometimes being creative works, and sometimes it can backfire.

8 LEARNING OUTCOME
Describe the three stages in the creative process.

creative process
The three stages are
(1) preparation,
(2) incubation and
illumination, and
(3) evaluation.

THE CREATIVE PROCESS. Intelligence and creativity are not highly correlated—that is, creative thinking hales from a broad continuum of people. It is also possible to enhance your own creative juices.[25] The three stages in the **creative process** are (1) preparation, (2) incubation and illumination, and (3) evaluation. Following these stages, which we discuss below and which are summarized in Exhibit 3–5, can help you get your creative juices flowing.

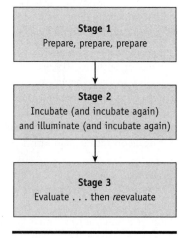

Exhibit 3–5
The Creative Process

1. *Prepare, prepare, prepare.* Get others' opinions, feelings, and ideas, but also get the facts. Look for new angles. Dream big (you can *always* scale back). At this stage it is important that you don't limit your thinking—take the attitude that everything goes. Also, don't judge your own ideas here or those of others—*nothing* throws cold water on creative brainstorming like criticism. (Criticism comes later.)

2. *Incubate (and incubate again) and illuminate (and incubate again).* Take a break; sleep on your idea. Not to worry—you *are* working on the problem, just subconsciously. Allowing your idea to incubate gives you insight you might not gain otherwise—call it peripheral vision. You may find the proverbial "lightbulb going off"—this is the illuminating part. And it never hurts to incubate your "lightbulb." Your subconscious workings are powerful—learn to trust them!

3. *Evaluate . . . then reevaluate. Now* you and your team can criticize. But rethink what you mean by "criticize"—make *it* creative, and *never never never* let it get personal. Much has been written about constructive criticism. In one useful approach, playing **devil's advocate**, some group members defend the idea on the table while others try to come up with reasons why it won't work. Then the groups switch sides. The idea is to turn everyone's thinking upside down, thereby generating revelations that might not be reached otherwise.

devil's advocate
Group members defend the idea while others try to come up with reasons why the idea won't work.

Use Information, Use Technology

As a 21st-century manager, like generations of earlier managers, you will use information and knowledge to make decisions. Unlike previous managers, however, you have a new world of tools to throw at problems and at opportunities. You will also have a new problem, however—that of too much information and too many tools.

Take information. You will find when you are generating alternatives that the following question will come up frequently: How much information do we need and where should we get it? There is no simple answer. The more important the decision, the more information you need (generally). However, too much information can paralyze the decision process. That is, the decision becomes too complex, and you don't get to the optimal alternative. Therefore, it behooves you to think about what constitutes *useful* information.

Useful information has four characteristics: (1) timeliness, (2) quality, (3) completeness, and (4) relevance (see Exhibit 3–6). *Timely* information is information that you get in time to make your decision. *High-quality* information is accurate information. False information misleads (obviously). In short—It Is Dangerous. Sometimes, group members give false information. Why? To push the group toward the decision *they* want. *Complete* information is of course complete—no holes, no gaps. Members of a dysfunctional group may withhold information; this can be very disruptive. *Relevant* information pertains to the group's objectives. Having good criteria helps you chuck irrelevant information.

Technology, as you well know, has opened up a wealth of access to information and tools that were hitherto unavailable. This is the 21st-century advantage. *Use it.* But *also* know when it is not useful, when it is expensive, when simpler approaches will not only suffice, but may actually be better.

Getting Groups to Use Creativity and Innovation

As noted earlier, the pitfalls of group dynamics include satisficing, domination issues, and groupthink. As a manager, you can help your group avoid these difficulties. A variety of methods are available to help you make the group effective, and the experience a valuable one. Exhibit 3–7 lists five widely used methods.

BRAINSTORMING. In **brainstorming** group members generate as many alternatives as they can in a short time frame. Here is how it works. The group is presented with a problem and asked to develop as many solutions as possible. A short time period (10 minutes, 20 minutes) is specified. Members are encouraged to make wild, off-the-wall suggestions. They can build on suggestions made by others. They are not to react in any way—favorably or unfavorably—to any contribution. When selecting members for a brainstorming group, it is a good idea to include a diversity of people—your goal, after all, is to get a diversity of ideas. Five to twelve people make a good-sized group for brainstorming. Everyone is given an equal voice—status differences should be ignored. Janitors have just as much to contribute to this process as CEOs. Alternatives are evaluated only after idea generation slows

brainstorming
The process of suggesting many possible alternatives without evaluation.

Exhibit 3–6   Characteristics of Useful Information

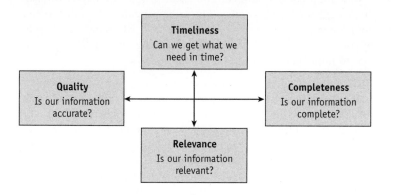

Exhibit 3–7   Methods That Foster Creativity and Innovation in Groups

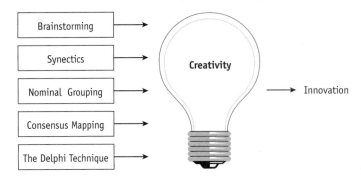

considerably. Companies commonly use brainstorming to generate out-of-the-box solutions and innovative new products.[26]

synectics
The process of generating novel alternatives through role playing and fantasizing.

SYNECTICS. In **synectics** novel alternatives are generated through role playing and fantasizing. Synectics focuses on generating novel ideas rather than a large number of ideas. The exact nature of the problem is purposefully not stated initially so that group members avoid preconceptions.

nominal grouping
The process of generating and evaluating alternatives using a structured voting method.

NOMINAL GROUPING. In **nominal grouping** a structured voting method is used to generate and evaluate alternatives. This process involves six steps:[27]

1. *List ideas.* Each participant generates ideas in writing.

2. *Record the ideas.* Each member suggests an idea. This continues in a round-robin manner until all ideas are posted. The leader then presents the ideas to the group.

3. *Clarify them.* Alternatives are clarified through a guided discussion, and additional ideas are listed.

4. *Rank them.* Each member rank-orders the top three ideas; low-ranked alternatives are eliminated.

5. *Discuss the rankings.* Rankings are discussed for clarification, not persuasion. During this step, participants explain their choices and their reasons for making them.

6. *Vote.* A secret vote is taken to select the alternative.

Used properly, nominal grouping minimizes domination, goal displacement, conformity, and groupthink.

consensus mapping
The process of developing group agreement on a solution to a problem.

CONSENSUS MAPPING. **Consensus mapping** develops group agreement on a problem solution. If a consensus cannot be reached, the group does not make a decision. It differs from nominal grouping because competitive battles in which votes are taken and a solution forced on members of the group are not allowed. The Japanese call this approach *ringi.*[28] Consensus mapping can be used after brainstorming. The principal difference is that in consensus mapping the group categorizes or clusters ideas rather than choosing a single solution. A major benefit of consensus mapping is that the group "owns" the solution, so members are more committed to implementing it.

TIMEOUT
Give examples of problems in your organization or team where brainstorming, nominal grouping, or consensus mapping would be appropriate.

_____

_____

_____

_____

THE DELPHI TECHNIQUE. In the Delphi technique a series of confidential questionnaires are used to refine a solution. Responses from the first questionnaire are analyzed and resubmitted to participants in a second questionnaire. This process may continue for five or more rounds before a consensus emerges. Delphi group members are typically recruited from the "best of the best," widely acknowledged as experts in their field, and—this is important—they are outsiders, not from the organization that is hiring them. Because of the nature of the process, they may never need to come together; this works well because getting that many high-powered people to take time out from their busy lives to solve your problem is, well, problematic. This is an expensive process, however—such people do not come cheap.

APPLYING THE CONCEPT   *Using Groups to Generate Alternatives*

For each situation, identify the most appropriate technique.

a. brainstorming   **c.** nominal grouping   **e.** Delphi technique

b. synectics   **d.** consensus mapping

_____ 11. A consultant leads company employees and young soccer players together to come up with ideas for new cleats.

_____ 12. Our team is suffering from morale problems.

_____ 13. We need new matching desks for the ten of us in this office.

_____ 14. We need to reduce waste in the production department to cut cost and increase productivity.

_____ 15. Top managers are projecting future trends in the retail sporting goods industry, as part of their long-range planning.

Upper-level managers commonly use synectics and the Delphi technique in their nonprogrammed decision making. Brainstorming, nominal grouping, and consensus mapping are frequently used at the department level with work groups. Whichever of these methods suits your decision situation, be sure to guard against responses that snuff out creativity. Exhibit 3–8 lists examples of "killer" statements. If a team member makes a killer statement, make sure everyone realizes that such negative attitudes are counterproductive.

Decision Trees

So you've got some alternatives—now what do you do? You might try making a decision tree. A *decision tree* is a diagram of alternatives. The tree gives you a "visual" to work with, which makes it easier for some people to analyze the alternatives.

To construct a decision tree, first write down every alternative that you can think of that could solve the problem you are grappling with. For each alternative, list potential outcomes. Next, list the choices (decisions) to be made with each alternative. Continue doing this, breaking each alternative into subalternatives, until you are satisfied you have explored each alternative in enough detail. A decision tree is shown for Michael Jordan's 2001 draft pick decision in the Case at the end of this chapter.

At **ADIDAS**, alternatives generated in the decision process included (among many others) doing nothing, developing a new advertising campaign, introducing new footwear products, creating new unrelated products, and creating new related products. **Why do you think doing nothing was considered an alternative? Play devil's advocate with this alternative, and defend doing it and rejecting it.**

Exhibit 3–8   Great Ways to Kill Creativity

- It can't be done.
- We've never done it.
- Has anyone else tried it?
- It will not work in our department/ company/industry.
- It costs too much.
- It isn't in the budget.
- Let's form a committee.

STEP 4: SELECT THE MOST FEASIBLE ALTERNATIVE

 LEARNING OUTCOME

9 Explain how quantitative techniques and cost-benefit analysis facilitate selecting alternatives.

At this point you may be wondering why steps 3 and 4 of the decision process (generating alternatives and selecting one) are two different steps. There is a good reason for this—trust us. Generating and evaluating alternatives at the same time often lead to satisficing and wastes time on poorly developed alternatives.

As you and your group evaluate alternatives, "think forward" and try to predict possible outcomes. Use the objectives and criteria you developed in step 2 of the decision process to critique each alternative. Then compare how each alternative measures up against your other alternatives. To assist you in this process, become familiar with (if not adept at) two types of techniques: quantitative analyses and cost-benefit analyses. To get you started, we present a brief overview here.

Quantitative Techniques

Quantitative techniques use mathematical analysis to assess alternative solutions.

BREAK-EVEN ANALYSIS. Break-even analysis calculates the volume of sales or revenue that will result in a profit. It involves forecasting the volume of sales and the cost of production. The break-even point occurs at the level where no profit or loss results. As it evaluated each alternative, **ADIDAS** no doubt computed how many pairs of Kobes would have to be sold to break even. To do this, Adidas factored in costs as diverse as the cost of Kobe Bryant's promotional contract, the cost of shipping the shoes from China, the research that went into their design, and so forth. **What other factors can you think of that might have been critical in Adidas's break-even analysis?**

CAPITAL BUDGETING. These techniques are used to analyze alternative investments. The *payback approach* calculates the number of years it will take to recover the initial cash investment. The goal here is to find the quickest payback. Another technique computes the *average rate of return.* It is useful when yearly returns of various alternatives differ. A more sophisticated technique, *discounted cash flow,* takes into account the time value of money. It assumes that a dollar today is worth more than a dollar in the future. To assess alternatives, organizations like **ADIDAS** often direct staff statisticians and financial analysts to perform discounted cash flow analyses. Adidas also uses capital budgeting techniques to decide what machines it should purchase for its factories. **Use the URL given in Reviewing Their Game Plan at the start of this chapter to look at the company's financial statements. Do the notes to the statements tell what type of analyses the accountants use?**

QUEUING THEORY. This technique addresses waiting time. Organizations often have numerous employees providing service to customers. Too many employees waiting on customers is an inefficient use of resources and is costly. Too few employees providing service can also be costly if poor service drives customers away. Queuing theory helps organizations balance these two costs. Event managers use queuing theory to determine the optimum number of ticket takers to reduce waiting time entering an event. Retail stores use queuing theory to determine the optimum number of checkout clerks; and production departments use it to schedule preventive maintenance on equipment.

PROBABILITY THEORY. Analysts use probability theory to help managers make decisions in risky environmental conditions. A probability for the chance of success or failure is assigned to each alternative. Expected value, which is the payoff or profit from each combination of alternatives and outcomes, is then calculated. Usually done on a payoff matrix or decision tree, the assigned probability of the outcome is multiplied by the assigned benefit or cost. Probability theory is used to determine whether and how much to expand facilities, to select the most profitable use of finances, or to determine the amount of inventory to stock. As an exercise in critical thinking, try using it to choose a hypothetical job.

TIMEOUT

Choose two or three decisions of various importance facing your team, and decide whether break-even analysis, capital budgeting, queuing theory, or probability theory is an appropriate technique to use in your decision process.

_____

_____

_____

_____

_____

APPLYING
THE CONCEPT   *Selecting a Quantitative Technique*

Choose the appropriate technique to use in each situation:

a. break-even   **c.** queuing theory

b. capital budgeting   **d.** probability theory

_____ 16. Claudia needs to repair the swimming pool's filtering system or to replace it with a new one.

_____ 17. Ben is investing money for the team.

_____ 18. Employees at a sporting goods store hang around with nothing to do and at other times they work for hours without stopping.

_____ 19. A bicycle shop owner wants to know how many times a bike must be rented out to make it worth purchasing.

_____ 20. Fans had to wait so long in the ticket line that they missed most of the first quarter of the game.

Cost-Benefit Analysis

Quantitative methods endeavor to objectify the comparison of alternatives by using various mathematical techniques. (An aside, no technique is ever *completely* objective; each method has to start with underlying assumptions that are, by their very nature, subjective.) As effective as these techniques are, and they can be extremely effective, circumstances don't always allow their use. Sometimes it is impossible to assign a probability to a benefit received for a cost. Cost-benefit analysis combines subjective methods and mathematical techniques to compare alternative courses of action. Also called pros and cons analysis, it looks at the advantages (benefits) and the disadvantages (costs) of each alternative. Exhibit 3–9 compares quantitative techniques and cost-benefit analysis.

Every coach worth his or her salt has sat an athlete down and laid out the pros and cons of his or her play, focus, attitude, or behavior on or off the field or court. Likewise, each of us has, at one time or another, thought about the pros and cons of a situation facing us without writing them down—and this works (often very well) for small, nonconsequential decisions. However, for important, nonprogrammed decisions, laying them out on paper and formalizing your analysis will improve the quality of your decision. (Try it on some current dilemma and see how it focuses your thinking and clarifies your courses of action.)

Cost-benefit analysis is more subjective than quantitative analysis. Therefore, groups that use cost-benefit analysis must consciously endeavor to sidestep group dynamics that can ambush subjective analysis. Playing devil's advocate, for example, can help groups avoid satisficing, dominance issues, and groupthink. Groups should also carefully consider how alternatives should be presented, because the order of discussion can affect decisions (people typically remember best what they hear first and last). Also, alternatives poorly or negatively presented tend not to be selected.

Exhibit 3–9   Comparison of Analysis Techniques

Quantitative Techniques	Cost-Benefit Analysis
←	→
(Objective)	(Subjective)
(Maximum use of math)	(Minimum use of math)

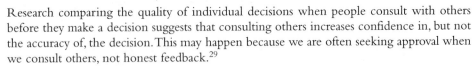

TIMEOUT

Describe a recent decision in your organization where cost-benefit analysis would have been particularly appropriate, and lay out a few of its pros and cons.

Research comparing the quality of individual decisions when people consult with others before they make a decision suggests that consulting others increases confidence in, but not the accuracy of, the decision. This may happen because we are often seeking approval when we consult others, not honest feedback.[29]

Whichever method you use to analyze alternatives, keep your end goal in mind—that of selecting the optimal alternative that meets the criteria you and your team have established. If none of the alternatives meet the criteria, you have two options: (1) Return to step 2 and change the criteria, or (2) return to step 3 and generate more alternatives. It appears **ADIDAS** has changed its criteria for selecting an athlete to endorse its footwear. The Kobe shoe line was quite successful, and it had a youthful, three-time world champion star as its sponsor. However, Kobe Bryant's contract with Adidas—worth an estimated $40 million over five years—came to an end. By not re-signing Bryant, Adidas made it clear that its new criteria involved finding a *potential* star player who would be satisfied with a less lucrative contract. Adidas would then generate new alternatives based on the new criteria. Possible alternatives were to sign the number one draft pick in 2002, Yao Ming. Another alternative might have been to sign Mike Dunleavey, who has a similar game to former superstar Larry Bird. Adidas ended up selecting Jay Williams of Duke University, who was picked number two overall (by the Chicago Bulls). Williams will cost Adidas only about $750,000 per year and has the potential to become the next Kobe Bryant or Michael Jordan.[30] **How accurate do you think general managers can be in deciding which player will become the next marketing superstar?**

STEP 5: IMPLEMENT THE DECISION
STEP 6: CONTROL THE RESULTS

The final two steps in the decision process are about implementing and controlling. Before you can implement a decision, you need a plan.

The Plan

Once you have chosen an alternative, it is time to develop a plan of action that includes a schedule for the implementation. We examine the details of planning in the next two chapters.

Implementing the Plan

How you implement your plan is crucial to its success or failure. The most promising alternative will fall flat on its paper face if its implementation is not carefully thought out and then carefully carried out. Communicating the plan to all employees is also critical. (We discuss effective communication in Chapter 11.) Delegating (discussed in Chapter 6) will also be key to a smooth implementation. You may need multiple implementation plans. **ADIDAS,** for example, developed a plan to sell TaylorMade golf clubs, a plan to advertise them, and a plan to distribute the clubs at the retail level. **Judging from the company's results with its TaylorMade clubs, do you think the implementation went smoothly?**

Controlling the Results

Control methods should be developed during planning. Establish checkpoints to determine whether the chosen alternative is solving the problem. If not, consider corrective action. More importantly, if the implementation continues to go poorly, don't remain married to your decision—that is, don't rule out a "divorce." You don't want to end up throwing good money after bad. When managers will not admit that they made a bad decision and take "evasive action" (to avoid the inevitable collision with failure), they are *escalating commitment*. When you make a poor decision, humble yourself. Admit the mistake and strive to rectify it. Go back over your decision process. It will be several years before **ADIDAS** management can determine whether its decision to diversify into new markets was a wise one. However, even though integrating the new products has gone more slowly than planned, the fit with Adidas's traditional lines of footwear appears to justify the company's entrance into growing markets such as golfing. Brazil, whom Nike backed, won the World Cup.[31] Germany, whom Adidas backed, lost. **Do you think Adidas's $36.8 million investment in the World Cup will pay off anyway? Was Adidas's decision to commit so many advertising dollars to the World Cup made in certain or risky conditions?** And analysts are starting to take notice—the company was recently mentioned as a promising stock pick for investors seeking safe harbor from the storm in U.S. markets.[32]

CHAPTER SUMMARY

1. Describe how meeting objectives, solving problems, and making decisions are connected.

Managers are responsible for setting and achieving organizational objectives. When managers do not meet objectives, problems result. When problems exist, decisions must be made about what, if any, action must be taken.

2. Explain how management functions, decision making, and problem solving relate.

When managers plan, organize, lead, and control, they make decisions. When managers are not proficient in these functions, they are part of the problem, not part of the solution.

3. Describe the six steps in the decision process.

The six steps in the decision process are (1) define the problem or opportunity, (2) set objectives and criteria, (3) generate alternatives, (4) select the most feasible alternative, (5) implement the decision, and (6) control the results.

4. Identify programmed and nonprogrammed decisions and recognize certain, uncertain, and risky business conditions.

Programmed and nonprogrammed decisions differ in how often they recur, whether they are routine, and in level of significance. Nonprogrammed decisions are nonrecurring, non-routine, highly significant decisions. Programmed decisions are recurring, routine, and less significant decisions.

Decisions are made in environmental conditions that are certain (you know the outcome of each alternative), that are risky (you can assign probabilities of success or failure to the outcomes), and that are highly uncertain (you cannot assign probabilities of success or failure to the outcomes).

5. Know when to use different decision models and when to make decisions as group or as an individual.

Use the rational model with group decision making when a nonprogrammed decision must be made in high-risk or uncertain conditions. Use the bounded rationality model when you work "solo" on programmed decisions made in low-risk and certain conditions. Note, however, that this is a general guide; there are always exceptions to the rule.

6. State the difference between an objective and "must" and "want" criteria.

An objective is the end result you want from your decision. "Must" criteria are the requirements that an alternative has to meet to be selected. "Want" criteria are desirable but are not absolutely necessary.

7. Explain how creativity and innovation differ.

Creativity is a way of thinking that generates new ideas. Innovation is the implementation of new ideas.

8. Describe the three stages in the creative process.

The three stages are (1) prepare, prepare, prepare; (2) incubate (take a break from the problem and let your subconscious work on it) and illuminate (recognize when your "lightbulb" goes on); (3) evaluate (critique your idea to make sure it is a good one).

9. Explain how quantitative techniques and cost-benefit analysis facilitate selecting alternatives.

Quantitative techniques use math to select objectively the alternative with the highest value. Cost-benefit analysis combines subjective analysis with some math, although alternatives don't necessarily have to be quantified to compare (as in the pros and cons approach).

10. Define the key terms discussed in the text.

Fill in the missing key terms from memory, or match the key terms from the list in the margin with their definitions below.

A _____ exists whenever objectives are not being met.

_____ is the process of taking corrective action to meet objectives.

_____ is the process of selecting an alternative course of action that will solve a problem.

A _____ involves making snap decisions without taking time to get all the information needed and without considering alternatives.

A _____ involves taking plenty of time to decide, gathering considerable information, and analyzing numerous alternatives.

A _____ involves taking time but not wasting time; knowing when more information is needed and when enough analysis has been done.

When making _____, with recurring or routine situations, the decision maker should use decision rules or organizational policies and procedures to make the decision.

When making _____, with significant and nonrecurring and nonroutine situations, the decision maker should use the decision-making model.

The three _____ include certainty, risk, and uncertainty.

_____ are the standards that must be met to accomplish an objective.

_____ is the implementation of a new idea.

_____ is a way of thinking that generates new ideas.

The three stages in the _____ are (1) preparation, (2) incubation and illumination, and (3) evaluation.

With the _____ approach, group members defend the solution while others try to come up with reasons why the idea won't work.

_____ is the process of suggesting many possible alternatives without evaluation.

_____ is the process of generating novel alternatives through role playing and fantasizing.

Key Terms

brainstorming

consensus mapping

consistent decision style

creative process

creativity

criteria

decision making

decision-making conditions

devil's advocate

innovation

nominal grouping

nonprogrammed decisions

problem

problem solving

programmed decisions

reflective decision style

reflexive decision style

synectics

_____ is the process of generating and evaluating alternatives using a structured voting method.

_____ is the process of developing group agreement on a solution to a problem.

REVIEW AND DISCUSSION

1. Why are problem solving and decision making important in sports?

2. Why is it necessary to determine the decision structure and the conditions surrounding the decision?

3. Why do organizations use groups to solve problems and make decisions?

4. Which pitfall of group problem solving and decision making do you think is most common?

5. Is a decrease in ticket sales or profits a symptom or a cause of a problem?

6. Would setting a maximum price of $1500 to spend on a lifecycle exercise machine be an objective or a criterion?

7. Are creativity and innovation really important to a soccer team?

8. We have all made decisions using information that was not timely, of quality, complete, and/or relevant—we are human, after all. Reflect on a decision your team made with poor information. What was the result?

9. What is the major difference between nominal grouping and consensus mapping?

10. Why are generating and selecting alternatives separate steps in the decision process?

11. Have you ever used any of the techniques discussed in the text to analyze an alternative? If so, which one? If not, how might you have improved on a recent decision using one of these techniques?

CASE

Draft Day for the Washington Wizards

In 2001, Michael Jordan, as the President of Basketball Operations for the Washington Wizards, faced a difficult decision. Should he use or trade away his overall number one draft pick, and which player should he pick if he elected to use the number-one slot? An overall number-one draft pick doesn't come along very often, and is not to be treated lightly. Which strategy would best help the Wizards turn around their losing record—one star player who might not be happy playing for a losing team *or* upgrading skill levels in several key positions?

Draft decisions require careful analysis, shrewd negotiations, and outside-the-box (in a word, creative) thinking. Choosing the correct strategy was crucial for the Wizards—they needed to get to a winning position in a finite period of time. Michael Jordan did not make this decision alone—this was *not* a programmed decision. The environmental conditions were anything but certain: Would the number one draft pick pan out? Would fans prefer a team of non-standout players who *might* win or a star player whom they would love but who might not be enough to turn the team around? Nothing less than the long-term success of the Wizards was depending on this decision—definitely not something to go solo on. Jordan of course knew this very well, and he no doubt huddled with the owner, general manager, scouts, draft specialists, and coaches for long hours into many nights before the Wizards announced their draft pick.

Michael Jordan developed four alternatives: (1) trade the top pick to a team like the Boston Celtics for their #10, #11, and #21 picks; (2) select high school center Kwame Brown; (3) select a college player such as forward Shane Battier; or (4) select a guard from a number of equally talented players. His decision tree might have looked like that shown in Exhibit 3–10.

So, what did the Wizards decide? The team went with high school student Kwame Brown. "This is a great beginning for this franchise and it starts with him," said Michael Jordan. "I'm not putting any added pressure on him, but all I ask him to be is be himself."[33]

For current information on the Washington Wizards, and to find out whether their draft day strategy appears to be working, go to http://www.nba.com/wizards/.

Exhibit 3–10   Jordan's Decision Tree

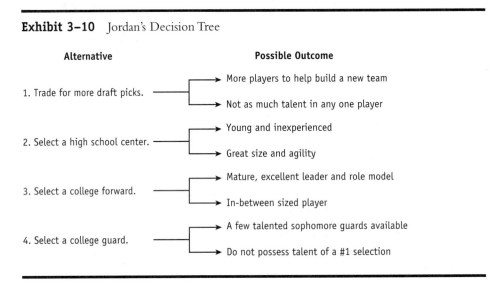

Alternative	Possible Outcome
1. Trade for more draft picks.	More players to help build a new team
	Not as much talent in any one player
2. Select a high school center.	Young and inexperienced
	Great size and agility
3. Select a college forward.	Mature, excellent leader and role model
	In-between sized player
4. Select a college guard.	A few talented sophomore guards available
	Do not possess talent of a #1 selection

CASE QUESTIONS

1. Michael Jordan's draft pick decision was a programmed decision.
   a. true   b. false

2. The rational model is appropriate for this decision.
   a. true   b. false

3. Michael needed to set objectives and criteria.
   a. true   b. false

4. Creativity and innovation are not crucial in the draft pick.
   a. true   b. false

5. The environmental conditions facing the Wizards were
   a. certain
   b. risky
   c. uncertain

6. The information given in the case discussion lacks the _____ that the Wizards needed to make their decision.
   a. timeliness
   b. completeness
   c. quality
   d. relevance

7. _____ would have been appropriate for generating alternatives for the Wizards.
   a. brainstorming
   b. synectics
   c. nominal grouping
   d. consensus mapping
   e. the Delphi technique
   f. none of these

8. Which method would have been most appropriate for Michael Jordan's decision process?
   a. a quantitative technique
   b. cost-benefit analysis

9. Do you believe that Michael Jordan was creative in selecting Kwame Brown?
   a. yes   b. no

10. Classify Michael Jordan's desire to improve his basketball team.
    a. objective
    b. criterion

11. List the pros and cons for each alternative from Michael Jordan's perspective, which may be different from yours. Be sure to state the pros and cons of trading the first pick versus using it.

12. Which alternative would you select if you were in Michael Jordan's shoes?

13. Is it ethical for an NBA team to draft a player fresh out of high school? Do you think there should be a minimum age for players? If so, what age would you choose, and why? If not, why not?

14. How has Kwame Brown worked out for the Washington Wizards?

15. Did Michael Jordan's return to playing in the NBA influence his draft decision? Was this factor part of the original decision-making process?

EXERCISES

Skill-Builder: Using the Six-Step Decision Process

Objective:

■ To hone your problem-solving and decision-making abilities.

Preparation:

Select a problem or opportunity that you would like to address. (Remember, a problem exists when your objectives are not being met. In other words, are what *is* happening and what you *want* to happen different?) Choose any aspect of your life—work, college, sports, a relationship, a purchase you wish to make, where to go on a big date, to name a few possibilities. Use the outline below to help you work through the decision process.

Step 1: Define the Problem or Opportunity

1. *Decision structure.* Is the decision programmed or nonprogrammed?

   _____

2. *Decision conditions.* Are they uncertain, risky, or certain?

   _____

3. *Decision model.* Which model is appropriate—rational or bounded rationality?

   _____

4. *Select the appropriate level of participation.* Should you make this decision solo or use a group?

   _____

5. *Distinguish symptoms from the cause of the problem*. List the symptoms and causes. Now state the problem simply.

_____

_____

_____

_____

_____

_____

_____

Step 2: Set Objectives and Criteria

6. What do you want to accomplish with this decision?

(a) My objective:

_____

_____

_____

(b) Must criteria:

_____

_____

_____

(c) Want criteria:

_____

_____

_____

Step 3: Generate Alternatives

7. What information do you need? (Remember, information must be timely, of quality, complete, and relevant to be useful.)

_____

_____

8. Will technology help you or hinder you?

_____

9. If you are using a group, will you brainstorm, use nominal grouping, or do consensus mapping?

_____

10. Generate at least three alternatives, and list them here.

_____

_____

_____

_____

_____

Step 4: Select the Most Feasible Alternative

11. Is quantitative or cost-benefit analysis appropriate?

12. List the pros and cons of each alternative.

13. On a separate piece of paper, make a decision tree.

Step 5: Implement the Decision

14. Write out a plan for implementing the decision (you may wish to skim Chapters 4 and 5). Be sure to state the control methods you will use to assess the results.

Step 6: Control the Results

15. Make notes about what (if any) progress you are making in solving your problem. Indicate whether corrective action seems advisable, and if necessary, return to prior steps in the decision process. Think about how can you avoid escalation of commitment.

In-Class Application

Complete the skill-building preparation noted above before class.

Choose one (one or two class periods):
- Break into groups of three to five members. One at a time, go through the six decision steps. At each step, group members give feedback by pointing out errors, suggesting how to improve the written statements, generating additional alternatives, listing pros and cons not thought of, stating which alternatives others would select, and so on.
- Informal, whole-class discussion of student experiences.

Wrap-up:

Take a few minutes and write down your answers to the following questions:

■ What did I learn from this experience?

_____

_____

_____

_____

■ How will I use this knowledge in the future?

_____

_____

_____

_____

As a class, discuss student responses.

Internet Skills: Analyzing Decision Making at the WNBA

Objective:

■ To analyze the WNBA's decision process during its first year (1996).

Preparation:

Visit http://www.wnba.com, click the *News and Features* link, then click *About Us,* and answer the following questions.

1. In 1996, did the WNBA face programmed or nonprogrammed decisions? Explain.

_____

_____

_____

_____

_____

2. How long did the WNBA have to organize the league? Did this length of time affect the quality of its decisions?

_____

_____

3. What did the WNBA adopt for its uniforms? What game rules did it decide on? Were compromises made as these issues were negotiated?

_____

_____

_____

_____

_____

_____

4. Visit http://www.businessweek.com and use the search engine to locate the June 20, 2001, article by Jay Weiner entitled "Growing Pains for the WNBA." Review the success or failure of various WNBA decisions over the past few years.

5. Who is highlighted in the *Career Counselor* link? What position do they hold? What level of education?

_____

_____

_____

_____

In-Class Application

Complete the questionnaire above.

Choose one:

- Break into groups of three to five, share your answers to the above questions, and try to come to a consensus on the effectiveness of the WNBA decision process. Select a spokesperson and present your findings to the class.
- Whole-class discussion of student responses to the four questions.

Wrap-up:
Take a few minutes and answer the following questions.

- What did I learn from this experience?

_____

_____

_____

- How will I use this experience in the future?

_____

_____

_____

As a whole class, share your thoughts and answers.

4 Strategic and Operational Planning

Learning Outcomes

After studying this chapter, you should be able to:

1. Explain how strategic and operational plans differ.

2. Describe corporate-, business-, and functional-level strategies.

3. Explain why organizations analyze industries and competitive situations.

4. Explain why organizations analyze the company situation.

5. Discuss how goals and objectives are similar yet different.

6. Write objectives.

7. Describe the four corporate-level grand strategies.

8. Describe the three growth strategies.

9. Discuss the three business-level adaptive strategies.

10. List four functional-level operations.

11. Define the following key terms (in order of appearance in the chapter):

- strategic planning
- operational planning
- strategic process
- strategy
- three levels of strategies
- corporate-level strategy
- business-level strategy
- functional-level strategy
- situation analysis
- SWOT analysis
- competitive advantage
- goals
- objectives
- management by objectives (MBO)
- grand strategies
- corporate growth strategies
- merger
- acquisition
- business portfolio analysis
- adaptive strategies
- operational strategies

REVIEWING THEIR GAME PLAN

FIFA Plans Strategically

Whole regions, peoples, and nations across the globe share neither mores, culture, language, nor religion, but they do share a passion—football. Not to be confused with *our* game of football, *football* (soccer to us neophyte Americans) is not only the world's number one game, it is also a "major player" on the international scene, and in commerce and politics. With over 200 million active players, it also constitutes a substantial chunk of the global leisure industry. Whole nations (from Yemen to Germany to Brazil to South Korea and Japan) dream about winning the World Cup, and their citizens pay money (and lots of it!) to travel to see matches, to play them at home, to wear shoes like their favorite players (whose status makes that of movie stars pale in comparison), and to buy numerous football products.

FIFA (Fédération Internationale de Football Association) is one reason for the world's love affair with football. Founded in Paris in 1904, it has survived the turmoil of two world wars and today includes 204 member organizations, making it the biggest and most popular sport federation in the world.

In 1998, at the 51st FIFA Ordinary Congress in Paris, Joseph Blatter (Switzerland) succeeded João Havelange (Brazil) as the eighth FIFA President. This victory elevated Mr. Blatter, who had served FIFA in various positions for 23 years, to the highest rung in the international football scene. Mr. Blatter is a versatile and experienced proponent of international sport diplomacy (this is crucial with a global sport like soccer) and is totally committed to serving football, FIFA, and the world's youth.

With the new president came a fresh strategic approach to issues facing world football. Mr. Blatter lost no time in presenting his vision of FIFA's future priorities, and has worked tirelessly to win widespread approval in FIFA's Congress and Executive Committee. His vision is wide-ranging and ambitious, and includes

- making the 2002 FIFA World Cup a huge success (do you think he succeeded at this one?)
- establishing FIFA for SOS Children's Villages
- improving FIFA's dialogue with governmental authorities
- improving relations with the IOC and other sport bodies
- creating a TV distribution policy for the World Cup
- improving refereeing standards

In pursuing these goals, Mr. Blatter speaks frequently of the need for a renewed sense of solidarity in the world of football. His House of FIFA, a "virtual house," features values crucial to FIFA's future (and future strength) as a global institution: Its *foundation* is the trust generated by the closely knit FIFA family; its *walls* are its efficiently managed organization based on the principles of democracy, solidarity, and quality whose goal is to support and protect the game; and its *roof* is its universality, which binds everything together. FIFA's slogan—For the Good of the Game—speaks to these ideas and guides its activities.

The two basic ideas that shape FIFA's mission—make the game better and take it to the world—are having an effect. Improvements can be seen in the coordination of the playing calendar, the professionalization of refereeing, and advances in medical research.

For current information on FIFA, visit http://www.fifa.com. (For ideas on using the Internet, see Appendix B.)

INTERNET RESOURCES

http://web.mit.edu/athletics/www/plan/index.html *Here you will find a strategic plan developed by MIT Athletics. In May 2000, the Department of Athletics, Physical Education, and Recreation decided to develop a strategic plan to analyze its current role and determine what direction the department should take in the future to be more responsive to the community's needs. The plan begins with the department's mission statement and proceeds to establish goals and make recommendations. It is a well-organized and thoughtful example of questioning the status quo. The plan was revised in the Spring of 2002.*

http://www.mindtools.com/spintro.html *The Sports Psychology section of the Mind Tools web site offers a great tutorial on how to decide on and achieve any sport-related goals you might have. Click the* Goal Setting *link, then* Deciding Goals, *to get started. By first asking you to determine how committed you are to your sport and what exact skills you will need to succeed, this site assures that whatever goals you set will be realistic. Mind Tools also offers a shareware program called LifePlan that will help you develop your plans and stay on course.*

http://www.mapnp.org/library/mrktng/cmpetitr/cmpetitr.htm *At this address, you'll find a collection of links to web sites that focus on competitive analysis. Use this site as a jumping-off point to explore benchmarking, competitive forces, customer satisfaction, product development, and a host of other related topics.*

DEVELOPING YOUR SKILLS   Effective managers develop sound strategic plans and set achievable objectives. This endeavor is part savvy business practice, part knowledge, part intuition, part experience, and part art. With patience and practice, you can learn to do this too. Does the organization you work for or play for have a plan? What are the objectives they intend to achieve this year? In two years? In five years?

STRATEGIC AND OPERATIONAL PLANNING

1 LEARNING OUTCOME
Describe the differences between strategic and operational plans.

Before we examine the planning process and the various levels of strategic planning, you need to know *why* managers plan. A great idea does not guarantee success. In fact, for every ten products introduced, *eight* fail. The reason for this high rate of failure? In two words—poor planning. A prime example is the now-defunct XFL, which was the World Wrestling Entertainment's attempt at developing a new professional football league.[1] Planning is one of the most important tasks managers do, and it is crucial today. Not only does the 1990s boom in the sport industry appear to be flagging, but economic woes and increasing competition will make success ever harder to attain. In this new environment, sport organizations will need innovative strategies if they wish to survive.[2]

The Strategic Process

In **strategic planning**, management develops a mission and long-term objectives and determines in advance how they will be accomplished. ("Long-term" generally means longer than one year.) In **operational planning**, management sets *short-term* objectives and determines in advance how they will be accomplished. ("Short-term" objectives are those that can be met in one year or less.) Strategic planning and operational planning differ primarily by time frame and by the management level involved. Strategic plans are typically developed for five years, and are reviewed and revised every year so that a five-year plan is always in place. Top-level managers develop strategic plans. Operational plans are developed for time frames of one year or less; middle managers or first-line managers develop operational plans.

TIMEOUT
State one objective from a strategic plan and one from an operational plan for a sport organization you are familiar with (preferably one you work for or play for). (You will be asked to analyze this same organization in other Timeouts in this chapter.)

_____

_____

_____

_____

_____

strategic planning
The process of developing a mission and long-term objectives and determining in advance how they will be accomplished.

operational planning
The process of setting short-term objectives and determining in advance how they will be accomplished.

The strategic process is about developing both the long-range and short-range plans that will enable the organization to accomplish its long-range objectives. Using the means and ends analogy (Chapter 2), top managers determine the ends and middle- and lower-level managers find the means to accomplish the ends.

In the **strategic process**, managers (1) develop the mission, (2) analyze the environment, (3) set objectives, (4) develop strategies, and (5) implement and control the strategies. Developing strategies takes place at three levels. As you can see from Exhibit 4–1, the process is not a linear one. Managers continually return to previous steps and make changes—planning is an ongoing process. Also note that management performs the four management functions—planning, organizing, leading, and controlling—in the strategic process.

> **strategic process**
> In this process, managers develop the mission, analyze the environment, set objectives, develop strategies, and implement and control the strategies.

Levels of Strategies

2 | **LEARNING OUTCOME**
Describe corporate-, business-, and functional-level strategies.

An organization's **strategy** is its plan for pursuing its mission and achieving its objectives. The **three levels of strategies** are corporate, business, and functional. We examine these three levels in more detail later in this chapter. Here we simply define them in order to give you an overview.

> **strategy**
> A plan for pursuing the mission and achieving objectives.

Corporate-level strategy is the organization's plan for managing multiple lines of businesses. Many large companies are actually several businesses. Adidas, for example, sells footwear, ski equipment, golf equipment, and cycling products—it treats each product line as a separate "line of business."[3]

> **three levels of strategies**
> Corporate, business, and functional.

Business-level strategy is the organization's plan for managing one line of business. Each of Adidas's businesses has its own strategy for competing in its market. Adidas used its Salomon division to acquire a Canadian company that specializes in equipment for mountain climbing and paddle sports such as kayaking (Arc'teryx Equipment Incorporated). Through this transaction Salomon expects to expand its presence in these fast-growing outdoor sports. Salomon's mission is to provide cutting-edge sport products for adventurous outdoor sports enthusiasts.[4]

> **corporate-level strategy**
> The plan for managing multiple lines of businesses.
>
> **business-level strategy**
> The plan for managing one line of business.

Functional-level strategy is the organization's plan for managing one area of the business. Functional areas include marketing, finance and accounting, operations/production, human resources, and others depending on the specific line of business. Managers in each of Adidas's business lines are involved with these functional areas. Exhibit 4–2 shows the relationship of corporate-, business-, and functional-level strategies.

> **functional-level strategy**
> The plan for managing one area of the business.

Exhibit 4–1   The Strategic Process

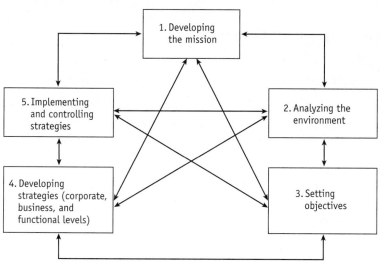

> **TIMEOUT**
> List the lines of business your organization is involved in.
> _____
> _____
> _____
> _____
> _____

Exhibit 4-2   Strategic Planning

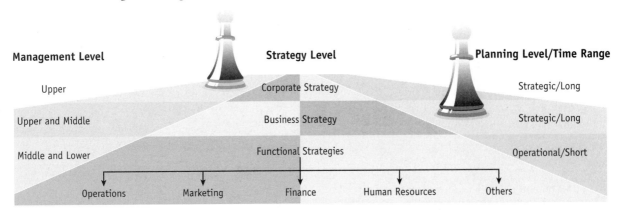

Management Level	Strategy Level	Planning Level/Time Range
Upper	Corporate Strategy	Strategic/Long
Upper and Middle	Business Strategy	Strategic/Long
Middle and Lower	Functional Strategies	Operational/Short

Operations   Marketing   Finance   Human Resources   Others

Developing the Mission

Developing the organization's mission is the first step in the strategic process. The mission provides the foundation on which the plan, via the four remaining steps, will be constructed. The organization's mission, as noted in chapter 2, is its purpose or reason for being. The mission states what business(es) the company is in now and will be in the future. It describes management's vision for the company—where the company is headed, and why. **FIFA's mission is to make the game of soccer better and to bring it to the world. Name three ways FIFA is fulfilling its mission and three areas it could improve in.** Over the past two decades, strategic planning has become an important tool for every sport organization as competition has grown keener.[5]

ANALYZING THE ENVIRONMENT

To create value, a strategy must fit with the capabilities of the firm and its external environment.[6] The organization's internal and external environmental factors (Chapter 2) are analyzed as step 2 in the strategic process, which determines the fit. Another term for analyzing the environment is situation analysis. A **situation analysis** draws out those features in a company's environment that most directly frame its strategic window of options and opportunities. The situation analysis has three parts: analysis of the company's industry and its competition, analysis of the company's particular situation, and analysis of the company's competitive advantage (or lack thereof). Companies with multiple lines of business conduct environmental analyses for each line of business.

situation analysis
Draws out those features in a company's environment that most directly frame its strategic window of options and opportunities.

Analysis of the Industry and the Competition

3 LEARNING OUTCOME
Explain why organizations analyze their industry and their competition.

Industries vary widely in their business makeup, competitive situation, and growth potential. To determine whether an industry is worth entering requires answers to such questions as: How large is the market? What is the growth rate? How many competitors are there? Callaway Golf Company, for example, faces strong competition from Acushnet (Titleist brand), Adams Golf (Tight Lies Fairway Woods), TaylorMade Golf, Orlimar Golf (TriMetal Fairway Woods), and SHC (formerly Spalding Sports Worldwide and owner of Top-Flite golf balls and Ben Hogan clubs).

FIVE COMPETITIVE FORCES. Michael Porter uses the idea of five competitive forces to analyze the competitive environment.[7]

1. Rivalry among competing firms. Porter calls this "the scrambling and jockeying for position."[8] How do businesses compete for customers—by price, quality, and speed (responding to new styles and models and getting these products quickly to retailers).

Nike, Reebok, Adidas–Salomon, and Fila are rivals in the athletic footwear industry. All four companies need to anticipate the moves of their competitors. They also need to be aware of newer competitors such as And1, which focuses on basketball footwear and apparel with an urban style.

2. *Potential development of substitute products and services.* This occurs when companies from other industries try to move into the market. Clothing manufacturers such as Tommy Hilfiger have attempted to enter the sneaker market using its fashion brand to its advantage. Also, "brown shoe" companies, such as Doc Martens, persuaded many younger buyers to buy hiking-style sneakers instead of the traditional sport sneakers. The brown shoe companies were quite successful in stealing away sales in the mid to late 1990s.

3. *Potential entry of new competitors.* How difficult and costly is it for new businesses to enter the industry? Does the company need to defend against new competition? And1, founded in 1993, has successfully entered the footwear and apparel industry.

4. *Bargaining power of suppliers.* How dependent is the business on its suppliers? If the business has only one major supplier, and no available alternatives, the supplier has great bargaining power. Nike doesn't actually make its own sneakers; it uses private contractors in Vietnam to produce them. Workers are paid very low wages, which indirectly gives Nike a great deal of power over these oftentimes helpless factory workers. In effect, since Nike can easily switch factories, it controls the suppliers.

5. *Bargaining power of consumers.* How much does the business depend on the consumer? Consumers of footwear have power because they can shift to other manufacturers on a mere whim, or because of a new style, better price, higher quality, greater convenience, and a host of other reasons. However, consumers lose power when they are loyal to a business like Nike and want to buy only Nike footwear. In effect, since there are many consumers who want Nike products, Nike is in a strong position as long as it continues to offer appealing products.

Companies use analyses of the industry and their competitors primarily at the corporate level when they are deciding which lines of business they should consider entering (or exiting) and how to allocate resources among their product lines. (We will return to this topic later in the chapter.) Nike bought Bauer, a hockey equipment manufacturer, because the company decided this was an attractive industry. See Exhibit 4–3 for a competitive analysis of Nike's decision.

TIME**OUT**
Using Exhibit 4–3 as a guide, do a simple five-forces competitive analysis for your organization.
_____
_____
_____
_____
_____

Exhibit 4–3   Nike's Five-Forces Competitive Analysis

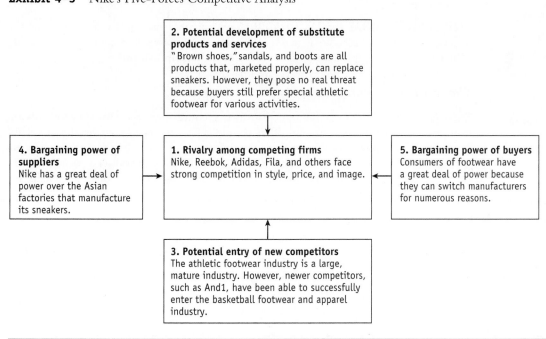

4 LEARNING OUTCOME
Explain why organizations analyze the company's situation.

Analysis of the Company Situation

Managers use analyses of the company situation when they develop business strategies and when they determine which issues need to be addressed in the next three steps of the strategic process. A complete company situation analysis has five steps, as shown in Exhibit 4–4.

STEP 1: ASSESS PRESENT STRATEGY. This assessment can be a simple comparison or a complex analysis of performance (wins, championships, attendance, market share, sales, net profit, return on assets, and so on) over the last five years. **How did Joseph Blatter assess FIFA when he took over the presidency of the association?**

SWOT analysis
Used to assess strengths and weaknesses in the internal environment and opportunities and threats in the external environment.

STEP 2: ANALYZE SWOTS. A highly recommended strategic tool, **SWOT** (**S**trengths, **W**eaknesses, **O**pportunities, **T**hreats) **analysis** is used to assess strengths and weaknesses in an organization's internal environment and opportunities in its external environment (see Chapter 2 for a discussion of internal and external environments).[9] Exhibit 4–5 shows Nike's SWOT analysis.

STEP 3: ASSESS COMPETITIVE STRENGTH. For a strategy to be effective, it must be based on a clear understanding of competitors. The emergence of motorsports (NASCAR) and professional wrestling (WWE), for example, as major competitors in the 1990s caught professional sport leagues such as the NBA and NFL by surprise and made an already competitive marketplace even tougher.[10] Their strategies and research missed the pent-up demand. In such situations, management has got to wonder, What else are we missing?

Looking at critical success factors can help improve a company's assessment of its competition. *Critical success factors* (CSFs) are key, pivotal activities that the business must do well at if it is to "win its race." It is imperative that management compare its CSFs for *each* product line to those of each of its major competitors. This takes a great deal of business acumen and objectivity. Organizations typically use one of two approaches. The first (and simpler) approach rates each CSF from 1 (weak) to 10 (strong) and tallies the ratings to rank competitors. The second approach uses the same rating system, but weights the CSFs by importance, with the weighted total equal to 1.00. The weight is multiplied by the rating to get a score for each firm on each factor. Scores are totaled to determine the final rankings. Exhibit 4–5 gives weighted CSF rankings for Nike, Reebok, and Adidas.

TIMEOUT
List three strengths and three weaknesses of your organization.

_____

_____

_____

_____

_____

_____

STEP 4: MAKE CONCLUSIONS. The questions here are simple to ask, not always so easy to answer. How is the business doing compared to its competition? Is our market share improving, or slipping?

STEP 5: DECIDE WHAT ISSUES TO ADDRESS. Using information developed in steps 1 to 4, management now asks, What needs to be done to improve our competitive position? **What issues did Joseph Blatter and FIFA decide to improve on?**

Competitive Advantage

competitive advantage
Specifies how the organization offers unique customer value.

Strategic planning helps organizations create a competitive advantage. **Competitive advantage** specifies how the organization offers unique customer value. It answers the following questions: What makes us different from our competition? Why should a person buy our product or service rather than the competition's? A sustainable competitive advantage (1) distinguishes the organization from its competitors, (2) provides positive economic benefits, and

Exhibit 4–4 Steps in the Analysis of the Company Situation

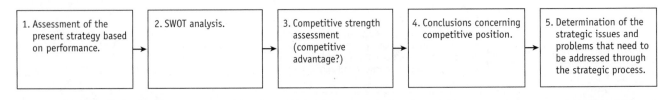

| 1. Assessment of the present strategy based on performance. | → | 2. SWOT analysis. | → | 3. Competitive strength assessment (competitive advantage?) | → | 4. Conclusions concerning competitive position. | → | 5. Determination of the strategic issues and problems that need to be addressed through the strategic process. |

Exhibit 4–5   Nike's Company Situation Analysis

1. Present Strategy Assessment

Nike's present strategy is working well. It is profitable and continues to be the leading company in the sport footwear and apparel industry. So far, it has been able to hold off strong competitors such as Reebok and Adidas.

2. SWOT ANALYSIS

Strengths. Nike's reputation for high-quality and innovative footwear. Nike is also known for its innovative marketing. Its ads are part of the pop culture—an impressive achievement. Famous campaigns feature Bo Jackson, Michael Jordan, and Tiger Woods. The Nike SWOOSH is highly recognizable worldwide. Its recent comeback has been greatly helped by increased sales of Nike apparel.[11]

Weaknesses. Slowdowns in the U.S. footwear business, as was the case in 2001. By 2002, though, Nike was able to improve inventory controls and order processing, and its market rebounded with a 7 percent increase in footwear sales.[12] Nike needs to continue to monitor and improve its inventory and ordering systems.

Opportunities. A continued increase in sales of golf equipment, football equipment, baseball products, socks, bags, and eyewear. The apparel business is expected to grow a healthy 4 to 5 percent in the year 2003.[13] However, Nike's most important opportunities may be Michael Jordan's return to the Washington Wizards and Tiger Woods's yearly attempt to win all four major golf tournaments.

Threats. Economic shock waves after 9/11 that have slowed retail shopping in general. More specifically, consumers may look for lower-priced products and be willing to sacrifice some quality. An industry-specific threat is the contracts that Reebok signed with the NBA and NFL for its apparel businesses. Another threat is the ongoing public relations problem pertaining to working environments in the factories producing Nike sneakers. Nike has striven to overcome images of sweatshop conditions, but the problem has been difficult to solve.

3. Competitive Strength Assessment

[Rating 1 (low) to 10 (high) for each firm—rating * weight.] Quality is determined to be the most important criteria with a weight of .50, followed by marketing and price at a weight of .25 each. In terms of quality, both Nike and Adidas have a perfect score of 10. 10 multiplied by the weight of .50 equals a score of 5.0. Reebok has a quality rating of 9 for a sum score of 4.5. Thus it is determined that Reebok's quality is slightly lower than that of its competitors. Overall, Nike is the strongest company at 9.75, followed by Adidas at 9.25 and Reebok at 8.75. It is important to note that scores are determined by executives at the companies, students in class, or (in this case) the authors. Scoring is based on completing a SWOT and should foster debate.

Critical Success Factors	Weight	Nike	Reebok	Adidas
Quality	.50	10—5.0	9—4.5	10—5.0
Marketing	.25	10—2.5	8—2.0	8—2.0
Price	.25	9—2.25	9—2.25	9—2.25
	1.00	9.75	8.75	9.25

4. Competitive Advantage Assessment

Nike's name recognition and quality image in many different markets. The Nike name and SWOOSH logo are worldwide status symbols.

5. Conclusions

Nike is the leading (and hence strongest) competitor and will remain so through continual improvement in the technology used in its footwear, equipment, and apparel lines. Continued growth in these divisions will be supported by new and creative marketing campaigns.

6. Issues

Nike needs to focus on (1) improving U.S. footwear sales, (2) continuing to increase international sales, and (3) building U.S. sales in its golf equipment and apparel lines.

TIMEOUT

Describe your organization's competitive advantage. If you don't think it has one, state how it resembles its competitors in its products or services.

(3) cannot be readily duplicated. The key to producing sustainable competitive advantage is effective management of people. Many organizations focus on quality as a means to beat the competition.

If you ever consider starting your own business, be sure to answer these questions: What will make my business different from the competition? Why should a person buy my product or service rather than the competition's? If you don't have answers to these crucial questions, go back to the drawing boards! Why? Because your business is *very* likely to join the ranks of failed businesses—20 percent of all small businesses fail in the first year, 60 percent after five years, and 75 percent after ten years.[14] Why? They *don't* have a competitive advantage, and they *don't* have a strategic plan for developing one. The Self Assessment at the end of the chapter helps you see if you have what it takes to be a successful entrepreneur, and in the Group Project you will develop a strategic plan for a hypothetical business.

Finding core competencies and benchmarking go hand in hand with developing competitive advantage. A *core competency* is what a firm does well—its strengths, in other words. Management that lasers in on core competencies can create new products and services that take advantage of their company's strengths. For example, Bally Total Fitness is *really* good at marketing fitness programs. Its high-quality and attractive national ad campaigns have attracted enough members to make Bally the largest and only nationwide operator of fitness centers in the United States.[15]

SETTING OBJECTIVES

For strategies to succeed, management must commit to a carefully thought-out set of objectives. Setting objectives is the third step in the strategic process. (Recall that developing the mission and analyzing the environment are the first two steps.) The idea is to set objectives that are compatible with the mission and that address strategic issues identified in the situation analysis. Objectives are then prioritized so that the organization can focus on the more important ones. (In Chapter 6 you will learn how to prioritize.)

Keep in mind that objectives are end results that you wish to attain—they do not tell others how to accomplish the objectives. Therefore, setting objectives is just the beginning of your task. That is also why you need to know the difference between goals and objectives, how to write objectives, criteria for effective objectives, and the concept of management by objectives (MBO), all of which we examine in the following discussion.

Goals and Objectives

5   LEARNING OUTCOME
Discuss how goals and objectives are similar yet different.

Some people use *goals* and *objectives* synonymously—this is not a good idea. Precise language makes for precision thinking, which of course enhances your ability to accomplish your organization's mission. **Goals** state general targets to be accomplished. **Objectives** state what is to be accomplished in specific and measurable terms by a certain target date. Goals are your target; objectives guide your development of operational plans and help you know if you are achieving the target. Goals thus translate into objectives. Exhibit 4–6 gives a hypothetical example of a few likely goals and objectives for Nike.

Writing Objectives

6   LEARNING OUTCOME
Write objectives.

Successful people set goals that they then strive to attain, and they write out explicit objectives to help them get there. The writing of the objectives is itself a clarifying and focusing endeavor, and is one reason why motivational gurus and career counselors swear by written objectives. Remember New Year's resolutions? Well, think about making some "career res-

goals
General targets to be accomplished.

objectives
State what is to be accomplished in specific and measurable terms by a certain target date.

Exhibit 4–6 Likely Goals and Objectives for Nike's Apparel and Footwear Divisions

GOALS

- To increase sales of international markets
- To increase sales in U.S. apparel business
- To revive growth in U.S. footwear business

OBJECTIVES

- We continue to be very pleased with the underlying strength of our international businesses. Our objective: To increase sales of our international business by 7 to 9 percent in each quarter of the next fiscal year (2003).

- As we expected, the U.S. apparel business improved last quarter, recording the first year-on-year increase in two years. Over the next year, we expect double-digit growth (10 to 13 percent) in U.S. apparel as our team sales continue to grow and we make further progress developing our women's apparel business. Our objective: To increase sales by 10 to 13 percent in U.S. apparel in 2003.

- U.S. footwear revenues fell 2 percent below last fiscal year. We still expect U.S. footwear revenues to pick up toward the end of the next fiscal year. Our objective for next year: To maintain sales revenues from the previous year (2003).

olutions." The *Wall Street Journal* notes that if you don't have career objectives, your resolution should be to get some.[16] The Skill-Builder at the end of this chapter will help get you started. To keep your focus on your end goals, post your objectives on your desk or wall.

So, you're chewing your pencil and can't quite get going? Here's a simple way (which we adapted from Max E. Douglas's model) to get your creative juices flowing.[17]

1. Start with the *infinitive* "to":	To—
2. Attach an *action verb*—typical ones are *increase, improve, enter, revive* (you get the picture):	—improve—
3. Now think up a *single, specific result* that you want to achieve and that can be *measured:*	—my xxxxx skills—
4. Choose a *target date.*	—by May 31, 200x.

TIME**OUT**
State one of your organization's goals, and list the objectives it is using to attain the goal. _____ _____ _____ _____ _____

This is too simple, you say? What do you think managers do when they write objectives? To prove our point, look at Exhibit 4–7, where we've diagrammed one of Nike's objectives from Exhibit 4–6. We'll show you some other examples when we discuss criteria.

Using Criteria to Write Objectives

All right, you've seen one of Nike's objectives diagrammed. Now let's look a little more critically at what makes an objective useful. The trick is to include four "must" criteria—we snuck them in steps 3 and 4 of writing objectives. They are (1) *single* result, (2) a *specific* one that is (3) *measurable,* and (4) a *target date.*

Exhibit 4–7 Writing Objectives

To write an objective:	Nike's objective:
1. Start with:	To—
2. Add an action verb:	—increase—
3. Insert a single, specific, and measurable result:	—sales in international markets by 7–9%—
4. Choose a target date	—in each quarter of the next fiscal year (2003).

A SINGLE RESULT. Write each objective so that it describes only one result. This prevents you from writing vague, meaningless objectives that are too complicated. You should aim for clarity, simplicity, and explicitness here. Vague or convoluted objectives can be misunderstood, and you want everyone who commits to achieving your objective to be on the same page. Later, you will have the luxury of stating Objective 1, met or not met—with multiple objectives listed as a single objective, you're going to sound wishy-washy and apologetic when you are reduced to saying, Objective 1, partially met, somewhat but not quite met, or almost met. And because there is nothing like examples to drive home a point, let's look at the objectives written by OB Iffy and OB Sharp, two young floating managers who work for various organizations.

OB Iffy: *To increase sales by 25 percent and to achieve a 5.4 percent market share.*

                  (Sales of what? Market share of what? And by when? What if Iffy meets one but not the other—is this objective met, or not met?)

OB Sharp: *To increase tennis racket sales by 25 percent by December 2005.*

                  To achieve a 5.4 percent market share of tennis rackets during 2005.

SPECIFIC RESULTS. State the exact level of performance expected. Research shows that people with specific goals perform better than those with general goals.[18]

OB Iffy: *To maximize profits in 2005.*

                  (How much is "maximize"? Is this gross profit or net profit?)

                  To recycle 40 percent by year-end 2005.

                  (40 percent of what—glass, paper, ideas?)

OB Sharp: *To earn a net profit of $15 million in 2005.*

                  To recycle 40 percent of all paper waste by year-end 2005.

MEASURABLE RESULTS. If you can't measure your progress, you're going to have trouble determining when—or whether—your objective has been met.

OB Iffy: *Perfect service for every customer.*

                  (Perfect by whose standards? How do you measure "perfect"?)

OB Sharp: *To attain 90 percent "excellent" in customer satisfaction ratings for 2005.*

RESULTS BY A TARGET DATE. Set a date for accomplishing the objective. Deadlines make all of us focus earlier and try harder.

OB Iffy: *To reach 4 million fans in attendance.*

                  (For every game? For all time?)

OB Sharp: *To reach 4 million fans in attendance by the end of the 2005 season.*

OB Iffy but Getting Better: *To double international business to $5 billion annually within five years.*

OB Sharp: *To double international business to $5 billion annually by year-end 2006.*

                  [*Note:* Some objectives are ongoing and therefore do not require a target date.]

OB Sharp: *To have 25 percent of sales coming from products that did not exist five years ago.*

In addition to the four "must" criteria, three "want" criteria help you achieve objectives.

REALISTIC OBJECTIVE. A number of studies show that people perform better when they work toward realistic objectives. That is, the objective should be somewhat difficult, but it must also be achievable. People do less well when the objective is too difficult (this is pretty obvious—we often give up when we think something is impossible), but they *also* don't do very well when the objective is too easy or when they are given an open-ended "do your best" instruction. (We examine this idea in more detail in Chapter 12.) Because what is realistic to one person is unrealistic to another, this criterion will always be subjective; therefore, it is a "want" criterion.

TIME OUT
Using the guidelines given above, write three objectives that you think your organization should pursue.

_____

_____

_____

_____

TEAM-SET OBJECTIVE. Work groups that set their own objectives generally outperform groups that are assigned objectives (Chapter 3). Be sure to use the appropriate level of participation for the group's capabilities. Because it is not always appropriate for groups to set objectives, this is also a "want" criterion.

TEAM COMMITMENT TO THE OBJECTIVE. A team that commits to an objective will work harder to achieve it. Participation in the decision-making and problem-solving process that usually precedes the setting of an objective is often key in attaining team commitment (Chapter 3). This is a "want" criterion because commitment will vary from individual to individual and sometimes you will have to set objectives that your group or team will not like.

For a review of these key criteria, see Exhibit 4–8.

Management by Objectives

Management by objectives (MBO) is the process by which managers and their teams jointly set objectives, periodically evaluate performance, and reward according to the results. Other names for MBO include work planning and review, goals management, goals and controls, and management by results.

MBO has met with both success and failure.[19] When it fails, researchers often find a lack of commitment and follow-through on management's part. MBO also fails when employees believe that management is insincere in its efforts to include them in the decision-making process. Such employees feel that management has already set the objectives and planned for implementation before involving them. MBO works when management truly involves employees. This is not always easy to do—what if they don't agree to your objectives?

There are three steps in the MBO process.

STEP 1: SET INDIVIDUAL OBJECTIVES AND PLANS. With each subordinate, the manager jointly sets objectives. These objectives are the heart of the MBO program and should meet the criteria discussed earlier.

STEP 2: GIVE FEEDBACK AND EVALUATE PERFORMANCE. Communication is a key factor in MBO's success or failure. Thus, the manager and employee must meet frequently to review progress. The frequency of evaluations depends on the individual and the job performed. However, most managers probably do not conduct enough review sessions.

STEP 3: REWARD ACCORDING TO PERFORMANCE. Employees' performance should be measured against their objectives. Employees who meet their objectives should be rewarded through recognition, praise, pay raises, promotions, and so on.

management by objectives (MBO) The process by which managers and their teams jointly set objectives, periodically evaluate performance, and reward according to the results.

7 LEARNING OUTCOME
Describe the four corporate-level grand strategies.

Exhibit 4–8   Key Criteria for Achieving Objectives

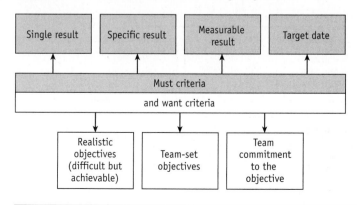

CORPORATE-LEVEL STRATEGY

After the mission is developed, the environmental analysis completed, and objectives set, the organization's strategy (step 4 in the planning process) is developed at the corporate, business, and functional levels. In this section you will learn about corporate-level strategy: grand strategy, corporate growth strategies, portfolio analysis, and product life cycles.

The Grand Strategies

grand strategies
The corporate strategies for growth, stability, turnaround, and retrenchment, or a combination thereof.

An organization's **grand strategies** are its corporate strategies for growth, stability, turnaround and retrenchment, or a combination thereof. Each grand strategy reflects a different objective.

GROWTH. Companies with a *growth strategy* aggressively attempt to increase their size through increased sales. We will return to growth strategies in a moment.

STABILITY. Companies with a *stability strategy* endeavor to hold and maintain their present size or to grow slowly. Many companies are satisfied with the status quo.

TURNAROUND AND RETRENCHMENT. A *turnaround strategy* is an attempt to reverse a declining business as quickly as possible. A *retrenchment strategy* is the divestiture or liquidation of assets. We list them together because most turnarounds involve retrenchment. Turnaround strategies attempt to improve cash flow by increasing revenues, decreasing costs, and selling assets. Converse, the longtime maker of athletic footwear, tried numerous turnaround strategies to save its failing company. Following years of declining sales, the company filed for Chapter 11 bankruptcy protection in 2001. Footwear Acquisition purchased the company, which intends to continue operations.[20]

COMBINATION. A corporation may simultaneously pursue growth, stability, and turnaround and retrenchment across its different lines of business. We discuss this idea in more detail under the portfolio analysis section.

> **TIMEOUT**
> State your organization's grand strategy.
> _____
> _____
> _____
> _____
> _____

Corporate Growth Strategies

8 LEARNING OUTCOME
Describe the three growth strategies.

corporate growth strategies
Concentration, backward and forward integration, and related and unrelated diversification.

Companies that want to grow have three major options. **Corporate growth strategies** include concentration, backward and forward integration, and related and unrelated diversification. Exhibit 4–9 summarizes an organization's choices when its grand strategy is growth.

Exhibit 4–9 Corporate Grand and Growth Strategies

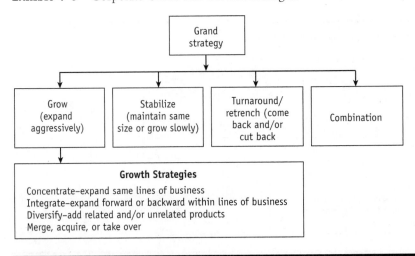

CONCENTRATE. An organization with a *concentration strategy* grows its existing line(s) of business aggressively. Dick's Sporting Goods, for example, continues to open new stores.

INTEGRATE. An organization with an integration strategy enters "forward" or "backward" lines of business. In forward integration the line of business is closer to the final customer. In backward integration the line of business is farther away from the final customer.[21] Some manufacturers, like Reebok, open factory stores and fitness centers to forward-integrate; that is, they bypass traditional retail stores and sell their products directly to the customer. News Corporation, which owns Fox networks, used a forward integration strategy when it bought the Los Angeles Dodgers of the MLB. To News Corporation, buying a baseball team gave it an opportunity to show its team on its television networks.[22]

DIVERSIFY. An organization with a diversification strategy goes into related or unrelated lines of products. Nike pursued related diversification when it decided to add sport clothing as a business line. Exhibit 4–9 summarizes the grand strategies used at the corporate level.

OTHER GROWTH STRATEGIES. Organizations also try to grow through mergers, acquisitions, and takeovers. In **mergers**, two companies form one new company. The New York Yankees and New Jersey Nets merged two teams to form YankeeNets. The objective of this MLB/NBA two-team merger is to increase operational revenue and build the value of each team.[23] YankeeNets has also acquired a third team, the New Jersey Devils of the NHL. In **acquisitions**, one business buys all or part of another business. Competing companies sometimes use mergers and acquisitions to compete more effectively with larger companies; to realize economies of size; to consolidate expenses; and to achieve access to markets, products, technology, resources, and management talent. Companies also use acquisitions to enter new lines of businesses—it is less risky to buy an established, successful business than it is to start a new one. YankeeNets acquired the Devils so that it could offer all three teams on their own television network (or another network). Also, having the combination of a basketball team and a hockey team will help validate the building of a new arena since both teams would use the site.[24]

When a target company's management rejects an offer to be bought out by another company, the purchasing company can make a bid to the target company's shareholders to acquire it through a takeover—these are typically not "friendly" actions (hence the term "hostile takeover"). Fortunately, YankeeNets was able to acquire the Devils without having to use unfriendly maneuvers. In friendly acquisitions, both companies see the value of becoming one company.

merger
Occurs when two companies form one corporation.

acquisition
Occurs when one business buys all or part of another business.

TIMEOUT
Identify the growth strategies that your organization uses. Are they working?

_____

_____

_____

_____

_____

APPLYING
THE CONCEPT   *Corporate Growth Strategies*

Identify the growth strategy used by each company.

a. concentration   **d.** related diversification

b. forward integration   **e.** unrelated diversification

c. backward integration

_____ 1. Spalding buys a rubber company to make the rubber it uses in its sneakers.

_____ 2. General Motors buys the Sea World theme park.

_____ 3. Dick's opens a new retail store in Worcester, Massachusetts.

_____ 4. Adidas opens its own retail stores.

_____ 5. Nike buys Bauer Hockey Equipment.

Business Portfolio Analysis

business portfolio analysis
The corporate process of determining which lines of business the corporation will be in and how it will allocate resources among them.

You are no doubt familiar with the idea of individual investment portfolios. Businesses use the term "portfolio analysis" somewhat differently than would an individual investor. In **business portfolio analysis**, corporations determine which lines of business they will be in and how they will allocate resources among the different lines. As noted at the beginning of the chapter, a *business line*—also called a *strategic business unit* (SBU)—is a distinct business with its own customers that is managed reasonably independently of the corporation's other businesses. What constitutes an SBU varies from company to company—SBUs are variously divisions, subsidiaries, or single product lines.[25] Adidas has divisions for footwear, ski equipment, cycling equipment, and golf equipment. Corporations use the environmental analysis they perform on each business line (step 2 in the strategic planning process) to analyze their portfolios. Another method, the BCG matrix, places each line of business in one matrix.

BCG GROWTH-SHARE MATRIX. One popular method for analyzing corporate business portfolios is the Boston Consulting Group's (BCG) growth-share matrix. A BCG matrix for Nike is shown in Exhibit 4–10. The four cells of the matrix are as follows:

- *Cash cows* generate lots of revenues. They may exhibit low growth, but they have high market share. (Examples: Air Jordan Sneakers[26] and Spalding basketballs.) Cash cows typically use stability strategies (why put a sure thing at risk?).

- *Stars* are emerging businesses with a rapidly growing market share. Corporations typically plow profits back into the star's product(s), in the hope that they will eventually garner enough market share to become a cash cow (example: Cybex International's steppers and upright cycles). Stars often use growth strategies (they aren't cash cows yet). Nike sees a future star in the golf line and has hired Tiger Woods to hawk its new Nike Tour Accuracy golf ball.[27] Nike's golf line has initially done very well, but Nike will need to monitor the Tour Accuracy's sales figures to make sure it is a star.

- *Question marks* are new lines of business with a low market share in an expanding market that the corporation believes can be grown into stars. To make question marks into stars, corporations must make significant cash outlays; this requires using profits from their other lines of business. This commitment of resources is, of course, not without risk because question marks can become dogs. Question marks use growth strategies (companies want them to get to profitability fast). For example, Nike has started to produce a line of sport watches with its logo on the face. Additionally, Nike is trying to sell electronic equipment such as portable radios and CD players to use while exercising. Nike will need to closely monitor sales of these products to determine if it has a star or a dog on its hands.

- *Dogs* are giving low returns in a low-growth market, and to add insult to injury, they have low market share—*nothing* is going right with a dog. Therefore, corporations often divest or liquidate their dogs at some point when they determine the dog is a hopeless case (example: The WWE's folding of the XFL in 2001). Dogs require turnaround and retrenchment strategies (or else they won't survive).

The business portfolio analysis helps corporate-level managers figure out how to allocate cash and other resources among the organization's business lines (as well as which corporate strategies to use). Managers use profits from cash cows to fund question marks and sometimes stars. Any cash from dogs is also given to question marks and stars, as well as any resources from their sale.

THE ENTREPRENEURIAL STRATEGY MATRIX. The BCG matrix works well with large companies with multiple lines of business. Sonfield and Lussier[28] developed the entrepreneurial strategy matrix (ESM) for small businesses. The ESM identifies different combinations of innovation and risk for new ventures and then suggests ways to optimize performance. The matrix answers such questions as, What venture situation are you in? and What are the best strategic alternatives for a given venture?

As we noted in an earlier chapter, *innovation* is the creation of something new and different. The newer and more different a product or service is, the higher its innovation. *Risk* is the probability of a major financial loss. Entrepreneurs need to determine the chances of their

Exhibit 4–10   Nike's BCG Matrix

Relative Market Share

	High	Low
High Market Growth Rate	**Stars** (growth) – Nike apparel – Golf equipment	**Question Marks** (growth) – Nike watches – Nike electronic products
Low	**Cash Cows** (stable) – Athletic footwear	**Dogs** (turnaround/retrenchment) – Sports Agency (which Nike sold)

venture failing and how serious the financial losses would be. Exhibit 4–11 shows how the ESM uses a four-cell matrix to assess innovation and risk.

The ESM then suggests appropriate strategies for each cell (also shown in Exhibit 4–11). Entrepreneurs use the first part of the matrix to identify which cell their firms are in. Then, based on their cell, they follow the suggested strategies.

BUSINESS-LEVEL STRATEGY

Each line of business must develop its own mission, analyze its own environment, set its own objectives, and develop its own strategy. Corporate- and business-level strategies for organizations with a single business are one and the same. For organizations with multiple lines of business, linking corporate strategy with operations at the business unit level is key to their success.

9 LEARNING OUTCOME
Discuss the three business-level adaptive strategies.

Adaptive Strategies

Each line of business needs its own strategy. Because it can be confusing to use similar names for corporate- and business-level strategies, business-level strategies are commonly called *adaptive strategies*. These correspond to the grand strategies, but their emphasis is on adapting to changes in the external environment and entering new markets. Exhibit 4–12 gives a brief overview of the criteria used to select the three **adaptive strategies**—prospecting, defending, and analyzing. Each adaptive strategy reflects a different objective.

adaptive strategies
Prospecting, defending, and analyzing.

PROSPECT NEW PRODUCTS OR MARKETS. The *prospecting strategy* calls for aggressively offering new products and/or entering new markets. Dick's Sporting Goods continues to open new stores to enter new markets. The prospector strategy corresponds to the growth grand strategy and is appropriate for fast-changing environments with high-growth potential.

DEFEND YOUR PRODUCTS OR MARKETS. When business segments employ a *defensive strategy*, they stay with their current product line and markets, and focus on maintaining or increasing market share. Defending resembles the stabilizing grand strategy, and is appropriate in a slow-changing environment with low growth potential.

ANALYZE NEW MARKETS. The *analyzing strategy* is a middle-of-the-continuum approach between prospecting and defending. Business segments that analyze move into new markets cautiously and deliberately, or they seek new opportunities to offer a core product group. Analyzing resembles the combination grand strategy, and is appropriate in moderately changing environments with moderate growth potential.

TIMEOUT
Identify the adaptive strategy that your organization pursues and describe how it uses the strategy.

Exhibit 4–11   The Entrepreneurial Strategy Matrix

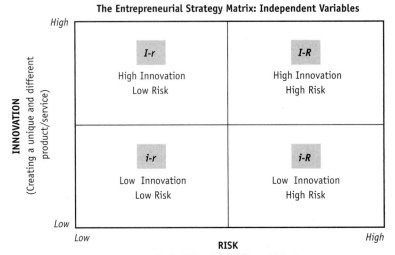

The Entrepreneurial Strategy Matrix: Independent Variables

INNOVATION (Creating a unique and different product/service)

High

I-r High Innovation Low Risk	**I-R** High Innovation High Risk
i-r Low Innovation Low Risk	**i-R** Low Innovation High Risk

Low

Low   **RISK**   High

(Probability of major financial loss)

The Entrepreneurial Strategy Matrix: Appropriate Strategies

INNOVATION

High

I-r
- Move quickly
- Protect innovation
- Lock in investment and operating costs via control systems, contracts, etc.

I-R
- Reduce risk by lowering investment and operating costs
- Maintain innovation
- Outsource high-investment operations
- Joint venture options

i-r
- Defend present position
- Accept limited payback
- Accept limited growth potential

i-R
- Increase innovation; develop a competitive advantage
- Reduce risk
- Use business plan and objective analysis
- Minimize investment
- Reduce financing costs
- Franchise option
- Abandon venture?

Low

Low   **RISK**   High

Source: "The Entrepreneurial Strategy Matrix Model for New and Ongoing Ventures" by M. C. Sonfield and R. N. Lussier from *Business Horizons* 40 (May–June), pp. 73–77, 1997. Reprinted by permission.

Exhibit 4–12   Choosing an Adaptive Strategy

Rate of Environmental Change	Potential Growth Rate	Adaptive Strategy	Corresponding Grand Strategy
Fast	High	Prospect	Grow
Moderate	Moderate	Analyze	Combination
Slow	Low	Defend	Stabilize

Although the adaptive strategies have no strategies similar to turnaround and retrenchment, business units do use this strategy when they cut back or stop selling dogs. If the firm does not replace its dogs with new products, it faces going out of business.

Competitive Strategies

Michael Porter identifies three effective business-level *competitive strategies:* differentiation, cost leadership, and focus.[29]

PRODUCT DIFFERENTIATION. Companies that differentiate stress the advantages of their products over those of their competitors. Nike, Spalding, Reebok, Adidas, and others use their logos in prominent places on their products in order to differentiate their products—indeed, the logos themselves become a selling feature. Differentiating strategies somewhat resemble prospecting strategies. According to Coca-Cola, the three keys to selling consumer products are "differentiation, differentiation, differentiation," which it does with great style with its scripted name logo and contour bottle.[30]

COST LEADERSHIP. Companies that use cost leadership strategies stress lower prices to attract customers. To keep prices down, such companies must have tight cost control and an efficient systems process.[31] Minor league baseball offers inexpensive tickets to quality baseball games in order to compete with major league baseball.

FOCUS. Companies that use a focus strategy laser in on a specific regional market, product line, or buyer group. Within the target segment, or market niche, the firm may use a differentiation or cost leadership strategy. The WNBA, the women's professional basketball league, supports various women's issues and causes in order to gain loyalty from women. The focus strategy resembles the analyzing strategy.

Product Life Cycle

The product life cycle is the series of stages—introduction, growth, maturity, and decline—that a product goes through over its "lifetime."[32] The speed at which products go through their life cycle varies. Many products, like wooden bats, stay around for many years, whereas fad products, like golfing products marketed to improve one's score, may last only a few months. Exhibit 4–13 gives appropriate portfolio analyses, grand strategies, and adaptive strategies for each life cycle stage for various Nike products.

Pricing strategies are important to growing and maintaining market share. They also change over the product's life cycle. Prices typically are higher at the product's introduction due to

---

APPLYING
THE CONCEPT   *Adaptive Strategies*

Identify the appropriate adaptive strategy for each situation.

a. prospector   **c.** analyzer

b. defender

_____ 6. Industry leader Gatorade's primary strategy in the U.S. sports drink market.

_____ 7. Reebok comes out with a new "zipper" sneaker to compete with Nike's "zipper" sneaker.

_____ 8. The Sports Authority opens restaurants in the State of Washington.

_____ 9. Wilson pioneers a baseball glove that can be folded up and put in your pocket.

_____ 10. Champion's strategy when other companies copied its sweatshirts.

Exhibit 4–13 Nike's Strategies for Products at Different Life Cycle Stages

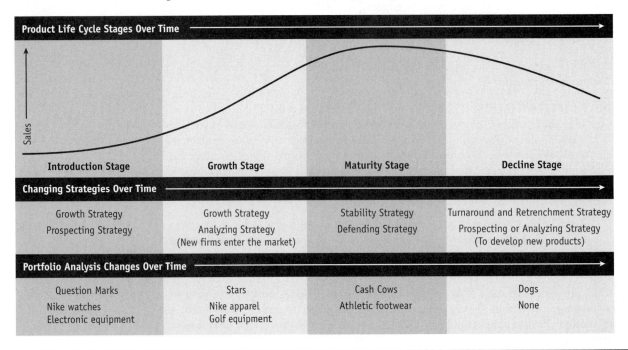

Product Life Cycle Stages Over Time			
Introduction Stage	Growth Stage	Maturity Stage	Decline Stage
Changing Strategies Over Time			
Growth Strategy Prospecting Strategy	Growth Strategy Analyzing Strategy (New firms enter the market)	Stability Strategy Defending Strategy	Turnaround and Retrenchment Strategy Prospecting or Analyzing Strategy (To develop new products)
Portfolio Analysis Changes Over Time			
Question Marks Nike watches Electronic equipment	Stars Nike apparel Golf equipment	Cash Cows Athletic footwear	Dogs None

the fact that there is little, if any, competition. Prices decline with product age, as new products are offered to consumers.

PRODUCT INTRODUCTION. When a new product (a question mark in the business portfolio) is introduced, a prospector company will endeavor to clearly differentiate it, but it will also use a focus strategy. That is, it will focus on getting customers to embrace the product. Resources will be used to promote (advertise) the product and to get production up and running. For example, the XFL embarked on a huge marketing blitz before the opening game of its new league. It used saturation advertising in its tv spots and drummed up the interest of sports magazines, who then created a buzz through their analyses of the new league and its teams.

GROWTH PERIOD. During the growth stage, sales expand rapidly. When analyzer companies see that a prospector company is doing well, they may endeavor to bring out their own version of the product. Analyzer companies may use differentiation, focus, or cost leadership to gain market share during their product's growth stage. They will focus on quality and systems process improvements to achieve economies of scale. They may lower prices, even though this reduces profit per unit, to gain market share. The WNBA (a new product) has now survived for a few years and may be heading into the growth stage—WNBA games are broadcast in 23 languages and in 167 countries.[33]

PRODUCT MATURITY. When a product is mature, sales growth continues (but more slowly), levels off, and may even begin to decline. In a saturated market, the company's strategy changes to one of stability (a defensive strategy). Cost becomes an issue, and cost-cutting efforts are emphasized. The NBA has been in a mature "product" for quite some time. Although the league has a loyal fan base, its TV ratings have decreased—that is, until Michael Jordan returned for the 2001 season.[34] Mature products are usually cash cows. **Determine at what stage in the product life cycle FIFA and soccer itself are located.**

PRODUCT DECLINE. As the product nears the end of its life cycle (it is aging), sales drop. The company's strategy changes from that of stabilizer-defender to turnaround and retrenchment and possibly back to prospector and analyzer as it begins to look for a replacement product. For example, if Major League Baseball doesn't start reinventing itself soon and solving its problems, it may start on a decline from which it cannot recover. The XFL went from question mark to dog, and skipped the growth period entirely as it went

TIMEOUT
Identify the life cycle stage for one of your organization's products. Is the strategy you identified in the Timeout on page 92 an appropriate strategy for this stage of the product's life cycle? Explain.

APPLYING
THE CONCEPT   *Product Life Cycle*

Select the life cycle stage of each product.

a. introduction   **c.** maturity

b. growth   **d.** decline

_____ 11. Baseball gloves

_____ 12. Racquetball rackets

_____ 13. Baseball caps

_____ 14. Skiing helmets

_____ 15. Recumbent exercise bicycles

from infant product to decline (one might say sudden death!). Television viewership plunged. Fans did not take to the XFL combination of football and wrestling.[35] The XFL performed like a fad and moved into its decline in only the second week of the season. A product can be in decline and remain profitable for many years. In the business's portfolio, aging products are considered dogs and may be divested. The company becomes a prospector or analyzer again and begins to develop new (infant) products.

Note that grand strategies and adaptive strategies complement one another. Companies select their strategies based on their mission, the external environment, and their objectives.

FUNCTIONAL-LEVEL STRATEGIES

10 LEARNING OUTCOME
List the four functional-level operational strategies.

Thus far we have been examining long-range strategic planning. We now turn our attention to functional-level planning. The primary task of functional-level departments is to develop and implement strategies that achieve the corporate- and business-level missions and objectives. These are the operational strategies that functional departments employ as they do their work, and they are also too numerous to describe here. Therefore, what we shall do is show you how the focus and emphasis of the functional departments change as corporate- and business-level strategies shift to address changes in the environment or mission. **Operational strategies** are used by every functional-level department—marketing, operations, human resources, finance, among others—to achieve corporate- and business-level objectives. Environmental analyses are performed at the functional levels to determine strengths and weaknesses. These departments then develop objectives and strategies for achieving them.

operational strategies
Strategies used by every functional-level department to achieve corporate- and business-level objectives.

The implementation of strategic plans is often a stumbling block as organizations have difficulty translating business strategies into cohesive competitive strategies (results). The need for greater integration of corporate-, business-, and functional-level strategies has long been recognized. Another thorny issue is achieving greater cooperation across functional departments. It has been suggested that functional-level strategies should be developed for each stage of a product's life cycle, then these strategies can be used to integrate the functional areas.[36] What follows is a brief overview of the functions, as you may have already taken (or will take) one or more entire courses devoted to each one.

Marketing Function

The marketing department's primary responsibility is defining the target market, finding out what the customer wants, and figuring out how to add customer value. It therefore is responsible for the four Ps—product, promotion, place, and price. In other words, it decides which products to provide, how they will be packaged, how they will be advertised, where they will be sold, how they will get there, and how much they will be sold for.

If the company is a prospector, marketing will plan for and implement new products and find new markets to enter. If the company is defending its products, marketing will focus on keeping them in the consumer's "eye and heart." If the company is an analyzer, marketing will endeavor to find a balance between prospecting and defending. If the company identifies a product as a dog, marketing will be involved in the turnaround/retrenchment process and will look for smart and/or graceful ways to drop the product or exit the market.

The Operations Function

The operations (or production) department is responsible for systems processes that convert inputs into outputs. Operations focuses on quality and efficiency as it produces the products that marketing determines will provide customer value. We will return to the operations function in Chapter 14.

If the company is prospecting for products, operations will help plan and produce the new products. Aggressive growth may require new operations facilities. If the company is defending its product(s), operations will endeavor to improve quality and efficiency and cut costs. If the company is an analyzer, operations will take its time and be sure a new product will be successfully manufactured. Analyzers take a midrange approach between prospecting and defending. If turnaround and retrenchment are necessary, operations will find ways to cut back systems processes.

Human Resources Function

HR departments work with all functional departments to recruit, select, train, evaluate, and compensate employees. We examine human resources more fully in Chapter 8.

If the company is a prospector, human resources will plan for, and then expand, the number of employees. In a stabilizer company, human resources will work on improving the quality and efficiency of the workforce through training and empowerment programs. If the company is in the analyzer mode, human resources will combine expansion and training activities. And, of course, in turnaround and retrenchment situations, human resources will plan for, and then implement, layoffs.

Finance Function

Finance departments perform at least two major functions: (1) They finance business activities by raising money through the sale of stock (equity) or bonds/loans (debt); they decide on the debt-to-equity ratio; and they pay off debt and pay out dividends (if any). (2) They record transactions, develop budgets, and report financial results (the income statement and balance sheet). A third function that finance departments perform in many organizations is optimizing the company's use of its cash reserves—that is, investing the company's cash as a means of making money. We discuss finance in Chapter 14.

If the company is a prospector, finance will raise money to cover the functional-area budgets, and dividends will be low, if any are given. If the company is defending its market share, finance will pay off debt and will also generally pay a dividend. If the company is an analyzer, finance will raise money and pay off debt. If the company finds itself in a turnaround situation, finance may endeavor to raise money and sell assets to pay for the comeback. In a retrenchment, finance will sell assets, but will not typically pay dividends, or they will be very low ones.

Other Functional Areas

Based on the type of business, any number of other functional departments will need strategies to achieve their objectives. One area that varies in importance depending on the nature of the company's business is research and development. Businesses that sell products usually allocate greater resources (budgets) for R&D than do service businesses.

TIMEOUT

Describe the operational strategy of a functional area in your organization.

_____

_____

_____

_____

_____

APPLYING THE CONCEPT — *Functional Strategies*

Identify the function described in each statement.

- **a.** marketing
- **b.** operations
- **c.** finance
- **d.** human resources
- **e.** other

_____ 16. Cleans up and repairs the arena.

_____ 17. Sends out the bills.

_____ 18. Transforms inputs into outputs.

_____ 19. Decides where the product will be sold.

_____ 20. Manages labor relations.

Implementing and Controlling the Strategies

The first four steps in the strategic process involve planning. The fifth and final step involves implementing and controlling the strategies to ensure that the organization's mission and objectives, at all three levels, are achieved. Top and middle managers are more involved with planning strategies, whereas the lower-level functional managers and employees *implement* the strategies on a day-to-day basis. Successful implementation of strategies requires effective and efficient support systems throughout the organization. Although strategic planning usually goes well, implementation is often a problem. Those in the trenches would say that if implementation isn't going well, strategic planners probably didn't do their job. Things that look good on paper are ultimately merely words, labels, or fancy terminology, and are not necessarily doable or practical. One reason strategic plans fail is that they often end up buried in bottom drawers and no action is taken to implement the strategy.[37] In Chapters 5 to 13, you will learn how to implement strategy.

As strategies are implemented, they must also be controlled. *controlling* establishes mechanisms to ensure that objectives are achieved in a timely and cost-efficient manner. Controlling also measures the department's progress toward achieving the objective and takes corrective action when needed. Budget issues are an important part of controlling, as is being flexible about the budget when necessary to meet new challenges in the environment. You will develop your controlling skills in Chapter 14.

TIMEOUT
Describe some of the controls used in your organization.

CHAPTER SUMMARY

1. Explain how strategic and operational plans differ.

They differ by time frame and management level involved. In strategic planning, a mission and long-range objectives and plans are developed. Operational plans state short-range objectives and plans. Upper-level managers develop strategic plans and lower-level managers develop operational plans.

2. Describe the differences between corporate-, business-, and functional-level strategies.

They primarily differ in focus, which narrows as strategy moves down the organization, and in the management level involved in developing the strategy. Corporate-level strategy focuses on managing multiple lines of business. Business-level strategy focuses on managing one line of business. Functional-level strategy focuses on managing an area of a business line. Upper-level managers develop corporate- and business-level strategy, and lower-level managers develop functional-level strategy.

3. Explain why organizations analyze industry and competitive situations.

The industry and competitive situation analysis is used to determine the attractiveness of an industry. It is primarily used at the corporate level to decide which lines of business to enter and exit, and how to allocate resources among the organization's lines of business.

4. Explain why organizations analyze company situations.

The company situation analysis is used at the business level to determine issues and problems that need to be addressed through the strategic process.

5. Discuss how goals and objectives are similar yet different.

Goals and objectives are similar because they both state what is to be accomplished. However, goals can be translated into objectives. They also differ in detail. Goals state general targets, whereas objectives state what is to be accomplished in specific and measurable terms with a target date.

6. Write objectives.

(1) Start with the infinitive "to," (2) add an action verb, (3) insert a single, specific, and measurable result to achieve, and (4) set a target date.

7. Describe the four corporate-level grand strategies.

Firms with a growth strategy aggressively pursue expansion. Firms with a stabilizing strategy maintain the same size or grow slowly. Firms with a turnaround strategy attempt a comeback; those that are retrenching decrease in size to cut costs so that they can survive. Firms with a combination strategy use all four strategies across different lines of business.

8. Describe the three growth strategies.

Firms that concentrate endeavor to grow existing line(s) of business aggressively. Firms that integrate grow their lines forward or backward. Firms that diversify grow by adding related or unrelated products.

9. Discuss the three business-level adaptive strategies.

A prospector company aggressively offers new products/services and/or aggressively enters new markets. Prospecting is a growth strategy used in fast-changing environments with high growth potential. A defender company stays with its product line and markets. Defending is a stable strategy used in slow-changing environments with low growth potential. An analyzer company moves into new markets cautiously and/or offers a core product group and seeks new opportunities. Analyzing is a combination strategy used in moderately changing environments with moderate growth potential.

10. List the four major functional operational strategy areas.

Companies develop operational strategies in four major functional areas: marketing, operations, human resources, and finance. Other functional-level strategies are developed as needed, depending on the organization's business and environment.

11. Define the key terms discussed in the text.

Fill in the missing key terms from memory, or match the key terms from the list in the margin with their definitions below.

_____ is the process of developing a mission and long-term objectives and determining in advance how they will be accomplished.

_____ is the process of setting short-term objectives and determining in advance how they will be accomplished.

In the _____, managers develop the mission, analyze the environment, set objectives, develop strategies, and implement and control the strategies.

Key Terms

acquisition

adaptive strategies

business-level strategy

business portfolio
    analysis

competitive advantage

corporate growth
    strategies

corporate-level strategy

functional-level strategy

goals

grand strategies

management by
    objectives (MBO)

merger

objectives

operational planning

operational strategies

situation analysis

strategic planning

strategic process

strategy

SWOT analysis

three levels of
    strategies

A _____ is a plan for pursuing the mission and achieving objectives.

The _____ are corporate, business, and functional.

The _____ is the plan for managing multiple lines of businesses.

The _____ is the plan for managing one line of business.

The _____ is the plan for managing one area of the business.

A _____ draws out those features in a company's environment that most directly frame its strategic window of options and opportunities.

Organizations use a _____ to assess strengths and weaknesses in the internal environment and opportunities and threats in the external environment.

_____ specifies how the organization offers unique customer value.

_____ state general targets to be accomplished.

_____ state what is to be accomplished in specific and measurable terms by a certain target date.

_____ is the process by which managers and their teams jointly set objectives, periodically evaluate performance, and reward according to the results.

_____ are the corporate strategies for growth, stability, turnaround, and retrenchment, or a combination thereof.

_____ include concentration, backward and forward integration, and related and unrelated diversification.

A _____ occurs when two companies form one corporation.

An _____ occurs when one business buys all or part of another business.

The _____ is the corporate process of determining which lines of business the corporation will be in and how it will allocate resources among them.

Prospecting, defending, and analyzing are _____.

_____ are used by every functional-level department to achieve corporate- and business-level objectives.

REVIEW AND DISCUSSION

1. Explain why strategic planning and operational planning are important.

2. How do plans and strategies differ?

3. Should all sport organizations have corporate-, business-, and functional-level strategies? Why or why not?

4. Should a mission statement for an athletic department be customer-focused? If so, why? If not, why not?

5. Why would a situation analysis be part of the strategic process of redesigning a sport organization?

6. Why is competitive advantage important to sport organizations?

7. Are both goals and objectives necessary for managing a health club? If so, why? If not, why not?

8. Why do managers write objectives?

9. As a manager or a coach, would you use MBO? If so, why? If not, why not?

10. Which growth strategy would you say is the most successful? Defend your answer.

11. What is the difference between a merger and an acquisition?

12. How do grand strategies and adaptive strategies differ?

13. Why would a sport organization use a focus strategy rather than try to appeal to all customers?

14. Give examples of "other" functional departments.

CASE

Strategic Planning at Disney

Companies of all sizes need to develop a corporate strategy. You can imagine how complex such strategies get when the organization is a media/sport conglomerate like Disney Corporation. Besides running the world's most popular theme parks, Disney acquired 80 percent of ESPN; a television network, ABC; an NHL hockey team, the Anaheim Ducks; and an MLB team, the Anaheim Angels.

Disney's strategic plan focused on a growth strategy of developing a media and entertainment empire. Its goal was a seamless distribution of sports and media to as many markets across the United States as possible. With regard to sports, Disney planned to forward-integrate and deliver the Disney themes through its new media outlets and sport teams. In many ways Disney CEO Michael Eisner and his team have achieved this goal. The purchase of ABC and ESPN has allowed these two Disney businesses to share both programming and broadcasting events. The Ducks and Angels, even though the Angels won the World Series in 2002, have allowed Disney to control their own programming. The Ducks have also helped Disney sell plenty of merchandise based on their playful name and logo.

Yet Disney's integration strategies have not worked out as well as industry analysts initially predicted. Disney offers a unique package of sports and entertainment, but tickets to its theme parks and sporting events are often expensive. The Ducks have tried to address high costs by reducing the price of season tickets for the 2002–2003 season.[38]

Competitors such as News Corporation (which owns Fox Networks and the Los Angeles Dodgers) and AOL (which owns the Atlanta Braves and the Atlanta Hawks) have also used integration strategies to combine their assets. Additionally, the Angels and the Ducks have had poor attendance. Disney has not really been able to attract a large audience to watch hockey games using its ESPN media outlets. Alas, the Ducks are better known as the hockey team in the Disney movie *The Mighty Ducks* than for their performance as a team in the NHL. At various times, Disney has been reported to be interested in selling both teams to allow the company to focus its attention on media instead of sport teams.

To find current information about the Disney Corporation, visit http://www.disney.com. Information about the Mighty Ducks can be found at http://www.mightyducks.com and the Anaheim Angels at http://angels.mlb.com.

CASE QUESTIONS

Select the best alternative for the following questions. Be sure you are able to explain your answers.

1. Disney does not have a competitive advantage over its competitors.
   a. true   b. false

2. Disney's move into multimedia and the sport industry shows their turnaround strategy.
   a. true   b. false

3. The information in this case refers primarily to
   a. strategic planning
   b. operational planning

4. Which of the five competitive forces is the strongest that Disney faces?
   a. competitive rivalry
   b. threat of substitute products
   c. potential new entrants
   d. power of suppliers
   e. power of buyers

5. Disney's global grand strategy is
   a. growth
   b. stability
   c. turnaround and retrenchment
   d. combination

6. Disney's corporate growth strategy is
   a. concentration
   b. forward integration
   c. backward integration
   d. related diversification
   e. unrelated diversification

7. The Disney and ABC/ESPN combination was
   a. a merger
   b. an acquisition

c. a turnaround
d. a divestiture

8. Disney's business-level adaptive strategy is
   a. prospecting
   b. defending
   c. analyzing

9. Disney's primary competitive strategy is
   a. differentiation
   b. cost leadership
   c. focus

10. The Ducks and Angels have both had trouble increasing attendance at their games. Determine at what stage of the product life cycle these teams are currently placed?
    a. introduction
    b. growth
    c. maturity
    d. decline

11. Conduct an industry and competitive situation analysis for Disney using the five-forces competitive analysis. Use Exhibit 4–3 as an example.

12. Conduct a SWOT analysis for Disney.

13. Write some possible goals and objectives for Disney.

VIDEO CASE

Burton Snowboards Responds to the Changing Environment

Introduction
Burton Snowboards is the leading designer and manufacturer of snowboards, boots, bindings, and snowboard apparel in the world. Burton's distribution strategy is simple: manufacturer to franchised dealers to customer. Retailers often place orders several months

in advance for the peak snowboarding season. An integrated information system allows the company to share and communicate all facets of the business together.

Focus Your Attention

To get the most out of viewing this Burton Snowboards video, think about the following issues: how strategic, business, and functional planning differ, how a marketing department helps an organization achieve its goals, and how relationships with a retailer can affect both organizations. Then answer the following questions after viewing the video:

1. Burton Snowboards uses a just-in-time distribution strategy. Does distribution strategy fall under strategic, business, or functional planning?

2. How has Burton's market (target customer) changed? What does Burton do to keep abreast of and adapt to its expanded customer base?

3. Why is Burton so selective when franchising retailers?

EXERCISES

Skill-Builder: Writing Objectives

Objective:

- To develop your ability to write effective objectives.

Preparation:

You will first analyze and rewrite several ineffective objectives, then you will write nine new objectives.

Part 1

Analyze the following objectives. First, note the missing components and the criteria that haven't been met. Then rewrite the objective so that it meets all "must" criteria. Make sure that your rewrites contain the four parts noted in the text (infinitive, action verb, result, and target date).

1. To improve our company image by year-end 2003.

    Criteria missing: _____

    Improved objective: _____

    _____

2. To increase the number of fans by 10 percent.

    Criteria missing: _____

    Improved objective: _____

    _____

3. To increase profits during 2003.

    Criteria missing: _____

    Improved objective: _____

    _____

4. To sell 5 percent more hot dogs and soda at the baseball game on Sunday, June 13, 2003.

    Criteria missing: _____

    Improved objective: _____

    _____

Part 2

Write three educational, personal, and career objectives that you want to accomplish. Your objectives can be as short-term as something you want to accomplish next week or as long-term as 20 years from now. Be sure your objectives meet the criteria given in the text for effective objectives.

Educational Objectives

1. _____

_____

_____

2. _____

_____

_____

3. _____

_____

_____

Personal Objectives

1. _____

_____

_____

2. _____

_____

_____

3. _____

_____

_____

Career Objectives

1. _____

_____

_____

2. _____

_____

_____

3. _____

_____

_____

In-Class Application

Complete the skill-building preparation noted above before class.

Choose one (10–30 minutes):

- Break into groups of three to five members, and critique each other's objectives.
- Informal, whole-class discussion of objective-writing.

SELF ASSESSMENT   *Are You an Entrepreneur?*

Objective:

To assess your entrepreneurial qualities.

Preparation:

Would you like to be your own boss? Ever thought about operating your own business? This Self Assessment will help you decide if you've got what it takes to be a successful entrepreneur.

ENTREPRENEURIAL QUALITIES

Check the number on the scale that best describes you.

1. I have a strong desire to be independent. / I have a weak desire to be independent.

   6   5   4   3   2   1

2. I enjoy taking reasonable risks. / I avoid risk.

   6   5   4   3   2   1

3. I usually don't make the same mistake twice. / I often make the same mistakes.

   6   5   4   3   2   1

4. I am a self-starter. / I need someone to motivate me to work.

   6   5   4   3   2   1

5. I seek out competition. / I avoid competition.

   6   5   4   3   2   1

6. I enjoy working long, hard hours. / I prefer taking it easy and having lots of personal time.

   6   5   4   3   2   1

7. I am confident of my abilities. / I lack self-confidence.

   6   5   4   3   2   1

8. I need to be the best/successful. / I'm satisfied with being average.

   6   5   4   3   2   1

9. I have a high energy level. / I have a low energy level.

   6   5   4   3   2   1

10. I stand up for my rights. / I let others take advantage of me.

   6   5   4   3   2   1

Scoring:

Add your assessment numbers. Your total score will be between 10 and 60. Place your score on the continuum below.

Entrepreneurial Qualities:

Strong   60—50—40—30—20—10   **Weak**

Generally, the higher/stronger your score in this Self Assessment, the better your chances of becoming a successful entrepreneur. Keep in mind, however, that simple paper-and-pencil assessments aren't always good predictors. If you scored low on this scale but you *really* want to start a business, you can still succeed. Just realize that you don't have all the qualities that *typically* mark entrepreneurs. That doesn't mean you can't work to consciously develop them.

IN-CLASS APPLICATION

Complete the skill-building preparation noted above before class.

Choose one (10–30 minutes):

■ Break into groups of three to five members, and discuss what you think makes for successful entrepreneurs.

■ Informal, whole-class discussion of the pros and cons of being an entrepreneur.

Wrap-up:

Take a few minutes and write down your answers to the following questions:

■ What did I learn from this experience?

_____

_____

■ How will I use this knowledge in the future?

_____

_____

Wrap-up:

Take a few minutes and write down your answers to the following questions:

- What did I learn from this experience?

  _____

  _____

  _____

- How will I use this knowledge in the future?

  _____

  _____

  _____

As a class, discuss student responses.

Group Project: Developing a Strategic Plan

Objective:

- To practice strategic planning.

Preparation:

Break into groups of five. Dream up a single-line *sport* business that you think *might* have possibilities (because this is a mere exercise, let your imaginations run to the out of the ordinary, even wild, here), and give it a name (preferably a strange one—it's time to have some fun) and a location. An important part of any business plan is, of course, determining startup costs, but because financial analysis is beyond the scope of this course, we've got some good news for you: Money is not an issue because you just won the lottery and you've got $50 million burning a hole in your corporate pocket! "All" you have to do is develop a strategy. Now, just so you know, this exercise is not all about fun—using a (possibly) preposterous idea simply lets you focus on the process itself.

So let's get started.

What is your company's name? _____

Are you going to provide a product or service? _____

Describe your product/service: _____

Step 1: Develop a Mission

Write a mission for your business._____

_____

_____

Step 2: Analyze the Environment

Do a five-forces competitive analysis on your industry's environment (model it after Exhibit 4–3).

Five-Forces Competitive Analysis

1. Rivalry among competitors _____

   _____

2. Threat of substitute products and services _____

   _____

3. Potential new entrants _____

   _____

4. Power of suppliers _____

_____

5. Power of buyers _____

_____

Now, do a company situation analysis.

Company Situation

1. SWOT analysis

Strengths	*Opportunities*
_____	_____
_____	_____
_____	_____
Weaknesses	*Threats*
_____	_____
_____	_____
_____	_____

2. Competitive advantage (if any). (Optional: Do a competitive strength assessment. Also, consider doing an ESM analysis, using Exhibit 4–11 as a guide.)

_____

_____

_____

_____

3. Describe your company's competitive position.

_____

_____

_____

_____

4. Determine issues and problems that you need to address through the strategic process.

_____

_____

_____

_____

Step 3: Set Objectives (list three)

_____

_____

_____

Step 4: Develop Strategies

You're in a single line of business, so you don't need a grand strategy or a portfolio analysis. Think about your product's life cycle, and develop competitive strategies and adaptive ones for your product's "infancy," growth period, maturity, and decline.

Strategy for the Infant Product

_____

_____

_____

_____

Strategy for the Growth Period

_____

_____

_____

_____

Strategy for the Mature Product

_____

_____

_____

_____

Strategy for the Aging Product

_____

_____

_____

_____

Step 5: Implement and Control Strategies

So, how are you going to make these strategies happen?

_____

_____

_____

In-Class Application

Complete the skill-building preparation noted above.

Choose one:

- As a group, present your strategic plan to the class. Plan and rehearse your presentation beforehand, and use whatever visual aids you think will enhance the presentation. (3 class periods)
- Informal, whole-class discussion of the pitfalls and strengths of strategic planning. (10–30 minutes)

Wrap-up:

Take a few minutes and write down your answers to the following questions:

- What did I learn from this experience?

_____

_____

_____

■ How will I use this knowledge in the future?

_____

_____

_____

As a class, discuss student responses.

Internet Skills: Analyzing Strategic Plans on the Internet

Objective:
■ To find strategic information about sport organizations on the Internet.

Preparation:
Visit http://www.hoovers.com and answer the following questions.

Discussion Questions

1. Search for GSI Commerce. What is the mission of GSI?

_____

_____

_____

_____

2. What companies are listed as top competitors for GSI?

_____

_____

_____

_____

3. Go to the *Financials* hyperlink and discuss profits at GSI.

_____

_____

_____

_____

4. What two footwear brands did GSI sell off?

_____

_____

_____

_____

5. Find the Internet sporting goods retailer that GSI bought in 2000. What do you think their reasoning was for this purchase?

_____

_____

_____

_____

In-Class Application

Complete the questionnaire above.

Choose one:

- Break into groups of three to five, share your answers to the above questions, and share your thoughts on what you think GSI's grand strategy is.
- Whole-class discussion of student findings.

Wrap-up:

Take a few minutes and write down your answers to the following questions:

- What did I learn from this experience?

    _____

    _____

    _____

- How will I use this experience in the future?

    _____

    _____

    _____

As a class, discuss student responses.

5 Facility and Event Planning

Learning Outcomes

After studying this chapter, you should be able to:

1. Describe what managing a sport facility entails.
2. Describe what is involved in event planning.
3. Explain how standing plans and single-use plans differ.
4. Explain when, and why, contingency plans are necessary.
5. Discuss how sales forecasts shape strategy.
6. Explain how qualitative and quantitative forecasting techniques differ.
7. Explain how the jury of executive opinion and the three sales composites differ.
8. Explain how past sales and time series forecasting techniques differ.
9. Know when to use planning sheets, Gantt charts, and PERT diagrams.
10. Use a time log.
11. Manage your time better.
12. Define the following key terms (in order of appearance in the chapter):

- standing plans
- policies
- procedures
- rules
- single-use plans
- contingency plans
- sales forecast
- market share
- qualitative forecasting techniques
- quantitative forecasting techniques
- time series
- scheduling
- planning sheets
- Gantt charts
- PERT diagrams
- critical path
- time management
- time management system

REVIEWING THEIR GAME PLAN

Making the Maccabi Games a Hit

Sport events don't just happen. Events that come off without a hitch mean that a whole team of event planners have been at work behind the scenes scrambling, smoothing, and problem solving for months, if not years. Events like the Senior Olympics, the Goodwill Games, and the **MACCABI GAMES,** which have dramatically expanded opportunities for people of all ages and all walks of life to participate in sports, exemplify event planning at its best. An offspring of the Israeli Maccabi Games—the Jewish Olympics held in Israel— the U.S. Maccabi games attract thousands of young athletes aged 13 to 16 to compete at different sites in the United States. The games help develop top Jewish American athletes, many of whom (Mark Spitz, 1971 Olympics; Mitch Gaylord, 1984 Olympics; and Lenny Krayzelburg, 2000 Olympics, to name a few) go on to achieve fame in the Olympics.[1]

Brazilian-born Assistant Games Director Claudia Fiks helps plan the U.S. Maccabi Games. Fiks, who has helped organize games in Florida and Massachusetts, works hard to make sure that each event, which takes more than a year to plan, is a success. First on her agenda is securing a host community center. Fiks negotiates with the management of potential host centers, alerts local governments so they can prepare for the influx of people, organizes volunteers, finds homes for the participants to stay in during the games, and secures sites at local colleges where games such as soccer and volleyball can be played. She has her committees in place by August of the previous year, a kick-off campaign ready two months later in October, and host families selected at least six months before the games begin.[2] Additionally, Fiks helps raise at least $300,000 to support the games.

The umbrella organization, the Maccabi World Union, is of great assistance to Fiks in these endeavors. The organization circulates a yearly planning calendar to assist in the design of the games. Although Fiks faces different issues with each site, she says the Union's calendar gives her a strong base on which she can build a great event.

For current information on Maccabi Games in your area, visit http://www.jccmaccabi. org. (For ideas on using the Internet, see Appendix B.)

INTERNET RESOURCES

http://www.onlinesports.com/sportstrust/sportsnewslist.html *At this site, you'll find a great collection of articles on a variety of issues pertinent to the sport industry. Under the Event Marketing heading, explore topics related to event planning. You'll discover what it takes to be a special events planner, special events broker, and corporate event marketer, and you'll learn how and why corporations sponsor sporting events. This site is also featured in Chapter 7.*
http://www.stadianet.com *This is the official site of more than 50 worldwide facilities, including most of the NFL and MLB stadiums. Here you can read facts about the facilities, and learn about stadium features (including web cameras in some cases) and upcoming events. It is a service of the Stadium Managers Association and also provides a "Pros Only" business-to-business function for all of that group's online news and communication. The site is updated directly by stadium personnel.*
http://www.heartland.org/studies/sports/sports-studies.htm *and* **http://www-personal.umich.edu/~jeremyjm/stadiums/index.html** *Public versus private funding of new stadiums is a controversial issue these days. The first site listed presents a series of policy studies to support the recent trend toward private financing. For a more optimistic look at public funding, visit the second site, where you'll find an examination of how new baseball stadiums in Detroit and Cleveland have helped to revitalize their downtown areas.*

DEVELOPING YOUR SKILLS   Never thought you'd need to know whether the college swimmers you're recruiting like liver mousse? Think again. If you want to manage a sport facility or work as an athletic director, you're going to plan events at one time or another. You've just entered a world not unlike the one wedding planners inhabit. A world of details and protocol, last-minute glitches, and clever solutions (and LOTS of people skills!). It's a fun world and will give you many anecdotes to tell your grandchildren, and you will sidestep many headaches and the dreaded "uh-ohs" *if* you become a skillful planner.

SPORT FACILITIES MANAGEMENT

1   LEARNING OUTCOME
Describe what managing a sport facility entails.

In Chapter 4 we examined strategic planning, which focuses on the long term. In this chapter we examine operational planning (also called short-term action planning) using event and facilities planning as our example because most sport managers at one time or another plan events and manage a facility.

Sport management professionals often find careers in managing various types of facilities. Such work varies from managing private health clubs, hotel fitness centers, YMCA or JCC athletic facilities, and indoor sporting centers to managing entire stadiums. Many colleges and universities have built new athletic facilities to attract top athletes, and many municipalities have built new stadiums and arenas to house pro sports. Critics of municipality-owned stadiums argue this is often little more than "blackmail" as owners threaten to take their teams elsewhere if such stadiums are not built, whereas proponents point out that new state-of-the-art stadiums attract business and tourists and therefore generate jobs and tax revenues. Thus, facility managers often find themselves on the political hot seat as they endeavor to juggle the needs of all the constituents in the stadium equation. Facility managers also help plan and design new facilities. They work to generate interest in both the organization and/or the local community for building the facilities—this is where they wear their public relations "hat."

In facility planning, experienced planners assemble a committee of interested and qualified people early in the process.[3] One critical and universal question is, How will we finance our new facility?[4] The committee and the facility planner will hire an architect and decide on facility criteria. After the building plans are approved and financing secured, a competitive bidding process helps ensure that building costs are contained. The building process itself requires the planner's constant attention.

If an existing facility is available, facility management may decide to remodel it to fit their criteria, or they may decide that moving to another existing facility is more cost-efficient. Twenty years ago, the Basketball Hall of Fame in Springfield, Massachusetts, moved from a small building on the Springfield College campus (the actual birthplace of basketball) to a larger building in downtown Springfield. It eventually outgrew the downtown facility, and in 2002 a brand-new Basketball Hall of Fame almost twice the size of the original facility opened its doors.[5] In the new Hall of Fame, fans enjoy multimedia tributes to the game's great players, coaches, and other figures of interest.

Once an athletic or recreational facility is open for business, the continual process of managing and training the people who will run the facility on a day-to-day basis begins. Planning daily operations also includes soliciting and scheduling various events to keep the facility's calendar full and revenues coming in.

A good example is Mike Crum, the director of Charlotte's Auditorium–Coliseum–Convention Center Authority since July 1998. The son of former University of North Carolina Chapel Hill head football coach Dick Crum, Mike presides over a $25 million budget, 200 employees (and another 1800 part-time workers), and all maintenance and operations for the Charlotte Convention Center, Charlotte Coliseum, Ovens Auditorium, and Cricket Arena. Although Mike seriously considered coaching, he eventually decided on sport management. He desired to be in the sport business but didn't like the insecurity of coaching. Crum spent eight event-filled (pardon the pun) years under former director Steve Camp learning the ropes. His responsibilities include expanding the convention center, building a new arena, and trying to keep the NBA's Charlotte Hornets in town (unfortunately, the Hornets did move the franchise to New Orleans). Crum characterizes his job as constantly putting out fires. The challenge is balancing political skirmishes with constantly changing demands. It also requires that he attend a never-ending series of meetings, conferences, and a large portion of the 450 concerts, ball games, and other events hosted by the arenas and auditoriums he manages. "You're never really off," Camp notes. "That takes awhile to get used to. It's a big job."[6]

Hiring Professional Facility Management Firms

In 1976, the Louisiana Superdome became the first major sporting facility to use outside professionals to manage its operations. (The owners pay a firm to manage facility operations.)[7] Today, the New Orleans Superdome is managed by SMG. The Philadelphia-based SMG is the world's leading company in the management of public facilities, including stadiums, arenas, theaters, and exhibition/convention centers.[8] It manages using long-term contracts and is responsible for both the financial and operating success of the facilities. Currently, SMG operates 156 facilities and works closely with Hyatt Hotels and ARA-MARK food services. SMG Europe manages eight facilities in the United Kingdom and elsewhere in Europe.

Facility managers are challenged daily as the facility management industry continues to grow. Managers are involved in the processes of scheduling events, arranging for transportation, managing event security, and making sure food concessions are ready for game time.

EVENT PLANNING

2 LEARNING OUTCOME
Describe what is involved in event planning.

Sport managers plan many types of events. They coordinate games, provide food for teams, arrange team transportation, hire officials, manage ticket sales, plan and monitor concession sales, schedule the various leagues, and organize tournaments. Exhibit 5–1 gives a partial list of the activities involved in planning a **MACCABI GAMES.**

Exhibit 5–1 Typical Activities in Planning a Maccabi Games

PEOPLE ACTIVITIES	ATHLETIC ACTIVITIES	FINANCIAL ACTIVITIES
Forming an administrative games management team (games director, assistant games director, etc.)	Training coaches and players on the rules of compassion for other coaches, athletes, and spectators	Securing sponsorship from businesses and individuals—sponsorship can be at the game sponsor level (top sponsors) and the gold, silver, bronze, or patron sponsor level
Forming operations committees to organize food, water, opening and closing ceremonies, transportation, and security	Conducting tryouts for teams	Developing budgets for all the administrative functions and athletic events
Recruiting coaches for each sport	Recruiting athletes for sports that do not have enough players	Managing cash activities ranging from the fees the athletes pay to the paying of suppliers (such as the bus company and security forces)
Developing public relations material (optional—only if you want the games to have media exposure)	Organizing a caring-and-sharing event to allow athletes to take time out from competition to volunteer within their community	Determining final revenue/cost comparison after the games have finished and the athletes have returned home

To prepare for a Maccabi Games for 1000 athletes, the event planner must:

- Set an event budget in line with the overall budget's allowances for events. For instance, how much money will be spent buying ping-pong tables or preparing the gymnasium floor for volleyball games?

- Find out whether the caterers being considered are licensed and insured. The caterer must be able to serve 1000 athletes and provide foods that will appeal to teens. Also, the caterer needs to serve food quickly since the athletes have a very busy schedule.

- Ask the caterer for a list of past clients and check with those clients to make sure the caterer is reliable.

- Find out whether the caterer can accommodate various dietary restrictions. For instance, the Maccabi Games need to have kosher foods available for athletes who follow Jewish dietary laws.

- Plan evening social activities. Visiting local amusement parks, museums, and dance clubs costs money and requires security and transportation.

- Arrange for security. Security measures have become much more important since 9/11. Police escorts to all events are required. Security at sporting events is monitored by having all athletes, coaches, and friends wear credentials around their necks at all times.

- Develop transportation networks to move all the athletes and coaches from venue to venue. All buses should be coordinated at a hub. Jewish Community Center buses need to run on tight schedules to ensure that athletes arrive at their events on time.[9]

 What activities do you think are involved in planning for parking at a Maccabi event?

PLANS

Planning Dimensions

Plans are characterized by five dimensions: (1) The *management level* that develops the plan. (2) The *type* of plan—is it strategic or operational? (3) The *scope* covered in the plan—is it broad in scope (for the entire organization or a business unit), or is it narrow (for a functional department or part of a department)? (4) The *timeframe*—it can be long range or short range. (5) *Repetitiveness*—is it a single-use plan or a standing plan? Chapter 4 covered the first four dimensions; here we cover the repetitiveness dimension. To get an overview of planning, examine Exhibit 5–2; note that upper-level managers employ single-use planning more frequently than first-level and middle managers, who typically use standing plans.

Standing Plans and Single-Use Plans

3 LEARNING OUTCOME
Explain how standing plans and single-use plans differ.

Plans are either *standing plans,* which are designed to be used repeatedly, or *single-use plans,* which are designed to be used just once. Exhibit 5–3 gives the different uses for standing and single-use plans.

Exhibit 5–2   The Five Dimensions of Plans

Management Level	Type of Plan	Scope	Time	Repetitiveness
Upper and Middle	Strategic	Broad	Long-Range	Single-Use Plan
Middle and Lower	Operational	Narrow	Short-Range	Standing Plan

Exhibit 5-3　Uses for Standing and Single-Use Plans

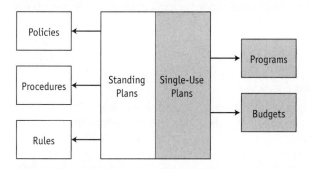

STANDING PLANS. To achieve the objectives laid out in their strategy, organizations develop standing plans, which saves everyone involved valuable time (because the plans are used over and over). **Standing plans** are the policies, procedures, and rules for handling situations that arise repeatedly. These plans guide future decision making. Union contracts in professional leagues like the MLB, NBA, and NHL are standing plans. Standing plans, properly used, help organizations meet objectives.

Policies are general guidelines for decision making. Policies exist at all levels of organizations. Boards of directors develop broad policies, with the input of top management, for entire organizations. Managers then implement these policies. In doing so, they often establish more detailed policies for their own work groups. External groups such as local and state governments, labor unions, and accrediting associations also dictate certain policies. For example, the federal government stipulates that organizations offer equal opportunity to every employee, and labor unions require collective bargaining. Typical policy statements include "We promote qualified employees from within" and "Employees will receive due process in grievances." Notice that policy statements are intentionally general—managers have much discretion in how they implement them. As a manager, your daily decisions will be guided by policies. It will be your job to interpret, apply, and explain company policies to your team.

Procedures (also called standard operating procedures [SOPs] and methods) are sequences of actions to be followed in order to achieve an objective. Procedures are more specific than policies; they entail a series of decisions and may involve more than one functional area. For example, to meet a client's needs, sales, accounting, production, and shipping personnel may follow a set procedure. Procedures ensure that recurring, routine situations are handled in a consistent, predetermined manner. Large organizations typically develop procedures for ticket sales, purchasing, inventory, grievances, and so forth. Small firms usually follow set procedures, but they don't always formalize them in a procedure manual.

Rules state exactly what should or should not be done. As you can see from the following examples, rules do not allow for discretion or leeway: "No shoes on the ice." "No smoking or eating in the locker room." "Hard hats required on the construction site." Violations of rules involve penalties that vary in severity according to the seriousness of the violation and the number of offenses. As a manager, you will be responsible for establishing and enforcing rules in a uniform manner.

Policies, procedures, and rules are all standing plans. They differ in terms of their scope—policies provide general guides, procedures set a sequence of activities, and rules govern specific actions—but they all guide behavior in recurring situations. It is important that you distinguish between them so that you know when can do something your way and when you cannot.

SINGLE-USE PLANS. Single-use plans include programs and budgets that address nonrepetitive situations. Single-use plans, unlike standing plans, are developed for a specific purpose and probably will not be used again in the same form. However, an effective single-use plan may become a model for future programs, budgets, or contracts. The union contracts discussed under a standing plan are originally a single-use plan, and when implemented they are a standing plan. A strategy is also a single-use plan.

standing plans
Policies, procedures, and rules for handling situations that arise repeatedly.

policies
General guidelines for decision making.

procedures
Sequences of actions to be followed in order to achieve an objective.

rules
State exactly what should or should not be done.

single-use plans
Programs and budgets developed for handling nonrepetitive situations.

TIMEOUT
Give an example of a policy, procedure, and rule from an organization you work for or play for.

_____

_____

_____

_____

_____

A *program* describes a set of activities designed to accomplish an objective over a specified period, which can be as short as one to three months or as long as several decades. Programs are set up for objectives as varied as developing products, expanding facilities, and taking advantage of new opportunities in the environment.

When you're developing a program, these steps should be followed: (1) Set broad program objectives. (2) Break the project down into specific objectives and goals. (3) Assign responsibility for each objective/goal. (4) Establish starting and ending times for each one. (5) Determine the resources needed for each one.

We will examine budgets in greater detail in Chapter 14, but the following definition will suffice for our purposes here: *Budgets* are the funds allocated to operate a department or program for a fixed period. Many people dread budgeting activities because their math and accounting skills are not their strong suit. In reality, budgets are as much (or more) about planning as they are about accounting. Budgets are crucial tools in both planning (they help you develop realistic plans) and control (they help you assess how implementation is going). One of **CLAUDIA FIKS'S** most important responsibilities is to ensure that each Maccabi Games is brought in within its budget. **What sorts of planning activities might she engage in to accomplish this objective?**

Contingency Plans

4 LEARNING OUTCOME
Explain when, and why, contingency plans are necessary.

No matter how effective your plan, there will be times when things go wrong. Maybe the computer where all the ticket information is stored will go down or your star player will be sidelined for the season due to injuries. Just because something is uncontrollable doesn't mean it is not foreseeable. Effective managers have contingency plans "in their pockets" for just such situations. **Contingency plans** are alternative plans that can be implemented if uncontrollable events occur. Therefore, wise coaches/managers take great pains to develop backup players/employees who can and will be ready to step in should a first-string

contingency plans
Alternative plans that can be implemented if uncontrollable events occur.

TIMEOUT
Give an example of a program your firm or team has in place and assess whether it was set up following the guidelines described above.

_____

_____

_____

_____

_____

APPLYING THE CONCEPT   *Categorizing Plans*

Categorize each of the following statements by whether it is

a. an objective   **c.** a procedure   **e.** a program

b. a policy   **d.** a rule   **f.** a budget

_____ 1. Programs that build healthy spirit, mind, and body for all (YMCA).

_____ 2. An athletic director's plan to improve the performance of the college's women's swim team.

_____ 3. To increase our attendance by 10 percent next year.

_____ 4. Employees having babies will be given a two-month maternity leave.

_____ 5. Next month's cost to operate your department.

_____ 6. Safety glasses required to tour the new sport arena's construction site.

_____ 7. Leaves of absence must be approved by the manager and the forms submitted to the personnel office one month in advance of their effective dates.

_____ 8. Maintain the reject rate on sneakers under 1 percent.

_____ 9. $1000 allotted for conducting a facilities management seminar.

player/employee get injured or call in sick. For example, MLB managers keep close tabs on promising minor league players, who are their "contingency plans" for sidelined stars.

To develop a contingency plan for your department or team, answer these three questions:

1. What might go wrong?

2. How can I prevent it from happening?

3. If it does occur, what can I do to minimize its effect?

Make sure you ask everyone involved questions 1 and 2. Your answer to question 3 is your contingency plan. It is also a good idea to talk to others both in- and outside your organization who have implemented similar plans. They may have encountered problems you haven't thought of, and their contingency plans can serve as models for yours.

Why Managers Don't Plan

CLAUDIA FIKS notes that by far the most common reason managers don't plan is lack of time—this is one reason she makes sure to allot time for this all-important activity. **How would you address this lack-of-time issue if you were in her shoes?** This is one reason we cover time management in this chapter. Many crises can be avoided if you carve out time for planning. Managers who always find time to do a job over but don't find the time to do it right the first time (plan, in other words) are not doing the right job. Managers who plan have fewer crises; they are in better control of their departments. Managers who don't plan find themselves scrambling from one "fire" to the next. Keep in mind that planning is a continuous activity. Plans don't have to be complicated or take lots of your time. Make planning an integral part of your "managing life." Remember the old adage when you are tempted to skip the planning stage: "When you fail to plan, you plan to fail."

Flags That Indicate Poor Planning

Signs of poor planning include the following:

- *Objectives that are not met.* Missed deadlines, delivery dates, and schedules.

- *Continual crises.* When every job is a rush job and overtime is overused to complete jobs.

- *Idle resources.* Physical resources idle, financial resources accumulating interest and not being put to immediate use, or staff kept waiting for the manager to assign tasks.[10]

- *Lack of resources.* Resources not available when needed.

- *Duplication.* The same task done more than once.

SALES FORECASTING TECHNIQUES

5 LEARNING OUTCOME
Discuss how sales forecasts shape strategy.

Forecasting is the process of predicting what will happen in the future. Organizations engage in continual forecasting as they scan the environment. For example, they forecast where the economy is headed, how new innovations in technology may affect their market share or internal processes, and how new government regulations will impact labor relations, to name a few. But they pay particular attention to sales forecasts.

A **sales forecast** predicts the dollar amount of product that will be sold during a specified period. Accurate sales forecasts are crucial in planning because many activities hinge on them—staffing up and laying off workers, ordering in adequate supplies to meet production needs, avoiding overstocking, and so forth. Marketing departments typically forecast short-term sales out for one year. They are then gone over by the sales manager, who submits them for approval and possible adjustment by upper management.[11] Marketing then uses the forecasts to set sales quotas. Operations uses them to decide how much product or service to produce. Marketing also monitors inventory levels (production and customer) to adjust the

TIMEOUT
Describe a situation in which a contingency plan is appropriate, then briefly describe a possible plan for it.

_____

_____

_____

_____

_____

TIMEOUT
How would you rate the planning ability of a current or past boss or coach? Give examples of flags that indicate inadequate planning.

_____

_____

_____

_____

_____

sales forecast
Predicts the dollar amount of a product that will be sold during a specified period.

forecasts as needed. Finance uses them to determine how much money the organization will take in so that Finance can budget expenditures and also how much money the organization will need to borrow to cover short-term and long-term expenses. Human Resources uses the forecasts to increase staffing or plan for layoffs. For example, the Boston Red Sox can forecast annual ticket sales of approximately 2.5 million.[12] The team will use this number to forecast its net revenues (which will also include advertising and media sales forecasts and team merchandise sales forecasts). Revenue forecasts will help the team determine how much budget it can allocate to acquiring new talent.

market share
An organization's percentage of total industry sales.

Companies use total industry sales to calculate their *market share.* **Market share** is the organization's percentage of total industry sales. For example, Nike's market share of the U.S. athletic shoe market is currently more than 35 percent.[13] Professional and trade publications forecast industry sales numbers to help organizations analyze the environment and forecast their own sales. Organizations also take local conditions, especially local competition, into account when they forecast sales.

Accurate forecasts often determine whether an organization survives tough times and whether it thrives in good times. The recent decline in the U.S. economy, increased competition, the sport industry's heavy debt, and the poor relations that pro sports has with consumers are putting heavy demands on forecasts.[14] The Starter Corporation, once the industry leader in sports-licensed apparel, declared bankruptcy in 1999, when the overall economy was still going strong. Starter depended heavily on the health of professional leagues to sell its licensed apparel. However, players' strikes and lockouts created a shaky business environment. Starter also faced new competition in the apparel industry from well-financed footwear companies.[15]

Sales forecasts are a key part of the business-level strategy. Organizations that use a prospector strategy are predicting they can grow sales at aggressive rates. Organizations that use an analyzer or defender strategy are forecasting that their sales will grow slowly or stay about the same. Companies that are retrenching have predicted that sales will fall precipitously.

6 LEARNING OUTCOME
Explain how qualitative and quantitative forecasting techniques differ.

qualitative forecasting techniques
Use subjective judgment, intuition, experience, and opinion to predict sales.

quantitative forecasting techniques
Use objective, mathematical techniques and past sales data to predict sales.

Sales forecasting techniques are either qualitative or quantitative. **Qualitative forecasting techniques** primarily use subjective judgment, intuition, experience, and opinion to predict sales. (Some math is also used.) **Quantitative forecasting techniques** use objective, mathematical techniques and past sales data to predict sales. Organizations typically combine quantitative and qualitative techniques to increase accuracy.[16]

Qualitative Sales Forecasting

As Exhibit 5–4 shows, qualitative techniques include individual opinion, a jury of executive opinion, sales force composites, customer composites, operating unit composites, and surveys. Note that only qualitative techniques can be used for new products or by new companies because they have no past sales data on which to base a quantitative forecast (although they can be influenced by all sorts of quantitative data if they are going into an established industry).

INDIVIDUAL OPINION. We all use our personal experience, intuition, and past events to predict what we think will happen in the future. A person starting a new business alone has no other option but to make an educated (based on industry analysis) individual opinion.

7 LEARNING OUTCOME
Explain how the jury of executive opinion and the three sales composites differ.

JURY OF EXECUTIVE OPINION. In this technique, a group of managers and/or experts pools their opinions to forecast sales. The typical format is a group meeting in which ideas are shared and an attempt is made to reach consensus on the sales forecast. The Delphi technique is commonly used here. However, the organization must first decide whether group decision making is appropriate for the situation (see Chapter 3). A jury of executive opinion is often used among partners.

Exhibit 5–4   A Summary of Common Sales Forecasting

Qualitative (subjective)	Quantitative (objective)
Individual opinion	Past sales
Jury of executive opinion	Time series
Sales force composite	Regression
Customer composite	
Operating unit composite	
Survey	

SALES FORCE COMPOSITE. This technique combines forecasts made by each sales rep. Each rep predicts his or her sales for the future period; these are then totaled to give the composite forecast. Sales reps tend to know their customers and can be a good source. However, many company managers believe that their salespeople are too optimistic, so they balance the composite with other forecast techniques.[17] Sales force composites work well when sales reps sell relatively expensive products (or total orders) with a clear-cut customer base or territory.

CUSTOMER COMPOSITE. In this technique the purchase forecasts of major customers are combined. This approach is frequently a solid bet because customers typically assess their buying needs very accurately. Customer composites work well when an organization has relatively few customers with large-volume sales. Nike, with large retail accounts like Dick's Sporting Goods and The Foot Locker, no doubt uses customer composites, among other techniques, to build forecasts.

OPERATING UNIT COMPOSITE. This is the total sales forecast for multiple units. Businesses with multiple operating units, such as chain stores like The Foot Locker, commonly predict the sales for each operating unit, then add them to forecast total company sales.

In *department composites,* a business with multiple departments (such as a sporting goods store with golf, fitness, footwear, and clothing departments) can treat each department as an operating unit. In *product composites,* a business with multiple products forecasts sales for each product or service and combines them to create a total forecast. Adidas might choose to do this with its footwear, golf, skiing, and cycling divisions.

SURVEY. This forecasting technique uses mail questionnaires or telephone or personal interviews to predict future purchases. A sample of a population (for example, people whose hobby is kayaking) is surveyed and a forecast for the entire population is made based on the responses. Businesses commonly use surveys to forecast sales for a new product or service. Surveys are also used in the development phase of a new product to maximize its quality or fit with the target consumer before the final product comes to market. **CLAUDIA FIKS** and the administrative committee of the Maccabi Games interviewed the leaders of a local community to gauge their interest in hosting the games. The interview results indicated the community wasn't sure if they were large enough to host an event of this magnitude. From this information, Claudia determined that her strategy would be to develop the mind-set in the community that by working together they would be able to properly host the games. **In what situations do you think the Maccabi Games staff would use qualitative forecasting techniques?**

> **TIMEOUT**
> Describe a situation in which your firm or team might forecast sales or team growth using qualitative techniques.
> _____
> _____
> _____
> _____
> _____

Quantitative Sales Forecasting

LEARNING OUTCOME
8
Explain how past sales and time series forecasting techniques differ.

Quantitative techniques include past sales, time series, and regression. Qualitative techniques can be combined with quantitative ones as long as the products and companies have existed long enough to accrue an adequate data base for sales. Time series and regression techniques need at least a year of data, and a longer period will give better results.

PAST SALES. This technique assumes that past sales will be repeated, or can be subjectively adjusted for environmental factors. For example, the Red Sox have sold around 2 million tickets annually for the last 20 years no matter how well the team performed on the field. Its past sales therefore indicate a strong likelihood of this pattern continuing.

time series
Predicts future sales by extending the trend line of past sales into the future.

TIME SERIES. Time series predicts future sales by extending the trend line of past sales into the future. Sales data is collected weekly, monthly, quarterly, or yearly, and then plotted to find the trend. The trend line can be extended by hand (an upward trending line implies increasing sales; a horizontal line implies flat sales; and a downward trending line implies decreasing sales) and the sales estimated manually, but computer time series programs are much more accurate. Time series is also used to plot seasonal trends. With time series, adjustments for environmental factors are still made, but are more objective.

REGRESSION. Beyond the scope of this book, *regression* (also called line of best-fit) is a mathematical modeling technique that helps you minimize error as you find a line that best fits your sales data. Regression analysis therefore makes forecasts more accurate. As a manager, you will find regression analysis very useful (simple regression analysis is not especially difficult); make sure you master it in your statistics classes. **CLAUDIA FIKS** uses her experience at previous Maccabi Games to forecast what will be needed at upcoming games. For instance, she can use past data on the number of athletes at previous games and the amounts of food, housing, security, and venues that were used. She can adjust these amounts based on the number of athletes that will be competing in the upcoming games. **In what situations do you think Maccabi Games staff would use quantitative forecasting techniques?**

SCHEDULING TOOLS

9 LEARNING OUTCOME
Know when to use planning sheets, Gantt charts, and PERT diagrams.

**APPLYING
THE CONCEPT**   *Sales Forecasting Techniques*

Choose the most appropriate forecast technique(s) for the following organizations.

a. Individual opinion	**f.** Survey
b. Jury of executive opinion	**g.** Past sales
c. Sales force composite	**h.** Time series analysis
d. Customer composite	**i.** Regression analysis
e. Operating unit composite	

_____ 10. The Sports Authority footwear chain.

_____ 11. And1 sports apparel with a sales force that calls on specific stores in the sales area.

_____ 12. A sole proprietor who sells his own new, very different sports cream.

_____ 13. Jim and Betty's "mom-and-pop" sports store.

_____ 14. Nike sneakers.

_____ 15. Ticket sales to a game between your championship team and last year's second-place finisher.

After marketing completes its sales forecast and receives customer orders for the product, operations begins to produce the product. To ensure ready availability of their products without excessive carrying costs (inventory costs), many organizations include customer input in their scheduling activities. This is particularly important with just-in-time (JIT) operations, which is a widely used method of reducing carrying costs.

Scheduling is the process of listing essential activities in sequence with the time needed to complete each activity. The details of the schedule answer the *what, when, where, how,* and *who* questions. For example, what is the goal that Claudia Fiks needs to achieve in setting up transportation for the **MACCABI GAMES?** When will the games take place (exact dates and times)? Where are the venues located? What size of buses will be needed? Who will greet the athletes and make sure they are picked up and dropped off properly? Effective schedulers define the objective to be accomplished, break it into finite, doable tasks, and make sure resources are available when needed. All managers schedule resources, including their own time, which we discuss in the next section.

Today, organizations routinely use computers to schedule resources. A wide variety of scheduling software is available, which you will certainly investigate in advanced courses. However, just as with math skills, it strengthens your scheduling skills if you understand the underlying concepts *before* you turn to computers. Therefore, to get you started, we will explore simple planning sheets, Gantt charts, and PERT diagrams using the old-fashioned paper and pencil in this section. But first let's discuss two simple, fundamental tools we use daily—our calendars and to-do lists. Don't underestimate their value in maximizing your efficiency. Planning calendars can be bought in every office supply store, and a to-do list is as close as a scrap of paper and your focused mind. *Use them.* Learn to schedule well and wisely *now,* while you are in school and your life (believe it or not) is fairly simple. This habit will stand you in good stead in every endeavor you undertake, and should be one you constantly hone.

Planning Sheets

Planning sheets state an objective and list the sequence of activities, when each activity will begin and end, and who will complete each activity to meet the objective. Exhibit 5–5 shows a planning sheet for a monthly marketing letter, developed by **CLAUDIA FIKS** for staff and volunteers involved in the Maccabi Games. **Before continuing, review Exhibit 5–5 and identify the five planning dimensions involved in this plan (Exhibit 5–2). (The answers are at the bottom of the exhibit.)** Planning sheets work best with activities that are accomplished in independent sequential steps. Use Exhibit 5–5 as a template for the planning sheets you use.

SET OBJECTIVES. Obviously, the first step in planning is to clearly state the end result you desire, using the writing objectives guidelines we presented in Chapter 4. Next, fill in who will be responsible for achieving the objective, starting and ending dates, the priority (high, medium, low), and control checkpoints for monitoring progress.

PLAN AND SCHEDULE. List the sequence of steps stating what, where, how, resources needed, and so on in the first column. In the "when" column, place the start and end time for each step. The third column contains the party responsible for each step. Note that steps 2 to 4 can be eliminated if the letters are printed on the word processor. (Which is more time- and cost-efficient?) Maccabi staff use printed correspondence (even though it is more expensive) because it helps set the personal tone that is so important in nonprofit organizations, which need to establish close relationships with their constituencies.

GANTT Charts

Popularized by Henry Gantt in the early 1900s, **Gantt charts** use bar graphs to illustrate progress on a project. Activities are shown vertically, and time horizontally. The resources to be allocated, such as people or machines, are shown on the vertical axis. Alternatively, a variety of department projects can be shown on the same chart. Gantt charts, like planning sheets, are appropriate for plans with independent sequential steps. Two advantages of Gantt charts over planning sheets are that their control is built-in (progress can be seen at a glance)

---

scheduling
The process of listing essential activities in sequence with the time needed to complete each activity.

planning sheets
State an objective and list the sequence of activities, when each activity will begin and end, and who will complete each activity to meet the objective.

Gantt charts
Use bars to graphically illustrate progress on a project.

Exhibit 5–5   Maccabi Operational Plan

OBJECTIVE: To mail a personalized letter to everybody involved in the Maccabi Games by the 15th of each month

Person responsible: Joel   **Starting date:** 1st of each month

Due date: 15th of each month   **Priority:** High

Control checkpoints: 7th and 12th of each month

	WHEN		
ACTIVITIES	**START**	**END**	**WHO**
1. Write letter.	1st	2nd	Claudia
2. Deliver letter to printer.	3rd	4th	Joel
3. Print letters on Maccabi stationery.	5th	6th	printer
4. Pick up letters at printer.	6th	7th	Joel
5. Use mail merge to type names and addresses on letters and envelopes.	7th	9th	Joel
6. Each letter is signed by Claudia; Joel does the envelope stuffing.	10th	11th	Joel
7. Bundle to meet bulk-mailing specifications.	12th	13th	Joel
8. Deliver to U.S. Postal Bulk Mail Center.	13th		Joel
9. Mail letters.	14th	15th	U.S.P.S.

Based on the five planning dimensions: (1) This plan was developed by Claudia and Stuart. Stuart is the top-level manager who works closely with Claudia Fiks. (2) Plan type—operational. (3) Narrow scope. (4) Time frame—short range. (5) Repetitiveness—standing plan.

TIMEOUT

Give an example of one of your team's plans that could be tracked effectively using a Gantt chart.

_____

_____

_____

_____

_____

and you can view multiple projects on one chart. This is very helpful when prioritizing and scheduling activities that use the same resources.

Gantt charts are used extensively for allocating resources. A planning sheet can be turned into a Gantt chart simply by changing the "when" columns to day columns and inserting Gantt bars in the rows. Although not shown in Exhibit 5–6, Gantt charts can also have "who" and "what" columns just like planning sheets.

Exhibit 5–6 is a hypothetical Gantt chart for multiple orders at a manufacturing company in their operations department. Each bar represents the start to end time, and the filled-in part represents order completion to date. The chart shows at a glance how orders are progressing. Knowing instantly when a project is behind schedule is crucial for taking corrective action. Assume that "today" is day 1 of week 3 in May (end of dark color of bar should be directly under 3 to be on schedule). What is the status of each of the four projects on the chart in Exhibit 5–6? The answer is at the bottom of the figure.

Performance Evaluation and Review Technique

Multiple activities are independent when they can be performed *simultaneously;* they are dependent when one activity must be completed *before* the next activity can begin. The planning sheet and Gantt chart are useful tools when the activities follow each other in a dependent series. However, when activities are both dependent and independent of each other, PERT diagrams are more appropriate. **PERT (Performance Evaluation and Review Technique) diagrams** highlight the interdependence of activities by diagramming their "network." Exhibit 5–7 shows a PERT diagram.

The key components in a PERT diagram are activities, events, time, the critical path, and possibly cost. With complex programs, it is common for one "event" to represent multiple activities. For example, in producing a racing car, building the engine (which requires multiple tasks) might be represented as one event. Time can be measured in a variety of units from seconds to decades, depending on the tasks being tracked. The strength of PERT diagrams is

PERT (Performance Evaluation and Review Technique) diagrams
These diagrams highlight the interdependence of activities by diagramming their network.

Exhibit 5–6   Multiple-Project Gantt Chart (Order by Week)

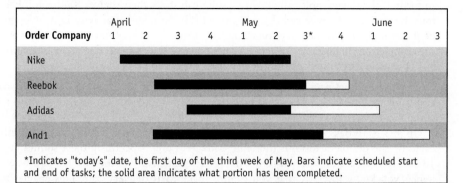

*Indicates "today's" date, the first day of the third week of May. Bars indicate scheduled start and end of tasks; the solid area indicates what portion has been completed.

The Nike project is done; Reebok is right on schedule and should be completed this week; Adidas is behind schedule and should be a high priority if it is to be completed by the end of the fourth week in May; And1 is ahead of schedule and should be completed during the first week of June.

Exhibit 5–7   PERT Diagram

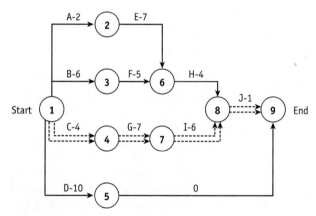

Circles = Events

Arrows and Letters = Activities

Numbers = Time in days

Double Arrows = The critical path, or how long it should take to complete the project

that they show which tasks form the project's "critical path." The **critical path** tracks the most time-consuming series of activities and therefore determines the length of time it will take to complete a project. The double arrows in Exhibit 5–7 show this particular project's critical path. Any delay in completing the critical path delays the entire project. Many organizations are focusing on shortening the time it takes to complete each activity to save time (time-based competition).[18] Cost for each activity can also tracked in a PERT diagram.

DEVELOPING A PERT DIAGRAM. The following steps explain how the PERT diagram in Exhibit 5–7 was completed:

1. *List every activity (event) that must be completed to reach the objective.* Assign each event a letter. Exhibit 5–7 shows ten activities labeled A to J.

2. *Determine the time it will take to complete each event.* In Exhibit 5–7, time is measured in days—A-2 (event A is slated to take 2 days); B-6 (event B, 6 days); C-4 (event C, 4 days); and so on.

critical path
The most time-consuming series of activities in a PERT network.

3. *Arrange the events in the sequence in which they must be completed.* In Exhibit 5–7, event A must be completed before event E can begin; event E before event H can begin; and so forth. If these were golf balls, before a store can stock their shelves (J), the golf balls must be ordered (A), received (E), and priced (H). Notice that activity D is independent. Arrows point in the direction of the event that follows. Numbered circles signify the completion of an event. All activities originate and terminate at a circle. In Exhibit 5–7, 1 represents the start of the project and 9 its completion.

4. *Determine the critical path.* To do this, the time it takes for each path from start (1) to end (9) is totaled. Path 1–2–6–8–9 takes 2 + 7 + 4 + 1 days, or a total of 14 days to complete. Path 1–3–6–8–9 takes 6 + 5 + 4 + 1 = 16 days, path 1–4–7–8–9 takes 4 + 7 + 6 + 1 = 18 days, and path 1–5–9 takes 10 + 0 = 10 days. The critical path (indicated by the double arrows) is therefore path 1–4–7–8–9. So this project should take 18 days to complete. If your customer has requested delivery of the product two weeks hence, you know instantly that you cannot make their delivery date. This enables to you to consider other strategies early on, including renegotiating the delivery date.

TIMEOUT
Give an example one of your team's plans that could be tracked effectively using a PERT diagram.

_____

_____

_____

_____

_____

In summary, planning sheets and Gantt charts are typically used to develop procedures for routine standing plans, whereas PERT diagrams are used with single-use plans for complex projects with dependent activities. However, all three can be used for standing and single-use plans. There are computerized versions of Gantt charts and PERT diagrams. The first Skill-Builder at the end of the chapter gives you practice in constructing a Gantt chart and PERT diagram by hand.

TIME MANAGEMENT

time management
Techniques that enable people to get more done in less time with better results.

Time used wisely is your friend—time used poorly places you at a distinct disadvantage. Time is also a crucial aspect of every organization's competitive advantage. Time management skills can therefore have a direct effect on your productivity and on your career.[19] **Time management** enables people to get more done in less time with better results. Although time is probably a manager's most valuable resource, many managers don't use this resource effectively. They don't prioritize activities and they don't use time management techniques. A 1999 study of the directors of 37 Canadian intercollegiate athletic departments showed that the directors perceived their most important and most time-consuming activities to be financial management, leadership, policy making, disturbance handling, revenue generation, and athletic affairs.[20] Developing time management skills is also an effective way to reduce stress (Chapter 9), increase personal productivity, and experience inner peace.

APPLYING THE CONCEPT   *Scheduling Tools*

Select the most appropriate scheduling tool for each situation.

a. planning sheet   c. PERT diagram

b. Gantt chart

____ 16. A high school with six teams and three practice fields.

____ 17. Planning the construction of a new sports arena.

____ 18. Developing procedures for a new way to track ticket sales.

____ 19. A plan to restructure the athletic department at a university.

____ 20. Scheduling the use of the YMCA's weight-training rooms and courses.

Analyzing Your Use of Time

The first step to successful time management requires that you figure out how you spend (and waste) time. Working long hours can be a sign that you are managing your time poorly, although it can also mean you have taken on too much or that your organization is trying to do too much with too few people. We often don't realize how much time we waste until we analyze how we use our time. For example, managers spend an average of 15 minutes a day on hold on the telephone; this adds up to *two weeks* a year.[21] Knowing this enables you to consider how you can double-task such dead time—read your mail, clean out a drawer, organize a file, and so forth. Don't think you need to analyze your use of time? Think again. *Everyone* can benefit from this endeavor. If you are an effective user of time, you will become more effective. If you are ineffective, well, it's time to get effective.

10 LEARNING OUTCOME
Use a time log.

KEEP A TIME LOG. The *time log* tracks your daily activities and helps you figure out "where all the time goes." Exhibit 5–8 can be used as a template for creating your own time logs. Track your time every day for one or two weeks. (Make sure these are typical weeks. Tracking atypical weeks won't be of much use.) Take the time log with you throughout the day, and fill in each 15-minute time slot, if possible.

ANALYZE IT. After logging your time for five to ten typical working days, it's time to analyze your data. Here is what you will do next—using the evaluation column and the abbreviations noted in parentheses below, you will review your logs and answer the following questions. We will give you possible solution ideas in the following discussion, but first take a moment and annotate your time logs.

- How did you spend most of your time? Note how much time you spent on your high priorities (HP) and on your low priorities (LP).

- Where did you spend too much time (TT)?

Exhibit 5–8   Daily Time Log

Daily Time Log for: Day _____ Date _____		
Starting Time	**Description**	**Evaluation of Time Use**
8:00 8:15 8:30 8:45		
9:00 9:15 9:30 9:45		
10:00 (etc., to ending time)		

- Where could you have spent more time? That is, you didn't spend enough time (NT).

- What major interruptions kept you from doing what you wanted to get done? How could you eliminate them in the future?

- What tasks could you delegate to someone else (D)? To whom can you delegate these tasks? (You will develop delegation skills in Chapter 6.)

- How much time does your boss control (B)? How much time do your employees control (E)? How much time do others outside your department control (O)? How much time do you actually control (M)? How can you gain more control of your own time?

- Look for crisis situations (C). Were they caused by something you did or did not do? Do you have recurring crises? What changes can you make to help eliminate recurring crises? Do you have effective contingency plans?

- Look for habits, patterns, and tendencies. Do they help you or prevent you from getting the job done? How can you change them to your advantage?

- List three to five of your biggest time wasters (W). What can you do to eliminate them?

- Ask yourself, "How can I manage my time more efficiently?"

TIMEOUT

Use your time log data to identify your three biggest time wasters. Read the following discussion and develop some strategies for minimizing them.

A Time Management System

11 LEARNING OUTCOME
Manage your time better.

Time management is a daunting challenge for people in unconventional work contexts. The time management system we present here has a proven track record with thousands of managers. Try it for three weeks. After that, you can custom-tailor it to your own needs.

The problem we all face is not a shortage of time, but using our time effectively. Think you could use an extra two hours every day? Experts say that we *waste* at least this much time every day. This means that on average we can improve our time use by 20 percent.

The four key components of an effective time management system are

- *Prioritize.* In other words, get realistic. Seldom—if ever—do we have enough time to do everything we *want* to do. However, there is usually enough time to do what we really *need* to do. Prioritizing tasks helps you decide where you should be spending your time and prevents you from squandering it on trivial matters.

- *Set objectives.* we've been here before (chapter 4), but it's true. *People who get things done set objectives.*

- *Plan.* Plan how you are going to get your objectives done. Don't skip this step.

- *Make a schedule.* Use planning sheets, Gantt charts, and/or PERT diagrams. Schedule each week and work day.

time management system
Planning each week, scheduling each week, and scheduling each day.

Time management systems all boil down to two things—develop a game plan and stick to it. Every **time management system** involves planning each week, scheduling each week, and scheduling each day.

1. *Plan each week.* On the last day of each week, plan the coming week. On Monday, you will be all set and ready to go. Do this each and every week. Using Exhibit 5–9 as a template, think about your objectives and list the ones you think you can accomplish next week. Focus on nonroutine tasks, not routine ones you do weekly or daily.

After setting a few major objectives, list the activities you need to accomplish for each objective in column 1. If an objective calls for multiple activities, use one of the three scheduling tools given earlier. Prioritize each activity. High priorities must be done that week; medium and low priorities can be pushed into the next week if necessary.

In the last two columns, fill in the time you think you will need and the most promising day to do each task. Total the time you have allotted for your objectives for the week. Is this time realistic considering you still need to do routine tasks and deal with unexpected events?

Exhibit 5–9   Weekly Planner

Plan for the week of: _____			
Objectives:			
Activities	**Priority**	**Time Needed**	**Day to Schedule**
Total time for the week			

With experience, you will become pretty accurate about what you can and cannot accomplish in a given week. Planning to do more than you can actually get done is not only frustrating, it guarantees failure. Not planning enough activities, of course, wastes time.

2. *Schedule each week.* Scheduling your work gets you organized and focused.[22] Make your schedule as you plan your week or do it afterward, whichever you prefer. These two tasks should take about 30 minutes. Using Exhibit 5–10, fill in time slots that are already spoken for, such as standing weekly meetings. Next, schedule events over which you have control, like performance appraisals. Most managers leave about 50 percent of their week unscheduled to accommodate unexpected events. Your job may require more or less unscheduled time. With practice, you will find the balance that works for you.

The key to time management is not to prioritize your schedule, but to schedule your priorities.[23] In other words, control your schedule, don't let it control you.

3. *Schedule each day.* At the end of each day, schedule the following day. Or you can schedule your day first thing in the morning. This should take 15 minutes or less. Base the

Exhibit 5–10   Weekly Schedule

Schedule for the week of: _____					
Time	**Mon.**	**Tues.**	**Wed.**	**Th.**	**Fri.**
8:00					
8:15					
8:30					
8:45					
9:00 (etc., to ending time)					

day's schedule on your plan and schedule for the week, using Exhibit 5–11 as a template. Daily schedules help you adjust for unplanned events. Pencil in already scheduled activities like meetings. Strive to keep your daily schedule flexible. As we noted earlier, most managers leave 50 percent of their time unscheduled to handle unexpected events. Here are some other scheduling tips:

- Don't be too optimistic; schedule enough time to do each task. Many managers find that *doubling* their initial estimate works well. Don't despair, you will improve with practice.

- You've got your priorities straight and your schedule in hand. Now focus *on only one task* at a time. Some people seem to get an incredible number of things done— if you watch them closely, you will see they have the discipline to laser in on one task at a time.

- Schedule high-priority items during your "prime time," the time when you are at your best. For most people it is early in the morning. Others start slow and build momentum through the day. Figure out your MO and use your prime time to work on tasks that require your full attention. Do routine tasks, such as checking your mail, at other times.

- Try to schedule a time for unexpected events. Tell employees to see you with routine matters during a set time, such as 3:00 P.M. Have people call you, and call them, during this set time.

- Don't perform an unscheduled task without determining its priority. If you are working on a high-priority item and a medium-priority matter arises, let it wait. Even so-called urgent matters can often wait.

Time management works well for managers whose jobs entail a variety of nonrecurring tasks. For managers and employees who deal primarily with routine tasks, the time management system we've outlined above may not be necessary. For those of you in routine situations, a good to-do list that prioritizes items may be all you need. We'll return to the proverbial to-do list in Chapter 6. The second Skill-Builder at the end of the chapter helps you analyze your time use. Forms similar to Exhibits 5–8 through 5–11 can be purchased in pad, book, and even computer versions. And you can always create your own versions of these examples.

Time Management Techniques

The Self Assessment on page 133 contains 50 time management techniques arranged by management function. Planning and controlling are placed together because they are so closely related. Organizing and leading are separated.

> **TIMEOUT**
> Using your answers from the Self Assessment, choose the three most important techniques you "should" be using. Explain how you will implement each technique.
> _____
> _____
> _____
> _____
> _____

Exhibit 5–11 Daily Schedule

Schedule for the day of: _____
Time
8:00
8:15
8:30
8:45
9:00
(etc., to ending time)

SELF ASSESSMENT   *Time Management Techniques*

Here are 50 ideas that you can use to improve your time management skills. Check the appropriate box for each idea.

	Should Do	Could Do	Do Not Do	Does Not Apply to Me
Planning and Controlling Management Functions				
1. I use the time management system presented in the text.	☐	☐	☐	☐
2. I use a to-do list and prioritize items on it. I do the important things rather than the urgent ones.	☐	☐	☐	☐
3. I get an early and productive start on my top-priority items.	☐	☐	☐	☐
4. I do only high-priority items and unpleasant or difficult tasks during my prime time.	☐	☐	☐	☐
5. I don't spend time on unproductive activities to avoid or escape job-related anxiety. I get the job done.	☐	☐	☐	☐
6. Throughout the day I ask myself, "Should I be doing this now?"	☐	☐	☐	☐
7. I plan before I act.	☐	☐	☐	☐
8. I do contingency planning—that is, I have plans in place for recurring crises.	☐	☐	☐	☐
9. I am decisive. It is better to make a wrong decision than none at all.	☐	☐	☐	☐
10. I schedule enough time to do the job right the first time. I try to be realistic about the amount of time it takes to do a job.	☐	☐	☐	☐
11. I schedule a quiet hour that my staff interrupts only for true emergencies. I have someone take messages, or I ask people to call me back.	☐	☐	☐	☐
12. I've established a quiet time for my team. I've found that the first hour of the day works best.	☐	☐	☐	☐
13. I schedule large blocks of uninterrupted (emergencies-only) time for projects and so forth.	☐	☐	☐	☐
14. If this doesn't work, I hide somewhere.	☐	☐	☐	☐
15. I break big tasks into smaller, more doable tasks.	☐	☐	☐	☐
16. Before I stop work on a scheduled item to do something unscheduled, I ask: "Is doing this unscheduled task more important than the scheduled event?"	☐	☐	☐	☐
17. I schedule a time for doing similar activities (making and returning calls, writing letters and memos).	☐	☐	☐	☐
Organizing Management Function				
18. I schedule time for unexpected events (my "office hours") and let people know when I'm "open" for calls and questions. I ask people to see me or call me during those hours, unless it's an emergency. I answer mail and do other routine tasks during this time. If people ask to see me—"Got a minute?"—I ask them whether it can wait until my "office hours."	☐	☐	☐	☐
19. I schedule a time, set up an agenda, and set a time limit for all visitors, and keep on topic.	☐	☐	☐	☐

(continued)

SELF ASSESSMENT (*continued*)

	Should Do	Could Do	Do Not Do	Does Not Apply to Me
20. I keep a clean, well-organized work area/desk.	☐	☐	☐	☐
21. I remove all non-work-related or distracting objects from my work area/desk.	☐	☐	☐	☐
22. I do one task at a time.	☐	☐	☐	☐
23. With paperwork, I make a decision at once. I don't reread it later and decide later.	☐	☐	☐	☐
24. My files are systematically arranged and labeled as active or inactive. When I file an item, I note a throwaway date on it.	☐	☐	☐	☐
25. When appropriate, I call rather than write or visit.	☐	☐	☐	☐
26. I delegate appropriate tasks when I can.	☐	☐	☐	☐
27. I use form letters and a word processor.	☐	☐	☐	☐
28. I answer letters (memos) on the letter itself.	☐	☐	☐	☐
29. I have someone read and summarize appropriate things for me.	☐	☐	☐	☐
30. I divide reading requirements with others and share summaries.	☐	☐	☐	☐
31. I have calls screened to make sure the right person handles it.	☐	☐	☐	☐
32. I plan before I call. I have an agenda and all pertinent information handy; and I take notes on the agenda.	☐	☐	☐	☐
33. I ask people to call me back during my "office hours." I also ask about the best time to call them.	☐	☐	☐	☐
34. I have a specific objective or purpose for every meeting I conduct. If I can't state the meeting's purpose, I don't have the meeting.	☐	☐	☐	☐
35. When I do hold meetings, I invite only the necessary participants and I keep them only as long as needed.	☐	☐	☐	☐
36. I always have an agenda for a meeting and I stick to it. I start and end as scheduled.	☐	☐	☐	☐
37. I set objectives for travel. I list everyone I will meet with, and I e-mail them agendas. I have a file folder for each person with all the necessary data for our meeting.	☐	☐	☐	☐
38. I combine and modify activities to save time.	☐	☐	☐	☐

Leading Management Function

	Should Do	Could Do	Do Not Do	Does Not Apply to Me
39. I set clear objectives for my staff with built-in accountability; I give them feedback often.	☐	☐	☐	☐
40. I don't waste others' time. I don't make my team wait idly for decisions, instructions, or materials in meetings. I wait for a convenient time—I don't interrupt team members/others and waste their time.	☐	☐	☐	☐
41. I train my staff carefully. I don't do their work for them.	☐	☐	☐	☐

SELF ASSESSMENT (*continued*)

	Should Do	Could Do	Do Not Do	Does Not Apply to Me
42. I delegate activities in which I don't need to be personally involved.	☐	☐	☐	☐
43. I set deadlines earlier than the actual deadline.	☐	☐	☐	☐
44. I use the input of my staff. I don't try to reinvent the wheel.	☐	☐	☐	☐
45. I teach time management skills to my team.	☐	☐	☐	☐
46. I don't procrastinate; I do it.	☐	☐	☐	☐
47. I'm not a perfectionist—I define "acceptable" and stop there.	☐	☐	☐	☐
48. I've learned to stay calm. Getting emotional only causes more problems.	☐	☐	☐	☐
49. I've found ways to reduce socializing without rocking the team spirit.	☐	☐	☐	☐
50. I communicate well. I don't confuse my staff with vague, poorly thought-out directives.	☐	☐	☐	☐

After you have completed the Self Assessment, implement your "should do" items. Next, work on your "could do" items. Try to keep a mind-set of continually improving your time management skills. Once in a while, reread the "does not apply to me" column to see if any of these items apply now.

CHAPTER SUMMARY

1. Describe what managing a sport facility entails.

Sport management personnel frequently help plan, design, and manage new facilities. A crucial part of their job is to generate interest in the organization and/or the local community for the new facility. Forming a committee of interested people early in the process ensures doing the right job. Once the facility is open for business, the job shifts to managing and training staff to run the facility on a day-to-day basis.

2. Describe what is involved in event planning.

Sport managers plan many types of events. They coordinate games, provide food for teams, arrange team transportation, hire officials, manage ticket sales, plan and monitor concession sales, juggle league schedules, and organize tournaments.

3. Explain how standing plans and single-use plans differ.

They differ in repetitiveness. Standing plans are policies, procedures, and rules for handling repetitive situations. Single-use plans are programs and budgets for handling nonrepetitive situations.

4. Explain when, and why, contingency plans are necessary.

Contingency plans are plans that may need to be implemented if uncontrollable events occur. There are many events that managers cannot control that can prevent achieving objectives. By identifying what can go wrong and planning how to handle it if it should happen, managers increase their chances of successfully achieving objectives.

5. Discuss how sales forecasts shape strategy.

Sales forecasts sometimes determine strategy. If forecasts indicate a slowdown in the economy (environment), companies can elect to defend market share. If forecasts indicate stable demand for a product or service, companies may choose to use a cash cow to fund new products. If sales forecasts indicate the economy is turning up, companies may choose to market aggressively in order to open up new markets.

6. Explain how qualitative and quantitative forecasting techniques differ.

Qualitative forecast techniques use subjective judgment, intuition, experience, and opinion, with some math. To make predictions, quantitative techniques use past sales data and mathematical (objective) analysis to predict sales. However, the two methods are often used in combination to improve forecasting.

7. Explain how the jury of executive opinion and the three sales composites differ.

The jury of executive opinion seeks a consensus from managers and/or experts. Composite methods combine the independent forecasts of salespeople, customers, or operating units to predict total company sales without reaching consensus. The composite techniques are more objective than the jury of executive opinion.

8. Explain how past sales and time series forecasting techniques differ.

With past sales, future sales are predicted to be the same or are subjectively adjusted for environmental factors. With time series, future sales are predicted by extending the trend line over time.

9. Know when to use planning sheets, Gantt charts, and PERT diagrams.

Planning sheets and Gantt charts work best for plans with independent, sequential activities. Gantt charts have two advantages over planning sheets: They show progress directly on the chart and they can show multiple projects on one chart. PERT diagrams are more appropriate when activities are both dependent on each other.

10. Use a time log.

A time log is a daily diary that shows how we use our time. It identifies areas to work on to improve time use.

11. Manage your time better.

The basic steps in the time management system are (1) plan each week, (2) schedule each week, and (3) schedule each day.

12. Define the key terms discussed in the text.

Fill in the missing key terms from memory, or match the key terms from the list in the margin with their definitions below.

_____ are policies, procedures, and rules for handling situations that arise repeatedly.

_____ provide general guidelines for decision making.

_____ are the sequences of actions to be followed in order to achieve an objective.

_____ state exactly what should or should not be done.

_____ are programs and budgets for handling nonrepetitive situations.

Key Terms

contingency plans
critical path
Gantt charts
market share
PERT diagrams
planning sheets
policies
procedures
qualitative forecasting techniques
quantitative forecasting techniques
rules
sales forecast
scheduling
single-use plans
standing plans
time management
time management system
time series

_____ are alternative plans that can be implemented if uncontrollable events occur.

A _____ predicts the dollar amount of a product that will be sold during a specified period.

_____ is an organization's percentage of total industry sales.

_____ use subjective judgment, intuition, experience, and opinion to predict sales.

_____ use objective, mathematical techniques and past sales data to predict sales.

A _____ predicts future sales by extending the trend line of past sales into the future.

_____ is the process of listing essential activities in sequence with the time needed to complete each activity.

_____ state an objective and list the sequence of activities, when each activity will begin and end, and who will complete each activity to meet the objective.

_____ use bars to graphically illustrate progress on a project.

_____ highlight the interdependence of activities by diagramming their network.

_____ is the most time-consuming series of activities in a PERT network.

_____ enables people to get more done in less time with better results.

The _____ involves planning each week, scheduling each week, and scheduling each day.

REVIEW AND DISCUSSION

1. What are the five planning dimensions?
2. What is the difference between a policy, a procedure, and a rule?
3. Why do some sport managers fail to plan?
4. Why is sales forecasting important?
5. What are some of the activities involved in planning a youth Olympics-style games?
6. What types of events do sport managers plan?
7. What do Gantt charts show that planning sheets and PERT diagrams don't?
8. When would you use a PERT diagram rather than a Gantt chart?
9. Why are time management skills important to a team manager?
10. What does a time log show?

11. What are the four key components of the time management system?

12. If you schedule each week, why do you also have to schedule each day?

CASE

When Civic Centers Get Old

What happens when you're no longer young, pretty, and sexy? We're not talking about movie stars here—we're talking about aging civic centers. Mid-sized civic centers are typically about 30 years old and they are showing their age. Often, arenas originally designed to hold 9000 got downsized at some point in the design/construction process to about 7000 seats. Planners thought they were saving money. Maybe they were—but only in the short run. Today it's hard to find a pro team that will play in these aging arenas. They don't have the seating capacity, they don't have luxury boxes, and let's face it, they don't have much pizzazz.

So how have management teams at these centers responded? They have thought outside the old arena, so to speak, and found new clients. Some centers have courted minor league teams like those found in the American Hockey League. And they've hit "arena gold" in hosting World Wrestling Entertainment (WWE) events. Once ridiculed for its circus-like antics and obviously staged wrestling bouts, the WWE is hot, and civic centers across the country are laughing all the way to the bank.

Centers are also building larger arenas around existing structures. Making these older centers bigger may hold the key to their long-term survival. If you can't beat 'em, maybe it's time to join 'em! Losing the revenues of local civic centers to larger cities with larger arenas is something many municipalities are fighting with creative financing and community support. Additionally, centers are hiring professional management companies to bring in fresh talent and fresh ideas.[24]

For more information on a thriving small civic center, visit http://www.ci.asheville.nc.us/civic/main.htm, the web site for Asheville's Civic Center in North Carolina. To compare, visit http://www.staplescenter.com, the web site of the famous Staples Center, home of the Los Angeles Lakers, Clippers, and Kings.

CASE QUESTIONS

Select the best alternative for the following questions. Be sure you are able to explain your answers.

1. Civic centers gain efficiency primarily from their
   a. standing plans
   b. single-use plans

2. To be the facility for mid-sized sporting events is a(n)
   a. objective
   b. policy
   c. procedure
   d. rule
   e. program
   f. budget

3. Finding new streams of revenue is a civic center
   a. objective
   b. policy
   c. procedure
   d. rule
   e. program
   f. budget

4. When looking for events that can attract an attendance appropriate for a midsize venue and that can generate profits for all involved parties, civic centers must be careful to stay within their
   a. objective
   b. policy

c. procedure

d. rule

e. program

f. budget

5. The planning tools that would be most effective in helping civic center managers schedule events are

   a. planning sheets

   b. Gantt charts

   c. PERT diagrams

6. Civic centers most likely use which quantitative sales forecasting technique?

   a. past sales

   b. time series

7. Civic centers most likely use which qualitative sales forecasting technique?

   a. sales force composite

   b. customer composite

   c. operating unit composite

   d. survey

8. Which of these teams might a smaller civic center schedule to gain a competitive advantage?

   a. a pro basketball team

   b. a pro hockey team

   c. a minor league hockey team

   d. a major NCAA basketball tournament

9. Time is a competitive advantage for a civic center.

   a. true   b. false

10. Time management skills are an important part of a civic center manager's skill kit.

    a. true   b. false

11. Civic centers that offer fitness center memberships to the public have a good long-term plan.

    a. true   b. false

12. What other events do you think could be appropriate for aging civic centers?

13. Describe the success (or struggles) of a midsize civic center in your area.

VIDEO CASE

Facility Planning at World Gym

Introduction

In this video segment, World Gym owner Joe Talvadge talks about the day-to-day activities of managing the gym, evaluating the different profit centers, and developing accounting and financial plans that respond to changes in demand from clients. When World Gym in San Francisco opened, Talvadge had to predict (forecast) sales for the first year.

Focus Your Attention

To get the most out of viewing this World Gym video, focus your attention on the following issues: the importance of accurate sales forecasting, why planning might be overlooked by a manager, and the relationship between time management and planning. Then answer the following questions after viewing the video:

1. In Chapter 5 the authors discuss the number-one reason why managers don't plan. What is that reason? In what areas did World Gym lack sufficient planning before opening? What might the result of the lack of planning have been?

2. What did World Gym predict for its sales (number of customers) in the first year? What were the actual results? What kind of problems might it have experienced by over- or under-forecasting?

3. What type of forecasting did World Gym probably employ? What does this type of forecasting consist of?

EXERCISES

Skill-Builder: Planning to Make a Dream Come True

Objective:

- To develop your planning skills using a Gantt chart and a PERT diagram.

Preparation:

You're about to take the plunge and realize your dream—your own sporting goods store: _____ (name it here). You've set April 1st for your Grand Opening. It is now late December. You need to move in one month before you open in order to set everything up. By March you need to have hired and trained an assistant. Your Aunt Matilda, who is financing this undertaking, has asked that you go over your plan with her on January 2. On January 3, you intend to put the plan in motion.

You're still new at this, so to be sure you've got everything covered, you're going to use both a Gantt chart and a PERT diagram. Construct them both, in your order of preference, using the guidelines given on pages 125–128. Make sure that you include the activities (plus others that you identify) and completion times listed below, which are not necessarily in sequence.

     a. Lease store fixtures for displaying sneakers, clothing, and sports equipment (2 weeks needed to receive and arrange them).

     b. Order and receive sneakers, clothing, and sports equipment (1 week).

     c. Recruit and select an assistant (3 weeks or less).

     d. Install the fixtures, paint, decorate, and so on (2 weeks).

     e. Form a corporation (4 weeks).

     f. Arrange to buy your merchandise on credit (2 weeks).

     g. Find a store location (6 weeks or less).

     h. Unpack and display merchandise (1 week).

     i. Train assistant (1 week).

     j. Select sneakers, clothing, and sports equipment (1 week).

     k. Determine start-up cost and cash outflow per month through April 30 (1 week).

GANTT CHART

When developing your Gantt chart, use the following week-based format. You may want to change the letter sequence to match starting dates.

Gantt Chart													
Activity (letter)	January				February				March				April	
	1	2	3	4	1	2	3	4	1	2	3	4	1	
_____														
_____														
_____														
_____														
_____														
_____														
_____														
_____														
_____														
_____														
_____														

PERT DIAGRAM

To construct your PERT diagram, first draw arrows from your start date, January 2, to circles for activities (events) that do not depend on other events—these are your independent events. Then work on dependent events. Place event letters inside each circle. On each arrow, place the number of weeks it will take to complete the event. Then draw an arrow to the end date, April 1. Once every event and the time to complete it are shown on the diagram, determine your critical path and add the second arrows to highlight this. *Hint:* Using the events listed above *only* (not including the events you have added), you should have five arrows coming from your start date to events. A promising place to start may be finding your store location.

PERT
(with critical path)

Start   End

In-Class Application

Complete the skill-building preparation noted above before class.

Choose one (10–30 minutes):

- Break into groups of three to five members, and critique each other's Gantt charts and PERT diagrams. Brainstorm ways to improve them.
- Informal, whole-class discussion of student charts and diagrams.

Wrap-up:

Take a few minutes and write down your answers to the following questions:

- Which is more appropriate for this situation—Gantt charts or PERT diagrams?

  _____

- What did I learn from this experience?

  _____

  _____

  _____

  _____

- How will I use this knowledge in the future?

  _____

  _____

  _____

  _____

  _____

Skill-Builder: Time Management

Objective:

- To learn to get more done in less time with better results.

Preparation:

For this Skill-Builder you will use Exhibits 5–9 through 5–11 as templates. Before using the time management system, it is helpful to keep a time log (Exhibit 5–8) for one or two (typical) weeks to identify areas where you would like to improve your use of time. (However, this is optional.)

Step 1: Plan Your Week

Using Exhibit 5–9, develop a plan for the rest of this week. Begin with today, and include the time you spend at work, at home, at school, and on recreational and sporting activities.

Step 2: Schedule Your Week

Using Exhibit 5–10, schedule the rest of this week. Be sure to schedule a 30-minute period to plan and schedule next week, preferably on the last day of this week.

Step 3: Schedule Your Day

Using Exhibit 5–11, schedule each day. Do this for every day at least until the class period when this Skill-Builder is due.

In-Class Application

Complete the skill-building preparation noted above before class.

Choose one (10–30 minutes):

- Break into groups of three to five members, and discuss your schedules and planning calendars. Pass them around so that you can compare time management styles. Brainstorm ways to improve each other's use of time.
- Informal, whole-class discussion of student findings.

Wrap-up:

Take a few minutes and write down your answers to the following questions:

- What did I learn from this experience?

_____

_____

_____

_____

_____

- How will I use this knowledge in the future?

_____

_____

_____

_____

_____

As a class, discuss student responses.

Internet Skills: What Do Corporate Event Planners Do?

Objective:

■ To get a feel for what event planners do.

Preparation (20 minutes):
Visit the American Sports Partners Inc. web site at http://www.americansportspartners. com. Explore the site's hyperlinks and answer the following questions.

1. What is the mission of American Sports Partners?

   _____

   _____

   _____

   _____

2. What events has Partners helped plan?

   _____

   _____

3. What services does Partners provide at golf tournaments?

   _____

   _____

4. What services does Partners provide at stadiums?

   _____

   _____

5. Use a search engine such as http://www.yahoo.com or http://www.google.com to locate a couple of Partners' competitors. What sort of services do they provide? How do they differ from the services that Partners offers?

   _____

   _____

   _____

   _____

6 Organizing and Delegating Work

Learning Outcomes

After studying this chapter, you should be able to:

1. Explain how flat and tall organizations differ.
2. Describe liaisons, integrators, and boundary roles.
3. Differentiate between formal and informal authority.
4. Explain the four levels of authority.
5. Describe the relationship between line and staff authority.
6. Describe organization charts.
7. Explain how internal and external departmentalization differ.
8. Describe matrix and divisional departmentalization.
9. Explain how job simplification and job expansion differ.
10. Describe the job characteristics model and what it is used for.
11. Set priorities.
12. Delegate.
13. Define the following key terms (in order of appearance in the chapter):

   - span of management
   - responsibility
   - authority
   - delegation
   - levels of authority
   - line authority
   - staff authority
   - centralized authority
   - decentralized authority
   - organization chart
   - departmentalization
   - job design
   - job enrichment
   - job characteristics model

REVIEWING THEIR GAME PLAN

Keeping a Fitness Center Healthy and Well

Stuart Greene is a past and current master of the four functions of management: A day doesn't go by that Greene doesn't plan, organize, lead, and control. Greene has managed the Health and Wellness Program at the Jewish Community Center (JCC) in Springfield, Massachusetts, for the past 20 years. He learned many years ago that to keep the Health and Wellness Program alive and well he would need a strategic plan. His state-of-the-art center has undergone more than four renovations to get to the tip-top condition that it is in today. Greene and the board of directors had a vision, and they laid careful plans for bringing their vision to fruition. First they built the Olympic-size pool, and then they built racquetball courts. Next they tackled the fitness center itself, and finally they modernized the center's locker rooms. Greene has succeeded so well in developing a broad and loyal customer base that the fitness center has since been enlarged to four times its original size.

As the program's director, Greene organizes *something* every day. The staff needs organizing to ensure that the fitness center, the membership desk, the health club, and the pool are well serviced. Then there are the special spinning classes, aerobic classes, preschool gym classes, and senior fitness classes to organize.

Greene's leadership skills were forged through many years of great customer service. Every member knows Stuart, because he is always around greeting, encouraging, mentoring, and coaching. He coaches the 100+-member swim team. He shows members proper techniques for weight training and cardiovascular exercise. Everyone who uses the wellness center admires Greene.

Control issues are just as important to Greene as they are to those in other organizations. So he carefully oversees the budgets that need to be prepared for the different areas of the program's operations. He and his staff determine membership rates for different usage levels. Greene knows that a knowledgeable, courteous, and enthusiastic staff are key to the center's success, so he pays special attention to developing his current staff and to hiring new employees. Being the director of a health and wellness center is a busy and fulfilling career.[1]

For more information about the Health and Wellness Program, please visit http://www.springfieldjcc.org. (For ideas on using the Internet, see Appendix B.)

INTERNET RESOURCES

http://www.tothenextlevel.org/docs/coach_development/delegate.html *To the Next Level offers a profusion of tools and tips for coaches and athletes. This article stresses the importance of delegation and offers numerous excuses for why some coaches are afraid to delegate, all of which are detrimental to the success of the team. Visit To the Next Level's home page (http://www.tothenextlevel.org) to access helpful features on how to better organize and structure your play. Recent topics have included constructing a coaching philosophy, becoming a leader, developing sport programs, and acquiring a championship attitude.*
http://www.bbhighway.com/talk/interactive_coach/JanssenPeak/ coercive%20or%20credible.asp *"Are You a Coercive or Credible Coach?" gives suggestions for becoming the type of coach whose players will want to run through a brick wall for you rather than scoffing at you behind your back. To win games, you must first win the respect of your athletes. To do this, you must treat your athletes with dignity, acting in a heartfelt and genuine*

manner toward them instead of belittling them when they make mistakes or imposing arbitrarily strict rules. This excerpt is from Jeff Janssen's book Seven Secrets of Successful Coaches. **http://www.augustachronicle.com/stories/073102/uga_124-3210.shtml** *An unwillingness to delegate cost Mark Richt a game in his first year as head coach of the University of Georgia's football team. He bit off more than he could chew, and his resulting lack of preparation led to a poor decision with seconds left on the clock. Don't let this happen to you.*

DEVELOPING YOUR SKILLS Setting priorities and delegating go hand in hand. Prioritizing requires you to conceptualize outcomes, tasks, and potential problems, and then make decisions. When you set priorities, you are also a resource allocator. Delegating uses your people skills and your communication skills. Effective managers do both of these tasks without having to think about them very much—they are part and parcel of their approach to their work. You, however, are new at this business, so we take some time here to break both these skills into steps that you can do—and should do—in order to see how prioritizing and delegating work and also so that you can hone your skills with these two key tools.

THE ORGANIZING FUNCTION

TIMEOUT
Follow the chain of command from your present position (or a past one) to the top of your organization. Identify anyone who reported to you and whom you reported to, list their title, their boss's title, and so on, all the way to the top manager.

_____

_____

_____

_____

_____

Organizing is the second function of management, and we defined it earlier (Chapter 1) as the process of delegating and coordinating tasks and resources to achieve objectives. Managers organize four resources—human, physical, financial, and informational. On a companywide basis, organizing is about grouping activities and resources. Effective managers know that organizing their team's resources carefully is instrumental in achieving objectives. Exhibit 6–1 lists various key aspects of the organizing function.

UNITY OF COMMAND AND DIRECTION. *Unity of command* means that each employee reports to only one boss.[2] *Unity of direction* means that all activities are directed toward the same objectives.

CHAIN OF COMMAND. *Chain of command,* also known as the *scalar principle,* is the clear line of authority from the organization's top to its bottom. Everyone in a company needs to understand the chain of command—that is, whom they report to and who, if anyone, reports to them. The chain of command also identifies the formal path for communications.[3] It forms the hierarchy described in organization charts, which we examine later in this chapter. **STUART GREENE** is part of the chain of command that extends above him (the director and assistant director of the JCC) and below him (fitness directors and instructors). **Draw boxes to show the chain of command at the JCC as described in this paragraph.**

Team captains are the part of the chain of command that links coaches and players. Team captains in the NHL often have as much influence over their teammates as the coaches.[4] Choosing the captain of a team, therefore, is not a decision to be taken lightly.

1 LEARNING OUTCOME
Explain how flat and tall organizations differ.

Exhibit 6–1   Different Aspects of Organizing an Organization

Unity of command and direction	Clarifying responsibilities and scope of authority
Chain of command	Delegation
Span of management/control (flat and tall organizations)	Flexibility
Division of labor (specialization)	Departmentalization
Coordination	Integration

SPAN OF MANAGEMENT. The **span of management** (also called the span of control) has to do with how many employees report directly to a manager. The fewer employees supervised, the smaller or narrower the manager's span of control, and vice versa. There is no optimal number of employees to manage. This span should be limited to a number that can be effectively supervised, and will depend on the nature of the work. Typically, however, lower-level managers have a wider span of control than do higher-level managers. (Of course, *directly* is the operative word here—second-level managers are responsible for first levels in their department, but also for all the staff under those first-level managers as well, even though they do not supervise them directly.)

Examining how an organization sets up its spans of management tells you a great deal about whether it is a flat or tall organization. *Flat organizations* have very few levels of management with wide spans of control. *Tall organizations* have many levels of management with narrow spans of control. Exhibit 6–2 illustrates these two different approaches. Notice that the flat organization has only two levels of management and the tall one has four.

In recent years, organizations have been flattening their hierarchies by cutting as many levels of management as they can. Why? For lots of reasons. (1) This is a crucial way to gain a competitive advantage—flat organizations respond more quickly to a rapidly changing environment because decisions have fewer layers to "trickle" through. (2) This is a great way to offer customer value through more efficient operations and reduced costs. (3) The workforce of today doesn't need its T's crossed and its I's dotted—high-functioning workforces are empowered to take charge and make things happen (without waiting around for someone to tell them what needs doing and how to do it)—and savvy organizations encourage this. Norman Blake, who hails from insurance giant USF&G, was recently hired to reorganize the U.S. Olympic Committee (USOC). Blake's going-in position? The USOC is "too hierarchical and too bureaucratic," and this facilitates its handing out money to Olympic sports without enough accountability. His solution? Flatten the USOC, move away from its management-by-committee style, and pay for performance.[5] "[Blake] recognizes that sports now has a very strong business tie and he's trying to take the USOC from a bureaucracy toward a business model," said Bob Colarossi, executive director of USA Gymnastics. "Ultimately, that benefits the [governing bodies] and the athletes."[6]

DIVISION OF LABOR. Division of labor occurs when jobs are organized by specialty—for example, accountants work in the accounting department, marketers and sales reps in the

span of management
The number of employees reporting to a manager.

TIMEOUT
Think about a current boss or coach and describe his or her span of control. Also, describe your own span of control if you are a manager or coach. How many levels of management exist in your organization, and would you characterize it as flat or tall?

_____
_____
_____
_____
_____

Exhibit 6–2   The Span of Control in Flat and Tall Organizations

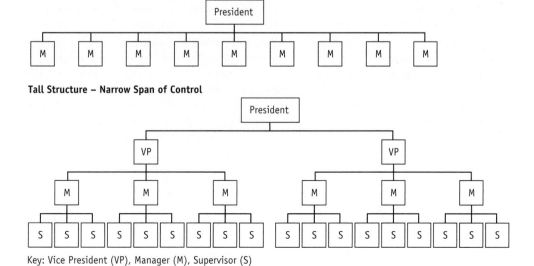

Flat Structure – Wide Span of Control

Tall Structure – Narrow Span of Control

Key: Vice President (VP), Manager (M), Supervisor (S)

marketing department, and so forth. Managers usually perform less specialized functions as they move up the management ladder. Paul Lawrence and Jay Lorsch coined the terms *differentiation* and *integration*.[7] Differentiation is about organizing work groups into departments, and integration is about coordinating departmental activities.

LEARNING OUTCOME

2 Describe liaisons, integrators, and boundary roles.

COORDINATION. *Coordination* is about departments and individuals in an organization working together to accomplish strategic and operational objectives. Coordination is the process of integrating tasks and resources to meet objectives. **STUART GREENE** needs to coordinate the physical site (i.e., the use of the gymnasium, pool, health club, and outdoor playing fields) as well as the staff and cleaning schedules. Remember that this coordination must be undertaken with the goal of meeting the needs of the members of the JCC. **What sorts of coordinating activities do you think would be involved in starting a swim fitness class for senior citizens at the JCC?** Note that every aspect of the organizing function involves coordination. Examples of coordinating activities include the following:

- *Direct contact* among people from the same department or from different departments.
- *Liaisons* who work in one department and coordinate information and activities with other departments.
- *Committees* formed to organize just about everything—for example, constructing a new fitness facility.
- *Integrators,* such as product or project managers, who don't work for a specific department but coordinate multiple-department activities.
- *Boundary roles* where staff (from sales, customer service, purchasing, and public relations, for example) work with people in the external environment.

Sporting events typically require a great deal of coordination. But not many event planners come up against the daunting challenges that the Salt Lake City 2002 Olympic Games faced after 9/11. On a visit to Salt Lake City prior to the games, Homeland Security Director Tom Ridge said that, during the Olympics, the city would be "one of the safest places on the globe."[8] And it was. Roughly 15,000 people—including 10,000 national guards, state and local police, and federal officers—handled security operations during the games. Metal detectors screened *every* visitor, and the airport screened *every* single piece of luggage. The airport was closed during the opening and closing ceremonies, airspace was heavily restricted, and vehicles could not get within 300 feet of any venue. At the time Ridge said, "This is the best planned, best coordinated, and best organized plan the world has ever seen. I think it sends a real strong message to the rest of the world. Terrorism will not prevail. Fear will not prevail. America will prevail and America will host the Olympics."[9]

The result of the massive precautions and amazingly efficient coordination? *Not a single* security issue occurred during the entire two-week experience. (Judging irregularities in figure skating caused a greater stir than security threats!) A senior official with the Utah Olympic Public Safety Command said that security plans and operations that could end up costing the federal government more than $400 million worked to near perfection and that no incident of any consequence threatened any Olympic sites or competitions.[10] The moral of this example may well be, If there is a will, there really is a way . . .

CLARIFYING RESPONSIBILITIES AND SCOPE OF AUTHORITY. Effective organizations know that in order to function well management must ensure that each person's responsibilities in the organization are clearly defined, that they are given the authority they need to meet these responsibilities (that is, that their scope of authority should match their responsibilities), and that they are held accountable for meeting them. **Responsibility** is one's obligation to achieve objectives by performing required activities. When strategic and operational objectives are set, the people responsible for achieving them should be clearly identified. Managers are responsible for the results of their organizations/divisions/departments even though they do not actually make the goods or provide the services.

responsibility
The obligation to achieve objectives by performing required activities.

Authority is the right to make decisions, issue orders, and use resources. As a manager you will be given responsibility for achieving departmental objectives. You must also be given a certain level of authority if you are to get the job done. Authority is delegated. CEOs are responsible for the results of their entire organization, and they delegate authority down the chain of command to lower-level managers who are responsible for meeting operational objectives. *Accountability* is the evaluation of how well individuals meet their responsibilities. *Everyone* in an organization from top management down should be evaluated periodically and held accountable for his or her performance.

As a manager, you will routinely delegate authority for performing tasks, but your accountability stays with *you*. For instance, Norman Blake was hired as president of the USOC, which holds the governing bodies of each Olympic sport accountable for establishing their funding needs, after an independent study found the USOC needed to be reorganized. Blake tried to reduce bureaucracy and increase accountability by linking funding for sport development programs with their performance. However, Blake's management style was not well received, and he resigned only eight months into his term.[11]

DELEGATION. Delegation has to do with assigning responsibility and authority for accomplishing objectives. Responsibility and authority are delegated down the chain of command. Delegation is an important skill for managers, and we examine it in some detail later in this chapter.

FLEXIBILITY. *Flexibility* has to do with understanding that there are often exceptions to the rule. Many managers focus on company rules rather than on creating customer satisfaction. Let's say your sporting goods store has a rule—no sales slip with returned merchandise, no cash refund, period. This is a good rule—it certainly protects your store from grifters who steal merchandise and return it for cash. But today, a well-known customer comes into the store and requests that you give him a cash refund for a baseball bat, even though he doesn't have a sales slip. Should you follow the rules and lose a good customer, or make an exception and make this customer happy?

authority
The right to make decisions, issue orders, and use resources.

delegation
The process of assigning responsibility and authority for accomplishing objectives.

TIMEOUT
Is your organization flexible? Explain why or why not.

_____
_____
_____
_____
_____

APPLYING THE CONCEPT   *The Organizing Function*

Note which aspect of the organizing function is operative in each situation.

a. unity of command and direction   **e.** coordination

b. chain of command   **f.** clarification of responsibility and authority

c. span of management   **g.** delegation

d. division of labor   **h.** flexibility

_____ 1. Karl told me to pick up the team mail. When I got to the post office, I didn't have a key, so the postal worker wouldn't give me the mail.

_____ 2. The players on the football team are either on the offensive squad or they're on the defensive squad.

_____ 3. My job can be frustrating. Sometimes my department manager tells me to do one thing, but my project manager tells me to do something else at the same time.

_____ 4. Middle manager: I want Sam, who works for Sally, to deliver this package, but I can't ask him to do it directly. I have to ask Sally to ask him.

_____ 5. There has been an accident in the game, and the ambulance is on the way. Jim, call Doctor Rodriguez and have her get to emergency room C in 10 minutes. Pat, get the paperwork ready. Karen, prepare room C.

Authority

Authority comes in many different forms, and in many different styles. Understanding them will help you become a more effective manager.

Formal and Informal Authority

3   LEARNING OUTCOME
Differentiate between formal and informal authority.

FORMAL AUTHORITY. Formal authority specifies relationships among employees. It is the sanctioned way of getting the job done. The organization chart outlines the lines of formal authority in the company.

INFORMAL AUTHORITY. Informal authority comes from the strength of relationships that evolve as people interact—it has a lot to do with trust and respect. If you note that someone is competent, dependable, and continually comes up with strategies that get the job done, you (and others) are very likely to turn to that person for leadership—this is informal authority. It can be as powerful as formal authority—indeed, many times it is more powerful. Although it is not sanctioned (formally specified), it is very real. Informal authority can be used to overcome the burdens and limitations that formal authority imposes on employees. Informal authority often gets the job done more quickly.

Exhibit 6–3
Scope of Authority

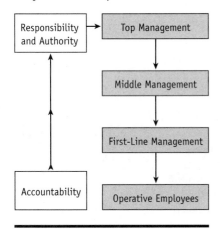

SCOPE OF AUTHORITY. People's scope of authority narrows the lower their job is in the organization chart. A CEO has more authority than a vice president, who has more authority than a manager, and so on. Responsibility and authority flow *down* the organization, whereas accountability flows *up* the organization, as Exhibit 6–3 illustrates.

Levels of Authority

4   LEARNING OUTCOME
Explain the four levels of authority.

levels of authority
Inform, recommend, report, and full.

Every manager needs to know the scope of his or her formal authority. For example, what authority would you as a coach have to alter a medical record that you believe to be in error? Levels of authority vary from task to task. The **levels of authority** are inform, recommend, report, and full.

1. *Inform authority.* At this level team members can inform their group leader of possible alternatives. The group leader then analyzes the alternatives and makes the decision. People in secretarial and clerical positions often have only inform authority because the job calls for gathering data for others. **Stuart Greene** has an administrative assistant who gathers and organizes data (writes schedules, updates brochures, and provides customer service to members).

2. *Recommend authority.* At this level, team members generate alternative actions, analyze them, and recommend action. However, the members may not implement the recommendation without the group leader's okay, who may require a different alternative if he or she doesn't agree with the recommendation. Committees are often given recommend authority. Instructors at the **JCC** can make recommendations on how to improve the daily operations of the fitness centers.

3. *Report authority.* At this level, each person in the group has the authority to select a course of action and carry it out. However, they routinely report their courses of action to their leader. The director of the fitness center, supervisor of the health club, and assistant director of physical education make decisions in their areas of expertise. However, they regularly report to **Stuart Greene**.

4. *Full authority.* At this level of authority, your boss may be coming to *you* for advice— you now have deep expertise in some area, and he or she trusts your judgment implicitly. You devise plans and carry them out with only a nod from your boss. You may have signing authority (for signing contracts or players). **STUART GREENE** has full authority to make decisions in the Health and Wellness area of the JCC. However, full authority does not give full leeway—the implication is that you will act with sound judgment and within the confines laid out by your group as the direction they have decided is best to go. **Does Stuart Greene have full authority over the entire JCC?**

Line and Staff Authority

5 LEARNING OUTCOME
Describe the relationship between line and staff authority.

Line authority is the responsibility to make decisions and issue orders down the chain of command. Operations and marketing are usually line departments, but some organizations also organize financial activities as line departments. Line managers are primarily responsible for achieving the organization's objectives, and their staff or team follows the directives the line manager develops to achieve those objectives. Coaches are line managers because they are responsible for leading their team to victory.

Staff authority is the responsibility to advise and assist other personnel. Human resources, public relations, and data processing are almost always staff departments. The line departments are internal customers of the staff departments. Therefore, the two types of departments have a collaborative partnership. Organizations whose line and staff departments have built strong relationships and trust are well on their way to developing a competitive advantage because their people see themselves as a team and will thus be more productive.[12]

FUNCTIONAL AUTHORITY. The staff's primary role is to advise and assist, but situations occur in which they can give orders to line personnel. *Functional authority* is the right of staff personnel to issue orders to line personnel in established areas of responsibility.

DUAL LINE AND STAFF AUTHORITY. Staff managers may have both staff and line authority. For example, some public relations (staff) managers advise and assist all departments in their organization. However, they also have line authority within their own department and issue orders (a line function) to their group.

GENERAL AND SPECIALIST STAFF. *General staff* work for only one manager. Often called "assistant to," they help the manager in any way needed. *Specialist staff* help anyone in the organization who needs it. Human resources, finance, accounting, public relations, and maintenance offer specialized advice and assistance.

line authority
The responsibility to make decisions and issue orders down the chain of command.

staff authority
The responsibility to advise and assist other personnel.

TIMEOUT
Think about a task you do routinely for your company or team and describe your level of authority for this task in detail.

_____
_____
_____
_____
_____

Centralized and Decentralized Authority

The major difference between centralized and decentralized authority is who makes the important decisions. With **centralized authority**, important decisions are made by top managers. With **decentralized authority**, important decisions are made by middle- and first-level managers. The major advantages of centralization include control (uniform procedures are easier to control, and fewer risks are taken) and reduced duplication of work (fewer employees perform the same tasks). The major advantages of decentralization are efficiency and flexibility (decisions are made quickly by people who have first-hand knowledge of the situation) and development (managers are challenged and motivated to solve their own problems). Which type of authority works best? There is no simple answer. Authority is a continuum, and most organizations function as a blend of centralized and decentralized authority. Flat organizations tend to have decentralized authority.

With the exception of very small companies, which tend to be centralized, most organizations lie somewhere between the two extremes. The key to success seems to be finding the right balance between the two, the one that serves the business's environment and its business functions best. For example, production and sales are often decentralized, whereas

centralized authority
Important decisions are made by top managers.

decentralized authority
Important decisions are made by middle- and first-level managers.

TIME**OUT**

Identify several line and staff positions in your company or team. State whether they are general or specialist staff.

_____

_____

_____

_____

_____

finance and labor relations are centralized to provide uniformity and control. Top managers are also decentralizing authority.[13] See Exhibit 6–4 for a review of authority.

ORGANIZATIONAL DESIGN

6 LEARNING OUTCOME
Describe organization charts.

It's time we address how entire firms are organized. *Organizational design* is the arrangements of positions into work units/departments and the relationships among them. Organization charts are a good place to examine a company's structure.

Organization Chart

organization chart
A graphic illustration of the organization's management hierarchy and departments and their working relationships.

The formal authority structures that define working relationships between the organization's members and their jobs are illustrated in organization charts. An **organization chart** lays out the organization's management hierarchy and departments and their working relationships. The boxes represent positions in the organization, and the lines indicate the reporting relationships and lines of communication. Note that organization charts do not show the day-to-day activities performed or the structure of the informal organization. Exhibit 6–5, a hypothetical organization chart for a university, illustrates four major aspects of organizations.

- *The level of management hierarchy.* The board of regents and president are the top two levels of management; the vice presidents are middle-level management; and department managers, such as Athletic Facilities, are first-level management.

- *Chain of command.* As you follow the lines, you will see that the president reports to the board of regents. The vice presidents report to the president, and the department managers report to the vice presidents.

- *The division and type of work.* The university divides itself by "product" by indicating different academic areas such as Health Sciences and Graduate Programs. Additionally, the university has divisions devoted to the administration such as University Relations and University Services. The university is also organized by functional area (Finance and Human Resources).

- *Departmentalization.* Organization charts show how the business of the firm is divided into permanent work units. The university's athletic departments are under the control of the Chief of Staff. The departments are Athletic Administration, Athletic Facilities, Men's Intercollegiate Athletics, Women's Intercollegiate Athletics, and Trademark and Licensing.

TIME**OUT**

What type of authority is most prevalent in your firm or team? Are there reasons that make this choice appropriate in this environment? Or is it not as effective as it could be? Explain.

_____

_____

_____

_____

_____

Exhibit 6–4 Authority

Authority			
Formal (sanctioned)	Line (issue orders)	Levels	Centralized (top management)
Informal (unsanctioned)	Staff (assist line)	1. Inform (present alternatives)	Decentralized (middle-and first-line managers)
		2. Recommend (present alternatives and suggest one)	
		3. Report (do and tell)	
		4. Full (do and don't tell)	

Exhibit 6–5 Hypothetical Organization Chart for a University: Highlighting Athletic Administration

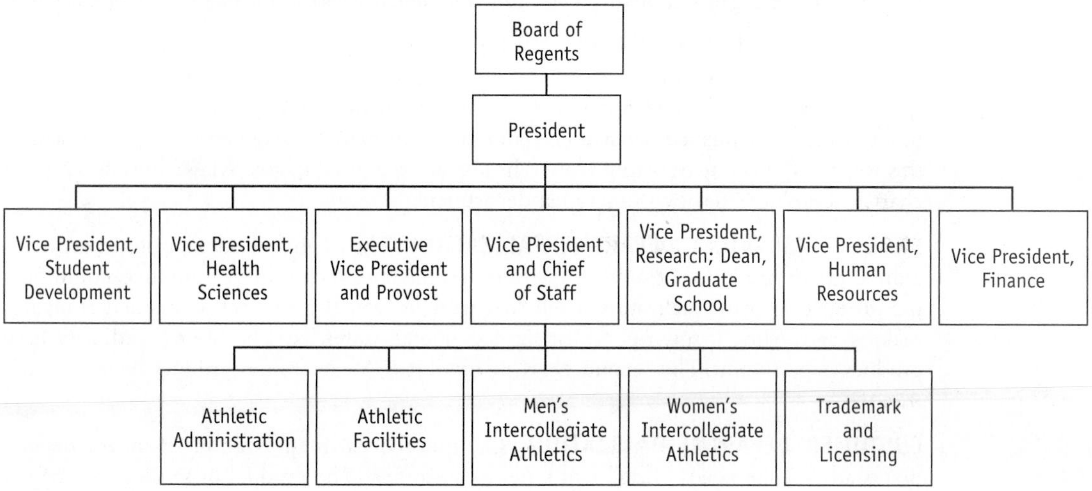
Board of Regents
President
Vice President, Student Development
Vice President, Health Sciences
Executive Vice President and Provost
Vice President and Chief of Staff
Vice President, Research; Dean, Graduate School
Vice President, Human Resources
Vice President, Finance
Athletic Administration
Athletic Facilities
Men's Intercollegiate Athletics
Women's Intercollegiate Athletics
Trademark and Licensing

To develop a mindset of better focus on the customer, some organizations use an "upside-down" chart with the customer at the top of the chart and management at the bottom. This reminds everyone in the organization that their job is to provide customer value, and informs managers that their role is to support their teams in providing that value.

Departmentalization

7 LEARNING OUTCOME
Explain how internal and external departmentalization differ.

Departmentalization is the grouping of related activities into work units. Departments may have an internal focus or an external one. Departmentalization around internal operations or

departmentalization
The grouping of related activities into work units.

APPLYING THE CONCEPT *Authority*

Identify the type of authority implied in each situation.

a. formal
b. informal
c. level
d. line
e. staff
f. centralized
g. decentralized

____ 6. I like my job, but it's frustrating when I recommend potential employees to the production and marketing managers and they don't hire them.

____ 7. It's great working for a team that encourages everyone to share information.

____ 8. Coaches here run their teams the way they want to.

____ 9. I'm not sure if I'm supposed to get a list of company cars for Wendy or recommend one to her.

____ 10. That is a great idea. I'll talk to Pete, and if he likes it, I'm sure he'll want us to present your idea to his boss, Jean.

functions and the resources needed to accomplish the unit's work is called *functional departmentalization*. External or output departmentalization is based on activities that focus on factors outside the organization; this is also called *product, customer, and territory departmentalization*.

FUNCTIONAL DEPARTMENTALIZATION. Functional departmentalization organizes departments around essential input activities, such as production, sales, and finance. Virtually all sport companies use some form of functional departmentalization and have specialized functions such as finance departments and sales and marketing departments. For instance, this is true of Spalding Sporting Goods, headquartered in Chicopee, Massachusetts. The first chart in Exhibit 6–6 shows functional departmentalization.

PRODUCT (SERVICE) DEPARTMENTALIZATION. This approach organizes departments around goods produced or services provided. Companies with multiple products commonly use product departmentalization. Each "department" can also be a self-contained company, making and selling its own goods or services. Retail stores like The Sports Authority have product departments. The second chart in Exhibit 6–6 exemplifies product departmentalization.

CUSTOMER DEPARTMENTALIZATION. Customer departmentalization organizes departments around the needs of different types of customers. The product or service may be the same or slightly different, but the needs of the customer warrant different marketing approaches (in the type of packaging, sales staff, and so on). If Nike used customer departmentalization, it would divide its divisions into professional and amateur athletes—for example, its golf division would be organized along the lines of selling golf equipment to professional golfers and amateur golfers. Organizations that offer a wide variety of products often use customer departments, as do some nonprofit organizations. The third chart in Exhibit 6–6 uses customer departmentalization.

GEOGRAPHIC (TERRITORY) DEPARTMENTALIZATION. This type of departmentalization organizes departments by each area in which the enterprise does business. For example, Nike divides its financial reporting into four geographic regions. The EMEA division consists of Europe, the Middle East, and Africa. The Americas division includes Canada, Mexico, and Central and South America. The other two divisions are Asia Pacific and the United States.[14] Each region reports numbers for sales, expenses, and so forth. The final chart in Exhibit 6–6 organizes by geographic area.

Multiple Departmentalization

Many organizations, particularly large, complex ones, use several departmental structures to create a *hybrid* organization. Any mixture of structures can be used. Some organizations use functional departments with manufacturing facilities, but organize sales by territory with separate sales managers and salespeople in different areas.

TIMEOUT

Draw a simple organization chart for your company or team. Identify the type of departmentalization and staff positions used.

_____

_____

_____

_____

_____

8   LEARNING OUTCOME
Describe matrix and divisional departmentalization.

MATRIX DEPARTMENTALIZATION. Matrix departmentalization combines functional and product departmentalization. That is, staff are assigned to a functional department but work on one or more products or projects. The advantage of the matrix approach is its flexibility—the enterprise can temporarily and quickly reorganize for high-priority projects. The disadvantage is that every person has two managers—a functional boss and a project boss—which can make coordination difficult and can cause conflicts to arise because of the different objectives of multiple managers. Exhibit 6–7 shows a matrix structure.

JOB DESIGN

job design
The process of combining tasks that each employee is responsible for completing.

The work performed by organizations is grouped into functional departments, which are further grouped into jobs. **Job design** is the process of combining the tasks that each employee is responsible for completing. Job design is crucial because it affects job satisfac-

Exhibit 6–6   Different Ways Nike Could Be Organized

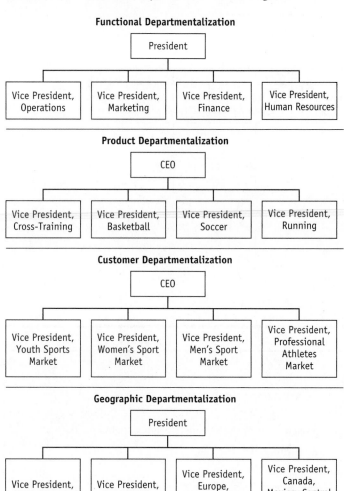

Functional Departmentalization

President
- Vice President, Operations
- Vice President, Marketing
- Vice President, Finance
- Vice President, Human Resources

Product Departmentalization

CEO
- Vice President, Cross-Training
- Vice President, Basketball
- Vice President, Soccer
- Vice President, Running

Customer Departmentalization

CEO
- Vice President, Youth Sports Market
- Vice President, Women's Sport Market
- Vice President, Men's Sport Market
- Vice President, Professional Athletes Market

Geographic Departmentalization

President
- Vice President, United States
- Vice President, Asia Pacific
- Vice President, Europe, Middle East, Africa
- Vice President, Canada, Mexico, Central and South America

tion and productivity.[15] Empowering employees by involving them in the design of their own jobs increases productivity.

As you will learn in this section, jobs can be simple (contain few tasks), or they can be expanded (contain many tasks). A job characteristics model is used to design jobs.

Job Simplification

9 LEARNING OUTCOME
Explain how job simplification and job expansion differ.

Job simplification makes jobs more specialized and efficient. It is based on the organizing principle of division of labor. The idea behind job simplification is to work smarter, not harder. *Job simplification* is the process of eliminating, combining, and/or changing the work sequence to increase performance. Thus, job designers would break a job into steps to see if they can:

- *Eliminate.* Does the task have to be done at all? If not, don't do it.

- *Combine.* Combining tasks often saves time. Make one trip to the mail room at the end of the day instead of several throughout the day, *if* this makes sense.

- *Change sequence.* Changing the order of tasks can save time.

Exhibit 6–7   Matrix Departmentalization

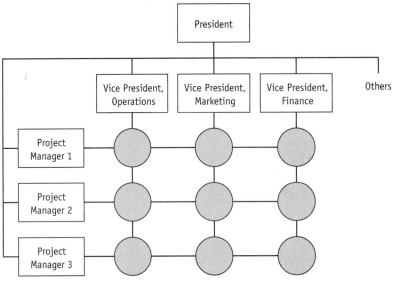

○ represents teams of functional employees working on a project

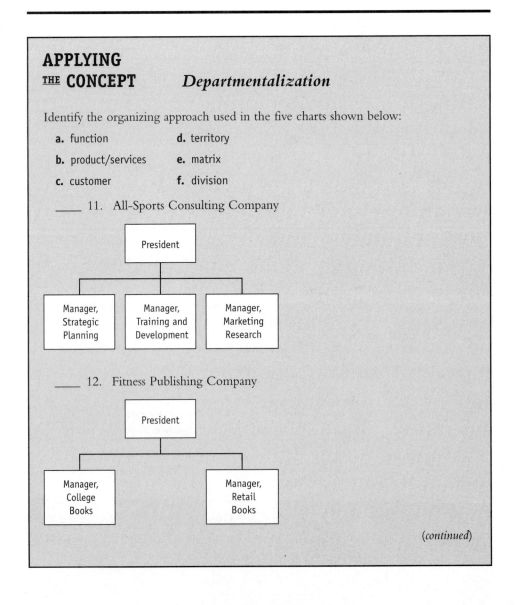

APPLYING
THE CONCEPT   *Departmentalization*

Identify the organizing approach used in the five charts shown below:

   a. function   **d.** territory

   b. product/services   **e.** matrix

   c. customer   **f.** division

_____ 11.   All-Sports Consulting Company

_____ 12.   Fitness Publishing Company

(continued)

APPLYING THE CONCEPT (continued)

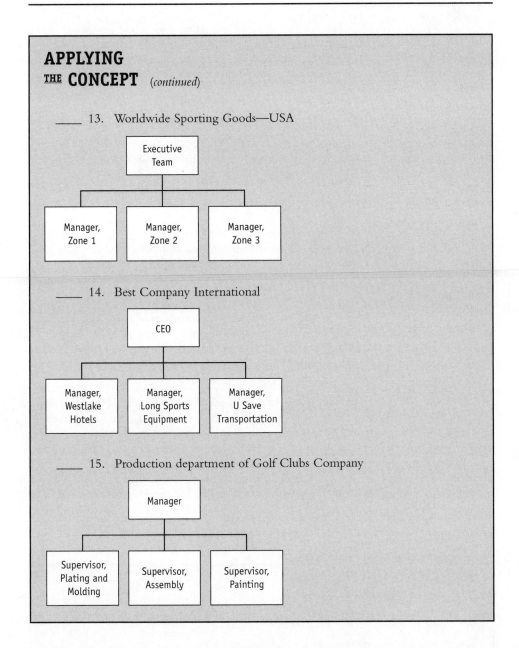

____ 13. Worldwide Sporting Goods—USA

Executive Team

Manager, Zone 1 | Manager, Zone 2 | Manager, Zone 3

____ 14. Best Company International

CEO

Manager, Westlake Hotels | Manager, Long Sports Equipment | Manager, U Save Transportation

____ 15. Production department of Golf Clubs Company

Manager

Supervisor, Plating and Molding | Supervisor, Assembly | Supervisor, Painting

A major caveat is in order here. Jobs that are too simple bore people, and bored workers are neither productive nor empowered. However, used appropriately, job simplification can motivate people. Often, people don't hate the job, just some aspect of it. Rather than ignoring or simply putting up with aspects of their job that they don't like, sometimes they can change them.

Job Expansion

Job expansion makes jobs less specialized in order to empower workers and to make them more productive. Jobs can be expanded through job rotation, job enlargement, and job enrichment.

JOB ROTATION. In this approach people perform different jobs for a set period of time. For example, employees making a sneaker on a New Balance assembly line could rotate so that they get to work on different parts. Many organizations develop conceptual skills in management trainees by rotating them through various departments.

Cross-training is related to job rotation. With cross-training, staff learn to perform different jobs so they can fill in when someone is on vacation or sick. This also functions to increase skills, which makes people more valuable to the organization.

JOB ENLARGEMENT. This approach to job design adds tasks in order to add variety. For example, rather than rotate jobs, the sneaker workers could perform four tasks instead of just two. There could be two jobs instead of four. However, only adding more simple tasks to an already simple job is not a great motivator.

job enrichment
The process of building motivators into a job by making it more interesting and challenging.

JOB ENRICHMENT. Job enrichment builds motivators into a job in order to make it more interesting and challenging. Job enrichment is a hot topic in flat organizations and works when employees want their jobs enriched. Some employees are happy with their jobs the way they are. A simple way to enrich jobs is for the manager to delegate more variety and responsibility to employees.

Work Teams

The traditional approach to job design has been to focus on individual jobs. Today, the trend is shifting to designing jobs for work teams, or rather, teams are redesigning members' jobs. Teamwork is as vital for successful companies as it is for successful football teams.[16] Moving to work teams is a form of job enrichment. The two common types are integrated teams and self-managed teams.

INTEGRATED WORK TEAMS. These teams are assigned a number of tasks, and the team itself then assigns specific tasks to members and is responsible for rotating jobs. For example, a college's athletic director (AD) has work teams coordinate facility management tasks. The teams decide who does what and how. The AD attends various meetings to see how the work is progressing, and checks on the quality of the finished process.

SELF-MANAGED WORK TEAMS. These teams are assigned an objective, and the team plans, organizes, leads, and controls their work in order to achieve it. Usually, self-managed teams operate without a designated manager; everyone on the team functions as both manager and worker. Teams commonly select their own members and evaluate each other's performance. The facility management group mentioned above can become a self-managed team by deciding what activities need to be coordinated and determining the most efficient sequence of activities. The team, not the AD, is responsible for checking its own progress.

Work teams have been quite successful. Team-based systems are emerging as a key source of sustained competitive advantage. However, members need to be carefully trained to work

TIMEOUT
Describe how you would expand a job at your company or team. Specify if you are using job rotation, job enlargement, or job enrichment.

TIMEOUT
Describe how your firm uses—or could use—work teams. Indicate whether the teams are integrated or self-managed.

APPLYING THE CONCEPT — *Job Design*

Identify the job design implied in each situation.

a. job simplification   c. job enlargement   e. work teams
b. job rotation   d. job enrichment

____ 16. Jack, I think you need a challenge, so I want you to develop some new offensive plays.

____ 17. Sales reps who have business lunches with clients that are under $20 no longer need to provide sales receipts.

____ 18. We'd like to change your fitness center job so that you can develop new skills, complete entire jobs by yourself so that the job is more meaningful, let you do the job the way you want to, and let you know how you are doing.

____ 19. To make your athletic assistant job less repetitive, we're adding three new responsibilities to your job description.

____ 20. I'd like you to learn how to run the stopwatch so that you can fill in for Ted while he's at lunch.

together effectively as a team. In Chapter 10 we examine ways to help teams succeed in greater detail. Exhibit 6–8 summarizes the types of job designs and the job characteristics model, which we discuss next.

The Job Characteristics Model

10 LEARNING OUTCOME
Describe the job characteristics model and what it is used for.

Developed by Richard Hackman and Greg Oldham, the job characteristics model provides a conceptual framework for designing enriched jobs.[17,18] Individuals or a team can use the model to enrich jobs. The **job characteristics model** addresses core job dimensions, critical psychological states, and employees' growth-need strengths to improve the quality of working life for employees and productivity for the organization.

CORE JOB DIMENSIONS. Five core dimensions determine a job's personal outcomes (quality of working life for employees) and work outcomes (productivity for the organization). By enhancing each dimension, you can increase both.

1. *Skill variety* is the number of diverse tasks required in the job and the number of skills used to perform the job.

2. *Task identity* is the degree to which employees perform a whole identifiable task. Does the worker put together an entire golf club, or just insert the grip on the end of the shaft?

3. *Task significance* is the perception of the task's importance to others—to the organization, the department, co-workers, and/or customers.

4. *Autonomy* is the degree to which employees have discretion to decide how to plan, organize, and control the task.

5. *Feedback* is the extent to which employees find out how well they perform their tasks.

CRITICAL PSYCHOLOGICAL STATES. As the three critical psychological states—developed through the five core job dimensions—improve, so do the job's personal and work outcomes.

■ *Experienced meaningfulness of the work* derives from (1) skill variety, (2) task identity, and (3) task significance. The greater these core dimensions, the greater the experienced meaningfulness of work.

■ *Experienced responsibility for outcomes of the work* derives from (4) autonomy. The greater the autonomy, the greater the experienced responsibility for outcomes of the work.

■ *Knowledge of the actual results of the work activities* derives from (5) feedback. The greater the feedback, the greater the knowledge of results of the work.

PERFORMANCE AND WORK OUTCOMES. Employees with the three critical psychological states benefit the organization because of their

■ high motivation

■ high performance

job characteristics model
Comprises core job dimensions, critical psychological states, and employee growth-need strength to improve quality of working life for employees and productivity for the organization.

Exhibit 6–8 Job Designs

Job Design Options

Job Simplification	Job Expansion	Work Teams	Job Characteristics Model
Eliminate	Job rotation, switch jobs	Integrated	Core dimensions
Combine	Job enlargement, more tasks	Self-managed	Critical psychological states
Change sequence	Job enrichment, delegate		Personal and work outcomes
			Employee growth-need strength

- high satisfaction with the work
- low absenteeism and turnover

EMPLOYEE GROWTH-NEED STRENGTH. A person's growth-need strength determines their interest in improving the five core dimensions. Exhibit 6–9 shows how this process works. Note that if a person is not interested in enriching his or her job, the job characteristics model will fail. We examine needs and motivation in more detail in Chapter 12.

ORGANIZING YOURSELF AND DELEGATING WORK

Successful managers set priorities and delegate work.[19] Recall that planning entails setting objectives and that organizing is the process of delegating and coordinating resources to achieve those objectives. Thus, prioritizing is important, because some objectives and tasks are more important than others, and delegating is important because this is how you get the work done.

Now that you understand how organizations and jobs are designed, it's time to learn how to organize yourself by setting priorities and delegating work. But first complete the Self Assessment on page 161 to determine the priorities that are important to you personally.

Setting Priorities

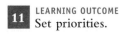 **LEARNING OUTCOME**
11 Set priorities.

As we have already noted, setting priorities is an important aspect of organizing *anything*— a department, a job, yourself.[20] At any given time, you and/or others must perform several tasks, often jointly. Prioritizing makes this easy. So how do you begin? With a to-do list. Yes, this sounds too simple, but simple is good here—getting to simplicity is extremely effective in becoming focused. So, here's what you do: List the tasks you need to do and then rank each one by importance *or* by a logical sequence (you can't tie your shoelaces until you put your shoes on!). *Then* focus on accomplishing only one task at a time by its priority.

To begin, ask yourself three questions:

1. *Do I need to be personally involved?* Often, you are the only one who can do the task, and you must be involved. If your answer here is no, you don't need to answer the remaining questions for this particular task.

Exhibit 6–9   The Job Characteristics Model

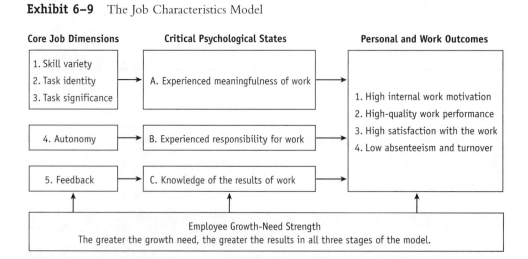

Core Job Dimensions

1. Skill variety
2. Task identity
3. Task significance

4. Autonomy

5. Feedback

Critical Psychological States

A. Experienced meaningfulness of work

B. Experienced responsibility for work

C. Knowledge of the results of work

Personal and Work Outcomes

1. High internal work motivation
2. High-quality work performance
3. High satisfaction with the work
4. Low absenteeism and turnover

Employee Growth-Need Strength
The greater the growth need, the greater the results in all three stages of the model.

SELF ASSESSMENT   *Your Personal Priorities*

For the following 16 items, rate how important each one is to you on a scale of 0 (not important) to 100 (very important).

Not important				Somewhat important					Very important	
0	10	20	30	40	50	60	70	80	90	100

_____ 1. An enjoyable, satisfying job

_____ 2. A high-paying job

_____ 3. A good marriage

_____ 4. Meeting new people, attending social events

_____ 5. Involvement in community activities

_____ 6. Relationship with God/religion

_____ 7. Exercising, playing sports

_____ 8. Intellectual development

_____ 9. A career with challenging opportunities

_____ 10. Nice cars, clothes, home, etc.

_____ 11. Spending time with family

_____ 12. Having several close friends

_____ 13. Volunteer work for nonprofit organizations like the Cancer Society

_____ 14. Meditation, quiet time to think, pray, etc.

_____ 15. A healthy, balanced diet

_____ 16. Educational reading, TV, self-improvement programs, etc.

Transfer your rankings for each item to the appropriate column below, then add the two numbers in each column.

	Professional	Financial	Family	Social
	1. ___	2. ___	3. ___	4. ___
	9. ___	10. ___	11. ___	12. ___
Totals	___	___	___	___
	Community	Spiritual	Physical	Intellectual
	5. ___	6. ___	7. ___	8. ___
	13. ___	14. ___	15. ___	16. ___
Totals	___	___	___	___

The higher your total in any area, the higher you value that area. The closer the numbers are in all eight areas, the more well-rounded you are.

Think about the time and effort you put into your top three priorities. Is your effort sufficient for you to achieve the level of success you desire in each area? If not, what can you do to change your level of effort? Is there any area that you feel you should value more? If yes, what can you do to give more priority to that area?

Food for thought. Consider how you value physical activity. Do you value exercise, playing sports, and eating properly as much as you thought you would? Do you think your valuing of physical activity can be transferred to community, spiritual, and intellectual pursuits? Is it realistic to expect that the values we learn in sports will transfer to other activities? Is sport, as Plato thought, a most valuable tool in instilling the right attitudes and values in young people? Or are we expecting too much from our national passion for sports?[21]

2. *Is the task my responsibility or will it affect the performance or finances of my department?* You must oversee the performance of your department and keep the finances in line with the budget.

3. *Is quick action needed (deadline)?* Should you work on this activity right now, or can it wait? Time is a relative term. The key is to start the task soon enough to meet the deadline. This may sound obvious, but people often miss deadlines simply because they start too late, so it bears repeating.

ASSIGN PRIORITIES. With your answers to the three prioritizing questions in mind, you can now assign each task a priority.

- *Delegate priority (D).* Delegate the task if your answer to question 1 is no. The task will go on your co-worker's to-do list with a priority.
- *High priority (H).* The task gets a high priority if you answered yes to all three questions.
- *Medium priority (M).* Assign a medium priority if you answered yes to question 1 but no to question 2 *or* question 3.
- *Low priority (L).* Assign a low priority if you answered yes to question 1 but no to *both* questions 2 and 3.

PRIORITIZED TO-DO LIST. Model 6–1 is a quick way to prioritize your to-do lists—make copies of it and use it on your job as follows:

1. *List the tasks to be performed.*

2. *Answer the three prioritizing questions.* Be sure to note the deadline and the time needed to complete the task. You may also want to note a deadline for starting the task as well as its completion date.

3. *Assign a priority (D, H, M, or L) to the task.* The top-left box helps you do this at a glance. If you wrote D, note when the task should be delegated by.

4. *Determine which task you should work on now.* You may have more than one high-priority task, so select the most important one. When you have completed your high-priority tasks, start on the medium-priority ones, and finally work on your low-priority tasks.

TIMEOUT
Make a copy of Model 6–1, and use it to list three to five tasks you must complete in the near future and prioritize them.

_____
_____
_____
_____
_____

It is important to realize that *you're not done* at this point. In fact, you've only just begun. You will need to continually *update* your list and *add* new tasks as they arise. As time passes, medium- and low-priority items will become high-priority items. How often should you update your list? Your particular job will give you that answer (since different jobs will place different demands on your time), but many people find that doing it daily works best.

As we noted in Chapter 5, if you deal with a wide variety of changing tasks and you need to carve out time for long-range planning, we strongly suggest that you use the time management system. Your prioritized to-do list dovetails neatly with that system. If your job is more routine and you basically plan for the short term, the to-do list will probably suffice to keep you both organized and focused. The first Skill-Builder at the end of the chapter uses the to-do list to help you develop your prioritizing skills.

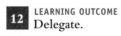

12 LEARNING OUTCOME
Delegate.

Delegating

When you delegate, you both assign the person responsibility for accomplishing a task and give him or her the authority to do what is needed. Directing people to do work that is part of their job description is *not* delegating. Delegating is about giving employees tasks that are not part of their regular job. The delegated task may eventually become a part of their job, or it may be a one-time task.

WHY SHOULD YOU DELEGATE? Because delegating gives you time to get your high-priority tasks done. When more tasks get accomplished, productivity rises. Delegating work that people don't ordinarily do stretches them and improves their self esteem, trains them for future opportunities, and eases the stress and burden on *you*.[22] Wise delegation of work enriches jobs and improves personal and work outcomes.

WHAT STOPS MANAGERS FROM DELEGATING? In two words, habit and fear. Managers get used to doing things themselves—that's the habit part of the problem (it's easy to fix). More importantly, managers fear two things: (1) that the employee will fail to accomplish the task (thereby making things worse, not better), and (2) that the person will show them up. As we've noted, managers can delegate responsibility and authority; they cannot delegate accountability. Managers who don't delegate well believe they can perform the task more efficiently than others. Perhaps they don't realize that delegating work is an important part

Model 6–1 Prioritized To-Do List

Assigning a Priority		Priority Determination Questions				
		#1	#2	#3		P r i o r i t y
D Delegate priority (N) No to question 1		1. Do I need to be personally involved?	2. Is it my responsibility or will it affect performance or finances of my department?	3. Is quick action needed?	Deadline/Time needed	
H High priority (YYY) Yes to all three questions						
M Medium priority (YNY or YYN) Yes to questions 1 and 2 or 3						
L Low priority (YNN) Yes to question 1 and no to questions 2 and 3						
Task						

of their job; others don't know *what* to delegate; and some don't know *how* to delegate. If you want to be an effective manager, make delegating part of your job. But first learn when, and what, to delegate, and to whom.

WHEN MANAGERS DELEGATE TOO LITTLE. Flags that indicate a manager is delegating too little include when (1) they take work home, (2) they perform employee tasks, (3) they are continually behind in their work, (4) they continually feel pressured and stressed, (5) they are always rushing to meet deadlines, (6) they rarely meet deadlines, and (7) their employees always seek approval before acting.

Getting to Delegating

An important part of delegating is knowing which tasks to delegate. Effective delegators know which work to delegate, when to delegate it, and the right person to delegate it to.[23]

WHAT AND WHEN TO DELEGATE. These two questions will make you very grateful that you have a prioritized to-do list. Why? Because their answers are natural fallouts of your list. Still, just to make sure you are approaching delegating correctly, here are the types of things you should consider delegating:

- *Paperwork.* Employees really can write reports, memos, and letters.
- *Routine tasks.* Employees really can check inventory, schedule, order, and so on.
- *Technical matters.* Your top employees really can deal with technical questions and problems. (If they can't, it's time to train them!)
- *Tasks with developmental potential.* Employees like learning new things (really!). Give them the opportunity to show the stuff they're made of.
- *Problem solving.* Train your people to solve their own problems. Your team will be more effective, and you will be less stressed.

WHAT YOU SHOULDN'T DELEGATE. This is pretty clear-cut—do *not* delegate the following:

- *Personnel matters.* Performance appraisals, counseling, disciplining, firing, and resolving conflicts.
- *Confidential activities.* Unless you have permission to do so.
- *Crises.* Crises are why you are a manager, and you don't have time to delegate them anyway.
- *Activities assigned to you personally by your boss.*

FIND THE RIGHT PERSON. This is where you earn your pay. You've got to know your people. If you choose wisely—that is, the person has the skills, the growth-need strength, *and* the time to get the job done right by the deadline, you will have a happy employee and a happy result. If you choose unwisely, the person may fail (because they aren't experienced enough, for example) through no fault of their own, *and* the job will still need doing. So, consider their skills and the requirements of the job very carefully. Also, consider their temperament—first and foremost you need the work done, and done right, or else you wouldn't be delegating. Make sure they have the temperament to work under pressure if a deadline is looming.

NOW IT'S TIME TO DELEGATE. The following four steps help ensure that the job you need done *gets* done, *and* done right. Note how these steps mesh with the job characteristics model, core job dimensions, and critical psychological states.

1. *Explain why you are delegating this job and your reasons for selecting the person.* We all like to know why—indeed, one can make a strong case that we *need* to know why. So tell your people why this job needs doing. Remember the "experienced meaningfulness of work"? Here is where you give work meaning. And telling people why they've been chosen is a very natural and genuine way to make them feel valued. Sometimes, you may have to tell it like it is—that is, "this is a lousy job but someone has to do it." Remember, employees *are* adults—they will know when you are trying to sugarcoat a lousy job. They will also, however, appreciate your honesty and trust you in the future because you are honest with them now.

2. *Clearly define the person's responsibility, the scope of their authority, and the deadline.* The key word here? "Clearly." Clarity is very important in this step.

3. *Plan the task.* Perhaps the person can plan the task themselves; perhaps they will need your help. This will depend on their experience, whether you are using this task to stretch them a bit, and so on. You (or they) may find it helpful to use a planning sheet (see Exhibit 5–5 in the previous chapter). The role-playing scenarios in the second Skill-Builder at the end of this chapter will give you some practice in delegating.

4. *Establish control checkpoints and hold employees accountable.* Obviously for short, simple tasks, you don't need to set controls or deadlines. That doesn't mean you shouldn't check progress on tasks that have multiple steps and/or that will take some time to complete. Consider the person's abilities and experience. The lower their abilities and/or experience, the more frequently you should check. The higher their abilities and experience, the less frequently you will need to check.

Of course, for complex tasks and projects, more formalized control and accountability are not only in order, they benefit everyone concerned. For one thing, this creates a healthy flow of information from the start. And discussing and agreeing on the form of progress checks (phone call, visit, memo, or detailed report) and their timeframe (daily, weekly, or after specific steps are completed) before work begins prevent future misunderstandings. It is also helpful to formalize control checkpoints in writing (possibly on the planning sheet itself), distributing copies of it so that everyone involved has a record. In addition, everyone should record pertinent control checkpoints on their calendars. If someone doesn't report as scheduled, you need to find out why. Be sure to evaluate performance at each checkpoint and also on completion of the task to provide immediate feedback (sound familiar?—this is the "knowledge of the results of work" that we discussed earlier). Praising progress and successful completion of the task is always a good motivator.[24] We will return to the subject of praise in Chapter 12.

Model 6–2 summarizes the delegation process.

> **TIMEOUT**
> Think about a manager or coach you have worked or played for and analyze how well he or she delegates. Which steps do they do well and which steps could they do better?
> _____
> _____
> _____
> _____
> _____

CHAPTER SUMMARY

1. Explain how flat and tall organizations differ.

Flat organizations have fewer layers of management with wide spans of control. Tall organizations have many layers of management with narrow spans of control.

2. Describe liaisons, integrators, and boundary roles.

Liaisons, integrators, and people in boundary roles are all coordinators. Liaisons and integrators coordinate internally, whereas people in boundary roles coordinate efforts with customers, suppliers, and other people in the external environment. Liaisons work in one department and coordinate with other departments, whereas integrators coordinate department activities without working for a specific department.

3. Differentiate between formal and informal authority.

Formal authority specifies relationships among employees. It is the sanctioned way of getting the job done. Informal authority comes from the strength of relationships that evolve as people interact—it works through trust and respect. With centralized authority top managers make important decisions; with decentralized authority middle- and first-line managers make important decisions.

4. Explain the four levels of authority.

(1) *Inform authority*—the person simply presents an alternative. (2) *Recommend authority*—the person presents alternatives and suggests one. (3) *Report authority*—the person can take action in their own area of expertise and regularly informs the boss. (4) *Full*

Model 6–2   How to Delegate

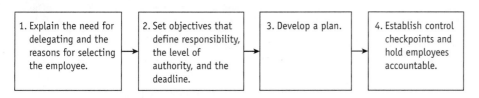

| 1. Explain the need for delegating and the reasons for selecting the employee. | → | 2. Set objectives that define responsibility, the level of authority, and the deadline. | → | 3. Develop a plan. | → | 4. Establish control checkpoints and hold employees accountable. |

authority—the person takes action in their area of expertise and usually does not have to inform the boss.

5. Describe the relationship between line and staff authority.

Staff advise and assist line personnel, who are responsible for making decisions and directing others down the chain of command.

6. Describe organization charts.

Organization charts show the organization's management hierarchy and departments and their working relationships. In so doing, they also show the chain of command and type of work.

7. Explain how internal and external departmentalization differ.

Internal departmentalization focuses on functions performed inside the organization. External departmentalization focuses on the product, customer, or territory in which the organization does business.

8. Describe matrix and divisional departmentalization.

Both are ways to set up departments. Matrix departments combine functional and product structures to focus on projects. Divisional departments are based on semiautonomous strategic business units and focus on portfolio management.

9. Explain how job simplification and job expansion differ.

Job simplification makes jobs more specialized by eliminating, combining, and/or changing the sequence of work. Job expansion makes jobs less specialized by rotating employees, enlarging the job, and/or enriching the job to make it more interesting and challenging.

10. Describe the job characteristics model and what it is used for.

This model is a conceptual framework for designing enriched jobs. It uses core job dimensions, critical psychological states, and employee growth-need strength to improve the quality of working life for employees and productivity for the organization.

11. Set priorities.

Setting priorities involves asking three questions: (1) Do I need to be personally involved? (2) Is the task my responsibility or will it affect the performance or finances of my department? (3) Is quick action needed? Delegate when you don't need to be personally involved. Assign a high priority when your answers to all three questions are yes (YYY). Assign a medium priority when your answers to questions 1 and 2 *or* 3 are yes (YNY or YYN). Assign a low priority when your answer to question 1 is yes and your answers to questions 2 and 3 are no (YNN).

12. Delegate.

To delegate effectively (1) explain why you are delegating the task and the reasons you chose this person to do the work; (2) clearly define responsibility, the person's scope of authority, and the deadline; (3) plan the task; and (4) establish control checkpoints and hold employees accountable.

13. Define the key terms discussed in the text.

Fill in the missing key terms from memory, or match the key terms from the list in the margin with their definitions below.

The _____ refers to the number of employees reporting to a manager.

_____ is the obligation to achieve objectives by performing required activities.

_____ is the right to make decisions, issue orders, and use resources.

Key Terms

authority
centralized authority
decentralized authority
delegation
departmentalization
job characteristics
   model
job design
job enrichment
levels of authority
line authority
organization chart
responsibility
span of management
staff authority

_____ is the process of assigning responsibility and authority for accomplishing objectives.

The _____ are inform, recommend, report, and full.

_____ is the responsibility to make decisions and issue orders down the chain of command.

_____ is the responsibility to advise and assist other personnel.

With _____, important decisions are made by top managers.

With _____, important decisions are made by middle- and first-level managers.

An _____ is a graphic illustration of the organization's management hierarchy and departments and their working relationships.

_____ is the grouping of related activities into work units.

_____ is the process of combining tasks that each employee is responsible for completing.

_____ is the process of building motivators into a job by making it more interesting and challenging.

The _____ comprises core job dimensions, critical psychological states, and employee growth-need strength to improve quality of working life for employees and productivity for the organization.

REVIEW AND DISCUSSION

1. What is the difference between unity of command and unity of direction?
2. What is the relationship between the chain of command and the span of management (span of control)?
3. What do the terms _differentiation_ and _integration_ mean?
4. What is the difference between responsibility and authority?
5. Can a coach delegate accountability to a player?
6. How does the scope of authority change through an organization and what is the flow of responsibility, authority, and accountability?
7. What is the difference between a general staff and a specialist staff?
8. What does an organization chart show? What doesn't it show?
9. What is the difference between product and customer departmentalization?
10. What is job design and why is it necessary?
11. What is the difference between an integrated and a self-managed work team?

12. What is the importance of employee growth-need strength to the job characteristics model?

13. Why is it important to update priorities on a to-do list?

14. What is the first and most important question you ask to determine what and what not to delegate?

15. Explain why each of the four steps of delegating is necessary.

CASE

Building a Champion Organization

Jerry Colangelo builds sport organizations, and lots of them. Gives them muscle, gives them focus, gives them a vision. And lets them do the rest. Take men's and women's pro basketball, where he's worked with the Chicago Bulls and the Phoenix Suns, *and* the Phoenix Mercury. Or football—his signature can be found on the Arizona Rattlers of Arena Football. Or baseball—oh yes, he's *also* worked with the Arizona Diamondbacks, the young upstarts who tumbled the dynastic New York Yankees in the 2001 World Series.

So what is this sport magician's multi-million-dollar secret?

Organization, organization, and more organization. He's been defining it, refining it, and tweaking it for years. Here is what Colangelo had to say about setting up the MLB team in Phoenix: "My first requirement was that the first place we would look to fill the jobs was from our other teams. We shifted people over from the basketball operation, and from other operations, and gave them a chance to move up the ladder." Colangelo gives his people a place to thrive and opportunities in which to shine. He gives them the ultimate compliment—trust, and the scope and the room to do what they need to do. Reward, compensation, community, opportunity, and responsibility are all part of his game plan.

The first thing that Jerry found that really counts in building organizations is assembling their leadership (carefully, shrewdly, and wisely). So when he set about building the Diamondbacks' organization, he went where the talent was and where he knew the people firsthand—he tapped into the Suns' management. His prize catch was Rich Dozer, who transferred to the new baseball group as president of the Diamondbacks. Originally from an accounting background, Dozer was thrilled to be part of the Diamondbacks' founding management team.

Marketing is another of Jerry's pet areas, areas that he knows make a big difference. His coaches and managers believe in marketing their team, and they're good at it. For the Arizona Rattlers, Colangelo hired Danny White, former Dallas Cowboys' quarterback, to manage the team. Because Danny White is an established name in football, fans were willing to check out what a local team might do in the little-known Arena Football League. White recently signed a two-year extension of his contract to continue coaching the Rattlers.

Colangelo has not hit a home run with every endeavor. His 1992–1994 entry into World Team Tennis failed. His Arizona Sandsharks of the Continental Indoor Soccer League also failed. Colangelo gives each new sport he buys into three years to prove itself. If the team can't build an audience in three years, Colangelo calls it quits. Why? Because good managers cut their losses, and move on to more promising prospects. This might be the destiny of the world champion Diamondbacks, who haven't generated the revenues that can pay their high salaries *and* put the bottom line in the green. This wouldn't be the first time a championship team ended up in the dustbin of sports history—the Florida Marlins disbanded after winning the World Series in 1997. As of this writing, Colangelo has kept the Diamondbacks together, and the team and organization are still winning.

For more information, please visit http://cbs.sportsline.com and search for "Jerry Colangelo." This site features numerous audio files—you can listen to Colangelo talk about his various professional teams.

CASE QUESTIONS

Select the best alternative for the following questions. Be sure you are able to explain your answers.

1. Jerry Colangelo's various endeavors in different professional sport leagues shows a great unity of direction.
   a. true   b. false

2. What level of authority does Colangelo have with the teams he owns?
   a. inform
   b. recommend
   c. report
   d. full

3. What type of authority does Danny White have as coach of the Arizona Rattlers?
   a. line
   b. staff

4. Within the organization, authority is
   a. centralized
   b. decentralized

5. Transferring managers from one team to another is an example of
   a. simplification
   b. rotation
   c. enlargement
   d. enrichment

6. Colangelo is reluctant to delegate.
   a. true   b. false

7. The Arizona Diamondbacks won the World Series in 2001. This is proof that a well-organized sport organization will always win the championship.
   a. true   b. false

8. Jerry Colangelo lacks the skills to properly coordinate his teams.
   a. true   b. false

9. Colangelo's teams are well suited to be organized using a matrix approach.
   a. true   b. false

10. Colangelo's teams are well suited to be organized by products/teams.
    a. true   b. false

11. Use the Internet to find out whether Colangelo has dismantled the Diamondbacks.

12. If professional teams are owned by wealthy businesspeople, would you expect most organizations to be centralized or decentralized?

EXERCISES

Skill-Builder: Setting Priorities

Objective:
- To hone your ability to set priorities.

Preparation:
Congratulations! You just made first-line management in golf ball production at A Birdie in the Hand. A prioritized to-do list with ten tasks is given on the next page. Assign priorities to each task using the steps outlined on page 162.

1. List each task. (The ten tasks for this Skill-Builder have been written in for you.)

2. Answer the three questions (see the box at the top left and use Y/N for yes/no). Because you aren't the actual manager of this department, do not fill in the deadline/time needed column.

Assigning a Priority		Priority Determination Questions				
		#1	#2	#3		P r i o r i t y
D Delegate priority (N) No to question 1		1. Do I need to be personally involved?	2. Is it my responsibility or will it affect performance or finances of my department?	3. Is quick action needed?	Deadline/Time needed	
H High priority (YYY) Yes to all three questions						
M Medium priority (YNY or YYN) Yes to questions 1 and 2 or 3						
L Low priority (YNN) Yes to question 1 and no to questions 2 and 3						
Task						
1. Tom, the sales manager, told you that three customers stopped doing business with the company because your products have decreased in quality.						
2. Your secretary, Michele, told you that there is a salesperson waiting to see you. He does not have an appointment. You don't do any purchasing.						
3. Molly, a vice president, wants to see you to discuss a new product to be introduced in one month.						
4. Tom, the sales manager, sent you a memo stating that the sales forecast was incorrect. Sales are expected to increase by 20% starting next month. There is no inventory to meet the unexpected sales forecast.						
5. Dan, the personnel director, sent you a memo informing you that one of your employees has resigned. Your turnover rate is one of the highest in the company.						
6. Michele told you that a Bob Furry called while you were out. He asked you to return his call, but wouldn't state why he was calling. You don't know who he is or what he wants.						
7. Phil, one of your best workers, wants an appointment to tell you about a situation that happened in the shop.						
8. Tom called and asked you to meet with him and a prospective customer for your product. The customer wants to meet you.						
9. John, your boss, called and said that he wants to see you about the decrease in the quality of your product.						
10. In the mail you got a note from Randolf, the president of your company, and an article from *Sports Business Journal*. The note says FYI (for your information).						

3. In the priority column assign a priority (D, delegate; H, high; M, medium; and L, low) to each task based on your answers to the three questions above.

4. Determine which task you should complete now. You may have more than one high priority, so select the most important one.

In-Class Application

Complete the skill-building preparation noted above before class.

Choose one (10–30 minutes):

- Break into groups of three to five members, and work to reach a group consensus on the ten priorities. As a group present your prioritized list to the class.
- Informal, whole-class discussion of student findings.

Wrap-up:
Take a few minutes and write down your answers to the following questions:

- What did I learn from this experience?

  _____

  _____

  _____

- How will I use this knowledge in the future?

  _____

  _____

  _____

As a class, discuss student responses.

Skill-Builder: Delegating

Objective:

- To develop your ability to delegate.

Preparation:
Review the material on delegating (pages 162 to 165), then familiarize yourself with the following scenarios.

Scenario 1
Camp Counselor Grace: You are the head camp counselor at your college's training camp for left-handed, right-footed male and female cheerleaders. You've got your hands full with these all-star wanna-bes, and you can't do *everything*. Think up some tasks you can delegate to Mandy that will help these kids develop a cool, new style that works with their inherent lack of grace.

Camp Counselor Mandy: You're new this year, and you've been stuck with the few good dancers in camp (who don't need any help), and you really want to show that you can make something out of the wrong shoes (so to speak).

Scenario 2
Sally: You manage Golfers Go for It, a retail store that sells to the local golf set and that is trying to move into the tennis market. Your favorite task is scheduling your salesclerks. You go to great lengths to accommodate everyone's requirements so you're "one happy crew," but it's taking more and more of your time. Your bosses have suggested that you delegate this task (you can't imagine why) to your assistant manager, Hector. Hector has never done any scheduling, but he appears to be willing and ready to take on the one task you really pride yourself on. Also, you've been reading this very useful book on Sport Management and are thinking that maybe its Chapter 6 on Organizing and Delegating Work has some pointers about delegating that you could use—especially the discussion on managers' fear of being shown up. Now you're thinking that it's very possible you've been hiding behind the "I'm *so* busy" excuse to avoid developing some new sales initiatives that might really make the new tennis section a go. With these issues in mind, use the planning sheet from Chapter 5 to plan how you will delegate staff scheduling to Hector.

Hector: You see this as an opportunity to streamline the system, but you also don't want to rock the boat.

Scenario 3

Seema: You and your two roommates, who are all star athletes, are looking for two more roommates. Your name is on the rental lease, and you've handled this pesky task in the past, but you're really swamped this quarter with the Little League softball team you've been coaching in your free time. None of you can cook, but you all like to eat and you're getting tired of takeout. Maybe the new roommates could teach you some things about cooking, or maybe they'll take over the cooking if you wash the dishes. Your rental house, The Castle, is the coolest and cheapest one near campus, so you expect a lot of calls. Plan how you will delegate this task to your roommates. Sara the basketball star is pretty shy, but Kate the soccer forward tends to procrastinate. You need two new renters in two weeks, or the three of you will have to make up the difference in the rent.

Sara: You know you've got to get over this shy business sometime, or you'll never make a good coach.

Kate: You see yourself as a successful international event planner but don't know how to get in gear.

In-Class Application

Choose one (10–30 minutes):

- Break into groups of three or four. Take turns being the delegator and the "delegatee" with each scenario. Those of you not doing the role play will observe the delegating process and provide an independent critique that might improve results.
- Three sets of students volunteer to role-play the three scenarios for the entire class, with informal discussion following.

Wrap-up:

Take a few minutes and write down your answers to the following questions:

- What did I learn from this experience?

  _____

  _____

  _____

- How will I use this knowledge in the future?

  _____

  _____

  _____

As a class, discuss student responses.

Internet Skills: Analyzing a Real Organizational Chart

Objective:

- To see how studying organization charts helps you understand the complex network of employee relationships in an organization.

Preparation (20 minutes):
The University of Minnesota's organization chart is over 25 pages long. Review the complete chart by visiting http://www.irr.umn.edu. To answer the following questions, find the Administrative Information heading and click on *University Organization Chart*.

1. According to its organization chart, how many levels of management does the University of Minnesota have?

_____

2. What are the different departments within the athletic area?

_____

_____

3. Is UM's organizational structure more or less extensive than your own college or university?

_____

4. To what person/position on UM's chart do the athletic departments report to?

_____

5. Looking at the chart, can you see ways in which UM's structure could be improved? If yes, what are they and why? If no, why not?

_____

_____

_____

7

Managing Change: Sport Culture, Innovation, and Diversity

Learning Outcomes

After studying this chapter, you should be able to:

1. Identify the driving forces behind change.

2. Describe the four variables of change.

3. Differentiate between facts, beliefs, and values.

4. Explain how the three components of organizational culture relate.

5. State the core values of TQM.

6. Describe a learning organization.

7. Explain how diversity can affect innovation and quality.

8. State how forcefield analysis and survey feedback differ.

9. Explain the difference between team building and process consultation.

10. Define the following key terms (in order of appearance in the chapter):

- variables of change
- management information systems (MISs)
- stages in the change process
- organizational culture
- components of culture
- core values of TQM
- learning organization
- organizational development (OD)
- OD interventions
- forcefield analysis
- survey feedback
- team building
- process consultation

The Manager Who Didn't Change

Under the leadership of **JOE TORRE,** the New York Yankees have snagged four more World Series championships and cemented their dynastic tradition as the reigning team in baseball. Torre made it look easy as he assembled a group of extremely talented players and molded them into formidable champions. But earlier in his career he managed the Mets, the Cardinals, and the Braves without much success—he was fired three times. The New York media and fans were not sure he was the manager the Yankees needed to rebuild the storied team. What did Joe Torre do to manage his own turnaround? What did he change? That answer is simple—he changed teams. What he *didn't* do was change his style—he had a vision, he just needed the right venue to see it bear fruit. So what's the moral of this story? Know *what* to change.

Joe Torre has always been a "players' manager." As an ex-player and the National League's Most Valuable Player in 1971, he certainly understands the needs of his players. Still, his early teams lost more often than they won. Both the media and his club owners put *(a lot)* of pressure on him to develop a more authoritarian style. Torre debated the merits of this advice and at one point even considered changing. Ultimately (and fortunately for the Yankees!), he stuck to his guns and to his own style. He learned to work closely with the members of the media and the owner of the team. Here is the first key (know your team's players) that Torre the manager lives by:

- *Know your players.* Know them inside and out—know their skills and abilities, their character and personal qualities, and their abilities to perform under pressure.

- *Make time for your players.* Make time for one-on-one talks/chats/discussions, help each player understand their importance to the team, let them know what you expect of them, bolster their confidence, answer every question and respond to every concern, and always, always, always offer support.

- *Enable success.* Give your players the opportunity to succeed, find the role that best matches each person's skills, and give them plenty of opportunities to fulfill that role.[1]

Joe Torre "walks his talk" (that is, he follows his own rules) and the Yankees win. He has put the total support of George Steinbrenner, the sometimes difficult owner of the Yankees, and the experience of two decades in baseball to good use. By knowing his players, he has earned their respect and devotion, and the adoration of millions of fans.[2]

For current information on Joe Torre and the New York Yankees, visit http://www.yankees.mlb.com. (For ideas on using the Internet, see Appendix B.)

INTERNET RESOURCES

http://web.mit.edu/aeroastro/www/labs/csi/gallery.html *Visit the Project Gallery at MIT's Center for Sports Innovation to learn about its latest research into sports technology. Here you will find information on the methodologies it uses to develop new products, its testing procedures, and study results. Click on the* Who We Are *and* Educational Initiatives *links to find out more about its objectives.*

http://www.onlinesports.com/sportstrust/sportsnewslist.html *This site provides "Sports News You Can Use." Under the Sport Management heading, click the* Women in Sport Management *and* Minorities in Sport Management *links to find statistics on these topics separated into three fields: athletic directors, professional sports, and Olympic sports.*

DEVELOPING YOUR SKILLS   Change is a fact of business life today. Your ability (or inability) to change with the ever-shifting demands of the business environment may make (or break) your career. And, if you are to succeed in management, one task you must learn to do—and do well—is to *implement* change. Change comes in many forms, and so does resistance to it. Learning to identify resistance to change can mean the difference between a successful transition and a failed one. Overcoming resistance to change will test and challenge your people skills, and hone them as well.

MANAGING CHANGE

Yogi Berra once said, "the future ain't what it used to be."[3] Managers face revolutionary change today as they endeavor to respond to the demands of the global marketplace. Today, an organization's long-term success stands directly on the shoulders of its ability to manage change. MasterCard is expanding its sponsorship interests to reinforce awareness of its brand image and to provide value to consumers. MasterCard's sponsorship of the World Cup of soccer is a marketing coup, making it a globally recognized brand, and it intends to capitalize on the passion this game arouses in its fans.[4] **How did Joe Torre change when he became the manager of the New York Yankees?**

Forces for Change

1 LEARNING OUTCOME
Identify the driving forces behind change.

ENVIRONMENTAL FORCES. Today's business environment presents many challenges, often daunting challenges, and as such it is a driving force behind change. As we noted in Chapter 2, organizations interact continually with their external and internal environments. Factors in both environments require all manner of change, and effective organizations endeavor to "change the change" to their advantage. That is, they try to anticipate and predict change, to shape it if they can, and to prepare for it if they cannot shape it. This is a proactive (rather than reactive) approach. Dr. David Hoch, Director of Athletics at Eastern Tech High School in Baltimore County, Maryland, suggests that athletic directors' problems created by change should be dealt with proactively without waiting until the change occurs.[5] An AD may face new budget restrictions, a new principal or superintendent, greater expectations from parents, or new technologies such as e-mail and the Internet.

ECONOMIC FORCES. Economic forces have changed so drastically that even players with average skills make millions of dollars per year. Also, baseball has become a sport where big-market teams like the New York Yankees and Boston Red Sox can generate more revenues and thus afford to spend more money to acquire star players. And more star players means more fan and media interest, which means even more money. Even though this economic change favors teams like the Yankees, they still need to properly evaluate the talent of available players. Because of the huge amount of money involved, **JOE TORRE** and his management team have very little margin for error when choosing players.

SOCIAL FORCES. Social forces also play an increasingly important role in managing a team. Most fans outside of the New York area consider the Yankees to be a bully of a team and not willing to share revenues with small-market teams. The Yankees are viewed as a team that gets to buy whatever players it wants. The result is that most non-Yankees fans dislike the team, which makes it hard for any Yankees player or manager to be accepted outside of New York. Even more socially significant, baseball has fallen behind football as America's favorite sport. Baseball fans have become leery of the game after the recent strikes, which were caused by anger and mistrust between players and owners. Meanwhile, fans love the physical contact and fast action found in football.

DEMOGRAPHIC FORCES. For the Yankees, operating in the racially mixed New York area, demographic forces are unique. **TORRE'S** team appears to have been built to resemble this racial mixture. Star center fielder Bernie Williams is from San Juan, Puerto Rico. Star relief pitcher Mariano Rivera is from Panama City, Panama. Pitcher Orlando Hernandez is from Havana, Cuba.

TECHNOLOGICAL FORCES. Technology is very different today than it was only a few years ago. The Yankees make a great deal more money from the media than any other team. More specifically the Yankees own YES, its own cable network. Some fans in the New York area do not receive Yankees games because their cable provider doesn't carry the YES network. These fans have become irate at the team for not allowing them television access to all the games.

Meanwhile, **JOE TORRE** thrives in the midst of these strong external factors. He handles the media with grace and ease, and gives interesting and thoughtful interviews. His own Italian ethnic background feels authentic to the people of New York. Although fans across the country may not like the Yankees and its owner, they still support Torre and his compassionate mannerisms.

THE MANAGEMENT FUNCTIONS AND CHANGE. Managers manage change every moment of their work day. Plans that they develop require changes. Organizing and delegating tasks often require the employees they lead to make changes. The hiring, orienting, and training of employees, and their performance evaluations, may indicate that aspects of their job, or their approach to it, must change. "Have you ever thought about the changes that athletic directors encounter every year and the impact that they usually have? New athletes? New parents? New coaches? They all spell change and the possibility of having to adjust and react differently."[6]

> **TIMEOUT**
> Think about a change the organization you work for or play for has faced recently, and identify the force driving the change.
> _____
> _____
> _____
> _____
> _____
> _____

2 | LEARNING OUTCOME
Describe the four variables of change.

Variables of Change

The four **variables of change**—strategy, structure, technology, and people—refer to what organizations must adapt, adjust, shift, or re-create to stay current, to keep or grow market share, or to remain viable as an organization, as they are bombarded with changes they must address in the marketplace. (See Exhibit 7–1.) Because of the systems effect, effective managers consider what repercussions a shift in one variable will have on the remaining variables and plan accordingly.

variables of change
Strategy, structure, technology, and people.

Exhibit 7–1   The Four Variables of Change

STRATEGY	STRUCTURE	TECHNOLOGY	PEOPLE
Corporate (growth, stability, and turnaround and retrenchment)	**Principles** (unity of command and direction, chain of command, span of management, division of labor, coordination, balanced responsibility and authority, delegation, and flexibility)	**Machines**	**Skills**
		Systems Process	**Performance**
		Information Process	**Attitudes**
Business Level (prospecting, defending, and analyzing)		**Automation**	**Behavior**
Functional (marketing, operations, finance, and human resources)	**Authority** (formal and informal, levels of, line and staff, and centralized and decentralized)		
	Organizational Design (departmentalization)		
	Job Design (job simplification, rotation, enlargement, enrichment, and work teams)		

STRATEGY. Organizations routinely adjust strategies at the corporate, business, and functional levels in order to adapt to changes in their external and internal environments. For example, Cybex International identified "expanding market share in the fitness industry" as a corporate objective. To do this, the company needed to broaden its line of fitness equipment, so it embarked on a friendly merger with Trotter Inc., an undisputed leader in cardiovascular research and products. The different experiences and the deep expertise both companies brought to the table have turned out to be a good "marriage." Since merging with Trotter, Cybex has been able to develop and offer the most advanced and complete line of equipment in its market.[7]

STRUCTURE. Structure typically follows strategy. In other words, a change in strategy causes a change in structure. Over time, organizational structures evolve to adapt to emerging needs. We examined organizational structure in Chapter 6; Exhibit 7–1 briefly summarizes key elements in organizational structure.

TECHNOLOGY. High-tech innovations—computers, faxes, e-mail, and the Internet—have increased the rate of change. (In a word—faster, faster, and, well, faster.) Technology increases productivity and thus helps organizations gain competitive advantage.[8] To gain this advantage, Olympic athletes, for example, look to their equipment suppliers to provide cutting-edge shoes, bats, skis, and bicycles, and to their trainers and therapists to provide cutting-edge technique and instant recovery from injuries that once sidelined players for a season, and now set them back mere days. All manner of sport organizations routinely use the Internet for all manner of reasons—from web sites for fans (check out http://www.nfl.com, http://www.nba.com, and http://www.mlb.com), to ideas on how to improve viewership or grow a fledgling swim team, to information on the latest coaching techniques. Once obscure sports like curling, fencing, and boomeranging have found new life through the Internet.[9]

Technology frequently drives change in strategy and structure. Here are a few examples of the innumerable ways technology affects changes:

- *Machines.* New machinery and equipment are introduced continually. In 2002, Cybex introduced the new Cybex Arc Trainer. This is a nonimpact aerobic exercise machine that is easier on the neck and back.[10]

- *Systems process.* How organizations transform inputs into outputs has been at the forefront of technological innovation. Companies use the latest in computer automation to build products free of defects.

- *Information process.* With the advent of the computer, organizations have radically changed the way they do business. **Management information systems (MISs)** are formal systems for collecting, processing, and disseminating information that aids managers in decision making. MISs centralize and integrate the organization's key information, such as finance, production, inventory, and sales. Departments plugged into MISs can better coordinate their efforts, and this translates into a more focused organization and higher productivity. For example, Information Communications Technology (ICT) helps P.E. teachers record students' physical activities and graph their progress. E-mail and databases also help P.E. departments with administrative duties.

- *Automation.* Computers and other machines have enabled organizations to replace people with robots. Automation takes away some jobs, and adds others. The jury is out as to whether the final numbers will be equivalent (that is, same ending number of jobs for people, just different ones), as we are still in the midst of this revolution—only time (measured in decades) will tell. Automation also changes the types of work people do. Pressing needs for better training, retraining, and higher levels of skill will continue for the foreseeable future. For example, Information Communications Technology (ICT) has enabled physical education teachers to allow their students to record their physical activities and graph their progress. Using e-mail and databases can also help physical education departments with administrative duties.[11]

PEOPLE. People have always been, and always will be, a key variable of change. Think of the ways changes affect you in your job, team, and school, *and* how you effect changes in your job, team, and school. The day-to-day tasks that we do to perform our jobs have changed

management information systems (MISs)
Formal systems for collecting, processing, and disseminating information that aids managers in decision making.

APPLYING THE CONCEPT   *The Variables of Change*

Identify the change variable involved in each situation.

   a. strategy   **c.** technology

   b. structure   **d.** people

_____ 1. We installed a new computer system to speed up the time it takes to bill ticket customers.

_____ 2. With the increasing number of pro basketball leagues, we're going to have to devote more time and effort to keeping our existing customers.

_____ 3. Jamie, I'd like you to consider getting a college degree if you're serious about a career in management with this team.

_____ 4. We're changing suppliers to get higher-quality components for our tennis rackets.

_____ 5. We are laying off some assistant coaches to increase the number of players reporting to one coach.

---

dramatically because of technology and the ensuing structural changes. As tasks change, our *skills* and *performance* have changed, and will continue to change. Organizations often attempt to change our *attitudes* and *behavior* to improve the bottom line, grow market niche, enhance productivity, among others.

Changes in organizational culture are also considered a people variable. Why? Because it is people who develop and implement changes in strategy and structure. We create, manage, and use technology; therefore, we are the organization's most important resource. This makes us both the organization's wild card and also its ace in the hole when it comes to implementing change. Changes in the other three variables cannot work without the commitment and energy and problem-solving abilities of people. So it is crucial to get input from those who will affected by a change, and also their commitment to its success. For example, an athletic director should inform and educate everyone involved with an upcoming change to help reduce fears and reservations.[12]

Stages in the Change Process

People in the midst of a change go through four distinct **stages in the change process**— denial, resistance, exploration, and commitment.[13]

1. *Denial.* When people first hear rumors that change is coming, they go into denial— "it won't happen here!" Prudent managers manage change proactively; they don't wait until change rudely knocks on their door. They start addressing the change and its ramifications early on to both lessen the impact of the change and smooth the transition.[14]

2. *Resistance.* Once people get over their initial shock and realize that change is inevitable, they resist it. It is important to understand that we *all*—in one way or another, and at one level or another—fear change. Change *always* takes us out of our comfort zone. Outside of our comfort zone, we may grow—yes, but we may also fail.[15]

3. *Exploration.* When implementation is launched, people explore the change, often through training, and they begin to better understand how it will affect them. It helps to solicit input from affected individuals. Inviting and encouraging them to be part of the change process is key to successful implementation.[16]

TIMEOUT

Describe a recent change in your organization or team and identify the variable(s) of change affecting it, or affected by it.

_____

_____

_____

_____

_____

_____

stages in the change process
Denial, resistance, exploration, and commitment.

Exhibit 7–2   Stages in the Change Process

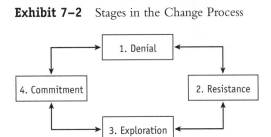

4. *Commitment.* Through exploration, people commit (or don't commit) to making the change a success. One's level of commitment can also change. Be alert for naysayers, and carefully and patiently address statements like, "It's always been done this way." **JOE TORRE** is a genuinely nice guy, and his players respond by being committed to doing whatever it takes to win. Besides being a nice guy, Joe Torre also uses specific techniques to gain a high level of commitment from his players. Can you think of some of them?

Exhibit 7–2 illustrates the change process. We present the stages as occurring in a circular fashion because change is rarely linear. People go back and forth—they waver in their resistance and commitment, as the arrows show.

Resistance to Change and How to Overcome It

Most change programs fail because the people involved resist—even sabotage—change. As a manager, your job is to understand why, and then to find ways to counter resistance. See Exhibit 7–3 for an overview. So, why do we resist change?

- *We fear uncertainty.* Remember, fear of the unknown is a universal human trait. People resist change in order to cope with their anxiety and fear of the unknown.[17] Learning anxieties underlie many people's resistance to change—the prospect of learning something new can conjure up old memories of failure and reminds people that failure (however unlikely it might be) is still a very real prospect.

- *We don't like to be inconvenienced.* We often don't want to disrupt our routines or the way things are because they are comfortable. At a minimum, change means having to learn new ways, and may mean extensive training. **JOE TORRE** works hard to keep his pitching rotation in proper order so that his pitchers can maintain a regular routine between appearances.

- *We always move to protect our self-interest.* This is also a universal human trait, and it can be both productive and conducive to change, and it can be counterproductive. *Of course* people will resist change if it threatens their self-interest. And we are usually more concerned about our own best interest than that of the organization. Effective organizations and effective managers know how to marry the two interests.

- *We fear loss.* Change often brings loss of jobs. Or it may require pay cuts—witness older players who can no longer demand high salaries like they did when they were rising stars. A change in work assignments or schedules may mean losing valued social relationships. The aging athlete is often happy to prolong his or her career for a year or two just to spend more time with teammates.

- *We like to be in control.* (Or at least feel like we're in control.) Actual or perceived losses in power, status, security, and especially control often come with change programs. It's all too easy to resent the someone or the entity that controls our destiny.

OK, now you know why people resist change. The good news is, there are ways to alleviate their fears and overcome their resistance. Here are some key ones:

1. *Create a trust climate.* Put money in the bank, so to speak. How, you ask? By carefully developing good relations with your team or work group. And don't forget to main-

Exhibit 7–3   Overcoming Resistance to Change

WHY PEOPLE RESIST CHANGE	HOW TO OVERCOME RESISTANCE
Uncertainty creates fear.	Create a trust climate.
Inconvenience is off-putting.	Develop a change plan.
Their *self-interest* is threatened.	State why change is needed and how it affects them.
We all fear *loss.*	Create a win-win situation.
Lack of *control* is often an issue.	Involve people, and provide support.

tain them. This is your "capital," and someday you may have to call it in. That is, you may have to ask your group to trust you to lead it through a change program for which initial resistance is especially strong. Make sure your group understands that you have everyone's best interests in mind. Constantly look for better ways to do things. Encourage people to suggest changes and implement their ideas. They are valued members of your team—show it! It is evident that **JOE TORRE'S** players trust him to make the right moves during games.

2. *Develop a change plan.* Successful implementation of change is no accident. Behind every successful implementation stands a good plan. Develop one, then *use* it. Identify possible resistance to change and plan ways to overcome it. View change from your team's position. Set clear objectives so that everyone knows exactly what he or she will do during and after the change. And make sure your plan addresses the next four issues.

3. *State why the change is necessary and how it will affect your group.* Communication is the key here. People need to know all the whys and they need to know all the hows. *Why* are we doing this? *How* will it affect me? Give them the good news, and the bad news. Be open and honest. You've taken great care to build trust—don't squander it. Giving the facts as early as you can not only allays everyone's fears, it also helps them feel in control. (Now *they* can make plans.) If a negative grapevine kicks in and starts spreading incorrect facts, correct the information quickly and firmly.

4. *Create a win-win situation.* If you can—obviously, you can't always do this. That said, with a little thought and consideration, you will often find that you really can meet employee needs *and* achieve the objectives you've been given. Think about how you can answer the question everyone is thinking but nobody is asking: "What's in it for me?" People who see how they will benefit from a change will be more open to it. So, how do you create this win-win scenario? Read on . . .

5. *Involve people.* It's a fact—a group's commitment to change is critical to its success. Here's another fact—people who help develop changes are more committed to their success than those who don't. It's about ownership and it's about control. Why do we like to own houses, cars, ice skates, golf clubs (rather than renting them, for example)? Because we can control their quality, their availability, and so on. The same goes for change at work, on the playing field—anywhere, in fact. If we feel we "own" the change, we feel in control, and we'll work like crazy to make it succeed.

6. *Provide support.* Training is very important to successful change; therefore it behooves you and your organization to provide as much training as you can before, during, and often afterward. Thorough training reduces anxieties, alleviates frustration, and helps people realize they will "have a life" after the change. Treat mistakes as learning experiences—as "gifts," in fact: "Good thing this happened here—now we'll know what to do when it comes up for real!" **Describe how Joe Torre would use the strategies found in Exhibit 7–3 to overcome his players' resistance to change.**

> **TIME**OUT
> Describe an instance when you resisted change. Specify which of the five reasons were behind your resistance. Now, be your own manager, and describe some proactive ways you could have overcome your initial reluctance.
> _____
> _____
> _____
> _____
> _____
> _____

A Model for Identifying and Overcoming Resistance

Before initiating change of any sort, savvy managers anticipate how their team will react. Looking at three key components of the resistance itself—intensity, source, and focus—will help you understand why certain members of your group may be reluctant to change.[18]

INTENSITY. We all view change differently. Some of us thrive on it even as others are upset by it. Most of us resist it at first but gradually we come to accept it ("somewhere in between" intensity), yet some of us resist it forever ("strong" intensity). And we view different changes differently. Some of us think nothing of taking up bungee jumping, but would "die" before we got up and addressed our work group. As a manager of change, you need to assess what you think will be the *intensity* of your group's response. Will their response be a strong one, a weak one, or will it be somewhere in between? Your can lower the intensity if you follow the six guidelines given above.

3 **LEARNING OUTCOME**
Differentiate between facts, beliefs, and values.

SOURCE. Resistance to change arises from three sources:

1. *When facts are used selectively.* All of us at one time or another have used facts selectively to prove our point. Facts used correctly help overcome our fear of the unknown.

2. *When beliefs color the facts.* Facts can be proven; beliefs cannot. Beliefs are subjective opinions that can be shaped by others—they are, in a word, our perceptions. How we perceive a situation colors whether we *believe* a change will be beneficial or detrimental, an improvement, or a step backward.

3. *When values trump the facts.* Values are what we believe are worth pursuing or doing. What we value is extremely important to us. Sometimes the facts directly collide with our values—in such situations, values often win.

FOCUS. When we resist change, we do so from three viewpoints—that is, we choose a focus:

1. *Ourselves.* All of us naturally want to know, What's in it for me? What will I gain or lose? When we perceive (correctly or incorrectly) that a proposed change will affect us negatively, we will resist the change.

2. *Significant others.* After considering what's in it for us, or when the change does not affect us, we next consider how the change will affect our friends, peers, and colleagues. If we believe the change will affect important others negatively, we may also be reluctant to embrace the change.

3. *Our work environment.* We like to be in control of our situation, whether it is our home, team, or work environment, and we resist changes that take away our feelings of control.

The resistance matrix in Model 7–1 gives examples for each component. Use the matrix to identify the intensity, source, and focus of your team or work group. This will help you

TIMEOUT

Think about the situation you identified in the preceding Timeout (page 181), then use the resistance matrix in Model 7–1 to determine your level of intensity, the focus of your resistance, and its source.

_____

_____

_____

_____

_____

Model 7–1   Resistance Matrix

Sources of Resistance (fact → belief → value)

1. Facts about self • I have never done the task before. • I failed the last time I tried.	**4. Beliefs about self** • I'm too busy to learn it. • I'll do it, but don't blame me if it's wrong.	**7. Values pertaining to self** • I like the way I do my job now. Why change? • I like working in a group.
2. Facts about others • She has the best performance record in the department. • Other employees told me it's hard to do.	**5. Beliefs about others** • He just pretends to be busy to avoid extra work. • She's better at it than I am; let her do it.	**8. Values pertaining to others** • Let someone else do it; I do not want to work with her. • I like working with him. Don't cut him from our department.
3. Facts about the work environment • We are paid only $7 an hour. • It's over 100 degrees.	**6. Beliefs about the work environment** • This is a lousy job. • The pay here is too low.	**9. Values pertaining to the work environment** • I don't care if we meet the goal or not. • The new task will make me work inside. I'd rather be outside.

Focus of Resistance (work → other → self)

Intensity (high, medium, or low for each box)

decide which strategies will be effective in getting people to buy into making the change work. Note that intensity is outside the matrix because it can be strong, moderate, or weak for the other nine components. In the Skill-Builder on change at the end of the chapter, you will use the resistance matrix to identify the source and focus of resistance to various changes.

ORGANIZATIONAL CULTURE

Organizational culture is the set of values, beliefs, and standards for acceptable behavior that an organization's members share. Understanding an organization's culture helps you understand how it functions and how you should do things "to fit in," and also helps you predict how it will do in good times and in bad ones. Think of culture as the organization's personality. Sport team culture adds a special dimension to the idea of organizational culture. Why? Because teams form a special bond that is often very strong. With this bond come special ways of behaving, goofing off, a special determination to win, "team ways" of dealing with winning and losing—in short, all the bonding mechanisms are in full display. Add to this mix fans who closely identify with and/or idolize a particular team's culture/image/personality, and you have many strong forces at play. Think of "good guy" teams like the Seattle Mariners and "bad guy" teams like the Oakland Raiders.

Not a few extremely successful businesses have taken sport team culture as their ideal model. They do this because it helps them win in the marketplace. "Sport team culture originated from the establishment and development of sports teams. The sport team culture with which all members voluntarily comply is the total of common faith, morality, spirit, ceremony, intelligence factor, and entertainment life. The function of the sport team culture is found in instructing people, construction of team standards, recovery, spiritual adjustment, and meeting psychological and social demand."[19] **Does Joe Torre have a "good guy" or "bad guy" image? What is the image for the New York Yankees as a team? The New York Yankees as an organization?**

organizational culture
The shared values, beliefs, and standards for acceptable behavior.

Three Components of Culture

4 LEARNING OUTCOME
Explain how the three components of organizational culture relate.

The three **components of culture** are behavior, values and beliefs, and assumptions.[20] Exhibit 7–4 shows the three components divided by level.

LEVEL 1: BEHAVIOR. *Behavior* is observable action—what we do and say. *Artifacts* are the results of our behavior and include written and spoken language, dress, material objects, and so on. Behavior also includes rites, celebrations, ceremonies, heroes, jargon, myths, and stories. When you examine an organization's culture, you will find that rites, corporate myths, jargon, and all the rest play an important part in defining its culture. Managers, particularly the founders, have a strong influence on their organization's culture. The late Tom Yawkey of the Boston Red Sox, the late George Halas of the Chicago Bears, and Al Davis of the Oakland Raiders were legends in their own time, and are legends still to fellow players, colleagues, and fans alike who relish the tales and anecdotes surrounding these enduring personalities.

LEVEL 2: VALUES AND BELIEFS. *Values* represent the way we think we ought to behave and identify what we think it takes to be successful. *Beliefs* represent "if-then" statements. (If I do X, then Y will happen.) Values and beliefs are the operating principles that guide decision making and behavior in an organization. We observe values and beliefs only indirectly, through the behaviors and decisions they drive. Values and beliefs are often described in an organization's mission statement, but take care here—sometimes an organization's "talk" (its *stated* values and beliefs) doesn't match its "walk" (values and beliefs put into action).

Tom Yawkey and his family walked their talk. They believed in giving to charity, and they made sure their team gave both money and personal time to the Dana Farber Institute. Before the 2002 baseball season, the Yawkey family sold the Red

components of culture
Behavior, values and beliefs, and assumptions.

Exhibit 7–4
The Three Components of Culture

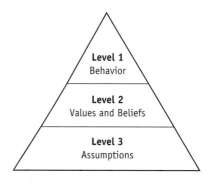

Sox to John Henry. This new management is carrying forward the Red Sox tradition by helping the Joey Fund.[21] And even though Al Davis values his team's maverick image and goes to great lengths to maintain it, "bad boys" Oakland Raiders also donate substantial time to worthwhile causes in the Oakland area.[22]

LEVEL 3: ASSUMPTIONS. *Assumptions* are deeply ingrained values and beliefs whose "truth" we never question. Because our assumptions are the very foundation of our belief system, they are "patently obvious" to us—and we assume to everyone else—so we rarely discuss them. They are the automatic pilots that guide our behavior. Naturally, when our assumptions are challenged, we feel threatened. Question teammates on why they do things certain ways—if they often respond with statements like, "That's the way it's always been done," you have probably run into an assumption. Assumptions are often the most stable and enduring part of culture and the most difficult to change. For instance, although the Boston Red Sox were known for their charity, the new owners challenged basic assumptions on how the team treated its fans and the media. Consequently, it has embraced both the media and the fans with new events that encourage players to get closer to both groups.[23] However, things don't always go this smoothly—changing assumptions is rarely an easy task.

Strong Cultures and Weak Cultures

Organizational cultures range from strong to weak. In organizations with *strong cultures,* people unconsciously share assumptions and consciously know the organization's values and beliefs. That is, they agree with the organization's assumptions, values, and beliefs—and behave as expected. In organizations with weak cultures, many employees don't behave as expected—they don't share underlying assumptions. When people don't agree with the generally accepted values and beliefs, they may rebel and fight the culture. This can be destructive or constructive. Culture is both an entrenched phenomenon and a fluid one. Hence cultures resist change, but they also continually adapt to the times.

There is good news and bad news about strong cultures. Strong cultures make communication and cooperation easier and better. Unity is common, and consensus is easier to reach. The downside is potential stagnation and a lack of diverse opinion (the "other side" never gets told because people don't see it). The continually changing environment requires that assumptions, values, and beliefs be questioned occasionally and changed when they no longer adequately address the needs of the marketplace.

Successful organizations realize that managing culture is not a program with a starting and ending date. It is an ongoing endeavor called *organizational development* (OD). You will learn about OD later in this chapter.

A change in culture is a *people* change. To be effective, changes in culture have to occur in all three components (people's behavior, values and beliefs, and assumptions). A culture of success allows for change, and businesses that fail to move with the times lose their competitive advantage.

Culture is an important consideration when companies merge or acquire a business. A mismatch in cultures often leads to failed mergers and acquisitions. When larger businesses acquire smaller companies, they often try to bring the smaller company's culture into alignment with their own culture, usually without much success. When developing or changing culture, remember that what you as a manager *say* doesn't count as much as what you *measure, reward,* and *control*—these three actions are powerhouses in influencing behavior. For example, management that *says* ethics are important, but fiddles suspiciously with their financial statements, will have a hard time establishing a trust climate.

> **TIMEOUT**
> Give examples of behaviors that accurately show your organization's culture working. What are the values, beliefs, and assumptions underlying these behaviors? Does the organization have a strong culture or a weak one?
>
> _____
> _____
> _____
> _____
> _____
> _____

INNOVATION

In Chapter 3 we noted that *creativity* is a way of thinking that generates new ideas and that *innovation* is the implementation of a new idea. Two important types of innovations are product innovation (new things) and process innovation (new ways of doing things).

Product innovation abounds in the sport industry. Take NASCAR, for example. Safety has been a major concern for NASCAR, accelerated by the death of Dale Earnhardt on the last lap of the 2001 Daytona 500. A new product innovation, shock-absorbing "soft walls," are

APPLYING
THE CONCEPT   *Strong Cultures and Weak Cultures*

Identify each statement as being characteristic of an organization with (a) a strong culture or (b) a weak culture.

_____   6. Walking around this athletic department during my job interview, I realized I'd have to wear a jacket and tie every day.

_____   7. I'm a little tired of hearing about how our team founders conducted business. We all know the stories, so why do people keep telling them?

_____   8. I've never met with so many people who all act so differently. I guess I can just be me rather than trying really hard to fit in.

_____   9. It's hard to say what is really important in our department. Management *says* quality is important, but they force us to work too fast and they know we send out defective athletic equipment all the time just to meet orders.

_____ 10. I started to tell this ethnic joke and the other employees all gave me a dirty look.

being used to protect drivers. Soft walls are constructed of steel tubing and foam pads in front of concrete. They are known as the SAFER (Steel and Foam Energy Reduction) barrier system and were developed by engineers at the University of Nebraska. The soft walls are 20 inches thick and cover 1100 feet at each corner of the track.[24] The walls will provide a cushion to any driver who happens to crash into them. Soft walls were used in the 2002 Indianapolis 500 and were successful in reducing the impact on two drivers who hit the walls at speeds of almost 200 mph.[25]

As with other industries caught up in the information/Internet revolution of the late twentieth century, the sport industry includes many examples of process innovation. Process innovation occurs when coaches bring in new concepts regarding how games are played or trained for. For example, the use of computers has become elaborate during preparation for football games, eliminating much of the time-consuming gathering of video and organizing of notes. Brian Billick, head coach of the Baltimore Ravens, is known to be a real innovator in this area. His coaches can call up any play on the computer that either their own team or a competitor has run in previous games. They can retrieve all plays called for a certain down/yardage combination (e.g., third down and eight yards to gain) and what defense the other team played (e.g., a dime defense). Teams now hire video/computer personnel to document every play.

Organizations are always on the lookout for innovations that will help them hold their own against the competition and, hopefully, stay ahead of it. Successful companies know that innovation can be a powerful competitive advantage. The multimillion-dollar question that every one of them asks is, How do we develop a culture that stimulates creativity and innovation? **What product innovations have occurred in baseball in the last ten years?**

> **TIMEOUT**
> Describe an innovation from an organization you have worked for or played for. Was it a product innovation or a process innovation?
>
> _____
> _____
> _____
> _____
> _____
> _____

Getting to Innovation

Business's current answer to the multimillion-dollar question we asked above is the "flat" organization. As noted in Chapter 6, flat organizations limit their bureaucracies ("tall" organizations have superfluous layers of management, which slows them down and makes them less able to move quickly on opportunities); divide labor along generalist lines (not by specialties); and routinely use cross-functional teams to get the work done, to solve problems, and to identify opportunities. Flexibility is the name of their game. Systems are informal and authority is decentralized. Jobs are designed to be "richer" in content and in responsibility, and work teams based on sociotechnical systems.

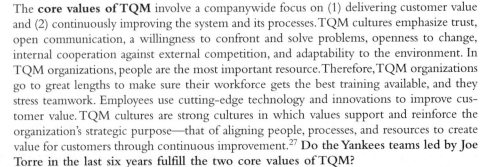

APPLYING
THE CONCEPT   *Getting to Innovation*

Check each statement that describes an innovative corporate culture.

_____ 11.   We have a very tall organization in our local soccer league.

_____ 12.   I tried for months to develop a stronger skate blade for hockey, but it didn't work. However, my boss thanked me profusely for trying.

_____ 13.   It drives me nuts when I'm given a task and my boss tells me *exactly* how to do the job, down to crossing the T's and dotting the I's. Why can't I meet the objective *my way* for a change?

_____ 14.   This athletic footwear company has a policy, procedure, and rule for everything under the sun.

_____ 15.   We strive mightily to make sure that our coaches' jobs are broad in scope and that they have a lot of autonomy to get the job done their way.

Large companies commonly create the small units so essential to innovation within the framework of their divisions. Innovative organizations commonly create separate systems for innovative groups, such as new venture units within the HR function. They also recruit creative people *and* they train their work force to think creatively (yes, this can be done!). Their reward system encourages people to think about new ways to do things and to think outside the box. Many organizations reward individuals and groups who come up with innovative ideas both financially and in other ways (recognition is important). Cash, prizes (such as trips), praise, and (always) recognition encourage people to explore the less traveled path.

Quality

High-performing organizations believe that innovation and quality go hand in hand. In fact, the characteristics that make a corporate culture innovative are essentially the same characteristics found in organizations that pursue total quality management (TQM). Outdoor sports and mail-order catalog firm L.L. Bean established a total quality and human resources (TQHR) department to lead the company's efforts to improve quality, efficiency, and customer service. The TQHR has saved the company millions of dollars annually from process improvements.[26]

5 LEARNING OUTCOME
State the core values of TQM.

core values of TQM
A companywide focus on (1) delivering customer value and (2) continuously improving the system and its processes.

The **core values of TQM** involve a companywide focus on (1) delivering customer value and (2) continuously improving the system and its processes. TQM cultures emphasize trust, open communication, a willingness to confront and solve problems, openness to change, internal cooperation against external competition, and adaptability to the environment. In TQM organizations, people are the most important resource. Therefore, TQM organizations go to great lengths to make sure their workforce gets the best training available, and they stress teamwork. Employees use cutting-edge technology and innovations to improve customer value. TQM cultures are strong cultures in which values support and reinforce the organization's strategic purpose—that of aligning people, processes, and resources to create value for customers through continuous improvement.[27] **Do the Yankees teams led by Joe Torre in the last six years fulfill the two core values of TQM?**

The late W. Edwards Deming developed 14 points that are pivotal in creating a TQM culture (see Exhibit 7–5). Deming's points improve people's job satisfaction, as well as product quality, productivity, effectiveness, and competitiveness.[28]

Exhibit 7–5   Deming's 14 Points for Creating the TQM Culture

1. Create constancy of purpose toward improvement of product and service, with the aim to become competitive, to stay in business, and to provide jobs.

2. Adopt a new philosophy. We are in a new economic age created by Japan. We can no longer live with commonly accepted styles of American management, nor with commonly accepted levels of delays, mistakes, or defective products.

3. Cease dependence on inspection to achieve quality. Eliminate the need for inspection on a mass basis by building quality into the product in the first place.

4. End the practice of awarding business on the basis of price tag. Instead, minimize total cost.

5. Improve constantly and forever the system of production and service to improve quality and productivity, and thus constantly decrease costs.

6. Institute training on the job.

7. Institute supervision. The aim of supervision should be to help people, machines, and gadgets to do a better job. Supervision of management is in need of overhaul, as well as supervision of production workers.

8. Drive out fear so that everyone may work effectively for the company.

9. Break down the barriers between departments. People in research, design, sales, and production must work as a team to foresee problems of production and use that may be encountered with the product or service.

10. Eliminate slogans, exhortations, and targets for the workforce that ask for zero defects and new levels of productivity. Such exhortations only create adversarial relationships. The bulk of the causes of low productivity belong to the system, and thus lie beyond the power of the workforce.

11. Eliminate work standards that prescribe numerical quotas for the day. Substitute aids and helpful supervision.

12. Remove the barriers that rob the hourly worker of his or her right to pride of workmanship. The responsibility of supervisors must be changed from sheer numbers to quality. Remove the barriers that rob people in management and engineering of their right to pride of workmanship. This means abolishment of the annual rating, or merit rating, and management by objectives.

13. Institute a vigorous program of education and retraining.

14. Put everybody in the company to work to accomplish the transformation.

Source: "Deming's 14 Points for Creating the TQM Culture" from *Out of the Crisis* by W. Edwards Deming, pp. 23–24. Reprinted by permission of The MIT Press.

THE LEARNING ORGANIZATION

6 **LEARNING OUTCOME**
Describe a learning organization.

The concept of the learning organization developed out of the systems view of organizations. In a learning organization, everyone understands that the world is changing rapidly, and that they must not only be aware of these changes, they must also adapt to the changes and, more important, be forces for change. The **learning organization** has a capacity to learn, adapt, and change as its environment changes to continuously increase customer value.

Organizations need to focus on building "corporate learning," which is a much broader idea than simply developing individual skills and knowledge. The learning organization appears to be an effective model for a fast-changing work environment. Learning organizations thus focus on developing good HR policies that will ensure that they can recruit, retain, and develop the best and the brightest. Learning organizations see that knowledge flows "horizontally"—this "grows" corporate learning as everyone in the organization participates in the transfer, sharing, and leveraging of individual knowledge and expertise. Trust is a crucial part of the learning culture because only by trusting one another can the workforce fully exploit its own knowledge and expertise. Creating a learning organization demands strong leadership, team-based structures, a commitment to empower its people, open information, strategies built through full employee participation, and a strong, adaptive culture.[29]

Peter Senge is often credited with popularizing the concept of learning organizations.[30] He cites an "event-management" example to demonstrate a learning situation. In an effort to control fan rowdiness at a football game, event planners stopped serving alcoholic beverages at half-time. Unfortunately, the rowdiness had started earlier in the game, and the gesture was too little and too late, and the rowdiness got out of hand. Later, in the cooler and calmer

TIMEOUT
Identify whether TQM values are operative in your organization or team. Give specific examples to support your conclusions.

_____

_____

_____

_____

_____

_____

learning organization
An organization that learns, adapts, and changes as its environment changes to continuously increase customer value.

morning after, a sobered stadium management looked at the problem more systematically, and realized that the real issue was excessive before-game drinking. Event staff decided to deny stadium access to every fan who was already obviously inebriated. Consequently, rowdiness subsided to manageable levels, and the event planners learned to look at the big picture before taking action.[31]

DIVERSITY

7 LEARNING OUTCOME
Explain how diversity can affect innovation and quality.

Today, diversity programs have replaced most equal employment opportunity (EEO) and affirmative action (AA) programs. EEO stressed treating all employees equally, whereas AA was created to correct the past exclusion of women and minorities from the workforce. AA established percentages and quotas. Although quotas are no longer used, many organizations actively recruit a diverse workforce, because they now realize that such a workforce responds better to problems. In other words, diversity is a good strategy in gaining competitive advantage. People with diverse backgrounds bring diverse experiences and viewpoints to bear on problems, and more creative solutions are often the result. Diversity programs thus help the individual, the group, and the organization. Championship Auto Racing Teams Inc. (CART), as one example, has implemented strong initiatives to promote diversity. CART seeks to bring members of the minority community and women into CART racing as drivers, engineers, mechanics, and administrative personnel. One of the most famous female drivers, Lyn St. James, ran CART seasons from 1992 to 1995, and she thinks that "every sanctioning body is recognizing the importance of diversity and representation; not equal representation, but just representation of something other than just white males," St. James observed. "Opening the doors to women is just one of the ways of demonstrating that."[32]

"Diversity is important to racing in the long haul. It can affect the sponsors we attract," St. James notes. "It can affect the fan base that we attract. So it makes good business sense. It's truly a reflection of what our sport is all about. So every sanctioning body, in my opinion, should be thinking about diversity and pay attention to it and be proactive."[33]

Danica Patrick is another female CART driver. She will be driving for Team Rahal in the 2002 to 2005 seasons. Bobby Rahal gave her a deal with the belief that she had the ability to qualify for and win an Indianapolis 500.[34]

Diversity and Culture

Effective organizational cultures value innovation, quality, *and* diversity. Quality and diversity have a special relationship. In order to improve the quality of their products and services, organizations must first understand and address the needs of their workforce, and this includes valuing diversity. Innovative organizations have long recognized the realities of the new workforce and how this affects efficiency and effectiveness.[35]

When we talk about diversity, we mean characteristics of individuals that shape their identities and their experiences in the workplace. *Diversity* refers to the degree of differences among members of a team or an organization. If you are questioning whether diversity is really all that important in the workplace and whether it will ever directly affect you, the answer is—no matter your race, religion, or ethnic background—*yes, yes,* and *yes.* By 2030 Caucasians will simply be the largest minority in a populace comprised of numerous minorities, but the most striking difference will be the burgeoning diversity of ethnic, racial, and religious groups. We will be a highly spiced, teeming stew of once-obscure (at least to Americans) peoples and religions, and we may finally become better versed in geography, if only to better understand our new neighbors and colleagues. The state of California is already less than 50 percent Caucasian, as are some major cities. In 2000, the foreign-born working and living in America were a record 28.3 million strong, with most of the immigrants coming from Latin America and Asia. Immigrants living in the United States in 2000 comprised some 10.4 percent of our population.[36] And—specific to our industry—the number of minorities playing, watching, and attending sports events continues to increase.

As you can well imagine, with statistics like these, diversity in the marketplace and in the workplace is a major concern that organizations are grappling with and endeavoring to turn to their advantage. People are diverse in many ways. As workers, we are commonly classified by our race/ethnicity, religion, gender, age, and "other." A few of the "other" categories include military status, sexual preference, lifestyles, socioeconomic class, and work styles. As both an employee and manager, you have a responsibility to deal with all people in an ethical and legal manner.

Valuing Diversity

When organizations value diversity, they focus on training everyone in their workforce—from all the different races and ethnicities, religions, genders, ages, abilities, and so forth—to function together effectively. The goal is a climate of dignity and trust. In such a climate and culture everyone wins. The organization wins because its workforce has a synergy that is fertile ground for creativity and innovation, and this can only help the organization in its ultimate goal of continuously improving customer value. The workforce wins because work becomes a place people can enjoy and value for its fairness and team spirit, and on which they can build a good life.

But to attain this ideal, organizations need to find ways to manage diversity. Why? Because with diversity come numerous belief systems, mores, and culturally acceptable and unacceptable ways of behaving that sometimes conflict. Think about something as "simple" as pointing your finger. This is OK in some cultures—that is, it is just a way to identify what you're referring to. But it is considered rude in other cultures and even obscene in some. Or take personal space—this varies from inches to feet around the world, and when it is violated, people get very uncomfortable. But we don't go around asking our colleagues, Am I in your personal space? Or take winning in a team sport—different cultures also handle winning and losing very differently. This is where diversity management and training come in. Don't look at diversity training and management as a pesky task to be merely tolerated—it is an opportunity to understand our world better and an opportunity for personal, professional, and organizational growth.

As shown in Exhibit 7–6, a solid diversity management program requires four building blocks. The first, and most important, building block is the support and commitment of *top management*. People throughout the organization look to management to set the example. If top management is committed and actively supports diversity programs, others will follow its lead—hence the term *diversity leadership,* which refers to the leadership that top-level managers provide in managing diversity. Diversity leaders and their teams develop the *diversity policies and practices* that the entire organization commits to. The final building block is, of course, *diversity training.* The Skill-Builder on diversity training at the end of the chapter will help examine your values and belief system about working in a diverse workforce.

Gender Diversity

Before we discuss gender issues, complete the Self Assessment to determine your attitude toward women in the workplace. (Yes, you female readers should complete this assessment also; you may be surprised at what you learn!)

Issues of gender equity have a special history in the sport industry. Perhaps most of you take for granted that female sports writers should routinely interview male athletes and that sports programs for females in high school and college should receive equal funding as those

Exhibit 7–6 Managing Diversity

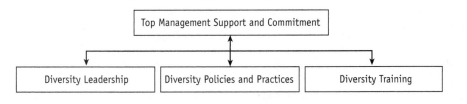

SELF ASSESSMENT

Women at Work

For each statement, select the response that best describes your belief. (Be honest!)

5—Strongly agree   4—Agree   3—Not sure

2—Disagree   1—Strongly disagree

_____ 1. Women lack the education necessary to get ahead.

_____ 2. Women entering the workforce has caused rising unemployment among men.

_____ 3. Women are not strong enough or emotionally stable enough to succeed in high-pressure jobs.

_____ 4. Women are too emotional to be effective managers.

_____ 5. Women managers have difficulty in situations calling for quick and precise decisions.

_____ 6. Women work to earn extra money rather than to support a family.

_____ 7. Women are out of work more often than men.

_____ 8. Women quit work or take long maternity leaves when they have children.

_____ 9. Women have a lower commitment to work than men.

_____ 10. Women lack the motivation to get ahead.

_____ **Total**

To determine whether you have a positive or negative attitude, total your score and place it on the following continuum.

10	20	30	40	50
Positive attitude			Negative attitude	

Each statement represents a commonly held attitude about women in the workplace. However, research has been shown all of these statements to be false. Such statements stereotype women unfairly and create glass ceilings.

---

for males, but this hasn't always been so. In 1972, a law with wide ramifications for the sport industry, Title IX of the Amendments to the Higher Education Act, was passed. Title IX requires equal access to education, including athletics, for women. Since that time the number of women playing on college teams has increased from 32,000 to about 163,000.[37] Why does this have ramifications for the sport industry? For one thing, because all these female athletes are current (and future) consumers of sporting equipment, attendees of—and participants in—sporting events, and current and potential athletic directors, sport writers, and sport business executives.

Complying with Title IX has led to the reduction of some men's programs to augment financial support for new women's teams. For instance, UCLA added varsity women's crew not only to provide sporting opportunities, but also to comply with one of the key requirements of Title IX, "proportionality." A landmark court decision in 1995 involving Brown University's athletic program defined proportionality as ensuring that the percentage of women in a school's athlete population matches the percentage of women in the overall student body.[38] Between 1981 and 1999, more than 400 collegiate men's teams were dropped. 171 wrestling programs and 84 men's tennis teams were dropped.[39]

Do women get equal treatment at work today? According to the Census Bureau, in spite of the Equal Pay Act, which requires equal pay for the same job, women's average hourly earnings are still only 70 percent of men's. Although organizations have made progress in promoting minorities and women, the glass ceiling is still a fact of business life.[40] For example, women by and large have been limited to coaching other women, whereas men commonly coach both men and women. Men coach women's NCAA basketball and the WNBA, but women do not tend to coach men's NCAA basketball or the NBA. Women are also more commonly sexually harassed than men at work. *Sexual harassment* is any unwelcome behavior of a sexual nature.

MENTORING. A word about mentoring is pertinent here. *Mentors* are highly skilled people who prepare promising employees for advancement; they function at every level of the organization.[41] Mentoring enhances management skills, encourages diversity, and improves productivity.[42] Mentoring programs also help women and minorities break the "glass ceiling"

APPLYING THE CONCEPT   *Sexual Harassment*

Check each behavior that would be considered sexual harassment in the workplace.

_____ 16. Ted tells Claire she is sexy and he'd like to take her out on a date.

_____ 17. Sue tells Josh he'll have to go to a motel with her if he wants that promotion.

_____ 18. Joel and Kathy have pictures of nude men and women in their office cubicles where everyone walking by can see them.

_____ 19. For the third time, after being politely told not to, Pat tells Chris an explicitly sexual joke.

_____ 20. Ray puts his hand on his secretary Lisa's shoulder as he talks to her.

(the invisible barrier that prevents minorities and women from advancing beyond a certain level). Skilled mentors can help you develop expertise, poise, confidence, and business savvy. It therefore behooves you to ask about mentoring opportunities at work. If your organization doesn't have a mentoring program, seek out a person whose professional attributes you admire and would like to emulate and ask him or her to mentor you.

ORGANIZATIONAL DEVELOPMENT

Now that you know something about the inner workings of change, it's time to examine organizational development, which is commonly used to manage change. **Organizational development (OD)** is the ongoing planned change process that organizations use to improve performance. HR departments (discussed in Chapter 8) are usually responsible for OD. *Change agents* are people selected by HR management to be responsible for the OD program. Change agents may be members of the organization or hired consultants.[43]

organizational development (OD)
The ongoing planned change process that organizations use to improve performance.

Change Models

LEWIN'S CHANGE MODEL. In the early 1950s, Kurt Lewin developed a model that is still used today to change people's behavior and attitudes.[44] Lewin's change model consists of three steps (see Exhibit 7–7).

1. *Unfreezing* lessens the strength of the forces that maintain the status quo. Organizations often accomplish unfreezing by introducing information that shows discrepancies between desired performance and actual performance.

2. In *moving,* behavior begins to shift to the desired one. That is, people begin to learn the new desired behavior, and they also begin to embrace the values and attitudes that go with it. Shifts in strategy, structure, technology, and people and/or culture may be needed here to attain the desired change.

3. In *refreezing,* the desired change becomes the new status quo. Reinforcement and support for the new behavior are often required for refreezing to take place.

A COMPREHENSIVE CHANGE MODEL. Today's rapidly evolving business environment has necessitated expanding Lewin's original model. Using the expanded model (also listed in Exhibit 7–7) as a change agent, you would

1. *Recognize the need for change.* Clearly state the change needed—set objectives. Don't forget the systems effects—that is, how will the proposed change affect other areas of the organization?

2. *Identify possible resistance to the change and plan how to overcome it.* Use the resistance matrix given in Model 7–1, then follow the guidelines given in Exhibit 7–7.

Exhibit 7–7   Two Change Models

LEWIN'S CHANGE MODEL	A COMPREHENSIVE CHANGE MODEL
Step 1. Unfreezing.	*Step 1.* Recognize the need for change.
Step 2. Moving.	*Step 2.* Identify possible resistance to the change and plan how to overcome it.
Step 3. Refreezing.	*Step 3.* Plan the change interventions.
	Step 4. Implement the change interventions.
	Step 5. Control the change.

3. *Plan the change interventions.* A careful diagnosis of the problem (step 2) often indicates the appropriate intervention(s). Interventions are discussed below.

4. *Implement the interventions.* Change agents oversee the interventions (from start to finish) to bring about the desired change.

5. *Control the change.* Follow up to ensure that the change is implemented and maintained. Make sure the objective is met. If not, take corrective action.

Change Interventions

OD interventions
Specific actions taken to implement specific changes.

OD interventions are specific actions taken to implement specific changes. What follows is a brief survey of common interventions (see Exhibit 7–8).

Most interventions include some form of *training and development*. Training is the process of developing skills, behaviors, and attitudes that will enhance performance. Baseball players, for example, spend the month of March in Florida and Arizona in spring training. During this time teams work on developing hitting, pitching, and fielding skills. (We examine training and development in more detail in Chapter 8.)

8   LEARNING OUTCOME
State how forcefield analysis and survey feedback differ.

Exhibit 7–8   OD Interventions

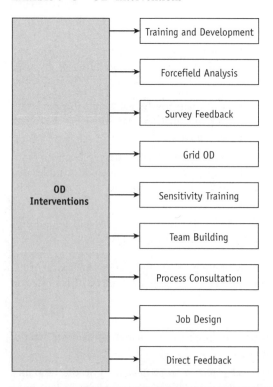

FORCEFIELD ANALYSIS. Particularly useful for small-group (4 to 18 members) problem solving, **forcefield analysis** first assesses current performance, then identifies the forces hindering change and those driving it. The result is a diagram that gives an overview of the situation. The process begins with an appraisal of current performance—this assessment appears in the middle of the diagram. Forces that are holding back performance (hindering it) are listed at the top or left side of the diagram. The forces driving change are listed at the bottom or right side. Diagramming the situation clarifies thinking and helps change agents develop strategies. The basic thrust is to find ways to strengthen the driving forces and simultaneously diminish the hindering forces. The diagram often points the way to a promising strategy. As an example, we created a forcefield diagram (see Exhibit 7–9) for a hypothetical footwear company, which has been losing market share. Our analysis indicates that the footwear company should develop interventions that focus on production and sales forecasting. **Draw a forcefield analysis for the New York Yankees at the time Joe Torre took over as coach of the team.**

SURVEY FEEDBACK. One of the oldest and most popular OD techniques, **survey feedback** uses a questionnaire to gather data to use as the basis for change. Survey feedback is commonly used in step 1 of the change model. Different change agents use slightly different approaches; however, a typical survey feedback includes six steps:

1. Management and the change agent do preliminary planning to develop an appropriate survey questionnaire.
2. The questionnaire is administered to all members of the organization or unit.
3. The survey data is analyzed to uncover problem areas for improvement.
4. The change agent presents the results to management.
5. Managers evaluate the feedback and discuss the results with their teams.
6. Corrective intervention action plans are developed and implemented.

GRID OD. Robert Blake and Jane Mouton have developed a "packaged" approach to OD.[45] *Grid OD* is a six-phase program, with a standardized format, procedures, and fixed goals, designed to improve management and organizational effectiveness. The six phases are as follows:

- *Phase 1: Training.* Teams of five to nine managers, ideally from different functional areas, are formed. During a week-long seminar, team members assess their own leadership style by determining their position on the grid. (You will learn about the grid in

forcefield analysis
Assesses current performance, then identifies the forces hindering change and those driving it.

survey feedback
An OD technique that uses a questionnaire to gather data to use as the basis for change.

Exhibit 7–9   Forcefield Diagram for a Footwear Company

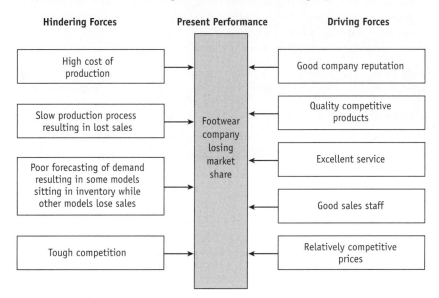

Chapter 13.) They work at becoming "9,9 managers" (who show high concern for production and people) by developing skills in team building, communication, and problem solving.

- *Phase 2: Team development.* Managers return to the job and use their new skills as 9,9 managers.
- *Phase 3: Intergroup development.* Work groups improve their ability to cooperate and coordinate their efforts. This is fostered by joint problem-solving activities.
- *Phase 4: Organizational goal setting.* Management develops a model for the overall organization that it will strive to achieve.
- *Phase 5: Goal attainment.* The changes needed to become the model organization are determined and implemented.
- *Phase 6: Stabilization.* The first five phases are evaluated to determine whether implementation is working, to stabilize positive changes, and to identify areas that need improving or altering.

SENSITIVITY TRAINING. Sensitivity training includes a training group (a "T-group") of 10 to 15 people. The training sessions have no agenda. People learn about how their behavior affects others and how others' behavior affects their own. Understanding each other's styles and qualities help people get along better.[46] The popularity of T-groups peaked in the 1970s as organizations questioned the on-the-job value gained through the training. Although T-groups are still used, they have largely been replaced by team building and process consultation.

9 LEARNING OUTCOME
Explain the difference between team building and process consultation.

team building
Helps work groups increase structural and team dynamics performance.

TEAM BUILDING. Team building is probably the most widely used OD technique today, and its popularity will continue to grow as more companies use teams. **Team building** helps work groups increase structural and team dynamics performance. It is a powerful tool, and crucial as well, because team effectiveness and ineffectiveness, both within teams and between teams, affect the results of the entire organization. Team building can be used as a comprehensive program, in which top executives first go through the program, then go through it with their middle managers, who then go through it with their groups, and so on throughout the organization. However, team building is more widely used as a "pinpoint" exercise by new or existing groups that need to improve effectiveness.

Team-building activities are quite diverse—indeed, they use many techniques developed in coaching sports. Teams may play in a golf tournament, play a single game of baseball or rugby, or participate in an "autocross" competition in which teams are timed as they drive cars through obstacle-course drills until a winning team is determined.[47,48] The activities are tied to classroom instruction on the principles of effective team building.

Team-building goals. The goals of team-building programs also vary considerably, depending on the group's needs and the change agent's skills. Typical goals include the following:

- To clarify the objectives of the team and the responsibilities of each team member.
- To identify problems preventing the team from accomplishing its objectives.
- To develop team problem-solving, decision-making, objective-setting, and planning skills.
- To develop open, honest working relationships based on trust and an understanding of group members.

The team-building program. Team-building agendas and the length of time vary with team needs and the change agent's skills. Typical programs go through six stages:

1. *Climate building and goals.* The program begins with change agents establishing a climate of trust, support, and openness. Change agents discuss the program's purpose and goals based on data gathered prior to the program. Team members learn more about each other and share what they would like to accomplish through team building.

APPLYING THE CONCEPT   *OD Interventions*

Identify the appropriate OD intervention(s) for each situation.

a. training and development
b. forcefield analysis
c. survey feedback
d. grid OD
e. sensitivity training

f. team building
g. process consultation
h. job design
i. direct feedback

_____ 21. We're not winning, our fans are leaving in droves, our costs are skyrocketing, the voters are unhappy about funding expensive stadiums that are often empty at games, and the players are about to go on strike.

_____ 22. Everyone can see that team morale is at an all-time low—but why?

_____ 23. We need a new scouting system; our present one isn't delivering the goods.

_____ 24. We've got a cutting-edge fitness machine and no one to run it.

_____ 25. We've got a lot of prima donna star athletes who are more interested in publicity than in winning.

---

2. *Structure and team dynamics evaluation.* Team building endeavors to improve both how the work is done (structure) and how team members work together as they do the work (team dynamics). The team evaluates its strengths and weaknesses in both areas.

3. *Problem identification.* Change agents use interviews and/or feedback surveys to help the team identify first its strengths, then its weaknesses (areas it would like to improve). The team next lists several areas where it can improve. Then it prioritizes them in terms of how improving each area will help the team improve performance.

4. *Problem solving.* The team takes the top priority and develops a solution. It then moves down the priorities in order of importance. Forcefield analysis may be used here for problem solving.

5. *Training.* Team building often includes some form of training that addresses the problem(s) facing the group.

6. *Closure.* The program ends with a summarization of what has been accomplished. Team members commit to specific improvements in performance. Follow-up responsibilities are assigned, and a future meeting is set to evaluate results. **Discuss a part of the team-building program that Joe Torre uses successfully.**

PROCESS CONSULTATION. Process consultation is often used in the second stage of team building, but it is also commonly used as a separate, more narrowly focused intervention. **Process consultation** improves team dynamics. Whereas team building frequently focuses on how to get the job itself done, process consultation focuses on how people interact as they get the job done. Team dynamics (or processes) are about how the team communicates, allocates work, resolves conflict, and handles leadership, and how it solves problems and makes decisions. Change agents observe team members as they work in order to give them feedback on the operative team processes. Under the change agent's guidance, the team discusses its processes and how to improve them. Training to improve group processes may also be conducted at this point. The ultimate objective is to train the group so that process consultation becomes an ongoing team activity. (We will examine team dynamics in more detail in Chapter 10.)

JOB DESIGN. Job design, discussed in Chapter 6, is also an OD intervention. Job enrichment is the commonly used intervention.

TIME**OUT**

Give an example of an OD intervention used recently in your firm or team. Was it effective? If so, why? If not, why not?

_____
_____
_____
_____
_____
_____

process consultation
An OD intervention designed to improve team dynamics.

DIRECT FEEDBACK. Situations occur, particularly with rapidly changing technologies, where a quick solution that is outside the company's core expertise is required. In these situations, outside consultants are often brought in to act as change agents and to recommend action directly.

CHAPTER SUMMARY

1. Identify the driving forces behind change.

The forces for change come from the external and internal environment. Changes in economic, social, demographic, and technological forces require organizations to adapt to their environments.

2. Describe the four variables of change.

Change occurs in strategies, structures, technologies, and people.

3. Differentiate between facts, beliefs, and values.

Facts are provable statements that identify reality. Beliefs cannot be proven because they are subjective, not objective. Values address what is important to people.

4. Explain how the three components of organizational culture relate.

The three components are (1) behavior (the actions people take), (2) values (the way we think we ought to behave) and beliefs (if-then statements), and (3) assumptions (those values and beliefs that are so deeply ingrained that we never question their truth). The values, beliefs, and assumptions of an organization guide its decision making and behavior.

5. State the core values of TQM.

The core values of TQM involve a companywide focus on (1) delivering customer value and (2) continuously improving the system and its processes.

6. Describe a learning organization.

Learning organizations consciously create a culture that has the capacity to learn, adapt, and change with its environments in order to continuously increase customer value.

7. Explain how diversity can affect innovation and quality.

A diverse workforce can be more innovative and also more effective at achieving quality.

8. State how forcefield analysis and survey feedback differ.

Forcefield analysis is used by small groups to diagnose and solve specific problems. Survey feedback uses questionnaires with large groups to identify problems; the group does not work together to solve the problem. Forcefield analysis is used to solve problems identified through survey feedback.

9. Explain the difference between team building and process consultation.

Team building is broader in scope than process consultation. Team building improves both how the work is done and how team members work together as they do the work (team dynamics). Process consultation improves team dynamics.

10. Define the key terms discussed in the text.

Fill in the missing key terms from memory, or match the key terms from the list in the margin with their definitions below.

The _____ are strategy, structure, technology, and people.

_____ are formal systems for collecting, processing, and disseminating information that aids managers in decision making.

The _____ are denial, resistance, exploration, and commitment.

Key Terms

components of culture

core values of TQM

forcefield analysis

learning organization

management
 information systems
 (MISs)

OD interventions

organizational culture

organizational
 development (OD)

process consultation

stages in the change
 process

survey feedback

team building

variables of change

_____ consists of shared values, beliefs, and standards for acceptable behavior.

The three _____ are behavior, values and beliefs, and assumptions.

The _____ are a companywide focus on (1) delivering customer value and (2) continuously improving the system and its processes.

A _____ learns, adapts, and changes as its environment changes to continuously increase customer value.

_____ is the ongoing planned change process that organizations use to improve performance.

_____ are specific actions taken to implement specific changes.

_____ assesses current performance, then identifies the forces hindering change and those driving it.

_____ is an OD technique that uses a questionnaire to gather data to use as the basis for change.

_____ helps work groups increase structural and team dynamics performance.

_____ is an OD intervention designed to improve team dynamics.

REVIEW AND DISCUSSION

1. How do the management functions relate to change?
2. How does the systems effect relate to the four variables of change?
3. List the four stages in the change process.
4. Which of the five reasons for resisting change do you believe is most common?
5. Which of the six ways to overcome resistance to change do you believe is the most important?
6. Select two sport organizations and discuss the differences between their cultures.
7. Discuss how the two types of innovations could be used by a manufacturer of golf balls.
8. Discuss how you would use team building to improve the effectiveness of a team you are playing on or have played for.
9. Do you agree with the core values of TQM? If not, how would you change them?
10. Which change model do you prefer? Why?

CASE

The Changing Job of ADs

Until the late 1970s the job of a college athletic director (AD) was an easy one. In the old days, colleges often gave the AD job to the football coach when he retired. Playing golf with alumni was a big part of the job then.[49] The times, how they change . . .

To say that ADs have many more job responsibilities today is a bit of an understatement. ADs supervise coaching staff and teams, oversee million-dollar budgets and requisitions, work with coaches to schedule events and travel itineraries, help plan facilities, issue contracts for home contests, watchdog player eligibility, maintain records of players and insurance coverage for all athletes, manage crowd behavior at events (are you tired yet?), fund-raise, attend booster club meetings, supervise the sports information director, maintain marketing publications, attend professional meetings, develop staff—oh, and they also conduct weekly meetings to monitor progress![50]

The AD job is just one of many positions in large collegiate organizations—college sports are big business today. The AD may have an associate director, sport information director, academic advisors, ticket managers, and event managers. For instance, at Ohio State, Andy Geiger oversees a department of 105 coaches, 156 full-time staff, 720 undergraduate part-time workers, 1400 seasonal employees, and more than 900 varsity athletes. His major constraint (besides human ability)—the National Collegiate Athletic Association rulebook. Ohio State must comply with these rules or face sanctions.[51]

AD jobs are also more complicated because external factors are changing so rapidly. ADs must keep up with legal issues such as Title IX, which (as we noted earlier) requires equal access to education (including athletics) for women. Recruiting athletes is increasingly competitive because more colleges actively pursue athletes as they endeavor to build winning teams. And, unfortunately, athletes (like the wider population) face a wide variety of social problems such as AIDS, drug addiction, and sexual harassment.

Fund raising is a constant endeavor—athletic operations are extremely expensive. The athletic department at Ohio State is expected to operate like a business and at least break even. Geiger uses the sales and marketing strategies of professional sports: seat licenses, luxury boxes, corporate sponsorships, new arenas, and high ticket prices. In fiscal year 2001, Ohio State's athletic department earned a profit of $3.51 million on revenues of $53.4 million, 47 percent of which came from its football team.[52]

Would you like to be an athletic director? An assistant AD? A coach? A sports information director? Visit http://www.ohiostatebuckeyes.com/school-bio/osu-staff-directory.html for information on jobs in Ohio State's athletic department.

CASE QUESTIONS

Select the best alternative for the following questions. Be sure you are able to explain your answers.

1. The forces for change in an AD's job came from which environment?
   a. external
   b. internal
   c. both

2. The change variable in AD jobs has primarily been what type of change?
   a. strategy
   b. structure
   c. technology
   d. people

3. ADs are not obliged to provide equality for women's sports.
   a. true   b. false

4. Part of the reason for change in an AD's job responsibilities was to develop the athletic department to be more cost effective.
   a. true   b. false

5. The primary way to overcome resistance to change as an AD is by
   a. developing a trust climate
   b. planning
   c. stating why change is needed and how it will affect employees
   d. creating a win-win situation
   e. involving employees
   f. providing support
   g. all of the above

6. An AD's job should be organized around the principles of TQM.
   a. true   b. false

7. Ohio State has learned to use professional marketing techniques such as corporate sponsorships to keep up with increasing costs in running an athletic department.

    a. true   b. false

8. ADs perform which of the following job responsibilities?

    a. helping plan facilities

    b. watchdogging player eligibility

    c. scheduling events

    d. organizing travel itineraries

    e. all of the above

9. Managing diversity is an important part of an AD's job.

    a. true   b. false

10. ADs are in a position to mentor many employees.

    a. true   b. false

11. In what sorts of situations do you think ADs use team-building skills?

VIDEO CASE

Innovation: Ping Out-Thinks the Competition

Introduction

Karsten Manufacturing, located in Phoenix, Arizona, was founded in 1959 by Karsten Solheim. With its 900 employees in 35 buildings on 30 acres, Karsten Manufacturing produces Ping golf clubs. It is the largest manufacturer of putters in the world and has shifted golf club design in new directions.

Focus Your Attention

To get the most out of viewing this Ping video, think about the following issues: the impact of innovation on an organization, the importance of a unifying organizational culture, and the process of continuous improvement. Then answer the following questions after viewing the video:

1. What is innovation? How has Karsten Manufacturing used innovation in its design and production of Ping golf clubs?

2. What is organizational culture? Name several components of Karsten Manufacturing's organizational culture.

EXERCISES

Skill-Builder: Identifying Resistance to Change

Objective:

- To develop your ability to identify resistance to change.

Preparation:

Below are ten statements made by people asked to make a change. Identify the source and focus of their resistance using the matrix given in Model 7–1. (Because it is difficult to identify intensity of resistance "on paper," skip the intensity factor in this Skill-Builder. However, when you deal with people on the job, *don't* skip this step, as it is often very important.) Select the number (1–9) of the resistance matrix box that best describes their response.

_____ 1. "But we've *never* done the butterfly stroke that way before—can't we just do it the way we've been doing it?"

_____ 2. Star tennis player Jill is asked by her coach to try Louise as her doubles partner. Jill's response: "Come on, Coach, Louise is a *lousy* player. Betty is much better; *please* don't break us up."

_____ **3.** Team manager Winny tells Mike to stop letting everyone on the team take advantage of him by sticking him with extra work. Mike's response: "But I want the team to like me—if I don't help people they might not like me."

_____ **4.** "I can't learn to use the new computer—I'm just a jock, and I'm not smart enough."

_____ **5.** Star defensive back Chris is asked to help develop a rookie player: "Do I have to? I broke in our last rookie, Wayne. He and I are getting along _really_ well."

_____ **6.** Rookie Tina has an idea for a new soccer play. Coach Chuck quickly dismisses it—"Learning this new play would be a waste of time; our current plays are fine."

_____ **7.** Diane organizes ticket sales. Her manager, Sue, directs her to take on a new responsibility—arranging the softball team's travel itinerary. Diane's response: "The job I'm doing now is more important."

_____ **8.** "I don't want to play with that team. It has the lowest performance record in the league."

_____ **9.** "Keep me in the kitchen part of the sports bar. I can't work the bar because drinking is against my religion."

_____ **10.** "But I don't see why I have to stop showing pictures of racing car accidents to help sell tickets to our racing events. I don't think it's unethical. Our competitors do it."

In-Class Application

Complete the skill-building preparation noted above before class.

Choose one (10–30 minutes):
- Break into groups of three to five members, and present your findings to the above questions. Try to reach a group consensus on the most probable resistance for each statement.
- Informal, whole-class discussion of student findings

Wrap-up:
Take a few minutes and write down your answers to the following questions:

- What did I learn from this experience?

_____

_____

_____

_____

- How will I use this knowledge in the future?

_____

_____

_____

_____

As a class, discuss student responses.

Skill-Builder: Diversity Training

Objective:
- To increase your appreciation for the value of diversity and your understanding for what it feels like to be different.

Preparation:

Fill in the blanks. (*Note:* You can elect not to share your responses in your group.)

Race and Ethnicity

1. My race: _____. My ethnicity(ies): _____.

2. My name is _____. It is significant because it means _____ and/or I was named after _____.

3. One positive thing about being a _____ is _____.

4. One difficult or challenging thing about being a _____ is _____.

Religion

5. My religion: _____.

6. One positive thing about being a _____ is _____.

7. One difficult or challenging thing about being a _____ is _____.

Gender

8. My gender: _____.

9. One positive thing about being a _____ is _____.

10. One difficult or challenging thing about being a _____ is _____.

11. Men and women are primarily different in _____ because _____.

Age

12. My age: _____.

13. One positive thing about being my age is _____.

14. One difficult or challenging thing about being my age is _____.

Ability

15. I am of _____ (high, medium, low) ability in college and on the job. I do/don't have a disability.

16. One positive thing about being of _____ ability is _____.

17. One difficult or challenging thing about being of _____ ability is _____.

Other

18. One major way in which I'm different from other people is _____.

19. One positive thing about being different in this way is _____.

20. One difficult or challenging thing about being different in this way is _____.

Prejudice, Stereotypes, Discrimination

21. Describe ways in which you have been pre-judged, stereotyped, or discriminated against.

_____

_____

_____

_____

_____

In-Class Application

Complete the skill-building preparation noted above before class.

Do each activity (10–30 minutes for each):

- Break into groups of three to five members. Strive to make your group as diverse as possible. If necessary, your instructor will reassign students to improve group diversity. Present your findings to the above questions. Select a spokesperson to present one or two of your group's best examples for item 21 to the class.
- In your group, role-play the stereotyping situation assigned to you by your instructor. Discuss how it feels to be on the receiving end of stereotyping.
- Informal, whole-class discussion of student findings

Wrap-up:

Take a few minutes and write down your answers to the following questions:

- What did I learn from this experience?

_____

_____

_____

_____

- How will I use this knowledge in the future?

_____

_____

_____

_____

As a class, discuss student responses.

Internet Skills: The Impact of the Equal Pay Act and Title VII

Objective:

- To understand the enforcement guidance on sex discrimination in the compensation of coaches in educational institutions.

Preparation (20 minutes):

Visit http://www.eeoc.gov. Use the search engine to find articles about "coaching." Click on the article titled "Enforcement Guidance on Sex Discrimination in the Compensation

of Sports Coaches in Educational Institutions" (notice number 915.002; date 10/29/97).
Use this EEOC article to answer the following questions.

1. What two laws remove sex discrimination in the compensation of sport coaches?

   _____

   _____

2. An NCAA study found that men's sports receive what percent of head coach
   salaries and what percent of assistant coach salaries in Division I institutions?

   _____

   _____

3. A U.S. General Accounting Office (GAO) survey found that head coaches for
   women's basketball earn what percentage of the average additional benefits
   earned by head coaches for men's basketball?

   _____

   List several of these benefits.

   _____

   _____

   _____

   _____

   _____

   _____

4. Women have by and large been limited to coaching women, whereas men coach
   both men and women. What percentage of the head coaches of women's
   intercollegiate teams at NCAA schools were females in 1996?

   _____

   What percentage of the head coaches of men's teams were females?

   _____

5. Review one of the examples cited on the web site and give your opinion of
   whether discrimination exists.

   _____

   _____

   _____

   _____

   _____

   _____

8 Human Resources Management

Learning Outcomes

After studying this chapter, you should be able to:

1. Describe the four parts of HR management.
2. Differentiate between a job description and a job specification and explain why they are needed.
3. State the two parts of attracting employees.
4. Explain how hypothetical questions and probing questions differ.
5. State the purposes of orientation and training and development.
6. Describe job instructional training.
7. Define the two types of performance appraisals.
8. Explain the concept, "You get what you reward."
9. State the two major components of compensation.
10. Describe how job analyses and job evaluations are used.
11. Give a brief history of labor relations in Major League Baseball.
12. Define the following key terms (in order of appearance in the chapter):

- human resources management
- bona fide occupational qualification (BFOQ)
- strategic human resources planning
- job description
- job specifications
- recruiting
- selection
- assessment centers
- orientation
- training
- development
- vestibule training
- performance appraisal
- compensation
- job evaluation
- comparable worth
- labor relations
- salary caps
- reserve clause
- free agent
- collective bargaining
- strike
- lockout

REVIEWING THEIR GAME PLAN

Cap Management in the NFL

Ever heard of **"CAPTOLOGY"**? Ask any NFL manager what it means—they know, because it is one of the most important "games" they play as they endeavor to create winning teams. Captology is the art/science/game that NFL team managers get good at, or their team loses. Unlike in most pro sports, NFL teams have salary caps—a dollar figure set by the league beyond which the team cannot go. This means that each year each team faces difficult decisions on which players it will keep and which ones it will let go. Captology is an art, the art of human resource (HR) management; it's a science, of data collection and statistics and probabilities; and it's

a game played for big stakes. Managers must balance each player's talent against the player's going rate. "So-and-so may win games, but can the team afford him given he is getting old, we've got an up-and-comer who is looking good in his spot and goes for less, *and* we really need to spend our resource dollars on strengthening our defense?"

The salary cap for the 2001– 2002 NFL season was $67.4 million. That is, each team could spend up to this amount for its total roster, but no more. A complicated process of dividing television revenue, merchandising, and gate receipts for all teams goes into choosing this number. One key area is the signing bonus, which can be prorated over the life of the player's contract. Thus, a player receiving a $12 million bonus gets his money up front, but for four years thereafter the team must count $3 million of his bonus toward their cap. However, if the player retires or is traded in the middle of the four-year period, the remainder of the signing bonus goes against the team's cap all at once.[1]

Now you know why NFL management signs players for what appear to be such huge signing bonuses. Players benefit—the signing bonus is guaranteed money, in fact their *only* guaranteed money (after all, they can get a career-ending injury in the first game). Managers benefit also—if they release players before their contracts expire, only the remaining bonus money counts toward the cap. Salary caps cause other results too. Older high-priced players may have had a great season the year before, but teams have to release some of them every year, as they look for the winning balance between high-priced known quantities and lower-priced unknowns who show promise.

For current information on how NFL teams live with the salary cap, visit http://www.nfl. com and http://www.askthecommish.com. (For ideas on using the Internet, see Appendix B.)

INTERNET RESOURCES

http://www.bls.gov/oco/ocos251.htm *The "Athletes, Coaches, Umpires, and Related Workers" page of the* Occupational Outlook Handbook *offers a comprehensive survey of what it takes to work in the sport industry. Read about working conditions, employment opportunities, required training, job outlook, and earnings potential. Click the* Management *link on the left side of the page to explore various careers in the field of management.*

http://www.bls.gov/opub/cwc/1998/Spring/art1full.pdf *For a nice overview of how salary caps function in the NBA and NFL, read the article found at this site. "Salary Caps in Professional Team Sports" also discusses the debate raging in the MLB and NHL over this issue, compares labor relations models among the four sports, and analyzes the interaction between salary caps and free agency. Note that the details of labor relations change frequently—this article is intended to help you understand the general issues involved with salary caps.*

http://www.starvingartistslaw.com/industries/sports.htm *Here is the Sports Law page of StarvingArtistsLaw.com. Scroll down to the Labor Relations in Sports heading, where* *you'll find links to several interesting articles from* Sports and Entertainment Law Journal. *Topics include collective bargaining in the NFL and labor troubles in the MLB, among more general scholarly articles on labor and sports.*

http://www4.hr.com/HRcom/index.cfm *Sign up for a free membership to HR.com to access the many useful features of this human resources clearinghouse—current HR news, interviews, research reports, advice, online discussion groups, a career center, and even HR-themed cartoons and horoscopes.*

DEVELOPING YOUR SKILLS   Organizations without good human resources fail—it's as simple as that—and organizations without good HR systems in place or HR staff to man them don't have an easy time either. Human resources is a vast subject and getting more complex every day. This field is so complicated that HR majors often specialize in labor issues, liability issues, developing benefits packages, employee training and development, and so on. In this chapter we give you a mere taste of this key maker and breaker of organizations. Managing your human resources will call into play every skill you have—your people skills, your communication skills, as well as your conceptual and decision-making skills. It's a challenging game, but one well worth playing to win.

THE HR MANAGEMENT PROCESS

1 **LEARNING OUTCOME**
Describe the four parts of HR management.

human resources management
Planning, attracting, developing, and retaining employees.

Managing human resources is an ongoing process that successful organizations pay close attention to. Every organization, after all, is only as good as its workforce. **Human resources management** (also known as staffing) consists of planning, attracting, developing, and retaining employees. Exhibit 8–1 gives an overview of this four-part process; the arrows indicate how the parts mesh to create a systems effect. For example, how an organization compensates its employees affects the caliber of people it will attract, labor relations affect planning, job analysis affects training, and so on. Irene Tanji was with the HR department of the Los Angeles Dodgers from 1958 to 1998. She started as a secretary and worked her way up through the ranks to become Director of Human Resources. Tanji believes that pro sports HR people face a variety of challenges in the present business environment. Issues include educating young players regarding their benefits and providing services for ethnically diverse players.[2]

THE LEGAL ENVIRONMENT

The external environment, especially the competitive environment and the legal environment, affects human resources practices in significant ways. When organizations don't match the pay and benefits of their competitors, good people can leave in search of better opportunities elsewhere. Neither are organizations completely free to hire whomever they want. The HR department must see that the organization complies with the law.[3] Irene Tanji believes the main challenge that HR departments face is keeping up with legal issues. She includes updating benefits; monitoring new medical insurance regulations, and administering the Dodgers' 401k retirement plan as complex issues with serious legal implications.[4]

Two laws, Equal Employment Opportunity (EEO) and executive orders on Affirmative Action (AA), have significant implications for hiring practices. EEO, a 1972 amendment to the Civil Rights Act of 1964, prohibits discrimination in the workplace on the basis of sex, religion, race or color, or national origin and applies to virtually all private and public organizations that employ 15 or more employees. Who is considered a minority by the EEO? Just about anyone who is not a white male, of European heritage, or adequately educated. Thus, Hispanics, Asians, African-Americans, Native Americans, and Alaskan natives are

Exhibit 8–1 Managing Human Resources

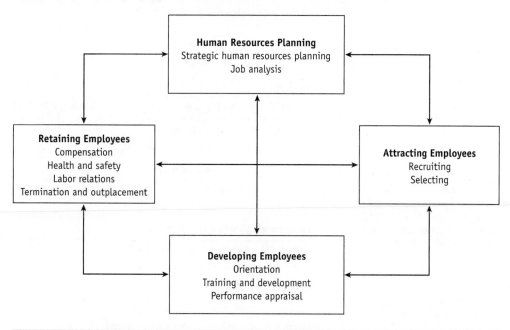

minorities. The EEO also protects disadvantaged young people, disabled workers, and people over 40 years of age.[5] Although the law protects women from discrimination in employment, they are not considered a legal minority because they make up half of the population, and in some situations comprise a majority.

The Equal Employment Opportunity Commission (EEOC), which is responsible for enforcing EEO mandates, has 47 field offices across the nation, and it operates a WATS line (1-800-USA-EEOC) around the clock to provide information on employee rights. If you are not sure if what you are about to do, or are doing, is legal, call them.

Violation of the antidiscrimination laws can lead to investigation by the EEOC or to class action or individual lawsuits. Courts find discrimination when selection criteria are vague, elusive, unstructured, undefined, or poorly conceived. As a manager, you should be familiar with your organization's EEO and AA program guidelines.

Preemployment Inquiries

No one in your organization—not recruiters, not interviewers nor other HR staff, not line managers—can legally ask discriminatory questions, either on the application or during interviews.[6] Here are two rules of thumb to guide you: (1) Every question you ask should be job-related. When developing questions, make sure you have a purpose for using the information. Ask only legal questions you plan to use in your selection process. (2) General questions should be asked of all candidates.

Exhibit 8–2 lists what you can (lawful information you can use to disqualify candidates) and cannot (prohibited information you cannot use to disqualify candidates) ask during the selection process. In all cases, the assumption is that the information asked for is not a bona fide occupational qualification (BFOQ) for the job. A **bona fide occupational qualification** allows organizations to base their hiring decisions on otherwise discriminatory attributes where it is reasonably necessary to the normal operation of a particular organization. For instance, a health and exercise study determined that chronological age, by itself, is seldom a reliable index of an individual's ability to perform strenuous physical work.[7] Therefore, age should not be viewed as a bona fide occupational qualification for physically strenuous occupations. Instead, each individual should be judged on the basis of his or her functional capabilities. That said, **CAP MANAGEMENT** appears to force NFL managers to release older players with higher salaries in favor of younger players who are paid less. **Do you believe cap management practices discriminate against older players? If so, can you think of a feasible solution?**

TIMEOUT

Have you or anyone you know ever been asked for discriminatory information when you were screened for a job? If yes, explain the situation.

_____

_____

_____

_____

_____

_____

---

bona fide occupational qualification (BFOQ)
Allows discrimination where it is reasonably necessary to normal operation of a particular organization.

Exhibit 8–2 Preemployment Inquiries

NAME

Can ask: Current legal name and whether the candidate has ever worked under a different name.

Cannot ask: Maiden name or whether the person has changed his or her name.

ADDRESS

Can ask: Current residence and length of residence.

Cannot ask: If the candidate owns or rents his or her home, unless it is a BFOQ.

AGE

Can ask: If the candidate is between specific age groups, 21 to 70, to meet job specifications. If hired, can you furnish proof of age? (For example, an employee must be 21 to serve alcoholic beverages.)

Cannot ask: How old are you? (Or to see a birth certificate.) How much longer an older person plans to work before retiring.

SEX

Can ask: One's sex *only if* sex is a BFOQ.

Cannot ask: One's sex if sex is not a BFOQ. Questions (or make comments) remotely considered flirtatious. Sexual preferences.

MARITAL AND FAMILY STATUS

Can ask: If the candidate can meet the work schedule. Whether the candidate has activities, responsibilities, or commitments that may hinder meeting attendance requirements.

Cannot ask: Marital status or any questions regarding children or other family issues.

NATIONAL ORIGIN, CITIZENSHIP, RACE, OR COLOR

Can ask: If the candidate is legally eligible to work in the United States, and if this can be proven if hired.

Cannot ask: Candidate to identify national origin, citizenship, race, or color (or that of parents and other relatives).

LANGUAGE

Can ask: Which languages the candidate speaks and/or writes fluently. If candidate speaks and/or writes a specific language if it is a BFOQ.

Cannot ask: The language spoken off the job, or how the applicant learned the language.

CONVICTIONS

Can ask: If the candidate has been convicted of a felony and other information if the felony is job-related.

Cannot ask: If the candidate has ever been arrested. (An arrest does not prove guilt.) For information regarding a conviction that is not job-related.

HEIGHT AND WEIGHT

Can ask: If the candidate meets or exceeds BFOQ height and/or weight requirements, and if it can be proven if hired.

Cannot ask: Candidate's height or weight if it is not a BFOQ.

RELIGION

Can ask: If the candidate is of a specific religion when it is a BFOQ. If the candidate can meet work schedules. If candidate must be absent for religious reasons (holidays, etc.).

Cannot ask: Religious preference, affiliations, or denominations.

CREDIT RATINGS OR GARNISHMENTS

Can ask: If this is a BFOQ.

Cannot ask: If this is not a BFOQ.

EDUCATION AND WORK EXPERIENCE

Can ask: For information that is job-related.

Cannot ask: For information that is not job-related.

REFERENCES

Can ask: For information that is job-related.

Cannot ask: For a reference from a religious leader.

MILITARY

Can ask: For information on job-related education and experience gained in the military.

Cannot ask: Dates and condition of discharge. Draft classification or other eligibility for military service. National Guard or reserve units of candidates. About experience in foreign armed services.

ORGANIZATIONS

Can ask: About membership in job-related organizations, such as union, professional, or trade associations.

Cannot ask: About membership in any non-job-related organization that would indicate race, religion, and so on.

DISABILITIES

Can ask: If the candidate has any disabilities that would prevent him or her from performing the specific job.

Cannot ask: For information that is not job-related. (Focus on abilities, *not* disabilities.)

THE HUMAN RESOURCES DEPARTMENT

One of the four major functional departments in organizations, human resources is a staff department that advises and assists all other departments. In companies large enough (usually about 100 or more employees) to have a separate HR department, HR develops the human resources plans for the entire organization:

- It recruits employees for line managers to select from as they hire new people.

- It conducts orientation sessions for new hires and trains many of them to do their jobs.

- It develops the performance appraisal system and forms used by managers throughout the organization.

APPLYING THE CONCEPT   *Legal or Illegal Questions*

Use Exhibit 8–2 to identify the ten preemployment questions as:

a. legal (can ask)   **b.** illegal (cannot ask)

_____ 1. What languages do you speak?

_____ 2. Are you married or single?

_____ 3. How many dependents do you have?

_____ 4. So you want to be a race-car driver. Are you a member of the union?

_____ 5. How old are you?

_____ 6. Have you been arrested for stealing on the job?

_____ 7. Do you own your own car?

_____ 8. Do you have any form of disability?

_____ 9. What type of discharge did you get from the military?

_____ 10. Can you prove you are legally eligible to work?

- It determines compensation guidelines.
- It develops employee health and safety programs, works on labor relations, and assists in the termination of employees.
- It keeps employment records.
- It is often involved with legal matters.

TIMEOUT
Describe your experiences with the HR department in the organization you work for or play for.

_____

_____

_____

_____

_____

_____

HUMAN RESOURCES PLANNING

Strategic human resources planning is the process of staffing the organization to meet its objectives. The job of the HR department is to provide the right kinds of people, in the right quantity, with the right skills, at the right time. HR plans use the organization's strategy as their base. If its strategy is growth, then employees will need to be hired. If its strategy is retrenchment, then there will be a layoff. Strategic HR management has become increasingly important.[8] The Director of Player Development for the Dallas Cowboys typically spends his time finding replacements for injured players, working on problems with the coaching staff, and preparing for contract negotiations.[9]

HR managers analyze the organization's current human resources with an eye on its strategy, environment, and sales forecasts. They then forecast specific HR needs. And finally, they plan how to provide the employees necessary to meet the organization's objectives. HR consultant Priscilla Florence has served as the HR person for two international sports events: the 1984 Los Angeles Olympics and the World Cup USA 1994. Priscilla's responsibilities involve recruiting, hiring, training, and organizing paid employees and volunteers.[10] General managers of NFL teams also need to be involved in strategic human resource management. When does a team release an aging quarterback? When is a player no longer worth a long-term contract? What free agents are worth spending large amounts of **CAP** money for? If a general manager doesn't answer these questions correctly, he or she will lose his or her job.[11]

strategic human resources planning
The process of staffing an organization to meet its objectives.

JOB ANALYSIS

2 LEARNING OUTCOME
Differentiate between a job description and a job specification and explain why they are needed.

Strategic HR planning determines the number of people and skills needed, but it does not specify how each job is to be performed. An important part of HR planning is reviewing information about the job itself. *Job design* is the process of developing and combining the tasks and activities that comprise a particular job. *Job analysis* is the process of determining what the position entails and the qualifications needed to staff the position. As you can see, job analysis is the basis for the job description and the job specifications.

job description
Identifies the tasks and responsibilities of a position.

The **job description** identifies the tasks and responsibilities of a position. In other words, it identifies what employees do to earn their pay. The trend is to describe jobs more broadly in order to design enriched jobs. Exhibit 8–3 is a sample job description for an Athletic Director of a Division III college.[12]

Exhibit 8–3 Sample Job Description

DIVISION III COLLEGE
POSITION DESCRIPTION
JOB TITLE: Athletic Director

Exempt (Y/N): Yes	**Salary Level:**
Department: Athletics	**Supervisor: Dean of Institutional Advancement**
Approved:	**Date: Spring 2002**
Incumbent:	**Status: Full-time, 12-month**

GENERAL RESPONSIBILITIES

The Director is responsible for administering and developing the athletic programs and policies while supporting student athletes and coaches. Responsible for all areas of compliance as applied to a Division III program.

SPECIFIC RESPONSIBILITIES

- Administration of all athletic programs.
- Development of athletic programs that reflect the vision outlined by the College.
- Recommendations for the quality of all athletic programs.
- Ensure consistency between athletic programs, College policies, and strategic plan.
- Monitor compliance as it applies to the student athlete concept, the principles governing intercollegiate athletics, gender equity, NCAA Division III and conference regulations, and legislation.
- Develop marketing concepts in collaboration with the College Marketing Department.
- Develop and implement promotions and public relations programs in collaboration with the College Marketing Department.
- Plan and participate in fund-raising efforts.
- Work with the Dean of Academics and the Dean of Students to integrate and administer a complementary high-quality athletics program.
- Supervision of all summer sports camps for children.
- Manage and oversee department budgets.
- Lead and supervise direct reports.
- Develop and implement student athlete recruiting strategies that demonstrate a cohesive approach and philosophy with the Admissions Office.
- Monitor and adjust, as needed, recruiting efforts by coaches.
- Monitor and adjust, as needed, coaching styles to reflect the College philosophy surrounding student athletes.
- Work collaboratively with the Human Resources Office to ensure College personnel policies/issues are handled with consistency of practice.

This list is representative of those duties and responsibilities that are required of this position. However, the list is not to be considered all-inclusive. Other responsibilities and duties may be assigned to meet mission/strategic plan requirements of the College, and cooperation of all personnel is expected.

(continued)

Exhibit 8–3   (*continued*)

SUPERVISORY RESPONSIBILITIES

- Administrative Assistant
- Contest Management
- Director, Sports Information
- Athletic Trainers
- Full-time and part-time coaches

QUALIFICATIONS REQUIREMENTS

Education, Experience, Skills:

The ideal candidate for this position will have demonstrated skills and experience in strategic leadership, written and oral communications, creative approaches, and problem solving, plus operations and administrations management. Qualifications include: master's degree in Athletic Administration, Sports Management, Physical Education, or a related field; five years of related experience in a college athletic department; conference, coaching, and NCAA experience.

STANDARDS OF PERFORMANCE

- Flexibility/Adaptability—Ability and willingness to work cohesively in support of the strategic plan, mission, and vision of the College.
- Judgment/Decision Making—Demonstrates a proactive role in judgment and decision processes.
- Communication—Maintains effective internal and external communication mechanisms.
- Planning and Organizing—Demonstrates skills in managing all aspects of the Athletic Department.
- Procedural Expertise—Adheres to the procedures and processes as established by the College.
- Management of Projects—Demonstrates leadership skills in meeting desired outcomes and in oversight of projects.
- Goals and Objectives—Develops and implements strategies that support the goals and objectives as established by the Athletic Department and the College.
- Use of resources—Demonstrates a prudent use of all resources.
- Safety, Security, Environmental Awareness—Consistently exhibits behavior and department oversight that promote the safety and security of people and facilities while ensuring responsible behavior for our environment, both on and off campus.
- General knowledge and promotion of the College's mission, purpose, goals, and the role of this position in achieving those goals.

PHYSICAL DEMANDS AND WORK ENVIRONMENT

The physical demands described here are representative of those that must be met by an employee to successfully perform the essential functions of this job. Reasonable accommodations may be made to enable individuals with disabilities to perform the essential functions. The incumbent is exposed to a typical, climate-controlled office environment and various weather-related conditions (extreme temperature ranges, rain, etc.), typical office equipment (computer, printer, fax machine, telephones, etc.), usual sports equipment, and associated items. This position requires sitting, standing, bending, reaching, vision (near, distance), walking, lifting, climbing stairs, and manual dexterity to perform essential job functions.

Source: "Sample Job Description for Athletic Director" reprinted by permission of Elms College.

Realistic Job Preview

An essential part of job analysis is developing a realistic job preview (RJP). The RJP provides the candidate with an accurate, objective understanding of the job. Research indicates that employees who feel they were given accurate descriptions are more satisfied with the organization, believe the employer stands behind them and is trustworthy, and express a lower desire to change jobs than do those who feel they were not given an accurate job description.[13]

Based on the job description, the next step is to determine job specifications. **Job specifications** identify the qualifications needed to staff a position. The job specifications thus identify the types of people needed.

job specifications
Qualifications needed to staff a position.

TIMEOUT

Perform a job analysis on your current job or one you recently held. Use your analysis to write a simple job description and job specifications.

_____

_____

_____

_____

_____

_____

Job analysis is an important HR activity because it is your basis for attracting, developing, and retaining employees. If you don't understand the job, how can you select employees to do it? How can you train them to do the job? How can you evaluate their performance? How do you know how much to pay employees?

ATTRACTING EMPLOYEES

3 LEARNING OUTCOME
State the two parts of attracting employees.

After hiring needs have been determined and jobs analyzed, the HR department typically recruits promising applicants, and line managers select people to fill positions. Thus, it is a good idea for you to understand recruiting, the selection process, and how to conduct interviews, even if you don't choose human resources as your career.

Recruiting

recruiting
The process of attracting qualified candidates to apply for job openings.

Recruiting is the process of attracting qualified candidates to apply for job openings. To fill an opening, possible candidates must first be made aware that the organization is seeking employees. They must then be persuaded to apply for the jobs. For instance, recruiting and retaining sport management professors has been challenging in recent years. Professors with sport management doctorates are in short supply and in high demand as numerous colleges add new sport management programs to their offerings. Administrators will have to use all types of recruitment methods to attract qualified sport professors. Advertising in magazines and newspapers will not suffice because the pool of sport management professors is so small.[14] Recruiting is conducted both internally and externally; Exhibit 8–4 lists possible recruiting sources.

Exhibit 8–4   Recruiting Sources

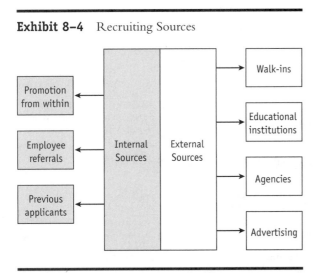

INTERNAL RECRUITING. _Internal recruiting_ involves filling job openings with current employees or personal referrals. Promotion from within and employee referrals are two common types of internal recruiting. Others include previous employees, and previous applicants who can still be contacted.

- _Promotions from within._ Many organizations post job openings on bulletin boards, in company newsletters, and so on. Current employees can then apply or bid for the open positions.

- _Employee referrals._ When job openings are posted internally, employees may be encouraged to refer friends and relatives for the positions. Typically, employees will refer only good candidates. However, the government has stated that this referral method is not acceptable when current employees are predominantly white or male because it tends to perpetuate the present composition of the workforce, which results in discrimination.

EXTERNAL RECRUITING. The following are external recruiting sources:

- _Walk-ins._ Sometimes, good candidates come to the organization "cold" (that is, without an appointment) and ask for a job. However, professionals tend to send résumés and cover letters requesting an interview.

- _Educational institutions._ Organizations recruit at high schools, vocational/technical schools, and colleges. Many schools offer career planning and placement services to aid students and potential employers. Educational institutions are good places to recruit people without prior experience.

- _Agencies._ There are three major types of agencies: (1) Temporary agencies, like Kelly Services, provide part- or full-time help for limited periods. They are useful for replacing employees who will be out for a short period of time or for supplementing the

TIMEOUT

Reflect for a moment on the job you analyzed in the preceding timeout. Were you given a realistic job preview when you were hired? Explain.

_____

_____

_____

_____

_____

_____

APPLYING THE CONCEPT   *Recruiting Sources*

Select the recruiting source that would be most appropriate for the five job openings described.

a. promotion from within   **d.** educational institutions   **g.** executive recruiters

b. employee referrals   **e.** advertising

c. walk-ins   **f.** agencies

_____ 11. You need a one-month replacement for Jason, who was hurt on the job manufacturing hockey skates.

_____ 12. Bonnie, a first-line supervisor in the fitness center, is retiring in two months.

_____ 13. You need an engineer to design new fitness equipment with very specific requirements. There are very few people with the qualifications you want.

_____ 14. Your sales manager likes to hire young people without experience in order to train them to sell insurance to athletes.

_____ 15. The maintenance department for your athletic center needs someone to perform routine cleaning services.

---

regular workforce during busy periods. (2) Public agencies are nationwide state employment services. They generally provide job candidates to employers at no, or very low, direct cost. (3) Private employment agencies are privately owned and charge a fee for their service. Agencies are good for recruiting people with prior experience. Executive recruiters are a type of private agency often referred to as "headhunters." They specialize in recruiting managers and/or those with high-level technical skills, like engineers and computer experts, and tend to charge the employer a large fee.

■ *Advertising.* It is important to use the appropriate media source to reach qualified candidates. A simple help-wanted sign in the window may be appropriate for some positions, but newspaper ads will reach a larger audience. Professional and trade magazines are more suitable for specific skill categories.

Technology is changing how organizations recruit and select employees. Employers now routinely advertise on the Internet. Numerous web sites match applicants and job opportunities. For instance, ESPN and Monster.com have formed an alliance in which Monster.com will create an ESPN/Monster dual-named job-search site for people interested in sports-oriented careers.[15] Make sure to visit http://espn.monster.com to find sports-related job openings in your area.

The Selection Process

4 LEARNING OUTCOME
Explain how hypothetical questions and probing questions differ.

Selection is the process of choosing the most qualified applicant recruited for a job. Selection is a crucial activity because bad hiring decisions haunt an organization for years. One study analyzed the staff recruitment and selection methods used by summer camp directors. Although camp directors endeavor to hire high-quality counselors, there are few guidelines available to help them. To fill this gap, researchers examined the relationship between motivating factors that led counselors to apply for a position at camp and their ensuing job performance. They recommended that camp administrators structure selection interviews so that they could ascertain specific capabilities of interviewees. The results indicated a strategic

TIMEOUT
Identify the recruiting source(s) used to hire you both for your current job and for previous jobs.

selection
The process of choosing the most qualified applicant recruited for a job.

interviewing technique would likely result in a staff who displayed a range of desirable capabilities relevant to the job.[16]

Organizations don't follow a universal, set sequence in their selection process. Nor do they use the same selection process for different jobs. That said, the selection process is typically composed of the application form, screening interviews, testing, background and reference checks, interviewing, and hiring. The selection process can be thought of as a series of hurdles that the applicant must overcome to be offered the job.

APPLICATION FORM. The first hurdle is typically the application. Job seekers are usually asked to complete a job application. The data that applicants provide are compared to the job specifications. If they match, the applicant may progress to the next hurdle. Organizations use different application forms for different jobs. For professional jobs, résumés may replace the application form.[17]

assessment centers
Places where job applicants undergo a series of tests, interviews, and simulated experiences to determine their managerial potential.

Organizations also often use computers to scan application forms and résumés. Before sending in a résumé, you may want to check to see if the company you are applying to does this. If so, the HR department can give you specific instructions to make sure your information is scanned accurately.

SCREENING INTERVIEW. Specialists in HR departments often conduct interviews to screen candidates—those they think are promising will continue on in the selection process. This saves line managers precious time. Organizations also now use computers to conduct screening interviews.

TESTING. Tests can be used by organizations when the tests meet EEO guidelines for _validity_ (people who score high on the test do well on the job and those who score low don't do well on the job) and _reliability_ (people taking the same test on different days get approximately the same score each time). Illegal tests can result in lawsuits. Testing achievement, aptitude, personality, and interest have all been deemed appropriate, as have physical exams.

Both internal and external candidates for management positions are tested through assessment centers. **Assessment centers** are places where job applicants undergo a series of tests, interviews, and simulated experiences to determine their managerial potential.

BACKGROUND AND REFERENCE CHECKS. Organizations that carefully check references to verify the information on a candidate's application form and résumé find that this helps them avoid poor hiring decisions. Unfortunately, all too many applications contain false material. It is not uncommon for applicants to falsely state that they have earned college degrees.

INTERVIEWING. The interview is the most heavily weighted selection criterion. Why? Because interviews are often worth the proverbial thousand words. Interviews are also usually the final hurdle in the selection process. Interviews give candidates a chance to learn about the job and size up the organization firsthand. (Is this a place where I really want to work?) Interviews give managers a chance to size up candidates in ways that applications, tests, and references just don't do. (Is he a people person? Is she a leader? Would he be more productive as a team player or as an independent contributor?) Because job interviewing is so important, we take you through the dos and don'ts of preparing for and conducting job interviews in some detail in the next section.

HIRING. After reviewing the information gathered from candidates' applications, references, and interviews, managers then compare the candidates without bias, and decide who is best suited for the job. They consider many criteria—qualifications, salary requirements, availability, issues of diversity in the department or organization. The chosen candidate is then contacted and offered the job. If he or she doesn't accept the offer—or accepts but leaves after a short period of time—the next-best candidate is offered the job.

INTERVIEWING

As we noted earlier, interviews are heavily weighted in most selection processes. It therefore behooves you to become a skillful interviewer. This is a skill you will use over and over, both as an interviewer and as an interviewee. So, study this section carefully, and be sure to do the

Skill–Builder on page 233. Exhibit 8–5 lists the types of interviews and the types of questions used in them.

The three types of interviews are based on structure: (1) *Structured* interviews use a list of prepared questions to ask all candidates. (2) *Unstructured* interviews do not use preplanned questions or a preplanned sequence of topics. (3) *Semistructured* interviews ask questions from a prepared list but also ask unplanned questions. That is, interviewers depart from their decided-upon structure when they feel it is appropriate. HR people generally prefer semistructured interviews because they not only help ensure against discrimination (the prepared questions are asked of all candidates), they also give interviewers flexibility in pursuing lines of questioning and conversation that give them accurate assessments of candidates' motivation and attitudes. At the same time, the standard set of questions makes it easier to compare candidates. The amount of structure you should use in interviews depends on your experience and on the situation. The less experienced you are, the more structure will help you conduct effective interviews.

QUESTIONS. The questions you ask give you control over the interview; they allow you to ferret out the information you need to make your decision. Make sure your questions all have a purpose and are job-related. Ask all candidates for the same information.

Interviewers use four types of questions: (1) *Closed-ended* questions require a limited response, often a yes or no answer, and are appropriate for dealing with fixed aspects of the job. "Do you have a class I license and can you produce it if hired?" (2) *Open-ended* questions require an unlimited response and are appropriate for determining abilities and motivation. "Why do you want to be a general manager for our company?" "What do you see as a major strength you can bring to our team?" (3) *Hypothetical* questions require candidates to describe what they would do and say in a given situation; these questions help you assess capabilities. "What would you do if a free-agent baseball player wanted his own private locker room?" (4) *Probing* questions require candidates to clarify some aspect of their background or some aspect brought up by the interview and help you understand an issue or point. Probing questions are not planned. "What do you mean by 'it was tough'?" "What was the dollar increase your team achieved in ticket sales?"

Preparing for the Interview

Going through the formalized procedure shown in Model 8–1 will help you improve your interviewing skills.

1. *Review the job description and specifications.* You cannot conduct an effective interview if you do not thoroughly understand the job for which you are assessing applicants. Study the job description and job specifications. If they are outdated, or don't exist, conduct a job analysis.

TIMEOUT
What types of job interviews have you participated in?

TIMEOUT
List the types of questions you have been asked when you interviewed for jobs, and give an example of each one.

Exhibit 8–5   Types of Interviews and Questions

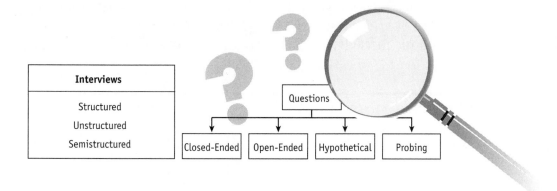

Interviews
Structured
Unstructured
Semistructured

Questions

Closed-Ended   Open-Ended   Hypothetical   Probing

Model 8–1   Preparing to Interview

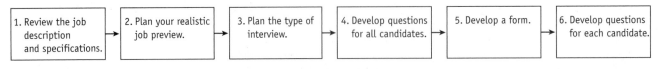

2. *Plan your realistic job preview.* One of your jobs as interviewer is to help applicants understand what the job is and what they will be expected to do. They should know the job's "good news" and its "bad news." Use the job description to plan a realistic job preview. It often helps to give candidates a tour of the work area.

3. *Plan the type of interview.* What level of structure will you use? The interview should take place in a private, quiet place, without interruptions. It may be appropriate to begin in an office and then tour the facilities while asking questions. Plan when the tour will take place and what questions you will ask. Take your form if you intend to ask several questions.

4. *Develop questions for all candidates.* Use the job description and specifications to develop questions that relate to each job task and responsibility. Use a mixture of closed-ended, open-ended, and hypothetical questions. Don't be concerned about the order of questions; just write them out at this point. Now check that your questions are job-related and nondiscriminatory. Ask them of all candidates.

5. *Develop a form.* Once you have a list of questions, determine the sequence. Start with the easy questions. One approach starts with closed-ended questions, moves on to open-ended ones, and then to hypothetical ones, using probing questions as needed. Another approach structures the interview around the job description and specifications, explains each, and then asks questions relating to each responsibility.

   Write out your questions in sequence, leaving space for checking off closed-ended responses, for making notes on the responses to open-ended and hypothetical questions, and for follow-up questions. Add information gained from probing questions where appropriate. Recording the candidate's responses on this form will help guide you through the interview and help keep you on topic. Make a copy of the form for each candidate, and a few extras to use when filling the same job in the future, or to help you develop forms for other jobs.

6. *Develop questions for each candidate.* Review each candidate's application and résumé. You will most likely want to verify or clarify some of the information given during the interview. "I noticed that you did not list any employment during 1995; were you unemployed during that time?" "On the application you stated you had computer training; what type of computer are you trained to operate?" Check that these individual questions are not discriminatory—for example, don't ask only women whether they can lift 50 pounds; ask every candidate this question.

You can either note individual questions on the standard form, writing them in where they may be appropriate to ask, or you can add a list at the end of the form.

CONDUCTING THE INTERVIEW. Following the steps in Model 8–2 will help make you an effective interviewer.[18]

Model 8–2   Steps in a Good Interview

1. *Open the interview.* Endeavor to develop rapport with applicants. Put them at ease by talking about some topic not related to the job. Maintain eye contact in a way that is comfortable for you and for them.

2. *Give your realistic job preview.* Be sure applicants understand the job requirements. Answer any questions they have about the job and the organization. If the job is not what they expected, or want to do, allow applicants to disqualify themselves and close the interview at that point.

3. *Ask your questions.* Steps 2 and 3 can be combined if you like. To get the most out of a job interview, take notes on applicants' responses to your questions. Tell each applicant that you have prepared a list of questions you will be asking, and that you plan to take notes.

   During the interview, applicants should do most of the talking. Give them a chance to think and respond. If someone doesn't give you all the information you need, ask an unplanned probing question. However, if it's obvious that the person doesn't want to answer the question, don't force it. Go on to the next question or close the interview. End with a closing question such as, "I'm finished with my questions. Is there anything else you want to tell me about, or ask me?"

4. *Introduce top candidates to coworkers.* Introduce top candidates to people with whom they will be working to get a sense of their interpersonal skills and overall attitude. Introductions can also give you a sense about whether the person is a team player.

5. *Close the interview.* Be honest without making a decision during the interview. Don't lead candidates on. Thank them for their time, and tell them about the next step in the interview process, if any. Tell candidates when you will contact them—be specific, and *keep your word.* You might say, for example, "Thank you for coming in for this interview. I'll be interviewing over the next two days and will call you with my decision by Friday of this week." *Don't* forget to make that call, whether it is a pleasant one or an unpleasant one. Simple courtesy demands that you give applicants closure. After the interview, be sure to jot down general impressions not covered by specific questions. When you are interviewing several people, you owe it to the applicants and to your organization to keep accurate documentation of your impressions, concerns, and so forth.

Selecting the Candidate

After all interviews are completed, compare each candidate's qualifications to the job specifications to determine whom you think will be best for the job. Gather coworkers' impressions of each candidate.

PROBLEMS TO AVOID. Here are some "don'ts" to avoid during the selection process:

- *Don't rush.* Take your time—this is an important decision. Don't be pressured into hiring just "any" candidate. Find the best person available.

- *Don't stereotype.* Don't prejudge. Don't leap to conclusions. Be objective *and* subjective. Use analysis to match the best candidate to the job, but also trust your gut.

- *Don't fall into the "like me" trap.* Remember the benefits of diversity. A department of your clones will not be an effective one.

- *Don't look for halos and horns.* Don't judge a candidate on the basis of one or two favorable *or* unfavorable characteristics. Look at the total person, and at the entire pool of candidates.

- *Don't jump prematurely.* Don't make your selection based solely on the person's application/résumé or right after interviewing a candidate who impressed you. Don't compare candidates after each interview. The order in which you interview applicants can be strongly influential. Be open-minded during all interviews and make a choice only after you have finished all interviews. Compare each candidate on each job specification.

TIME OUT
Use Model 8-2 to analyze an interview in which you were the job *seeker.* Did your interviewer use all the steps we have examined? If not, why might he or she have skipped some steps?

_____

_____

_____

_____

_____

_____

DEVELOPING EMPLOYEES

After an organization has attracted employees (recruited and selected them), the organization must then develop them (orient and train them).

Orientation

5 LEARNING OUTCOME
State the purposes of orientation and training and development.

orientation
Introduces new employees to the organization, its culture, and their jobs.

Orientation introduces new employees to the organization, its culture, and their jobs. Orientation is about learning the ropes. Effective orientation reduces the time needed to get new hires up to speed, reduces their new-job jitters, and gives them an accurate idea from the start of what is expected of them. Good orientation programs reduce turnover and improve attitudes and performance.[19] One researcher notes that "allowing coworkers to help with orientation is a good idea since they can be good coaches in passing along unwritten rules of behavior and cultural norms in the organization."[20]

Although orientation programs vary in formality and content, the five elements listed in Exhibit 8–6 are shared by effective programs. Basically, orientation is an opportunity (1) to sell the company to new hires (where the organization sees itself in five years, why people would want to stay with the organization, and what type of culture the organizations has); (2) for the organization to focus on key issues the organization wants made crystal clear (issues of honesty, diversity, sexual harassment, among others); and (3) for you to explain what your department does, how the new hire's job relates to other jobs in the department, and how the different departments relate. Be sure to clearly explain the new hire's responsibilities and the standing plans that need to be followed. Give new hires a tour of the facilities and introduce them to coworkers. Priscilla Florence, the HR consultant hired by the 1994 World Cup USA, hired another consultant to provide orientation and training. The consultant was responsible for the orientation of 1,500 workers at each of the nine sites across the United States that held World Cup games.[21] Professional leagues such as the NBA conduct orientation programs with rookie players to help them understand the complexities of being a professional player. The orientation includes discussions on the use of illegal drugs and fiscal responsibility. **How would the Buffalo Bills' orientation program differ for its first-round draft pick (Mike Williams) compared with that of its newly acquired free-agent star quarterback (Drew Bledsoe)? How would the orientation program for a new player development director differ?**

Exhibit 8–6
Orientation Programs

Organization and department functions
Job tasks and responsibilities
Standing plans
Tours
Introduction to coworkers

Training and Development

training
Acquiring the skills necessary to perform a job.

development
Ongoing education that improves skills for present and future jobs.

vestibule training
Develops skills in a simulated setting.

New hires need to be taught how to perform their new job. Orientation and training often take place simultaneously. **Training** is about acquiring the skills necessary to perform a job. **Development** is ongoing education that improves skills for present and future jobs. Less technical than training, development endeavors to strengthen people skills, communication skills, conceptual abilities, and decision-making skills in managerial and professional employees. Training and development are good investments—they benefit individuals, their organizations, and the economy as a whole.

OFF THE JOB AND ON THE JOB. As the name implies, *off-the-job training* is conducted away from the work site, often in some sort of classroom setting. A common method is vestibule training. **Vestibule training** develops skills in a simulated setting. It is used to teach job skills when teaching at the work site is impractical. *On-the-job training (OJT)* is done at the work site with the same resources the employee uses to perform the job. Managers, or employees selected by the managers, usually conduct the training. Because of its proven track record, job instructional training (JIT) is a popular method worldwide. Baseball players attend spring training in Florida and Arizona every spring to practice running, hitting, pitching, and fielding skills.[22] This training stands them in good stead during the regular-season games. Spring training helps develop teams that are well coached and players that have fewer errors and fewer injuries. **What sorts of training do you think NFL managers**

might undergo to enhance their understanding and use of captology? Because both rookie and experienced players fall behind when they miss training camp while holding out for a larger contract, do you think management would be better off if they just offered more money at the start of negotiations?

6 LEARNING OUTCOME
Describe job instructional training.

JOB INSTRUCTIONAL TRAINING (JIT). JIT is composed of four steps (see Model 8–3). Remember that what *we* know well seems very simple to us, but new hires don't yet share this perspective.

1. *Preparation of the trainee.* Put trainees at ease as you create interest in the job and encourage questions. Explain the quantity and quality requirements and their importance.

2. *Presentation of the task.* Perform the task yourself at a slow pace, explaining each step several times. Once trainees seem to have the steps memorized, have them explain each step as you perform the job at a slow pace. Write out complex tasks with multiple steps, and give trainees a copy.

3. *Performance of the task by the trainee.* Have trainees perform the task at a slow pace, explaining each step. Correct any errors and be willing to help them perform any difficult steps. Continue until they can perform the task proficiently.

4. *Follow-up.* Tell trainees whom to go to for help with questions or problems. Gradually leave them alone. Begin by checking quality and quantity frequently, then decrease the amount of checking based on the trainee's skill level. Watch them perform the task and correct any errors or faulty work procedures before they become a habit. Be patient and encouraging.

Model 8–3   Steps in JIT

| 1. Preparation of the trainee. | → | 2. Presentation of the task. | → | 3. Performance of the task by the trainee. | → | 4. Follow-up. |

The Training Cycle

Following the steps in the training cycle (see Exhibit 8–7) ensures that training is systematic. Systematic training is always more effective.

1. *Conduct a needs assessment.* Before you begin training, you must determine your staff's training needs. Common needs assessment methods include observation, interviews, and questionnaires. These needs will differ depending on whether you are training new or existing employees. An assessment center may also be used to determine training needs.

2. *Set objectives.* Any training program should have well-defined, performance-based objectives. As with all plans, begin by determining the end result you want to achieve. The criteria for your objectives should meet the criteria discussed in Chapter 4.

3. *Prepare for training.* Before conducting a training session, have written plans and all the necessary materials ready. If you have ever had an instructor come to class unprepared, you know why preparation before training is necessary for success. Remember, as many as 30 hours of preparation are needed for one hour of training.

Exhibit 8–7   The Training Cycle

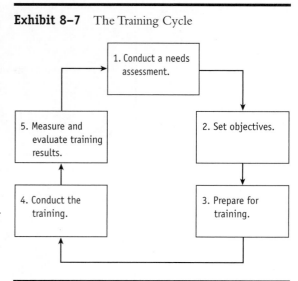

> **TIMEOUT**
> Describe an orientation you participated in recently. Which elements of effective programs did it include? Which ones did it exclude?
>
> _____
> _____
> _____
> _____
> _____
> _____

> **TIMEOUT**
> Identify which JIT steps your trainer used to teach you on your current job. Was the training on or off the job?
>
> _____
> _____
> _____
> _____
> _____
> _____

Selecting the training method is an important part of your preparation. You have already learned about JIT. Exhibit 8–8 (in the next section) lists various training methods. Whatever method you develop, break the task into steps. What we do as part of our routine seems simple, but it can appear very complicated to a new employee. Write out each step and go through the steps yourself to make sure they work.

4. *Conduct the training.* Have your written plan with you, as well as any other materials you will need.

5. *Measure and evaluate training results.* Linking training outcomes and results can only make you more effective as a trainer. During training and at the end of the program, measure and evaluate the results to determine whether you achieved your objectives. If you met your goals, training is over. If you didn't meet your goals, either continue the training until your objectives are met or take employees off the job if they cannot meet the standards. Revise and improve your written plans for future use.

Training Methods

Exhibit 8–8 lists the various training methods available, many of which can be used as part of JIT. The third column lists the primary skill developed. However, some of the technical methods can be combined. Technical skill also includes acquiring knowledge that can be tested.

When selecting a training method, keep the following statistics in mind: People learn 10 percent of what they read, 20 percent of what they hear, and 30 percent of what they see. People learn 50 percent of what they see and hear. They learn 70 percent of what they talk over with others. People learn 80 percent of what they use and do in real life. They learn 95 percent of what they teach someone else. We learn by doing.[23] And the level of skill needed to succeed in the global village will continue to increase.[24]

WHEN MANAGERS TRAIN PEOPLE. Managers typically use reading, lectures, videos, question-and-answer sessions, discussion, programmed learning, demonstrations, job rotations, and projects to train employees. Managers do not commonly use role-playing and behavior modeling. However, these two methods are appropriate when you need to teach people skills. Managers also use management games, in-basket exercises, and cases to train managers.

TIMEOUT
Describe the methods used to train you in your current job.

_____

_____

_____

_____

_____

_____

APPLYING THE CONCEPT　　*Training Methods*

Select the most appropriate training method for the following situations.

a. written material	**f.** programmed learning	**k.** behavior modeling
b. lecture	**g.** demonstration	**l.** management games
c. video	**h.** job rotation	**m.** in-basket exercise
d. question-and-answer session	**i.** projects	**n.** cases
e. discussion	**j.** role-playing	

_____ 16. Your large department has a high turnover rate. Staff must know the rules and regulations in order to sell high-quality bicycles.

_____ 17. In the athletic center you manage, you occasionally need to teach new employees how to handle typical problems they face daily.

_____ 18. Your boss has requested a special report.

_____ 19. You need your staff to be able to cover for each other as lifeguards at the center's swimming pool.

_____ 20. Your staff needs to know how to handle customer complaints about weather conditions at the ski resort you manage.

Exhibit 8–8 Training Methods

METHOD	DEFINITION	SKILL DEVELOPED
Written material	Manuals, books, and so on.	Technical
Lecture	Spoken word, class lectures.	Technical
Video	Television, class videos.	Technical
Question and answer	After other methods, the trainer and trainees ask questions about what they read, heard, and watched.	Technical
Discussion	A topic is presented and discussed.	Technical
Programmed learning	A computer or book is used to present material, followed by a question or problem. Trainees select a response, then are given feedback on their answers. Depending on the material presented, programmed learning may possibly develop people skills and conceptual skills.	Technical
Demonstration	Trainers show trainees how to perform the task. This is step 2 in JIT. Demonstrations can also be used to develop people skills and decision-making skills.	Technical
Job rotation	Employees learn to perform multiple jobs.	Technical and conceptual
Projects	Special assignments, such as developing a new product or a new team. Projects that require working with people and other departments also develop people skills and conceptual skills.	Technical
Role playing	Trainees act out a possible job situation, such as handling a customer complaint, to develop skill at handling similar situations on the job.	People and communication
Behavior modeling	(1) Trainees observe how to perform the task correctly. This may be done via a live demonstration or a videotape. (2) Trainees role-play a situation using the observed skills. (3) Trainees receive feedback on how well they performed. (4) Trainees develop plans for using the new skills on the job. (Behavior modeling is a feature of this book.)	People and communication
Cases	Trainees are presented with a situation and asked to diagnose and solve the problems involved. They are usually asked to answer questions. (Cases are included at the end of each chapter of this book.)	Conceptual and decision making
In-basket exercise	Trainees are given actual or simulated letters, memos, reports, telephone messages, etc. typically found in the in-basket of a person holding the job they're being trained for. Trainees are asked what, if any, action they would take for each item, and to assign priorities to the material.	Conceptual and decision making
Management games	Trainees manage a simulated company. They make decisions in small teams and get the results back, usually on a quarterly basis, over a period of several game "years." Teams are in an "industry" with several competitors.	Conceptual and decision making
Interactive video	Trainees sit at a computer and respond as directed.	Any of the skills

PERFORMANCE APPRAISALS

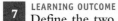

LEARNING OUTCOME
7
Define the two types of performance appraisals.

After people are hired and trained, organizations need to know how they are working out. Is their performance outstanding or merely adequate? Are they embracing the organization's culture and strategy? How might we help them develop their full potential? Here is where performance appraisals enter the picture.

Performance appraisal is the ongoing process of evaluating employee performance. Performance appraisals (PAs) come in two types—developmental and evaluative. *Developmental PAs* are used to improve performance. *Evaluative PAs* are used to decide pay raises, transfers and promotions, and demotions and terminations. Evaluative PAs focus on the past, whereas developmental PAs focus on the future. However, developmental plans are always based on evaluative PAs. The primary purpose of both types is to help employees continuously improve their performance.

performance appraisal
The ongoing process of evaluating employee performance.

When developmental and evaluative PAs are conducted together—which they commonly are—the development PA is often less effective, especially when an employee disagrees with the evaluation. Most managers are not good at being both a judge and a coach. Therefore, separate meetings make the two uses clear and make the process more productive for both employee and manager.

The Performance Appraisal Process

Exhibit 8–9 shows the connection between the organization's mission and objectives and the performance appraisal process. The feedback loop indicates the need to control human resources performance. Based on the organization's mission and objectives (Chapter 4), employees' performance should be measured against the achievement of these goals.

1. *Job analysis.* The job analysis includes working up the job description and job specifications. The responsibilities laid out in the job description should be ranked in order of importance.

2. *Develop standards and measurement methods.* After determining what it takes to do the job, standards and methods for measuring performance can be developed. (In the next section we describe several common measurement methods; we discuss how to set standards in Chapter 14.)

3. *Informal PA—coaching and discipline.* Effective PA systems encompass more than just the once-a-year formal interview. As we stated above, appraising performance is an ongoing process. We all benefit from regular informal feedback on our performance.[25] Coaching involves giving praise for a job well done to maintain performance, and taking corrective action when standards are not met. Someone performing below standard may need daily or weekly coaching or discipline to meet standards.[26] In Chapter 14, we will examine coaching and discipline in more detail.

4. *Prepare for and conduct the formal PA.* Follow the steps in Models 8–1 and 8–2.

Developing Performance Standards

As a manager, your employees need to know what the organization's standards are, and what your standards are. If you give an employee an average rating rather than a good one, you must be able to clearly explain why. The employee then needs to understand what he or she can do during the next appraisal period to earn a higher rating. If your standards are clear and your coaching effective, there should be no surprises during the formal performance appraisal. In Chapter 14, you will learn how to set standards in the areas of quantity, quality, time, cost, and behavior.

Exhibit 8–9 The Performance Appraisal Process

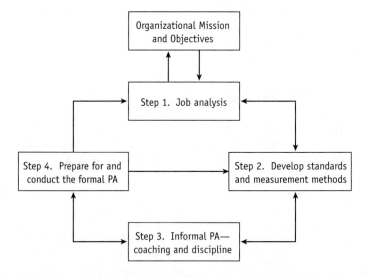

8 LEARNING OUTCOME
Explain the concept, "You get what you reward."

You Get What You Reward

One of the most important things you should take away from this course is that all of us will do what we are rewarded for doing. We seek information concerning what activities are rewarded and then endeavor to do (or at least pretend to do) those things, often to the exclusion of activities not rewarded. The extent to which this occurs depends on the attractiveness of the rewards. For example, if a professor gives a class a reading list of several sources, but tells students (or they realize without being told) they will not discuss them in class or be tested on them, how many students will acquire and read this list? How about if we tell you A, B, and C from this chapter are important and we'll test you on them, but X, Y, and Z are not. Would you spend equal time studying both groups?

Measurement Methods

People giving formal PAs often use a standard form (typically rating scales or BARS—see Exhibit 8–10) developed by the HR department to measure employee performance. Exhibit 8–10 lists commonly used PA measurement methods. Which PA method is best? This depends on your objectives, on the type of people in your group, on the work being evaluated, and on your organization's culture. Combinations usually work better than any one method. For developmental PAs, critical incidents and MBO work well because they are tailored to the individual. For evaluative PAs, ranking methods work well because they help you select the best. Successful PAs depend on your people skills as a manager, and on your fair and objective analysis.

The Personal Appraisal Interview

Always, always, always plan before you conduct PA interviews. You owe this to your employees, and you owe it to the organization. (And you will be a lot happier too!) *Everybody* comes out ahead when you are well prepared. Model 8–4 gives you the steps you should follow in your all-important preparation and in the interview itself. When you conduct the interview, encourage the employee to talk. You want the person to feel free to talk, free to share their own concerns—their feeling of freedom (or lack thereof) builds the trust (or distrust) that makes them more open (or closed) to viewing the evaluation objectively. Note that Model 8–4 presents the preparation and conduct of the evaluative and developmental PAs separately. We do this in order to show you how they differ and also how they resemble each

Exhibit 8–10 Performance Appraisal Measurement Methods

Critical incidents file: Managers note an employee's positive and negative performance behavior throughout the performance period. This form of documentation is particularly necessary in today's litigious environment.

Rating scale: Managers simply check off the employee's level of performance. Typical areas evaluated include quantity of work, dependability, judgment, attitude, cooperation, and initiative.

Behaviorally anchored rating scales (BARS): This method combines rating and critical incidents. It is more objective and accurate than the two methods separately. Rather than using excellent, good, average, and poor ratings, managers choose from several statements the one that best describes the employee's performance for that task. Good BARS make standards clear.

Ranking: Managers rank employee performance from best to worst. That is, managers compare employees to each other, rather than comparing each person to a standard measurement. An off-shoot of ranking is the forced distribution method, which resembles grading on a curve. A predetermined percentage of employees are placed in performance categories: for example, excellent—5%, above average—15%, average—60%, below average—15%, and poor—5%.

Management by objectives (MBO): Managers and their employees jointly set objectives for the employee, periodically evaluate his or her performance, and reward according to the results (see Chapter 4 for details).

Narrative: Managers write a statement about the employee's performance. The system varies. Managers may be allowed to write whatever they want, or they may be required to answer specific questions about performance. Narratives are often combined with another method.

APPLYING THE CONCEPT   *Selecting Performance Appraisal Methods*

Use Exhibit 8–10 to select the most appropriate PA method for the given situation.

a. critical incidents   **d.** ranking

b. rating scales   **e.** MBO

c. BARS   **f.** narrative

_____ 21. The roller-skating rink you started six years ago now has 10 employees. You're overworked, so you want to develop one PA form that you can use with every employee.

_____ 22. You've been promoted to middle management at Golf Balls Deluxe. You've been asked to select your replacement.

_____ 23. Winnie, who markets the new line of basketballs, isn't performing up to standard. You decide to talk to her about ways she can improve her performance.

_____ 24. You want to create a system for helping employees realize their potential.

_____ 25. Your roller-skating rink has grown to 50 employees. Some of them are concerned that the form you're using doesn't work well for the various jobs, so you've hired a professional to develop a PA system that is more objective and job-specific. You have specifically asked her to develop more focused PA forms.

other. Note the collaborative tone in the steps. Remember, you and the employee are on the same side here—maximizing their potential is in *both* your best interests.

RETAINING EMPLOYEES

Besides attracting and developing their workforce, organizations must have HR systems in place that will help them retain this extremely valuable resource. High turnover rates reduce productivity and profitability, and cause morale to plummet. Replacing a good employee can cost half to several times a year's pay, depending on the job. Thus, organizations go to great lengths to keep the employees they have. There are numerous strategies for doing this: People who believe they are being justly rewarded tend to stay. A culture of respect and valuing people and their contributions keeps people. A good work environment keeps people. So does challenging work and good feedback. And so does an informed and highly skilled HR department. Therefore, in this section we examine compensation, health and safety, labor relations, and termination and outplacement.

Compensation

9 LEARNING OUTCOME
State the two major components of compensation.

compensation
The total cost of pay and benefits to employees.

Compensation is the total cost of pay and benefits to employees. Compensation is pivotal in both attracting and retaining employees. An important strategic decision is the organization's pay level. *Pay level* refers to whether the organization aims at being a high-, medium-, or low-paying organization. Low-paying firms may save money by low-balling wages, but such savings can be lost to the high cost of turnover.

PAY SYSTEMS. There are three general compensation methods, and organizations use all three. (1) *Wages* are paid on an hourly basis. (If you work 45 hours, you get paid your hourly

Model 8–4   Steps in Solid Performance Appraisals

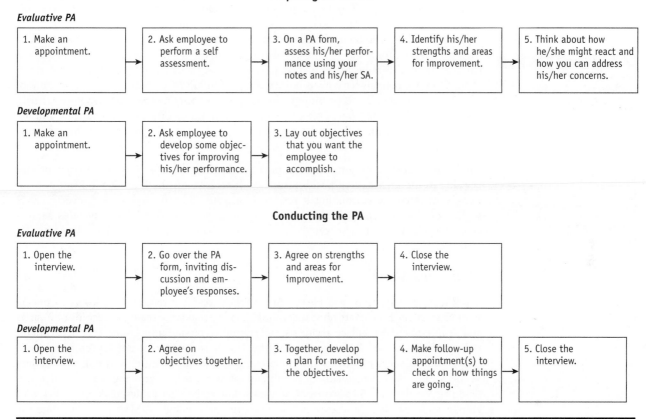

Preparing for the PA

Evaluative PA

| 1. Make an appointment. | → | 2. Ask employee to perform a self assessment. | → | 3. On a PA form, assess his/her performance using your notes and his/her SA. | → | 4. Identify his/her strengths and areas for improvement. | → | 5. Think about how he/she might react and how you can address his/her concerns. |

Developmental PA

| 1. Make an appointment. | → | 2. Ask employee to develop some objectives for improving his/her performance. | → | 3. Lay out objectives that you want the employee to accomplish. |

Conducting the PA

Evaluative PA

| 1. Open the interview. | → | 2. Go over the PA form, inviting discussion and employee's responses. | → | 3. Agree on strengths and areas for improvement. | → | 4. Close the interview. |

Developmental PA

| 1. Open the interview. | → | 2. Agree on objectives together. | → | 3. Together, develop a plan for meeting the objectives. | → | 4. Make follow-up appointment(s) to check on how things are going. | → | 5. Close the interview. |

wage times 45 hours.) (2) *Salary* is figured weekly, monthly, or annually, but does not take into account the number of hours worked. (If you work 30 hours or 45 hours, your weekly salary stays the same.) (3) *Incentives* are pay for performance. Incentives include piece rate (pay based on production), commissions (pay based on sales), merit raises (the more productive workers get paid more), and bonuses. Two common bonuses include a specific reward for reaching an objective and profit sharing in which employees get a part of the profits.[27] Pay for performance is also commonly used.[28] Professional athletes sometimes receive enormous salaries—recall that in an earlier chapter we mentioned MLB player Alex Rodriguez, who is paid about $22 million a year. However, many more athletes are paid a base amount, then get incentive pay if they perform well—that is, if they reach a certain number of hits, touchdowns, quarterback sacks, or games played. General managers believe that incentive pay motivates players to excel—"give it their all."

10 LEARNING OUTCOME
Describe how job analyses and job evaluations are used.

DETERMINING PAY. How much to pay each employee is a difficult decision organizations face year in and year out. Some organizations use an external approach—they find out what other organizations pay for the same or similar jobs and set their pay based on that. Other organizations use an internal approach that involves job evaluation. **Job evaluation** determines the worth of each job relative to other jobs in the organization. Organizations commonly group jobs into pay grades. The higher the worth or grade of the job, the higher the pay. Both approaches are frequently used together. *Comparable worth* is yet another approach that has been around for a while but remains controversial. In **comparable worth** jobs that are distinctly different but that require similar levels of ability, responsibility, skills, working conditions, and so on are valued equally and paid equally. This means

job evaluation
The process of determining the worth of each job relative to other jobs in the organization.

comparable worth
Jobs that are distinctly different but that require similar levels of ability, responsibility, skills, working conditions, and so on are valued equally and paid equally.

that a lot of jobs traditionally held by women would rise in pay, even though we have previously valued them less than certain jobs traditionally held by men.

BENEFITS. *Benefits* are the part of a compensation package that is not direct wages. They are also not merit-based. Legally required benefits include *workers' compensation* to cover job-related injuries, *unemployment compensation* for when people are laid off or terminated, and *Social Security* for retirement. Employers match the amount the government takes out of each person's pay for Social Security. Benefits that are *technically* optional but that are offered almost universally are health insurance; paid sick days, holidays, and vacations; and pension plans. Optional benefits have been historically paid in full by employers, but today some of them (health insurance and pension plans) are split between employee and employer or paid completely by the employee. Other benefits less commonly offered include dental and life insurance, membership to fitness centers, membership in credit unions, and tuition reimbursement.[29]

TIMEOUT
Describe the compensation package offered by your current employer.

The benefits portion of compensation packages has been increasing over the years, primarily due to the high cost of health insurance. It varies with the level of job from one- to two-thirds of compensation, but it has been estimated that the average employee receives slightly over 40 percent of their compensation from benefits. Work-family benefits, such as elder and childcare, are also on the increase, as organizations focus on work-family life issues.[30]

Health and Safety

The Occupational Safety and Health Act (OSHA) of 1970 requires employers to pursue workplace safety. Employers must meet OSHA safety standards, maintain records of injuries and deaths due to workplace accidents, and submit to on-site inspections. HR departments commonly are responsible for ensuring the health and safety of employees. They work closely with other departments and often conduct new-hire training and ongoing training in this area, as well as maintaining health and safety records. A growing area of concern is workplace violence.[31] As a manager, you must know the safety rules, make sure that your employees know them, and enforce them to prevent accidents. OSHA is investigating the death of Minnesota Vikings offensive lineman Kory Stringer, who died of heatstroke during practice. OSHA is trying to determine whether the Vikings adequately discussed workplace hazard issues.[32] **Do you think NFL teams consider OSHA when selecting players to fit under the salary cap?**

Labor Relations

labor relations
Interactions between management and unionized employees.

Labor relations are the interactions between management and unionized employees. Labor relations are also called union-management relations and industrial relations. There are many more organizations without unions than there are with unions. Therefore, not all organizations include labor relations as part of their HR systems. Unions are organizations that represent employees in collective bargaining with employers. They are also a source of recruitment. The National Labor Relations Act (also known as the Wagner Act, after its sponsor) established the National Labor Relations Board (NLRB) in 1935; this board conducts unionization elections, hears unfair labor practice complaints, and issues injunctions against offending employers.

UNION-ORGANIZING. There are typically five stages in forming a union, as Exhibit 8–11 shows.

11 LEARNING OUTCOME
Give a brief history of labor relations in Major League Baseball.

How Baseball Players Joined the Union

"For all the hand-wringing and laments for the good old days, baseball has outlasted sky-is-falling owners, spoiled players, scandal, and embarrassment for more than 100 years," says Alan Schwarz, *New York Times* columnist and avid fan.[33] Our national pastime thus provides

Exhibit 8-11   The Union-Organizing Process

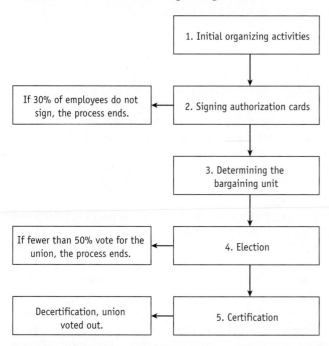

a rich example of labor relations. Conflicts between baseball players and owners date back to the 1880s. Fans have endured five strikes since 1966 and the owners have locked players out three times (1973, 1976, and 1990).[34] The following brief history will give you a feel for where labor issues are coming from in pro sports. As Steve Greenberg (former deputy commissioner and son of the legendary Hank Greenberg) notes, "You can't get the full picture without understanding the history of vitriol and animosity."[35]

Salary caps are the maximum amount of money a team can spend on players. In the 1880s MLB owners established the first salary cap in pro sports—their $2,000 salary cap was not peanuts, although it seems paltry today, even taking into account inflation.[36] A 1914 *Baseball Magazine* editorial blasted the players' "recent evil tendency to purchase and maintain automobiles."[37]

MLB's first challenge to its hold on the sport came in 1913 when Federal Base Ball (FBB) tried to start a new league. Eventually, FBB's major investors joined up with Major League Baseball. However, one owner objected to the deal and sued under antitrust law. The case made it all the way to the Supreme Court, which ruled that baseball was exempt from federal antitrust law. This landmark decision essentially made MLB a federally sanctioned monopoly.[38]

Player/owner spats continued unabated, however. Remember the "Black Sox" scandal? Eight White Sox players threw the 1919 World Series, supposedly because of owner Comiskey's stinginess.[39] Players who dared to criticize management's infamous reserve clause (which basically married players to their clubs for life with no chance of divorce) were called "persons of avowed Communist tendencies" by 1949 Brooklyn Dodgers executive Branch Rickey.[40] The **reserve clause** allowed teams to automatically re-sign their players at the end of the season.

By the 1950s star players were creating their own associations to discuss such issues as minimum salaries and retirement pensions. However, these associations were not real unions, so the owners didn't take them seriously.[41]

By the 1960s baseball players began to believe that a players' union was the only way to negotiate better benefits. LA Dodgers star pitchers Sandy Koufax and Don Drysdale held out before the 1966 season. When they did sign, both players received substantial salary increases. Koufax settled for one year at $125,000 and Drysdale for $110,000.[42]

salary caps
The maximum amount of money a team can spend on players.

reserve clause
Allowed teams to automatically re-sign their players at the end of the season.

The late 1960s and early 1970s saw the players' union trying to break management's infamous reserve clause, which "treated players as chattel," according to Albert Hunt.[43] In 1969, St. Louis Cardinals star player, Curt Flood, asked for a substantial salary increase but instead found himself promptly traded to the Philadelphia Phillies. He sued to stay in St. Louis. This case also went all the way to the Supreme Court, which ruled against Flood, citing the Federal Base Ball decision of 1915. The Flood case showed the Supreme Court was unwilling to change the reserve system.[44]

free agent
A player who is free to negotiate a contract with any team.

A successful challenge to the reserve clause didn't occur until the 1970s. The first case came when Charles Finley, owner of the Oakland Athletics, withheld part of Catfish Hunter's $100,000 salary. Hunter's contract stipulated that half of his salary go toward purchasing an annuity in an insurance fund. Finley didn't pay because of a tax question, so he had not fulfilled the contract, and this allowed Hunter to become a free agent.[45] A **free agent** is a player who is free to negotiate a contract with any team. Catfish Hunter went on to sign a huge contract with the New York Yankees, and it was the beginning of the end for the reserve system.

Rather than sit out the 1975 season, Andy Messersmith of the Los Angeles Dodgers played under the standard contract that was renewed by the Dodgers, but he never signed it. Courts later ruled that when Messersmith chose to play at the Dodgers' option, but without signing the new contract, he became a free agent.[46] Today, after several versions of free agency, free agents can sign with any team that will sign them, and the original team receives a draft pick.

MLB's unique exemption from antitrust laws under the 1915 Federal Base Ball decision prevails to this day, even though there are periodic rumblings in Congress about changing it. But owners and players still tangle periodically.[47] The 1976 baseball season started without a contract, so owners locked players out of spring training that year. Owners were subsequently found guilty in court of collusion three times (1987, 1988, and 1990).[48] *Collusion* meant the owners were guilty of working together to organize how they would bid or not bid for free agent ballplayers. The 1994–1995 baseball season ended in a strike, and the World Series was cancelled.[49] Even the 2002 season was played under the shadow of labor tensions and threats of a strike. Fortunately, both sides were able to negotiate a last-minute settlement, and the 2002 season was completed as scheduled.

Collective Bargaining

collective bargaining
The negotiation process resulting in a contract that covers employment conditions at the organization.

Collective bargaining is the process of unions and management negotiating a contract that covers employment conditions at the organization. Contracts typically stipulate compensation, hours, working conditions, and health benefits. But contracts can include other issues—job security, for example, which is a hot issue for unions today. Pro sports and business organizations are not the only groups that deal with labor issues. Colleges and other nonprofits also find themselves sitting at the collective bargaining table. For example, it took three years of negotiations for the union that represents nonfaculty coaches who work for the Pennsylvania State Athletic Conferences (PSAC) to reach a collective bargaining agreement with the Pennsylvania state system of higher education. The contract increases minimum salaries to $30,000 for full-time head coaches and $25,000 for full-time assistants.[50]

strike
When employees refuse to go to work.

lockout
When management refuses to let employees in to work.

To avoid a **strike** (employees refuse to go to work), or a **lockout** (management refuses to let employees in to work), and to handle *grievances* by either side, involved parties sometimes agree to use neutral third parties, called mediators, from the Federal Mediation and Conciliation Service. *Mediators* are neutral parties who help management and labor settle disagreements. In cases where the two parties are unwilling to compromise but still want to avoid a strike or lockout, they may choose to call in an arbitrator. *Arbitrators* differ from mediators in that arbitrators' decisions are binding (must be followed). Arbitrators more typically work to settle grievances; mediators deal with impasses in collective bargaining.

A recent example of arbitration involves NHL player Billy Guerin, who plays wing for the Boston Bruins. An all-star in the 2000–2001 season, with 40 goals and 45 assists, Guerin has had a difficult negotiation history with previous teams. When negotiations broke down yet again going into the 2001–2002 season, Guerin chose arbitration. The Bruins offered $3.4 million, a small increase from his previous contract. Guerin countered with $5.9 million. The arbitrator sided with Guerin and awarded him the $5.9-million contract.[51] This golden boy went on to have an all-star 2001–2002 season. The Dallas Stars then signed Guerin as a free agent following the 2001–2002 season—the Bruins gambled and lost one of their key players. Interestingly, one study of Major League Baseball notes that the performance of free agents frequently declines after they move to new teams. (Ken Griffey Jr. comes to mind.) This study suggests that if MLB teams were to pay free agents based on their future performance (that is, their first year on the new team), players might not be so eager to become free agents.[52]

Termination and Outplacement

Employees leave organizations for three primary reasons: (1) voluntarily (for other jobs or for other reasons like retirement or health issues); and involuntarily—(2) because they are fired and (3) because they are laid off. Whatever causes attrition (voluntary termination), these employees often need to be replaced. Employees who leave voluntarily are often interviewed to find out why they are leaving. The *exit interview*, usually conducted by the HR department, helps identify problem areas that may be causing turnover. Involuntary termination occurs in one of two ways—firing (when employees break important rules and are otherwise found wanting) and layoffs (which occur because of downturns in the economy or problems in the organization, and through mergers and acquisitions). In 1998 Nike laid off about 1,600 people worldwide due to unexpected high levels of inventories.[53] Nike's CEO Philip Knight observed, "The job reductions were difficult to undertake, but necessary to make the company competitive."[54] When companies undergo layoffs, they sometimes offer *outplacement services,* the purpose of which is to help employees find new jobs. Why would companies bother, you ask? The reason is simple—for goodwill (they may want to hire those people back someday) and to avoid wrongful-termination lawsuits.

CHAPTER SUMMARY

1. Describe the four parts of HR management.

The four parts are (1) human resources planning, (2) attracting employees, (3) developing employees, and (4) retaining employees.

2. Differentiate between a job description and a job specification and explain why they are needed.

Job descriptions identify what a worker does on the job, whereas job specifications list the qualifications needed to do the job. Job analysis is an important basis for attracting, developing, and retaining employees.

3. State the two parts of attracting employees.

The two parts are recruiting and selecting. Recruiting is about persuading qualified candidates to apply for job openings. Selecting is about choosing the most qualified applicant recruited for a job.

4. Explain how hypothetical questions and probing questions differ.

Hypothetical questions are planned; they require candidates to describe what they would do and say in a given situation. Probing questions are not planned and are used to clarify responses.

5. State the purposes of orientation and training and development.

Orientation introduces new employees to the organization, its culture, and their jobs. Training and development help employees acquires new skills that they will use to perform present and future jobs.

6. Describe job instructional training.

(1) Preparation of the trainee, (2) presentation of the task, (3) performance of the task by trainee, and (4) follow-up.

7. Define the two types of performance appraisals.

Developmental PAs are used to improve performance. Evaluative PAs are used to give pay raises, transfers and promotions, and demotions and terminations.

8. Explain the concept, "You get what you reward."

People seek information concerning what activities are rewarded, and then endeavor to do those things, often to the exclusion of activities not rewarded.

9. State the two major components of compensation.

The two components are pay and benefits.

10. Describe how job analyses and job evaluations are used.

Job analyses determine what the job should entail and the qualifications needed to staff the position. Job evaluations determine how to pay employees for their work.

11. Give a brief history of labor relations in Major League Baseball.

MLB labor relations have been difficult for over 100 years. Both managers and players have tangled over such issues as salary caps, reserve clauses, free agency, and benefits. The result has been a series of strikes and lockouts. The two sides tiptoed past another strike in 2002.

12. Define the key terms discussed in the text.

Fill in the missing key terms from memory, or match the key terms from the list in the margin with their definitions below.

Key Terms

assessment centers

bona fide occupational
  qualification (BFOQ)

collective bargaining

comparable worth

compensation

development

free agent

human resources
  management

job description

job evaluation

job specifications

labor relations

lockout

orientation

performance appraisal

recruiting

reserve clause

salary caps

selection

strategic human
  resources planning

strike

training

vestibule training

_____ consists of planning, attracting, developing, and retaining employees.

A _____ allows discrimination where it is reasonably necessary to normal operation of a particular organization.

_____ is the process of staffing an organization to meet its objectives.

The _____ identifies the tasks and responsibilities of a position.

_____ identify the qualifications needed to staff a position.

_____ is the process of attracting qualified candidates to apply for job openings.

_____ is the process of choosing the most qualified applicant recruited for a job.

In _____ job applicants undergo a series of tests, interviews, and simulated experiences to determine their managerial potential.

_____ introduces new employees to the organization, its culture, and their jobs.

_____ helps people acquire the skills necessary to perform a job.

_____ is ongoing education to improve skills for present and future jobs.

_____ develops skills in a simulated setting.

_____ is the ongoing process of evaluating employee performance.

_____ is the total cost of pay and benefits to employees.

_____ determines the worth of each job relative to other jobs in the organization.

In _____ jobs that are distinctly different but that require similar levels of ability, responsibility, skills, working conditions, and so on are valued equally and paid equally.

_____ are the interactions between management and unionized employees.

_____ are the maximum amount of money a team can spend on players.

A _____ allowed teams to automatically re-sign their players at the end of the season.

A _____ is a player who is free to negotiate a contract with any team.

_____ is the negotiation process resulting in a contract that covers employment conditions at the organization.

When employees/players _____, they refuse to go to work.

When management calls a _____, they refuse to let employees in to work.

REVIEW AND DISCUSSION

1. How do you feel about bona fide occupational qualifications?

2. What are the components of a job analysis?

3. What do you think about promoting from within for pro baseball teams? Why would this work or not work?

4. Should the interview be the primary criterion in selecting a coach? If so, why? If not, why not?

5. What web site helps people find jobs in sports?

6. Suppose the firm you work for has an HR department. What does this mean for you as a manager? What services will it typically provide? What will you still need to do?

7. How does setting objectives affect measuring and evaluating training results for a general manager? For a coach? For an athlete?

8. How does compensation help attract and retain employees? In view of your answer, why do some organizations elect as their strategy to be low-paying organizations, while others elect to be high-paying ones?

9. Why don't most employees realize how expensive benefits are and how much they contribute to compensation cost?

10. Are player unions greedy because they expect more than they are worth? Or do management/owners take too large a share of the profits for themselves? What do their stances imply for the future of pro sports?

11. What is the difference between mediators and arbitrators?

12. Define the reserve clause and free agency.

13. What is the difference between a strike and a lockout?

CASE

Coach Jekyll and Coach Hyde

Bobby Knight is not an easy coach to fathom. One of the youngest coaches ever to achieve 700 wins in NCAA college basketball, Knight argues that his style may not be pretty, but his teams win. He is right about that. His coaching style is *not* pretty—in fact, put mildly, it is vocal, confrontational, and loaded with controversy. Mention Bobby Knight, and chair throwing comes to mind (Indiana vs. Purdue, 1984–1985 season)—the dilemma is, so does winning (Indiana was NCAA champion in 1976, 1981, and 1987).

Fans like winners, and Knight, a true basketball genius, built a large and loyal following in the state of Indiana. Knight was very successful at externally recruiting players. But there can be costs to winning, and sometimes they are too high. Knight's costs came home to roost in March 2000 when his high-visibility style got him in hot coaching water. Knight's coaching style is to be highly energized and to control his team as much as possible. However, a former player, Neil Reed, asserted that Knight choked him on the court. Allegations by other former Indiana players began to surface. Knight held onto his coaching position for a while but was fired in September 2000 for what university president Myles Brand considered a pattern of unacceptable behavior. Knight had violated a zero-tolerance policy the university had implemented to control his actions.

Of course, much of Knight's personnel information at Indiana is private. But it behooves us to wonder. Where was HR as his behavior began to deteriorate? Are some people above human resources? Are some positions above the behavior parameters set for others? If so, is the organization still liable for unacceptable behavior from people in such positions? Did HR let Knight and the university down? Did Knight receive fair treatment? Was a program of progressive discipline and/or counseling undertaken before he was fired? Does he have a case against Indiana if he didn't receive counseling? Do his former players have a case against Indiana for allowing them to be endangered? Did the fact that Knight brought fame and fortune to the Indiana campus enter into Indiana's winking at his behavior? Should it have?

In 2001 Texas Tech reached outside its university in its search for candidates to coach the men's basketball team. Tech selected Knight, and he has already led the team to an NCAA tournament appearance. So far, at Tech Knight has led by being a positive example.

For current information on Bobby Knight, use Internet address http://texastech.fansonly.com/sports/m-baskbl/text-m-baskbl-body.html. There is also a multimedia presentation at http://sportsillustrated.cnn.com/multimedia_central/news/2000/03/15/knight_mmc.

CASE QUESTIONS

1. Which area of training would benefit Bobby Knight?
   a. technical training
   b. people and communication skills
   c. conceptual and decision-making skills

2. At Indiana, Knight's primary recruiting source for players was
   a. internal
   b. external

3. There were good employee relations between Knight and Indiana University.

   a. true   b. false

4. Coach Knight received a reserve clause after he was terminated.

   a. true   b. false

5. Coach Knight's management style was to let his players run the team.

   a. true   b. false

6. Knight left Indiana University for which reason?

   a. retirement

   b. another job

   c. breaking the rules

   d. layoffs

7. Internal recruiting occurred when Knight accepted the position at Texas Tech.

   a. true   b. false

8. Suppose Indiana's replacement for Knight was his assistant coach; this would be an example of what recruiting method?

   a. walk-in

   b. educational institutional

   c. agency

   d. promotion from within

9. Apparently, Texas Tech was comfortable with Knight's past record at Indiana with regard to behavior and coaching. This is an example of

   a. application form

   b. screening interview

   c. testing

   d. background check

10. Knight eventually met with Texas Tech's president to discuss the possibility of him taking the coaching position. This is an example of which stage of the selection process?

    a. application form

    b. interview

    c. testing

    d. background check

11. Why do you think there is such a high turnover rate among college coaches?

12. Do you believe that Indiana University gave Bobby Knight enough chances before they fired him?

EXERCISES

Skill-Builder: Selecting a Tennis Coach

Objective:

■ To perform a job analysis and to develop your interviewing skills.

Preparation:

You're in your first year as athletic director at a local high school, and you have an opening for a tennis coach. Compensation, which is competitive with the pay of other tennis coaches in the area, is set in the budget and will be paid in one lump sum at the end of the season. You don't have a recruiting budget, so you do some internal recruiting and contact some athletic directors in your area to spread the word about the opening.

Your efforts yield three candidates. Here are their qualifications:

■ Candidate A has taught history at your school for ten years. He also coached tennis for two years, but it's been five years since he coached the team. You don't know why he stopped coaching or how good a job he did. He never played competitive tennis. However, someone told you he plays regularly and is pretty good. You guess he's about 35 years old.

- Candidate B supervises the graveyard shift for a local business. She has never coached before, but she was a star player in high school and college. She still plays in local tournaments, and you see her name in the paper now and then. You guess she is about 25 years old.
- Candidate C has been a basketball coach and physical education teacher at a nearby high school for the past five years. She has a master's degree in physical education. You figure it will take her 20 minutes to get to your school. She has never coached tennis, but she did play high school tennis. She plays tennis about once a week. You guess she is about 45 years old.

Preparing for the interviews:
Follow the steps given in Model 8–1. For step 1, there are no job descriptions or specifications. Because there are only three candidates, you've decided to interview them all.

In-Class Application

Complete the skill-building preparation noted above before class, and bring your interview questions to class.

Choose one (1–2 hours):
- Break into groups of three, and present the questions you developed. As a group, critique the various lists, and then use the best questions to develop a PA form that you think best serves this situation. Now meet with another group and take turns using your master list to interview the three "candidates" from the other group. Allot no more than 15 minutes per interview (even though this is unrealistic in a real-world setting). (Make sure you follow the steps outlined in Model 8–2.) Observing members give feedback after each interview.
- Informal, whole-class discussion of students' interview questions.

Wrap-up:
Take a few minutes and write down your answers to the following questions:

- What did I learn from this experience?

  _____

  _____

  _____

- How will I use this knowledge in the future?

  _____

  _____

  _____

As a class, discuss student responses.

Internet Skills: The History of Labor Relations in MLB

Objective:
- To use your research skills to find out more about the history of labor relations in Major League Baseball.

Preparation (50 minutes):
Visit http://bigleaguers.yahoo.com, the official web site of the Major League Baseball Players Association (MLBPA). Explore the site looking for information on salary caps and use this information to answer the following questions.

1. When was the MLBPA created?

   _____

2. What does the MLBPA do?

   _____

   _____

   _____

3. When was the first collective bargaining agreement (CBA) negotiated between the players and owners?

   _____

4. What is the record between players and owners in salary arbitration cases?

   _____

5. When does a player become eligible for free agency?

   _____

   _____

9

Behavior in Organizations: Power, Politics, Conflict, and Stress

Learning Outcomes

After studying this chapter, you should be able to:

1. Describe the Big Five personality traits.

2. Understand the perception process and the two factors it is based on.

3. Explain how personality, perception, and attitude are related, and why they are important.

4. State what job satisfaction is and why it is important.

5. Define power and the difference between position and personal power.

6. Explain how reward, legitimate, and referent power differ.

7. Understand how power and politics are related.

8. Explain what networking, reciprocity, and coalitions have in common.

9. Describe the five conflict management styles.

10. Use collaboration to resolve conflict.

11. Explain the stress tug-of-war analogy.

12. Define the following key terms (in order of appearance in the chapter):

- organizational behavior
- win-win situation
- personality
- perception
- attribution
- attitudes
- Pygmalion effect
- power
- politics
- networking

- reciprocity
- coalition
- conflict
- dysfunctional conflict
- functional conflict
- initiators
- BCF statements
- mediator
- arbitrator
- stress
- stressors

Applying Legitimate Power at the NCAA

The NCAA (National Collegiate Amateur Association) is a powerful and well-funded sport organization that accredits college athletic programs. A voluntary association of about 1,200 organizations, the NCAA focuses on better ways to administer intercollegiate athletics. It is the mouthpiece through which our colleges and universities speak out on athletics. Its mission is to see that intercollegiate athletics are an integral part of every college's educational program and that athletes are high-functioning members of every student body. One of its main objectives is to promote good conduct in intercollegiate athletics.[1]

No one will debate that the NCAA does a good job in many areas. The NCAA funnels much of the money it generates through NCAA basketball and football to fund NCAA sports that are not self-supporting. Once Title IX was passed, the NCAA worked tirelessly to get to gender equity in college sports. The result? Women now participate equally with men in many college sports. In fact, the Women's Final Four NCAA tournament has more fans and media coverage every year.

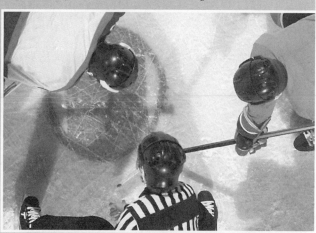

The NCAA is also mired in controversy. Some say that the NCAA uses its power coercively by abandoning its amateur status in favor of the commercial success of big-time sports.[2] The NCAA rules (indeed, they must rule on these issues, as they are the governing body) on all manner of issues—from how to recruit students to whether students can use sports agents to whether student athletes should receive a salary for playing a game that many millions spend (good) money to watch. Many charge that their rules are too restrictive. Others (like the Knight Commission on Intercollegiate Athletics, formed in 1990 and reconvened in 2000) often criticize the Association for failing to maintain academic standards, for not being more fiscally responsible, for commercializing collegiate sports, and for college presidents not being accountable for their policies.[3] For example, the Knight Commission determined that college presidents should control their schools' involvement with television.[4] Also, that coaches are paid millions of dollars and that college teams receive payments from the likes of Nike and Adidas to wear their athletic apparel give many pause for thought. Are college sports for all intents and purposes no longer amateur sports? That is, are they professional sports in all but name?

That is only a small sampling of the difficult issues facing the NCAA. Here are a few others. Revamping their programs to satisfy Title IX has left universities with little choice but to eliminate various men's programs. Wrestling, tennis, swimming, and gymnastics have often been eliminated.[5] And, although basketball and football revenues support many lesser-known collegiate sports, they also graduate a smaller percentage of players than those sports.[6] The Knight Commission proposed that schools graduate at least half their players or be eliminated from postseason competition. Such a position would have eliminated many of the teams who participated in the 2002 NCAA basketball tournament.[7]

Understanding the role the NCAA plays in collegiate sports is crucial for those of you who intend to pursue a career in collegiate sports administration. For more information about the NCAA, visit http://www.ncaa.org. Search the site for information about the Knight Commission Report to gain insight into important issues facing the NCAA. (For ideas on using the Internet, see Appendix B.)

INTERNET RESOURCES

**http://www.bbhighway.com/Talk/Coaching_Box/Clinics/ALambert/
conflict_management.asp** *Another great article from the Basketball Highway—"The*

Importance of Conflict Management in Coaching" helps you determine the cause of conflict within your team or management, gives you the tools to resolve conflict in a way that will be beneficial to all involved, and offers suggestions for establishing rules that will keep you focused on finding a solution rather than flying off the handle. By building from these simple rules, perhaps you will eventually learn how to create an atmosphere of open communication in which conflicts are resolved before they become major issues.

http://www.humanmetrics.com/cgi-win/JTypes2.asp *Take Humanmetrics' Jung Typology Test to determine your personality type. The 72 questions are based on the works of Carl Jung as well as the Myers-Briggs typology. Take your time to consider each question—and make sure your answers reflect who you really are, not who you'd like to be in an ideal world. After you submit your answers, which personality type you most closely fit will be revealed. Although the categories are somewhat different from those given in the first Self Assessment in this chapter, on the Humanmetrics web site you will be given the opportunity to read in more depth about the factors that make up your personality.*

http://www.pp.okstate.edu/ehs/links/stress.htm *To learn more about how stress affects your daily performance and to discover a range of techniques to relieve your tension, visit Oklahoma State University's online Stress Management library. Here you'll find links to articles and organizations that can help you bring your stress down to a manageable level so that you can breathe easily again.*

DEVELOPING YOUR SKILLS   Your people skills and communication skills are the most important management skills you can develop. Getting your management job done, and done well, requires that you get work done through others. Effective leaders share at least one thing in common—they all have amazing people skills. We will discuss these in great detail in the leadership section, Chapters 9–13, but first it behooves us to stand back for a moment and look at organizational behavior. Why? Because understanding how people behave in the workplace helps you see how you should be leading your "troops." It will also help you understand how to use power and negotiation to get the job done.

ORGANIZATIONAL BEHAVIOR

Have you ever wondered why coworkers behave the way they do? This is what organizational behaviorists look at. Our behavior consists of what we say and do—in a word, our actions. **Organizational behavior (OB)** is the study of actions that affect performance in the workplace. Organizational behaviorists endeavor to explain and predict actions in the workplace and show how such actions affect performance. They attempt to create win-win situations. **Win-win situations** occur when organizations and their employees get what they want. OB has three levels of focus: individual, group, and organizational. In this chapter we examine individual behavior; in Chapter 9 we look at group behavior; and we discussed the organizational level in Chapter 7 (as organizational development).

The better you understand OB, the more effective you will be at working with others both as a manager and as a worker. Three components—our personality, perception, and attitudes—drive our behavior. They are the foundations on which our behavior is built, and they are observable through our every action. Understanding how personality, perception, and attitude drive behavior gives you insight into how people will behave in certain situations.

PERSONALITY

Look around you. You will see outgoing, shy, loud, quiet, warm, cold, aggressive, and passive people—we come in all flavors and stripes. These "stripes and flavors" are what behaviorists call individual traits. **Personality** is the combination of traits that characterizes individuals. Our personality affects our behavior, our perceptions, and our attitudes. Because of this, organizations routinely consider personality as they place people to ensure a proper match between workers and jobs. Take sports announcers. Quiet announcers—no matter how

organizational behavior
The study of actions that affect performance in the workplace.

win-win situation
A situation in which both parties get what they want.

personality
The combination of traits that characterizes individuals.

good their knowledge or skill—would be the death knell for *Monday Night Football* or *NBA on NBC*. No, only extroverts—and preferably idiosyncratic ones—need apply for announcer jobs. Think about the late Howard Cosell, Billy Packard, John Madden, Charles Barkley, and Deion Sanders—where would their viewership be if they didn't have lively on-air personalities? CBS Sports President Sean McManus believes that today, with channels crammed with sports content and the resulting fragmentation in audience loyalties, announcer personalities are pivotal in garnering viewership.[8]

Our personalities are shaped by our genes and by the environment. Our genes we are born with—the environment that forms us is composed of our families, our friends, and our life experiences. Researchers have developed numerous ways to classify personality. Two widely recognized ones are the single traits system and the Big Five personality traits. To get a feel for how organizational behaviorists use these traits, complete the Self Assessment on page 241. But first review the brief summary of each given here.

Single Traits System of Personality

Key traits in the single traits system are locus of control, optimism, risk propensity, Machiavellianism, self-esteem, and self-efficacy. (Self-esteem and self-efficacy are based on perception, so they are discussed with perception.) This system places each trait on a continuum.

LOCUS OF CONTROL. This trait, which deals with who we believe controls our destiny, lies on a continuum with externalizers at one end and internalizers at the other. Externalizers believe that they have no control over their fate and that their behavior has little to do with their performance. Internalizers believe just the opposite—that they control their fate and that their behavior directly affects their performance. Internalizers obviously tend to perform better.

OPTIMISM. The continuum here is between optimists and pessimists. Optimists believe that things will go well, and they approach life with a can-do attitude. Pessimists believe that everything that can go wrong will go wrong, and this infuses their approach to life. Optimists take action to meet objectives because they believe they can make a difference, whereas pessimists give up easily and are defeated much earlier than optimists.

RISK PROPENSITY. This trait lies on a continuum between risk takers and risk avoiders. Entrepreneurs are risk takers. Successful organizations seek managers who take reasonable risks, risks that they can justify based on market research and their reading of the environment. Organizations whose managers avoid reasonable risk too much of the time can find themselves closing their doors. Don Ohlmeyer, who produced *Monday Night Football* during its highest ratings in 1970s, took a big risk when he hired abrasive nonathlete Howard Cosell. That move paid off generously. However, after Ohlmeyer had been away from Monday Night Football for many years, he returned for one year in 1999 and hired comedian Dennis Miller. The move did not go over well with viewers.[9] Decision makers must realize all their risky decisions will not be huge successes. *Monday Night Football* has since replaced Miller and hired John Madden, a popular sports announcer previously on the FOX television network.[10]

MACHIAVELLIANISM. This trait has to do with the degree to which we believe that the ends justify the means and thus how much we are willing to use (or abuse) power to get what we want. The term comes from the sixteenth-century Renaissance philosopher Niccolo Machiavelli. Behavioralists have found that "high Machs" can be effective in situations in which bargaining and winning are important, such as jobs that require negotiating (purchasing/labor) or as commissioned sales reps. However, high Machs are more concerned about meeting their needs than helping the organization. Thus, they tend to create win-lose situations and may use unethical behavior to achieve their ends.

The Big Five Personality Traits

1 LEARNING OUTCOME
Describe the Big Five personality traits.

The Big Five trait system is the most widely accepted way to classify personalities. The five traits are also defined as continuums.

EXTROVERSION. This trait lies on a continuum between extroverts and introverts. Do you like to meet new people? You may be an extrovert. Extroverts often do well in sales and management.

AGREEABLENESS. This trait lies on a continuum between cooperators and competitors. Do you cooperate with your coworkers or do you compete with them? Teams whose members cooperate with each other and compete with external teams show higher levels of performance than when the competition goes "inside." This may also be true of professional sports. Can you name some teams that have high-stature star players who are not team players? How are those teams doing?

EMOTIONALISM. The continuum here is between emotionally stable and emotionally unstable. Stable people are calm, secure, and positive, whereas unstable people are nervous, insecure, and negative. Do you typically behave with a positive attitude or a negative one? Like the optimism continuum in the single trait system, workers with positive attitudes generally perform better.

CONSCIENTIOUSNESS. This continuum has responsible/dependable at one end and irresponsible/undependable at the other. It has also been portrayed as being a planner (organized) or not (unorganized). Obviously, responsible employees outperform irresponsible ones.

OPENNESS TO EXPERIENCE. This aspect of ourselves varies from being very willing to try new things to being very afraid to try new things. Do you like change, or do you prefer routines? If change is not your cup of tea, find ways to loosen up—especially if you want to succeed. Change is a fact of business life today, and people who embrace learning new things are sought after.

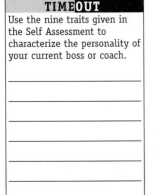

TIMEOUT

Use the nine traits given in the Self Assessment to characterize the personality of your current boss or coach.

_____

_____

_____

_____

_____

_____

Let's be blunt. From an individual perspective, there are no simple "right and wrong" ways to be, but from the organization's perspective, there are. Organizations therefore go to great lengths to recruit and retain people with traits from the left-hand side of these continuums (see the Self Assessment on page 241) because people with these traits are far more productive than people whose traits fall on the right-hand side. The good news is, you very likely already pretty much fall on the left side. Why? Because people who score on the *far* right side in *every* trait don't get very far in life (for example, extreme pessimists/externalizers don't have the "stick-to-itness" to get into college, let alone succeed there). The bad news is, you're not perfect, so there are probably aspects of yourself that you need to work on. As you assess each trait in the Self Assessment, realize that you *can* change. Also realize that your answers are telling you something very important. This is the real you that you are looking at—do you really *want* to change? Perhaps we can paraphrase here to make our point: To each trait there is a season. There *are* places and times to be an introvert (ask a long-distance runner or any writer worth his or her salt) or not be open to change (ask the Enron executives who were so intoxicated by the new economy!). There *are* times to avoid risk (ask all the stockholders of dot.coms). And if you are an athlete, you *know* there are times to be competitive!

PERCEPTION. Why do some people think George Steinbrenner is a nice guy while others think he is a jerk? Why do some of us view a referee's videotaped decision as fair while others do not? We all see the same videotaped play, don't we? Yes, but we don't *perceive* it the same, and therein lies not only the tale, but volumes and volumes of research literature. **Why is it debated whether the NCAA is *perceived* to be doing a good job of managing collegiate sports?**[11] Why spend so much time and money researching perception? That answer, at least, *is* simple—because needs and perception are the starting point of behavior. The tail really does wag the dog here. Our behavior follows our perceptions of people, of events, of learning, of work, of organizations—you name it, our perception of it colors it. We treat people we perceive as likable differently from people we perceive as unlikable. We work harder for someone we perceive as a good manager than for someone we perceive as ineffective. Perception is our individual interpretation of reality. Right or wrong, rational or irrational, it is the lens through which we view life. Thus, some see the **NCAA** as doing a great job, and others see the NCAA as too powerful. **What is your perception of how powerful the NCAA is in collegiate sports? How much power can the NCAA exert upon individual conferences, the media, and college presidents?**

SELF ASSESSMENT   *Personality Traits*

For each trait, check the level that you believe best characterizes you. Be honest. Also, to see how others perceive you and how this fits with your perception of yourself—and to prepare for our next topic (perception)—have people who know you well assess your personality using this form.

Single Traits of Personality

Locus of Control

I'm an internalizer.   _____ _____ _____ / _____ _____ _____   I'm an externalizer.

Optimism

I'm an optimist.   _____ _____ _____ / _____ _____ _____   I'm a pessimist.

Risk Propensity

I'm a risk taker.   _____ _____ _____ / _____ _____ _____   I'm a risk avoider.

Machiavellianism

I'm not a power user.   _____ _____ _____ / _____ _____ _____   I'm a power user.

The Big 5 Personality Traits

Extroversion

I'm an extrovert.   _____ _____ _____ / _____ _____ _____   I'm an introvert.

Agreeableness

I'm cooperative.   _____ _____ _____ / _____ _____ _____   I'm competitive.

Emotionalism

I'm stable/positive.   _____ _____ _____ / _____ _____ _____   I'm unstable/negative.

Conscientiousness

I'm dependable.   _____ _____ _____ / _____ _____ _____   I'm not dependable.

Openness to Experience

I try new things.   _____ _____ _____ / _____ _____ _____   I avoid doing new things.

The Perception Process

2 LEARNING OUTCOME
Understand the perception process and the two factors it is based on.

Perception is the process through which we select, organize, and interpret information from the surrounding environment. Because this perception process colors everything, no two people experience anything exactly the same. Why are organizational behaviorists so interested in perception? Because how we perceive work is colored by our perception of work. How we select, organize, and interpret information is based on numerous internal individual factors—our personality, self-esteem, attitudes, intelligence, needs, values, and so on. These comprise the internal component of perception. *Self-esteem*, or self-concept, is our perception of ourself. As we noted earlier, self-esteem is also a personality trait; it varies between high/positive/ and low/negative. Do you like yourself? Do you consider yourself a valuable person/employee? Do you believe you are a capable person? Organizations endeavor to recruit people with positive self-esteem. The "why" is pretty obvious—people with high self-esteem perform better on the job.

The second component of this process is the information itself—this is the external component. The more accurate our information, the more closely our perception will resemble

perception
The process through which we select, organize, and interpret information from the surrounding environment.

reality. Inaccurate rumors thus cause our perceptions to veer wildly from reality and can be a serious problem for organizations. The **NCAA** must deal with all types of rumors (e.g., recruiting violations and academic irregularities) and determine whether they are violations of NCAA rules. **Do you believe the NCAA should investigate a university based on rumors?**

attribution
The process of determining why people behave certain ways.

ATTRIBUTING REASONS FOR BEHAVIOR. **Attribution** is the process of determining why people behave certain ways. Every one of us tries to find reasons behind behavior every day—our own, those around us, football players on TV—in fact, we do this continually. The process (shown in Model 9–1) begins when we observe an act directly or indirectly (through reading or friends reporting it). We want to know if the person's intent was situational (accidental or beyond the person's control) or intentional (within the person's control). (We may not use these words, but this is what we are doing.) We judge intent (or lack thereof) by three variables: distinctiveness (does Dennis Rodman behave this way in other situations?), consensus (does his whole team behave this way?), and consistency (does Rodman behave this way most—or all—of the time?). We also look for reasons for the behavior (did Rodman decide that publicity, even negative publicity, was a good way to set himself apart—that is, a good career strategy?). Lastly, we decide on a response—we may abhor Rodman's behavior or be amused by it or even admire it. Or we may simply not care. All of these responses will drive our behavior—we may abstain from watching any game he is in, we may drive long distances to see him play, or we may affect his style of dress and buy T-shirts emblazoned with his name.

TIME OUT
Explain how you used the attribution process (a) in a recent incident in professional sports and (b) in a recent incident at work.

As we have noted, attribution is how we determine reasons for our behavior and that of others. However, most of us spend more time mulling over why other people behave the way they do. We spend less time examining our own behavior, but when we do look at our own behavior, we tend to credit our successes as being intentional. Conversely, when we fail, we tend to blame the situation. We also tend to reverse intention (Sally failed because she didn't practice enough) and situation (Brian just got lucky) when we attribute reasons for other people's behavior. This is a classic example of perception differences.

Bias in Our Perception

As noted above, all of us perceive the same behavior differently. But *why* do we do this? In two words, personal bias. Bias has several components: selectivity, frame of reference, stereotypes, and expectation. Keep in mind that we are all subject to these biases.

Selectivity is the manner in which we screen information to favor the outcome we desire. We often go to great lengths to find information that supports our point of view, yet ignore information that does not. In other words, we hear only what we want to hear. For example, we might hear ten good points about the **NCAA** and only one bad point. If we want the outcome of receiving this information (our response) to square with the fact that we like to disparage the NCAA, we will focus on the one negative point and disregard the other positive information. This enables us to conclude that the NCAA doesn't do a good job of managing college sports. A related bias is the *halo/horns effect* in which we judge others based on our perception of a single trait of theirs. (A person with a halo can do no wrong—likewise a person with horns can do no right.) **Do you tend to select positive or negative information about the NCAA?**

Model 9–1 The Attribution Process

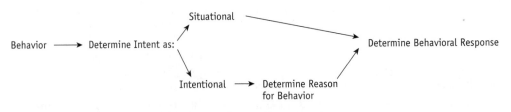

Our *frame of reference* is our bias of seeing things from our own point of view. This one is pretty hard to overcome, and it tends to make situations into win-lose propositions. As employees we will view management decisions quite differently than we will as managers. As manager or employee we would use the same data during contract negotiations. However, as managers we may perceive that employees want more pay and are not willing to work to increase productivity, but as employees we may perceive managers as greedy and not willing to share the wealth, which we—as employee—perceive that we create. The MLB players' union and the owners display classic frame-of-reference problems. Players claim that MLB teams are very profitable—owners claim continual brink of bankruptcy.[12] Thus, as a manager, don't be surprised if your group doesn't perceive things the way that you do. Remember, it is not your perception but the employees' perception that will influence their behavior and performance. Try to see things from the employees' perspective and create a win-win situation so that all parties get what they want. **Could colleges and universities create a win-win situation by complying with Title IX requirements?**

Stereotyping happens when we project the characteristics or behavior of an individual onto a group. Think about breakthrough athletes like Hank Greenberg or high school female wrestlers. All faced stereotypes that charged (falsely) that they couldn't be good at what they did. Stereotyping gets in your way of seeing true strengths and true weaknesses—don't let it.

Read the phrase in the triangle below.

Did you read the word "the" twice? Or, like most people, did you read what you expected to read, only one "the"? Our *expectations* also bias our perceptions. Many of us, especially when we know each other well, don't really listen to each other. We hear what we expect to hear.

Another expectation bias is the "like us" assumption—that others perceive things as we do because they are *like us*. Don't expect others to behave as you do or perceive things the way you do, and don't judge others' behavior as wrong on the sole basis that it differs from yours. Remember to value diversity. It is argued that the benefits of cultural diversity in sport organizations (e.g., creativity, challenge, constructive conflict) will be realized when managers and organizations value diversity.[13]

ATTITUDES

LEARNING OUTCOME
Explain how personality, perception, and attitude are related, and why they are important.

Attitudes are positive or negative evaluations of people, things, and situations. Attitude is a major factor in determining performance. Your self-esteem has a significant effect on your attitude. Organizations look for people with high self-esteem and positive attitudes toward their careers and personal lives, because such people tend to be loyal and reliable workers. Our perceptions and input from others (family, friends, teachers, coworkers, the mass media, and so on) form our attitudes. And our attitudes affect our behavior. When we have positive attitudes toward a person or a situation, we often behave differently than if our attitude is a negative one. Fortunately, diversity training is changing attitudes by helping to eliminate negative stereotypes. In this section we examine how the attitudes of management affect performance and job satisfaction.

How the Attitudes of Management Affect Performance

The **Pygmalion effect** has to do with how management's attitude toward workers, their expectations of them, and their treatment of them affect workers' performance. It's pretty simple—how you view your staff is what you get! That is, your attitude toward your staff

---

TIMEOUT
Think about a misunderstanding that arose when you and another person perceived the same situation differently. Which perceptual biases do you think contributed to the misunderstanding?

_____

_____

_____

_____

TIMEOUT
Relate incidents in which your attitude affected your workplace behavior negatively and positively.

_____

_____

_____

_____

_____

attitudes
Positive or negative evaluations of people, things, and situations.

Pygmalion effect
Manager's attitudes and expectations of employees and how they treat them affect workers' performance.

TIME OUT

Describe how someone's (parent, friend, teacher, coach, boss) expectations of you strongly affected your success or failure.

directly affects the quality of their work. There is much research to show this.[14,15] When you as a manager view your staff as competent and highly skilled (*even though* they might not be initially) they will rise to the occasion (it may be slow at first, but it *will* happen). Likewise, when you, because of an underlying attitude, don't believe your staff to be competent or trustworthy, guess what—they won't surprise you! Management's attitudes become a *self-fulfilling prophecy*. In summary, then, your attitude is an essential part of your effectiveness as a manager. John Wooden, the legendary basketball coach at UCLA (now retired), expected excellence from every player. The result? *Ten* NCAA national championships. Wooden constructed his "pyramid of success" (check it out at the web site given in the endnote) out of such concepts as "keep it simple" and "teamwork is not a preference, it's a necessity."[16]

All this said about the Pygmalion effect and self-fulfilling prophecies, you as both an employee and an eventual manager are still responsible for your own actions. Yes—others' attitudes *can* affect your behavior and performance, but that doesn't mean you have to *let* them. Ignore negative comments, stay away from people with negative attitudes, and get good at what you do. Look at a negative boss as a gift—you need to learn how to work with difficult people; just don't let them defeat you.

Attitudes and Job Satisfaction

4   LEARNING OUTCOME
State what job satisfaction is and why it is important.

Job satisfaction is how content we are (or are not) with our jobs. The continuum, of course, ranges from high satisfaction (positive attitude) to low satisfaction (negative attitude). Organizations measure job satisfaction in OD surveys (Chapter 7). Why? Because job satisfaction affects employee absenteeism and turnover, morale, and performance. Optimists who have positive self-esteem tend to have greater job satisfaction, but organizational behaviorists have long debated whether a happy worker is a productive worker. However, a positive relationship appears to exist between job satisfaction and productivity.[17] Also, job satisfaction affects our satisfaction with life—finding jobs that satisfy us affects the way we view our lives outside work.

What determines job satisfaction? Find out for yourself—take the Self Assessment on page 245. Note that it is quite normal to have high job satisfaction and not like some aspects of your job.

Remember that job satisfaction is based on personality and perception; it can therefore be changed. See the Self Assessment for more details. If you work at being more positive by focusing on the good parts of your job, and spend less time thinking about and especially complaining to others about your job, your job satisfaction will improve. People with negative attitudes often change jobs because they are not satisfied. They think that the "grass will be greener" on another job. Unfortunately, they often find that the new job is no better than the old one. One exception is when the real cause of dissatisfaction is the work itself. However, some people with truly negative personality types never find a job they are satisfied with no matter how many job changes they make.

Thus, remember to recruit and retain employees with positive attitudes. If you ask job candidates about their prior jobs and they make negative statements, cannot think of anything good to say, or hesitate, they may have a negative personality and job attitude. Improving your human relationship skills can help you get along better with coworkers and managers and increase your job satisfaction, as well as increase your chances for growth and opportunity for advancement and higher compensation.

POWER

5   LEARNING OUTCOME
Define power and the difference between position and personal power.

To be effective in an organization, you need to understand how people gain power and how they use power. Therefore in this section we examine power—its importance, its bases, and its implications.

SELF ASSESSMENT   *Job Satisfaction*

Select a present or past job. For each of the following determinants of job satisfaction, identify your level of satisfaction by placing a check on the continuum.

Personality

I have a positive self-esteem.   ____ ____ ____ / ____ ____ ____   I have a negative self-esteem.

Work Itself

I enjoy doing the tasks
I perform.   ____ ____ ____ / ____ ____ ____   I *do not* enjoy doing
the tasks I perform.

Compensation

I am fairly compensated.   ____ ____ ____ / ____ ____ ____   I am *not* fairly compensated.

Growth and Upward Mobility

I have the opportunity to learn
new things and get better jobs.   ____ ____ ____ / ____ ____ ____   I have *no* opportunity to learn
new things and get better jobs.

Coworkers

I like and enjoy
working with my coworkers.   ____ ____ ____ / ____ ____ ____   I *do not* like and enjoy
working with my coworkers.

Management

I believe that managers
are doing a good job.   ____ ____ ____ / ____ ____ ____   I *do not* believe that managers
are doing a good job.

OVERALL JOB SATISFACTION

When determining overall job satisfaction for yourself, you cannot simply add up a score based on the above six determinants, because they are most likely of different importance to you. Thus, thinking about your job and the above factors, rate your overall satisfaction level with your job.

I am satisfied with my
job (high level of satisfaction).   _6_ _5_ _4_ / _3_ _2_ _1_   I am dissatisfied with my
job (low level of satisfaction).

Organizational Power

Power is often viewed as one's ability to make people do something, or as one's ability to do something *to* people or *for* them. These definitions are true, but they also cast power as manipulative, or even destructive, as does Lord Acton's saying, "Power tends to corrupt and absolute power corrupts absolutely." It is important to look at power as a constructive tool, as a way to organize action and get something done. For our purposes, then, **power** is the ability to influence the actions of others. Myles Brand, president of the NCAA, is thus a powerful person, as is every effective coach and athletic director. FIFA is a powerful organization because of the influence it wields around the world. Nike is a powerful organization because of its ability to shape culture (also around the world) through its products. The caveat, of course, is to use power wisely. Some charge that the **NCAA** uses its power coercively; others say the NCAA is just doing what needs to be done. **How might the NCAA use its power constructively to solve some of the troubling issues facing college sports?**

power
The ability to influence the actions of others.

Without power, organizations and managers cannot achieve objectives. Leadership and power go hand in hand. Employees are not influenced without a reason, and the reason is often the power a manager has over them. You don't always have to *use* your power to direct people. Often it is the "perception" of power, rather than the wielding of it, that influences others. Power starts at the top of the organization, and today shrewd organizations take great pains to empower their employees.[18]

Power can be derived from one's position and/or from one's personal attributes. Management thus has the power of position. Charismatic leaders have personal power. Position power is more effective when it is accompanied by personal power.[19] Just as it can be gained, every type of power can also be lost (ask Kenneth Lay, former CEO of Enron).

The Bases of Power

The seven bases of power, along with their sources, are shown in Exhibit 9–1. People who get results and who have good people skills are often granted power (either formally by promotion or informally by general agreement of the group). Note that building a power base does not necessarily mean taking power away from others.

COERCIVE POWER. Coercive power is position power; it uses threats and/or punishment to achieve compliance. It gets its effectiveness from our fear of humiliation (in the form of reprimands, probation, suspension, or dismissal). Coercion is not quite the monster that these words imply, and yes, it does have appropriate uses—indeed, we are all under coercive power every day in one manner or another. None of us wants a speeding ticket. None of us wants to lose our jobs either. The **NCAA** uses coercive power routinely, as do innumerable governing bodies. To name but one example from many, the NCAA recently placed Kentucky State University on two years of probation and imposed a number of penalties because of numerous violations in KSU's cross country, track and field, men's basketball, and baseball programs, including bylaws governing eligibility, recruiting, and a lack of institutional control. The initial violation occurred in 1998 when the head track and field coach directed an ineligible student athlete to compete under the name of another student athlete.[20] Coercive power also uses verbal abuse and ostracism (both dramatic but not very productive). Group members may use coercive power to enforce norms. **Do you agree the NCAA should have coercive power over its members?**

CONNECTION POWER. When someone uses a relationship with influential or important people to influence your behavior or attitudes, he or she is using connection power. Connection power is therefore a combination of position and personal power, and it can be a very useful thing to have. Connections can help you find work. They can also get the resources you need and increase your business. Think about how important networking is—networking is nothing more than working to increase connection power.

 6 LEARNING OUTCOME
Explain how reward, legitimate, and referent power differ.

REWARD POWER. As a manager, you will have the ability to praise, to recognize achievement, to raise wages, and to promote people. This is reward power—the ability to influence others by giving them something they value. As we noted in Chapter 8, as a manager you will get what you reward. Genuine (deserved) praise is a powerful tool in every manager's "kit." It is also the one you will use most often, because you (obviously) can't give out award dinners, raises, and promotions every day. Make sure your praise is honest praise—giving false praise is patronizing and tears down whatever trust you have built up.

LEGITIMATE POWER. Power given to people by organizations or by society is legitimate power. Managers have legitimate power. So do policemen. (And both have coercive power as well.) Legitimate power is position power, and it is, well, powerful. Use it well, use it sparingly—in today's era of work teams gratuitous use of legitimate power actually diminishes your personal power.

Exhibit 9–1   Sources and Bases of Power

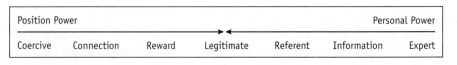

Position Power						Personal Power
Coercive	Connection	Reward	Legitimate	Referent	Information	Expert

REFERENT POWER. Referent power is about voluntarily giving someone power over you—you hand them authority because you admire them, because you want to emulate them in some fashion. Therefore, in your behavior you will *refer* to what you think the *referent*, the power holder, would do or would want you to do. Rock stars and star athletes have referent power over their fans. This is personal power, of course. It is about the referent's charisma, their interpersonal openness, their experience as someone older and wiser or more successful and more skilled. Managers gain this power when they are respected by their work group.

INFORMATION POWER. In this age of information people who have knowledge or data that others need have information power. This is personal power, although sometimes it is also position power, because you happen to be in the right place (position) to acquire the knowledge or gather the data. As a manager you will need to rely on information supplied by others. They will therefore have power over you because your work can only be as good as the information it is based on. You will also be a conveyer of information—to your staff and to your bosses—and as such will also have information power.

EXPERT POWER. People who have expertise or specialized skills that others need have expert power. This too is personal power. Michael Jordan, Ichiro Suzuki, Emmitt Smith—all have expert power that their teams need. The fewer people who possess a particular expertise, the more power the expert has (not unlike a monopoly). Experts are often promoted to management positions; whether this is a wise decision depends on the field and on the person. The best managers are not always experts. Experts by definition have a very specialized focus. The best managers endeavor to have a broader focus, called vision. Expert power is essential to people who work with other departments and other organizations. They have no direct position power, but being seen as an expert gives them credibility and standing.

Why do some people want and seek power whereas others refuse it even if it's pressed on them? In his acquired needs theory of motivation (Chapter 12), McClelland states that the answer is based on one's need for power.[21] (You can measure your need for power in the Self Assessment on page 337 in Chapter 12.)

So, you are asking, how can I increase my power? Well, first and foremost ask yourself why you want more power (does your current job really require it) and whether you are ready (mature enough, experienced enough, seasoned enough) to handle it well. Think about this carefully—if you handle power poorly, your staff will revolt, your objectives will not be met, and it could take you years and many sleepless nights to regain your former credibility. The odd thing is, if you have to ask how you can increase your power, you probably aren't seasoned enough to handle it. Why? Because power is the ultimate apprenticeship. There are no quick routes to attaining power—no Power 101 courses. Power is gained only with time, with experience, with success, with the increasing respect of your colleagues. Power grabbers may succeed for a while, but they usually ultimately fail. People have divining rods about power—they know when it is legitimate and when it is not. And they are easy to lead when they believe you have legitimate power and impossible to lead when they sense that you are a power grabber. Be patient—if you excel, power will find you.

> **TIMEOUT**
> Think about several bosses or coaches whom you are in a position to observe. Describe the types of power they have and the ones that they use. Do you think they use their power well? If so, why? If not, why not?
>
> _____
> _____
> _____
> _____
> _____

POLITICS IN THE OFFICE AND ON THE FIELD

Before you read further, complete the Self Assessment on page 249.

7 | LEARNING OUTCOME
Understand how power and politics are related.

The Nature of Politics in the Workplace

Politics are the efforts of groups or individuals with competing interests to obtain power and positions of leadership. Like power, office politics have negative connotations because they can be manipulative and destructive. And there is no doubt that office politics run

politics
The efforts of groups or individuals with competing interests to obtain power and positions of leadership.

APPLYING THE CONCEPT   *Using Power*

Identify the appropriate power to use in each situation.

a. coercive   **c.** reward or legitimate   **e.** information or expert

b. connection   **d.** referent

_____ 1. Bridget, one of your top people, normally needs very little direction. However, recently her performance has faltered. You suspect that Bridget's personal problems are affecting her work.

_____ 2. You need a new computer to help you organize ticket sales more efficiently. Computers are allocated by a committee, which is very political in nature.

_____ 3. Jean, a promising assistant coach, wants a promotion. Jean has talked to you about getting ahead in sport management and has asked you to help prepare her for when the opportunity comes.

_____ 4. John, one of your worst players, has ignored one of your directives once again.

_____ 5. Whitney, who continually needs direction and encouragement, is not working to standard today. As she does occasionally, she claims that she doesn't feel good but can't afford to take time off. You have to get an important customer order for golf clubs shipped today.

amok do great harm. For example, the AIAW (Association for Intercollegiate Athletics for Women) represented women's collegiate sports from 1971 until it folded in 1982. Observers blame the NCAA's move into women's sports for the fall of AIAW. However, the blame should also be placed on internal politics and the policies of the AIAW itself. AIAW had problems with its own members with regard to the organization's lack of support for athletic scholarships for women.[22]

Politics are also a fact of organizational life. Why, you say, if they are so destructive? Because there is much more to office politics than the clichés so gleefully skewered by cartoonists and so bemoaned by people on the losing side of a political struggle. In fact, politics are a *healthy* part of life in the organization! Surprised? Don't be. Politics are about give and take, about everyone having their say, and about the stronger argument winning—or the more skilled players winning. Politics are another facet of capitalism, which as you recall is about competition and survival of the fittest—be the "fittest" a product, a company, a team, a strategy, or an idea. As the groups or individuals politicking move higher in the organization, the more their political skills count because the stakes get higher. Which strategy, which product, which team to turn our company around—answers to these questions are rarely clear-cut. And when situations are not clear, politicking is one way to get to resolution.

Political Behavior

8 LEARNING OUTCOME
Explain what networking, reciprocity, and coalitions have in common.

networking
Developing relationships in order to gain social or business advantage.

reciprocity
Using mutual dependence to accomplish objectives.

Networking, reciprocity, and coalitions are important political behaviors. **Networking** is about developing relationships in order to gain social or business advantage. Management activities can be divided into four areas: traditional management, communication, human resources management, and networking. Successful managers spend around twice as much time networking as average managers.[23]

Reciprocating is about returning in kind. **Reciprocity** thus involves using mutual dependence to accomplish objectives. When someone does something for you, you incur an obli-

SELF ASSESSMENT   *Political Behavior*

Select the response that best describes your behavior on your job or team.

(1) rarely   (3) occasionally   (5) usually

(2) seldom   (4) frequently

_____ 1. I get along with everyone, even difficult coworkers.

_____ 2. I avoid giving my personal opinion on controversial issues, especially when I know others don't agree with them.

_____ 3. I try to make people feel important by complimenting them.

_____ 4. I often compromise when I work with others, and I also avoid telling people they are wrong.

_____ 5. I try to get to know key managers and find out what is going on in every department.

_____ 6. I dress like people in power dress and pursue the same interests (watch or play sports, join the same clubs, etc.) as they do.

_____ 7. I network with higher-level managers so they will know who I am.

_____ 8. I seek recognition and visibility for my accomplishments.

_____ 9. I get others to help me get what I want.

_____ 10. I do favors for others and ask favors from them in return.

To determine your score, add your answers. The higher your score, the more political your behavior in the workplace. Place your score here ____ and on the continuum below.

Nonpolitical   10–20–30–40—50   Political

gation that they may expect to be repaid in kind. Likewise, when you do something for someone, you create a debt that you may be able to collect later when you need a favor.

A **coalition** is an alliance of people with similar objectives who together have a better chance of achieving their objectives. Reciprocity is a work in continual progress. In contrast, coalitions come together temporarily, then dissolve once their objectives are accomplished. Reading the "political landscape" correctly and choosing appropriate allies can help you form coalitions to accomplish unpopular or difficult objectives.

coalition
An alliance of people with similar objectives who together have a better chance of achieving their objectives.

Developing Political Skills

If climbing the corporate ladder is a goal of yours, political skills should be in your tool kit. Review the statements in the Self Assessment on this page and strive to become comfortable with networking, reciprocating, and working with coalitions. Absorb your organization's culture, and make it *your* strength as well. Learn what it takes in the organization where you work as you follow the guidelines in Exhibit 9–2.

LEARN THE ORGANIZATIONAL CULTURE. By now, you know how important organizational culture is (Chapter 7). Make sure you learn yours well—culture defines the ground rules for politicking at work.[24] Networking might be encouraged at one company and considered obsequious at another. Learn to read between the lines. Promote yourself in politically acceptable and ethical ways. Remember, there is always more than one way to accomplish your objectives, and the method you use may be what determines your success.

LEARN THE POWER PLAYERS. Who are the power players? Your boss for one. Power players are people who have the ability to help you in your career. When you understand the power players in your group, department, and organization, you can tailor your presentations to meet their pet criteria. For example, some managers want details; others are impatient with the details and just want you to give them the big picture.

DON'T SURPRISE YOUR BOSS. If you want to get ahead, have good working relationships with your superiors. Know what they expect from you and do it. Get their advice when you think forming a coalition is the best strategy. Give them the good news—and the bad

TIMEOUT
Give examples of how your firm or team uses networking, reciprocity, and coalitions to achieve objectives.

_____

_____

_____

_____

_____

_____

Exhibit 9–2   Developing Political Skills

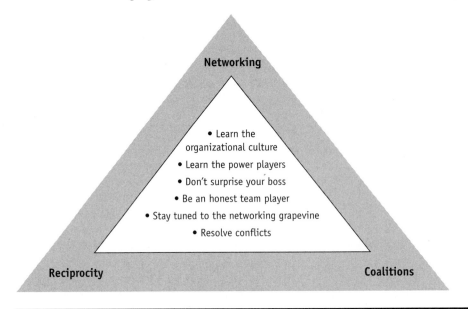

news. Let them know early on from *you* if you're having a problem. No boss wants to find out about your problem from somebody else. And *never* show up a boss in public.

BE AN HONEST TEAM PLAYER. High-functioning organizations are built on respect, confidence in coworkers, and trust. Self-discipline, teamwork, and fair play are great values to take from the playing field to the office. Some values should be left on the field—uncritical obedience to the coach, a predisposition to win at all costs, and an exaggerated competitive spirit.[25]

STAY TUNED TO THE NETWORKING GRAPEVINE. The grapevine can be a good thing— it can help you learn your organization's culture and who the key players are. It can also be a bad thing—it can be feverish with untrue rumors. Think about making your own grapevine, of people whom you respect and trust, that includes people both inside and outside your organization. Get active in trade or professional associations. The North American Society for Sport Management (http://www.nassm.org) is a good place to start.

RESOLVE CONFLICTS. As you climb the corporate ladder, take care not to get thrown off. Choose your stands carefully. Avoid fights you can't win. If you find yourself suddenly out of the information loop, or if your coworkers or boss start treating you differently, find out why. Use your network or grapevine to find out whether someone is trying to undermine you and why. Understand where your enemies are coming from, how they operate, who's behind them, and what "weapons" they might use. Confront individuals or groups suspected of instigating conflict. If you did something to offend a coworker, an apology from you may be in order. In any case, approach your adversary and try to resolve the conflict using the ideas in the next section.

TIMEOUT
Which suggestion(s) for developing political skills feel *least* comfortable to you? Explain.

MANAGING CONFLICT

conflict
Exists whenever disagreement becomes antagonistic.

A **conflict** exists whenever argument (which is an agreement to disagree) becomes antagonistic. Conflict is inevitable in business. Well-meaning people differ all the time. When the issues are important, and the opposing opinions strong, temperatures rise—and conflict can ensue. Thus, effective conflict resolution and negotiation skills are imperative if you want to succeed as a manager. How well you handle conflict also affects your own job satisfaction and stress levels.

Remember, conflict occurs everywhere, even in golf—the last genteel pro sport, where players are known for their manners and sportsmanship. The Professional Golf Association (PGA)

APPLYING THE CONCEPT   *Political Behavior*

Identify each behavior as (a) effective or (b) ineffective.

_____ 6. Jill is taking golf lessons so she can join the Saturday golf group that includes some higher-level managers.

_____ 7. Paul tells his boss's boss about mistakes his boss makes.

_____ 8. Sally avoids socializing so that she can be more productive on the job.

_____ 9. John sent a very positive performance report to three higher-level managers to whom he does not report. They did not request copies.

_____ 10. Carlos has to drop off daily reports by noon. He brings them around 10:00 on Tuesday and Thursday so that he can run into some higher-level managers who meet at that time near the office where the report goes. On other days, Carlos drops the report off around noon on his way to lunch.

---

is seeing increased conflicts among players on tour. Star golfers want to discuss being paid for Ryder Cup play (a team competition where the golfers selected represent the United States). Also, the PGA wants caddies to immediately generate such information as each shot's length, lie, location, and club choice, which would then be displayed instantly on TV and on the Internet. Tiger Woods disagrees—he believes the club he uses on a particular shot is a "trade secret."[26]

So, how do people go about resolving conflict? First, they try to understand the ground rules.

The Ground Rules

Implicit in all of our interactions with others is a contract that we'll call the ground rules.[27] These are our—and others'—expectations. At work, we all have a set of expectations about what we will contribute to the organization (effort, time, skills) and what it will provide us (compensation, job satisfaction, status). These are our unspoken, invisible ground rules, and we don't want them violated. The trouble is, we're not always aware of all of our expectations until the moment they're not met, so we don't set them out in front of everyone so that everyone knows what the score is. However, we *believe* that there is already mutual agreement on the ground rules. Maybe we think they are "so obvious—how could anyone not get it" or "this is the only way it could be." And therein lies the problem.

Conflict arises because our ground rules get broken. We fail to make explicit our own expectations and we fail to inquire into the expectations of other parties. We further assume that other parties hold the same expectations as we do. As long as people meet our expectations, everything is fine, but when they don't, the result is very often conflict. Thus, sharing expectations—figuring out all the hidden agendas—and carefully negotiating explicit ground rules are key to avoiding conflict.[28]

Functional and Dysfunctional Conflict

Mention conflict and people think of fighting and disruption. This is **dysfunctional conflict**—conflict that prevents groups from achieving their objectives. **Functional conflict** fosters disagreement and opposition that actually help achieve a group's objectives. The question then is not whether conflict is negative or positive, but how to manage conflict so that it benefits the organization. The **NCAA** needs to resolve two very important but conflicting goals—the increasing commercialism of college sports and the development of young amateur athletes. If growing revenue through sponsorships and commercials becomes the NCAA's primary goal, it will be harder and harder to square this with keeping college athletes

dysfunctional conflict
Conflict that prevents groups from achieving their objectives.

functional conflict
Disagreement and opposition that help achieve a group's objectives.

in amateur status. This is a dilemma the NCAA has grappled with for many years.[29] The longer it goes unresolved, the more likely the conflict will become dysfunctional. The NCAA has some tough decisions to make; it will be interesting to watch what happens. **Do you believe the balance between commercialism and amateurism in the NCAA is a dysfunctional or functional conflict?**

We would all agree that too much conflict is always dysfunctional. It so happens that so is too little conflict. Too little conflict means that not enough differing viewpoints are being heard. Too few viewpoints mean that not enough alternatives are being explored and that opportunities in the environment are being overlooked. Functional conflict is one way to get to innovation and increased performance.

9 LEARNING OUTCOME
Describe the five conflict management styles.

Styles of Conflict Management

Conflict management is based on two dimensions (concern for others' needs and concern for your own needs), which result in three types of behavior (passive, aggressive, and assertive). Taken together, these five components combine to give us five different styles of conflict resolution, which are presented in Exhibit 9–3.

AVOIDING. People who ignore conflict rather than face and resolve it try to manage conflict by avoiding it. They refuse to take a stance, withdraw mentally, or simply leave. This approach is neither assertive nor cooperative, and resolves nothing. Both sides lose.

The advantage of avoidance is that it maintains relationships that would be hurt by resolving the conflict. The first disadvantage, of course, is that nothing gets resolved.[30] The second disadvantage is that habitual avoiders become "rugs," and people who get walked on internalize a lot of conflict and stress. People walk all over avoiders. This can cause passive-aggressive behavior (where the avoider "loses it" and really turns up the heat by getting in a yelling match), which is destructive. Avoider managers allow employees to perform poorly without confronting them. This, of course, just makes the problem worse. The longer people wait to confront others, the more difficult the confrontation.[31]

All this said, there are times when avoidance *is* appropriate: (1) when the conflict is trivial (trivial issues are not worth conflict); (2) when your stake in the issue is not high (you have everything to lose and nothing to win); (3) when confrontation could damage an important relationship (no sense burning big bridges); (4) when you don't have time to resolve the conflict (hurried resolutions are rarely good resolutions); and (5) when emotions are high (wait until heads are cooler). Commissioner Tim Finchem may have been consciously

Exhibit 9–3 Styles of Conflict Management

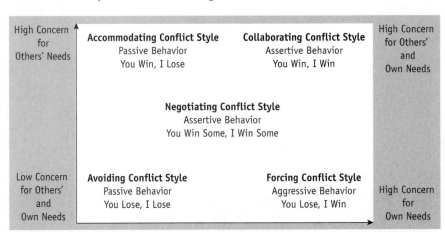

avoiding conflict in the PGA instant-data wrangle when he answered Tiger Woods' concern with "There are challenges, but what are the alternatives?" and "I'll take the superstar, no doubt."[32] Finchem probably didn't feel the issue was important enough to risk the animosity of the players.

ACCOMMODATING. People who resolve conflict by passively giving in are managing conflict by accommodation. Accommodators satisfy the other party, but neglect their own needs in the process. The opposing party wins; the accommodator loses.

Avoidance and accommodation differ in one significant way. Avoiders basically do nothing, but accommodators have to do something. Habitual accommodation maintains relationships (ostensibly) by doing things the other person's way. However, relationships built on one side's continual capitulation tries are not healthy ones and don't last. And giving in is counterproductive if the accommodator has the better solution. As with avoiders, people also take advantage of accommodators.

Accommodation, however, is appropriate in certain situations: (1) when you enjoy being a follower; (2) when maintaining the relationship outweighs all other considerations; (3) when the changes agreed to are not important to you, but are to the other party; (4) when time is limited; and (5) when you have an autocratic boss who resolves conflicts by force.

FORCING. People who use aggression to get their way resolve conflict by "going to combat." Forcers are uncooperative and aggressive—they do whatever it takes to satisfy their needs at the expense of others. Forcers threaten, intimidate, and call for majority rule when they know they will win. They also enjoy dealing with avoiders and accommodators because they are easy wins. Forcers win; everyone else loses.

When forcers have the better idea, the organization wins but it comes at a cost—in the form of low morale and "wounds" that may haunt later situations. Plus, forcers make enemies right and left. Forceful managers use position power to force others to do things their way.

Force is appropriate in conflict resolution (1) when unpopular action must be taken on important issues; (2) when maintaining relationships is not critical; and (3) when the conflict resolution is urgent.[33]

NEGOTIATING. People who resolve conflict through assertive give-and-take sessions are managing conflict by negotiation (also called compromise). Negotiators are both assertive and cooperative. Everyone wins some and loses some.

Negotiators typically resolve conflict quickly, and because everybody has given and gotten something, working relationships are maintained. The disadvantage is that the compromises negotiated may be suboptimal decisions. Negotiators often ask for more than they need in order to get what they want, particularly in collective bargaining.

Negotiation is appropriate to use (1) when the issues are complex and critical and there is no simple, clear-cut solution; (2) when parties have about equal power and are interested in different solutions; (3) when a solution will be only temporary; and (4) when time is short.

COLLABORATING. People who jointly and assertively try to get to the best solution, one that all parties can buy in to, resolve conflict by collaboration. Collaborators are problem solvers. They are both assertive and cooperative. Of the five styles, only collaborators focus on finding the best solution. Avoiders and accommodators focus on avoiding conflict at all cost, and forcers focus on winning at all cost. Collaborators are also willing to change positions if a better solution is presented.[34] Negotiation is often based on secret information, whereas collaboration is based on open and honest communication. This is the only conflict management style in which all parties win.[35]

Collaboration often leads to strong solutions. The disadvantage is that greater skill, more effort, and more time are required to get there. Collaboration is difficult in the three situations mentioned for negotiation, and also when a forcer blocks the process. Collaboration offers the most benefits to individuals, groups, and organizations.

Collaboration is appropriate (1) when an important issue requires an optimal solution and compromise would result in a suboptimal solution; (2) when people place the group goal before self-interest; (3) when maintaining relationships is important; (4) when time is available; and (5) when the conflict is among peers.

APPLYING THE CONCEPT   *Selecting Conflict Management Styles*

Identify the most appropriate conflict management style for each situation:

a. avoidance   **c.** forcing   **e.** collaboration

b. accommodation   **d.** negotiation

_____ 11. While serving on a committee that allocates athletic funds for building a new football stadium, you make a recommendation that another member opposes quite aggressively. Your interest in what the committee does is low. You can see quite clearly that yours is the better idea.

_____ 12. The task force you've been assigned to has to select new fitness equipment. The four alternatives will all do the job. Members disagree on their brand, price, and service.

_____ 13. You manage golf cart sales for the Hole In One stores. Beth, who makes a lot of the sales, is in the midst of closing the season's biggest sale, and you and she disagree on which strategy to use.

_____ 14. You're late and on your way to an important meeting. As you leave your office, at the other end of the work area you see Chris, one of your employees, goofing off instead of working.

_____ 15. You're over budget for labor this month. It's slow, so you ask Kent, a part-time employee, to leave work early. Kent tells you he doesn't want to because he needs the money.

> **TIMEOUT**
> Which style of conflict management does your current boss or coach use most often? Explain using a typical example.
>
> _____
> _____
> _____
> _____
> _____
> _____
> _____

There is no one best style for resolving conflict. The style we prefer personally may meet our needs but not the needs of the situation. If you wish to become a truly effective manager, you will become proficient at all five styles. And you will learn to judge a conflict and select the style that will best resolve it. Avoidance, accommodation, and force are the easiest to learn—indeed we've been using them for a long time (since childhood). Most people find negotiation and collaboration the hardest to learn—perhaps this is because they are the most nuanced and "mature." They are the last styles we learn as people maturing into fully functioning adults, and hence the ones we have least practice with. Therefore, we shall explore negotiation and collaboration in more depth in the next two sections.

NEGOTIATION

> **TIMEOUT**
> Which one style of conflict management do you use most often? Why? Give several examples.
>
> _____
> _____
> _____
> _____
> _____
> _____
> _____

As we noted above, negotiating is about trying to get what you want. Negotiators attempt to hammer out agreements in which everyone gets something and everyone gives something. Negotiation is used to complete business deals, resolve disagreements, and reduce conflicts. Negotiation is appropriate and common in collective bargaining, buying and selling goods and services, (sometimes) in getting a raise—none of these have a fixed price or deal. "Take it or leave it" situations, of course, leave no room for negotiation. Power and politics are important negotiating tools.

Creating "I Win Some, You Win Some" Situations

Negotiation often occurs in zero sum conflicts, in which one party's gain is the other party's loss. For example, each knockdown in price that a sports director can negotiate for a new scoreboard is her gain and the seller's loss. Thus, negotiators must sell the other party on their ideas, or they must exchange something for what they want. For the deal that is struck to work over a period of time, all parties in the negotiation need to believe they got a good deal. If a players' union believes that management "won," player morale may dip, which could affect performance. Also, if fans (who are the nonrepresented third party in the wrangle between the MLB and the players' union) believe *they* got a bad deal, attendance might drop dramatically, as it has in past strikes.

The Negotiation Process

As Model 9–2 shows, negotiations often involve three—and sometimes four—steps: plan, negotiate, (sometimes) postpone, and agree or fail to agree.

PLANNING. Solid preparations, or lack thereof, can mean the difference between success and failure.[36] Be clear about what it is you are negotiating—is it price, options, delivery time, sales quantities, or all four? Planning entails four steps:

1. *Research the other party(s).* Know the key players, know the issues, know the context. *Before* you negotiate, try to find out what the other parties want and what they are and are not willing to give up. Use your networking grapevine to size up negotiators' personalities and negotiation style. The more you know about the other side, the better your chances of reaching an agreement. Think about what worked and did not work in previous negotiations with these parties.

2. *Set objectives.* Based on your research, what can you expect?

   ■ Set a lower limit below which you are willing to fail to agree.

   ■ Set a target objective—what you believe is a fair deal.

   ■ Set an objective for the opening offer that is higher than you expect you could conceivably get. Remember, the other party is doing the same thing, so don't view their opening offer as final.

   The key to successful negotiations is for all parties to get between their minimum and their target. This is the "I win some, you win some" situation that negotiations strive to achieve. It is helpful to have must and want criteria (Chapter 3).

3. *Try to develop options and tradeoffs.* Suppose you are a free-agent NBA player. If you have multiple offers from other teams, you are in a stronger power position to get your target salary. Remember context, however. If the job market is soft or you really want this particular job for whatever reason, dickering over salary may not be in your best interest.

   If you have to give up something, or cannot get exactly what you want, be prepared to ask for something else in return. If you cannot get the size raise you want, maybe you can get more days off or more in your retirement account.

Model 9–2   The Negotiation Process

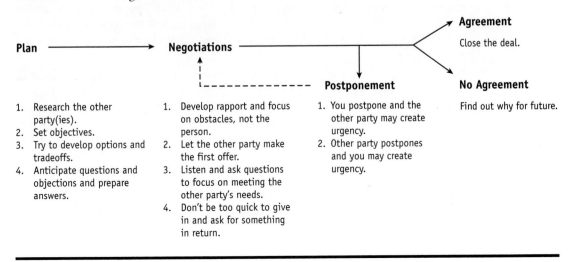

4. *Anticipate questions and objections and prepare answers.* The other team may want to know why you are looking for a job with their team. Be prepared to answer the unasked question—what's in it for me? Don't focus on what you want but on how your deal will benefit the other team. Talk in "you" and "we" terms, not "I" terms, unless you are telling others what you're going to do for them.

There is a good chance that the other side will raise objections—reasons the negotiations won't result in agreement. When an agent asks for a raise, management typically says the team can't afford it. Agents who have done their homework strengthen their case if they can quote profit numbers to prove their point. Unfortunately, parties don't always come out and state their real objections. Thus, you need to listen and ask questions to find out what is preventing the agreement.

Make sure you fully understand yourself, your position, and your deal, and project confidence. If the other team doesn't trust you, or believes the deal is not a good one, you won't reach an agreement. Thus, during the selection process, it is your job to convince the general manager that you can do the job.

NEGOTIATING. Now you are ready to negotiate the deal. Face-to-face negotiations are preferable because you can assess nonverbal behavior (discussed in Chapter 11) and better understand objections. However, telephone and written negotiations work, too. Again, know the other party's preference.

1. *Develop rapport and focus on obstacles, not the person.* Smile and call the other party by name as you greet them. A smile tells people you like them, are interested in them, and enjoy them.[37] Open with some small talk. How much time to wait until you get down to business depends on the other party's style. Some people like to get right down to business, but others want to get to know you before they discuss business. However, you want the other party to make the first offer, so don't wait too long or you may have to make the first move.

Never attack anybody on the other side or put them down with negative statements like, "You're being unfair to ask for such a salary cut." The other party will become defensive, you will end up arguing, and prospects for agreement will dim if not go away altogether. Instead, make statements like, "You think my salary request is too high?" Then state your competitive advantage in a positive way. If people perceive that you're pushing, threatening, or belittling, they won't trust you and negotiations will stall or reach an impasse.

2. *Let the other party make the first offer.* Why? Because there is always the possibility that they will offer you more than your target objective—you can then close the deal and be on your way. On the other hand, if they offer less than your target, you can work from the assumption that this is their lowball offer and negotiate up by asking questions like "What is the salary range for this position?"

When others pressure you to make the first offer with questions like "Give us your salary requirement, and we'll tell you whether we'll take it," put the ball back in their court with, "What do you expect to pay?" If things go well during steps 1 and 2, you simply close the deal—you agree to agree. If you're not close to agreement, all is not yet lost.

3. *Listen and ask questions to focus on meeting the other party's needs.* Create opportunities for them to reveal their reservations and objections. Remember, when you're speaking you may be revealing more than you want to, but when you're listening, *they* are doing the talking, which is what you want. That is, you are receiving information that will help you to overcome their objections. If you go on and on about what you have to offer, you're not finding out what they are really interested in, and you may be killing the deal. Ask questions—"Is the salary out of the ballpark?" "Is it a reasonable amount?"—and then listen. *Don't* forget to listen. Perhaps their objection is a want criteria, such as two years of experience and you have only one—well, then, play up the features you have that they do want and you may get an agreement. If their objection is a must criteria that you cannot meet, at least you know and you can stop chasing a deal that is not going to happen.

4. *Don't be too quick to give in and ask for something in return.* Those who don't ask, don't get. Don't give away the farm. You want to satisfy the other party without giving up too much, and you want to get something in return.[38] Don't go below your minimum objective—if it is realistic, you may have to walk away. If you do walk away, realize that you may or may not be called back, and if not, you may be able to come back for the same low salary, but not always. If the other party knows you are weakening and will accept a low agreement, they are less likely to move from their stance. Think about "Must sell—need cash" signs. What type of price do you think they get? Don't let comments such as "Are you kidding me, that's too much" intimidate you. Also, when you are not getting what you want, having other options in your "bag"—fallback positions—can give you bargaining power.

There are, however, situations in which making the first concession is a good strategy—for example, when you're negotiating a contract with numerous complexities and tradeoffs. This strategy can make the other party feel obligated and then you can ask for something that is larger than what you gave up.

Avoid giving unilateral concessions. Recall your planned tradeoffs. If the other team asks for a lower salary, ask for a concession such as an extra year added to the contract. Send the message—you don't give something for nothing.[39]

POSTPONING. When you are not making progress, it is often wise to postpone the negotiations.

They postpone—you create urgency. The other team says, "I'll get back to you." When you're not getting what you want, you can create urgency—for example, "This specific deal ends today." But don't be dishonest. The primary reason negotiations work is because of mutual trust and respect. Establishing a relationship of trust is key to closing a deal. Indeed, honesty and integrity are the most important assets a negotiator can possess.[40] That doesn't mean you can't look at your options. Maybe you do have other job offers from other teams—in which case, it's perfectly acceptable to ask: "I've got another job offer pending. When will you let me know what you've decided?"

But what if urgency doesn't fit and they say, "I'll think about it"? Your response? "That's a good idea." *But* you also work in a quick review of the parts of your deal that they do like—leave them thinking about what they are walking away from. Putting them in the position of having second thoughts may keep the door open. If not, then don't let them leave you without pinning them down: "When can I expect to hear if I got the job?" Ask for a specific time and note that if you don't hear from them by that date, you will call. Follow up with a letter, e-mail, or fax of thanks for their time and highlight again the features they liked.

When the other party becomes resistant, the hard sell won't work. Take the pressure off by backing off. Ask where they want to go from here, but don't press for an answer. This is the place to leave things open-ended. Waiting and giving them some breathing room may keep the door open. This is where you say, "Why don't we think about it and discuss it some more later?" Learn to read between the lines. Some people will not come right out and tell you "no deal."

You postpone—they create urgency. If you're not satisfied with the deal, or want to shop around, tell the other party that *you* want to think about it. You may also need to check with your agent for advice before you can finalize the deal. If the other team is creating urgency, be sure it is real. In many cases, you can get the same deal at a later date, so don't be pressured into making a deal you are not satisfied with or may regret later. If you do want to postpone, give a specific time that you will get back to them, and do so with more prepared negotiations or simply tell them you cannot make an agreement.

AGREEING. Once you've got an agreement, restate it and/or put it in writing. It is common to follow up an agreement with a letter of thanks that restates the agreement to ensure the other party has not changed their mind regarding the terms. After the deal is made, stop selling it. Change the subject to a personal one and/or leave, whichever is appropriate.

FAILING TO AGREE. Rejection, refusal, and failure happen to everyone. The difference between also-rans and successful people lies in how they respond to failure.[41] Successful people keep trying, they learn from their mistakes, and they continue to work hard. If you cannot come to an agreement, analyze the situation and determine why.

COLLABORATION

 LEARNING OUTCOME
10 Use collaboration to resolve conflict.

initiators
People who approach other parties to resolve conflicts.

BCF statements
Statements that describe conflicts in terms of behavior, consequences, and feelings.

Successful collaborations keep people open to working together to find solutions. To understand how this works, we need to define two new terms. **Initiators** are people who approach other parties to resolve conflicts. Skillful initiators use BCF statements, and then get involved parties to respond in BCF statements. **BCF statements** describe conflicts in terms of behavior, consequences, and feelings. That is, when you do B (behavior), C (consequences) happens, and you feel F (feelings). An example of a BCF statement is "When you smoke in the locker room (behavior), I have trouble breathing and become nauseous (consequence), and I feel uncomfortable and irritated (feeling)." The sequence can be varied to fit the situation "I fear (feeling) that the advertisement is not going to work (behavior), and that our hockey team will lose money (consequences)."

The idea is to keep people from becoming defensive. When we become defensive, we go into behavior modes that are counterproductive. Two things are sure to make people defensive—when you don't let them talk and when you fix blame. Therefore, when you develop your opening BCF statement, be descriptive, not evaluative. Keep your opening statement short. The longer your statement, the more defensive you are likely to make the other party. And *don't* assess blame. Timing is also important. If people are busy, make arrangements to see them later to discuss the conflict. In addition, don't confront a person on several unrelated issues at once.

Now that you know what BCF statements are, you can use them to collaboratively resolve conflict. Model 9–3 outlines the process, and the Skill-Builder on pages 270–272 gives you practice using the process.

1. *Plan a BCF statement that maintains your ownership of the problem.* First let's look at what "ownership of the problem" means. Suppose you don't smoke and someone who is visiting you starts smoking. Who "owns" this problem? The smoke bothers you, not your visitor. It's your problem. BCF statements that ask respondents to help you solve your problem don't assess blame, yet state the problem clearly. This approach reduces defensiveness and establishes an atmosphere of problem solving that keeps doors open.

   Put yourself in the other person's position. What presentation would keep you most open to solutions? Show concern for their issues, as well as concern for your issues.

Model 9–3   Resolving Conflict by Collaboration

Initiating Conflict Resolution	Responding to Conflict Resolution	Mediating Conflict Resolution
Step 1. Plan a BCF statement that maintains ownership of the problem.	Step 1. Listen to and paraphrase the conflict using the BCF model.	Step 1. Have each party state his or her complaint using the BCF model.
Step 2. Present your BCF statement and agree on the conflict.	Step 2. Agree with some aspect of the complaint.	Step 2. Agree on the conflict problem(s).
Step 3. Ask for and/or give alternative conflict resolutions.	Step 3. Ask for and/or give alternative conflict resolutions.	Step 3. Develop alternative conflict resolutions.
Step 4. Make an agreement for change.	Step 4. Make an agreement for change.	Step 4. Make an agreement for change.
		Step 5. Follow up to make sure the conflict is resolved.

TIMEOUT
List the steps in collaboration.

_____

_____

_____

_____

_____

_____

_____

Finally, practice your BCF statement before you approach the other party—you don't want to lose your cool here.[42]

2. *Present your BCF statement and agree on the conflict.* After you make your statement, let the other party respond. If they don't understand or refuse to acknowledge the problem, persist gently, but firmly. You can't resolve a conflict if the other party won't acknowledge its existence. Explain the problem in different terms until you get an acknowledgment or realize that it's hopeless. But don't give up too easily.

3. *Ask for and/or give alternative conflict resolutions.* Ask the other party what they think can be done to resolve the conflict. If you agree, great; if not, offer your solution. The idea here is to get to collaboration. If the other party acknowledges the problem, but is not responsive to resolving it, appeal to common goals. Make them realize the benefits—to themselves and to the organization.

4. *Make an agreement for change.* Find specific actions you can both take. Clearly state, or for complex agreements, write down the specific changes that all parties must do to resolve the conflict. Follow up to make sure the conflict is resolved.

<table><tr><td>**TIMEOUT**
Use Model 9–3 to outline how you could have resolved a conflict you recently faced.

_____
_____
_____
_____
_____
_____</td></tr></table>

Mediating Conflict

Frequently, parties in conflict cannot resolve their dispute alone. In these cases, mediators can be very helpful. **Mediators** are neutral third parties who help resolve conflict. In nonunionized organizations, managers are commonly the mediators. But some organizations have trained staff who are designated mediators. In unionized organizations, mediators are usually professionals from outside the organization. However, resolution should be sought internally first.[43] As a manager you may be called upon to mediate a conflict. In this case, remember that you are a mediator, not a judge, and your job is to remain impartial. Get the employees to resolve the conflict, if possible.[44]

mediator
Neutral third party who helps resolve conflict.

As a mediator, don't place blame. If either party blames the other, make statements like, "We're here to resolve the conflict; placing blame is not productive." Focus on how the conflict affects their work. Discuss the issues, not personalities.[45] If someone says, "We can't work together because of a personality conflict," ask him or her to describe the specific issues. Endeavor to make parties aware of their behavior and its consequences.[46]

If the conflict has not been resolved, an arbitrator may be used as a follow-up.[47] **Arbitrators** are neutral third parties whose decisions are binding. Arbitration should be kept to a minimum because it is not a collaborative style. Arbitrators commonly use negotiation. Mediation and then arbitration tend to be used in management–labor negotiations when collective bargaining breaks down and the contract deadline is near.

arbitrator
Neutral third party whose decisions are binding.

Dealing with different personality types, varying perceptions and attitudes, power, politics, and conflict can be very stressful. Therefore, in the next section we examine the causes and consequences of stress and how to manage it.

STRESS

Our lives today abound with tension—deadlines, traffic jams, long hours at work, the need to excel in an uncertain business climate, always short of time—the list is seemingly endless sometimes. **Stress** is our body's internal reaction to external stimuli coming from the environment. Our emotional reactions drive our bodies' physical reactions. Because stress is everywhere and because it dramatically affects performance, numerous organizations offer stress management programs to help employees handle stress better.

stress
Our body's internal reaction to external stimuli coming from the environment.

Functional and Dysfunctional Stress

Stress is functional when it helps us perform better by challenging and motivating us to meet objectives. Truth be told, we all perform best under some pressure. When deadlines approach and the clock is ticking, our adrenaline flows and we often rise to the occasion with better-than-usual performance. The operative word here is, *some* pressure.

Too much pressure is a different story altogether, and it is a serious, endemic problem in today's workplace. Too much pressure turns into more stress than our bodies can handle. This

stressors
Situations in which people
feel overwhelmed by anxiety,
tension, and pressure.

is dysfunctional stress, and it causes irritability, headaches and muscle tension, stomach problems (poor digestion, heartburn, and ulcers), disease (weakened immune system; elevated blood sugar levels, blood pressure, and cholesterol levels; and heart problems), and premature death. Mild signs of stress include an increased breathing rate and an excessive amount of perspiration. **Stressors** are situations in which people feel overwhelmed by anxiety, tension, and pressure.[48]

Stress that is constant, chronic, and severe can cause burnout. *Burnout* is the constant lack of interest and motivation to perform one's job due to stress. Burnout results in physical and/or emotional exhaustion and the more severe stomach problems and diseases listed above. From the organizational side, high stress results in job dissatisfaction, absenteeism, turnover, and lower levels of productivity.

Our abilities to handle pressure vary.[49] In the same situation one person will be comfortable and stress-free and another will be overwhelmed and stressed out.

Causes of Stress

There are five common job stressors. Before you read further, complete the Self Assessment on page 261 to determine your stress personality type.

So, are you a Type A or a Type B personality? This is an important question for your health. Why? Because how much stress we personally set up in our lives is due, in part, to our personality type. *Type A personalities* are characterized as fast-moving, hard-driving, time-conscious, competitive, impatient, and preoccupied with work. And as you have no doubt discerned, Type As set up fast-moving, hard-driving lives. They choose stressful lives. *Type B personalities* are just the opposite of Type As. As you can well imagine, Type As are more stressed than Type Bs. Therefore, if you are a high Type A personality, it behooves you to find ways early on in your career to deal with stress. And it's OK to take time out to recharge your batteries. Take Jerry West, who retired at 62 in 2000 as the executive vice president of the Los Angeles Lakers. He was at the top of his game, having overseen the Lakers' acquisition of Kobe Bryant and Shaquille O'Neal and the team's return to the top. Although some in the Lakers organization no doubt hoped West was taking a "sabbatical," West did return, but as manager of the NBA's Memphis Grizzlies.[50] Obviously, one way Type As recharge their batteries is to take on different challenges!

So, what causes stress in the workplace? What follows is a brief summary of the different contributors to stress in the workplace.

ORGANIZATIONAL CULTURE. Employee stress levels are directly affected by whether the culture is a cooperative one or an autocratic one and whether morale is high or low. The more positive an organization's culture, the less stress employees experience. Organizations that push their people to high levels of performance create stress, of course, but also give them high job satisfaction, which is de-stressing, so the best strategy is to strike a balance.

MANAGEMENT'S SKILL AT MANAGING. The better managers supervise their employees, the less stress there is. Calm, participative management styles are less stressful. Workers with bad bosses are five times as likely to report stress-related lost sleep, headaches, and upset stomachs.[51]

WORK PERFORMED. Some work is more stressful than other work. (Just ask policemen and ambulance workers!) For most of us, however, not a small amount of our stress comes from whether we enjoy our work. Those of us who enjoy the work itself handle stress better than those of us who don't. Thus, finding work that you enjoy is a wise move. In 1997, when University of Kentucky coach Rick Pitino became the Boston Celtics' coach, he was the highest-paid coach in history at $7 million annually. However, Pitino discovered that his coaching style, which had worked so well in college basketball, did not fit pro players. His response? Return to what he did well—he left the Celtics in 2001 and is now (happily) in Louisville doing what he loves, and what he does best.

HUMAN RELATIONS. When people don't get along, stress rises. Our relationships with our coworkers are a very important factor in our job satisfaction. People who don't like their work but enjoy the people they work with can be very happy at work. However, when both

SELF ASSESSMENT

Stress Personality Type

Identify how frequently each item applies to you at work or when you are playing on a team.

(5) usually   (4) often   (3) occasionally

(2) seldom   (1) rarely

_____ 1. I enjoy competition and I work and play to win.

_____ 2. I skip meals or eat fast when there is a lot of work to do.

_____ 3. I'm in a hurry.

_____ 4. I do more than one thing at a time.

_____ 5. I'm aggravated and upset.

_____ 6. I get irritated or anxious when I have to wait.

_____ 7. I measure progress in terms of time and performance.

_____ 8. I push myself to work to the point of getting tired.

_____ 9. I work on days off.

_____ 10. I set short deadlines for myself.

_____ 11. I'm not satisfied with my accomplishments for very long.

_____ 12. I try to outperform others.

_____ 13. I get upset when my schedule has to be changed.

_____ 14. I consistently try to get more done in less time.

_____ 15. I take on more work when I already have plenty to do.

_____ 16. I enjoy work/school more than other activities.

_____ 17. I talk and walk fast.

_____ 18. I set high standards for myself and work hard to meet them.

_____ 19. I'm considered a hard worker by others.

_____ 20. I work at a fast pace.

_____ Total. Add up your scores (1–5) for all 20 items. Your total score will fall between 20 and 100. Place an X on the continuum that represents your score.

Type A personality   Type B personality

100–90–80–70–60–50–40–30–20

---

components are missing—we don't like the work *and* we don't fit with our coworkers, high absenteeism and turnover are often the result.

Signs of Stress

Mild signs of stress include an increased breathing rate and an excessive amount of perspiration. When stress continues for a period of time, disillusionment (*yes,* this can be a sign of stress!), irritableness, headaches and other body tension, a feeling of exhaustion, and stomach problems can result. When you continually feel pressured and fear that you aren't going to meet deadlines or that you are failing, you are experiencing stress. People in stress do many things to find relief. They watch TV/movies (too much), drink (too much), eat (too much), sleep (too much), and take drugs. Alcoholism costs American businesses over $86 billion annually in lost production, absenteeism, and health costs.[52]

Managing Your Stress

When you *manage* your stress, you find ways to eliminate or reduce it. Three steps are involved: First, you have to identify *your* stressors, the ones in *your* life. Next, you look at what's causing them and the consequences of living with (and without—maybe you really don't want to quit college!) them. Finally, you find ways to eliminate or decrease the stressors that work for *you*. The stress management techniques we present here are widely effective.

MANAGE YOUR TIME. Generally, people with good time management skills experience less job stress. Chapter 5 gives details on time management.

RELAX. This, of course, is an excellent stress management technique. People who don't balance career and personal life commonly suffer burnout. OK, so maybe you'll have to practice relaxing consciously at first—do it, you really can! Get enough rest and sleep; have some fun and laugh. Slow down and enjoy yourself. You will find that time down and time off make you more effective at school and at work, and may actually *save* you time! Find some enjoyable off-the-job interests, and pursue them. Socializing with friends, prayer, meditation, music—all of these work for different people. Find the ones that work for you. In a survey sponsored by ESPN Sports, 61 percent (up from 48 percent in an earlier survey) of 1,020 randomly polled respondents said watching sports on TV is more important post-9/11 than it was before as a source of relieving stress. Some 82 percent of respondents said advertisers should maintain or increase their spending in sports.[53]

USE RELAXATION EXERCISES. When you feel stress, simple relaxation exercises can give you relief. One of the most popular and simplest is deep breathing because it relaxes the entire body. Consciously relaxing your entire body going from toe to head is another. Exhibit 9–4 lists "quick-trick" relaxation exercises that you can do almost anywhere.

Deep breathing can be done during and/or between the other exercises. Simply take a slow deep breath, preferably through your nose, hold it for a few seconds (count to five), then let it out slowly, preferably through lightly closed lips. Make sure that you inhale by expanding the stomach, not the chest. Breathe in without lifting your shoulders and/or expanding your chest. Think of your stomach as a balloon. Slowly fill it, then empty it. As you inhale, visualize breathing *in* healing energy that makes you feel better, more energetic, and less pained. As you exhale, visualize breathing *out* the tension, pain, illness, and other stress. Use this visualizing technique during the other relaxation exercises.

GIVE YOURSELF THE GIFT OF ENERGY. Stress depletes your energy. Even worrying about a *future* stressor depletes your energy. Mental stress is often more exhausting than physical stress. Breathing, relaxation (especially sleep), and nutrition are major ways to replenish energy. And as you all know, exercise also increases energy levels.[54]

EAT RIGHT. Good health is essential to everyone's performance, and nutrition is a major factor in health.[55] Obesity is a pervasive health problem in United States.[56] Stress often leads to overeating and compulsive dieting, and being overweight is itself stressful. Good, solid information about nutrition and healthy eating habits is widely available. It's also knowledge most of us already have—eat breakfast; don't eat junk food; eat less fat, sugar, caffeine, and salt; eat more fruits and vegetables, and so forth. If you have an eating disorder, acknowledge it (being proud here can kill you!) and get professional help.

EXERCISE. As you all know, it is well established that physical exercise has numerous beneficial effects on our health.[57] Releasing stress is one of these benefits. Always check with a doctor before starting an exercise program. Remember, your objective here is to relax and reduce stress, *not* increase it. The no pain–no gain mentality? Leave that on the court or playing field; it does *not* apply to stress management.

THINK POSITIVELY. Don't laugh—rather, *do* laugh! Optimists have less stress than pessimists. Get rid of your negative self-talk. Talk to yourself in the affirmative: "This is easy" or "I can do this." Repeat positive statements while doing deep breathing, but be realistic. Positive thinking doesn't guarantee that you will be free of stress headaches, but pessimism and negative self-talk push many people into headaches and other illnesses.

DON'T PROCRASTINATE. Don't be a perfectionist. Procrastinating is stressful. Perfectionism is stressful. Get beyond them.

BUILD A SUPPORT NETWORK. Talking to others helps reduce stress. Friends, family, and friendly coworkers—talk to them—that's what they are there for. That doesn't mean you should continually lean on others, but don't be too proud when things are getting you down.

The Stress Tug-Of-War

11 LEARNING OUTCOME
Explain the stress tug-of-war analogy.

TIMEOUT
Choose a major stressor in your life right now, and develop a plan to manage it, using the suggestions noted above, or others that you think would work well for you.

_____

_____

_____

_____

_____

_____

TIMEOUT
Which of the stress management techniques noted above are you best at and worst at? Develop a plan to improve your weakest stress management skills.

_____

_____

_____

_____

_____

_____

Exhibit 9–4   Quick Tricks for Relaxation

MUSCLES RELAXED	EXERCISE*
All	Take a deep breath, hold it for around 5 seconds, then let it out slowly. See the deep breathing discussion in the text for specific details. Deep breathing may be performed during and/or between other relaxation methods.
Forehead	Wrinkle your forehead by trying to make your eyebrows touch your hairline for 5 seconds. Relax.
Eyes, nose	Close your eyes tightly for 5 seconds. Relax.
Lips, cheeks, jaw	Draw the corners of your mouth back tightly (grimace) for five seconds. Relax.
Neck	Drop your chin to your chest, then slowly rotate your head without tilting it backward. Relax.
Shoulders	Lift your shoulders up to your ears and tighten for five seconds. Relax.
Upper arms	Bend your elbows and tighten your upper muscles for five seconds. Relax.
Forearms	Extend your arms out against an invisible wall and push forward with your hands for five seconds. Relax.
Hands	Extend your arms in front of you; clench your fists tightly for five seconds. Relax.
Back	Lie on your back on the floor or bed and arch your back up off the floor, while keeping your shoulders and buttocks on the floor, and tighten for five seconds. Relax.
Stomach	Suck in and tighten your stomach muscles for five seconds. Relax. Repeating this exercise several times throughout the day can help reduce the size of your waistline.
Hips, buttocks	Tighten buttocks for five seconds. Relax.
Thighs	Press your thighs together and tighten them for five seconds.
Feet, ankles	Flex your feet with toes pointing up as far as you can and tighten for five seconds, then point your feet down and tighten for five seconds. Relax.
Toes	Curl your toes under and tighten for five seconds, then wiggle them. Relax.

*Tighten all your muscles as much as you can without straining, and perform as many tightening–relaxing repetitions as needed to feel relaxed without straining.

Think of stress as a tug-of-war with you in the center, as shown in Exhibit 9–5. On your left are ropes (causes of stress) pulling you to burnout. Stress that is too powerful will pull you off center. On your right are ropes (stress management techniques) that you can *choose* to use to pull you back to the center. The stress tug-of-war is an ongoing game. On easy days you move to the right, and on overly tough days you move to the left. Your objective in this game? Find ways to stay centered.

Managing stress well doesn't mean that you have to use all the techniques. Use what works best for you, but be aware that taken together, the techniques add up to a pretty good definition of a healthy life. Okay, you say—I *am* using these techniques and my stress levels are *still* off the charts. *Now* what do I do? Consider getting out of the situation. Seriously. Ask

Exhibit 9–5   The Stress Tug-of-War

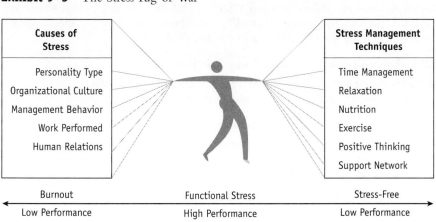

Causes of Stress		Stress Management Techniques
Personality Type		Time Management
Organizational Culture		Relaxation
Management Behavior		Nutrition
Work Performed		Exercise
Human Relations		Positive Thinking
		Support Network

Burnout	Functional Stress	Stress-Free
Low Performance	High Performance	Low Performance

APPLYING THE CONCEPT *Stress Management Techniques*

Identify the technique being used in each statement.

   a. time management   **c.** nutrition   **e.** positive thinking

   b. relaxation   **d.** exercise   **f.** support network

_____ 16. I talk to myself to be more optimistic about my foul shooting.

_____ 17. I've set up a schedule for myself to meet season ticket sales goals.

_____ 18. I get up earlier and eat breakfast to improve my performance.

_____ 19. I'm talking to my partner about my problems in acquiring funding for our athletic department.

_____ 20. I pray.

yourself two questions: "Is my long-term health important?" and "Is this situation worth hurting my health for?" Did you answer yes and no, in that order? It's time to drop the ropes and walk away.

CHAPTER SUMMARY

1. Describe the Big Five personality traits.

Five continuum traits exist: extrovert and introvert (the extroversion trait); cooperative and competitive (the agreeableness trait); stable and unstable (emotionalism); dependable and not dependable (conscientiousness); and willingness and unwillingness to try new things (openness to experience).

2. Understand the perception process and the two factors it is based on.

Perception is the process of selecting, organizing, and interpreting information from the external environment. How we do this is based on internal individual factors that include our personality and our attitudes. The second factor in the perception process is the information itself.

3. Explain how personality, perception, and attitude are related, and why they are important.

Our personalities affect our perceptions and our attitudes. Perception affects attitudes, and vice versa. Changing self esteem and adjusting attitudes actually change single personality traits such as optimism. Personality, perception, and attitude are important because combined they directly affect behavior and performance.

4. State what job satisfaction is and why it is important.

Job satisfaction is a person's attitude toward his or her job. Job satisfaction is important because it has a direct relationship with absenteeism, turnover, and performance.

5. Define power and the difference between position and personal power.

Power is the ability to influence others' behavior. Position power is derived from top management and delegated down the chain of command, whereas personal power is derived from the followers based on the individual's behavior.

6. Explain how reward, legitimate, and referent power differ.

The difference is based on how the person with power influences others. Reward power is the user's ability to influence others with something of value to them. Legitimate power is given by the organization and is a type of position power. Referent power has to do with the user's personal power relationship with others.

7. Understand how power and politics are related.

Power is the ability to influence the behavior of others. Politics is the process of gaining and using power. Therefore, political skills are a part of power.

8. Explain what networking, reciprocity, and coalitions have in common.

Networking, reciprocity, and coalitions are all political behaviors. Networking develops relationships in order to gain social or business advantage. Reciprocity creates obligations and develops alliances and uses them to accomplish objectives. Coalitions are alliances of people with similar objectives who together have a better chance of achieving their objectives.

9. Describe the five conflict management styles.

Avoiders passively ignore conflict rather than resolve it. *Accommodators* resolve conflict by passively giving in to the other party. *Forcers* use aggressive behavior to get their own way. *Negotiators* resolve conflict through assertive give-and-take concessions. *Collaborators* resolve the conflict by finding the best solution that is agreeable to all parties.

10. Use collaboration to resolve conflict.

Collaboration involves (1) planning a BCF statement that maintains your ownership of the problem; (2) presenting your BCF statement; (3) agreeing on the conflict; (4) asking for, and/or giving, alternative solutions; (5) making an agreement for change; and (6) following up to see whether the conflict was truly resolved.

11. Explain the stress tug-of-war analogy.

The stress tug-of-war puts us in the center between stressors that try to pull us off balance and stress management techniques that can keep us centered so that our stress is at functional levels and our performance high. If the causes of stress pull us off center, we burn out and our performance suffers.

12. Define the key terms discussed in the text.

Fill in the missing key terms from memory, or match the key terms from the list in the margin with their definitions below.

_____ is the study of actions that affect performance in the workplace.

A _____ occurs when both parties get what they want.

_____ is a combination of traits that characterizes individuals.

_____ is the process through which we select, organize, and interpret information from the surrounding environment.

_____ is the process of determining why people behave certain ways.

_____ are positive or negative evaluations of people, things, and situations.

The _____ states that managers' attitudes and expectations of employees and how they treat them affect workers' performance.

_____ is the ability to influence the actions of others.

Key Terms

arbitrator

attitudes

attribution

BCF statements

coalition

conflict

dysfunctional conflict

functional conflict

initiators

mediator

networking

organizational behavior

perception

personality

politics

power

Pygmalion effect

reciprocity

stress

stressors

win-win situation

_____ are the efforts of groups or individuals with competing interests to obtain power and positions of leadership.

_____ develops relationships in order to gain social or business advantage.

_____ involves using mutual dependence to accomplish objectives.

A _____ is an alliance of people with similar objectives who together have a better chance of achieving their objectives.

A _____ exists whenever disagreement becomes antagonistic.

A _____ prevents groups from achieving their objectives.

A _____ fosters disagreement and opposition that help achieve a group's objectives.

_____ are people who approach other parties to resolve conflicts.

_____ describe conflicts in terms of behavior, consequences, and feelings.

A _____ is a neutral third party who helps resolve conflict.

An _____ is a neutral third party whose decisions are binding.

_____ is the body's internal reaction to external stimuli coming from the environment.

_____ are situations in which people feel overwhelmed by anxiety, tension, and pressure.

REVIEW AND DISCUSSION

1. Are the conflicts that the NCAA faces functional or dysfunctional?
2. How could the NCAA use negotiation to solve some of their conflicts?
3. Could the NCAA use mediation to solve some of their conflicts?
4. Can college athletes use stress management to improve their performance?
5. What are the Big Five personality traits?
6. What are the four biases in perception?
7. What determines job satisfaction? Are they of equal importance to everyone?
8. What are the seven bases of power?
9. Can management order the end of power and politics in the organization? Should they? Why or why not?
10. Why should you learn your organization's culture and identify power players where you work?
11. How do you know when you are in conflict?
12. What is the difference between functional and dysfunctional conflict and how does each affect performance?

13. What is the primary reason for your personal conflicts? Your work conflicts?

14. What is meant by "ownership of the problem"?

15. How are BCF statements used?

16. What is the difference between a mediator and an arbitrator?

17. What are the characteristics of Type A personalities?

18. What are some stress management techniques?

CASE

Little League Baseball Gets Political

We Americans like to view youth sport organizations like Little League Baseball (LLB) as places where the spirit of sport grows pure and strong. Alas, as we all know all too well, this is no longer true. Scandal dogs these organizations, too, as the media constantly reminds us—parents out of control, "young" athletes who are really too old; the list is depressing, and long. In LLB's 2000–2001 season, conflicts arose between *countries*. Clearly this is no longer the Little League Baseball of yesteryear. Indeed, LLB has come a long way since 1938 when a dad (Carl E. Stotz) organized a boys' baseball program. Stotz's program grew because it was a good thing, and generations of boys grew up loving sports, loving baseball, and practicing good sportsmanship and learning to play by the rules.

But LLB has changed with the times. In 1963, ABC's Wide World of Sports televised for the first time the Little League World Series championship game. This brought Little League baseball into prime-time TV and garnered it national viewership. With national viewership came money, and lots of it, and LLB is now Big Business. When Title IX came along, LLB opened the game to girls. Today, not only is there Little League *Softball* but there is also *Senior* League Softball.[58]

Sponsors line up to use LLB as a vehicle to hawk their wares: Bubblicious Bubble Gum; Honda ("Official Vehicle of Little League Baseball"); New Era ("Official Cap"); RC Cola ("Official Carbonated Beverage"); Russell Corporation ("Official Uniform"); Wilson Sporting Goods Company ("Official Baseball & Softball"). Is this a good thing? Should LLB be laughing all the way to the bank? Or has it lost its way? Is this a good thing for the main constituency of LLB—young athletes? Are young athletes *even* LLB's main constituency today?

LLB's 2001 World Series cast more light on the flip side of the coin. A star pitcher for the New York–based Paulino Little League team, Danny Almonte became a media star after pitching a perfect game. What should have been a wonderful experience for all concerned quickly turned nightmarish when it was established that Danny was 14, not 12 as his father had claimed. Although no punitive action was taken against Danny, the Bronx league's founder, Rolando Paulino, was banned for life from any association with LLB (the team's charter was not revoked), as was Danny's father, Felipe de Jesus Almonte. LLB is working closely with the local league to help it reorganize with credible leadership so that history does not repeat itself. Separately, Dominican authorities plan to prosecute Danny's father, charging him with falsifying Danny's birth records.[59]

So, what's the moral of the story here? Would that we knew. Is winning everything? A Jewish immigrant, Saul Steinberg (famed for his *New Yorker* covers), once said, "It is impossible to understand America without a thorough knowledge of baseball."[60] What does the game of baseball say about us today?

For more information on Little League Baseball visit http://www.littleleague.org. To watch video files from Little League Baseball, President George W. Bush, and the Rolando Paulino team regarding the Danny Almonte controversy, visit http://espn.go.com/moresports/llws01/s/2001/0831/1246234.html.

CASE QUESTIONS

Support your answers to the following questions with specifics from the case and text, or with information you get from the web and other sources.

1. Which type of power base did Little League Baseball use when it banned Rolando Paulino?
   a. coercive
   b. connection
   c. reward
   d. legitimate
   e. referent
   f. information

2. Which type of power did Danny Almonte's father use (ultimately unsuccessfully) to establish his son's age as 14 years old?
   a. coercive
   b. connection
   c. reward
   d. legitimate
   e. referent
   f. information

3. The traditional perception of LLB has nothing to do with organizational politics.
   a. true   b. false

4. Are attitudes an issue in the Almonte case?
   a. yes   b. no

5. What style of conflict management was LLB forced to use to resolve the problem with Danny's father?
   a. avoiding
   b. accommodating
   c. forcing
   d. negotiating

6. Which trait from the single trait system did Danny Almonte's father exhibit the most in this case?
   a. locus of control
   b. optimism

   c. risk propensity
   d. Machiavellianism

7. Did Rolando Paulino's team and the national Little League achieve a win-win situation?
   a. yes   b. no

8. What type of conflict was involved in the Almonte case?
   a. functional
   b. dysfunctional
   c. resolve
   d. psychological

9. What type of stress was placed on Danny Almonte?
   a. functional
   b. dysfunctional
   c. management
   d. organizational

10. Danny's father had what level of "Mach" behavior?
    a. high   b. low

11. Why do conflicts arise in youth leagues?

12. Should leagues validate birth records? (Consider the costs involved in such a venture.)

13. Violence among parents at youth leagues is on the increase. What steps do you think youth league management could take to curb the violence?

14. Is office politics avoidable? If not, why not? If so, how?

EXERCISES

Skill-Builder: Contract Negotiation

Objective:

- To develop negotiation skills.

Preparation:
Re-read the section on the negotiating process (pages 255–258).

In-Class Application

Activity (10–20 minutes):

- Break into groups of two.
- One of you is Butch Steel, your team's star football player, and one of you is the general manager. You are about to begin negotiations to re-sign Butch with your team.
- Your instructor has just handed you your confidential sheets. Read them and jot down some plans (your basic strategy, what you will say) for the lunch meeting you are about to have.
- As part of your preparation, read the following negotiating checklist, and keep it by you during the negotiations for reference and note taking:

1. The appropriate plan for this situation:

    _____ general single-use project plan   _____ detailed standing-policy plan

2. Your basic plan:

    _____

    _____

    _____

3. Your lower limit, target, and opening salary:

    _____

    _____

4. Can you imply that you have other options and/or tradeoffs? _____ If so, what are they?

    _____

    _____

    _____

5. Can you anticipate questions and objections? _____ If so, what are they, and what are your answers?

    _____

    _____

    _____

6. Did you develop rapport and focus on obstacles, not the person? _____ If not, why not?

    _____

    _____

    _____

    _____

7. Did you let the other party make the first offer? _____ If not, why not?

    _____

    _____

    _____

    _____

8. Did you listen? _____ Did you ask questions that focused on meeting the other party's needs? _____ Did you ask for something in return for concessions? _____ If so, what?

_____

_____

_____

9. Were you able to use postponement as a strategy? _____ If so, how did the other side create urgency?

_____

_____

_____

10. Did you reach agreement? _____ If so, state the final offer: _____ If not, why not?

_____

_____

_____

- You do not have to finalize the contract. Begin negotiations.
- After you sign the contract, or agree not to sign, read your partner's confidential sheet and discuss the experience.

Choose one (10–20 minutes):
- Volunteers present their negotiations, and class critiques them.
- Informal, whole-class discussion of student experiences.

Wrap-up:
Take a few minutes and write down your answers to the following questions:

- What did I learn from this experience?

_____

_____

_____

- How will I use this knowledge in the future?

_____

_____

_____

- Had the stakes been real would this task have caused you some stress?

_____

As a class, discuss student responses.

Skill-Builder: Initiating a Collaboration

Objective:
- To develop your ability to resolve conflict.

Preparation:
During class you will role-play a conflict you are currently facing, or have faced. Students have told us that this exercise helped them successfully resolve real conflicts with roommates, coworkers, and teammates. Fill in the following information before class:

Other party(ies)
(use fictitious names):

Pertinent information (relationship to you,
knowledge of the situation, age, background, etc.):

_____   _____

_____   _____

Describe the conflict:

_____

_____

_____

The other party's possible reaction to your initiating a discussion to resolve the conflict (how receptive will they be to collaborating? what might they say or do during the discussion to resist change?):

_____

_____

_____

How will you overcome this resistance to change?

_____

_____

_____

Write out your opening BCF statement (keep it short, maintain ownership of the problem, and don't assess blame):

B: _____

C: _____

F: _____

In-Class Application

Complete the skill-building preparation noted above before class. Break into groups of three, and use the conflict papers you prepared before class to role-play a possible resolution. Take turns acting as initiator, responder, and observer. Observers will make notes on the feedback sheets provided in class (or use the form provided below), and then lead a short discussion on the collaboration's effectiveness. Change groups and role-play the same conflicts with different people.

Choose one (10–15 minutes):

- Volunteers present examples of effective and ineffective resolutions.
  Select one student's example and as a group present it to the entire class.
- Informal, whole-class discussion of student experiences.

Wrap-up:

Take a few minutes and write down your answers to the following questions:

- What did I learn from this experience?

_____

_____

- How will I use this knowledge in the future?

_____

_____

As a class, discuss student responses.

Observer's Feedback Form

Note comments for improving each step in the collaboration. Cast them in positive terms, if you can. Be *descriptive* and *specific,* and for all improvements have an alternative positive behavior (APB) (if you would have said/done . . . , it would have improved the conflict resolution by . . .).

Was initiator's opening BCF statement well-planned and effective? _____ Give specifics on how to improve it:

_____

_____

_____

Did the initiator present the BCF statement effectively? _____ If so, why? If not, why not?

_____

_____

Did the initiator and responder agree on the conflict? _____ If not, why not?

_____

_____

Who suggested alternative solutions? _____ Was it done effectively? _____ How could it have been improved?

_____

_____

_____

Was there an agreement for change? _____ If so, was it a reasonable resolution? _____ If not, why not?

_____

_____

_____

Other suggestions:

_____

_____

_____

Internet Skills: Stress Management Techniques

Objective:

- To use your research skills to find information about reducing stress at work, at home, or in your sport.

Preparation:

Go to the web site http://www.fennsports.com. Answer the following questions regarding managing stress in your life.

1. What is the Stress and Sports Center of America?

_____

_____

2. How can you use visualization to improve your performance?

_____

_____

_____

3. What is the Zone?

_____

_____

_____

4. How would you use visualization and the Zone as an athlete and a sport manager?

_____

_____

_____

5. Complete the free stress test titled "How Stressful Is Your Life?" Total your score. Do you agree with these results?

_____

_____

_____

_____

10 Team Development

Learning Outcomes

After studying this chapter, you should be able to:

1. Understand how groups and teams differ.
2. State the group performance model.
3. Categorize groups by their structure.
4. Define the three major roles group members play.
5. Explain how rules and norms differ.
6. Describe cohesiveness and why it is important to teams.
7. Describe the five major stages of group development and the leadership style appropriate for each stage.
8. Explain how group managers and team leaders differ.
9. Lead a meeting.
10. Define the following key terms (in order of appearance in the chapter):

- group
- team
- group performance model
- group structure dimensions
- group types
- command groups
- task groups
- group composition
- group process
- group process dimensions
- group roles
- norms
- group cohesiveness
- status
- stages of group development

Getting Kids to Team Play

Playing together, learning together, working together. These activities start early in life and continue throughout our lives. They are something every one of us does, and they shape us in crucial and fundamental ways into functioning adults, functioning communities, and functioning societies. Set them up wrong and you can take out the word "functioning" from the preceding sentence. Our society endeavors in numerous ways to keep the "functioning" in our nation's description. Groups like the **BOYS & GIRLS CLUBS OF AMERICA,** the YMCA (Young Men's Christian Association), the Jewish Community Centers (JCCs), town sport leagues, and Little League Baseball—to name only a very few—all work to shape kids into team players and high-functioning adults.

The mission of the Boys & Girls Clubs of America is simple—be available for kids. As the organization notes in its mission statement: "In every community, boys and girls are left to find their own recreation and companionship in the streets. An increasing number of children are at home with no adult care or supervision. Young people need to know that someone cares about them." Boys & Girls Clubs offer that, and more. Club programs and services instill a sense of competence, usefulness, belonging, and influence. "Boys & Girls Clubs are a safe place to learn and grow—all while having fun. They are truly The Positive Place for Kids."[1]

Whether it is basketball at the YMCA, softball at the JCC, or leading a Boy Scout or Girl Scout troop, the men and women in these organizations devote their lives to helping kids and being positive role models. Their dream? That eventually the kids they coach will carry forward the torch of good sports conduct, the value of integrity and hard work, and a love of sports as coaches, parents, teammates, teachers, and community leaders.

These organizations also need you. Join them—it's time for you to pass the torch forward. You will find that this is a boomerang endeavor. What you give "away" will come back in deep satisfaction, in surprising joy, in strength you never knew you had, and in wisdom you won't gain anywhere else. For example, MasterCard donated $500,000 to the Boys & Girls Clubs to help empower our kids.[2]

For current information on local recreation centers, use the Internet address http://www. bgca.org for the Boys and Girls Clubs of America. Use http://www.ymca.net for the Young Men's Christian Association (YMCA), and use http://www.jcca.org for the Jewish Community Centers (JCCs) of North America. (For ideas on using the Internet, see Appendix B.)

INTERNET RESOURCES

http://www.positivecoach.org/leaders/ *Check out the Positive Coaching Alliance's Leaders page for some great resources geared toward fulfilling the organization's motto: "Transforming youth sports so sports can transform youth." In particular, click on the* Roadmap to Excellence *and* Guidelines for Honoring the Game *links to read about ways to help kids understand that having fun and respecting each other while playing sports can be more rewarding than winning. Also, click on* Useful Links *to discover other organizations that are working toward the same goal.*

http://www.psychedonline.org/Articles/Vol2Iss2/TeamBuilding.htm *There are many useful articles to be found on the Psyched—Athletic Performance Enhancement Web site. "Building a Sports Team" starts off by defining what a sports team is before running through the components that make a team successful—from situational factors to personal and leadership factors.*

Along the way, topics such as cohesiveness, roles, and norms are discussed. The article finishes up with a list of ways a manager can improve communication and create harmony among the coaches and athletes on the team.

http://4h.unl.edu/volun/arlen/small.htm *The Small Group Dynamics page of A Toolkit for Volunteer Leaders (brought to you by the University of Nebraska–Lincoln) reinforces many of the ideas for conducting productive meetings covered in this chapter, including exercises and questions for discussion. Particularly helpful is the summary found at the bottom of the page, which contains a list that offers suggestions for what type of discussion to use to accomplish various meeting goals.*

DEVELOPING YOUR SKILLS   Savvy group leaders analyze their group's development stage and select the leadership style appropriate to the stage. Group skills are an important part of management's leadership function. Group leaders must in turn be leaders and liaisons; monitors, information disseminators, and spokespersons; and disturbance handlers, resource allocators, and negotiators.

THE LESSON OF THE GEESE

Ever wondered why geese fly south for the winter in "V" formations? What scientists have found has implications teams would do well to learn.

- Each bird flapping its wings creates an uplift (thrust) for the bird following. Flying in Vs adds *71 percent greater* flying range than flying in disorganized clusters or flying alone.

  Lesson: Travel on the thrust of each other (synergy). A common direction and a sense of community can get your team to the finish line faster and easier.

- Falling out of formation causes individual birds to feel the sudden drag and the higher (and more difficult) resistance of going it alone. This helps them continually adjust their flying to keep the formation.

  Lesson: There is strength and power and safety in members who travel in the same direction.

- When lead birds get tired, they rotate to the back of the formation and another goose flies "point."

  Lesson: Take turns doing the hard jobs.

- Geese at the back of the V honk to encourage front flyers to keep speed.

  Lesson: We all need to be acknowledged with active support and praise.

- When a goose gets sick or is wounded and falls out of the V, two geese follow it down to help it and protect it. They stay with the downed goose until the crisis is resolved, and then they launch out on their own in a V formation to catch up with their group.

  Lesson: Stand by each other in times of need.

TEAMS AND PERFORMANCE

Did you ever experience a great sense of teamwork when you belonged to a youth organization? Kids learn to work with each other when they join a youth organization like the **BOYS & GIRLS CLUBS.** They learn there are good times (winning games and laughing) and bad times (losing games and getting hurt), but either way they learn to stand with each other. Sports has a lot to teach business, and business has been listening. The very idea of teams—work teams, that is—obviously is a lesson that business has learned from the world of sports. The issue is whether managers really understand what is required to run their businesses like great sports teams, and then whether they have the guts to "go for it."[3]

Groups, be they departments or teams, are the backbone of organizations, and managers report spending most of their time in some form of group activity.[4] Performance is a "circling-back" pyramid, built on the "shoulders" of those below you in the organization, but lead forward by the "heads" above. That is, your performance as a manager depends on your team's performance, but your team's performance depends on your leadership. Under this principle, for example, PE teachers need to set high, but achievable, expectations for every student, but their teaching strategies must also consistently support progress toward these expectations.[5] Consequently, the better you understand the connectivity of groups and performance, the more effective you will be both as a group member and as a group leader.[6] And team experience on your résumé is a sure winner.

---

1 LEARNING OUTCOME
Understand how groups and teams differ.

There Are Groups and There Are Teams

Although we often use *group* and *team* interchangeably, they are different. All teams are groups, but not all groups are teams. **Groups** have a clear leader and two or more members who perform independent jobs with individual accountability, evaluation, and rewards. **Teams** are groups whose members share leadership and whose members perform interdependent jobs, with individual and group accountability, evaluation, and rewards. Exhibit 10–1 further distinguishes between groups and teams.

As we noted in Chapter 7, Joe Torre's phenomenal success leading the New York Yankees is the stuff legends are made of. Torre no doubt has other pro teams scratching their heads. Yankee star players get paid *63 times more* than Yankee backup players, yet the Yankees are a team of team players. There is no resentment at the end of the day in the clubhouse. How does he do it? As writer Geoffrey Colvin notes, "The truth is, everyone on the team knows who the stars are and embrace those stars. A lot of corporate teams try to suppress that reality. Winning athletic teams embrace it."[7] Such gracious acknowledgment of star players doesn't happen all that frequently on other teams. Nor does it happen as much as it should in work groups. What is the key to making teams in pro sports and in business work? Valuing *everyone's* contribution. This means that team members must understand and accept the idea that some players, "star workers," are key to the team's success. Of course, the flip (and equally important) side is that star players and star workers need to understand that they can't win alone—the team must work together seamlessly.

Evaluating Team Worth

Determining the value of pro teams is a sport unto itself these days. Recently, Forbes valued the Yankees at $730 million, behind only the Washington Redskins ($796 million) and the Dallas Cowboys ($743 million).[8] Why is this of such interest? Because pro sports teams are first and foremost businesses, and increasing the value of a franchise is, well, good business. Thus, as Gladden, Irwin, and Sutton say, "We contend that 2000 to 2010 will be the decade in which team management activities evolve from a focus on winning as a means of realizing short-term profits to a focus on strategic management of the team brand as a means of realizing long-term appreciation in franchise value."[9] Building a strong team brand is a sure-fire way to increase the value of a franchise. Why? Because each league can produce only one champion a year. Losing teams need to make money too.

As Exhibit 10–1 shows, it's not always easy to clearly distinguish when a group is also a team. This is because there are shades of team/group structures—a continuum—and most groups lie somewhere in between "extreme groups" (with little latitude in autonomy) and "extreme teams" (with great latitude in autonomy). The terms *management-directed, semi-autonomous,* and *self-managed* (or directed) are commonly used to differentiate groups along this continuum.[10] Management-directed groups are clearly groups, self-directed groups are clearly teams, and semi-autonomous groups are somewhere in between.

group
Two or more members with a clear leader who perform independent jobs with individual accountability, evaluation, and rewards.

team
A group with shared leadership whose members perform interdependent jobs with both individual and group accountability, evaluation, and rewards.

> **TIMEOUT**
> Describe a current work group or team you play for in terms of the six characteristics given in Exhibit 10–1. Use this group or team for the remaining Timeouts in this chapter.
>
> _____
> _____
> _____
> _____
> _____
> _____

---

2 LEARNING OUTCOME
State the group performance model.

Exhibit 10–1   Differences between Groups and Teams

CHARACTERISTICS	GROUPS	TEAMS
Size	Two or more; can be large.	Typically 5–12 members.
Leadership	One clear leader makes decisions.	Leadership is shared among members.
Jobs	Jobs are distinct and clear-cut; individual members do one independent part of the work.	Jobs are fluid and overlap in responsibility and tasks performed. Members perform numerous interdependent tasks with complementary skills; the team completes an entire task or project.
Accountability and evaluation	Leader evaluates each member's performance.	Members evaluate each other's individual performance and the group's performance.
Rewards	Rewards are based on individual performance.	Rewards are based on both individual and group performance.
Objectives	Set by the organization and group leader.	Set by the organization and the team.

Level of Autonomy

Group Management-Directed	Semi-Autonomous	Team Self-Directed

THE GROUP PERFORMANCE MODEL

group performance model
Group performance is a function of organizational context, group structure, group process, and group development stage.

The performance of groups is based on four factors (as shown in Exhibit 10–2). In the **group performance model**, performance is a function of organizational context, group structure, group process, and group development stage.

Organizational Context

A number of factors in the organization and the environment—called context—affect how groups function and their level of performance.[11] We have discussed these factors in previous chapters.

GROUP STRUCTURE

group structure dimensions
Include group type, size, composition, leadership, and objectives.

Group structure dimensions include group type, size, composition, leadership, and objectives. (See Exhibit 10–3.)

3 LEARNING OUTCOME
Categorize groups by their structure.

APPLYING THE CONCEPT *Is It a Group or Is It a Team?*

Identify each statement as characteristic of (a) groups or (b) teams.

_____ 1. My boss conducts my performance appraisals, and I get good ratings.

_____ 2. We don't have departmental goals; we just do the best we can to accomplish our mission.

_____ 3. My compensation is based primarily on my club's performance.

_____ 4. I get the assembled tennis racket from Jean; I paint it and send it to Tony for packaging.

_____ 5. There are about 30 people in my department.

Exhibit 10–2   Group Performance Model

Group Performance	(f)	Organizational Context	Group Structure	Group Process	Group Development Stage
High to low		Environment	Type	Roles	Orientation
		Mission	Size	Norms	Dissatisfaction
		Strategy	Composition	Cohesiveness	Resolution
		Culture	Leadership	Status	Production
		Structure	Objectives	Decision making	Termination
		Systems and processes		Conflict resolution	

(f) = a function of

Group Leadership

To a large extent, leaders both provide and determine group structure.[12] Exhibit 10–1 highlighted the fact that the leadership requirements for groups and teams are different. As you have already seen and as you will see, leadership is often a *response* to environment, context, group size, composition, and objectives.

Types of Groups

Groups can be formal or informal, functional or cross-functional, and command or task.

FORMAL OR INFORMAL. *Formal groups,* such as departments and departments within departments, are created by organizations as their official structures.[13] *Informal groups* are not part of the organization's official structure. They are spontaneous creations that occur when members come together voluntarily because of similar interests. Kids join a formal team when they join a **LITTLE LEAGUE BASEBALL** team. They join an informal team when they play a pick-up game of baseball at a Boys & Girls Club. **Do you recall having a better experience on formal or informal teams when you were younger?**

FUNCTIONAL OR CROSS-FUNCTIONAL. Groups organized by function (vertically) perform work of one type. Accounting, human resources, and sales departments are functional groups. Groups whose members come from different functional areas are cross-functional (horizontal) groups. Groups organized around projects are typically cross-functional groups. Managers coordinate activities between functional and cross-functional groups and thus serve as their links (see Exhibit 10–4). Rensis Likert calls this the *linking-pin role.* The use of cross-functional groups is on the rise because of the need to coordinate functional areas.[14]

group types
Formal or informal, functional or cross-functional, and command or task.

Exhibit 10–3   How Groups Are Structured

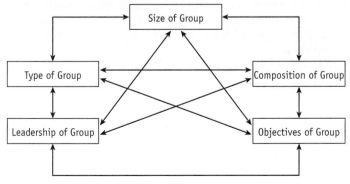

The arrows indicate the effect (or systems interrelationship) each dimension has on the others.

Exhibit 10–4   Functional and Cross-Functional Groups

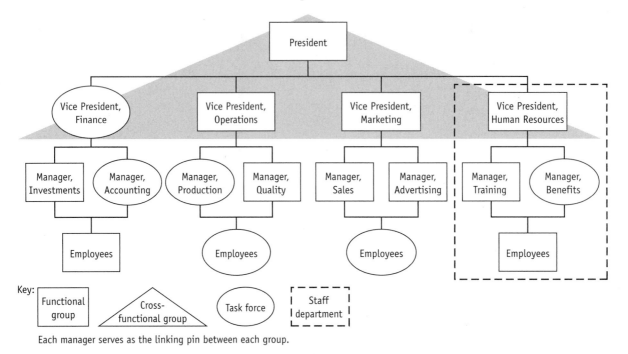

Each manager serves as the linking pin between each group.

command groups
Consist of managers and their staffs.

COMMAND OR TASK. Command groups consist of managers and their staffs, and get the job done—whatever the job is. People are hired to be a part of a command group. Command groups can be either functional or cross-functional. The president and vice presidents in an organization form a cross-functional command group; each vice president and his or her managers are a functional command group.

task groups
Consist of employees who work on a specific objective.

Task groups are composed of staff who work on a specific objective. Task groups are *committees.* As more and more organizations adopt sport terminology, they have taken to calling their committees *teams.*[15] There are two primary forms of task groups: task forces and standing committees.

Task forces are temporary groups formed for a specific purpose. Project teams and ad hoc committees (Chapter 6) are task groups in which members have a functional leader and work with cross-functional departments as needed. One person from each functional area involved in the work serves on the task force. Volunteers in sport organizations are often placed in task forces (temporary committees) to help on specific tasks. For instance, at the Senior Olympics, volunteers coach, perform marketing activities, and distribute food and water at events. One study found that members of task forces have an increased sense of commitment to the organization as long as their group functions well.[16]

Standing committees are permanent groups that work on ongoing organizational issues. Membership in standing committees is often rotated every year so that new ideas and fresh perspectives are brought in. For example, membership may be for three years, with one-third of the committee replaced every year.

Command groups and task groups differ in several ways. One difference is the membership. Command groups are usually (although not always) functional, whereas task groups are typically cross-functional.[17] Another difference is in who belongs to which type of group. Everyone in an organization belongs to a command group, but employees often work for organizations for many years without ever serving on a cross-functional task group. Generally, the higher the level of management, the more time is spent serving in task groups.

TIMEOUT
Identify the task groups in the organization you work for or play for. Specify whether they are task forces or standing committees.

_____
_____
_____
_____
_____
_____
_____

Group Size

There is no ideal group size. Its size varies depending on its purpose. Accounting departments can number in the hundreds, but they can also be a department of two. Groups that are too small limit ideas and creativity. Small groups tend to be too cautious. Issues of over-work and burnout can also arise because the workload is not distributed over enough members. On the other hand, groups that are too large tend to be slow, and individuals don't always get to contribute as much as they can in smaller groups.

Groups tend to be larger than teams. Groups with 20 or more members are definitely groups rather than teams because there are too many members to reach consensus on issues and decisions. Also, such large-group members tend to form subgroups, which is counter to the team concept. Free-riding is another problem.[18] Free-riding occurs when members rely on others to carry their share of the workload.

HOW SIZE AFFECTS LEADERSHIP. Group size affects group process, so leadership style must be tailored to the size of the group. The larger the group, the more formal or auto-cratic leadership should be. Why? Because larger groups are harder to keep on task, harder to keep headed in one direction, and harder to keep momentum going. "Generals" are needed in large groups just to get *anything* done. Large-group members are often grateful, even relieved, for (reasonable) autocratic leadership. (It's frustrating to see time and resources dithered away.) Smaller groups need less formal and more participative management styles. Larger groups inhibit equal participation. Generally, participation is most equal in groups of around five. This is why teams are small in size. The larger the group, the more the "troops" need "support" in the form of formal structured plans, policies, procedures, and rules.

Managers typically have no say in the size of the groups they manage. However, managers of large departments can choose to organize their department into teams. Committee chairs are often able to select the group's size, and in doing so should keep the group size appropriate for the task.

Teams are often small (10 to 15 players) when kids join a formal **LITTLE LEAGUE BASE-BALL** team. The small number of players on the team allows the players to get to know each other very well over the course of a season. Kids would not be able to feel as close to all of their classmates in a physical education class at school with 100 students. **Did you like smaller or larger groups in your youth?**

Composing the Group

Group composition is the mix of members' skills and abilities. Obviously, composition directly and strongly affects performance.[19] Without the right mix of skills and abilities, groups cannot excel.[20]

group composition
The mix of group members' skills and abilities.

To make the team and to stay on the team, players—be they gymnasts, swimmers, fencers, and shortstops *or* accountants, managers, HR people, and engineers—must maintain their skills and abilities at high levels. Winning teams are made up of the best available people. Teams that aren't, don't succeed as well as they might, and businesses that aren't, fall short of their potential. And losing competitive advantage can be a death knell in today's business environment. CEOs like GE's legendary Jack Welch consciously set up competitive internal environments, with great returns on their efforts. Not everyone has had Welch's success, however.[21] By their very nature, organizations aren't as lean and mean as sports teams, and can't always assemble teams made up of the best of the best.

The **BOYS & GIRLS CLUBS** promote an atmosphere of team spirit. In contrast, coaches in town leagues choose players based on their ability. The more talented players are selected to represent their towns. This selection process makes the kids feel competitive toward each other. **Did you prefer to belong to more competitive teams when you played sports as a youth?**

People with a high need for affiliation tend to make better team players than people with a high need for power, who work better in groups. Managers typically have a high need for power and a low need for affiliation, which contributes to their use of groups and their resistance to changing to teams.

HOW COMPOSITION AFFECTS LEADERSHIP. Attracting, selecting, and retaining the best people for the job is one of your most important functions as a manager, and this really hits home when building teams. Try to assemble a diverse group. Your management skills may be stretched, but it will be worth it; as we have noted previously, diverse groups often outperform homogeneous groups. When assembling teams, look for people with complementary skills.

Objectives

In Chapter 4 we explored the benefits of setting objectives. It is important to understand that these benefits apply to both individuals and groups. In groups, objectives are commonly very broad—usually about fulfilling the organization's mission. Teams frequently develop their own objectives. One reason teams often outperform groups is that having developed their objectives, they "own" them in a way that groups do not. Objectives provide the structure required to identify organizational need.[22] A sports team, for example, might set objectives to improve community and media relationships, to strengthen team chemistry, to best last year's win-loss record, to win as many games as they lose, to finish first, to make the playoffs, to play in the championship game, or to win the championship. Recreational sport teams might emphasize teamwork and exercise. Work teams might set objectives to increase customer satisfaction, team rapport, sales, or profits.

HOW OBJECTIVES AFFECT LEADERSHIP. Effective managers pay close attention to objective setting. They guide their team in setting objectives that can be met, that are clear, and that can solve the problem.[23]

GROUP PROCESS

group process
The patterns of interactions that emerge as group members work together.

Group process is the patterns of interactions that emerge as group members work together. Group dynamics is another word for group process. Group process often changes over time, and it is not something people figure out on their own. Careful and thoughtful training in group process is crucial for teams to be effective. Close attention to this important aspect of groups is also key to improving team performance.

group process dimensions
Include roles, norms, cohesiveness, status, decision making, and conflict resolution.

The six components of **group process dimensions** are roles, norms, cohesiveness, status, decision making, and conflict resolution.

4 LEARNING OUTCOME
Define the three major roles group members play.

Group Roles

group roles
Expectations shared by the group of how members will fulfill the requirements of their various positions.

As a group works to achieve its objectives, certain functions emerge. Members develop roles in order to fulfill these functions. **Group roles** are expectations shared by the group of how members will fulfill the requirements of their various positions. Effective groups develop clear roles for members.[24] Careful descriptions of members' jobs help to clarify group roles. People often perform multiple jobs within their group. For example, the manager of a local soccer club may take on the jobs of teacher, counselor, recruiter, and scout.

Group roles are different from the jobs themselves. In groups, members basically perform task roles, maintenance roles, and self-interest roles. In Chapter 1, you learned that when managers interact with employees, they can use task behavior or maintenance behavior. These same two dimensions are performed by group members as they interact.[25]

Group members play *task roles* when they do and say things that help to accomplish the group's objectives.[26] Task roles are often described as structuring, job-centered, production, task-oriented, and directive. Group members play *maintenance roles* when they do and say things that shape and sustain the group process.[27] Maintenance roles are described as consideration, employee-centered, relationship-oriented, and supportive (the four terms are interchangeable).

Members play *self-interest roles* when they do and say things that help the individual but hurt the group. When members put their own needs before those of the group, the group's performance can suffer. For example, hockey players who strive to score the most goals themselves are acting in their own self-interest, not necessarily that of the team. Such athletes might actually be costing the team goals because they don't pass to teammates who are in better positions to score.

To be effective, groups need their members to focus on both their task roles and their maintenance roles, while minimizing self-interest roles. When members focus only on tasks, per-

**APPLYING
THE CONCEPT**   *Roles*

Identify the role fulfilled in each statement:

a. task   **b.** maintenance   **c.** self-interest

_____   6.   Wait. We can't decide yet—we haven't heard Rodney's idea.

_____   7.   I don't understand. Could you explain why we're practicing our
              power play *again*?

_____   8.   We've tried that play before; it doesn't work. My play is much better.

_____   9.   What does who's going to the dance have to do with the game
              tonight? We're getting sidetracked.

_____   10. Ted's solution is much better than mine. Let's go with his idea.

formance can suffer because maintenance roles not only help members deal with conflict effectively, they also develop an *esprit de corps*. Group process without maintenance roles may even become dysfunctional. Obviously, groups whose members focus solely on having a great time don't get the job done. And groups whose members place self-interest ahead of group interest don't produce to their fullest potential.

There are, of course, many situations that benefit both the individual and the group. Therefore, as you strive to achieve objectives, you need to distinguish between self-interests that benefit both the individual and the organization (win–win situations) and those that benefit the individual but hurt the organization (win–lose situations). Group performance typically increases dramatically when members aren't concerned about who gets credit for this accomplishment or that one.

LEADERSHIP IMPLICATIONS. Savvy group leaders watch the roles being played in their group. They step in to guide the group back to balance when members shift too far to a task focus or a maintenance focus, and they reign in "star" members who put their self-interest ahead of the group's interest.

5 LEARNING OUTCOME
Explain how rules and norms differ.

Group Norms

Whether or not policies, procedures, and rules are in place to guide behavior, every group eventually develops group norms, unwritten "rules" about how things are done. **Norms** are the group's shared expectations of members' behavior. Norms determine what should, ought, or must be done in order for the group to maintain consistent and desirable behavior.[28] In one study, researchers found that team norms developed in four situations: during practices, during competition, in social situations, and in the off-season. Norms were most strongly associated with productivity (giving 100 percent during competition, working hard at practice, and training during the off-season). Norms frequently associated with group maintenance were also popular. Norms such as maintaining contact with team members in the off-season, attending social functions, and respecting teammates at social functions were frequently cited. The authors summarized that, in short, norms evolve around matters of importance to group members.[29]

Norms develop spontaneously as members interact.[30] Each group member brings cultural values and past experience (beliefs, attitudes, and knowledge) to the group that shapes norms. The composition of the group is therefore key to the type of norms that the group will develop. If being a hard worker becomes a group norm, the entire group will perform to that expectation; likewise, if on-the-job socializing becomes the number one group

TIMEOUT
State the primary group roles played in your current work group or team.

_____

_____

_____

_____

_____

_____

norms
The group's shared expectations of members' behavior.

norm, performance will suffer. Groups develop their own "rules" for what is acceptable (and not acceptable) in humor, socializing, ways of talking, ways of letting new members know what is acceptable and not acceptable—the list is endless, and encompasses obvious behavior and subtle, nuanced behavior. Norms can change over time to meet the changing needs of the group. And dysfunctional norms can be reshaped as well—for example, diversity training helps to discourage ethnic jokes.

Depending on the group and its culture, members who don't adhere to the norms often find themselves pressured to comply.[31] Strategies used to induce compliance with sport association policies and rules normally fall within a framework of two categories: sanctions or compensation.[32] B. Goff notes that "evidence concerning negative exposure derived from NCAA sanctions against a university athletic program suggests it will have negative consequences."[33] The threat of sanctions should be enough to induce universities to follow the NCAA rules.

LEADERSHIP IMPLICATIONS. Group norms can help or hinder a group. Norms can promote healthy group process—for example, when helping each other, working hard, being the best performers, and not being prima donnas are group norms. Or, they can sabotage performance—for example, when bending the rules, heavy social drinking, and underperforming are the group norms. As a group leader, be aware of your group's norms. Work to develop positive norms and try to eliminate negative ones.

LEARNING OUTCOME
6
Describe cohesiveness and why it is important to teams.

Group Cohesiveness

group cohesiveness
The extent to which members stick together.

The extent to which a group will abide by and enforce its norms depends on its cohesiveness. **Group cohesiveness** is the extent to which members stick together. The more cohesive the group, the more it sticks together as a team. The more desirable membership in the group, the more willing members will be to comply with the group's norms. In highly cohesive groups all members will follow the norm, even if the norm is "produce less than required" or "work a lot harder than the company expects." This won't happen in moderate- or low-cohesive groups—these members will produce at varying levels, and the norms will not be strongly enforced. This has important consequences—for example, if a highly cohesive group's norm is social drug use, some group members will do drugs that they wouldn't do on their own, simply to be accepted by the group. One study interviewed athletes and coaches from eight teams in the Atlanta Olympics about their performance. The four teams that failed to meet performance expectations had problems with team cohesion. They also lacked experience, faced travel problems, experienced coaching problems, and encountered problems related to focus and commitment.[34]

What makes groups cohesive? Six factors influence cohesiveness:

1. *Objectives.* The stronger the agreement and commitment made to achieving the group's objectives, the higher the group's cohesiveness.

2. *Size.* The smaller the group, the higher the cohesiveness. Three to nine members appear to be a good group size for cohesiveness.

3. *Homogeneity.* Generally, the more similar group members, the higher the group's cohesiveness. (People tend to be attracted to people who are similar to themselves.) The dilemma here is that diverse groups usually make better decisions.

4. *Participation.* The more equal member participation, the higher the group's cohesiveness. One recent study that examined cohesion and performance in team sports concluded that a "positive cohesion-performance relationship was linked to a stronger perception that athletes would train in the off-season."[35]

5. *Competition.* The focus of the competition affects cohesiveness. If the group focuses on internal competition, members will try to outdo each other, and low cohesiveness results. If the group focuses on external competition, members tend to pull together as a team to beat out rivals.

TIMEOUT
Identify at least two norms in your current work group or team. How do you know these are norms? How does the group enforce these norms?

6. *Success.* The more successful a group is at achieving its objectives, the more cohesive it becomes. Success breeds cohesiveness, which breeds more success. People want to be on a winning team.

HOW COHESIVENESS AFFECTS GROUP PERFORMANCE. Many studies have compared cohesive and noncohesive groups. The general conclusion is that cohesive groups have a higher level of success and greater satisfaction. Cohesive group members tend to miss work less often, are more trusting and cooperative, and have less tension and hostility. One study found that "NBA teams with a high-shared experience and a low turnover tended to improve their win-loss records significantly."[36] To measure a team's shared experience, the authors looked at both members' overall tenure on the team and their actual on-court minutes. "Managing a lower turnover of players led to improved win-loss records for both winning teams and losing teams. This is important since it would appear that losing teams have little reason for keeping their roster intact. Teams with more losses than wins in one year won an average of 5.7 more games in the following year if their level of shared experience also rose. However, teams won only 1.2 more games on average if they had shuffled their rosters. In other words, teams that stayed together tended to play a lot better together."[37]

Cohesiveness is associated with performance in the following ways:

- Groups with the highest productivity were highly cohesive and accepted management's directives on productivity levels.

- Groups with the lowest productivity were also highly cohesive, but rejected management's directives on productivity levels; they set and enforced their own levels, which were below those of management. This can happen in organizations with unions that have an "us against them" attitude.

- Groups with intermediate productivity were low-cohesive groups, irrespective of their acceptance of management's directives. The widest variance of individuals' performance was among the groups with the lower cohesiveness. They tended to be more tolerant of nonconformity with group norms.

LEADERSHIP IMPLICATIONS. Your goal as a leader is to develop cohesive groups that hold high productivity as a group norm. Participative management style helps groups develop cohesiveness and builds agreement on, and commitment toward, objectives. Coaching also encourages cohesiveness. Some intragroup competition may be helpful, but leaders should focus primarily on intergroup competition. Winning teams become cohesive very naturally, which in turn motivates the group to higher levels of success. The trick is to develop a cohesive but diversified group. **Were the teams you played on as a youth cohesive? Were they diversified?**

Status within the Group

As group members interact, they develop respect for one another in numerous ways. The more respect, prestige, influence, and power a group member has, the higher his or her status within the group. **Status** is the perceived ranking of one member relative to other members in the group. Status is based on several factors—one's performance, job title, salary, seniority, expertise, people skills, appearance, and education, among others. Depending on the group's norms, what sports members play affects their status. Go into a high-end men's clothier sometime and look at their neckties. If wearing your sport on an expensive tie indicates anything, it appears that fishing, tennis, sailboating, golfing, and polo are high-status sports.[38] On the other hand, working-class people in Britain are more likely to grant high status to someone who plays rugby and football (soccer to us).

Group status depends on the group's objectives, norms, and cohesiveness. Members who conform to the group's norms typically have higher status than members who don't. Conversely, a group is more willing to listen to and overlook a high-status member who breaks the norms. High-status members also have more influence on the development of norms and on decisions made by the group. Because members with less status often find their ideas ignored, they tend to copy high-status members' behavior. They also find acceptance by agreeing with their suggestions.

TIMEOUT
Identify your work group or team's cohesiveness as high, medium, or low. Support your assessment with examples.

_____
_____
_____
_____
_____
_____

status
The perceived ranking of one member relative to other members in the group.

Exhibit 10–5   Six Group Processes

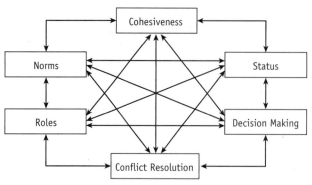

The arrows indicate the effect (or systems interrelationship) each dimension has on the others.

TIMEOUT
List each member in your current work group or team, including yourself, and identify each person's status in the group. Support your assessment with reasons.

HOW STATUS AFFECTS GROUP PERFORMANCE. High-status members have a major impact on the group's performance. If high-status members support positive norms and high productivity, chances are the group will, too.

Another important factor influencing group performance is status congruence, which is the acceptance and satisfaction members receive from their status in the group. Members dissatisfied with their status may not participate as actively as they would if they were satisfied with their status. Dissatisfied members may therefore physically or mentally escape from the group and not perform to their full potential. Or they may cause conflict as they strive to gain status.

LEADERSHIP IMPLICATIONS. To be effective, leaders need high status. Therefore, it behooves leaders to maintain good relations with the group, particularly with high-status informal leaders, to be sure they endorse positive norms and objectives. In addition, leaders should be aware of conflicts that may be the result of status incongruence. Equal or close to equal status is most productive.

Decision Making and Conflict Resolution

How decisions are made by groups and teams directly affects performance. As we noted earlier, with groups, decision-making authority is held by the manager.[39] However, with teams, decision-making authority is held by members.[40] One study found that "professionals and volunteers at sporting events felt that some areas of decision making were perceived to be the domain of either the professionals or volunteers. Professionals wanted the relationship to be more equal. One implication of this finding is the potential for improved organizational decision making between professionals and volunteers at sporting events."[41]

Conflict is common in groups and teams, and unresolved conflicts can have a negative effect on performance. In Chapter 9 you developed your skills at resolving conflict. Understanding group processes will make you a more effective group/team member and leader. Exhibit 10–5 summarizes the six group processes.

7 | **LEARNING OUTCOME**
Describe the five major stages of group development and the leadership style appropriate for each stage.

STAGES OF GROUP DEVELOPMENT AND LEADERSHIP STYLES

stages of group development
Orientation, dissatisfaction, resolution, production, and termination.

As we have noted, groups have organizational contexts, structures, and processes. They also go through developmental stages as they grow from a collection of individuals to a smoothly operating and effective group or team. The **stages of group development** are orienta-

---

APPLYING
THE CONCEPT   *Group Process*

Identify the group process operative in each statement:

a. roles   **c.** cohesiveness   **e.** decision making

b. norms   **d.** status   **f.** conflict resolution

_____ 11. Although we do have occasional differences of opinion, we really get along well and enjoy playing together.

_____ 12. When you need advice on how to do things, go see Shirley—she knows the ropes around here better than anyone.

_____ 13. I'd have to say that Carlos is the peacemaker around here. Every time a disagreement occurs, he gets the players to work out the problem.

_____ 14. Kenady, you're late for the team meeting. Everyone else was on time, so we started without you.

_____ 15. What does fundraising for a new scoreboard have to do with solving the problem? We're getting sidetracked.

---

tion, dissatisfaction, resolution, production, and termination. Savvy managers change their leadership style as the group develops.

Stage 1: Orientation

Command groups are rarely started with all new members. Therefore, the orientation stage is more characteristic of task groups that are clearly beginning anew. Orientation, also known as the forming stage, is characterized by low development (D1, high commitment and low competence). When people first form a group, they often come with a moderate to high commitment to it. However, because they haven't worked together, they lack competence as a team, even though they may be highly competent individuals.

During orientation, members must work out structure issues about leadership and group objectives.[42] The size of the group and its composition are checked out. Members may be anxious over how they will fit in (status), what will be required of them (roles and norms), what the group will be like (cohesiveness), how decisions will be made, and how members will get along (conflict). These issues must be resolved if the group is to progress to the next developmental stage. Training camps held before a season begins are an important mechanism not only for deciding which players will make the team but also for developing group norms and for resolving orientation issues. Thus, a swimming league not only will train before school starts, it will also have barbecues and other social functions so that parents and swimmers can get to know each other.

LEADERSHIP STYLE. The appropriate leadership style during orientation is autocratic (high task/low maintenance). When groups first come together, leaders need to help the group clarify its objectives, and provide clear expectations for members. Leaders can also set a friendly tone that helps members start to get to know one another.

Stage 2: Dissatisfaction

This stage, also known as the storming stage, is characterized by moderate development level (D2, lower commitment and some competence). After working together for a time, members typically become dissatisfied in some way with the group.[43] Uncomfortable questions arise: Why am I a member? Are we ever going to accomplish anything? Why don't other members do what's expected of them? Often the task is more complex and difficult than anticipated; members mask their own feelings of incompetence with frustration. The group has developed some competence to perform the task, but not as much as they would like, so there is impatience here as well.

During dissatisfaction, the group needs to resolve its structure and process issues before it can progress to the next developmental stage. This is a dangerous stage because groups can get stuck in dissatisfaction and never progress to becoming a fully functioning team. Coaches in the swimming league may be frustrated with certain players because they are trying to balance swim practice with band camp, and beginning swimmers may question whether they will ever get in good enough shape.

LEADERSHIP STYLE. The appropriate leadership style during the dissatisfaction stage is consultative (high task/high maintenance). When satisfaction drops, leaders need to focus on the maintenance role to encourage members to continue to work toward the objectives. At the same time, leaders must continue to focus on the task—swimming skills and endurance, in our example—to help the group rise to the level of competence it is capable of.

Stage 3: Resolution

Resolution, also called the norming stage, is characterized by a high development level (D3, variable commitment and high competence). With time, members often resolve the incongruence between their initial expectations and the realities that the objectives, tasks, and skills represent. As members develop competence, they typically grow more satisfied with the group. Relationships develop that satisfy group members' affiliation needs. Members learn to work together as they develop a structure and process with acceptable leadership, norms, status, cohesiveness, and decision-making styles. During periods of conflict or change, the group will return to resolve these issues yet again.

Commitment will vary from time to time as the group interacts. If the group does not deal effectively with its process issues, it may regress to stage 2 (dissatisfaction) or it may "plateau" and stagnate in both commitment and competence. If the group succeeds at developing positive structures and processes, it will develop to the next stage. The swimming league developed a series of organized practices that fit all of the swimmers' schedules. This resolution was not an easy task, but accomplishing it made the team close-knit as it worked together to find ways to carpool.

LEADERSHIP STYLE. The appropriate leadership style during resolution is participative (low task/high maintenance). Once group members know what to do and how to do it, there is little need to direct their task behavior. Groups in resolution need their leaders to focus on maintenance.

When commitment varies, it is usually due to some problem in group process, such as a conflict. Leaders should then focus on maintenance behavior to get groups through the issue(s) they face. If leaders continue to overmanage task behavior, groups can become dissatisfied and regress or plateau at this level.

Stage 4: Production

The production stage, also called the performing stage, is characterized by a high level of development (D4, high commitment and high competence). At this stage commitment and competence don't fluctuate much. Groups function smoothly as teams with high levels of satisfaction. They maintain positive structures and processes. The fact that members are very productive further fuels positive feelings. Group structure and process may change with time, but issues are resolved quickly and easily; members are open with each other. The swimming team did move into the production stage and routinely takes swimmers to national competitions.

LEADERSHIP STYLE. The appropriate style during the production stage is empowerment (low task/low maintenance). Groups that achieve this stage play appropriate task and maintenance roles; by this stage leaders don't need to play either role, unless there is a problem, because the group is effectively sharing leadership.

Stage 5: Termination

Termination, also called the adjourning stage, is not reached in command groups unless there is some drastic reorganization. However, task groups do terminate. During this stage,

Exhibit 10–6   Group Development Stages and Leadership Style

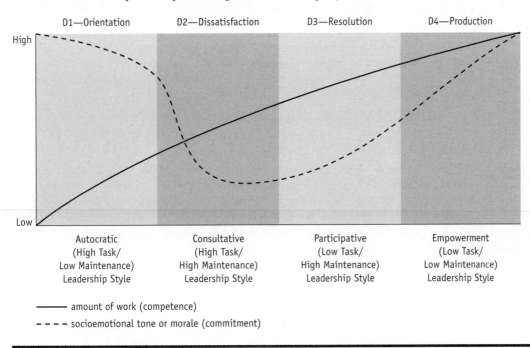

members experience feelings of loss as they face leaving the group. Closure is important. The swimming league's annual awards dinner, which carefully honors every team member, helps swimmers who are going on to college—and their parents—say goodbye to members who have become friends.

CHANGES IN GROUP DEVELOPMENT AND LEADERSHIP STYLE. Two key variables identified through each stage of group development are work on the task (competence) and the socioemotional tone or morale (commitment). These two variables do not progress in the same manner. As Exhibit 10–6 shows, competence continues to increase steadily through stages 1 to 4, whereas commitment fluctuates—it starts out high in stage 1, drops in stage 2, then rises through stages 3 and 4.

8 LEARNING OUTCOME
Explain how group managers and team leaders differ.

TIME**OUT**
Identify your work group or team's developmental stage and the leader's management style. Is his or her style appropriate for your group's stage? What do you think could be done to improve your group's structure and process?
_____
_____
_____
_____
_____
_____
_____

DEVELOPING GROUPS INTO TEAMS

As Exhibit 10–1 showed, groups and teams are different. The trend is to empower groups to become teams because teams are more productive than groups.[44] As you work to make groups teams, consider the size of the department/group. If your group has 20 or more members, break the group into two or three teams. In this section we examine training, planning, organizing and staffing, leading, and controlling teams and how group managers and team leaders differ.

Training

If teams are to succeed, members need training in group process skills so they can make decisions and handle conflict.[45] A team-building program, as discussed in Chapter 7, is also very helpful in turning groups into teams.[46]

The Management Functions

The management functions are handled differently in groups and teams. In this section, we discuss how the manager's job changes with teams.

PLANNING. Setting objectives and decision making are important parts of planning. In teams, team members set objectives, develop plans, and make the decisions. The manager's role is one of involving and coaching members and making sure they understand the objectives, accept them, and are committed to achieving them.

ORGANIZING AND STAFFING. Team members participate in the selection, evaluation, and rewarding of members.[47] Jobs are more interchangeable and are assigned by members as they perform interdependent parts of the task.

LEADING. Although teams share leadership, most teams do identify someone as leader; the difference is, they lead with the permission of the team and they are leading a group of leaders, so to speak. Thus, the official team leader doesn't tell people what to do or assign people tasks, unless the team gives the leader this authority for process reasons. Effective team leaders are highly skilled in group process and team building. Leaders spend a great deal of time developing group structure and process. Effective leaders work to bring the team to the production stage, and they change leadership styles with the team's developmental stage.

CONTROLLING. Team members monitor their own progress, take corrective action, and perform quality control.

In summary, the roles of group manager and team leader differ in significant ways. Group managers perform the four functions of management. Team leaders empower members to perform the management functions and focus on shaping group structure and group process, and getting the team to the "mature" developmental stage, that of production.

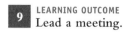

9 LEARNING OUTCOME
Lead a meeting.

GETTING TO BETTER MEETINGS

Teams typically have daily meetings. With the increasing use of teams, meetings take up an increasing amount of time in organizations.[48] Therefore, leading effective meetings is an important skill to have. Successful meetings depend on the leader's skill at managing group process. People commonly complain that there are too many meetings, they are too long, and they are unproductive. Therefore, in this section, we give you pointers on how to plan and conduct meetings and how to handle problem group members.

Planning Meetings

Your preparations and that of your team are crucial for conducting effective meetings. Unprepared leaders conduct unproductive meetings. Planning is needed in at least five areas: (1) setting objectives; (2) selecting participants; (3) making assignments; (4) setting the agenda and the time and place for the meeting; and (5) leadership. A written copy of the plan should be sent to members prior to the meeting (see Exhibit 10–7).

OBJECTIVES. Have one—or don't call a meeting. Amazing numbers of meetings are called without a clear purpose. So, before you call a meeting, *clearly* define its purpose and set out the objectives that you wish to accomplish. Linda Higgison is an event planner who feels that people who plan association meetings never see their marketing potential. She notes that "the Olympics have been successful in attracting global corporate sponsorships. Better yet is that these sponsors end up spending much more on events, ads, and consumer contests to reinforce the Olympic affiliation."[49] Linda suggests listing and advertising one objective of your meeting to attract sponsors and to promote your organization.

PARTICIPANTS AND ASSIGNMENTS. Before you call a meeting, decide who *needs* to attend the meeting. When too many people attend, your ability to complete the work slows down considerably. Look at your objectives and decide who is affected by them and who should have input. Do you need an outside specialist to provide expertise? It is often advis-

Exhibit 10–7   Meeting Plans

CONTENT

- *Time*. List date, place (if it changes), and time (both beginning and ending).
- *Objectives*. State the objectives and/or purpose of the meeting. The objectives can be listed with agenda items, as shown below, rather than as a separate section. Make sure that objectives are specific.
- *Participation and assignments*. If all members have the same assignments, list them. If different members have different assignments, list their names and assignments. Assignments may be listed as agenda items, as shown below for Ted and Karen.
- *Agenda*. List each item to be covered in priority order with its approximate time limit. Accepting the minutes of the last meeting may be an agenda item.

EXAMPLE

BOYS CLUB BASEBALL TEAM MEETING

December 15, 2006, Boys Club Central Office, 1:00–2:00 P.M.

Participation and Assignments

All members will attend and should have read the list of players available for each of the six teams before the meeting. Be ready to discuss your preferences for selecting players.

Agenda

1. Ted will lead a discussion of the process to be utilized in selecting players—20 minutes.
2. Karen will lead the process of selecting players—60 minutes.
3. Ted and Karen will present dates for teams to hold practice without discussion—5 minutes. Discussion will take place at the next meeting after you have given the possible practice dates some thought.

able to discuss controversial issues with key members before the meeting. Participants should know in advance what is expected of them. Be sure to give adequate notice if any preparation is required on their part (read material, do research, make a report, and so forth).

AGENDA. Before you call a meeting, identify the activities that will take place and list them in order—this is your agenda. Agendas tell people what is expected and how the meeting will progress. Setting time limits for each item keeps everyone on task, and avoids the needless (and endless) discussion and getting off topic that are so common at meetings. When digression occurs, take the group back to topic. However, you need to be flexible and allow more time when really needed. Members may also submit agenda items they want included.

List items in order of priority. Then, if the group doesn't get to every item, the least important items will carry forward.

DATE, PLACE, AND TIME. To determine which day(s) and time(s) of the week are best for meetings, get members' input. Members tend to be more alert early in the day. When members work in close proximity, it is better to have more frequent, shorter meetings that focus on one or just a few items. However, when members have to travel, meetings must be fewer and longer. Select an adequate place for the group, and plan for its physical comfort. Make sure that seating provides eye contact for small discussion groups, and plan enough time so that the members don't have to rush. If the meeting place needs to be reserved, check very early on how far ahead you need to reserve the room. A current trend is to hold important meetings at sports stadiums. Conference rooms in newer stadiums are often larger than those available at hotels. Then there is the prestige of holding an event at a sports stadium such as the new Bolton Wanderers' Reebok Stadium (which features the 125-room De Vere Whites hotel and offers group rates per person per night for bed and breakfast); this ensures attendance. However, make sure you tour the facilities if you are considering this option; make sure the conference room's size suits the size of the group attending. Too large a room can cast a pall over a meeting.[50]

LEADERSHIP. Think about what leadership style best fits your objectives for the meeting. Each agenda item may need to be handled differently. For example, some items will simply call for disseminating information, but others may require a discussion, vote, or consensus; still other items require a simple quick report from a member, and so forth. Develop your team members' leadership skills by rotating meeting leaders.

TECHNOLOGY. E-mail, teleconferences, and videoconferences have cut the need for some meetings. They save travel costs and time, and they may result in better and quicker decisions. Personal computers are said to be the most useful tool for running meetings since Robert's Rules of Order. PCs can be turned into large-screen "intelligent chalkboards" that can dramatically enhance meeting results. Minutes (notes on what took place during a meeting) can be taken on laptops, and hard copies or e-mails can be distributed at the end of the meeting.

Conducting Meetings

THE FIRST MEETING. Remember that at a group's first meeting, the group is in the orientation developmental stage. Therefore, develop objectives, but give members time to get to know one another. Introductions set the stage for subsequent interactions. A simple technique is to start with introductions, then move on to the group's purpose, objectives, and members' jobs/assignments. Sometime during or following this procedure, take a break to enable members to interact informally. If members see that their social needs will not be met, dissatisfaction may occur more quickly.

Effective meetings have three parts:

1. *Identify objectives.* Begin meetings on time.[51] Waiting for late-arriving participants penalizes those who are on time and develops a norm for coming late. Begin by reviewing progress to date, the group's objectives, and the meeting's purpose or objective. If minutes are recorded, they are usually approved at the beginning of the next meeting. For most meetings, it is recommended that a secretary be appointed to take minutes.

2. *Cover agenda items.* Cover agenda items in priority order. Try to keep to the approximate times, but be flexible. If the discussion is constructive and members need more time, give it to them. However, if the discussion begins to digress or becomes a destructive argument, move on.

3. *Summarize and review assignments.* End the meeting on time. Whoever is leading the meeting should summarize what took place. Were the meeting's objectives achieved? Review the assignments given. The secretary and/or leader should record all assignments. This sets up accountability and follow-up on assignments.

LEADERSHIP. Meeting leaders need to focus on group structure, process, and development. As stated, leadership needs change with the group's developmental level. Assess the stage your group is in as you decide how to lead meetings. Provide appropriate task and/or maintenance behavior only as it is needed.

Handling Problem Members

As groups and teams develop, certain personalities emerge that can cause the group to be less efficient. They are Silent Ones, Talkers, Wanderers, Arguers, and the Bored.

SILENT ONES. In effective groups, every member participates. Silent Ones do not give the group the benefits of their input. Encourage Silent Ones to participate, without being obvious or overdoing it. One technique that works well is rotation, in which all members take turns giving input. Rotation is generally less threatening than being called on directly. However, rotation is not appropriate all the time. To build up Silent Ones' confidence, call on them with questions they can easily answer. If you are a Silent One, push yourself to participate. You can change, and you can find your voice. Nobody said it was going to be easy, but look at it simply as another challenge—take baby steps if need be. With practice it will not only become natural, you will wonder why you didn't start earlier.

TALKERS. Talkers have something to say about everything. They dominate discussions and drown out other voices. Talkers can cause intragroup problems such as low cohesiveness and conflicts. Your job is to slow Talkers down, not to shut them up. Above all, don't let them dominate. Rotation works well here too because it limits Talkers' amount of "floor." When rotation isn't appropriate, gently interrupt Talkers and present your own ideas or call on other members to present theirs. If you are a Talker, consciously slow down. Be quiet—consciously. Remember, powerful people *listen*.

APPLYING
THE CONCEPT   *People Who Sabotage Meetings*

Identify the person in each statement as

a. a Silent One   **c.** a Wanderer   **e.** an Arguer

b. a Talker   **d.** a Bored One

_____ 16.   Charlie is always first or second to give his ideas. He elaborates and expounds and then elaborates again.

_____ 17.   One of the usually active team members is sitting back quietly today for the first time. The other members are doing all the discussing and volunteering for assignments.

_____ 18.   As the team discusses game strategy for next Saturday, Billy asks if they heard about the team owner and the mailroom clerk.

_____ 19.   Eunice usually shrinks from giving her ideas. When asked to explain her position, she often changes her answers to agree with others in the group.

_____ 20.   Dwayne loves to challenge members' ideas. He likes getting his own way. When someone doesn't agree with Dwayne, he makes wisecracks about the person's prior mistakes.

WANDERERS. Wanderers are distracters. They digress, they joke, they change the subject, and they are general roadblocks to getting anything done. Your job is to keep the group on track. If Wanderers want to socialize, cut it off. Be kind, thank them for their contribution, and then throw out a question to the group to get it back on track. If you are a Wanderer, change your habits. Check your urge to stray from topic. Think about why you wander—are you trying subconsciously to sabotage the group?

ARGUERS. Like Talkers, Arguers like to be the center of attention. For Talkers, arguing is an end in itself. Whether it is constructive or destructive doesn't concern them. They view everything as win-lose situations, and they cannot stand losing. Your job is to resolve conflict, but not in an argumentative way. Don't get into an argument with Arguers; that is exactly what they want. Should they start an argument, bring others into the discussion. If the argument gets personal, cut it off, period. Make it clear that you will not tolerate personal attacks. Keep the discussion moving; keep it on target. If you are an Arguer, practice backing off. Lose on purpose—it is *not* the end of the world. Think about why you have to be the center of attention. What makes you so insecure? Strive to change your win-lose view of life. (Win-win is much more pleasant.) Learn to convey your views assertively, not aggressively—besides, it's good for your blood pressure! All of us get to be wrong—and not only sometimes; we are all wrong a lot. Learn to do it gracefully.

THE BORED. The Bored are not interested in the meeting, the group, or its objectives. Maybe they are preoccupied. Maybe they feel superior. Whatever their reason, they don't pay attention and they don't participate. Assign the Bored tasks. Have them record ideas on the board or record minutes. Call on the Bored; bring them into the group. Don't allow the Bored to sit back—boredom is contagious and as such it can spread. If you are one of the Bored, think about why. Should you be changing jobs? No, you say? Then *participate*—you owe this to your team, and you owe this to yourself. Remember, motivation comes from within.

WORKING WITH PROBLEM MEMBERS. Here are the rules you do not break: Do not embarrass, do not intimidate, and do not argue with any members, no matter how much they provoke you. If you do, they will be martyrs and you will be a bully. If you have serious problem members who don't respond to the preceding techniques, it's time to talk with them individually outside the group. Review the BCF statements in Chapter 9, and maintain ownership of the problem. Be honest, be firm, lay your cards on the table.

TIMEOUT
Recall a recent meeting you attended. Write a critique of the meeting, laying out what went well and why, and what went wrong and why. Were there problem members? How did the leader handle them?

_____

_____

_____

_____

_____

_____

CHAPTER SUMMARY

1. Understand how groups and teams differ.

Groups and teams differ by size, leadership, jobs, accountability and evaluation, rewards, and objectives. Groups have a clear leader and two or more (possibly many more) members who perform independent jobs with individual accountability, evaluation, and rewards. Teams typically have fewer members who share leadership and who perform interdependent jobs with both individual and group accountability, evaluation, and rewards.

2. State the group performance model.

Group performance is a function of organizational context and the group's structure, process, and developmental stage.

3. Categorize groups by their structure.

Groups can be structured as formal or informal, functional or cross-functional, and command or task. Formal groups are part of the organizational structure; informal groups are not. Functional group members come from one area; cross-functional members come from different areas. Command groups are comprised of managers and their staff working to get the job done—whatever the job is; task groups work on specific objectives. Task forces are temporary; standing committees are ongoing.

4. Define the three major roles group members play.

Group task roles are played when members do and say things that directly aid in the accomplishment of the group's objectives. Group maintenance roles are played when members do and say things that develop and sustain the group process. Self-interest roles are played when members do and say things that help the individual but hurt the group.

5. Explain how rules and norms differ.

Rules are formally established by management or by the group itself. Norms are the group's shared but unspoken expectations of its members' behavior. Norms develop spontaneously as members interact.

6. Describe cohesiveness and why it is important to teams.

Group cohesiveness is the extent to which members stick together. Group cohesiveness is important because highly cohesive groups that accept management's directives for productivity levels perform better than groups with low levels of cohesiveness.

7. Describe the five major stages of group development and the leadership style appropriate for each stage.

(1) Orientation is characterized by low development level (D1)—high commitment and low competence, and the appropriate leadership style is autocratic. (2) Dissatisfaction is characterized by moderate development level (D2)—lower commitment and some competence, and the appropriate leadership style is consultative. (3) Resolution is characterized by high development level (D3)—variable commitment and high competence, and the appropriate leadership style is participative. (4) Production is characterized by outstanding development level (D4)—high commitment and high competence, and the appropriate leadership style is empowerment. (5) Termination is not reached in command groups unless there is some drastic reorganization. However, task groups do terminate.

8. Explain how group managers and team leaders differ.

The group manager takes responsibility for performing the four functions of management. The team leader empowers the members to take responsibility for performing the management functions, and focuses on developing effective group structure, group process, and group development.

9. Lead a meeting.

Make sure the meeting has a purpose. Begin meetings by covering the objectives for the meeting. Cover agenda items in priority order. Keep people on track. Conclude with a summary of what took place and assignments to be completed for future meetings.

10. Define the key terms discussed in the text.

Fill in the missing key terms from memory, or match the key terms from the list in the margin with their definitions below.

A _____ has two or more members with a clear leader who perform independent jobs with individual accountability, evaluation, and rewards.

A _____ is a group with shared leadership whose members perform interdependent jobs with both individual and group accountability, evaluation, and rewards.

In the _____, group performance is a function of organizational context, group structure, group process, and group development stage.

_____ include group type, size, composition, leadership, and objectives.

_____ include formal or informal, functional or cross-functional, and command or task.

_____ consist of managers and their staff.

_____ consist of employees who work on a specific objective.

_____ is the mix of members' skills and abilities.

_____ refers to the patterns of interactions that emerge as group members work together.

_____ include roles, norms, cohesiveness, status, decision making, and conflict resolution.

_____ are expectations shared by the group of how members will fulfill the requirements of their various positions.

_____ are the group's shared expectations of members' behavior.

_____ is the extent to which members stick together.

_____ is the perceived ranking of one member relative to other members in the group.

_____ are orientation, dissatisfaction, resolution, production, and termination.

Key Terms

command groups
group
group cohesiveness
group composition
group performance
    model
group process
group process
    dimensions
group roles
group structure
    dimensions
group types
norms
stages of group
    development
status
task groups
team

REVIEW AND DISCUSSION

1. Which are usually larger, groups or teams?

2. Give one reason the New York Yankees are a successful team.

3. One study found that NBA teams with a high-shared experience and a low turnover tended to have significantly better win-loss records. Why?

4. Why is diversity important to group composition?

5. Why are objectives important to groups?

6. How do groups enforce norms?

7. Recall the study cited in the text that examined the performance of eight U.S. teams in the 1996 Olympics at Atlanta. What were some of the reasons that four of the teams failed to meet expectations?

8. Does members' commitment to the group continue to increase through the first four stages of group development?

9. Are the four functions of management important to both groups and teams?

10. Why is it important to keep records of meeting assignments?

11. Describe the five types of problem members in meetings. How do they cause problems?

CASE

Summer at Sport Camp

Summer sport camps are growing in leaps and bounds—literally and figuratively. Name the sport, and there are people providing sport camps and parents lining their children up to participate. Roller-skating rinks offer roller hockey leagues. Gymnastics schools offer gymnastics programs organized around summer vacations. Colleges are using their success in various sports to move aggressively into the summer sport camp market. Well-known local athletes who manage soccer and hockey camps garner incredibly loyal followings. One parent was so dedicated to his favorite soccer camp that he drove his son from site to site, wherever the roving soccer camp was located for next week's program.

Golf camps have become increasingly popular due to Tiger Woods's success. Coaching golf for kids under ten years old is especially rewarding. Kids in summer golf programs play two holes at local golf courses and practice the rest of the week at driving ranges and mini golf courses.

The growth of summer sport programs has created a hot job market for camp directors.[52] Not only is it fun work and rewarding work, it's also a good place to hone your team-building skills and your people skills, and perhaps find your career fit. One assistant camp director coached the boys basketball team at an overnight camp that included his younger brother. The first year the team did well but lost the championship game. The same group of kids returned the following summer and rallied around the theme of winning the championship. The coach worked to help each player focus on what he or she could do to make the team champions. Foremost in everyone's minds was working on becoming a team of team players. Much like a movie, the team got to the championship game, and this time it won. The young coach went on to complete a doctorate in Sports Psychology with a focus on team behavior.

CASE QUESTIONS

1. The campers playing basketball at the sports camp were primarily a
   a. group   b. team

2. The basketball team exhibited a high level of cohesiveness.
   a. true   b. false

3. The coach had to teach the players their individual roles.
   a. true   b. false

4. At what developmental stage was the team the summer it lost the championship game?
   a. orientation   d. production
   b. dissatisfaction   e. termination
   c. resolution

5. At what developmental stage was the team the summer they won the championship game?
   a. orientation   d. production
   b. dissatisfaction   e. termination
   c. resolution

6. Tiger Woods has increased the popularity of golf. Is golf primarily a team sport?
   a. yes   b. no   c. both yes and no

7. Being the director of an overnight camp is a position that requires little teamwork.
   a. true   b. false

8. Managing a soccer camp is a position that requires little teamwork.
   a. true   b. false

9. Owning and managing a hockey camp is a position that requires little teamwork.
   a. true   b. false

10. Owning and managing a roller-skating rink is a position that requires little teamwork.
    a. true   b. false

11. Describe any team experiences you have had attending or working at a camp. Are these experiences something you would like to build a career upon?

12. Describe team experiences you have had attending or working at a summer sport camp. Are these experiences something you would like to build a career upon?

VIDEO CASE

Teams, Conflict, and Compromise: Cannondale's Model

Introduction
In this segment, you will see how effective teamwork improves the design, manufacturing, and marketing of the Cannondale "Jekyll" model. A team of ten individuals irons out design, safety, and cost concerns. Cannondale fosters a horizontal, special-purpose team approach leaving lines of communication open. You will see how skillful teamwork ultimately benefits this company and the consumer.

Focus Your Attention
To get the most out of viewing this Cannondale video, think about the following issues: how team structure can affect the success or failure of a project, how diversity can be used positively in a team environment, and how conflict can lead to better decisions. Then answer the following questions after viewing the video:

1. According to the director of product management, what kind of relationship among team members makes the best team? Why would this be beneficial?

2. How does Cannondale resolve conflicts among teams?

3. The Cannondale Jekyll team does not hold traditional meetings. Explain their meeting style and why it is encouraged in this company.

EXERCISES

Skill-Builder: Group Performance

Objective:

■ To use group structure, process, development, and meetings to improve group performance.

Note:

This exercise is designed for class groups that have worked together for some time. (Five or more hours of prior classwork are recommended.)

Preparation:

Answer the following questions as they apply to your class group/team.

1. Using Exhibit 10–1, would you classify your members as a group or a team? Why?

_____

_____

_____

_____

Group Structure

2. Our group/team is structured (circle one in each category):

   formally / informally

   functionally / cross-functionally (by majors)

   by command / by task.

3. There are _____ students in our group/team, which is (circle one):

   too large   too small   just right

4. Describe the composition of your group/team.

_____

_____

_____

5. Is there a clear group/team leader? Name the leaders.

_____

_____

_____

6. List your group/team's objectives.

_____

_____

_____

7. List some ways in which your group/team's structure could be improved to achieve its objectives.

_____

_____

_____

Group Process

8. List each member of your group/team (including yourself) and the major role(s) you each play.

    1. _____   4. _____

    2. _____   5. _____

    3. _____   6. _____

9. Identify at least three group/team norms. Are they positive or negative? How does the group/team enforce them?

    _____

    _____

    _____

    _____

10. Is your group/team a high-, moderate-, or low-cohesive group?

    _____

11. List each group/team member, including yourself, in order of status. If this does not apply, tell why.

    1. _____   4. _____

    2. _____   5. _____

    3. _____   6. _____

12. How does your group/team make decisions?

    _____

    _____

    _____

13. How does your group/team resolve conflict?

    _____

    _____

    _____

14. List some ways in which your group/team's group process could be improved to achieve its objectives.

    _____

    _____

    _____

    _____

Developmental Stage

15. At what stage of group development is your group/team? Explain.

    _____

    _____

    _____

16. List some ways in which your group/team can move to a higher developmental stage in order to increase group performance.

    _____

    _____

    _____

Meetings

17. List some ways in which your group/team meetings could be improved to increase group performance.

_____

_____

_____

_____

18. Does your group/team have any problem members? What can be done to make them more effective?

_____

_____

_____

_____

In-Class Application

Complete the skill-building preparation noted above before class.

Choose one (10–30 minutes):
- Meet with your assigned group/team and present your findings to the above questions. Brainstorm ways to improve your group/team's structure, process, developmental stage, and meetings.
- Informal, whole-class discussion of student findings.

Wrap-up:
Take a few minutes and write down your answers to the following questions:

- What did I learn from this experience?

_____

_____

_____

_____

- How will I use this knowledge in the future?

_____

_____

_____

_____

Internet Skills: Improving Team Performance

Objective:
- To use a team test to improve performance.

Preparation:
Go to the Leadership Strategies home page at http://www.leaderx.com. Click the _Click to Try Our Coaching_ link. Enter the required data and submit it. Click _Is Your Team Following?_ Take the test by answering the questions as they relate to the team you selected in step 1, then click _Submit_ for scoring. The results of your quiz will be e-mailed to you.

1. Read your quiz results, which give you feedback on how your team can improve. Note that this score is not a reflection of you alone; it relates to the whole team. Read the results a second time and list tips below that pertain to developing your individual leadership style.

   _____

   _____

   _____

2. What do you agree with in the results? What do you disagree with? Why?

   _____

   _____

   _____

3. What, if anything, in the results surprised you? Why?

   _____

   _____

   _____

4. What findings are most important to you individually? Why?

   _____

   _____

   _____

5. How can your team use this information to improve its performance?

   _____

   _____

   _____

11 Communicating for Results

Learning Outcomes

After studying this chapter, you should be able to:

1. Understand how communication flows through organizations.

2. List the four steps in the communication process.

3. Use transmission channels well.

4. Communicate effectively in person.

5. Select appropriate channels for your messages.

6. Solicit feedback properly.

7. Explain how we receive messages.

8. Choose appropriate response styles.

9. Calm an emotional person.

10. Define the following key terms (in order of appearance in the chapter):

- communication
- vertical communication
- horizontal communication
- grapevine
- communication process
- sender
- encoding the message
- receiver
- transmitting the message
- decoding the message
- nonverbal communications
- feedback
- paraphrasing
- message-receiving process
- listening
- reflecting
- empathy

REVIEWING THEIR GAME PLAN

Courting the Changing Media

We are a media-driven nation of sport enthusiasts. Think about your favorite "viewer sports" (the ones you like to watch) for a moment. Short of envisioning yourself playing them, you are just as likely to conjure up a TV image or favorite radio announcer's voice as you are to think of a game or tournament you watched live. Like eyeglasses and contact lenses for those of us who don't have perfect vision, TV, radio, and print media are the lenses through which most of us view most of the sports we follow. This makes the media especially important to sport organizations. Sport organizations that don't have great relationships with their market's media aren't doing their job.

Today, often the first way that fans and customers access an organization's products, whether the product is a star shortstop or a hotly desired catcher's mitt, is through the media. The conduits of sport information that first come to mind are, of course, television, radio, and print media. However, media sources are proliferating. Online magazines, chat networks, e-mail marketing, and web sites buzz 24 hours a day, seven days a week— all over the globe. Radio stations broadcast over our radios, but also through our computers via the Internet. Savvy organizations monitor a great variety of media to see how their team or company is being portrayed. "Dish" is ever more important. If a false rumor spread on the Internet can send a company's stock plummeting, think about what a crank fan's web site or a cranky sports columnist can do. Media conglomerates such as AOL/Time Warner, which owns *Sports Illustrated, Time Magazine,* CNN, TBS, TNT, WB, and Warner Brothers Music and Movies, wield great power. In an entertainment-driven world, *not* talking about your team—the silent treatment—can be just as devastating as false buzz.

Company web sites allow customers and fans to e-mail comments and suggestions. Customers get to vent *and* applaud, and fans get to feel like they are part of the action. Not surprisingly, more and more fans and customers are hitting the Send button. The response has been so great that companies have had to hire new personnel to support their web sites.

The importance of building strong relationships with the media, then, cannot be stated too strongly. Your organization, be it the Seattle Mariners, a local high school, or a private youth sport league, needs to garner the interest of local newspapers in order to continually generate public interest. Watching children play in local leagues is a wonderful experience, but without media attention few people beyond the players' families know about these games. That may be okay. Then again, it may not if you need to grow your team. This may mean courting local reporters to help them cover your team extensively and responsibly. It may mean courting local sports talk shows to rev up excitement in the team.

A positive example of using sports talk shows to keep fans at a fever pitch is the long-running afternoon radio talk show **MIKE AND THE MAD DOG** on New York's WFAN radio station. This show consistently garners a Number 1 in its ratings slot and has a huge listenership. Mike (Francesa) and the Mad Dog (Chris Russo) are voted two of the most powerful sports figures in New York year in and year out. The simple (and brilliant) idea behind the their show is basically two guys in a bar, talking sports. "The words tumble out of [Mad Dog's] mouth in a strange stew, the L's and R's smoosh into W's particularly when he's talking fast. Which is most of the time."[1]

Of course, the Olympics, NCAA, NFL, NBA, and MLB are covered widely by ESPN, ABC, CBS, NBC, and FOX. Think about some American traditions. Where would football be without *Monday Night Football* and friendly crowds at local sports bars watching their alma maters ravage a long-time rival on fall Saturdays? Will the WNBA, women's professional basketball, become an American tradition? If it does, it will be in large part because its games are shown on NBC and, now with their new agreement, also on ESPN and ESPN2.[2] The jury on the WNBA's fate is still out at this writing—not a few viewers are opting to watch NFL European football games instead of WNBA games.[3]

Large organizations have PR departments to court the media, talk to them, keep their interest up, and occasionally put a "spin" on things. In small organizations, however, the PR hat is worn by many and, sometimes, by everyone. In one sense, every person in an organization represents the company—people need to realize this and be trained in communications.

For current information on two media outlets, use the Internet addresses http://www.espn. com and http://www.wfan.com. (For ideas on using the Internet, see Appendix B.)

INTERNET RESOURCES

http://www.sportslinkscentral.com/Sports_Media/sports_radio.htm *To further investigate sports talk shows, visit Sports Links Central.com's collection of links to sports radio networks, stations, and programs/personalities. Find a station that broadcasts in your area, or explore the national networks and programs listed on this site.*
http://infosports.net/baseball/arch/650.htm *and*
http://www.amateurumpire.com/mech/signs.htm *These two sites will help you understand how nonverbal communication is employed in baseball from two different perspectives: that of the coaches/players and that of the umpires. How does a coach, without saying a word, communicate to the player on first base that he or she should attempt to steal second? How does the opposing team's second baseman let the shortstop know who needs to cover the bag on the steal? InfoSports.net's Youth Baseball Knowledge Base will answer these questions and more. And every umpire has his or her own unique way of calling a strike—from quietly extending the right arm to violently shaking the right fist in the air and yelling "stee-rike!" Check out the Umpire Signs and Signals page to learn about the pros and cons of these different approaches and the many other signals umpires use to get their point across.*

DEVELOPING YOUR SKILLS   We humans are all about talk, and, frankly, the best managers talk better than the rest of us. They are message makers and message senders who stay on target, and who get their messages across time and again to all manner of recipients, from staff to stockholders to the news media. Fortunately, this is a skill you can develop and hone to levels you don't think yourself capable of. Do it. This will stand you in good stead in every aspect of your life and your career.

THE IMPORTANCE OF GOOD COMMUNICATION

Good communication skills are an important part of every manager's tool kit—that goes without saying, of course, but we're saying it here (as we have done elsewhere) to underscore its importance. The world of work *revolves* around communications—effective communications may mean a problem solved in its infancy or sidestepped altogether. Ineffective communications may mean a problem created. Each of us in every job we hold must do everything we can to communicate clearly, effectively, accurately. Additionally, good communication between groups that historically have been at odds with each other (such as unions and management) can mean good things for the bottom line.

communication
The process of transmitting information and meaning.

Communication is the process of transmitting information and meaning. For our purposes, there are two types of communication: organizational and interpersonal. Organizational communication takes place between organizations and among an organization's divisions/departments/projects/teams. Interpersonal communication takes place between individuals.

1 LEARNING OUTCOME
Understand how communication flows through organizations.

ORGANIZATIONAL COMMUNICATIONS

If an organization is to thrive, its mission, its strategy, its goals, and its culture all must be communicated effectively. Kathleen Hessert of Sports Media Challenge, a speaking, training, and consulting company based in Charlotte, North Carolina, says, "For today's athlete and coach, winning is no longer enough. The stakes have risen considerably, and so has the scrutiny on every aspect of their lives. Those who excel as communicators distinguish themselves from the rest."[4] The same can be said of organizations as well—organizations that excel at communicating with their constituencies gain a competitive advantage. ESPN is known for being a cable television station that communicates well with sports fans. It uses creative, humorous advertisements to gain attention for its shows and to reinforce the idea that true sports fans must watch ESPN SportsCenter to know what is happening in sports.

Think about how communications flow through an organization. The first thing that comes to mind are the formal channels. These can be vertical—down from the top (from the CEO and corporate executives on down the chain of command) and up from the bottom (from staff at the "front line" of the organization's work). They can also be horizontal—same-level communications between salespeople and between vice presidents, for example. Then there are the informal channels (the grapevine) that every organization has—these channels resemble the ricochet of bullets.

Formal Communication

Vertical communication is the downward and upward flow of information through the organization. It is *formal* communication because it is officially sanctioned transmission of information. Top management's strategies, policies, and procedures are communicated down the chain of command to instruct employees—this is the process of higher-level managers telling those below them what to do and how to do it.[5] The delegation process is downward communication.

Upward communication, on the other hand, involves staff sending information up through the different management levels. Managers often learn about what is going on in the organization and with customers through staff on the front lines.[6] To facilitate upward communication (because it is often people on the front line who first sense changes in the business climate), most organizations encourage "open door" management styles and communications, the idea being to make people feel at ease in going to managers. *Management by walking around (MBWA),* which involves getting out of the office and talking frequently and informally with staff, is another way to strengthen upward communication. Coaches often meet with their teams when they are performing subpar to get feedback from players on how the team can get to winning. Depending on the issue, the coach's style, and the team's culture, the information flow will be downward (the coach tells players what they need to do), upward (players tell the coach what needs to happen), or (hopefully) both.

Horizontal communication is information shared between peers. Horizontal communication is the coordination that goes on within a department, among team members, and among different departments.[7] Teleconferencing links staff participants in different areas of the country and sometimes of the world. Managers meet with people from different departments to coordinate their efforts and resolve conflicts between them. More experienced players encourage each other and rev up their teammates for a big game. **MIKE AND THE MAD DOG** "chewing the fat" is also horizontal communication with the listener (the audience), which is why their fans love the show so much. **Can you provide an example of horizontal communication for a sports talk radio show you listen to?**

Informal Communication—Getting the Lowdown through the Grapevine

The **grapevine** is the flow of information through informal channels. It is informal communication because it isn't official or sanctioned communication.[8] This rumor mill begins anywhere in the organization and flows in any direction. Grapevines spread false good news

vertical communication
The downward and upward flow of information through an organization.

horizontal communication
Information shared between peers.

grapevine
The flow of information through informal channels.

APPLYING THE CONCEPT   *Communication Flow*

Identify each communication as:

a. downward   **c.** horizontal

b. upward   **d.** grapevine

_____ 1. Hey, Carl, did you hear that our two linebackers, Paul and Frank, were drinking at the prom last week?

_____ 2. Juanita, you know when you hand the baton off to me, you need to quickly move out of my way.

_____ 3. Tom, here's the team roster you needed. Check it, and I'll make changes.

_____ 4. Robin, I've got two new customers who want to set up charge accounts. Please rush the credit check so we can increase ticket sales.

_____ 5. Ted, please run this letter over to the athletic funding committee before noon.

TIMEOUT

Give examples of vertical communication and horizontal communication, and list a piece of information you got from your organization's grapevine.

_____

_____

_____

_____

_____

_____

(fabulous retirement deals on the horizon) and true bad news (layoffs that really are on the horizon) with equal aplomb, and always ahead of when the formal information is put out.

Grapevines are a powerful means of communication. They can be useful, and they can be destructive. Organizations sometimes use them to their advantage as well. Reining them in during times of uncertainty can be a daunting undertaking. Unlike many talk show hosts, **MIKE AND THE MAD DOG** carefully verify the information they receive, and this has paid off handsomely. One reason they are so highly regarded is that fans know they aren't dishing out unsubstantiated rumors.

2 LEARNING OUTCOME
List the four steps in the communication process.

communication process
The transmission of information, meaning, and intent.

sender
Initiates communication by encoding and transmitting a message.

encoding the message
The sender's process of putting the message into a form that the receiver will understand.

receiver
The person to whom the message is sent.

transmitting the message
The process of using a form of communication to send a message.

decoding the message
The receiver's process of translating the message into a meaningful form.

GETTING THE COMMUNICATION PROCESS RIGHT

The **communication process** (the transmission of information, meaning, and intent) is both simple and complex (see Exhibit 11–1).

1. A **sender** (the person initiating the communication) **encodes the message** (puts it into a form the **receiver** of the message will understand).

2. The sender **transmits the message** (by using a form of communication such as talking, phoning, or e-mailing) to the person or group receiving it.

3. The receiver **decodes the message** (translates it into a meaningful form).

4. The receiver may (or may not) give feedback.

Of course, in this "simple" process lies the potential for the whole range of human communication, from the sublime nuances of our best communications to the most garbled tangles of our worst ones.

Encoding Your Message

As the *sender* of your message, you are initiating the communication. Your *message,* of course, is the information/meaning/intent you want to get across to the receiver. Make sure you have a clear intent for your messages—if *you* don't have a clear idea of what you want to get

Exhibit 11-1   The Communication Process

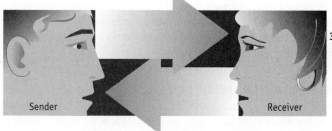

2. Message transmitted through a channel.

1. Encodes the message and selects the transmission channel.

Sender

3. Decodes the message and decides if feedback is needed.

Receiver

4. Feedback, response, or new message may be transmitted through a channel.

The sender and receiver may continually change roles as they communicate.

across, neither will the receiver.[9] To do this, consider your receivers, and determine what *they* need to hear to understand your message. Avoid barriers that block communication (see Exhibit 11–2). **MIKE AND THE MAD DOG** basically encode the content (message) of their show in typical New York working-class speech, accent, and slang. Why? Because this not only creates the ambience (two guys shooting the breeze in a bar) the producers want listeners to imagine, it also *cinches* a broad listenership. New Yorkers from Wall Street power brokers to taxi cab drivers have great affection for this accent; it is part of the mystique, and they are very comfortable with it. **What sort of audience do you think Mike and the Mad Dog would attract if they spoke with the accent and language of Prince Charles? In Texas drawl?**

FIRST BARRIER—THE WORDS WE CHOOSE. *Semantics* and *jargon* can be formidable barriers for your receivers, because words mean different things to different people (semantics) and jargon excludes people outside its originating group. Thus, "breaking his ankles" (an expression for moving very quickly past an opposing basketball player) will be totally misinterpreted by receivers who are unfamiliar with it and will cause them to puzzle futilely over your message.

To overcome problems of misinterpretation, consider what your receiver needs in the way of language to understand your message and tailor the language you choose to fit their needs. This means your choice of words in any communique is important—you knew this already, now just remember it! Thus, effective communicators don't use jargon with people who are not familiar with the terminology and especially with people from different cultures. Think for a moment about the many ways we use sport terms. For example, take the expressions "sure shot" (pool), "slam dunk" (basketball), "tap in" (golf)—used outside sports they are all metaphors for "sure success." **Brainstorm with your roommates to come up with as many sport metaphors as you can think of. Compare your lists during class—**

Exhibit 11-2   Barriers That Block Communication

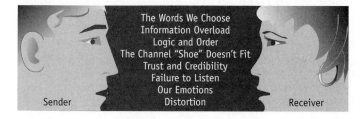

The Words We Choose
Information Overload
Logic and Order
The Channel "Shoe" Doesn't Fit
Trust and Credibility
Failure to Listen
Our Emotions
Distortion

Sender

Receiver

it's an amazing number, isn't it? Sport metaphors are so embedded in our everyday language we don't give them a second thought. People trying to learn our language for the first time, however, don't have a clue as to what these sayings mean—so much so that numerous Web sites are devoted to explaining in great detail the games of baseball, football, and basketball to English-language students just so that they can understand us. One sport management study determined that perceptual barriers can be overcome by including individuals with specific characteristics (examples: various ethnicities, genders, target age groups) as spokespersons in an organization's persuasive communications (advertisements, promotional messages, development campaigns, and announcements) to appeal to and influence the attitudes and behaviors of its intended audience.[10]

SECOND BARRIER—INFORMATION OVERLOAD. All of us have limits on the amount of information we can take in and process at any given time. A couple of examples come to mind, and you no doubt have several of your own: New employees commonly experience information overload during their first few days at work, because new information is coming fast and furiously, and it is all important. With so much information available so instantly via the Internet, we are often dazzled and overwhelmed and don't know what to do with it all.[11]

To minimize information overload, limit the information in your message to an amount the receiver can reasonably take in. For example, don't do monologues—check periodically to be sure the receiver is keeping up with you. Give the receiver a chance to process the message and feed it back to you so that you can check for misunderstandings or lapses in attention. If you talk for too long, the receiver will become bored or lose the thread of the message.

THIRD BARRIER—LOGIC AND ORDER. Make your message make sense. One of the simplest ways to do this is to check the order of your points. Your receivers can't "make the basket" (get your point) if you haven't given them a "ball" to shoot with. Outlines really help here. **What other encoding barriers can you think of?**

Transmitting Your Message

After you encode your message, you must select the transmission channel (oral or written, phone or e-mail, videoconference or face-to-face meeting) through which you will transmit the message.

BARRIER—THE CHANNEL "SHOE" DOESN'T FIT. Different channels work for different messages. Use of an inappropriate channel can kill a communication. E-mails or cold calls just won't work, thank you. Using phone calls to clinch a deal with a multimillion-dollar player isn't the same as meeting with him or her in person. So before you send an important message, give careful thought to which channel will help you get across your message. In the next section, we examine various channels in detail.

Decoding the Message

Decoding, as we noted above, occurs when receivers translate or interpret your message. They will mix the content in your message with other ideas or information they have and with emotions they are feeling at the time, and they will also look at your message through the lenses of their own perceptual filters. All of these can be barriers (see Exhibit 11–2) to receiving your message accurately.

FIRST BARRIER—TRUST AND CREDIBILITY. All of us as receivers—sometimes unconsciously, sometimes very consciously, sometimes in a split-second judgment, sometimes mulled over for days or weeks—consider whether we trust the sender and whether the sender has credibility. When we don't trust the sender—for whatever reason (they don't know what they're talking about, they don't have all the facts, they don't have good judgment, they've betrayed others before)—we are reluctant to accept the message at face value. Once doubt enters the equation, it is extremely difficult to rebuild trust. So, be honest first and foremost and everywhere in between. *If you can't be honest about something (and this happens), don't* send the message! Know what you're talking about. Get the facts straight

APPLYING
THE CONCEPT   *Barriers That Block Communication*

Identify the barriers in the following messages or responses as:

a. perceptual filter   **d.** emotions   **g.** failure to listen

b. information overload   **e.** trust and credibility

c. wrong transmission channel   **f.** distortion

_____   6.   Relax. You shouldn't be so upset that our young team didn't win the championship.

_____   7.   No questions. (Really thinking, "I was lost back on step one and don't know what to ask.")

_____   8.   We are right on schedule building our new athletic facility. (Really thinking, "We are actually behind, but we'll catch up.")

_____   9.   I said I'd do it in a little while. It's only been 15 minutes. Why do you expect it to be done by now?

_____   10.   You don't know what you're talking about when you give your opinions on how to play defense. I think we will do it my way.

before you send your message, not after. Trust and credibility are precious and sacred; don't squander them.

SECOND BARRIER—FAILURE TO LISTEN. We are all guilty of this. Our attention wanders. We're more interested in what we're going to say than in hearing what the sender is really saying (we've thought of something clever to say, and we stop listening and start framing it). We want to get to the "end of the story"—we don't want to hear the details, or they bore us. So, help your receivers receive your message—by this we mean help them listen. Question them in such a way that they must paraphrase your message back to you. Stop during a long message and give receivers a chance to ask questions and to think about what you've just said. Ask for their thoughts on what you've said so far. Make your message interesting.

THIRD BARRIER—OUR EMOTIONS. Guess what—our emotions color how we decode messages. When we are angry, sad, or irrationally attached to an idea, concept, or person, we find it difficult to be objective and to hear the real message. Take the fans who call the **MIKE AND THE MAD DOG** show. These folks by definition are not exactly objective about their favorite teams and favorite players or teams and players they love to hate and hate to love—they will hear an honest but negative appraisal as an attack or as anything but the truth. So, take this into consideration when you have to send a difficult message. Also, don't forget to look at how your own emotions are coloring the message you are sending. Later in this chapter we give you ways to calm emotional people. **What other decoding barriers can you think of?**

FOURTH BARRIER—DISTORTION. *Distortion* occurs when we alter or distort information we receive. We do this for innumerable reasons, and we've all done it. We don't like the truth, so we twist a message to fit our version of the incident and the "facts"—we believe what we want to believe. How many times have you heard someone say, "I just can't believe it"? Likewise, when receiving messages, we hear what we want to hear. In these situations, you may have to repeat your message. You may have to reframe it. Asking for feedback helps you discern what the receivers are hearing. Listen carefully.

3   LEARNING OUTCOME
Use transmission channels well.

USING THE CHANNELS

Failed communications and those that hit their mark—sometimes what makes the difference is your choice of channel. The channels through which we transmit our messages today are either oral, written, or visual (see Exhibit 11–3).

nonverbal communications
Messages sent without words.

An aside about nonverbal communication is in order here. *Every time* we talk to someone face to face, yes, we use words, but we also communicate nonverbally. **Nonverbal communications** are the messages we send without words. Nonverbal communication is thus our *body language,* and we humans have developed a rich vocabulary in this "language." Try talking without body language of any kind. Go ahead. You can't do it, can you? Or if you did manage to talk like a zombie, the color and richness of your message went down the proverbial drain, didn't it? Now try to send a message using *only* body language—you can send some pretty complex messages nonverbally. Yes, our frowns, chuckles, hand gestures, posture, and tone of voice all signal excitement, purpose, despair, confidence or lack thereof, disapproval, affection, enthusiasm, and the whole host of human responses. In fact, psychologists claim that 56 percent of any communication is transmitted through body language.[12] Take the old adage "Actions speak louder than words." Well, it's true, and it will always be true. So be aware of your nonverbal signals. Make them consistent with your message or, rather, make your message consistent with your body language because it is always the "iceberg under the water" of your message. All of us have a bred-in-our-bones ability to read body language, and when yours is inconsistent with your message, your receiver will know instantly. Likewise, use this ability yourself to tip you off to people's "real" messages.

And another thing—how you arrange your office signals numerous things (nonverbally) about your management style. Are you an autocrat? Or a team leader? Look at your office; the answer is probably "sitting" in its arrangement. If you want open communication, make your office conducive to open communication. Don't sit behind your desk and have the other person in front of the desk, *unless* you really do need to signal that you are the person holding all the cards. Sitting side by side signals, on the other hand, that you are willing to be egalitarian, that you are willing to meet the person halfway, and that you respect what he or she has to contribute.

Oral Channels

We transmit messages orally by talking with each other directly (face to face), in meetings, in presentations, by telephone, and by voice mail. Using oral channels is easy and fast and gives immediate feedback. The disadvantages are that such channels are often less accurate and they provide no record. Many studies have shown that the single most important factor in professional success is oral communication skills.[13] It is fair to say that we are all in the same business—that business is communication. Excellence in sports does *not* guarantee excellence in oral communication—these are two very different skills. Depending on your career path, you may or may not need to excel at sports, but you will need to excel at presenting your ideas, be it face to face, in meetings, or in presentations.

4 LEARNING OUTCOME
Communicate effectively in person.

Exhibit 11–3   Channels for Transmitting Messages

ORAL CHANNELS	WRITTEN CHANNELS	VISUAL CHANNELS
Face to face	Memos	Television
Meetings	Letters	Posters
Presentations	Reports	
Telephone	Bulletin boards	
Voice mail	Newsletters	
	New tech (e-mail, fax machines, AOL instant messages)	

FACE TO FACE. Face-to-face communications are appropriate for delegating tasks, coaching, disciplining, sharing information, answering questions, checking progress toward objectives, and developing and maintaining rapport. Here are a few pointers to keep in mind in face-to-face communications.

1. *Develop rapport.* Put the receiver at ease. The easiest way to do this is with small talk.

2. *State your point (your message's objective).* Tell the receiver why you are communicating (what you want to accomplish). As a manager, tell receivers what you want them to do. Give instructions and set deadlines for completing tasks.

3. *Check the receiver's understanding.* Ask direct questions and paraphrase. Simply asking, "Do you have any questions?" does *not* check understanding. (We examine paraphrasing in more detail later in the chapter.)

4. *Get a commitment and follow up.* When your goal of communication is to inform, obviously a commitment is not necessary. However, when your goal is to influence or direct, don't leave without a commitment.

TIMEOUT
Think about a task your boss or coach recently assigned you. Note which of the preceding steps were taken, which ones were not taken, and how the message could have been sent more effectively.

_____

_____

_____

_____

_____

_____

MEETINGS. Meetings are appropriate for coordinating team activities, delegating tasks to groups, and resolving conflicts. The most common meeting is the brief, informal get-together with two or more employees. With the increased use of teams, much more time is spent in meetings, and the ability to lead effective meetings (Chapter 10) is an important skill to acquire.

PRESENTATIONS. Whether accepting an award, promoting a charity, or fulfilling sponsor requirements, the ability to use words gracefully, lucidly, and accurately and then to deliver them well is a sure way to garner positive attention from your colleagues and from your bosses. Speaking skills are needed in virtually every job. And don't save your presentation skills only for formal speeches. Use the grace and confidence you gain in giving presentations as an essential ingredient of your work with staff and customers, and also in negotiating, resolving conflicts, training, presenting products and reports, and running meetings. Here are a few basic pointers.

Begin speeches with an attention-grabbing opener—a quote, a joke, or an interesting story that ignites interest in your topic. Your presentations should have three parts: (1) a beginning—a purpose statement and an overview of the main points to be covered; (2) a middle—the discussion of the main points in enough detail to get the message across (but not so much detail that you lose your audience); and (3) an end—a summary of the purpose, main points, and any action required of the audience. If you are uncomfortable giving presentations, don't be proud—practice. Then practice some more. Join your local Toastmasters club—these clubs have shaped many an effective speaker from the clay of pure terror. There are numerous books on giving effective presentations. Browse your favorite bookstore to find one that fits your needs. Read it as many times as it takes to embed its message in your psyche. Keep it at work. And use it—make it your "bible of presenting."

TELEPHONE/CELL PHONE. The amount of time you will spend on the phone will depend on your job. First of all, remember that phones are inappropriate for personal matters. The telephone/cell phone *is* appropriate for quick exchanges of information and for checking up on things. They are especially useful for saving travel time.

Here are a few pointers to keep in mind when you "live on the phone" at work. Before making calls, set an objective and list what you plan to discuss. Use your list for jotting notes during the call. When receiving calls, determine the caller's purpose and decide whether you or another person should handle it. When calls come in at inconvenient times, arrange to call the person back. Take care to use your cell phone responsibly and politely. Other people in the airport really don't want to hear your business talk, and they will if you're not considerate because cell phone users always talk louder than normal, even though they are not aware of it. And avoid using your cell phone when you're driving—it isn't "just" *your* life that is on the line.

VOICE MAIL. Voice mail is one of the godsends of the modern world. Productivity took a giant leap forward when we stopped having to call back innumerable times because someone was away from his or her desk or on the phone.

Written Channels

Today, every organization demands good writing skills in its people. Why? Because *nothing* reveals your weaknesses more clearly (and more permanently!) than poorly written communications. Poor writing signals—all too loudly—fuzzy thinking, and there is no place for that in today's highly competitive business climate. So learn to write effectively. As you well know, written communications are used because they allow for accuracy and precision and they provide the all-important record. Of course, it also takes longer to write a letter than it does to just pick up the phone, and feedback is not immediate. So, written communications are not the best choice when time is short or when you need an answer on the spot.

Here are the channels you will continually use in your work.

1. *Memos*—commonly used to send intraorganizational messages
2. *Letters:*
   - "snail mail" for getting your formal messages to people outside the organization
   - e-mail for instant 24/7 communications with inter- and intraorganizational messages (both formally and informally)
   - faxes for when the instant communication needs to be hard copy
3. *Reports* for formally conveying information, evaluations, analyses, and recommendations
4. *Newsletters* for conveying general information to the entire organization
5. *Bulletin-board notices* for supplementing other channels and for wide dissemination of public information
6. *Signs* for permanent reminders of important information, such as mission statements, safety instructions, and so on

Use written channels for all manner of communications—to send general information, to send specific and detailed information, to thank people, for messages that require future action, or for messages that affect several people in a related way, to name but a few.

Here is a (very) short course for improving your writing.

LACK OF ORGANIZATION IS THE NUMBER-ONE WRITING PROBLEM. Therefore, before you write, organize your thoughts. Give them the "golf clubs" (content that will help them understand your point) before you show them how to take the swing. Outlines are good for this—use them. Check the message that you've laid out in your outline for focus. Weed out ideas and information they don't need this time around. Keep your receivers in mind—what do you want them to hear, to think, to do? Now write from your outline. As with effective presentations, effective communications have a beginning (the purpose of this communication), a middle (support for the purpose—facts, figures, reasoning, and so on), and an end (a summary of the major points and a clear statement of conclusions or of action, if any, to be taken by you and the receivers). If you want your message to sizzle, reread it and rewrite it. Do it again. If great writers can "stoop" to multiple drafts, so can you.

Write to communicate clearly, not to impress. Keep your message short and simple. Limit each paragraph to a single topic and an average of five sentences. Sentences should average 15 words. Vary paragraph and sentence length, but never let a paragraph exceed half a page. Write actively (I recommend . . .), not passively (it is recommended . . .).

Pare, hone, polish. Look for verbs with character. Tired verbs (overused verbs) are wonderful sleeping pills; carefully chosen verbs are the espresso of effective messages. Check your work for spelling and grammar errors. Have others edit your work. Depending on your audience and your message, don't shy from the dramatic. Drama *is* memorable, and it has its place. And finally, read outstanding writing—search out *anything* written or said by the Sage of Omaha (Warren Buffet); he is one of the most memorable and savvy writers in business today.

Combining Channels

Repetition helps ensure that important messages are received and their meaning understood and remembered. This is where combining channels can be very useful. Therefore, for

---

APPLYING THE CONCEPT   *Choosing Channels*

Select the most appropriate channel for transmitting the messages below (which haven't been encoded yet). When combined media is the most effective choice, indicate which ones.

a. face to face	**e.** memo	**h.** bulletin board
b. meeting	**f.** letter	**i.** poster
c. presentation	**g.** report	**j.** newsletter
d. phone call		

_____ 11. You want to know whether an important shipment of uniforms has arrived.

_____ 12. You want staff and players to turn the lights off in the locker room when no one is in it.

_____ 13. You need to explain the new community relations program to your team.

_____ 14. John has come in late for work again; you want him to shape up.

_____ 15. You've exceeded your ticket sales goals and want your boss to know about it, because it should have a positive influence on your upcoming performance appraisal.

---

important messages you will find yourself sending a memo (sometimes several), then following up with personal visits or phone calls to see if receivers have questions. There are times when you will want to formally document a face-to-face meeting, particularly in disciplinary situations (our litigious society demands this, so for your protection and your organization's protection and in fairness to the person, take careful notes and record them promptly while they are fresh). **MIKE AND THE MAD DOG** use multiple channels to distribute their show. The daily radio broadcast is on WFAN; the television broadcast is on the YES network. The show is simultaneously broadcast using both mediums to enrich the experience for viewers. **Do you think broadcasting the *Mike and the Mad Dog* show on television reduces or enhances the normal communication process of radio?**

5 LEARNING OUTCOME
Select appropriate channels for your messages.

Choosing Channels

To choose the best channel for a given message, look at the media's richness. *Media richness* is the amount of information and meaning that the channel can convey. The more information and meaning, the "richer" the channel. Face-to-face talk is therefore the richest channel because the full range of oral and nonverbal communication is used. Phone calls are less rich than face-to-face meetings because many nonverbal cues are lost. Written messages can be rich, but they must be very well written to qualify. Television is rich because body language is back in the picture (forgive the pun). So, key your channel choice to how difficult/complex, simple/routine, and/or important your message is.

A Summary of Encoding and Transmitting

Let's summarize some of the key points made above by restating them slightly differently. (Remember, repetition ensures that the message gets through—note that we're using this concept right here.)

TIMEOUT

Identify the channel used for an oral message and a written one that you recently received at work or on your team. State whether the sender's choice of channel was effective and, if it was not, which channel would have been better and why.

_____

_____

_____

_____

_____

_____

So, before you send a message, use this short checklist to make sure your message is on target. Ask yourself, What? Who? How? Which? and When?

- *What* is my goal in this message? (What do you want the end result of the communication to be? Set an objective.)

- *Who* should receive my message?

- *How* should I encode my message?

- *Which* channel is appropriate for my message, my receivers, and the situation? (Think creatively here, too—Dallas Mavericks' owner Mark Cuban often uses the Internet to communicate with fans.) (*Where?* is another question to ask here. Is it your office, the locker room, or the receiver's work place? Choose a place that keeps distractions to a minimum.)

- *When* should I transmit my message? Timing is important. (Think about your receiver and be considerate—for example, don't approach someone 5 minutes before quitting time to transmit a 15-minute message. Make appointments when appropriate.)

6 LEARNING OUTCOME
Solicit feedback properly.

Getting Receivers to Get It

For communication to take place, at some point you and your receiver must reach a mutual understanding about your message's meaning. Therefore, after you transmit your message, you will need to know whether the receiver "gets it." This is where you check understanding by soliciting feedback.

feedback
The process of verifying messages.

Senders use *feedback* to verify that their meaning has been communicated (understood). **Feedback** literally feeds back to the sender the original information/meaning/intent transmitted in the message. Questioning, paraphrasing, and soliciting comments and suggestions are all ways senders can check understanding through feedback. Requiring feedback from receivers motivates them to achieve high levels of performance and improves their attention *and* their retention.[14] (Ask any professor who continually asks his or her student audience questions!) Indeed, the most common cause of messages *failing* to communicate information/meaning/intent is a lack of feedback.[15] But before we look at effective ways to solicit feedback, let's look at what can go wrong.

HOW *NOT* TO SOLICIT FEEDBACK. One sure way to block feedback is to send your entire message and then ask, "Do you have any questions?" Most of the time, you have very effectively killed any chances for discussion. Why? Because very few people will ask questions. Here is why they don't.

1. *They* feel *ignorant.* No one wants to look like the dim bulb in the group.
2. *They* are *ignorant.* Sometimes we don't know enough about the topic to ask questions. That is, we don't know whether the information given is complete, correct, or subject to interpretation. Sometimes it takes an in-depth background just to get to a level of understanding from which one can form questions.
3. *They don't want to point out* your *ignorance.* This commonly occurs when the sender is a manager and the receivers are staff. Asking a question in this situation may suggest that you have done a poor job of preparing and sending the message. Or that you are wrong. Neither is a comfortable situation for your receivers.
4. *They have* cultural *barriers.* In many Asian countries, for example, it is impolite to disagree with the boss, so receivers will answer "yes" when asked by a manager/sender if the message was understood.

After senders ask if there are questions (and thereby end the discussion), they often make yet another leap in the wrong direction. They assume that no questions means receivers understand the message. Would that this were true! When "this isn't what I asked for" happens, the message has to be sent again, that task has to be done again, and time, materials, and effort have been wasted in the meantime.

SO HOW SHOULD YOU SOLICIT FEEDBACK? Proper questioning and proper paraphrasing help ensure that your receivers get your message. In **paraphrasing** receivers restate the message in their own words.

1. *There are no dumb questions. Never* sneer at a question (no matter how stupid you think it is). *Always* answer patiently and explain clearly. If people sense impatience in you, you've just stopped any question-asking dead in its tracks. To encourage good questions, praise good questions.

2. *Tune into your own nonverbals.* Match your walk to your talk. If your nonverbal messages are discouraging feedback, no amount of verbal pleading on your part will bring forth the harvest of questions you desire.

3. *Tune into your receivers' nonverbals.* Seeing a lot of puzzled or blank looks out there? It's time to stop, backtrack, and clarify.

4. *Ask your receivers questions.* Go ahead. Ask anything. (*Except* of course "Do you have any questions?") Ask for specific information you have given. If responses are off track or muddled, repeat the message, give more examples, or elaborate further.[16] Ask indirect questions: "How do you feel about such and such?" Ask "if you were me" questions. (That is, "If you were me, how would you solve our lack of focus during games?") Ask third-party questions, such as "How will players respond when they have to bring their grades up to stay on the team?" The point is, if you get them talking, the feedback sluice gates will open.

5. *Have receivers paraphrase your message.* Paraphrasing is a valuable way to check understanding. Soliciting it gracefully is also an art. Clumsy soliciting of paraphrasing makes people feel stupid. "Joan, tell me what I just said so that I can be sure you won't make your typical mistakes" is *not* going to work—in fact, it's going to backfire big time! This is something you need to practice. In the beginning, before it becomes second nature, have some paraphrasing questions worked out beforehand; with practice they will eventually roll off your tongue. "Now tell me what you are going to do so that we will be sure we are in agreement." "Would you tell me what you are going to do so that I can be sure that I explained myself clearly?"

RECEIVING MESSAGES

So far, we've been discussing the communication process from the viewpoint of the sender. We've done everything we can to make you a solid sender. Now it's time to become a solid receiver. Look around you. What do the best receivers *all* do? They *listen.* Well, duh, you say—*I* listen! Do you? Take the Self Assessment on page 317 to find out.

We shouldn't have to say this, but listening is important. We spell it out here for one simple reason. Most of us are pretty poor listeners. It's easy to slip into bad listening habits—tuning out, letting our minds wander, jumping to what we *think* they're going to say, thinking more about what *we're* going to say rather than what they *are* saying. Because these habits are so pervasive and so insidious, it is essential to circle back every once in a while and critically assess your listening habits. This will sharpen your concentration skills in school and your performance on the field and in the office. Careful listening clues you in to others' needs and desires and to important information that can make you more effective and more skillful. This is why salespeople, negotiators, and conflict resolution experts are such good listeners.

Before we sharpen your listening skills, let's step back for a moment and consider how we receive messages (summarized in Exhibit 11–4). The **message-receiving process** includes listening, analyzing, and checking understanding. To receive the real message the sender is transmitting, you have to do all three. Receiving doesn't end with good listening. Listening is just the beginning.

Becoming a Listener

So, let's get down to the business of listening. We examined checking understanding earlier, and you got a great deal of practice in analysis (although we give you a quick course in

paraphrasing
The process of having receivers restate the message in their own words.

TIMEOUT
Think about an especially effective boss or coach you've had. Did he or she solicit feedback? If so, how? If not, why not?

_____
_____
_____
_____
_____
_____
_____

message-receiving process
Includes listening, analyzing, and checking understanding.

Exhibit 11-4   The Message-Receiving Process

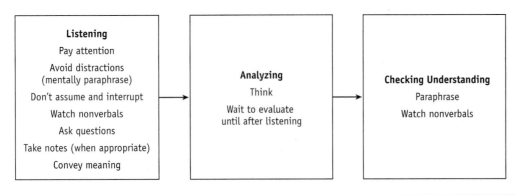

---

analysis below). However, failure to listen is the silent killer of many an effective communication, and it's time to stamp this virus out.

Here is what you are going to do. You are going to spend one week focusing on listening. This is going to be a *very* quiet week for you. Talk as little as possible, and listen, listen, listen. When your attention wanders, bring it back. Get quiet. Take special pains to concentrate on what other people say and on the nonverbal signals they send. To keep your focus, keep a diary of your observations. Jot down some notes when you see verbal and nonverbal messages that are particularly consistent and when you see ones that are blatantly out of sync. Note when nonverbals reinforce the speaker's words and when they detract from them. Talk *only* when necessary. (You can do this, *really*—it's just for a week!)

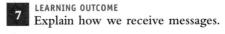

LEARNING OUTCOME
7
Explain how we receive messages.

listening
The process of giving the speaker your undivided attention.

Okay, now let's go back to square one. **Listening** is the process of giving the speaker your undivided attention. Remember this—when we say *undivided,* we mean *undivided.* Poor listening is caused in part by the fact that we speak on average about 120 words a minute, but we can comprehend 600 or so words a minute. Our ability to comprehend words five times more quickly than speakers can talk results in—you guessed it—wandering minds. Our minds don't like to be empty, so they pack in meandering and ricocheting thoughts. The result, of course, is that with all the background chatter, the sender's message loses out. Here are some reminders on how to get to undivided attention:

■ *Pay attention.* It's that simple—and that hard, because this *is* hard, or we would all be great listeners. So, relax (quickly) and clear your mind, then focus on the sender. This gets you on track *right now,* not five minutes from now. If you miss the first few words, you may miss the whole gist of the message. Practice this. The next time someone interrupts your doing some task in order to talk, stop whatever you are doing *(now)* and give them your full and complete attention immediately. Do this a lot over the next week.

■ *Avoid distractions.* Keep your eyes on the speaker. Do *not* fiddle with pens, papers, your belt loop, or your new haircut. Put your phone on "take a message" mode. If it's noisy or distracting, move to a quiet spot.

■ *Stay tuned in.* Don't let your mind wander to personal topics. If it does (and it will), gently bring it back. Continue to bring it back every time you notice yourself straying. Don't tune out because you don't like something about the speaker or because you disagree with what he or she is saying. Don't tune out because the topic is difficult—ask questions instead. Don't think about what you're going to say in reply. Stay tuned in by silently paraphrasing the message.

■ *Don't assume and don't interrupt.* Guess what—you *really* do not know what the speaker is going to say. (You're not prescient.) Most mistakes in receiving messages are made when we hear the first few words of a sentence, think we *know* what is about to be

SELF ASSESSMENT   *Listening*

Select the response that best describes the frequency of your behavior.

A—almost always   U—usually   F—frequently
O—occasionally   S—seldom

_____ 1. I encourage others to talk by showing interest, by asking them questions about themselves, and by smiling, nodding, and so forth.

_____ 2. I pay closer attention to people who are similar to me than those who are different from me.

_____ 3. I evaluate people's words and nonverbal signals as they talk.

_____ 4. I avoid distractions; if it's noisy, I suggest moving to a quiet spot.

_____ 5. When people interrupt me when I'm doing something, I put what I was doing out of my mind and give them my complete attention.

_____ 6. When people are talking, I allow them time to finish. I don't interrupt them, anticipate what they're going to say, or jump to conclusions.

_____ 7. I tune people out who don't agree with my views.

_____ 8. My mind wanders to personal topics when someone else is talking or professors are lecturing.

_____ 9. I pay close attention to nonverbal signals to help me fully understand what the other person is really saying.

_____ 10. When the topic is difficult, I tune out and just pretend I understand.

_____ 11. When the other person is talking, I'm thinking about what I'm going to say in reply.

_____ 12. When I think something is missing or contradictory in a discussion, I ask questions to get people to explain their ideas more fully.

_____ 13. I let the other person know when I don't understand something.

_____ 14. When listening to other people, I try to put myself in their place and see things from their perspective.

_____ 15. When I'm given information or instructions, I repeat back to the other person what they said in my own words to be sure I understand.

Now have some of your friends fill out this assessment, giving their impressions of your listening habits.

Scoring. For statements 1, 4, 5, 6, 9, 12, 13, 14, and 15, give 5 points for A answers, 4 for Us, 3 for Fs, 2 for Os, and 1 for Ss. For items 2, 3, 7, 8, 10, and 11, the score reverses: 5 points for Ss, 4 for Os, 3 for Fs, 2 for Us, and 1 for As. Place these scores on the lines next to your responses and add them to get your total. Your score should be between 15 and 75. Place your score on the continuum below.

Poor listener   Good listener
15–20–25–30–35–40–45–50–55–60–65–70–75

said, finish it in our own minds, then miss the real message. Listen to the entire message. Don't string your own beads on the speaker's "necklace" (message); let the speaker finish the necklace with his or her own beads.

■ *Watch nonverbals.* Understand the speaker's walk as well as his or her talk. People sometimes say one thing and mean something else. So, watch as you listen to be sure that the speaker's eyes, body, and face are sending the same message as the verbal message. If something seems out of sync, ask questions to clarify.

■ *Ask questions.* When you feel something's missing or contradictory, or you just don't understand, don't be afraid to ask for clarification. Not only will the speaker be grateful, so will other listeners. Chances are, they are not understanding it either.

■ *Take notes.* Write down important things. Not only does this help you concentrate on what is being said, it helps you remember later. The prepared mind has something to write on and something to write with.

- *Convey that you are listening.* Let the speaker know you are listening. Use verbal clues ("you feel . . . ," "uh huh," "I see," "I understand") and nonverbal cues (eye contact, nodding your head, leaning slightly forward) to indicate that you are interested and listening.

Once you've put in your week of listening, take some time and think about what it felt like to listen more than you talked. Was it hard? Now take the Self Assessment on page 317 *again.* Did your answers change? Do you still talk more than you listen? To be sure your perception is correct, ask your boss, coworkers, and friends who will give you an honest answer. If you spend more time talking than listening, you are not only *not* receiving messages you need to hear, you are probably also boring people. (Let's face it—none of us are profound and clever all the time.) Regardless of how much and how well you listen, if you follow these guidelines, you will improve your conversation and become someone people want to listen to instead of a person they feel they have to listen to. To become an active listener, take responsibility for ensuring mutual understanding. Work to change your behavior to become a better listener. Review the 15 statements in the Self Assessment. Make a habit of doing items 1, 4, 5, 6, 9, 12, 13, 14, and 15. And avoid doing items 2, 3, 7, 8, 10, and 11.

Analyzing the Message

When we *analyze a message,* we think about it, decode it, and evaluate it. Therefore, as speakers send their messages, you should be

- *Thinking.* Use your excess capacity for comprehending to listen "actively." Silently paraphrase, organize, summarize, review, interpret, and critique. This marshals all your forces for decoding the message.

- *Waiting to evaluate.* When people try to listen and evaluate what is said at the same time, they miss part or all of the message. So listen to the entire message, *then* make your conclusions. When you evaluate the message, base your conclusions on the facts presented rather than on stereotypes and politics.[17]

RESPONDING TO MESSAGES

Not every message requires a response, of course, but many do. With each response, the communication process both begins again (you encode and transmit, and the receiver decodes) and continues (because this is a response, not the initiating message). The roles of receiver and sender continue to flip throughout every conversation.[18]

8 LEARNING OUTCOME
Choose appropriate response styles.

Response Styles

It is important to understand that how you as receiver respond to a message directly affects the communication process. You, of course, want to respond appropriately, and you basically have five response styles from which to choose (see Exhibit 11–5). To demonstrate the dif-

---

Exhibit 11–5   Response Styles

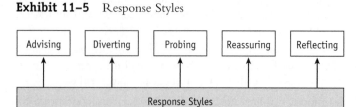

---

ferent response styles, let's look at five responses to a rather confrontational message from a person on your team:

"You supervise me so closely that I can't do my job—I have *no* breathing room."

ADVISOR'S RESPONSES. "You need my directions to do a good job; you lack experience." "I disagree. You need my instructions and for me to check your work." (Note that advice was not asked for, but it was given anyway.)

Advisors evaluate, give their personal opinion, direct, or instruct. Advisors tend to close, limit, or direct the flow of communication away from the sender to the receiver.

When is advising appropriate? Giving advice is appropriate when you are asked for it. Remember, however, that giving advice too quickly builds dependence. Developing your staff's ability to think things through and to make decisions is an important part of your job. When asked for advice by employees who you believe don't really need it, instead ask questions like "What do you think is the best way to handle this situation?"

DIVERTER'S RESPONSES. "You've reminded me of a manager I once had who . . ." "Did you see the game last night?"

Diverters switch the focus to a new message—we commonly call diverting "changing the subject." Diverters tend to redirect, close, or limit the flow of communication. Diversions used early on may cause senders to feel that their message is not worth discussing or that the other party's message is more important.

When is diversion appropriate? When either party is uncomfortable with the topic. Diversion may be helpful when sharing personal experiences or feelings that are similar to those of the sender but that edge the conversation away from something too personal, too embarrassing, or too "close."

PROBER'S RESPONSES. "What do I do to cause you to say this?" (*Not* "Why do you feel this way?") "How long have you felt this way?"

Probers ask the sender to give more information about some aspect of the message. It can be useful to get a better understanding of the situation. When probing, "what" questions are preferred to "why" questions.

When is probing appropriate? Probe during the early stages of the message to ensure that you fully understand the situation. After probing, the other response styles are often needed.

REASSURER'S RESPONSES. "Don't worry, I won't do it for much longer." "Your work is improving, so I may be able to provide less direction soon."

Reassurers endeavor to reduce the intensity of the emotions associated with the message. They're saying, "Don't worry; everything will be okay." "You can do it." They are pacifying the sender.

When is reassuring appropriate? When the other person lacks confidence. Encouraging responses that give praise can help people develop confidence.

REFLECTOR'S RESPONSES. "My checking up on you annoys you?" "You don't think I need to check up on you; is this what you mean?" (Note that these responses allow people to express their feelings and direct the path of the exchange.)

Reflecting paraphrases the message and telegraphs understanding and acceptance to the sender. When reflecting, be sure *not* to use the sender's exact words or the sender will feel that you are mimicking (and thus patronizing) him or her—that you neither understand nor have listened closely. This is tricky and requires some practice before it works gracefully. Reflecting in your own words can often lead not only to successful exchanges but also to solid relations with your coworkers. Female managers tend to favor reflecting and probing responses; male managers tend to favor evaluative advising responses.[19]

When is reflecting appropriate? Basically, when you coach and when you counsel. When reflecting is used gracefully, senders will feel listened to, understood, and free to explore the topic in more depth. As the exchange progresses, however, do change to other response styles. The caveat is that reflecting used obviously or inappropriately makes senders feel patronized and manipulated.

TIMEOUT

State two oral messages you received recently and your responses to them. Identify your response style for each message. Give two different responses using other styles and state why each is appropriate or inappropriate.

_____
_____
_____
_____
_____
_____

reflecting
Paraphrasing the message and communicating understanding and acceptance to the sender.

APPLYING THE CONCEPT   *Identifying Response Styles*

Identify each response to the given situation as:

a. advising   **c.** probing   **e.** reflecting

b. diverting   **d.** reassuring

Irate parent: Coach, do you have a minute to talk?

Coach: Sure, what's up?

Irate parent: Can you do something about all the swearing that players do on the team? It's disgusting. I'm surprised you haven't done anything.

Coach:

_____ 16. I didn't know anyone was swearing. I'll look into it.

_____ 17. You don't have to listen to it. Just ignore the swearing.

_____ 18. Are you feeling well today?

_____ 19. So you find this swearing offensive?

_____ 20. What words are they saying that offend you?

DEALING WITH EMOTIONAL PEOPLE

One thing is certain—sometime, and most likely many times, someone with whom you work—player, coach, parent of player, boss, work group member, customer, the list is endless—is going to start an emotional exchange with you. Emotions can shut down accurate message-receiving, they can garble the message, and they can divert receivers from the real message, but they can also be catalysts that bring new ideas and new ways of doing things to the table. So, if you want to succeed as a leader and as a manager, understand emotions and learn to deal with them. Realize that feelings are

- subjective—they reveal people's attitudes and needs
- often disguised as factual statements
- neither right nor wrong

People cannot choose their feelings, nor can they control the feelings themselves. However, they can control how they *express* their feelings. For example, if Rachel the Bad Winner in the heat of a win exults in Louise's humiliating loss in their tennis match, Louise can choose to lower herself to Rachel's level with a confrontational and emotional response. *Or* she can rise to the occasion and show grace, dignity, and the courage to face her loss as a Good Loser. Depending on her choice of expression, the exchange can deteriorate from here or it can remind Rachel by Louise's grace in losing well that some things are more important than winning. **Who is the leader here—and why? The lesson here?** *Each of us* chooses our responses in emotional exchanges, and we *always* have a chance to shape them into something positive. Effective managers/coaches/leaders don't get caught up in others' emotions.

9 LEARNING OUTCOME
Calm an emotional person.

Throwing Cool Water on Hot Words

So, someone comes to you boiling over—what do you do? Fortunately, the answer is, lots of things. But first, here is what you *don't* do (and frankly these are more important than what you *do* do):

- Don't put them down.
- Don't deny their anger.
- Don't accuse back.
- Don't patronize them.
- Don't show them who is boss.

This means the following statements must *never* be said (even if you are thinking them):

- "You shouldn't be angry." (How do you know—maybe they *should* be angry.)
- "Don't be upset." (Too late—they are *already* upset.)
- "You're acting like a baby." (Like this is going to get you somewhere?)
- "Just sit down and be quiet." (Right. You may get to this point in the exchange, but starting here is a sure way to flame the fire.)
- "I know how you feel." (No, you don't.)

Can you list other statements that you should *not* make when you're trying to calm someone?

These statements only raise the temperature of the exchange. And you're trying to get away from "exchange" and into "communication."

Like we said, fortunately for your career and for their peace of mind, there are many productive ways you can respond. For one thing, make sure you know Chapter 9 inside and out. For another, learn to empathize. **Empathy** is the ability to understand and relate to someone else's situation and feelings. Empathic responders deal with feelings, content, and the underlying meaning being expressed in the message. Your ability to empathize will stand you in good stead as a coach, as a leader, as a manager, and as an employee dealing with your boss. Why? For one thing, if your work relationships are based on trust, you have many cards to play in heated moments. For another, if you are an empathizer, you didn't begin empathizing in *this* heated moment; you've been empathizing with many different people in many different situations for a while, and you bring this knowledge and insight to the exchange. And finally, empathic people are good listeners—in fact, with good listening comes empathy; they are natural by-products of each other. So, remember the good listening skills and use them here. Pay attention to what people are saying, don't assume and don't interrupt, let them know you are listening (honor their feelings, in other words), and hold your evaluation back. Let them let their steam out. Emotions need steam to keep running; letting the steam out causes the kettle to stop boiling over.

Later, carefully reflect their feelings back to them. "You were *hurt* when you didn't get first-string position." "You *resent* Charlie for not pulling his weight on the team—is that what you mean?" "You're *doubtful* that the job's going to get done on time—is that what you're saying?" You will find that very often simply understanding the sender's feelings *is* the solution, that only venting is wanted, not advice. Other times solutions must be found. As emotions cool (and they will if you give them enough time), you can proceed to the crux of the problem and to solving it. Sometimes, if emotions continue to run high, you may have to wait until a later time before you get to considering solutions.[20]

empathy
The ability to understand and relate to someone else's situation and feelings.

TIMEOUT
Recall an emotional exchange that you witnessed at work or on your team. Did the responder calm the person effectively? Write a paragraph about the exchange showing where the responder went right or went wrong.

_____
_____
_____
_____
_____
_____

Criticism

Criticism. In this life, you're going to give some and you're going to get some. As with other important endeavors, you may well do both well. Just for a moment, let's look at how to give it (only briefly—we'll explore this in greater detail in Chapter 14). It's easier to give it than to get it, isn't it? Remember this when you're giving criticism. (Your empathy? Use it here.) Personal criticism? Avoid it. (Like the plague!) Public criticism? Not *ever*. (Criticism of work reports, progress on schedules, and the like, of course, are different animals.) Remember, giving (and taking) criticism is just another tool in your tool kit—one that you can learn, that you can hone, and that you can turn to your competitive advantage.

Now about getting criticism. You're going get some, so you might as well take it well. In fact, if you are wise, you will *want* it. (How else are you going to realize your full potential?) So, to begin with, view criticism through the perceptual lens of wanting it (constructive criticism, that is—we are *not* talking about destructive criticism here). This will put you in a position to use it constructively and to see it *not* as a personal attack on you but as what it is—help, encouragement, and teaching. Let's say this again: *Think of criticism as what it is*—feedback to improve your performance.[21] Even extraordinary talents get their share of criticism. New York Yankees manager Joe Torre has praised Alfonso Soriano, his young second baseman, numerous times for his ability to take criticism. "That's not to say the message gets through instantly each time. Soriano still struts a bit when he hits a deep ball, and when the ball doesn't go out, a double or triple can become a single."[22] That said, we will never tell you that this is an easy thing to do. You will need a few calluses on your ego. (And, by the way, they are a good thing to have!) If you are overly sensitive, people will avoid giving you the criticism you need if you are to grow. None of us enjoy being criticized, even when it is constructive.[23] Think about the gain you will get when you take the pain. And one last word—taking it gracefully gives you power.

CHAPTER SUMMARY

1. Understand how communication flows through organizations.

Formal communications flow vertically (down and up through the chain of command) and horizontally (between coworkers). Informal communication flows through the grapevine in many directions.

2. List the four steps in the communication process.

The sender (1) encodes a message, then (2) transmits it. (3) The receiver decodes the message. (4) The receiver decides if feedback is needed and, if it is, encodes a message (a response) and transmits it—and the process begins again.

3. Use transmission channels well.

Although oral communication is easy and fast and encourages feedback, it is also less accurate and provides no record. Written communication is more accurate and provides a record, but it also takes longer, and feedback is not immediate.

4. Communicate effectively in person.

(1) Develop rapport. (2) State your message using a beginning/middle/end format. (3) Check the receiver's understanding. (4) Get a commitment and follow up.

5. Select appropriate channels for your messages.

As a general guide, use rich oral channels for sending difficult and unusual messages, written channels for transmitting simple and routine messages to several people, and combined channels for important messages.

6. Solicit feedback properly.

Do not simply ask if anyone has questions. *Do* ask receivers to paraphrase. Ask them for specific information you have given. Ask indirect questions, "if you were me" questions, and third-party questions. Just get them talking.

7. Explain how we receive messages.

To receive a message well, we listen (give the speaker our undivided attention), analyze (think about, decode, and evaluate the message), and check our understanding (often by giving feedback).

8. Choose appropriate response styles.

Heated exchanges are best handled by advising, diverting, probing, reassuring, and reflecting, but not in this order. Depending on the exchange, reflecting, reassuring, or diverting are typically good first responses. Probing is appropriate later in the process, and advising is typically the last step if it is used at all.

9. Calm an emotional person.

To calm an emotional person, avoid statements that put the person down, patronize them, show them who is boss, and so forth. Instead, pay attention, don't assume and don't interrupt, let them know you are listening (honor their feelings), and hold your evaluation back. Let them vent. Later, carefully reflect their feelings back to them.

10. Define the key terms discussed in the text.

Fill in the missing key terms from memory, or match the key terms from the list in the margin with their definitions below.

_____ is the process of transmitting information and meaning.

_____ is the downward and upward flow of information through an organization.

_____ is information shared between peers.

The _____ is the flow of information through informal channels.

The _____ is the transmission of information, meaning, and intent.

A _____ initiates communication by encoding and transmitting a message.

When _____, the sender puts the message into a form that the receiver will understand.

A _____ is the person to whom the message is sent.

_____ is the process of using a form of communication to send a message.

When _____, the receiver translates the message into a meaningful form.

_____ are messages sent without words.

_____ is the process of verifying messages.

In _____, receivers restate the message in their own words.

The _____ includes listening, analyzing, and checking understanding.

_____ is the process of giving the speaker your undivided attention.

_____ paraphrases the message and communicates understanding and acceptance to the sender.

_____ is the ability to understand and relate to someone else's situation and feelings.

Key Terms

communication
communication process
decoding the message
empathy
encoding the message
feedback
grapevine
horizontal
    communication
listening
message-receiving
    process
nonverbal
    communications
paraphrasing
receiver
reflecting
sender
transmitting the
    message
vertical communication

REVIEW AND DISCUSSION

1. What is the difference among vertical, horizontal, and grapevine communications?

2. What is the difference between encoding and decoding?

3. What is distortion?

4. Give an example of nonverbal communication in baseball, in poker, and in soccer.

5. What forms of communications do you personally use to gather information about sports?

6. On average, how many words do effective sentences have? How many sentences do effective paragraphs typically have?

7. What is media richness?

8. What should you include when you send an oral message? A written one? What makes each effective and why?

9. Which response style do you use most often?

10. When we calm emotional people, why don't we simply show them who is boss?

CASE

Handling the Pro Athlete's Handler—the Famous (and Infamous) Agent

Do you think you would be good at babysitting egos? Think you can handle the fickle media, long hours, and first-class seats on airplanes and at sporting events? Then become a sport agent—it's good work if you can get it. And life will never be dull again. Yes, some very large sport agencies—IMG and Pro Serv are two that come to mind—represent professional athletes in all sports. But many pro players use independent agents, and a growing number of these are lawyers.[24]

Agents handle all or part of a professional athlete's business affairs, including contract negotiations, product endorsements, licensing arrangements, personal appearances, public relations, and financial counseling.[25] Although agents don't like to reveal the commissions they get on the contracts they negotiate for their players, it appears to range between one and six percent.[26] Pretty "pennies" when you're talking about millions of greenbacks!

Agents get regulated fairly carefully because the opportunities for defrauding players or misrepresenting them are legion. Regulators include state and federal governments, the agents themselves, the National Collegiate Athletic Association (NCAA), and players' associations. All of these groups have, with varying success, adopted certification programs in attempts to monitor player agents.[27] The record is spotty at best. The NCAA's endeavor to establish a uniform system for regulating athlete agents—the Uniform Athlete Agents Act (UAAA)—has been passed by only 14 states. Eighteen states have existing, non-UAAA legislation for regulating agents, but 11 states have no such legislation either pending or in place.[28]

Agents who represent MLB players must jump through a few hoops. To be certified by the Players' Association, for example, an agent must represent at least one member on a 40-man roster of an MLB club.[29] The association has over 300 agents on record.

Why all the emphasis on regulating agents, you ask? Because there are a lot of rules and regulations to get around. And big bucks attract rule-benders galore. So, yes, unfortunately, there is too much monkey business in the business of sport agency. Agents are not supposed to communicate with players while they are in college. But they do. And when they get caught, everyone pays—the athletes, the colleges, the sports programs, and the fans. Athletes such as basketball players Marcus Camby (University of Massachusetts) and Ricky Moore (University of Connecticut) received gifts while in college. Gifts can range from money to airline tickets.[30]

College athletes do need to select an agent when they turn professional. When first-round NFL draft pick Ricky Williams hired Leland Hardy (who worked for rapper Master P), industry watchers assumed that Williams and Hardy would really click since Hardy had done so well for Master P.[31] The assumption was that Hardy would get better deals for Williams because they had the same type of social and economic background. However, the Hardy deal turned out to be full of incentive clauses and did not work out well for Williams. Williams soon dropped Hardy for Leigh Steinberg, a much more experienced agent. As with any business decision, choosing one's agent requires a shrewd reading of the business environment and of one's own strengths and weaknesses. Sometimes cooler heads are needed instead of a close personal friend—or one's father. Take Eric Lindros, whose father Carl and lawyer Gord Kirke represent him.[32] The Philadelphia Flyers and the Lindros duo rarely saw eye to eye, and (truth be known) they did more head butting than effective communicating. Finally, in the summer of 2001 the Flyers traded Lindros to the New York Rangers with a great sigh of relief.

For more information about becoming an agent, review the rules of being an agent as outlined by the NCAA. Visit http://www1.ncaa.org/membership/enforcement/agents/uaaa/history.html for more information. Additionally, information about becoming an MLB agent can be found at http://bigleaguers.yahoo.com/mlbpa/faq.html.

CASE QUESTIONS

Answer the following questions about an agent communicating with a player.

1. College athletes are not allowed to communicate with which of the following professionals during his or her collegiate career?
   a. baker   c. agent
   b. postman   d. media personnel

2. Ricky Williams and Leland Hardy made a great team because they came from the same socioeconomic background.
   a. true   b. false

3. Ricky Williams's first contract was poorly designed because
   a. he rushed into picking an agent.
   b. he was hurt during his rookie season.
   c. his contract contained too many incentives.
   d. his contract was for too much guaranteed money.

4. Ricky Williams switched to agent Leigh Steinberg because he was more experienced in the process of communicating with professional teams.
   a. true   b. false

5. IMG is an independent agency that represents
   a. football players
   b. baseball players
   c. tennis players
   d. all sports

6. No rules govern the conduct of sport agents.
   a. true   b. false

7. Marcus Camby was found to have communicated with agents while he was an amateur player in college.
   a. true   b. false

8. Eric Lindros and his agent communicated very well with the Philadelphia Flyers.
   a. true   b. false

9. What step of the communication process is being used if a player's agent and the team are working on the wording of the first draft of the player's contract?
   a. encoding   c. decoding
   b. transmitting   d. feedback

10. What step of the communication process is being used if Pro Serv faxes a copy of a revised player contract back to the team?
    a. encoding   c. decoding
    b. transmitting   d. feedback

11. Name two other athletes who have had problems with their agents. What sort of communication barriers do you think were operative in each case?

EXERCISES

Skill-Builder: Strong Messages, Strong Receivers

Objective:

- To hone your ability to send and receive messages.

Preparation:

Review the points made in the chapter on encoding and receiving messages. Your instructor will inform you as to which one or more of the three messages you will be transmitting. Message 1 will be given in class. Messages 2 and 3 will require some research and brainstorming.

IN-CLASS APPLICATION

Choose one or more of the three messages:

- For message 1, break into pairs. You will each be sender and receiver in turn.
- For messages 2 and 3, break into groups of five to eight members and transmit your messages to the group. Select one of the group's messages for presentation to the class. If this is a message 3, your group will present their "decoding" to the class as well.

Message 1. Your instructor will be passing out drawings of sports objects. Your job as encoder is to direct your receiver to draw the object. Your receiver may not look at the drawing. You are not to tell them what the object is nor the sport in which it is used. You may not use hand signals or drawings of your own—only words are "legal." You have 15 minutes to get the drawing done.

Message 2. Find a sport-related message by a coach, athlete, player's agent, MLB manager, head of the NFL, etc. that was difficult to deliver or hard to receive. This could be a coach who lost his or her cool, a coach who rallied a team that was on its knees, a player retiring, a leader involved in a strike, or a parent found out in a youth league scandal—there are many possibilities. Use the Internet, old copies of *Sports Illustrated,* or your favorite biographies of sport figures to find the exact quote, the context in which it was delivered, and the receivers of the message. Deliver this message to your group as it was originally delivered (to the best of your imagination) and as it *could* have been delivered. Perhaps lesser communicators would have delivered it poorly and this person did a great job of encoding a difficult message; if so, show the more likely encoding first, then the great rendition. Perhaps the original message was encoded very poorly; if so, your job then is to show how it could have been delivered—what would have made it much more effective.

Message 3. Research an obscure sport or game (such as curling or boomeranging), one you are pretty sure your classmates don't know how to play. Develop some interesting ways to explain the rules (in 10 minutes or less) of this sport or game to your receiving group. You may not tell the name of the sport or the names of objects used in the sport. Your receivers will demonstrate that they received your message by giving a very quick demonstration of the game. Whichever one is presented to the entire class, ask the class to guess the sport if it is really obscure.

Wrap-up:

Take a few minutes and write down your answers to the following questions:

- What did I learn from this experience?

_____

_____

_____

■ How will I use this knowledge in the future?

_____

_____

_____

As a class, discuss student responses.

Internet Skills: Getting to Great Talks

Objective:
■ To help you find tips on the Internet for giving great speeches.

Preparation (20 minutes):
Visit the web site http://www.sportsmediachallenge.com. Search the site and answer the following questions.

1. Use the Quick Clicks and go to *Speech* in the PLAYBOOK section. What are the eight most common speech slipups?

   _____

   _____

   _____

   _____

   _____

2. What are the Tips for D-Day (Speech Delivery Day)?

   _____

   _____

   _____

   _____

   _____

3. Review the Speech Gut Check! What are these steps?

   _____

   _____

   _____

   _____

   _____

4. What are the 9 Steps to Working a Crowd?

   _____

   _____

   _____

   _____

   _____

5. What do you say when you're receiving an award?

   _____

   _____

   _____

   _____

   _____

12 Motivating to Win

Learning Outcomes

After studying this chapter, you should be able to:

1. Explain how motivation works.

2. Use the performance equation.

3. Discuss the four content-based motivation theories.

4. Discuss the three process-based motivation theories.

5. Discuss reinforcement theory.

6. Compare content, process, and reinforcement theories.

7. Define the following key terms (in order of appearance in the chapter):

- motivation
- motivation process
- performance equation
- content-based motivation theories
- hierarchy of needs theory
- ERG theory
- two-factor theory
- acquired needs theory
- process-based motivation theories
- equity theory
- goal-setting theory
- expectancy theory
- reinforcement theory

REVIEWING THEIR GAME PLAN

Pat Summitt: Lady Motivator

Sometimes hyperbole is warranted. When **PAT SUMMITT** comes to mind, so does "living legend." Pat Summitt is not only a remarkable athlete (silver medalist in women's basketball in the 1976 Olympics), an extraordinary coach (six NCAA national championships and the gold medal in U.S. women's basketball in the 1984 Olympics), and a breaker of new ground for women and women athletes (as a young player she started 30-plus years ago when college women athletes were not only a lonely group, they were coached entirely by men), but first and foremost she is a motivator—of herself and of a myriad of colleagues and athletes (11 of her athletes have gone on to win Olympic gold). And as the 27-year coach of the University of Tennessee's famed Lady Volunteers, she is also the most well-known female coach in all of sports.

Her accolades boggle. She is a Hall of Fame coach and one of the "25 Most Influential Working Mothers" (*Working Mother* magazine, 1997). As co-chair of the 1996 United Way Campaign in Knoxville, she cut no corners and logged enormous amounts of time visiting the United Way agencies even as she recruited, ran camps, and directed UT's women's basketball program, arguably the most successful program in the nation. And in the past few years she has given motivational speeches to everyone from the CIA to Victoria's Secret to Federal Express to the Federal Reserve Board. The lady doesn't stop!

Then there is the incredible graduation rate of her players. This may well be her most remarkable achievement. It is one thing for your teams to win, but what better legacy can there be than to know you have shaped and formed winners in every aspect of your players' lives as they leave your stewardship and go out on their own? Summitt walks her own talk. Her players know this and go to the wall to emulate her integrity, her competitive spirit, and her standards of excellence in every endeavor they undertake.

Change is a cornerstone of her coaching style. So are work ethic and respect. She strives to help her athletes embrace change and see that it is a good thing, not something to be feared. She respects athletes who give it their all, but she is not afraid to show wrath. She treats her athletes as adults, and they hear about it when they don't act like adults. Her philosophy? "Discipline is all about structure. It is the bare-bones architecture of your organization, the beams and joists that hold everything together. Maintaining the integrity of your interior philosophy is crucial. Even if it costs you a valued member of your team. Otherwise your structure will collapse."[1]

When words of wisdom are given by one so successful, it pays to listen. In Summitt's book, *Reach for the Summit,* she outlines 12 steps for success. These steps include discipline, loyalty, taking full responsibility, being a competitor, and handling success and failure.[2] Heed them well.

For further information on the legendary "Summitt," visit the web site http://www.coachsummitt.com. (For ideas on using the Internet, see Appendix B.)

INTERNET RESOURCES

http://www.aahperd.org/naspe/template.cfm?template=domainsStandards.html
To find a summary of standards for what coaches should know and be able to do, visit this web site. The National Association for Sport & Physical Education (NASPE) based its National Standards for Athletic Coaches around eight domains: Injuries—Prevention, Care, and Management; Risk Management; Growth, Development, and Learning; Training, Conditioning, and Nutrition; Social/Psychological Aspects of Coaching; Skills, Tactics, and Strategies; Teaching

and Administration; and Professional Preparation and Development. Click on the National Standards for Athletic Coaches *link at the bottom of the page to purchase the full text of the standards in book form.*

http://www.competitivedge.com/peak.html *All of the Competitive Advantage Peak Performance Guides found on this page offer useful tips for motivating athletes to function at their highest level. In particular, check out* A Coach's Guide to Winning at the Motivation Game *and* A Coach's Guide to Developing Self-Esteem. *If you're a coach, use the practical, step-by-step recommendations to help your team perform its best. If you're an athlete, look over these steps to understand what it takes to get and stay motivated.*

http://www.geocities.com/Colosseum/Bench/6823/goals.html *When setting a goal, you need to make sure that the goal is challenging yet realistic and that, once accomplished, the goal will contribute to your self-esteem and future performance. For coaches, it is important to set goals that keep the team perfectly balanced between under- and over-aroused.* Goal-Setting for Athletes *will help you achieve all these objectives and more.*

 DEVELOPING YOUR SKILLS   Giving praise is a big deal. Why? Because praise motivates. More than raises. More than *anything else.* It is not used nearly enough. Savvy managers give it generously. Get comfortable with giving praise. Make sure yours is genuine and apt.

Motivation and Performance

1 **LEARNING OUTCOME**
Explain how motivation works.

Why is motivation important? Because without it, we are ineffectual. And with it, we are just about invincible. Motivation is what drives every one of us to satisfy our unsatisfied needs. We do what we do to meet our "I need . . ." and "I want . . ." lists. From a management perspective, **motivation** is the willingness to achieve organizational objectives.

motivation
The willingness to achieve organizational objectives.

motivation process
Process through which people go from need to motive to behavior to consequence and finally to either satisfaction or dissatisfaction.

Motivation is also a process. Through the **motivation process**, people go from need to motive to behavior to consequence and finally to either satisfaction or dissatisfaction. Let's say you work up a powerful thirst (need) while skateboarding and want some water (motive). You get a drink (behavior) that quenches (consequence) and thus satisfies your thirst. It's a funny thing about us humans. In many endeavors, our satisfaction is often short lived. (Perhaps we should say *thank goodness*—or else we would not continue to strive to survive and prevail!) For this reason, the motivation process loops back, and the process begins anew:

Need ⟶ Motive ⟶ Behavior ⟶ Consequence ⟶ Satisfaction or Dissatisfaction

← Feedback ←

Our needs and wants thus motivate *every aspect* of our behavior. Because our needs and wants are typically infinitely more complex than our thirst after a skateboarding session, we don't always know what they are and therefore—and this is the important part—we don't always know *why* we do what we do. That is why organizational behaviorists study needs—understanding needs often explains behavior. We can't observe motives directly, but we can observe behavior and thereby infer motive. The "wrench" in this idea is that we humans are vastly trickier than this simple model. Why? Because different motives frequently drive the same behavior. Add to this murky mix the fact that we also endeavor to satisfy several needs at once, and you can fill a lot of libraries.

Alas, motivation is also *the number-one problem* facing businesses today, and it behooves every aspiring manager to wonder why frequently and to put not a small amount of energy into becoming skilled at motivating others. A motivated and satisfied workforce contributes big-time to the bottom line.[3] Poor performance? The answer is most likely motivation, motivation, motivation. . . .

So, how do organizations, managers, coaches, and other leaders motivate their people? We devote this chapter to providing a few answers.

Motivation is important not only to small businesses but also to major corporations and pro sport teams. Giving immediate, frequent, and direct feedback leads to higher motivation and performance. Recall from Chapter 9 that job satisfaction leads to lower absenteeism and turnover and higher levels of performance.[4] Generally, people who are satisfied with their jobs are more highly motivated.[5] To motivate employees, make work fun. Organizational cultures that approach work as fun fuel some of the most productive people and organizations in America. Companies that bring play and celebration into the workplace also often have higher profits. Do you think it would be fun to play for **PAT SUMMITT?** Have you ever had a job that was fun? How did it affect your motivation?

The Role of Expectations

What causes poor performance? Many things, but a key factor (key because you have control over it) is managers themselves. Don't look first at the inadequacies of your staff (poor skills, lack of experience, bad attitude—you know the list). Look first at your own expectations. Remember the Pygmalion effect (Chapter 9)? Yes, that's right—*your* expectations and *your* treatment of people affect their motivation and hence their performance. If you have high expectations for your staff and treat your workers as high achievers, you will get their best. **PAT SUMMITT** treats her players as champions, and her players make history season after season. What exactly does Summitt do to treat her players "as champions"?

All this said, *ineffective* stabs at motivation only make the problem worse. You have to do it right. So, first of all, check your frame of reference—you may have a perception problem. What works to motivate you may not work to motivate others. Thus, rule number one is Know Your People. Get to know them as individuals and learn what meets their unique and diverse needs. One study of aerobic participants suggests that it is crucial to instill a self-perception of competence in individuals who are low in self-determination.[6]

People's expectations of themselves also affect their performance. This is the *self-fulfilling prophecy.* We *will* live up—or down—to our own expectations, so each of us must seek ways to be positive, confident, and optimistic. A negative outlook is not cast in concrete, but positive ones are often "cast" in sweat and effort—that is, negativity can be changed; it just takes effort (Chapter 9). Henry Ford said that if you believe you can, or you believe you can't, you are right. If you think you will be successful, you will be. If you think you will fail, you will, because you will fulfill your own expectations.

2 LEARNING OUTCOME
Use the performance equation.

The Performance Equation

Yes, motivated people try harder, but this is not the complete solution to the performance problem. Performance is not just about motivation. The good news is that the "arithmetic" is pretty simple:

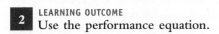

Performance = Ability × Motivation × Resources

This is the **performance equation**—ignore it at your organization's peril! To get maximum performance from your staff, you need high levels of ability *and* motivation *and* resources—it's that simple. It is also that complicated, because this is not easy to pull off, as every organization knows all too well. What this equation does is focus your thinking. Your group's performance is suffering? Then examine what is missing from the equation and why. Only when you know what is missing can you develop strategies that will solve the problem. **PAT SUMMITT** constantly looks for ways to improve her team's performance equation. For instance, if her team's ability is not up to snuff, she lasers in on specifics, adjusts their training accordingly, and recruits to fix holes in the net. What do you think Summitt might do if her *resources* are not as tip-top as she needs? What are her resources in the performance equation?

performance equation
Performance = Ability ×
Motivation × Resources

APPLYING THE CONCEPT   *The Performance Equation*

Identify which part of the performance equation is operative in each situation.

a. ability   **b.** motivation   **c.** resources

_____ 1. Calling on one of her golf club retailers, Latoya realizes belatedly that she has forgotten her product display book. No visuals—no interest. She loses the sale.

_____ 2. Frank is *definitely* the team's slacker—as Coach says, he's got the goods; he just doesn't use them.

_____ 3. I train longer and harder, but Heather and Linda continually beat my times.

_____ 4. Yeah, my grades could be better, but, hey, I made the team, so it's time to relax and have some fun.

_____ 5. FIFA would be more efficient if it cut down on waste.

_____ 6. Amateur athletes have to pinch pennies to pay for training.

_____ 7. Our athletic director says we need money for the lacrosse program.

_____ 8. When team cuts loom, players train harder.

_____ 9. Before Title IX, women did not enjoy equal opportunities to play collegiate sports.

_____ 10. Women collegiate basketball teams have plenty of applicants now that WNBA pro basketball is an option after players finish school.

Getting to Motivated People

This is the big question, isn't it? How do we motivate our workers, our players, and ourselves to be our best? Sorry, we can't offer a snappy sound bite here, because there is no single best way. This works in your favor, however, because you will need a lot of tools in this part of your kit (remember, different people motivate in different ways). So, it's time to look at some theories. To get an overview, peruse Exhibit 12–1.

3 LEARNING OUTCOME
Discuss the four content-based motivation theories.

CONTENT-BASED THEORIES

content-based motivation theories
Focus on identifying and understanding people's needs.

According to content-based theorists, to create a satisfied workforce, organizations must meet their employees' needs. **Content-based motivation theories** thus focus on identifying and understanding people's needs. When we are asked to meet objectives, our first (underlying) thought is, What's in it for me? The key to success for organizations, therefore, is to achieve resonance between the needs of the workforce and the objectives of the organization. As you strive to create this win-win situation, you need to sell the benefits that meet the employees' needs. For **PAT SUMMITT,** this part is pretty easy—she wants to win, and her players want to win. So how do you think Summitt's Lady Vols answer the "what's in it for me" question?

Exhibit 12–1   Major Motivation Theories

CLASSIFICATION OF THEORIES	SPECIFIC THEORIES
1. Content-based theories—focus is on identifying and understanding people's needs.	**Hierarchy of needs**—people are motivated by five levels of needs: physiological, safety, social, esteem, and self-actualization (Maslow).
	ERG—people are motivated by three needs: existence, relatedness, and growth (Alderfer).
	Two-factor theory—motivator factors (higher-level needs) are more important than maintenance factors (lower-level needs) (Herzberg).
	Acquired needs—people are motivated by their need for achievement, power, and affiliation (McClelland).
2. Process-based theories—focus is on how people choose behaviors to fulfill their needs.	**Equity**—people are motivated when their perceived inputs equal outputs (Adams).
	Goal-setting—difficult but achievable goals motivate people (Locke).
	Expectancy—people are motivated when they believe they can accomplish the task and the rewards for doing so are worth the effort (Vroom).
	Types of Reinforcement
3. Reinforcement theory—focus is on consequences for behavior (Skinner).	**Positive reinforcement**—attractive consequences (rewards) for desirable performance encourage continued behavior.
	Avoidance—negative consequences for poor performance encourage continued desirable behavior.
	Extinction—withholding reinforcement for an undesirable behavior reduces or eliminates that behavior.
	Punishment—undesirable consequences (punishment) for undesirable behavior prevent the behavior.

Hierarchy of Needs

Abraham Maslow developed the hierarchy of needs in the 1940s.[7] The **hierarchy of needs theory** proposes that people are motivated by five levels of needs: physiological, safety, social, esteem, and self-actualization. Maslow operated under four major assumptions: (1) Only unmet needs motivate. (2) People's needs are arranged in order of importance (a hierarchy) going from basic to complex. (3) People will not be motivated to satisfy a higher-level need unless their lower-level needs have been at least minimally satisfied. (4) People have five types of needs, presented here in order of importance from lowest to highest.

hierarchy of needs theory
Proposes that people are motivated by the five levels of needs: physiological, safety, social, esteem, and self-actualization.

1. *Physiological needs.* Our primary or basic needs are air (we can't live without it), food, shelter, sex, and relief from, or avoidance of, pain.

2. *Safety needs.* Our safety and security is our next level of need.

3. *Social needs.* After we establish a safe and secure life, we look for love, friendship, acceptance, and affection. MLB player Ken Griffey Jr. elected to play in Cincinnati, where he was raised, for his father, even though it meant walking away from $40 to $50 million.[8]

4. *Esteem needs.* We then focus on ego, status, self-respect, recognition for our accomplishments, and a feeling of self-confidence and prestige. Yes, pro athletes get paid *very* well, but that doesn't preclude their wanting to achieve excellence on the playing field for the excellence itself.

5. *Self-actualization needs.* This is our highest level of needs—our need to develop our full potential. And we will go to *incredible* lengths to do this. (Think about the people who pursue extreme sports!)

USING THE HIERARCHY OF NEEDS. Dr. Maslow noted that enlightened managers who truly understand that people are the organization's most valuable assets are rare, and, unfortunately, this is still true today.[9] Most managers continue to focus on maximizing productivity from a "work harder" viewpoint rather than from a "how do we get to self-actualization"

TIMEOUT
Where in the hierarchy of needs are you at this time for a specific professional aspect of your life? For a specific aspect of a sport? Explain why you are at this level.

_____
_____
_____
_____
_____
_____

Exhibit 12-2   How Organizations Satisfy the Hierarchy of Needs

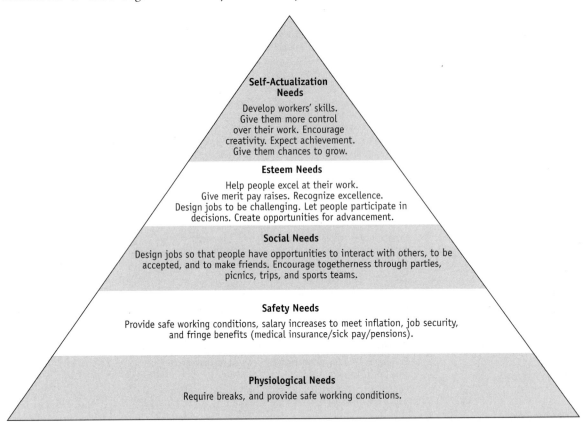

Self-Actualization Needs

Develop workers' skills. Give them more control over their work. Encourage creativity. Expect achievement. Give them chances to grow.

Esteem Needs

Help people excel at their work. Give merit pay raises. Recognize excellence. Design jobs to be challenging. Let people participate in decisions. Create opportunities for advancement.

Social Needs

Design jobs so that people have opportunities to interact with others, to be accepted, and to make friends. Encourage togetherness through parties, picnics, trips, and sports teams.

Safety Needs

Provide safe working conditions, salary increases to meet inflation, job security, and fringe benefits (medical insurance/sick pay/pensions).

Physiological Needs

Require breaks, and provide safe working conditions.

viewpoint. Interestingly, decades before self-directed teams became popular in the 1990s, Maslow called for them, because it is a straightforward way to meet self-actualization needs. Exhibit 12–2 lists ways in which managers attempt to meet these five needs.

ERG Theory

ERG theory
Proposes that people are motivated by three needs: existence, relatedness, and growth.

ERG is a well-known simplification of the hierarchy of needs. The **ERG theory** proposes that people are motivated by three needs: existence, relatedness, and growth. Clayton Alderfer reorganized Maslow's needs hierarchy into three needs: existence (physiological and safety needs), relatedness (social), and growth (esteem and self-actualization). He agreed with Maslow that unsatisfied needs motivate individuals, but disagreed that only one need level is active at a time.[10]

USING ERG THEORY. To use this theory, first determine which needs have been met and which ones have been frustrated. Then work on meeting the unsatisfied needs.

Two-Factor Theory

two-factor theory
Proposes that motivator factors, not maintenance factors, are what drive people to excel.

In the 1950s, Frederick Herzberg classified two sets of needs. Herzberg and his associates disagreed with the traditional view that satisfaction and dissatisfaction are at opposite ends of one continuum.[11] They proposed two continuums: One continuum is our satisfaction/dissatisfaction with the work environment; the other continuum is our satisfaction/dissatisfaction with the job itself. Herzberg called the first continuum the *maintenance* or *hygiene* factor (pay, job security, title, working conditions, fringe benefits, and relationships) and the second continuum the *motivator* factor (achievement, recognition, challenge, and advancement). In the **two-factor theory**, motivator factors, not maintenance factors, are what drive people to excel. (See Exhibit 12–3.) Maintenance factors are also called *extrinsic factors,*

Exhibit 12-3   Herzberg's Two-Factor Theory

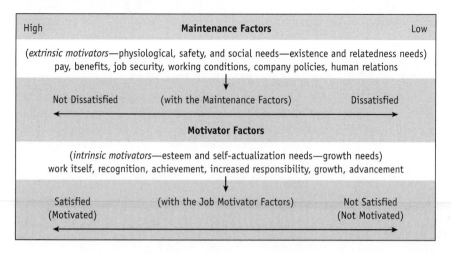

because they are outside the job itself. Motivators are thus *intrinsic factors,* because they derive from the work itself.

Herzberg contended that maintenance factors minimize or even prevent employee dissatisfaction, but they do not satisfy or motivate workers. Thus, dissatisfied employees who get a pay raise will, for a time, not fault their pay—they will be "*not* dissatisfied" for a while. Before long, however, they will grow accustomed to the new standard of living and dissatisfaction will creep back in. They will soon need another "hit" of money, which obviously cannot go on indefinitely. Something else must be operative in job satisfaction and in motivating people to excel. Herzberg's stance is that organizations must ensure that maintenance factors are adequate, but they do not have to go to excessive levels (in other words, maintenance needs to be only realistic and reasonable). Once employees are no longer dissatisfied with their environment, the intrinsic factors in their jobs will kick in and motivate them. The current view of money as a motivator is that, yes, money matters, but money does not in and of itself motivate people to work harder. Recall (Chapter 9) that people can experience *overall* job satisfaction without being satisfied with every determinant of job satisfaction, including that of pay.

Pro athletes are often very well paid today; many would argue that their compensation is excessive. In fact, to the consternation of their owners and managers, all too often athletes whose pay hits the stratosphere play flat the following season. Alex Rodriguez at $22 million a year doesn't need more money to motivate him. What will motivate him are such intrinsic factors as his reputation and the chance to win the World Series. The troubling issue facing pro sport organizations is not everybody gets to go to the "World Series" of their sport every year, yet lots of pro teams not only have superstar pay to justify to their shareholders, they also have restless superstars who are beyond motivating with mere pay. And fans are beginning to long for the days of lesser-paid stars who were not above signing autographs and paying attention to fans, who didn't get in trouble with the law, and who could even be held up as someone for their kids to aspire to be.

So, intrinsic factors loom large in the motivational equation. To motivate employees, make their jobs more interesting and challenging, give them more responsibility, provide them with opportunities for growth, and offer them recognition for a job well done. A recent study supports Herzberg's theory and concludes that enhanced and sustained job performance is directly related to the intrinsic factors that produce positive attitudes about the job.[12]

But let's focus on you for a moment. What motivates *you?* Take the Self Assessment on page 336 and find out.

USING THE TWO-FACTOR THEORY. This theory implies that the best way to motivate employees is to ensure that they are not dissatisfied with maintenance factors and then focus on motivator factors. This means building challenge and opportunity for achievement into

SELF ASSESSMENT

What Motivates You?

For the following 12 factors, rate how important each one is to you on a scale of 1 (not important) to 5 (very important).

_____ 1. An interesting job I enjoy doing

_____ 2. A good boss who treats people fairly

_____ 3. Getting praise, recognition, and appreciation for the work that I do

_____ 4. A satisfying personal life on the job

_____ 5. The opportunity for advancement

_____ 6. A prestigious or high-status job

_____ 7. A job that gives me freedom to do things my way

_____ 8. Good working conditions (safe environment, nice office, cafeteria, etc.)

_____ 9. The opportunity to learn new things

_____ 10. Sensible company rules, regulations, procedures, and policies

_____ 11. A job I can do well and can succeed at

_____ 12. Job security

Record your answers below and total each column.

Motivating Factors Score	Maintenance Factors Score
1. ___	2. ___
3. ___	4. ___
5. ___	6. ___
7. ___	8. ___
9. ___	10. ___
11. ___	12. ___
___ Total points	___

Are motivator factors or maintenance factors more important to you?

---

the job itself. Entrepreneurs often note that to stay motivated they find new challenges within their business.[13] Job enrichment (Chapter 6), one way to increase motivation, is increasingly being used today.[14] The job characteristics model (also in Chapter 6) has been shown to consistently predict outcomes such as internal work motivation, job involvement, and job satisfaction.[15]

Acquired Needs Theory

acquired needs theory Proposes that employees are motivated by their need for achievement, power, and affiliation.

The **acquired needs theory** proposes that employees are motivated by their need for achievement, power, and affiliation. Henry Murray developed the original general needs theory;[16] it was later adapted by John Atkinson and David McClelland (who developed a specific acquired needs theory).[17] We examine McClelland's work here. McClelland does not classify lower-level needs. His affiliation needs are the same as social and relatedness needs, and his power and achievement needs resemble esteem, self-actualization, and growth needs.

Unlike Maslow, McClelland believed that our personality determines our needs, which are further developed as we interact with our environment. All of us need some amount of achievement, power, and affiliation, just in varying degrees. One of the three needs tends to dominate in each of us and thus drives our behavior. (And this "feels" right—we all know nurturers, achievers, and perennial "captains.") Before we examine the three needs in detail, see which one is dominant in you by completing the Self Assessment on page 337.

THE NEED FOR ACHIEVEMENT (nAch). People with high nAch typically take personal responsibility for solving problems. They are goal oriented and set moderate, realistic, and attainable goals. They seek challenge and excellence, and choose the road less traveled (that is, they are often highly individualistic). They take calculated, moderate risk and desire concrete feedback on their performance. They are willing to work hard. High nAchs think about how they can do a better job, how they can accomplish something unusual or important, and how they can fast-forward their careers. They perform well in nonroutine, challenging, and competitive situations (in which low nAchs do not perform well).

McClelland's research showed that only about 10 percent of the U.S. population has a high dominant need for achievement. Evidence of a correlation exists between high achievement

---

TIMEOUT

List the maintenance and motivator factors in your current job or team and rate your level of dissatisfaction/satisfaction in each continuum. Give reasons for your rating.

_____

_____

_____

_____

_____

_____

need and high performance. High nAchs tend to enjoy sales and are often entrepreneurs. Managers tend to have high nAch, as do Olympic athletes.

Motivating high nAchs. Basically, don't get in their way—high nAchs motivate themselves! Assign them the nonroutine, challenging tasks that they crave. Give them frequent feedback on their performance. Increase their responsibility as they gain competence.

THE NEED FOR POWER (nPow). People with high nPow typically like to control situations. They want influence or control over others, they enjoy competition in which they can win (they do not like to lose), and they are willing to confront others. High nPows think about controlling situations and others, and seek positions of authority and status. They tend to have a low need for affiliation. Managers often have high nPow, as of course do CEOs and owners of pro sport teams.

Motivating high nPows. Let high nPows plan and control their jobs as much as possible. Try to include them in decision making, especially when the decision affects them. They tend to perform best alone rather than as team members. Try to assign them to a whole task rather than just part of a task.

THE NEED FOR AFFILIATION (nAff). People with high nAff seek close relationships with others. They very much want to be liked. They enjoy social activities and endeavor to fit in. They join groups and organizations. High nAffs think in terms of friends and relationships. They enjoy developing, helping, and teaching others. They derive satisfaction from working with the group rather than from the task itself. They typically have low nPow. They also tend to avoid management because they like to be "one of the regular folks"—they have no desire to be the group's leader.

High nAffs often work in human resources. Effective teams typically have a good number of high nAffs. Think about great sport teams. Very often the "heart" of these teams are "nonstar" players who are every bit as important as the stars. The nonstars are easy to get along

---

SELF ASSESSMENT

Which Acquired Need Drives You?

For the following 15 statements, rate how similar each one is to you on a scale of 1 (not like me) to 5 (very much like me).

_____ 1. I enjoy working hard.

_____ 2. I like to compete, and I like to win.

_____ 3. I take good care of my friends.

_____ 4. I don't shrink from difficult challenges.

_____ 5. I usually end up deciding which movie or restaurant we'll go to.

_____ 6. I want other people to really like me.

_____ 7. I check on how I'm progressing as I complete tasks.

_____ 8. I confront people who do things I disagree with.

_____ 9. I love parties.

_____ 10. I go to great lengths to set and achieve realistic goals.

_____ 11. I try to influence other people to get my way.

_____ 12. I belong to lots of groups/organizations.

_____ 13. The satisfaction of completing a difficult task is as good as life gets.

_____ 14. I take charge when a group I'm in is floundering.

_____ 15. I prefer to work with others rather than alone.

Enter your scores from above here and total each column. The column with the highest score is your dominant or primary need.

Achievement	Power	Affiliation
___ 1.	___ 2.	___ 3.
___ 4.	___ 5.	___ 6.
___ 7.	___ 8.	___ 9.
___ 10.	___ 11.	___ 12.
___ 13.	___ 14.	___ 15.
___	___	___ Totals

with, take good care of fans, and are willing to play numerous positions—they are the glue that makes the team a team. They are role players, and they emphasize their nAff, even though they obviously are pretty high nAch—or else they wouldn't be pro athletes.

Motivating high nAffs. You want these people on your team, because they will make your team effective. So make sure they are assigned to teams. Praise them and value them. Assign them the tasks of orienting and training new employees. They make great mentors. (Just remember, when you are assembling a team with too many nAchs, it can cause the team to be ineffective because teams need a certain amount of conflict in order to avoid groupthink and to be creative.)

Exhibit 12–4 compares the four content-based theories of motivation.

 LEARNING OUTCOME
4 Discuss the three process-based motivation theories.

PROCESS-BASED MOTIVATION THEORIES

process-based motivation theories
Focus on understanding how employees choose behavior to fulfill their needs.

Process-based motivation theories focus on understanding how employees choose behavior to fulfill their needs. Process-based theories are more complex than content-based theories. Content-based theories simply identify and then endeavor to understand our needs. Process-based theories go a step further and try to understand

- why we have different needs;
- why our needs change;
- how and why we choose to satisfy needs in different ways;
- the mental process we go through as we understand situations; and
- how we evaluate how well we are satisfying our needs.

Equity Theory

equity theory
Proposes that employees are motivated when their perceived inputs equal outputs.

Equity theory, primarily J. Stacy Adams's motivation theory, proposes that we seek social equity in the rewards we receive (output) for our performance (input).[18] **Equity theory** proposes that employees are motivated when their perceived inputs equal outputs. A knowledge of equity theory thus gives us insights into future behavior.

According to equity theory, all of us compare our inputs (effort, experience, seniority, status, intelligence, etc.) and outputs (praise, recognition, pay, benefits, promotions, increased status, supervisor's approval, etc.) to that of relevant others. A relevant other may be a coworker or group of employees from the same or different organization, or even from a hypothetical situation. Notice that the definition above says *perceived,* and not *actual,* in the comparison of inputs to outputs. Equity may actually exist. However, if we *believe* inequity

Exhibit 12–4   A Comparison of Content-Based Motivation Theories

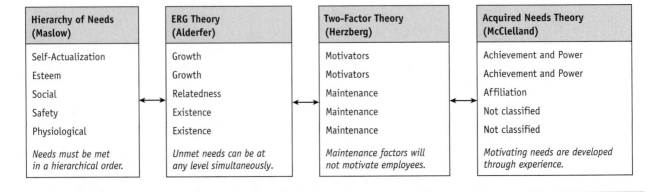

Hierarchy of Needs (Maslow)	ERG Theory (Alderfer)	Two-Factor Theory (Herzberg)	Acquired Needs Theory (McClelland)
Self-Actualization	Growth	Motivators	Achievement and Power
Esteem	Growth	Motivators	Achievement and Power
Social	Relatedness	Maintenance	Affiliation
Safety	Existence	Maintenance	Not classified
Physiological	Existence	Maintenance	Not classified
Needs must be met in a hierarchical order.	*Unmet needs can be at any level simultaneously.*	*Maintenance factors will not motivate employees.*	*Motivating needs are developed through experience.*

exists, we will change our behavior to create perceived equity. That is, we need to *perceive* that we are being treated fairly, relative to others.

Unfortunately, many of us tend to inflate our own efforts and performance when we compare ourselves to others. We also tend to overestimate what others earn. We may be very satisfied and motivated until we find out that a relevant other earns more for the same job or earns the same for less work. When we perceive inequity, we may try to reduce it by reducing input or by increasing output. A comparison with relevant others leads to three conclusions: We are underrewarded, overrewarded, or equitably rewarded.

1. *Underrewarded.* When we perceive that we are underrewarded, we may try to reduce the inequity by

   - increasing outputs (getting a raise);

   - reducing inputs (doing less work, absenteeism, long breaks, etc.);

   - rationalizing (finding a logical explanation for inequity);

   - changing others' inputs or outputs (getting them to do more or get less); or

   - leaving the situation (transferring or leaving for a better job) or changing the object of comparison (to a relevant other who makes less).

One reason Tennessee Titans management rewarded Jevon Kearse with an incentive-laden contract was to demonstrate the club felt he was underpaid compared to similar NFL players. Titans management chose to reward Jevon with an equitable contract in order to help negotiations with his future contracts.[19]

2. *Overrewarded.* Being overrewarded rarely disturbs most of us. However, research suggests that we may reduce perceived inequity by

   - increasing input (working harder or longer);

   - reducing output (taking a pay cut);

   - rationalizing (I'm worth it); or

   - trying to increase others' output (giving them the same as me).

Some pro athletes negotiate extremely lucrative contracts that suddenly become hard to fulfill because of injury, age, or declining skills. The athlete may still be motivated to excel, but physical ability no longer warrants his or her compensation. Management has to accept the responsibility of the large contract and find alternate methods to make the team competitive.

3. *Equitably rewarded.* Inputs and outputs are perceived as being equal; motivation exists. We may even believe that relevant others should have greater outputs if they have more experience, education, or skills.

MOTIVATING WITH EQUITY THEORY. Research supporting equity theory is mixed. One view proposes that equity theory parallels Herzberg's maintenance factors. When we are *not dis*satisfied, we are not actively motivated, but maintenance factors work against our motivation when we are dissatisfied. Thus, in equity theory, when we believe we are equitably rewarded, we are not actively motivated. However, when we believe we are underrewarded, our motivation suffers a hit.

Using equity theory in practice can be difficult, because you as a manager don't necessarily know the employee's reference group nor do you know his or her view of inputs and outcomes. However, equity theory does offer some useful general recommendations:

1. Be aware that equity is based on perception, which may not be correct. Managers sometimes create equity and inequity by favoring certain workers.

2. Go to great lengths to make rewards equitable. When employees perceive that they are not treated fairly, morale and performance suffer. Employees who produce at the same level should be given equal rewards.

3. Reward excellence. Make sure employees understand the inputs needed to attain certain outputs.[20] When using incentive pay, clearly specify the exact requirements needed to achieve the incentive. You should be able to objectively justify to others why one person got a higher merit raise.

Goal-Setting Theory

goal-setting theory
Proposes that achievable but difficult goals motivate employees.

Goal-setting theory is currently one of the most valid approaches to work motivation.[21] It complements Herzberg's and McClelland's theories because goals lead to higher levels of motivation and performance.[22] Goals challenge people; thus, high nAchs thrive in goal-setting situations.[23] **Goal-setting theory** proposes that achievable but difficult goals motivate employees. (Chapter 4 examined management by objectives (MBO) in detail.) The idea behind goal setting is that behavior has purpose—to fulfill needs. Goals help us marshal our resources to accomplish a given task. Setting goals helps us identify ways we can meet our needs, and attaining objectives reinforces effective behavior. Work expands to fill the time available for its completion. When we set difficult but achievable goals with reasonable deadlines (but that don't have much "slop"), we work efficiently and effectively in order to complete the task in the allotted time.

MOTIVATING WITH GOAL SETTING. Lou Holtz, coach of Notre Dame's 1988 championship football team, noted a "circular key ring" with three keys to success: a winning attitude, positive self-esteem, and high goals.[24] Winning attitudes lead to positive self-esteem, which in turn motivates us to set high goals, which in turn gives us an even more positive attitude and self-esteem. Every year Holtz had players set personal goals and the team set team goals, which he wrote in his notebook. All good performance starts with clear goals. When setting objectives, be sure that they are challenging, achievable, specific, measurable, have a target date for accomplishment, and are jointly set when possible (see Chapter 4 for details). However, remember that setting goals is not enough. You also need action plans (Chapter 5) to achieve the goals and measure progress.

Expectancy Theory

expectancy theory
Proposes that employees are motivated when they believe they can accomplish the task and the rewards for doing so are worth the effort.

Expectancy theory is based on Victor Vroom's equation:[25]

$$\text{Motivation} = \text{Expectancy} \times \text{Valence}$$

Expectancy theory proposes that employees are motivated when they believe they can accomplish the task and the rewards for doing so are worth the effort. This theory assumes the following: (1) Both internal (needs) and external (environment) factors affect our behavior. (2) Behavior is the individual's decision. (3) We have different needs, desires, and goals. And (4) we decide to pursue certain behaviors based on our perception of the outcome.

Two important variables, expectancy and valence, must be met for people to be motivated.

- *Expectancy* is our perception of our ability to accomplish an objective (that is, the probability that we will succeed). Generally, the higher our expectancy, the better our chances for motivation. When we don't believe we can accomplish objectives, we stop trying. Also important is our perception of the relationship between performance and the outcome or reward (called *instrumentality*). Generally, the higher our expectancy of attaining the outcome or reward, the higher our motivation.

- *Valence* is the value we place on the outcome or reward—that is, its importance. Generally, the higher we value the outcome or reward, the higher our motivation. If we don't value the reward, we are less likely to work hard for it.

MOTIVATING WITH EXPECTANCY THEORY. Expectancy theory accurately predicts work effort, satisfaction, and performance, but only if correct values are plugged into the equation. Obviously, coming up with correct values is difficult to do, since you as a manager can't go around measuring people's expectancy and valences all the time. Therefore, this theory works in certain contexts but not in others. However, the theory's implications are easy to put in place. Thus, people are motivated when

1. Objectives are clearly defined and they are doable.[26]

2. Performance is tied to rewards and high performance is rewarded.

3. Rewards have value to the employee. (It thus behooves you to know what makes workers or players on your team tick.)

4. Employees believe that you walk your talk. (As we have noted numerous times, trust is everything.)

TIMEOUT
Give an example of how your perception of equity or inequity affected your motivation and performance at your current job or team. Were you under-, over-, or equitably rewarded?

———————
———————
———————
———————
———————
———————

TIMEOUT
Give an example of how a goal affected your motivation and performance or that of someone with whom you work or play.

———————
———————
———————
———————
———————
———————

REINFORCEMENT THEORY

5 LEARNING OUTCOME
Discuss reinforcement theory.

B. F. Skinner, the famed psychologist and influential theorist of behaviorism, contended that to motivate people we don't need to identify and understand their needs (content theories) or understand how they choose behaviors to fulfill them (process theories). Instead, we must understand the relationship between behavior and consequence and then arrange contingencies that reinforce desirable behaviors and discourage undesirable ones. **Reinforcement theory** proposes that consequences for behavior cause people to behave in predetermined ways. The idea behind reinforcement then is that we learn what is, and is not, desired behavior as a result of consequences for our behavior. Because behavior is learned through experiences of positive and negative consequences, Skinner proposed three components.[27]

reinforcement theory
Proposes that consequences for behavior cause people to behave in predetermined ways.

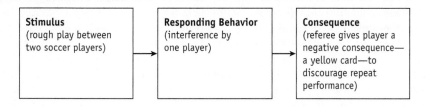

Different types of reinforcement done on schedules (operant conditioning) are used to modify behavior.

6 LEARNING OUTCOME
Compare content, process, and reinforcement theories.

Types of Reinforcement

POSITIVE REINFORCEMENT. This is a powerful way to attain desired behaviors. Basically, desired behaviors are encouraged, and negative ones are ignored. Attractive consequences (rewards) are thus offered for desirable performance. Here's a simple example: A habitually late employee arrives on time for a meeting and is rewarded with thanks. The praise reinforces punctuality. Other reinforcements include pay raises, promotions, time off, increased status—the list is endless. Positive reinforcement is an excellent way to increase productivity, and positive incentives are therefore routinely used today to motivate individuals, teams, and whole divisions.[28,29] Giving recognition for a job well done is another effective positive reinforcement that costs only your time. Giving players a day off from practice after a well-played game can also be an effective, no-cost positive reinforcement. Offering incentives is thus positive reinforcement. It is also a proven way of increasing motivation, as previously mentioned. NFL player Jevon Kearse signed a revised contract full of incentives to keep him performing in the last year of his multiyear contract. In Kearse's contract, different levels of incentives are triggered at different numbers of sacks. The incentives are also based on playing time, interceptions, fumble returns, Pro Bowl selection, the defensive player of the year award, and the Super Bowl MVP award. Jevon could earn between $1 and $2 million extra in the 2002 season if he achieves his incentives.[30]

NEGATIVE REINFORCEMENT. This is the flip side of positive reinforcement. There are three types of negative reinforcement.

■ *Avoidance* works because we all prefer to avoid negative consequences. With avoidance there is no actual punishment; it's the *threat* of negative consequences that controls our behavior. Habitually late employees see that their being late causes them to miss receiving some key data, and they think twice about being late in the future. Standing plans, especially rules, are designed to get us to avoid certain behavior. We don't break the rules because we don't want to get injured on the job or burn the building down.

TIMEOUT
Give an example of how your expectancy has affected your motivation at your job or team. Specify your expectancy and valence.

_____

_____

_____

_____

_____

_____

- *Extinction* attempts to reduce or eliminate an undesirable behavior by withholding reinforcement when the behavior occurs. The late employee is thus ignored rather than praised or reprimanded. Or you withhold a reward of value, a pay raise, until the employee performs to set standards. Managers can also inadvertently extinguish good performance if they do not reward it (that is, praise it, acknowledge it, or reward it).

- *Punishment* is an undesirable consequence and can thus be used to change undesirable behavior. So, rather than thanking the employee for being on time, the person is reprimanded for being late. The employee's desire to avoid the humiliation will cause him or her to be on time in the future. Punishments are legion—historically we humans have been very good at punishing—and include taking away privileges, probation, fining, demoting, and firing, to name but a few.

A few more words about punishment are in order here. Punishment is the least effective way to motivate people.[31] Why? There are several reasons. We get inured to punishment (weird, but true!). Punishment can also *cause* other undesirable behaviors, such as lowered productivity (because of resentment or poor morale) and theft or sabotage. One study found that athletes with high intrinsic (internal) motivation felt their coaches provided a higher amount of positive feedback and a lower amount of punishment and avoidance reinforcements.[32] However, **PAT SUMMITT** yells at her players, which is normally a form of punishment. However, in her case players understand it is her method of motivating players. A more typical form of punishment is what happened to Carl Everett. For being late to team buses and for arguing with the Boston Red Sox manager, the club punished Everett by ordering him to miss games and docking his pay. Unfortunately, the punishment did not change Everett's behavior; he continued to be a detriment to team morale, and he was eventually traded.[33] Exhibit 12–5 illustrates the four types of reinforcement. **Visit http://www.coachsummitt.com. Do you believe the pictures on her web site show a coach motivating or punishing her players?**

YOU GET WHAT YOU REINFORCE. Remember that employees will do what they are rewarded for doing. If managers say quality is important, but employees who do quality work are not rewarded, and nothing happens to employees (extinction or punishment) who do not do quality work, employees will not be motivated to continue to do quality work. If a professor tells students to read this book but does not test students on the book (reward or punishment based on test performance)—i.e., test questions come only from lectures—what percentage of students do you think will read and study this book versus those who will simply take notes and study them for exams?

Schedules of Reinforcement

The second consideration in modifying behavior is *when* to reinforce it. Behaviorists have developed two schedules: continuous reinforcement and intermittent reinforcement.

TIMEOUT
Illustrate the four types of reinforcements with examples from your current job or team.

_____
_____
_____
_____
_____
_____

Exhibit 12–5   Types of Reinforcement

As a manager, you have an employee who makes many errors when doing the finishing work on an expensive set of golf clubs. Your objective, which you discussed with the employee, is to decrease the error rate. There are four types of reinforcement you can use with the employee when you next review the work.

Employee Behavior	Type of Reinforcement	Manager Action (Consequence)	Employee Behavior Modification (Future)
Improved performance	Positive	Praise improvements	Repeat quality work*
Improved performance	Avoidance	Do not give any reprimand	Repeat quality work
Performance not improved	Extinction	Withhold praise/raise	Do not repeat poor work
Performance not improved	Punishment	Discipline action, i.e., written warning	Do not repeat poor work

*Assuming the employee improved performance, positive reinforcement is the best motivator.

- *Continuous reinforcement.* With continuous schedules, each and every instance of the desired behavior is reinforced. Thus, machines with automatic counters that let the workers know, at any given moment, exactly how many units have been produced function as continuous reinforcement, as would managers who comment on every customer report.

- *Intermittent reinforcement.* Intermittent schedules are of two types. Time-based schedules are called *interval* schedules. Output-based schedules are called *ratio* schedules. Ratio schedules are generally better motivators than interval schedules. Either type can then use a fixed interval or ratio or a variable interval or ratio.

TIMEOUT

Give examples of behavior at your current job or team that was modified by reinforcement. State the type of reinforcement used and the schedule used.

_____

_____

_____

_____

_____

_____

Motivating with Reinforcement

Positive reinforcement is by every measure the best all-around motivator.[34] Here are some general guidelines:

1. Make sure people know exactly what is expected of them.[35] Set clear objectives.

2. Select appropriate rewards. A reward to one person may be a punishment to another. Know your employees' needs.

3. Use an appropriate reinforcement schedule. (For example, continual praise doesn't sound genuine and is both smothering and patronizing.)

4. Do not reward mediocre or poor performance.

5. Look for the positive and praise it; don't focus on the negative and on criticizing. Use the Pygmalion effect—make people feel good about themselves.

6. Make sure your praise is genuine and generously given—don't be miserly with your praise.

7. Do things *for* your employees, not *to* them.

As a manager, positive reinforcement should be your reinforcement of choice. Positive reinforcement creates win-win situations by meeting both employees' and the organization's needs. Avoidance and punishment create lose-win situations for employees. The organization/manager may "win" initially by forcing people to do something they really don't want to do but ultimately loses if highly skilled and trained people quit.

Reinforcement for Attendance and Punctuality

The traditional method used to get employees to come to work and to be on time is avoidance and punishment. If employees miss a specific number of days, they don't get paid. If an employee is late, the time card indicates this, and the employee receives punishment. Many managers today use positive reinforcement by offering employees rewards for coming to work and being on time.

A popular technique used by many organizations, which reduces the problem of being late for work, is *flextime.* Flextime allows employees to determine when they start and end work, provided they work their full number of hours, with certain restrictions on working hours. A typical schedule permits employees to begin work between 6:00 and 9:00 A.M. and to complete their work day between 3:00 and 6:00 P.M. Flextime helps meet the goal of good human relations because it allows employees to schedule their time to accommodate their personal needs and job requirements.

Praise

In the 1940s, Lawrence Lindahl's research revealed that what people want most from their job is full appreciation for their work. Similar studies performed over the years confirm this.[36] Praise develops positive self-esteem and leads to better performance—the Pygmalion effect and self-fulfilling prophecy rolled into one tidy package. Praise motivates because it meets employees' needs for esteem/self-actualization, growth, and achievement. Giving praise creates win-win situations. It is probably the most powerful, most simple, least costly, and yet most underused motivational technique.

Model 12–1   Giving Praise

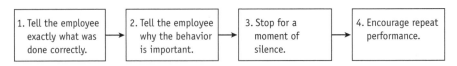

1. Tell the employee exactly what was done correctly.	→	2. Tell the employee why the behavior is important.	→	3. Stop for a moment of silence.	→	4. Encourage repeat performance.

Ken Blanchard and Spencer Johnson popularized praise through their best-selling book *The One-Minute Manager*. They show how to give one-minute feedback of praise. Model 12–1 adapts their method.

1. *Tell the employee exactly what was done correctly.* Be sincere; look the person in the eye. (Eye contact shows sincerity and concern.) Be specific and descriptive. General statements such as "you're a good worker" are not as effective. On the other hand, don't talk for too long, or the praise loses impact.

   Jose: "Al, I just watched you deal with that in-your-face reporter. Great job! You kept your cool; you were polite. That reporter came to the game angry and left happy."

APPLYING
THE CONCEPT   *Motivation Theories*

Identify the theory behind each statement.

a. hierarchy of needs	**d.** acquired needs	**g.** expectancy
b. ERG theory	**e.** equity	**h.** reinforcement
c. two-factor	**f.** goal-setting	

_____ 11. I make sure every job in our racquet stores is interesting and challenging.

_____ 12. I treat everyone in our sporting goods store fairly.

_____ 13. I know Kate likes people, so I give her jobs in which she works with other employees.

_____ 14. Carl yelled at umpires because he knew it bothered me. So I decided to ignore his yelling, and he stopped.

_____ 15. I know my employees, what they like to do, and what about work excites them. And I know what sorts of rewards light a fire under their performance.

_____ 16. Our sporting goods company now offers good working conditions, salaries, and benefits, so we are working at developing employee camaraderie by having TGIF parties at 4:00.

_____ 17. Whenever my staff at the fitness center does a good job, I thank them.

_____ 18. I used to try to improve working conditions to motivate my staff. But I now focus on giving people more responsibility so they can grow and develop new skills.

_____ 19. I realize I tend to be autocratic because this fills my needs. I'm working at giving the team that makes baseball gloves more autonomy.

_____ 20. I focus on three needs and realize that needs can be unmet at more than one level at a time.

2. *Tell the employee why the behavior is important.* State (briefly) how every-one benefits from the action. Also, tell the employee how you feel about the behavior. Be specific and descriptive.

> *Jose:* "Without reporters, we don't reach our fans. But one dissatisfied reporter can cost us thousands of dollars in lost sales. It really made me proud to see you handle that tough situation the way you did."

3. *Stop for a moment of silence.* Being silent is tough for many managers.[37] The rationale for the silence is to give the employee the chance to feel the impact of the praise. Think of this as "the pause that refreshes." When you are thirsty and take the first sip/gulp of a refreshing drink, it's not until you stop and say "ah" that you feel your thirst being quenched.

> (Jose silently counts to five.)

4. *Encourage repeat performance.* This reinforcement motivates the person to continue the desired behavior. Blanchard recommends touching the employee. Touching has a powerful impact. However, he recommends it only if both parties feel comfortable. Others say don't touch employees; it has too many other connotations and is dicey in this era of sexual harassment litigation.

> *Jose:* "Thanks, Al, keep up the good work" (while touching him on the shoulder or shaking hands).

As you can see, giving praise is easy, and it doesn't cost a penny. Managers who give praise genuinely and generously say it works wonders. It is also a much better motivator than raises or other monetary rewards. One manager stated that an employee was taking his time stacking tennis-ball cans on a display. He gave the employee praise for stacking the tennis-ball cans so straight. The employee was so pleased with the praise that the display went up about 100 percent faster. Note that the manager looked for the positive and used posi-tive reinforcement rather than punishment. The manager could have given a reprimand comment such as "quit goofing off and get the job done." That statement would not have motivated the employee to increase productivity. All it would have done was hurt human relations and could have ended in an argument. The cans were straight. The employee was not rebuked for the slow work pace. However, had the praise not worked, the manager could have then used another reinforcement method.[38]

PUTTING THEORY TO WORK

The motivation theories we've been discussing are important because they help us under-stand why people behave the way they do.[39] At this point, you're probably wondering, Do these theories fit together? Is one best? Or should I try to pick and choose for particular sit-uations? (The answers are Sort Of, No, and Yes.)

Yes, the theories "sort of" fit together in that they complement each other. That is, each cat-egory of theories focuses on a different stage in the motivation process. So they answer dif-ferent questions. Content-based theories address *what* needs do people have that should be met on the job? Process-based theories address *how* do people choose behavior to fulfill their needs? Reinforcement theory addresses *what* can I do to change undesirable behavior?

Earlier in this chapter, we discussed how the motivation process progresses from need to motive to behavior to consequence and then to satisfaction or dissatisfaction. The motiva-tion theories help us see the motivation process as a more nuanced process, as shown in Exhibit 12–6. Note the step-4-to-step-3 loop-back that occurs because behavior is learned through consequences (behavior modification). The final step-5-to-step-1 loop-back is always a given because meeting our needs is a never-ending process. Finally, step 5 is actu-ally two separate continuums (satisfied/not satisfied or dissatisfied/not dissatisfied), based on the need factor being met (motivator or maintenance).

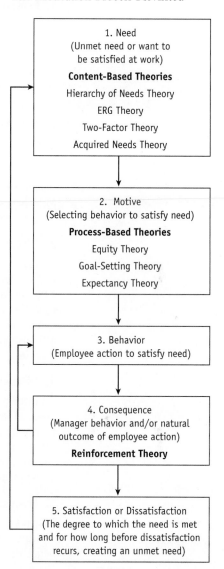

Exhibit 12–6
The Motivation Process Revisited

1. Need
(Unmet need or want to be satisfied at work)
Content-Based Theories
Hierarchy of Needs Theory
ERG Theory
Two-Factor Theory
Acquired Needs Theory

2. Motive
(Selecting behavior to satisfy need)
Process-Based Theories
Equity Theory
Goal-Setting Theory
Expectancy Theory

3. Behavior
(Employee action to satisfy need)

4. Consequence
(Manager behavior and/or natural outcome of employee action)
Reinforcement Theory

5. Satisfaction or Dissatisfaction
(The degree to which the need is met and for how long before dissatisfaction recurs, creating an unmet need)

CHAPTER SUMMARY

1. Explain how motivation works.

People go through a five-step process to meet their needs. This is a circular process because needs recur.

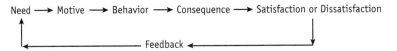

Need → Motive → Behavior → Consequence → Satisfaction or Dissatisfaction ← Feedback

2. Use the performance equation.

The performance equation states that

Performance = Ability × Motivation × Resources

If any one of these components is weak, performance is negatively affected. When performance stumbles, managers need to determine which component of the equation is causing performance to suffer and take action to correct the problem.

3. Discuss the four content-based motivation theories.

All four content theories identify and then seek to understand people's needs. They identify similar needs but differ in the classification of needs. Hierarchy of needs theory classifies needs as physiological, safety, social, esteem, and self-actualization. ERG theory classifies them as existence, relatedness, and growth. Two-factor theory lists motivator factors and maintenance factors. Acquired needs theory uses achievement, power, and affiliation needs. (See Exhibits 12–1 and 12–4 for a comparison of the four content-based theories.)

4. Discuss the three process-based motivation theories.

All three process theories seek to understand how people choose behaviors to fulfill their needs. The process theories differ in their explanations of what motivates people. Equity theory proposes that the perception of inputs equaling outputs motivates people. Goal-setting theory proposes that achievable but difficult goals are the driving factor in motivation. Expectancy theory proposes that motivation occurs when people believe they can accomplish the task and when the rewards for doing so are worth the effort.

5. Discuss reinforcement theory.

Positive reinforcement rewards the person for performing the desired behavior. Avoidance reinforcement encourages the person to perform the desired behavior in order to avoid a negative consequence. Extinction reinforcement withholds a positive consequence to get the person to stop the undesirable behavior. Punishment reinforcement gives the person a direct negative consequence to get him or her to stop the undesirable behavior.

6. Compare content, process, and reinforcement theories.

Content-based theories focus on identifying and understanding employees' needs. Process-based theories seek to understand how people choose behavior to fulfill their needs. Reinforcement theory is not concerned with need; it focuses on getting people to desirable behavior through consequences and reinforcement.

7. Define the key terms discussed in the text.

Fill in the missing key terms from memory or match the key terms from the list in the margin with their definitions below.

_____ is the willingness to achieve organizational objectives.

Through the _____, people go from need to motive to behavior to consequence and finally to either satisfaction or dissatisfaction.

Key Terms

acquired needs theory

content-based
   motivation theories

equity theory

ERG theory

expectancy theory

goal-setting theory

hierarchy of needs
   theory

motivation

motivation process

performance equation

process-based
   motivation theories

reinforcement theory

two-factor theory

The _____: Performance = Ability × Motivation × Resources.

_____ focus on identifying and understanding people's needs.

The _____ proposes that people are motivated by five levels of needs: physiological, safety, social, esteem, and self-actualization.

The _____ proposes that people are motivated by three needs: existence, relatedness, and growth.

In the _____, motivator factors, not maintenance factors, are what drive people to excel.

The _____ proposes that employees are motivated by their need for achievement, power, and affiliation.

_____ focus on understanding how employees choose behavior to fulfill their needs.

_____ proposes that employees are motivated when their perceived inputs equal outputs.

_____ proposes that achievable but difficult goals motivate employees.

_____ proposes that employees are motivated when they believe they can accomplish the task and the rewards for doing so are worth the effort.

_____ proposes that consequences for behavior cause people to behave in predetermined ways.

REVIEW AND DISCUSSION

1. What is motivation and why is it important to know how to motivate employees?
2. Do managers' attitudes and expectations affect employee motivation and performance? Explain your answer.
3. Do you agree with the performance equation? Will you use it on the job?
4. Do people really have diverse needs?
5. Apply Maslow's hierarchy of needs to a sport organization you are familiar with.
6. Which of the three process-based motivation theories do you prefer? Why?
7. What reinforcements have been used to get you to go to work and to be on time?
8. True or false: Reinforcement theory is unethical because it is used to manipulate employees. Explain your reasoning.
9. What athletes do you know who have been punished as a way to discourage a certain behavior? What was their punishment?
10. Which motivation theory do you plan to use on your job or as a coach? If you plan to use a "hybrid," explain which parts of which theories you will emphasize.

CASE

Living His Passion

Few of us are fortunate enough to build our lives around a passion. John Amaral is one of these fortunate few. His passions are teaching and soccer, and they dovetail neatly. A professional soccer player from 1977 to 1979, John is involved with soccer at all levels—youth, high school, college, and professional leagues. His youth soccer experience goes back 30 years, when he first coached in Texas, which is where he looked into the future and saw the answer. The future lay in the hands of the moms. Moms loved the safety of soccer. Moms loved the conditioning of soccer. Moms put in the time to bring their kids to this "new" sport (new to American families back then). Soccer would thrive because of moms.

And thrive it has—in California, in Washington, in Texas, and, in fact, all over the country. In John's opinion, Texas fields the best tournaments in the country today. John's involvement in soccer has grown as the sport has grown. Today he scouts high school players for both college and professional soccer teams. He mentors high school kids whom he believes have the talent to play at higher levels. This has been particularly rewarding. One of John's "kids" now plays professionally, and John is his trusted agent. John believes the key to a player's success is not ability—it's the motivation to succeed. Even if players play for a small school, they can still be noticed by scouts if they are motivated.

John also coaches men's soccer at Elms College in Chicopee, Massachusetts. He focuses on the self-esteem of each of his players, both on the field and off. Rule number one: His players do *not* neglect academics. He asks professors to contact him immediately if any of his players have problems in the classroom. He teaches players to not allow people to take advantage of them whether they are on or off the field. In return, student athletes need to exhibit good sports conduct and high levels of motivation both on and off the field. When coaching collegiate-level players, John focuses on their personal growth. He tries to build self-esteem (i.e., reaching personal and team goals, playing challenging teams, and trying to fulfill the opportunity to play for professional leagues), because his team consists of young men who are preparing for careers in and out of soccer.

It is interesting to watch John with his players. They love following his lead and are truly motivated to play for him. Why? He helps them grow as individuals. He is fair and distributes rewards equally to all players who deserve recognition. In summary, he uses positive reinforcement.

In past summers, John has coached a women's pro soccer team, the Springfield Sirens of the USL (United Soccer League). He uses the same principles as he does at the collegiate level. He expects his players to give the game everything they have in every game. John told one young woman that more men's teams could use her tenacity, fire, and leadership. Unfortunately, the Sirens did not play in the 2001–2002 season for financial reasons, but John expects to coach the team again in the 2002–2003 season.[40]

For more information on John Amaral and his college team, please visit http://www.elms.edu/campus/athletics/mensoc.htm#coach.

CASE QUESTIONS

1. John focuses on motivation and performance.
   a. true   b. false

2. John focuses on which factor in the performance equation?
   a. ability
   b. motivation
   c. resources

3. John's collegiate players appear to be on which level in the hierarchy of needs?
   a. physiological
   b. safety
   c. social
   d. esteem
   e. self-actualization

4. John focuses on which level of ERG needs with his college players?
   a. existence   c. growth
   b. relatedness

5. John's approach has less emphasis on meeting which need?
   a. achievement   c. affiliation
   b. power

6. Herzberg would say John is using
   a. maintenance   b. motivators

7. Vroom would agree that John uses expectancy motivation theory.
   a. true   b. false

8. Adams would say John offers
   a. equitable rewards
   b. underrewards
   c. overrewards

9. John uses goal-setting theory.
   a. true   b. false

10. John uses which types of reinforcement?
    a. positive   c. extinction
    b. avoidance   d. punishment

11. What type of motivation do you think John uses with his players? Do you know any sport organizations that use John's motivating techniques?

12. In a position of authority, would you use John's motivational style? Explain your answer.

13. Could John's technique work in all organizations? Explain your answer.

EXERCISES

Skill-Builder: Giving Praise

Objective:
- To hone your ability to praise.

Preparation:
Think of a situation in which you did something well in a sport, deserving of praise and recognition—you made a great save in a game, you turned an unhappy teammate into a happy one, and so on. Put yourself in your coach's position and write the praise you would give yourself.

- Briefly describe the situation.

_____

_____

_____

_____

1. Tell exactly what you did correctly.

_____

_____

_____

_____

2. Tell why your behavior was important.

_____

_____

_____

_____

3. Stop for a moment of silence. (Count to five silently.)

4. Encourage your repeat performance.

_____

_____

_____

_____

In-Class Application

Complete the skill-building preparation noted above before class. Break into groups of three to five members and take turns giving your praise to a member of the group.

1. Explain the situation.

2. Give the praise as you would in real life. (*Do not* read it off your paper.)

3. Group feedback:

   ■ Was the praise specific and descriptive? Did the giver look the getter of the praise in the eye?
   ■ Was the importance of the behavior clearly stated?
   ■ Did the giver stop for a moment of silence?
   ■ Did the giver encourage repeat performance?
   ■ Did the giver of praise touch the receiver (optional)?
   ■ Did the praise take less than one minute? Did the praise look sincere?

Wrap-up:
Take a few minutes and write down your answers to the following questions:

■ What did I learn from this experience?

_____

_____

_____

■ How will I use this knowledge in the future?

_____

_____

_____

As a class, discuss student responses.

Internet Skills: Motivating Pat Riley–Style

Objective:
   ■ To see how other coaches motivate their players.

Preparation (20 minutes):
Visit the web site http://speakers.com/riley.html. Search the site and answer the following questions.

1. What two management positions does Pat Riley hold with the NBA's Miami Heats?

_____

_____

2. Why has Riley earned the title "America's Greatest Motivational Speaker"?

_____

_____

_____

_____

3. What does Riley base his philosophy on?

_____

_____

_____

_____

4. Which of the theories discussed in this chapter do you think Riley uses most?

_____

_____

5. Which theories do you think he uses least?

_____

_____

13 Leading to Victory

Learning Outcomes

After studying this chapter, you should be able to:

1. Explain why managers are not always leaders.

2. Compare the trait, behavioral, and contingency theories of leadership.

3. Explain leadership trait theory.

4. Contrast two-dimensional leaders and Grid leaders.

5. Identify the management levels where charismatic, transformational, transactional, and symbolic leaders work best.

6. Contrast the various contingency models of leadership.

7. Critique the continuum and the path-goal models.

8. Describe normative leaders.

9. Define the following key terms (in order of appearance in the chapter):

- leaders
- trait theorists
- behavioral theorists
- leadership style
- two-dimensional leaders
- Leadership Grid
- charismatic leaders
- transformational leaders
- transactional leaders
- symbolic leaders
- contingency leaders
- situational favorableness
- continuum leaders
- path-goal leaders
- normative leaders
- substitutes for leadership

REVIEWING THEIR GAME PLAN

Charisma Builds a Skateboarding Empire

Tony Hawk is Mr. Skateboarding. Once a funny, quirky thing kids did to fill and kill time, skateboarding is a big sport today. How did this happen? What helped the "Hawk" single-handedly transform the rebel pastime into a mainstream sport? The answer is, in a word, charisma. **TONY HAWK** is a charismatic leader, which is to say he inspires loyalty, enthusiasm, and extraordinary effort from those around him. The Hawk fell in love with skateboarding in the late 1970s when the sport was not on the radar of very many folks. He turned pro at 14—and by 16 he was charming the wheels off fans everywhere. But pure charm and inventiveness alone do not make a charismatic leader. Something else is at work, and whatever it is it is operative in Tony Hawk.

Tony's capacity for leadership and vision did not emerge until the 1990s. But when he made his move—from player extraordinaire to businessman/leader extraordinaire—he never looked back, and the rest is the envy of every reader of *Fortune* magazine. He went into debt to start Birdhouse Skateboards, a board and accessories manufacturing company. At one point, Birdhouse almost went under as enthusiasm for skateboarding didn't merely wane—it collapsed. (Skateboarding has historically endured harsh cycles—hot stuff in the 70s, virtually ignored in the early 80s, hot again, and on the skids yet again in the early 90s.)[1] But Hawk and his enterprises held on, and he added new enterprises, Blitz Distribution and a board sports clothing line. Each venture eventually thrived and, as a not inconsiderable side effect, helped grow public awareness of the sport of skateboarding.

Today, Tony Hawk is a well-known marketer of well-known products. There is the series of video games *(Tony Hawk's Pro Skater)*. There is the licensing agreement with Mattel's Hot Wheels. There is the endorsement of Bagel Bites for Heinz. By 2001, Hawk's *Pro Skater* had generated retail sales in excess of $425 million and earned Mr. Skateboarding an estimated $6 million in royalties in 2001 alone.[2]

The lessons here are many: Have a dream—yes; follow your dream—sure; but most of all, have the wherewithal to make it happen.

For more information on skateboarding and Tony Hawk, visit http://www.tonyhawk.com, where you can check out Tony's touring schedule and find information on the Tony Hawk Foundation, which supports skateboard park construction. (For ideas on using the Internet, see Appendix B.)

INTERNET RESOURCES

http://www.fastcompany.com/online/resources/leadership.html *At this address, you will find* Fast Company *magazine's Leadership Style Online Guide. This guide offers links to hundreds of articles and features, from profiles of successful leaders in a wide range of activities to Leadership in Action, an online simulation created by Forio Business Simulations to test your capacity for leadership by having you direct a team through the design cycle of a fictional company's new product. Sport-related topics include Pat Gillick of the Seattle Mariners, Leigh Steinberg ("the most powerful agent in sports"), Nike's women's movement, the Japanese art of aikido, Indy driver Sarah Fisher, racing yacht crews, the Memphis Redbirds, Chorus (a snowboard company run by and geared toward women), NFL kickers, Patagonia Inc. (maker of adventure clothes and equipment), track coaching, America's Cup, and Ray Evernham (one of NASCAR's top crew chiefs).*
http://www.princeton.edu/~oa/manual/sect9.html *The Outdoor Action Guide to Group Dynamics & Leadership is taken from a manual written by Rick Curtis of the Outdoor Action Program at Princeton University. This program coordinates wilderness trips designed to help*

participants build their leadership and interpersonal skills. The resource found at this web address offers comprehensive guidelines for planning and conducting a successful wilderness learning experience, including discussions of some of the leadership theories covered in this chapter. Note: The links in the Table of Contents just take you to the organization's newsletter. Scroll down to find the text of the guide.

DEVELOPING YOUR SKILLS   Leadership is one of the most talked-about, written-about, and researched management topics. Ralph Stogdill's well-known *Handbook of Leadership* lists 3,000-plus articles on the topic, and Bass's revision of the *Handbook* lists well over 5,000 articles.[3] Leaders—obviously—substantively affect the performance of organizations.[4] Effective leadership is key to succeeding in good times, surviving in uncertain times, and thriving in the global arena. Thus, organizations are increasingly looking for ways to train and develop leaders, one current focus being team leadership as more and more organizations turn to teams. The good news is that everyone has leadership potential. This means that you, too, can become a leader.

LEADING THE TROOPS

Surprisingly, the study of leadership in athletics has been rather limited. As A. Kent and P. Chelladurai note, "While leadership has been an immensely popular area of study in industrial and organizational psychology, research on the topic of sport management has been largely focused on coaches rather than administrators."[5] In this chapter, we blend leadership theories with sport applications. In the Internet Skills exercise at the end of the chapter, you will examine the leadership skills of former UCLA basketball coach John Wooden. As you will see, Coach Wooden's approach to coaching is very similar to what traditional management researchers have determined to be extremely effective leadership. Management professor Dr. Judith Neal (University of New Haven) commented that what we once called coaching is now more appropriately called leadership.[6]

1 LEARNING OUTCOME
Explain why managers are not always leaders.

leaders
Influence employees to work to achieve the organization's objectives.

Leaders influence people to work to achieve the organization's objectives. We frequently use *manager* and *leader* interchangeably. We shouldn't, because they are not necessarily one and the same.[7] Leading *is* a management function (remember, there are four—planning, organizing, leading, and controlling). Unfortunately, not all managers are leaders. And, of course, there are leaders who are not managers. Many of us have worked in situations in which one of our peers had more influence in the department than did the manager. Effective managers focus less on "being the boss" and much more on having a vision, on having a direction and a destination, and on finding ways to get there—leading, in other words.

2 LEARNING OUTCOME
Compare the trait, behavioral, and contingency theories of leadership.

3 LEARNING OUTCOME
Explain leadership trait theory.

The Traits of Effective Leaders

Researchers first studied leadership in the early 1900s. They wanted to identify a set of characteristics or traits that distinguished leaders from followers and effective leaders from ineffective ones. Their investigations led to the trait, behavioral, and contingency theories of leadership, which have done much to help us understand what makes leaders tick and what makes them effective.

Early studies assumed that leaders are born, not made, but exactly what makes a person a leader has proved to be elusive. Today, research supports the idea that we can learn to lead: Leaders are made not born.[8] Using one of the original approaches, **trait theorists** look for characteristics that make leaders effective. Over the years in more than 300 studies, they analyzed numerous physical and psychological qualities, such as appearance, aggressiveness, self-reliance, persuasiveness, and dominance, in an effort to identify a set of traits that successful leaders possess.[9] The idea was that this list of traits would then guide the promotion of promising candidates to leadership positions.

trait theorists
Look for characteristics that make leaders effective.

The problem was that no one has been able to compile a list of traits that successful leaders universally possess. There are *always* exceptions. The lesson here, of course, is that leaders are an extremely diverse lot. Another aspect of the results of trait theory is perhaps even more perplexing. Not a few organizations installed people who possessed many, if not all, of the identified traits in positions of leadership, only to find that they could not lead. In addition, some people could lead in one position but not in another. Researchers began to question whether traits like assertiveness and self-confidence might not come about simply *because* one is placed in a position of leadership. Peter Drucker believes that there is no such thing as "leadership qualities or a leadership personality." So, if we don't come into the world with traits that "make" some of us leaders, how do those of us who are leaders become leaders? Trait theorists went back to the drawing board and shifted their thinking.

Today, even though it is generally agreed that no universal set of leadership traits exists, we continue to study and write about leadership traits. Why? Because we humans learn by categorizing things, for one reason. For another, even though leaders don't *universally* possess the same qualities, a lot of them do possess certain qualities. And the good news is that these qualities can be learned. Recall from Chapter 9 that continuums of various traits describe our personalities quite accurately. Thus, personality is an important part of trait theory, because organizations continue to select managers with certain personality traits. And, as you well know, organizations often give personality tests as part of their selection process (Chapter 8). So how does this information help you? To be an effective leader, you must understand how *you* function as a leader, as a coworker, as a member of a team, and as a manager. Get to know yourself through the various Self Assessments we provide in this book. Your personality affects your leadership style. You can strengthen desirable qualities in yourself and mitigate undesirable ones and still be yourself.

THE GHISELLI STUDY. As we noted Chapter 1, Edwin Ghiselli conducted a widely publicized study of leadership traits. He studied over 300 managers from 90 different U.S. businesses and published his results in 1971.[10] He concluded that certain traits are important to effective leadership, but not all of them are necessary for success. Ghiselli identified the following six traits, in order of importance, as being significant:

1. *Supervisory ability.* Leaders get the job done through others, using the four functions of management—planning, organizing, leading, and controlling—which you are learning about in this book.

2. *A need for occupational achievement.* Leaders seek responsibility. They work hard to succeed.

3. *Intelligence.* Leaders use good judgment and have the capacity to think through problems and reason them out.

4. *Decisiveness.* Leaders solve problems by making sound decisions.

5. *Self-assurance.* Leaders view themselves as capable of coping with problems. They behave in a manner that shows others they have self-esteem.

6. *Initiative.* Leaders are self-starters—they see what needs to be done and they get it done without prompting.

TIMEOUT
Which of the Ghiselli traits does your current boss or coach exhibit, and which ones does he or she lack?

_____

_____

_____

_____

_____

_____

ETHICS AND SPIRITUALITY IN THE WORKPLACE. Recall the importance of business ethics (Chapter 2). Our behavior, ethical or otherwise, derives from our personal values. Leading by example is important today. Related to ethics and values is spirituality. People are asking, "Why am I here?" They are looking for meaning in life at work. Organizations are offering programs to help employees find this meaning by engaging consulting firms such as Spirit at Work.[11]

THE BEHAVIOR OF EFFECTIVE LEADERS

By the late 1940s, most research into leadership had shifted from analyzing traits to analyzing what leaders do. In the continuing quest to identify which leadership styles work and which ones fail, researchers compared the behavior of effective and ineffective leaders.[12] **Behavioral theorists** look at the leadership style of effective leaders. This focus has also provided insights into the leader-follower dynamic. However, before we examine these theories, complete the Self Assessment on page 357 to determine your leadership style.

behavioral theorists
Look at the leadership style of effective leaders.

Basic Styles of Leadership

Leadership style is the combination of traits, skills, and behaviors managers use to interact with employees.

leadership style
The combination of traits, skills, and behaviors managers use to interact with employees.

In the 1930s, before behavior theory became popular, researchers at the University of Iowa studied leadership styles of managers and identified three basic styles:[13]

1. *Autocratic.* The manager makes the decisions, tells employees what to do, and closely supervises them—basically Theory X behavior.

2. *Democratic.* The manager encourages employee participation in decisions, works with them to determine what to do, and doesn't supervise them closely—Theory Y behavior.

3. *Laissez-faire.* The manager lets employees go about their business without much input—that is, employees decide what to do and take action, and the manager does not follow up.

Two-Dimensional Leaders

4 LEARNING OUTCOME
Contrast two-dimensional leaders and Grid leaders.

two-dimensional leaders
Focus on job structure and employee considerations, which results in four possible leadership styles.

Two-dimensional leaders focus on job structure and employee considerations, which results in four possible leadership styles. In 1945, Ralph Stogdill at Ohio State University and Rensis Likert at the University of Michigan began independent studies of leadership styles. Although the research teams used different terminology, they both identified the same two dimensions. UM's team called the two dimensions job-centered and employee-centered; OSU's team called them initiating structure and consideration. The OSU and UM leadership models also differed in structure: UM placed the two dimensions at opposite ends of the same continuum. OSU considered the two dimensions independent of one another. Both dimensions measure the manager's behavior when interacting with employees:

- *Initiating structure/job-centered.* The extent to which managers take charge to plan, organize, lead, and control as employees perform tasks. This dimension focuses on getting the job done.

- *Consideration/employee-centered.* The extent to which managers develop trust, friendship, support, and respect. This dimension focuses on developing rapport with employees.

In the two-dimensional model, managers get the job done by directing people and/or by developing supportive relationships. Combinations of the two dimensions result in four leadership styles, as shown in Exhibit 13–1.

The Leadership Grid®

In the 1960s, Robert Blake and Jane Mouton originally developed the Managerial Grid, which later became the Leadership Grid, with Anne Adams McCanse replacing Mouton.[14]

TIMEOUT
Which of the two-dimensional leadership styles does your coach or boss use? Describe his or her behavior using this model.

_____

_____

_____

_____

_____

_____

SELF ASSESSMENT   *Your Leadership Style*

Note the frequency with which you do (or *would* do, if you have not yet held a position of leadership) each action. Be honest. There are no right or wrong answers.

U—Usually   F—Frequently

O—Occasionally   S—Seldom

_____ 1. I set objectives for my department alone; I don't include staff input.

_____ 2. I allow staff members to develop their own plans, rather than develop them myself.

_____ 3. I delegate several of the tasks that I enjoy doing to staff, rather than do them myself.

_____ 4. I allow staff members to solve problems they encounter, rather than solve them myself.

_____ 5. I recruit and select new employees alone; I don't solicit input from staff.

_____ 6. I orient and train new employees myself, rather than have members of my team do it.

_____ 7. I tell staff members only what they need to know, rather than give them access to anything they want to know.

_____ 8. I praise and recognize staff efforts; I don't just criticize.

_____ 9. I set controls for the team to ensure that objectives are met, rather than allow the team to set its own controls.

_____ 10. I frequently observe my group to ensure that it is working and meeting deadlines.

For items 1, 5, 6, 7, 9, and 10, give U answers 1 point; Fs 2 points; Os 3 points; and Ss 4 points. For items 2, 3, 4, and 8, give S answers 1 point; Os 2 points; Fs 3 points; and Us 4 points. Total your score, which should be between 10 and 40. Place your score here _____. You have just measured your Theory X and Theory Y behavior. Douglas McGregor (1906–1964) developed Theory X and Theory Y. McGregor contrasted the two theories based on the assumptions managers make about workers. Theory X managers assume people dislike work and need managers to plan, organize, and closely direct and control their work for them to perform at high levels. Theory Y managers assume people like to work and do not need close supervision.[15] Place a check on the continuum below that represents your score.

Theory X   10 — 20 — 30 — 40   Theory Y

Behavior   Behavior

(Autocratic)   (Participative)

The lower your score (10), the more you tend toward Theory X behavior; the higher your score (40), the more you tend toward Theory Y behavior. A score of 20 to 30 shows a balance between the two extremes of the continuum. *Note:* Your score may or may not accurately reflect how you would behave in an actual job; however, it can help you understand your underlying attitudes.

The Leadership Grid uses the same dimensions as the two-dimensional model; in the Grid, these dimensions are called *concern for production* and *concern for people*. The **Leadership Grid** identifies the ideal leadership style as having a high concern for both production and people. Because the Grid measures the two dimensions on a scale from 1 to 9, 81 possible permutations are possible, from which Blake and McCanse categorized five major leadership styles.

> **Leadership Grid**
> Identifies the ideal leadership style as having a high concern for both production and people.

- (1,1) *Impoverished leaders* show low concern for both production and people. They do the minimum required to remain employed.

- (9,1) *Authority-compliance leaders* show a high concern for production and a low concern for people. They focus on getting the job done by treating people like machines.

- (1,9) *Country club leaders* show a low concern for production and a high concern for people. They strive to maintain a friendly atmosphere without much regard for production.

- (5,5) *Middle of the road leaders* balance their concerns for production and people. They strive for performance and morale levels that are minimally satisfactory.

- (9,9) *Team leaders* show a high concern for both production and people. They strive for maximum performance and maximum employee satisfaction.

Exhibit 13-1   The Two-Dimensional Model of Leadership

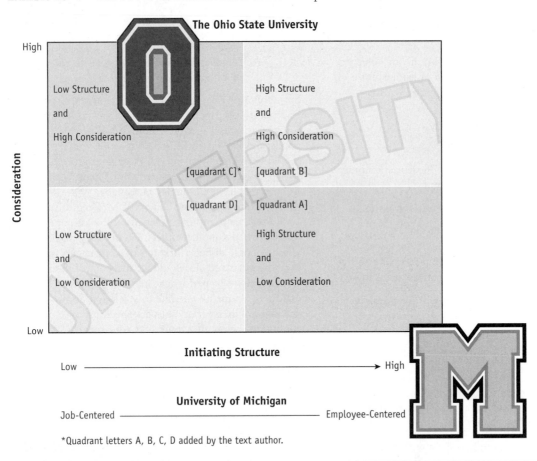

*Quadrant letters A, B, C, D added by the text author.

Exhibit 13-2

The Leadership Grid

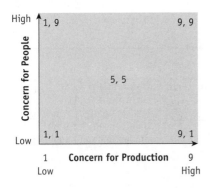

According to behavioral theorists, the team leadership style (9,9) is the most appropriate style to use in all situations. However, researchers have found this belief to be a myth.[16]

The trend toward teams has resulted in demands for leaders who have a balanced directive and supportive style but not necessarily high concern for both at the same time.[17] For example, a coach may focus on a skills drill, showing high concern for performance. At another time, the coach may give a motivational speech, focusing on players. As we discussed in Chapter 7, Joe Torre of the New York Yankees has come close to creating an overall 9,9 situation. The players are happy to play for the Yankees, and the team has been very productive on and off the field.[18] Exhibit 13-2 is an adaptation of the Leadership Grid.

CONTEMPORARY PERSPECTIVES

5   LEARNING OUTCOME
Identify the management levels where charismatic, transformational, transactional, and symbolic leaders work best.

Current researchers focus on which behaviors make top-notch managers outstanding, even though the managers' individual leadership styles may vary dramatically.[19] These researchers have identified charismatic, transformational, transactional, and symbolic leaders.

Charismatic leaders inspire loyalty, enthusiasm, and high levels of performance. Charismatic leaders have a vision and a strong personal commitment to their goals; they communicate their goals to others, display self-confidence, and are viewed as able to make the radical changes needed to reach the goals. In our media-driven age, *charismatic* fits many contemporary leaders, including Michael Jordan (basketball), Sammy Sosa (baseball), Ronaldo (soccer), and Brett Favre (football). Researchers A. Kent and P. Chelladurai found that charismatic leaders have a strong influence on employee commitment to the organization.[20] Followers buy into the belief systems of charismatics, feel affection for them, obey them, and develop emotional ownership of their goals, all of which lead to higher levels of performance. Researchers thus recommend that top-level managers emulate the charismatic leader and make the charismatic's mystique part of their organization's culture.

charismatic leaders Inspire loyalty, enthusiasm, and high levels of performance.

Transformational leaders emphasize change, innovation, and entrepreneurship as they continually take their organizations through three acts. Although every leader can be a transformational leader, these leaders are typically top-level managers. Transformational leaders create significant changes as they foster high-quality relationships and commitment from their employees.[21] They are good team leaders, because they allow employees to be proactive in change as they match personal values to organizational values.[22] They transform relationships, because they believe that people do not resist change per se but they do resist what they don't understand.[23] As we noted in Chapter 2, Pat Gillick of the Seattle Mariners is a transformational leader. When he arrived in 1999, the Mariners had just lost its three best and most popular players. Gillick was brought in to inspire the team and lead it to winning. He succeeded by finding players who were positive role models and who worked well together. Gillick also brought an attitude that winning should be fun—as he says, "Be positive. Be upbeat. Be supportive."[24]

transformational leaders Emphasize change, innovation, and entrepreneurship as they continually take their organization through three acts.

Transformational leaders take their organizations through three acts on an ongoing basis:

- *Act 1.* They recognize the need for revitalization. They understand that the organization has to change to keep up with the rapidly shifting environment and to keep ahead of the competition.

- *Act 2.* They create a new vision. They visualize the changed organization and motivate people to make it become a reality.

- *Act 3.* They institutionalize change. They introduce structure for change.

transactional leaders
Emphasize exchange.

Transactional leaders emphasize exchange. "Exchange" is about rewarding jobs well done. Such managers may or may not engage in both task and consideration behaviors with employees during the exchange. Transactional leaders are typically middle and first-line managers. However, top-level managers usually approve of the monetary rewards involved.

symbolic leaders
Establish and maintain a strong organizational culture.

Symbolic leaders establish and maintain a strong organizational culture. An organization's workforce learns the organization's culture (shared values, beliefs, and assumptions of how workers should behave in the organization) through its leadership.[25] Symbolic leadership starts with top management and flows down to middle and first-line managers. **Do you believe Tony Hawk is a charismatic, transformational, transactional, or symbolic leader?**

TIMEOUT
Think about the top manager in your firm or team. Is he or she a charismatic leader or a transformational leader? Why or why not?

_____

_____

_____

_____

_____

_____

CONTINGENCY LEADERSHIP MODELS

Both the trait and behavioral theories attempted to identify the best leadership style for all situations—a one-size-fits-all approach. In the late 1960s, it became apparent that this approach doesn't work very well. The surge in the popularity of teams has also demonstrated that leadership styles need to vary. Contingency leaders fit their leadership style to the situation.

Contingency Leaders

6 LEARNING OUTCOME
Contrast the various contingency models of leadership.

contingency leaders
Are task- or relationship-oriented, and their style should fit the situation.

In 1951, Fred E. Fiedler began to develop the first contingency leadership theory—the contingency theory of leader effectiveness.[26] Fiedler believed that our leadership style reflects our personality and remains basically constant. That is, leaders do not change styles.[27] **Contingency leaders** are task- or relationship-oriented, and their style should fit the situation. The first step is to determine whether your leadership style is task- or relationship-oriented. To do so, you would fill in the Least Preferred Coworker (LPC) scales. After determining your leadership style, you then look at situational favorableness.

situational favorableness
The degree to which a situation enables leaders to exert influence over followers.

Situational favorableness is the degree to which a situation enables leaders to exert influence over followers. The three variables, in order of importance, are as follows:

1. *Leader-member relations.* Is this relationship good or poor? Do followers trust, respect, accept, and have confidence in their leader? Is it a friendly, tension-free situation? Leaders with good relations have more influence. The better the relations, the more favorable the situation. Pat Gillick has a good relationship with the people who work for him.

2. *Task structure.* Is the task structured or unstructured? Do employees perform repetitive, routine, unambiguous, and standard tasks that are easily understood? Leaders in structured situations have more influence. The more repetitive the jobs, the more favorable the situation.

3. *Position power.* Is the manager's position power strong or weak? Does he or she have the power to assign work, reward and punish, hire and fire, and give raises and promotions? Leaders with position power have more influence. The more power, the more favorable the situation.[28]

WHICH STYLE IS APPROPRIATE? To determine whether a task or relationship orientation is appropriate, use the Fiedler contingency model and answer three questions (pertaining to situational favorableness) set up as a decision tree—Exhibit 13–3 shows an adapted model. That is, users answer question 1 and follow the decision tree to *good* or *poor* depending on their answer. After answering question 3, users end up in one of eight possible situations.

Exhibit 13–3   The Contingency Model of Leadership

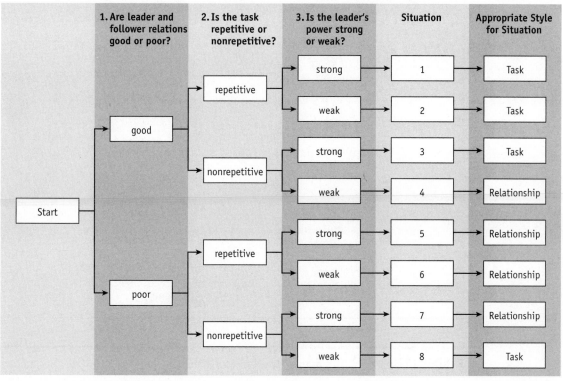

	1. Are leader and follower relations good or poor?	2. Is the task repetitive or nonrepetitive?	3. Is the leader's power strong or weak?	Situation	Appropriate Style for Situation

Decision tree:

Start → good →
- repetitive → strong → 1 → Task
- repetitive → weak → 2 → Task
- nonrepetitive → strong → 3 → Task
- nonrepetitive → weak → 4 → Relationship

Start → poor →
- repetitive → strong → 5 → Relationship
- repetitive → weak → 6 → Relationship
- nonrepetitive → strong → 7 → Relationship
- nonrepetitive → weak → 8 → Task

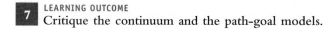

If the manager's preferred leadership style matches the situation, the manager does nothing. If the preferred leadership style does not match the situation, the manager changes the situation to match his or her preferred leadership style.

A major criticism of Fiedler's model concerns his view that leaders cannot change their style (task/job/production-centered or relationship/employee/people-centered) and that, if their style does not fit the situation, they should change the situation to fit their style.[29] The other contingency writers suggest changing leadership styles, not the situation.

Continuum Leaders

7 LEARNING OUTCOME
Critique the continuum and the path-goal models.

In Robert Tannenbaum and Warren Schmidt's model (developed in 1964), leadership occurs on a continuum from boss-centered (autocratic) to employee-centered (participative) leadership. Their model focuses on who makes the decisions. They identify seven major styles from which leaders can choose. Exhibit 13–4, an adaptation of their model, lists the seven styles.[30] **Continuum leaders** choose their style based on boss-centered or employee-centered leadership.

Before selecting one of the seven styles, managers consider the following three variables:

1. *The manager's preferred leadership style.* In this variable, experience, expectation, values, background, knowledge, feeling of security, and confidence in the subordinates are considered.

2. *The subordinates' preferred style for their leader.* Experience, expectation, and so on are again considered. Generally, the more willing and able the subordinates, the more leadership responsibilities they should take on and vice versa.

continuum leaders
Choose their style based on boss-centered or employee-centered leadership.

APPLYING THE CONCEPT   *Contingency Leaders*

Use Exhibit 13–3 to identify the appropriate leadership style (1–8) for each situation and whether the style is (a) task-oriented or (b) relationship-oriented.

_____ 6. Saul oversees the assembly of mass-produced golf tees. He has the power to reward and punish. He is considered a hard-nosed boss.

_____ 7. Karen manages corporate event planning. She helps other departments plan events. Karen is viewed as being a dreamer; she doesn't understand the various departments. Employees are often rude to Karen.

_____ 8. Juan manages the processing of checks. He is well liked by his staff. Juan's boss enjoys hiring and evaluating his employees' performance.

_____ 9. Sonia, the event manager, assigns dates and times for each event. The event-planning atmosphere is tense.

_____ 10. Louis owns a professional soccer team. He is highly regarded by volunteer members on the board of directors. The board members recommend ways to increase season-ticket sales.

Exhibit 13–4   The Continuum Model of Leadership

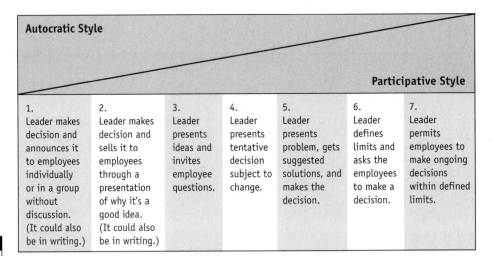

| 1. Leader makes decision and announces it to employees individually or in a group without discussion. (It could also be in writing.) | 2. Leader makes decision and sells it to employees through a presentation of why it's a good idea. (It could also be in writing.) | 3. Leader presents ideas and invites employee questions. | 4. Leader presents tentative decision subject to change. | 5. Leader presents problem, gets suggested solutions, and makes the decision. | 6. Leader defines limits and asks the employees to make a decision. | 7. Leader permits employees to make ongoing decisions within defined limits. |

3. *The situation.* Environmental considerations—such as the organization's size, structure, business climate, goals, and technology—and how much time is available are considered in this variable. The leadership style used by one's superiors in the organization heavily influences the styles of lower-level managers. For example, if your boss is autocratic, very likely you will be too.

Tannenbaum and Schmidt recommend (1) that leaders become a group member when the group needs to make decisions; (2) that leaders clearly state the style (subordinates' authority) being used; (3) that leaders not try to trick the group into thinking it made a decision that was actually made by the leader; and (4) that it's not the number of decisions the group makes but, rather, their significance that counts.[31]

Even though the continuum model was very popular in the 1960s, one major criticism of it charges that the model is too subjective. In other words, determining which style to use when is difficult.

> **APPLYING**
> **THE CONCEPT**   *Continuum Leaders*
>
> Use Exhibit 13–4 to identify the continuum leadership style (1–7) implied in each statement.
>
> _____ 11. Chuck, I recommended that you be transferred to the new public relations department, but you don't have to go if you don't want to.
>
> _____ 12. Sam, go clean the tables in the stadium restaurant right away.
>
> _____ 13. From now on, this is the way security at all games will be done. Does anyone have any questions about the procedure?
>
> _____ 14. These are the two weeks we can schedule the high school basketball tournament. You select one.
>
> _____ 15. I'd like your ideas on how to stop the bottleneck on the production line making hockey pucks. But I have the final say on the solution we implement.

Path-Goal Leaders

Robert House developed the path-goal leadership model in the 1970s. **Path-goal leaders** determine employee objectives and achieve them using one of four styles. The focus here is on how leaders influence employees' perceptions of their goals and the paths they follow to attain goals.[32] As shown in Exhibit 13–5 (an adaptation of the model), House's model uses situational factors to determine which leadership style best achieves goals by influencing employee performance and satisfaction.[33]

path-goal leaders
Determine employee objectives and achieve them using one of four styles.

SITUATIONAL FACTORS. *Subordinate* situational characteristics include: (1) authoritarianism—the degree to which employees defer and want to be told what to do and how to do the job; (2) locus of control—the extent to which employees believe they control goal achievement (internal) or whether goal achievement is controlled by others (external); and (3) ability—the extent of employee ability to perform tasks to achieve goals. *Environmental* situational factors include: (1) task structure—the extent of repetitiveness of the job; (2) formal authority—the extent of the leader's power; and (3) work group—the extent to which coworkers contribute to job satisfaction.

LEADERSHIP STYLES. Based on situational factors, managers select the most appropriate leadership style by following these general guidelines:

1. *Directive.* Leaders provide high structure. Directive leadership is appropriate when subordinates want authority, have external locus of control, and are of low ability. It is also appropriate when the task is complex or ambiguous, formal authority is strong, and the work group provides job satisfaction.

> **TIMEOUT**
> Which leadership style (1–7) in the continuum model does your boss or coach use? Is it the most appropriate style? Why or why not?
> _____
> _____
> _____
> _____
> _____
> _____

Exhibit 13–5 The Path-Goal Model of Leadership

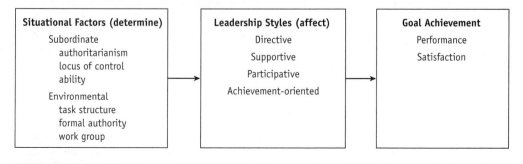

Situational Factors (determine)	Leadership Styles (affect)	Goal Achievement

Subordinate
  authoritarianism
  locus of control
  ability
Environmental
  task structure
  formal authority
  work group
	Directive
	Supportive
	Participative
	Achievement-oriented
		Performance
		Satisfaction

TIME OUT

Which path-goal leadership style does your boss or coach use? Is this the most appropriate style for the situation? Explain.

_____

_____

_____

_____

_____

_____

2. *Supportive.* Leaders provide high consideration. Supportive leadership is appropriate when subordinates do not want autocratic leadership, have internal locus of control, and are of high ability. This style is also appropriate when tasks are simple, formal authority is weak, and the work group does not provide job satisfaction.

3. *Participative.* Leaders solicit employee input. Participative leadership is appropriate when subordinates want to be involved, have internal locus of control, and are of high ability. This style is also appropriate when the task is complex, authority is either strong or weak, and job satisfaction from coworkers is either high or low.

4. *Achievement-oriented.* Leaders set difficult but achievable goals, expect subordinates to perform at their highest level, and reward them for doing so. That is, leaders provide both high structure and high consideration. Achievement-oriented leadership is appropriate when subordinates are open to autocratic leadership, have external locus of control, and are of high ability. Achievement-oriented leadership is also appropriate when the task is simple, authority is strong, and job satisfaction from coworkers is either high or low.

Normative Leaders

8 LEARNING OUTCOME
Describe normative leaders.

normative leaders
Use one of five decision-making styles appropriate for the situation.

In the 1970s, Victor Vroom and Philip Yetton attempted to bridge the gap between leadership theory and managerial practice by developing a normative leadership model.[34] **Normative leaders** use one of five decision-making styles appropriate for the situation. Vroom and Yetton identified the five leadership styles. Two are autocratic (AI and AII), two are consultative (CI and CII), and one is group-oriented (GII).

- *AI leaders* make decisions alone using available information.

- *AII leaders* get information from subordinates but make decisions alone. Subordinates may or may not be told what the problem is. They are not asked for input.

- *CI leaders* meet individually with subordinates, explain the situation, and get information and ideas on how to solve the problem. They make the final decision alone. They may or may not use subordinates' input.

- *CII leaders* meet with subordinates as a group, explain the situation, and get information and ideas on how to solve the problem. They make the decision alone after the meeting. They may or may not use subordinates' input.

- *GII leaders* meet with subordinates as a group and explain the situation, and the decision is made by the group with the help, but not the over-influence, of the leader.

To determine the appropriate style for a specific situation, users of the normative model answer eight questions (not discussed here), some of which may be skipped depending on prior answers. The questions are sequential and are presented in a decision-tree format similar to Fiedler's contingency model.

Vroom and Yetton's model is popular with academics because it is based on research.[35] However, the model is not as popular with managers, who find it cumbersome.

The late Vince Lombardi, the legendary football coach, often used AI-style leadership. Does the AI style work today? The answer is that it depends. Pat Summitt's leadership style (Chapter 12) is quite similar to Lombardi's. So is Bill Parcells's, who took the New York Giants to Super Bowl victories in 1986 and 1990.[36] Other coaches prefer GII-style leadership. Phil Jackson, coach of the NBA-champion Chicago Bulls and Los Angeles Lakers, uses Zen-like philosophy to motivate and train his players.[37] He has been blessed with superstar players, but he has also used a group attitude to produce results.

TIME OUT

Which normative leadership style does your boss or coach use? Is this the most appropriate style for the situation? Explain.

_____

_____

_____

_____

_____

_____

When Leaders Are Not Necessary

The leadership theories we've presented thus far assume that some type of leader should be directing every situation. What happens when leaders are not what the situation requires?

That is, given the circumstances or environment, they either *cannot* be effective or are simply not needed? Steven Kerr and John Jermier argue that certain variables prevent leaders from being effective.[38] **Substitutes for leadership** eliminate the need for a leader. In certain circumstances, three characteristics can counteract or neutralize the efforts of leaders or render them unnecessary.

substitutes for leadership
Eliminate the need for a leader.

The following variables can substitute for or neutralize leadership because they provide the needed direction or support:

1. *Characteristics of subordinates*—their ability, knowledge, experience, and training; their need for independence; their professional orientation; and their indifference toward organizational rewards.

2. *Characteristics of the task*—whether a sense of clarity and routine prevails, and whether the task is intrinsically satisfying.

3. *Characteristics of the organization*—its level of formalization (explicit plans, goals, and areas of responsibility); its inflexibility (rigid, unbending rules and procedures) or lack thereof; whether its advisory and staff functions are highly specified and active; whether work groups are loosely knit and cohesive; whether organizational rewards are within the leader's control; and the spatial distance between superiors and subordinates.

TIMEOUT
Do the characteristics of your peers, the work you do, or your organization's culture eliminate the need for a designated leader? In other words, is your boss necessary? Explain.

GETTING TO YOUR PERSONAL STYLE OF LEADERSHIP

So, as a fledgling manager, you may be wondering, Where do I start? Which style will work for me? How will I know which route to take in a given situation? These are reasonable questions. And we have no nifty sound-bite response for you. Leadership is a much-studied and not always well-understood phenomenon. Suffice it to say, you are not today the manager/leader you will be in the future. You will have many opportunities in your future jobs and teams to see which leadership shoe fits your foot, which shoe works really well for you in some situations but not in others, and which shoe should work for you but doesn't. True leadership is like a masterpiece painting. You can paint by the numbers (lead by the rules/theories/models), but your painting won't look like Rembrandt's or Picasso's. This doesn't mean that Rembrandt and Picasso—like other masters (be they legendary coaches or legendary entrepreneurs)—didn't know the rules. They knew them very well indeed—they were just able to take them to another level. That is what masterful leaders do—they take the rules, models, and theories to another level, and, when they do, they sometimes make history. (And then researchers study *them*—just ask Jack Welch next time you see him!) There's another thing: Masterful painters/coaches/leaders don't start out as masters—they all, each and every one of them, start out as apprentices, practicing, learning, and living the rules. So, let's start you out on earth—only time will tell how high you can fly.

TIMEOUT
State the leadership style you prefer and why.

Back on earth, to help you through this maze, we've gathered the various models and theories in Exhibit 13–6. Study it carefully. It will help you understand the similarities and differences in the approaches to leadership we've examined in this chapter.

TIMEOUT
Describe the type of leader you aspire to be.

CHAPTER SUMMARY

1. Explain why managers are not always leaders.

Just because someone is a manager doesn't mean he or she understands how to lead people.

2. Compare the trait, behavioral, and contingency theories of leadership.

Trait theorists look for distinctive characteristics of effective leaders. Behavioral theorists look at the behavior of effective leaders and try to find one leadership style that works for all situations. Contingency theorists try to fit leadership style to the situation.

Exhibit 13–6 A Comparison of Leadership Models

	Two-Dimensional Leadership Styles			
	HD/LS	HD/HS	LD/HS	LD/LS
I. Trait Leadership	X	X	X	X
II. Behavioral Leadership				
Basic Leadership Styles	Autocratic	Democratic		Laissez-faire
Two-Dimensional (13–1)*	Quadrant A	Quadrant B	Quadrant C	Quadrant D
Leadership Grid (13–2)	9,1 Authority	9,9 Team; moderate D&S 5,5 Middle of the Road	1,9 Country Club	1,1 Impoverished
Charismatic Leadership	X	X	X	X
Transformational Leadership	X	X	X	X
Transactional Leadership	X	X	X	X
Symbolic Leadership	X	X	X	X
III. Contingency Leadership				
Contingency Leadership (13–3)	Task		Relationship	
Leadership Continuum (13–4)	1	2 & 3	4 & 5	6 & 7
Path-Goal (13–5)	Directive	Achievement	Supportive	
			Participative	
Normative Leadership	AI & AII	CI & CII		GII
Leadership Substitutes	X	X	X	X

H = High; L = Low; D = Directive; S = Supportive

X = No two-dimensional leadership style used with this theory.

* Material in parentheses refers to model or exhibit in this text that illustrates theory.

3. Explain leadership trait theory.

Trait theory assumes that distinctive characteristics account for leadership effectiveness. According to Ghiselli, supervisory ability is the most important leadership trait. Supervisory ability is the aptitude to perform the four management functions (planning, organizing, leading, and controlling).

4. Compare two-dimensional leaders and Grid leaders.

These two types of leaders use the same two dimensions of leadership, but the two models describe and structure the dimensions somewhat differently. The two-dimensional model defines four leadership styles (high structure/low consideration, high structure/high consideration, low structure/high consideration, low structure/low consideration), whereas the Leadership Grid uses five leadership styles (1,1—impoverished; 9,1—authority-compliance; 1,9—country club; 5,5—middle of the road; and 9,9—team).

5. Identify the management levels where charismatic, transformational, transactional, and symbolic leaders work best.

Charismatic and transformational leaders are typically top-level managers. Transactional leaders are usually middle and first-line managers. Symbolic leaders work in top management, and, if successful, their vision flows down to middle and first-line management.

6. Contrast the various contingency models of leadership.

Fiedler's contingency model recommends changing the situation, not the leadership style. The other contingency models recommend changing the leadership style, not the situation.

7. Critique the continuum and the path-goal models.
Both models are subjective, making them difficult and cumbersome to use.

8. Describe normative leaders.
Normative leaders use one of five decision-making styles, depending on the situation.

9. Define the key terms discussed in the text.
Fill in the missing key terms from memory, or match the key terms from the list in the margin with their definitions below.

_____ influence employees to work to achieve the organization's objectives.

_____ look for characteristics that make leaders effective.

_____ look at the leadership style of effective leaders.

_____ is the combination of traits, skills, and behaviors managers use to interact with employees.

_____ focus on job structure and employee considerations, which results in four possible leadership styles.

The _____ identifies the ideal leadership style as having a high concern for both production and people.

_____ inspire loyalty, enthusiasm, and high levels of performance.

_____ emphasize change, innovation, and entrepreneurship as they continually take their organization through three acts.

_____ emphasize exchange.

_____ establish and maintain a strong organizational culture.

_____ are task- or relationship-oriented, and their style should fit the situation.

_____ is the degree to which a situation enables leaders to exert influence over followers.

_____ choose their style based on boss-centered or employee-centered leadership.

_____ determine employee objectives and achieve them using one of four styles.

_____ use one of five decision-making styles appropriate for the situation.

_____ eliminate the need for a leader.

Key Terms

behavioral theorists
charismatic leaders
contingency leaders
continuum leaders
leaders
Leadership Grid
leadership style
normative leaders
path-goal leaders
situational favorableness
substitutes for
   leadership
symbolic leaders
trait theorists
transactional leaders
transformational leaders
two-dimensional leaders

REVIEW AND DISCUSSION

1. What is leadership and why is it important?

2. What traits do you think are important to leaders?

3. Based on your responses to the Self Assessment on page 357, are you a Theory X or a Theory Y leader?

4. Name several pro athletes who are charismatic leaders and explain why.

5. What are the two dimensions of leadership and the four possible leadership styles?

6. Why do you think most sport management studies have focused on the leadership skills of coaches instead of those of athletic administrators?

7. Describe Joe Torre's and Phil Jackson's leadership styles in terms of the Leadership Grid. Defend your answers.

8. Describe and compare the two leadership styles of the contingency model of leadership.

9. Describe and compare the two dimensions of the continuum model of leadership.

10. Describe and compare the four leadership styles of the path-goal model of leadership.

11. Give examples of MLB general managers who are transformational leaders.

12. What are three substitutes for leadership?

13. Do you believe results differ when male coaches coach women's college teams? What about women coaching men's college teams? Defend your answers.

14. Review the coaching examples provided in the discussion of Vroom and Yetton's normative model of leadership. Do you agree with our analysis of the leadership styles of these coaches? Why or why not?

CASE

Leading a Production Facility out of Inefficiency

Wilson Sporting Goods's golf ball production facility in Humboldt, Tennessee, once held the dubious title of least efficient plant in the Wilson Corporation. The facility lost money year after year, and problems abounded—productivity, quality, cost, safety, morale, and housekeeping. Management and employees continually locked horns in a hopeless, self-defeating "us against them" atmosphere.

Today, the Humboldt plant sports a "Best Plants in America" plaque on its wall. What went right? Someone refused to throw in the towel. That someone was plant manager Al Scott.

There is a lesson here. The best leaders have the best visions, and they pursue them in spite of the odds. That's what Al Scott did. Terrible productivity, you say? Too bad—we'll get to great productivity. Terrible labor relations, you say? Too bad—we'll get our work-force on board. Totally outdated facilities, you say? Too bad—we'll make them better. Al Scott never stopped believing that inside Humboldt's beleaguered and seriously tattered skin was a butterfly just needing some nudging to emerge. He wanted Humboldt to make the best golf balls in the world and to have the most efficient production facilities in the world. It was that simple.

With this (some might have said impossible) vision in mind, Al developed a mission statement and talked it up to everyone who would listen: "Our mission is to be recognized . . . as the premier manufacturer of golf balls." To achieve the mission, Al developed five guiding philosophies—what he wanted to become shared values. They were—and are—employee involvement, total quality management, continuous improvement, lowest total manufacturing cost, and just-in-time manufacturing.

Al met with all those disgruntled employees and all those discouraged managers. He told them about his vision—the mission he thought Humboldt was capable of—and the values that would make the vision a reality. He asked people to change—radically change—their way of doing business. Al told managers that dictator-style management was out. Henceforth employees would be associates. Al told people that only by working together could managers and associates find new solutions to the stubborn problems facing them. Managers were trained in employee involvement and learned to include associates in decisions. The leadership style did change at Humboldt, and the payoff was enormous. Associate loyalty returned, morale shot up, enthusiasm grew, and performance surged.

One of Al's pet projects was his "Team Wilson," a voluntary associate participation program. The Humboldt plant assembled teams of associates to problem-solve in every problem area. To ensure success, every team member underwent team training.

Within a few years, 66 percent of associates had formed voluntary teams, which dramatically changed the Humboldt facility. Each team represented a specific area of the plant. The teams created their own logos, T-shirts, and posters to hang in the plant. Team Wilson held cookouts, picnics, and parties to recognize the contribution of these problem-solving teams. Awards were given out to three "Teams Wilson" each quarter.

So, you say, let's see the numbers. The numbers are remarkable—an increase in market share from 2 to 17 percent, an increase in the inventory turnover ratio from 6.5 to 85, a 67 percent reduction in inventory, a 67 percent reduction in scrap and rework, and a 121 percent increase in productivity. The Humboldt plant produces over one billion golf balls each year, and the volume is growing. And, of course, there is the Best Plants in America award from *Industry Week* magazine.

The other lesson may be that excellence is contagious.

To see how Wilson is performing, visit Wilson's web site at http://www.wilsonsports.com.

CASE QUESTIONS

1. Al Scott called for a change in basic management style from _____ to _____.
   a. democratic to laissez-faire
   b. autocratic to laissez-faire
   c. laissez-faire to democratic
   d. autocratic to democratic

2. Based on two-dimensional leadership (Exhibit 13–1), within the Team Wilson teams, the team leader primarily uses the _____ leadership style.
   a. telling—high structure/low consideration
   b. selling—high structure/high consideration
   c. participating—low structure/high consideration
   d. delegating—low structure/low consideration

3. Al Scott _____ be considered a charismatic leader.
   a. should   b. should not

4. Al Scott should be considered a _____ leader.
   a. transformational
   b. transactional

5. Al Scott _____ focus on symbolic leadership at the Humboldt plant.
   a. did   b. did not

6. Consider the original situation at Humboldt, and use Exhibit 13–3 to determine Al's situation and the appropriate style.
   a. 1—task
   b. 2—task
   c. 3—task
   d. 4—relationship
   e. 5—relationship
   f. 6—relationship
   g. 7—relationship
   h. 8—task

7. Using the continuum model (Exhibit 13–4), Al's leadership style is _____.
   a. 1   c. 3   e. 5   g. 7
   b. 2   d. 4   f. 6

8. Using path-goal leadership terminology, Al changed Humboldt's management style to a _____ style.

   a. directive
   b. supportive
   c. participative
   d. achievement-oriented

9. The normative leadership style used by Team Wilson is _____.
   a. AI   c. CI   e. GII
   b. AII   d. CII

10. Al _____ create substitutes for leadership at the Humboldt plant.
    a. did   b. did not

11. What role did leadership play in improving the Humboldt plant?

12. Would the methods used by Al Scott work at your organization? Why or why not?

VIDEO CASE

Sunshine Cleaning Wins with Innovative Leadership

Introduction

Sunshine Cleaning employs approximately 1,000 people with $10 million in annual sales. Sunshine offers janitorial, pressure-cleaning, and window-cleaning services to accounts that include the Miami Dolphins training center, the Orlando Arena (home of the Orlando Magic), and the Florida Citrus Bowl. The founder, Larry Calufetti, is a former catcher for the New York Mets and has coached in New York and Florida. His baseball experience influences his leadership style. Calufetti believes a happy employee makes a happy customer. To accomplish the goal of having satisfied employees and customers, Calufetti encourages a coaching leadership style.

Focus Your Attention

To get the most out of viewing the Sunshine Cleaning video, think about the following issues: how leadership and management are different, how different leadership styles might be appropriate in different areas of an organization, and how effective management and communication can impact an organization. Then answer the following questions after viewing the video:

1. How is "managing" different from Calufetti's "coaching" style?

2. What is leadership? How does Calufetti use leadership to achieve Sunshine's organizational objectives?

EXERCISES

Skill-Builder: Leadership Styles

Objective:

- To better understand what makes a leadership style effective or ineffective.

Preparation:
Recall the best coach or boss and the worst coach or boss you ever had and complete the assignment.

Best Coach or Boss

1. List leadership traits (i.e., Ghiselli's list) the coach/boss had and how they helped make the person an effective leader. *(trait theory)*

   _____

   _____

   _____

2. List the behavior (things said and done) of the coach/boss and how it helped make the person an effective leader. Was the coach/boss charismatic, transformational, transactional, and/or symbolic? *(behavioral theory)*

   _____

   _____

   _____

3. Identify the leadership style of the coach/boss and explain how the style helped make the person an effective leader. Did the coach/boss change leadership styles? *(leadership style)*

   _____

   _____

   _____

4. Which of the four Ohio State University leadership styles (refer back to Exhibit 13–1) did the coach/boss use? Give examples.

   _____

   _____

   _____

   _____

5. Which of the seven leadership continuum styles (refer back to Exhibit 13–4) did the coach/boss use? Give examples.

   _____

   _____

   _____

   _____

Worst Coach or Boss

1. List leadership traits (i.e., Ghiselli's list) the coach/boss lacked and how they helped make the person an ineffective leader. *(trait theory)*

   _____

   _____

   _____

2. List the behavior (things said and done) of the coach/boss and how it helped make the person an ineffective leader. Was the coach/boss charismatic, transformational, transactional, and/or symbolic? *(behavioral theory)*

   _____

   _____

   _____

3. Identify the leadership style of the coach/boss and explain how the style helped make the person an ineffective leader. Did the coach/boss change leadership styles? *(leadership style)*

_____

_____

_____

4. Which of the four Ohio State University leadership styles (refer back to Exhibit 13–1) did the coach/boss use? Give examples.

_____

_____

_____

_____

5. Which of the seven leadership continuum styles (refer back to Exhibit 13–4) did the coach/boss use? Give examples.

_____

_____

_____

_____

In-Class Application
Complete the skill-building preparation noted above before class.

Procedure 1 (10–15 minutes):
Break into groups of five to six members and come to an agreement on what makes a leader effective or ineffective based on your answers above. Focus on the most important traits, behaviors, and leadership styles that make the difference. Place the group summary below.

- Effective leaders:

_____

_____

_____

- Ineffective leaders:

_____

_____

_____

Procedure 2 (10–15 minutes):
Each group selects a spokesperson to present the group's answer to Procedure 1.

Wrap-up:
Take a few minutes and write down your answers to the following questions:

- What did I learn from this experience?

_____

_____

_____

_____

- How will I use this knowledge in the future?

  _____

  _____

  _____

  _____

As a class, discuss student responses.

Internet Skills: Leadership

Objective:
- To apply the leadership theories of John R. Wooden, former men's basketball coach at UCLA.

Preparation (20 minutes):
Visit the web site http://www.coachwooden.com. Search the site (you will have to click on each box to learn the underlying principle) and answer the following questions.

1. In your own words, describe The Pyramid of Success.

   _____

   _____

   _____

2. What two cornerstone blocks make true leaders?

   _____

   _____

   _____

3. Summarize Coach Wooden's views on leadership.

   _____

   _____

   _____

4. In your opinion, which cornerstone block is most important in making a leader a great leader and why?

   _____

   _____

   _____

5. Ultimately, what is needed for competitive greatness?

   _____

   _____

   _____

14 Controlling for Quality

Learning Outcomes

After studying this chapter, you should be able to:

1. Explain how controls function with the systems process.

2. Understand why feedback is a control.

3. Describe the control process.

4. List which control methods are used with which frequency.

5. Differentiate between static and flexible budgets, and incremental and zero-based budgets.

6. Explain how capital budgets and operating budgets differ.

7. State what the three basic financial statements entail.

8. Use motivational feedback.

9. Understand the role of EAP staff.

10. State three ways to increase productivity.

11. Define the following key terms (in order of appearance in the chapter):

- controlling
- preliminary controls
- concurrent controls
- rework controls
- damage controls
- standards
- critical success factors (CSFs)
- control frequencies
- management audits
- budgets
- operating budgets
- capital budgets
- financial statements
- coaching
- management by walking around (MBWA)
- management counseling
- employee assistance programs (EAPs)
- discipline
- productivity

REVIEWING THEIR GAME PLAN

It Takes Three to Golf

In the story of **THE RANCH GOLF CLUB** in Southwick, Massachusetts, the three protagonists are a dairy family, two Jiffy Lube owners, and a realtor. The dairy family owned the dream, the Jiffy Lube couple owned the willingness, and the realtor owned the expertise. How did this unlikely trio work a dream into reality and a fledgling golf club into a 4-Star course rating in less than a year of operation? The answer is expertise—in this instance, in the form of Rowland Bates, the realtor of the trio (of Golf Realty Advisors). The Hall family approached Bates with the idea that its family dairy was "good turf" for golf, and he liked the "tint of their lenses." The Halls would provide the land, and Bates would find the investors.

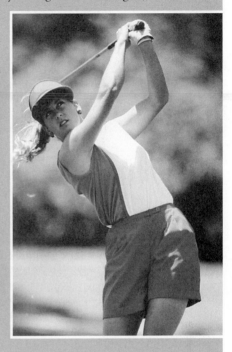

Enter Pete and Korby Clark, young part-owners of some 50 Jiffy Lubes in the Northeast, who had jingles in their pockets from a recent sale of most of their franchises and a desire to try something new. The Clarks had been looking at various ventures since 1991, but nothing much interested them until Rowland Bates approached them with his plan. What was different about Bates's proposal? Rowland offered the Clarks a hands-on deal—they would be in on the creation; he didn't want just their money.

The Clarks soon found that building a golf course requires money, and lots of it. And although banks were willing to lend them plenty of money *if* they built Jiffy Lubes, they could not get a dime for their golf course. Again, Bates's expertise, connections, and tireless beating of the investor bushes soon netted them enough investors to cut the deal. The final deal hammered out by Bates involved one-third ownership by the Halls, one-third by the Clarks, and one-third by other investors.[1]

The idea from the beginning was to create a state-of-the-art, premier golf course. The trio had plenty of natural advantages to work with in the Halls' dairy land, which was rich in beauty, vistas, woods, and the all-important differing elevations. The owners hired California architect Damian Pascuzzo to design a grand golf course. And design one he did. The Ranch boasts 7,100 yards in length and a 140 slope rating (a *very* good rating). Each Ranch golf car is equipped with a ParView GPS system that diagrams each hole along with current yardage from the pin and other helpful facts and figures.[2] Peak-season green fees are around $100 with unsurpassed service in New England, similar to that in Arizona where the Clarks played golf to learn about excellent service. On the course at all times, player assistants provide all types of service, including golf tips, the fetching of left-behind clubs, and cool towels on hot days. The two massive 19th-century barns have been completely remodeled and painted their original and distinctive yellow color, and now serve as clubhouse, restaurant and lounge, golf shop, and function facility.[3]

The Clarks wanted to create a new business—they didn't necessarily want to be involved in its day-to-day operation, so they turned to Willowbend, a professional golf management team (which Rowland Bates is now part of) for four reasons. (1) They needed expertise. (2) They had other things to do with their life—a family to raise, community service they are keenly committed to, and coaching, among others. (Pete is currently the head baseball coach and assistant football coach for Agawam High School and has also coached for Trinity College.) (3) The mix was right—Pete and Korby oversee the important strategic decisions and have input when they want, but Willowbend handles the day-to-day decisions. (4) The employees work for Willowbend, which offers a good benefits package. The key to successful co-managing for the Clarks and Willowbend has been clear, open communications of expectations.

Pete says there are more similarities than differences in running Jiffy Lubes, golf clubs, and baseball and football teams. The focus is the same—high-quality service. You have to treat the customer/player right. He uses the same "three I's" philosophy with Jiffy Lubes, The Ranch, and his coaching: *Intensity* to be prepared to do the job right, *Integrity* to do the right thing when no one is watching, and *Intimacy* to be a team player. The three I's are turning into the three $$$s. The Ranch is striving to be the best golf club in New England. Its 4-Star course rating is one of only four in New England.

For current information on The Ranch Golf Club, visit http://www.theranchgolfclub.com, which features a virtual visit of the golf course. (For ideas on using the Internet, see Appendix B.)

INTERNET RESOURCES

http://senate.ohio-state.edu/AthleticBudget.pdf *Here you'll find Ohio State University's approved 2001–2002 budget for its Department of Athletics. On page 1, check out how incomes compare for the various sports. As you might expect, men's football and basketball are the top income generators. On page 2, see how the department plans on spending its income. Note how close the total income and total expenditures were for the 2000–2001 budget and how the projected budget for 2001–2002 is balanced.*

http://beginnersinvest.about.com/library/lessons/bl-introduction.htm *Investing Lesson 4: Income Statement Analysis offers detailed instructions for understanding and utilizing the information found on an income statement. Segment 1 walks you through the elements that make up an income statement line by line, offering helpful explanations of equations, examples, and practical tips. Segment 2 analyzes Abercrombie & Fitch's 2001 annual income statement as well as the income statement of a fictional safety products company. An interactive quiz at the end tests your retention of what you've just learned. Click on the* Investing Lessons *link to the left to find other related instructions, including Investing Lesson 3: Analyzing a Balance Sheet.*

http://www.opm.gov/ehs/eappage.asp *The web site of the United States Office of Personnel Management offers a collection of guides, reports, and official documents that provide information about work/life programs. At the address given above, you'll find the Employee Assistance Program page, with links to several useful publications including* Your Federal Employee Assistance Program: A Question and Answer Guide for Federal Employees, Confidentiality and the Employee Assistance Program: A Question and Answer Guide for Federal Employees, *and* Handling Traumatic Events: A Manager's Handbook. *Although these resources are geared toward federal workers, they offer plenty of general information for any work situation.*

DEVELOPING YOUR SKILLS Every effective manager is a pro—a past master—at controlling. It is the *only* way you will know whether you and your department are on the right track. It is the *easiest* way to catch problems in their infancy. It tells you whether you work for an effective organization, which, by the way, is something you need to think about. What good will it do you as an effective manager and employee if you work for an ineffective organization? So, read this chapter carefully and take at least one accounting course—and don't fall asleep in it either! Accounting is the "biology" of business. It tells you where the "blood" (cash) flows and whence it flows, and what "cholesterol" may be clogging up the organization's "arteries" and where. Remember, you won't be in business for long if you can't generate profits, and controlling is your key to the kingdom of profits.

CONTROLLING FROM THE OUTSIDE

controlling
The process of establishing and implementing mechanisms to ensure that objectives are achieved.

As defined in Chapter 1, **controlling** establishes mechanisms that ensure that objectives are achieved. Many sport organizations are monitored and controlled by external bodies of governance. We have discussed many of these bodies: FIFA and its Executive Committee monitor all soccer activities; the International Olympic Committee (IOC) monitors all Olympic activities; the PGA is the regulating body for golf; each Jewish Community Center is monitored by the JCCA (Jewish Community Centers Association); likewise, each individual YMCA is governed by the YMCA of the USA (YUSA); and college athletics are governed by the rules and policies set forth by the NCAA.

These governing bodies are dedicated to their particular sport. They establish rules and regulations that every member must follow. For example, the IOC approves the sports and events in the Olympics. The IOC picks locales for the Summer and Winter Games seven years in advance. Cities bid for the right to hold games and must prove they have the necessary facilities to play the games, house the athletes and spectators, and provide officiating.[4]

Sometimes members of governing bodies disagree on an issue and decide to present the topic to the media. The media then tries to determine whether unethical acts occurred. For instance, if universities disagree with an NCAA policy, they will certainly complain to the governing body, but they may also take their case to the media.

CONTROLLING FROM THE INSIDE

1	LEARNING OUTCOME

Explain how controls function with the systems process.

To determine whether performance is up to expectations, it must be measured and controlled.[5] Because of the diversity in types of organizations and types of stakeholders, no performance measure or control system is universally applicable—the measure or system must be tailored to each situation. In this chapter, we focus on how various controls are used to measure and evaluate each stage of the system.[6] In Chapter 2, we examined the systems process; now we examine how controls are used at each stage to ensure that objectives are met. Exhibit 14–1 shows how this works.

Top managers use controls to guide and effect change in the organizations they lead. Controlling starts at the top with long-range strategic planning and flows down through every aspect of the organization until it reaches day-to-day operations. Four different types of controls are needed at different parts of the system.

Preliminary controls anticipate and prevent possible problems. One major difference between successful and unsuccessful managers is in their ability to anticipate and prevent problems, rather than solving problems after they occur. If preliminary controls work, a manager doesn't need to use concurrent, rework, or damage control to fix a problem.

Planning and organizing are key functions in preliminary control, which is also called *feedforward control*. The organization's mission and objectives guide the use of all of its resources. Standing plans control employee behavior in recurring situations to prevent problems, and contingency plans tell employees what to do if problems occur.

A typical preliminary control is preventive maintenance. Many production departments and transportation companies/departments routinely tune up their machines and engines to prevent breakdowns. Another preliminary control is to purchase only quality inputs in order to prevent production problems. The practice area, the golf course itself, golf cars, and tee times are the major inputs that require preliminary control at **THE RANCH**.

TIMEOUT
Use Exhibit 14–1 to identify the primary inputs, transformation, outputs, and customers of your firm or team. Also, identify the level of customer satisfaction. (Remember, "customers" can be fans, users of the golf course, buyers of your merchandise, players on your youth league soccer team, employees at your organization if your department is human resources, stockholders if you are the CEO, or suppliers of input to your company if you are the finance department that pays them. Employees, stockholders, and suppliers are also called stakeholders—stakeholders can thus be considered "customers" from certain viewpoints.)
_____
_____
_____
_____
_____
_____

preliminary controls
Anticipate and prevent possible problems.

Exhibit 14–1   Controlling the Systems Process

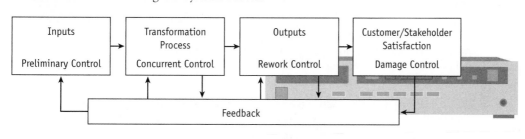

Inputs	Transformation Process	Outputs	Customer/Stakeholder Satisfaction
Preliminary Control	Concurrent Control	Rework Control	Damage Control

Feedback

concurrent controls
Actions taken during transformation to ensure that standards are met.

Concurrent controls are actions taken during transformation to ensure that standards are met. The key to success here is quality control. It is more efficient to reject faulty input than to rework output that does not work properly. Checking quality is also crucial during the transformation process and, of course, at the output stage. At **The Ranch,** the transformation is the actual playing of golf. A major concurrent control is player assistance out on the course. If players are not satisfied, player assistants know it early on and fix the problem before the game is over.

rework controls
Actions taken to fix output.

Rework controls are actions taken to fix output. Rework is necessary when preliminary and concurrent controls fail. Most organizations inspect output before it is sold or sent as input to other departments in the organization. Sometimes rework is neither cost effective nor possible, and outputs have to be accepted as is, discarded, or sold for salvage, all of which can be costly. For example, if Wilson Sporting Goods makes defective golf balls (outputs), it is too late; the company cannot change the past.

damage controls
Actions taken to minimize negative impacts on customers due to faulty output.

Damage controls are actions taken to minimize negative impacts on customers due to faulty output. When a faulty product or service gets to the customer, damage control is needed. Warranties (a form of damage control) refund the purchase price, fix the product or reperform the service (a form of rework), or replace the product with a new one. Note that damage control is important at every stage of the system, because each successive stage is the "customer" of the previous stage. Thus, output departments are customers of transformation departments, and transformation departments are customers of input departments. For example, handling customer complaints is a controlling technique. **The Ranch** goes to great lengths to ensure that if a player is not satisfied, the management hears about it. Customer evaluation cards are important; so are employees on the lookout for dissatisfied customers.

FEEDBACK. Feedback helps organizations continually increase customer satisfaction, so feedback is an important control and must be used at every stage of the system. Customer evaluation cards are only one example of feedback. **Can you think of other forms of feedback?** The Clarks spend much of their time at **The Ranch** talking to players about the service, looking for ways to improve The Ranch experience. Within an organization, output groups give feedback to transformation and input groups. Transformation groups give feedback to input groups for continuous improvement through the entire system.

THE WRONG FOCUS. Too many managers skip preliminary and concurrent controls and focus on rework and damage control. It is costly to do things twice in order to get them right. Using rework as the sole control of performance means wasted resources, unpredictable delivery schedules, and extra inventory (for "safety stock"). Effective managers never overlook the other two controls, because they cut down on rework and damage control. The customers win (they get what they want—a good product or service), and the organization wins (it minimizes warranty cost).

It should be noted that the four types of controls just discussed are interrelated. For example, damage control is used at every stage of the system.

Controlling Functional Areas

Recall from Chapters 1 and 6 that firms are commonly organized into four functional areas: operations, marketing, human resources, and finance. Information is a fifth functional area, which can be a stand-alone department or part of finance. Organizations have other departments as well; however, these five key functional areas serve our purposes here, as shown in Exhibit 14–2 on page 380.

Although in most organizations operations is the only functional area that transforms inputs into the external outputs of goods and services (products), all functional areas have inputs and outputs. Note that although external customer damage control is primarily the function of marketing, damage control is also necessary when internal outputs are faulty and thus is required in every functional area.

OPERATIONS. Operations (also called production and manufacturing) is the functional area that actually makes the goods or performs the service. For example, **Willowbend** uses a sophisticated scheduling system to maintain the golf course turf. When to seed, fertilize, water, mow, and so on are well planned and computerized.

APPLYING THE CONCEPT *Using Appropriate Controls*

Choose the appropriate control for each situation.

a. preliminary   **c.** rework
b. concurrent   **d.** damage

_____ 1. The new golf shirt I bought today has a button missing.

_____ 2. I just got my monthly budget report telling me how much of its budget marketing spent.

_____ 3. Coach is reviewing the plays he will use in Sunday's big game.

_____ 4. As I was jogging in my new nylon shorts, the shorts split down the side.

_____ 5. The manager uses the time management system on Fridays.

MARKETING. Marketing, which includes sales, is the functional area responsible for selling the organization's products and services. The four key areas (called the "four Ps") of marketing are pricing; promoting (personal selling and advertising); placing (sales locations); and product attributes (features, packaging, brands, installation, and instructions). Marketing also identifies target markets.

Marketing deals primarily with external customers and undertakes damage control outside the organization, whereas other departments perform damage control inside the organization. Marketing also distributes customer and competitor feedback to other departments.

THE RANCH markets in a variety of ways. First, its best marketing is the word-of-mouth kind. Golfers are always on the lookout for great courses, and players are pleased to recommend The Ranch. The Ranch also runs TV ads and print media ads in newspapers and golf magazines. And, as mentioned, at its cutting-edge web site (http://www.theranchgolfclub.com) professionals and amateur players can take a virtual tour of the course.

HUMAN RESOURCES. Inputs for human resources are the potential employees that HR attracts (recruits and selects). In HR's transformation process, it develops (orientation, training and development, and performance appraisal) and retains (compensation, health and safety, and labor relations) employees. Its outputs are new and more productive employees, which are also major inputs to every functional area.

For details on HR processes, see Chapter 8. Large organizations such as Wilson Sporting Goods fund a separate HR department. **THE RANCH** has approximately 70 employees with equal staffing numbers in its three major departments. People working at The Ranch are actually employees of Willowbend, which performs most of the HR functions for The Ranch.

FINANCE. Finance (which includes accounting) is the functional area responsible for recording all financial transactions (primarily paying for inputs and costs involved in the sale of outputs); obtaining funds needed to pay for inputs (loans plus sale of bonds and stocks); and investing any surplus funds (various forms of savings accounts and the purchasing of assets, such as another company's stock holdings). Finance also prepares the budgets and financial statements.

Inputs for finance include collected revenues, borrowed funds, and owners' funds. The transformation process includes recording transactions and overseeing the budgeting process. Outputs are budgets, financial statements, and other reports (such as tax returns, employee tax withholding, and annual reports). Its primary "customers" are other departments (through their budgets) and stakeholders (employees via their paychecks, and suppliers and lenders via payments to them).

TIMEOUT
Describe the controls you personally use in your department.

TIMEOUT
Use Exhibit 14–2 to diagram the systems process for the department you work in.

Exhibit 14–2   Functional-Area Systems Processes

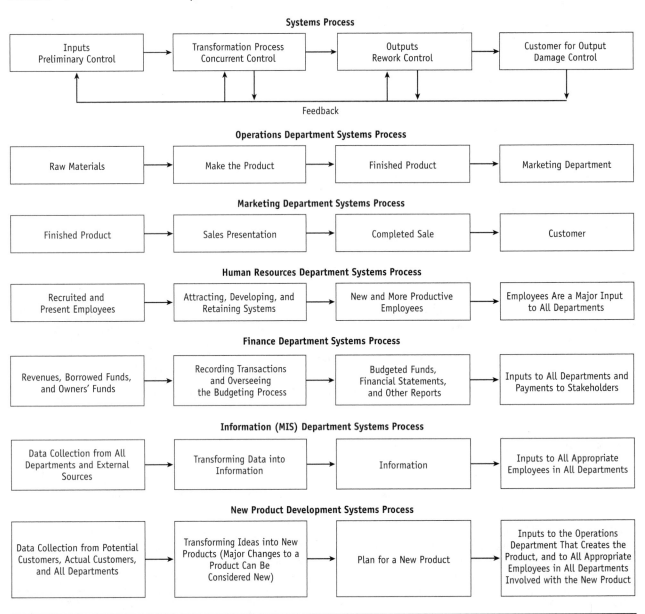

Systems Process

| Inputs
Preliminary Control | Transformation Process
Concurrent Control | Outputs
Rework Control | Customer for Output
Damage Control |

Feedback

Operations Department Systems Process

| Raw Materials | Make the Product | Finished Product | Marketing Department |

Marketing Department Systems Process

| Finished Product | Sales Presentation | Completed Sale | Customer |

Human Resources Department Systems Process

| Recruited and
Present Employees | Attracting, Developing, and
Retaining Systems | New and More Productive
Employees | Employees Are a Major Input
to All Departments |

Finance Department Systems Process

| Revenues, Borrowed Funds,
and Owners' Funds | Recording Transactions
and Overseeing
the Budgeting Process | Budgeted Funds,
Financial Statements,
and Other Reports | Inputs to All Departments and
Payments to Stakeholders |

Information (MIS) Department Systems Process

| Data Collection from All
Departments and External
Sources | Transforming Data into
Information | Information | Inputs to All Appropriate
Employees in All Departments |

New Product Development Systems Process

| Data Collection from Potential
Customers, Actual Customers,
and All Departments | Transforming Ideas into New
Products (Major Changes to a
Product Can Be
Considered New) | Plan for a New Product | Inputs to the Operations
Department That Creates the
Product, and to All Appropriate
Employees in All Departments
Involved with the New Product |

INFORMATION. Management information systems (MISs) control information in a central location and for networks. MIS departments are typically responsible for the organization's computers. MIS departments collect data from all departments and external sources as its inputs. ("Data" used in this context is unorganized facts and figures.) This department then transforms data into information. *Information* is data organized in a meaningful way that helps workers make decisions.

CROSS-FUNCTIONAL PRODUCT DEVELOPMENT. Not all organizations fund product development teams. Therefore, we don't list this as a major functional area. However, it is an important function in many firms and usually falls within the purview of either marketing or operations. Ideas for major improvements and new products often come from external sources, especially potential customers, as well as from other areas of the firm. For example, Nike's marketing department collects data so that product development can design a line of footwear that will appeal to new and existing customers. Operations looks into the practical aspects of producing the new footwear. Finance works up numbers on the cost and pricing effects. The final plan for producing the new footwear then goes to operations. The mar-

Exhibit 14–3   The Feedback Process

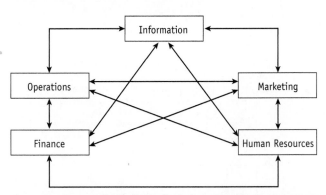

The arrows represent the flow of feedback throughout the systems process

keting department plans how to promote and sell the new footwear. Finance works up the costs and budget for the footwear and keeps records (information) on performance. The human resources department may need to make personnel changes or attract creative engineers or marketers to the company. Meanwhile, top managers control the entire process, making sure the new product development is completed successfully.

2 LEARNING OUTCOME
Understand why feedback is a control.

THE FEEDBACK PROCESS. Every employee in an organization transforms inputs into outputs in some way. For example, a production worker makes a part of a sneaker, which becomes input for the next person down the line and so on, until the footwear is completed. Every employee should therefore also use preliminary, concurrent, rework, and damage controls.

Feedback is essential if the system is to improve (see Exhibit 14–3).[7] Throughout the system, feedback circulating through all the functional areas improves inputs, transformations, and outputs while continually increasing customer satisfaction.[8] Note that operations, marketing, finance, and human resources provide feedback to each other and to MIS as well.

ESTABLISHING CONTROL SYSTEMS

3 LEARNING OUTCOME
Describe the control process.

The *control process* involves the four steps shown in Model 14–1. The steps are the same whether the control is an organization-wide control or a functional-area control, even though the controls themselves may be very different.

1. *Set objectives and standards.* Planning and controlling are inseparable. A key part of planning is to develop controls. Setting objectives (Chapter 4) is the starting point for both planning and controlling. Setting objectives and setting standards are part of the input process and are preliminary controls. Objectives, in a sense, are standards, but they are "big-picture" standards. Thus, detailed and specific standards (the "little picture" that makes the big picture work) are also needed to determine whether the objectives are being met.

    Objectives are often qualitative or, at least, "broad-brush" quantitative. Controls are "greater-detail" quantitative. To be comprehensive and complete, standards must address five criteria. **Standards** minimize negative impacts on customers due to faulty

standards
Minimize negative impacts on customers due to faulty output by controlling quantity, quality, time, cost, and behavior.

Model 14–1   The Control Process

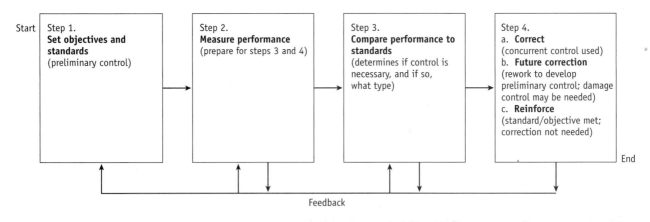

output by controlling quantity, quality, time, cost, and behavior. Incomplete standards often lead to negative results. For example, if production is asked to produce high quantities in too short a time frame, it may have to ignore quality to make the designated quantities and meet the schedule.

Workers respond to what is measured, so developing balanced standards is a key management function that drives business success.[9] At the same time, a word of caution is in order. When you establish control systems, especially the standards against which performance will be measured, it is important to consider employee reaction. If employees buy into the change, the odds of its succeeding increase dramatically; if they don't, your problems may multiply, not diminish. Therefore, before you set out new standards, always review how to manage change (Chapter 7) and involve your staff in developing and establishing the new controls.[10]

■ *Quantity.* How many units should someone produce to earn his or her pay? Examples of quantitative standards include number of sales made, home runs hit, quarterback sacks made, or classes taught. Measuring performance quantitatively is clear-cut and easy.

■ *Quality.* How well must a job be done? How many errors are acceptable? Qualitative standards are essential if the control is to be effective. Quality can often be measured quantitatively. Quantitative examples include the number of delinquent loans made, interceptions thrown, coaching mistakes made in games, and poor teaching evaluations received from students. But other aspects of quality are often difficult to establish and measure. How does an administrator determine how good the teachers are in a sport management program? It isn't easy, but quality must be measured and evaluated.

■ *Time.* When should the task be completed? How fast should it be completed? When you assign tasks, it is important to specify time frames. Deadlines are a time-honored, time-based standard. Performance is also measured against specific periods—goals scored per season, annual graduation rate, home runs in a season, profits per quarter, and so on.

■ *Cost.* How much should the job cost to do? This is part and parcel of the budgeting function. Some production departments use cost-accounting methods to ensure accuracy. Most departments have set budgets. Examples include expense account limits for entertaining customers, fixed overhead costs to keep expenses down (long-term rent agreements or outsourcing secretarial help), and so on. Cost standards for the professor may include a salary limit set by the state and a limit for overhead costs such as travel.

■ *Behavior.* Which behaviors are appropriate and which ones are not appropriate? Standing plans, especially rules, guide and control behaviors of workers. Professors are expected to refrain from dating current students. Players are expected to be on time for practice. Carl Everett, the former Boston Red Sox outfielder, was fined repeatedly for his outbursts.[11] Unable to control his behavior, Everett was eventually traded to the Texas Rangers. We have previously discussed various ways of controlling behavior, including through positive and negative reinforcement. Other methods to control behavior are also effective, and we discuss a few of them later in this chapter.

2. *Measure performance.* Measuring performance helps organizations determine whether they are meeting their objectives and also helps them find ways to beat their current performance and beat or match that of their competitors. An important consideration in the control process is what to measure and how frequently to measure it.[12]

During the objective- and standard-setting process, it is important to identify critical success factors. **Critical success factors (CSFs)** are pivotal areas in which satisfactory results will ensure successful achievement of the objective/standard. In other words, we cannot control everything, but as organizations, departments, teams, and individuals we *can* identify the few most important objectives/goals/standards without which we fail and with which we succeed. These are the CSFs, and you must control them very carefully. For example, possible CSFs for the WNBA include improving team competitiveness, maintaining national television exposure, and improving marketing.[13]

How often should performance be measured and which control methods are most effective? There is no simple answer here—different situations require different controls and different measurement periods. Performance is typically measured by frequency of use; thus, constant, periodic, and occasional usage all require different measurement periods.

3. *Compare performance to standards.* After determining what, when, and how frequently performance will be measured, the next step, of course, is to measure it and then compare it to the standards you've set.[14] This step is relatively easy if the first two steps have been done correctly. The results of this step determine what type of control, if any, is needed in step 4.

A performance or variance report, such as the one shown in Exhibit 14–4, is commonly used to measure performance. Performance reports typically show standards, actual performance, and deviations from the standards. In Exhibit 14–4, the golf club production results, although under the production goal and over cost, are good because they both deviate less than 1 percent from the standard. (Deviation is determined by dividing the variance by the standard.) When variances are significant, they should be examined carefully. We discuss this in more detail later in this section.

4. *Correct or reinforce.* During the transformation process, concurrent controls are used to correct performance to meet standards.

When the job is done (the product is made or the service is delivered), it is faulty, *and* it is too late to correct the problem, then it is time to (1) figure out why the standard was not met; (2) use the information to develop new preliminary controls; and (3) implement the new controls so that the standard is met next time. When performance affects others, damage control may also be required.

critical success factors (CSFs)
Pivotal areas in which satisfactory results will ensure successful achievement of the objective/standard.

> **TIMEOUT**
> Give several CSFs for your current job. Place them in order of importance and explain why they are critical.
> _____
> _____
> _____
> _____
> _____
> _____

> **TIMEOUT**
> Think about a situation in which you or your boss had to take corrective action to meet a standard. Describe the action taken.
> _____
> _____
> _____
> _____
> _____
> _____

Exhibit 14–4   Operations Performance Report

OUTPUTS AND INPUTS	STANDARD OR BUDGETED AMOUNT	ACTUAL	VARIANCE
Units produced (golf clubs—the outputs)	100,000	99,920	–80
Production cost (inputs)			
Labor, including overtime	$700,000	$698,950	+$1,050
Materials	$955,000	$957,630	–$2,630
Supplies	$47,500	$47,000	+$500
Totals	$1,702,500	$1,703,580	–$1,080

Of course, when the standard has been met, there is no need for corrective action. This does not mean that the control process ends here. It's time for a little gratitude—*don't* forget to praise your team for a job well done.

THE FREQUENCY OF CONTROLS

LEARNING OUTCOME
4   List which control methods are used with which frequency.

control frequencies
Constant, periodic, and occasional.

Ten methods, which can be categorized by frequency of occurrence, are used to measure and control performance. **Control frequencies** are constant, periodic, and occasional.

Constant Controls

Constant controls are in continuous use and include self-control, clan control, and standing plans. The three I's that Pete Clark uses at **THE RANCH** are constant controls. One constant-control standing plan at The Ranch is the 10-foot rule: If you come within 10 feet of customers, you *always* greet them cheerfully *and* ask whether they need any assistance. **How effective do you think the 10-foot rule is?**

METHOD 1: SELF-CONTROL. A big question facing every manager is, will your staff do their job if they are not monitored closely? The answer is that you must know your staff. Some groups need much less control than others. The issue here is one of balance—self-control (internal in employees) versus imposed control (external from managers). Too much external control causes problems and so does too little control.

METHOD 2: CLAN CONTROL. This control is about organizational culture and norms, which are powerful ways to shape desired behavior. Organizations that use teams often rely on clan control. See Chapter 10 for details on group control (another phrase for clan control). Self-control and clan control are used throughout the controls process and in conjunction with the four control types.

METHOD 3: STANDING PLANS. Policies, procedures, and rules exist in order to influence behavior in recurring predictable situations (Chapter 5). Standards can be thought of as a type of standing plan. When standing plans and standards are developed, they are preliminary controls. When standing plans and standards are implemented to solve problems, they become concurrent, rework, or damage controls.

Periodic Controls

Periodic controls are used on a regular, fixed basis, such as hourly, daily, weekly, monthly, quarterly, or annually. Periodic controls include regularly scheduled reports, budgets, and audits. **WILLOWBEND** management provides the owners with monthly reports. Together they develop annual and monthly budgets, and they have an annual audit performed.

METHOD 4: REGULARLY SCHEDULED REPORTS. Oral reports in the form of daily, weekly, and monthly meetings to discuss progress and problems are common in all organizations. Written reports required on a schedule are also common. At Wilson Sporting Goods, the sales manager gets weekly sales reports. Vice presidents get monthly income statements. Regularly scheduled reports are designed as a preliminary control. But the report itself is used (when there is a problem) as a concurrent, rework, or damage control, depending on the situation.

METHOD 5: BUDGETS. Budgets are a widely used control tool. They are also essential. In today's highly competitive environment and with global conditions that are driving labor costs and profit margins down, carefully controlling costs means the difference between thriving and surviving and stumbling and going out of business. Budgets need to be constructed carefully, always with an eye on where costs can be cut yet again, and actual costs need to measured against budgeted costs relentlessly. Think of budgets as your reality check.

New budgets are preliminary controls. As the year progresses, they become concurrent controls. At year-end, they are reworked for the next year. A budget may also require damage control if significant changes such as overspending take place for some reason. The damage control might involve disciplining or firing the employee who overspent.

METHOD 6: AUDITS. Organizations use two types of audits: internal and external. Part of the accounting function is to maintain careful and extremely detailed records of the organization's transactions and assets. (Accounting transparency is a cornerstone of the American economy, as we explain below—careful records are one way to ensure transparency.) Large organizations maintain internal auditing departments whose responsibility it is to make sure assets are reported accurately. Internal auditors also serve as watchdogs to keep theft (embezzlement and fraud) to a minimum. Most organizations hire outside auditors to verify their financial statements. Lastly, **management audits** look at ways to improve the organization's planning, organizing, leading, and controlling functions. This analysis examines the past and present so that it can improve the future. Management audits are conducted both internally and externally.

Audits are also occasional controls when used sporadically—for example, auditors sometimes make unannounced visits at irregular intervals. Audits are a preliminary control used to ensure accurate records and to control theft. When audits detect problems, other controls become necessary. Auditors are supposed to strive for exceptionally high standards of honesty, objectivity, and professional practice. Why? Because our entire economy—the business of America—is built on open (transparent) and objective accounting principles. The importance of this statement cannot be emphasized enough. Our accounting practices are one of the walls that stand between our being an economic power and becoming a banana republic. When questionable accounting practices creep in, confidence stumbles, investment capital dries up (no one wants to fund crooks), and our economy can spiral into recessions—and worse. It goes without saying that the scandals breaking at once-revered corporations such as Enron, WorldCom, Xerox, and Global Crossing are giving organizations across the country pause for thought. Pro sport teams are particularly affected because several of the corporations facing scrutiny for questionable accounting own pro sport teams. For instance, the NHL had to take over the Buffalo Sabres's daily operations because its owner, John Rigas, and two of his sons were charged with conspiracy for allegedly misusing money from their telecommunications company, Adelphia Communications. Rigas and his sons apparently hid $2.3 *billion* in liabilities from investors.[15]

Occasional Controls

Occasional controls are used on an as-needed basis. They include observation, the exception principle, special reports, and project controls. Unlike periodic controls, they are not conducted at set intervals. The Willowbend management team and the Clarks come in unannounced to observe operations at **THE RANCH** to ensure that everything is up to standard. The Clarks provide special reports to Willowbend managers to help them continually improve. Project controls are also in place for special golf events that involve corporate clients and other organizations.

METHOD 7: OBSERVATION. This is exactly what it sounds like—designated people, video cameras, and electronic devices observing work in progress, whether the work is a professor giving a lecture, a pro athlete in training, or a machine making a golf ball. Observation is used with all four types of control. Management by walking around (MBWA) is an especially effective method of observation that we will examine in more detail later in this chapter.

METHOD 8: THE EXCEPTION PRINCIPLE. This is about placing control in the hands of staff unless problems occur, in which case people go to their supervisors for help. Corrective action is then taken to get performance back to standard. However, people—be they production line workers or CEOs—often shrink from asking for help or reporting poor performing until it is too late to take corrective action. Therefore, it is important for managers and staff (or the board of directors, stockholders, and the CEO) to agree in great detail on what constitutes an exception.

METHOD 9: SPECIAL REPORTS. When problems or opportunities are identified, management often requests special reports, which may be compiled by a single employee, a

Exhibit 14-5 The Control System

TYPES OF CONTROLS	FREQUENCY AND METHODS OF CONTROL		
	Constant Controls	Periodic Controls	Occasional Controls
Inputs (preliminary)	Self	Regularly scheduled reports	Observation
Transformation (concurrent)	Clan	Budgets	Exception principle
Outputs (rework)	Standing plans	Audits	Special reports
Customer satisfaction (damage)			Project

committee, or outside consultants. The intent of such reports is to identify causes of problems and possible solutions.

METHOD 10: PROJECT CONTROLS. With nonrecurring projects, project managers still need to install controls to ensure that such projects are completed on time and on budget. Because planning and controlling are so closely linked, planning tools, such as Gantt charts and PERT networks (Chapter 5), are also project control methods. Project controls are designed as a preliminary control but can be used with any of the other three types of controls when schedules are not being met.

Organizations understand that controls are crucial to their success.[16] Therefore, it behooves you to get comfortable with the control process and learn to use controls well. Exhibit 14–5 summarizes the control process. The types, frequency, and methods of control are listed separately because all four types of control may be used with any method. Recall how a budget changes its type of control over time and that more than one control method can be used at once. You need to be aware of which stage of the system you are working in and the controls that will be most effective for what you are doing in that stage (Exhibit 14–1).

FINANCIAL CONTROLS

Budgets and financial statements are important tools. The information they contain is key in making decisions of all kinds. Therefore, go to some length to get very comfortable with budgets and financial statements. As organizations everywhere strive to slash costs and identify trends, this knowledge will stand you in good stead. You may find that not only must you bring your costs in line with budgets, you will be expected to develop budgets and to use spreadsheet software to present them. Don't think of this as a task to be endured. Accounting *is* the language of business and, as such, is a key way to understand your organization. Financial statements can tell you a great deal if you "speak their lingo."

The Master Budget

Exhibit 14-6 The Master Budget

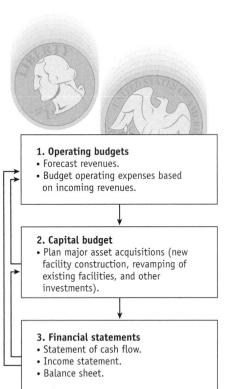

1. Operating budgets
- Forecast revenues.
- Budget operating expenses based on incoming revenues.

2. Capital budget
- Plan major asset acquisitions (new facility construction, revamping of existing facilities, and other investments).

3. Financial statements
- Statement of cash flow.
- Income statement.
- Balance sheet.

budgets
Plans for allocating resources to specific activities.

Preparing and following budgets are every manager's business. **Budgets** are plans for allocating resources to specific activities. Notice that our definition does not use terms of money. That is because organizations budget all types of resources—human resources, machines, time, space, and, yes, funds. However, in the following discussion our focus is on financial budgets, the "money part" of the picture.

To construct master budgets, organizations develop (1) operating budgets and (2) capital budgets; they then measure costs and revenue flow through (3) the income statement, the balance sheet, and the statement of cash flow. (See Exhibit 14–6.) Notice that information from two of the end products of the process, the income statement and the balance sheet, is used to construct future master budgets, because these two statements tell managers how

---

APPLYING THE CONCEPT   *Control Methods*

Identify the appropriate control method for each situation:

Constant	Periodic	Occasional
a. self	**d.** regularly scheduled reports	**g.** observation
b. clan	**e.** budgets	**h.** exception principle
c. standing plans	**f.** audits	**i.** special reports
		j. project

_____ 6. The boss asks the floor supervisor to meet to explain why imprinting the current golf ball run with the corporate logo is behind schedule.

_____ 7. Posted signs state that helmets are to be worn throughout the factory—no exceptions.

_____ 8. The manager's desk faces the work floor.

_____ 9. Accounting staff members are working on supply contracts alone today since the boss is out of the office.

_____ 10. The manager assembles the monthly operations performance report.

---

much money they have to work with and therefore how much they will need to borrow to cover operating expenses and capital expenditures.

Budgets usually cover one year, broken down by month. The *controller,* the chief finance officer (CFO), oversees the budgeting process that results in the master budget. In other words, the master budget is the end result of the budgeting process. Although organizations commonly follow the three steps we noted above, how each step is performed varies widely from organization to organization.

Each department submits a proposed budget to the controller/committee for approval. During the budgeting process—which by its very nature deals with scarce (not infinite) resources—power politics often come into play as managers defend their "turf" and their budgets. Budgeting is therefore also about negotiating (see Chapter 9) and hard bargaining.

Operating Budgets

Operating budgets use revenue forecasts to allocate funds to cover projected expenses. Only after organizations determine how much money they have and expect to have can they plan how it should be spent to make more money. Therefore, the first step in the master budgeting process is to forecast revenue.

operating budgets
Use revenue forecasts to allocate funds to cover projected expenses.

FORECASTING REVENUE. This is the forecast of total income for the year. Although sales are the most common form of revenue, many organizations also have revenue from investments. Revenue for nonprofit organizations consists of fees, donations, grants, and fundraising. Revenue forecasts project and then total all sources of income. Marketing commonly provides revenue figures for the entire firm.

Revenue forecasts are therefore primarily built on sales forecasts (Chapter 5). In one sense, the sales forecast is *the* building block on which all budgets are based. Major sources of revenue, by department, at **THE RANCH** include:

- Golf green and practice fees
- Crane's Kitchen Restaurant
- Phil's Pub
- Functions Golf Shop

BUDGETING EXPENSES. Operating budgets use expense projections to allocate total operating spending for the year. It is, of course, true that controlling expenses is important. Each functional area has an operating budget. Many managers dread budgets, because their math and accounting skills are weak. In reality, budgeting is more about planning than it is about math and accounting. Computers make the job even easier. Because of the systems effect, every functional-area budget affects the others. Operations needs sales forecasts to determine how many products or services to produce (and to estimate the related expenses of doing so). Human resources needs staffing requirements before it can determine how many people it needs to hire (and to estimate the related expenses of doing so). And so it goes through every functional area and every department. Therefore, it is imperative that managers share information.[17] Major expenses at **THE RANCH** include:

- Golf course maintenance
- Building maintenance
- Purchasing for all three departments—fertilizer/chemicals, food and beverages, clothes and golf equipment
- Management and administrative expenses
- Employee compensation

Types of Operating Budgets

5 LEARNING OUTCOME
Differentiate between static and flexible budgets, and incremental and zero-based budgets.

Two costs are important in operating budgets. *Fixed costs* are costs that don't change as business activity fluctuates. The rent remains the same regardless of whether the facility is used once a year or every day. *Variable costs,* however, do change as business activity fluctuates. The total cost of sales catalogs and mailing increases or decreases as the number printed and mailed increases or decreases.

STATIC VERSUS FLEXIBLE BUDGETS. *Static budgets* have only one set of expenses, whereas *flexible budgets* have a series of expenses for a range of activities. Static budgets are appropriate in stable environments in which demand for the product is unchanging. Flexible budgets are appropriate in turbulent environments in which demand for the product varies dramatically. **THE RANCH** has a static budget for each month, which it tries hard to meet.

INCREMENTAL VERSUS ZERO-BASED BUDGETS. These two budgets differ in how allocations are justified. With *incremental budgeting,* justification of funds from past budget periods and approval of previously allocated expenses are not required; only new expenses are justified and approved. With *zero-based budgeting (ZBB),* all expenses are justified and approved with each new budget. That is, ZBB assumes that the previous year's budget should not be the base on which next year's budget is constructed. Zero-based budgets focus on the organization's mission and objectives and what it will cost to achieve them. ZBB is especially appropriate in turbulent environments in which some departmental activities/products are increasing dramatically and others are decreasing.

ACTIVITY-BASED COST ACCOUNTING (ABC). Activity-based cost accounting allocates costs by tasks performed and resources used. ABC is a relatively new method and is not as widely used as the preceding approaches. However, it is particularly useful to organizations that produce numerous goods and services that require a wide diversity of tasks and resources to produce them. For example, recreation facilities offer a variety of services. Some are simple activities that use few resources and take little time (such as a weekly exercise class for ten adults—about three hours a week). Others use many resources and take a lot of time (such as a sports camp for 300 campers—an all-summer endeavor). How does the facility calculate the cost of these two services? Eight times the cost of the weekly exercise class does not accurately describe the expenses that will be incurred in the more complex summer camp.

TIMEOUT
Identify the major sources of revenue and expenses at your firm or team.

_____

_____

_____

_____

_____

_____

Capital Budgets

LEARNING OUTCOME
Explain how capital budgets and operating budgets differ.

The second step in constructing the master budget is to estimate funds for capital expenditures. **Capital budgets** allocate funds for improvements. Capital expenditures—expenditures for improvements—make assets perform better than before by increasing their life, reducing their operating cost, or increasing their rate of output.[18] Capital expenditures are used to purchase or improve *long-term assets*—these are the assets from which the organization expects to receive benefits for several years, that are paid for over several years, and that are depreciated over several years. They include land, new buildings, new stadiums and arenas, and—today—existing companies that the organization acquires. They also include replacements for expensive machinery or arenas that are now outmoded and must be updated if the organization is to remain competitive. In every case, the objective is to earn a satisfactory return on invested funds. Raising money to buy capital assets is an important function of finance.

capital budgets
Allocate funds for improvements.

Financial Statements

LEARNING OUTCOME
State what the three basic financial statements entail.

The third step in the master budgeting process is the preparation of the financial statements. The financial statements lay out for the world to see the organization's financial health or lack of health. As such, they are used internally (as the organization monitors its own health) and externally (as investors decide whether they will invest in the firm, creditors decide whether they will lend it money, and suppliers decide whether the firm will stand good on its credit line). As you can see, financial statements are pretty important pieces of paper. Well done, they are *transparent* and allow stakeholders (investors, credit markets, and suppliers) to evaluate a company's performance, its growth rate, and its reserve funds. Poorly done (at least from the standpoint of stakeholders), they are *opaque* and can even perpetrate fraud, as Enron and all too many others did during the halcyon days of the "new economy."

The three **financial statements** are the income statement, the balance sheet, and the statement of cash flow. We present them in the order in which they appear in companies' annual reports.

THE INCOME STATEMENT. The *income statement* shows the company's revenues and expenses and its profit or loss for the stated period. In annual reports, income statements show year-to-year figures. Why? Because a $10 million profit is meaningless unless you know that the company made $5 million last year and $20 million the year before that. (Stakeholders need a context, and year-to-year numbers give them this context so that they can identify trends.) Organizations also use monthly and quarterly income statements to measure interim performance and to catch performance problems early on. Exhibit 14–7 shows an abbreviated income statement and balance sheet for Callaway Golf Company.

So, what are the two primary ways organizations increase net income? They increase revenues and decrease expenses. Unfortunately, this is more easily said than done. Capital expenditures are one way companies endeavor to increase revenues; they use operating budgets to see where they can decrease costs.

It is important to note here that profit is not the same as cash. In fact, a company can be earning substantial profits and still need to borrow cash to operate. Cash therefore does not appear on the income statement as revenue. Cash appears on the balance sheet and the statement of cash flow.

THE BALANCE SHEET. The *balance sheet* lists assets, liabilities, and owners' equity. Assets are what the organization owns. Liabilities are what it owes to others. Subtract the organization's liabilities from its assets and you have the owners'/stockholders' equity (that share of

financial statements
The income statement, the balance sheet, and the statement of cash flow.

TIMEOUT
Identify several of your firm's or team's capital expenditures.

_____

_____

_____

_____

_____

_____

Exhibit 14–7   Income Statement and Balance Sheet for Callaway Golf Company

CALLAWAY GOLF COMPANY		YEAR	
Income Statement	Dec. 01	Dec. 00	Dec. 99
Revenue*	816.2	837.6	714.5
Cost of Goods Sold	374.1	399.9	336.5
Gross Profit	442.1	437.7	378.0
Gross Profit Margin	54.2%	52.3%	52.9%
SG&A (Selling, General, and Administrative) Expenses	292.1	275.5	258.4
Depreciation & Amortization	37.5	40.2	39.9
Operating Income	112.5	122.0	79.7
Operating Margin	13.8%	14.6%	11.2%
Total Net Income	58.4	81.0	55.3
Net Profit Margin	7.2%	9.7%	7.7%
Balance Sheet	Dec. 01	Dec. 00	Dec. 99
Cash	84.3	102.6	112.6
Net Receivables	48.7	58.8	54.3
Inventories	167.8	134.0	97.9
Total Current Assets (= Cash + Receivables + Inventories + Other Current Assets)	354.7	342.5	310.5
Total Assets	647.6	630.9	616.8
Short-Term Debt	2.4	0.0	0.0
Total Current Liabilities	101.9	109.3	105.3
Long-Term Debt	3.2	0.0	0.0
Total Liabilities	133.4	119.2	116.9
Total Equity	514.3	511.7	499.9

* All amounts (except percentages) are in millions of U.S. dollars.

Source: http://www.hoovers.com, as of June 14, 2002.

the assets owned free and clear). This statement is called a balance sheet because assets *always* equal liabilities plus owners' equity for a particular point in time (see Exhibit 14–7).

Operating costs affect current (less than a year) assets and liabilities. Capital expenditures affect long-term assets and liabilities in the form of property/plant and equipment. *Long-term liabilities* are the payments (such as mortgage payments and bond debt) that the organization has contracted for in order to purchase major assets.

THE STATEMENT OF CASH FLOW. This statement shows cash receipts and payments for the stated period. It commonly has two sections: operating and financial activities. Checks are considered cash. Statements of cash flow typically cover one year. However, monthly and quarterly statements of cash flow are also computed to measure interim performance and to stop cash flow problems in their tracks. Operating costs and capital expenditures affect the statement of cash flow as revenue is received and cash expenditures are paid for.

The financial statements are prepared last because they use information from the operating and capital budgets. Cash flow is prepared first because it is used to prepare the other two. The income statement is prepared next because its information is used on the balance sheet. If the financial statements do not meet expectations, next year's capital budget and/or operating budgets will need to be revised—hence the feedback loop in the master budget process in Exhibit 14–6. Revisions are common when a net loss is projected.

Pro forma statements are special financial statements prepared using certain assumptions. The assumptions fall into categories: (1) Past transactions—what the numbers would look like if certain transactions had *not* occurred. For example, if a large one-time expense is excluded, the bottom line in the pro forma statement will look a lot better. (2) Assumptions about the future—what the numbers would look like if historical patterns (growth rates or rates of return) continue *or* if new assumptions about growth rates are used.[19] **THE RANCH** develops pro forma financial statements for the year and for each month.

TIMEOUT
Does your organization make its financial statements available to the public? If so, get a copy and review them. Also, does it develop operating and capital budgets? Try to get copies of those as well. If you are not sure, ask your boss.

HUMAN CONTROLS

Coaching

8 LEARNING OUTCOME
Use motivational feedback.

Coaching gives motivational feedback to maintain and improve performance. Employees who are given immediate, frequent, and direct feedback perform at higher levels.[20] Many people who hear the word *coaching* immediately think of athletes. If so, they are on the right track (excuse the sport pun!). Why? Because it has (finally) dawned on the business community that coaches are incredible motivators. If you have ever had a good coach, think about what he or she did to maintain and improve your performance and that of other team members. The next time you watch a sporting event, keep an eye on the coaches and watch their technique. Before reading further, think about the best and worst boss or coach you ever had and keep him or her in mind as you progress through this section.

Employees are key in increasing productivity.[21] Coaching is an especially effective way to improve performance, and highly successful organizations all over the business map use it today.[22] Football coach Lou Holtz continually set higher standards for each of his players while at the University of Arkansas and later at Notre Dame. Training is an important part of coaching, because coaches train their athletes continuously. Coaching can also be used to confront employees should the need arise (and it doesn't very often).

Coaching is more art and attitude than it is specific technique. **THE RANCH'S** approach to motivation is a coaching approach. Each employee goes through an extensive orientation and training program. Managers continue to motivate staff by working on the basics to continually improve performance through (Coach) Pete Clark's three I's.

THE IMPORTANCE OF MOTIVATIONAL FEEDBACK. As implied in our definition of coaching, feedback is the "main entree" of coaching, and it should be motivational.[23] The idea is to give more positive feedback than negative feedback. A culture of positive feedback creates an abundance of enthusiasm and energy in an organization. So, cheer your people on with an immediate response to their excellent work. What happens when athletes make good plays? The coach and team cheer them on! The same technique motivates people in the workplace—try it.

Only ineffective and frustrated managers spend more time criticizing than praising. Managers who only criticize staff are shooting themselves in the proverbial foot by *demotivating* their people. Demotivated workers play it safe, do the minimum, focus on not making errors (rather than taking reasonable risks to venture into creative territory), and cover up errors to avoid criticism—not exactly the way you want your team to work. If you find yourself doing more criticizing than praising—it's time to consider what *you* are doing wrong, not what your staff is doing wrong.

Now think about your best and worst bosses and coaches. Who gave you more positive feedback? For whom did you do your best work? (We think we already know the answer.) So, remember the Pygmalion effect and give praise (Chapter 12). Use this coaching technique daily.

COACHING CORRECTIVE ACTION. As you no doubt know by now in this course, ability and motivation directly affect performance. When people are not performing to their potential, even if their work is acceptable, it's time to look a little deeper. Remember the performance equation (Chapter 12)? Use it to think about the situation:

Performance = Ability × Motivation × Resources

When ability is holding back performance, consider training. When motivation is lacking, find out why. Talk to the person—he or she may have some insight—and develop a plan together. If motivation does not work, you may have to use discipline, which we discuss below. When resources are lacking, work to obtain them. Management by walking around (discussed in the section after next) increases your knowledge and thus will give you ideas for possible solutions, whether they are resource problems or ability or motivation problems.

coaching
Gives motivational feedback to maintain and improve performance.

TIMEOUT

Rate your current boss's coaching ability, using specific incidents to defend your answer.

_____

_____

_____

_____

_____

_____

A Coaching How-To Primer

What do managers most often shrink from doing? In three words, advising problematic employees.[24] Managers all too often hesitate to sit down with people who need help, even to the point of jarred nerves and sleepless nights.[25] They hope that the person will somehow turn around on his or her own, only to find that the situation often worsens. Part of the problem is that managers don't know how to coach. Coaching gets simple if you view it as a way to provide ongoing feedback. Model 14–2 is a good place to start.

1. *Describe current performance.* Using specific examples, describe the current performance that needs to be changed. Tell the person exactly what he or she is doing wrong, but couch it as, "You're not doing XXX as well as you can." *Do* tell the positive parts; *don't* tell only the negative side.

   - *Don't* say: "You're picking boxes up wrong."
   - *Do* say: "Billie, there's a more effective and safer way to pick boxes up than bending at the waist."

2. *Describe desired performance.* Tell the person in detail *exactly* what the desired performance is. If the problem is *ability* related—that is, lack of knowledge or experience—demonstrate the proper way. If the problem is *motivational,* simply describe the desired behavior as you ask the person to state *why* the behavior is important.

   - *Ability:* "If you squat down and pick up the box using your legs instead of your back, it is easier and there is less chance of injuring yourself. Let me demonstrate for you."
   - *Motivation:* "Why should you squat and use your legs rather than your back to pick up boxes?"

3. *Get a commitment to the change.* When the issue is *ability,* it usually isn't necessary to get a verbal commitment to the change if the person seems willing to make it. However, if the person defends his or her way and you're sure it's not as effective, explain why your proposed way is better. If you cannot get the person to understand and agree, get a verbal commitment. This step is also important if the issue is *motivation,* because if the employees are not willing to commit to the change, they will most likely not make the change.

   - *Ability:* In our box example, the employee will most likely be willing to do it correctly, so skip the step.
   - *Motivation:* "Will you squat rather than use your back from now on?"

4. *Follow up.* Remember, very few employees (those with low and moderate self-control) will do what managers *inspect* (imposed control), not what they *expect.* Therefore, you're doing both yourself and the employee a favor by following up to ensure that change is occurring as desired.

   In *ability* situations (and the person was receptive and you skipped step 3), say nothing—just watch to be sure the task is done correctly in the future. Coach again, if necessary. In *motivation* situations, clearly state that you will follow up and that there are consequences if performance doesn't improve.

   - *Ability:* Say nothing, but observe.
   - *Motivation:* "Billie, picking up boxes with your back is dangerous; if I catch you doing it again, I will take disciplinary action."

Model 14–2   How to Coach

1. Describe current performance.	→	2. Describe desired performance.	→	3. Get a commitment to the change.	→	4. Follow up.

Management by Walking Around

Management by walking around (MBWA) is about listening, teaching, and facilitating.

LISTENING. If you want to find out what's going on, listen more than you talk and be open to feedback. Learn to talk last, not first. Open with a simple question like, "How are things going?" Then use the communication skills you honed in Chapter 11.

TEACHING. Teaching is *not* about telling people what to do—that is training (Chapter 8). It *is* about helping people do a better job by empowering them to solve their own problems. Therefore, coaches say, "What do *you* think should be done?"

FACILITATING. *Facilitating* is about taking action that helps people do their jobs. The focus here is on improving the system. Your team members know their jobs *and* they know (often all too well) the stumbling blocks in their way. Why? Because they deal with them every day—*trust their expertise.* *Your* job is to run interference and to remove those pesky stumbling blocks so that the team can get on with its business.

Now it's *your* turn to give feedback. Tell the team what is going to be done about the problem—if anything—and when. If you listen but don't facilitate, your staff will stop talking and you will lose your most important source for improving the system. The **CLARKS AND WILLOWBEND** managers are classic MBWA-ers. The result? A 4-Star golf course almost from the get-go *and* a highly motivated staff.

management by walking around (MBWA)
Is about listening, teaching, and facilitating.

PROBLEM EMPLOYEES

When you coach people, you are fine-tuning the performance of someone who *wants* to improve. When you counsel and discipline people, you are dealing with a very different situation—a problem employee who is not performing to standard or who is violating standing plans. Organizations realize that part of their job is to help employees deal with their problems.[26] A growing number of organizations today train managers in counseling as a way to improve performance.

Who are the problem employees? They fall into four categories: (1) People who don't have the *ability* to meet standards. This is an unfortunate situation, but, after you have trained such employees and realized that they are *unable* to do a good job, they should be dismissed.[27] Employees are often hired on a trial basis—this is the time to say, "Sorry, but you have to go." (2) People who lack *motivation.* (3) People who intentionally *violate standing plans.* As a manager, it is your job to enforce the rules through disciplinary action. (4) People with *problems.* These people are the ones whom counseling targets. They may have the "goods," but they also have a personal problem that is hurting their performance. Personal problems are numerous and wide ranging: from child care to anger management to elder care to relationship/marital problems to health issues to drug use—the list is long and surprising in its diversity.

Before we examine your options as a manager dealing with a problem employee, take a moment to study Exhibit 14–8 and think about its implications. As you can see, it is not always easy to identify into which category a problem employee fits. Therefore, think coaching and/or counseling first. Discipline is your fallback position and your last resort—use it carefully or it loses its power to shape change.

TIME**OUT**
Think about a problem employee or teammate whom you are aware of. Describe how the person affected your department's or team's performance.
_____
_____
_____
_____
_____
_____

When Managers Are Counselors

9 LEARNING OUTCOME
Understand the role of EAP staff.

When most people hear the term *counseling,* they think of professional therapy—as well they should. People who are *not* professional counselors—and that includes managers—should *not* attempt this level of help. (Unless, of course, you relish lawsuits!) Management counseling is something very different; in fact, it is not really counseling at all. When you hear the term *management counseling,* think of recognition and referral, because that is what it is and

Exhibit 14–8 Problem Employees

The late employee
The absent employee
The dishonest employee
The violent or destructive employee
The alcoholic or drug user
The nonconformist
The employee with a family problem
The insubordinate employee
The employee who steals
The sexual or racial harasser
The safety violator
The sick employee
The employee who's often socializing or doing personal work

management counseling
Helps employees recognize that they have a problem, and then refers them to the employee assistance program.

employee assistance programs (EAPs)
Help employees get professional assistance in solving their problems.

that is all it is. **Management counseling** helps employees recognize that they have a problem, and then refers them to the employee assistance program. **Employee assistance programs (EAPs)** help employees get professional assistance in solving their problems. More and more companies are offering EAPs, because they improve employee retention and productivity. Former Cleveland Indians pitcher Sam McDowell became a certified and licensed therapist in sport psychology and addiction after his retirement in 1975. For 14 years, he was the director of EAPs and sport psychology programs for the Texas Rangers and Toronto Blue Jays.[28]

Management counseling requires a great deal of tact, restraint, wisdom, insight, and timing. It is *not* about delving into someone's personal life. There is a line here that must not be crossed—for the employee's sake and also for yours. You don't need to know the details; in fact, it is better that you not know them. Knowing too much can hurt your effectiveness as a manager, and *it is not your job.* Issues of privacy play a big role here; that's why your organization has a separate department—the assistance program. Your role is simply to help the person realize that he or she has a problem and that it is affecting his or her work. You are pointing employees to a track where they can get help; you are not going on the track with them. The counselors in the assistance program will do that.

So, *don't give advice.* If you do, you are putting both yourself and your organization at risk for litigation. To make the referral, you *can* say something like, "Are you aware of our employee assistance program? Would you like me to set up an appointment with Jean in HR to see if they can help?" If job performance continues to suffer, then and only then does discipline become an appropriate choice.

Remember, your first obligation is to your organization—it is *not* to individual employees. Not taking action because you feel uncomfortable approaching individuals, because you feel sorry for them, or because you like them helps neither you nor the employees. Don't forget that problem employees are not only not as productive as they should be, they are also causing more work for you and for the rest of the team. This is not good for morale. Taking action is the right thing to do; just make sure it is the right action.

TIMEOUT
Explain the manager's role in counseling.

Discipline

You've taken the coaching route. You've taught and facilitated and fed back positive reinforcements. And you've been down the EAP road. Nothing has worked. *Now* what do you do? You think about taking disciplinary action.

discipline
Corrective action to get employees to meet standards and to follow the rules.

Discipline is corrective action to get employees to meet standards and to follow the rules. Discipline can be effective if it makes the person realize the seriousness of the situation. The first objective of discipline is to change behavior. There are some important secondary objectives. One is to let employees know that action will be taken when rules are broken or performance is not met. A key example is fraud. Unfortunately, this is a troubling and growing problem. Companies who punish perpetrators swiftly and publicly (by taking them to trial) reduce the incidence of fraud by orders of magnitude. The second one is to maintain your authority when challenged.

When you find yourself having to consider disciplinary action, it's time to involve your HR department. Why? For lots and lots of reasons. Today, there are many rules and regulations surrounding what disciplinary action you can and cannot take. Unless you are a walking encyclopedia of labor law, you aren't going to know the legality or illegality of any given action you might think up. Gone are the days of Theory X managers who could take it upon themselves to send an employee home without pay for a couple of days. Gone too are the days when you could fire someone on your own. HR departments typically handle many of the disciplinary details today, and they also provide written guidelines. *Read them.* HR procedures outline grounds for specific sanctions and dismissal based on the violation. Common offenses include theft, sexual or racial harassment, verbal or substance abuse, and safety violations. Exhibit 14–9 gives guidelines for legal and effective discipline.

PROGRESSIVE DISCIPLINE. Many organizations use a series of escalating actions. Progressive discipline occurs in this order: (1) oral warning; (2) written warning; (3) suspension; and finally (4) dismissal. For most violations, all four steps will be followed. However, for certain violations, such as theft or sexual or racial harassment, offenders may be dismissed immediately. Documenting each step is extremely important. At **THE RANCH,** employees are well trained and clearly told expectations. Employees who do not meet the standards are warned and terminated if they don't perform to standard. The Willowbend managers, with the Clarks, are involved in performance appraisals, discipline, and termination.

Exhibit 14–9   Guidelines for Legal and Effective Discipline

A. Clearly communicate the standards and standing plans to all employees.
B. Be sure that the punishment fits the violation.
C. Follow the standing plans yourself.
D. Take consistent, impartial action when the rules are broken.
E. Discipline immediately, but stay calm and get all the necessary facts before you discipline.
F. Discipline in private.
G. Document discipline.
H. When the discipline is over, resume normal relations with the employee.

When You Have to Discipline Someone

The steps shown in Model 14–3 set up an effective model for you to use if you ever need to discipline an employee. These steps would also serve a team well if it is faced with low performance by a team member.[29]

1. *Refer to past feedback.* Begin the interview by refreshing the employee's memory. Refer to the coaching or counseling the person has received or to the fact that the person has been warned about breaking the rule in question.

   - *Prior coaching:* Billie, remember my showing you the proper way to lift boxes with your legs?
   - *Rule violation:* Billie, you know the safety rule about lifting boxes with your legs.

APPLYING THE CONCEPT *Guidelines for Effective and Legal Discipline*

Use Exhibit 14–9 to identify which guideline is or is not being followed in each situation (A–H).

_____ 11. The coach must have been very upset about us not trying hard enough to yell that loudly.

_____ 12. It's not fair. The star players come back from winter break late all the time; why can't I?

_____ 13. When I miss my defensive assignment, Coach reprimands me. When Chris does it, nothing is ever said.

_____ 14. Coach gave me a verbal warning for smoking inside the locker room, which is a restricted area, and placed a note in my file.

_____ 15. I want you to come into my office so that we can discuss this matter.

Model 14–3   Steps in Disciplining

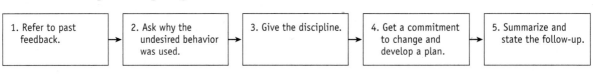

| 1. Refer to past feedback. | → | 2. Ask why the undesired behavior was used. | → | 3. Give the discipline. | → | 4. Get a commitment to change and develop a plan. | → | 5. Summarize and state the follow-up. |

2. *Ask why the undesired behavior was used.* Give the person a chance to explain the behavior. He or she may or may not have justification for the behavior.

   ■ *Example:* Two days ago you agreed to lift boxes by the rules. Is there a reason you're still using your back?

   If the explanation is reasonable, end this conversation with a comment that it's time to get back on track. If you have "been here before," so to speak, and it is time to move beyond excuses, do *not* ask the person why he or she is still using the undesirable or prohibited behavior. Now is *not* the time to be patronizing—loss of face is not going to help anyone. Asking why he or she is still doing XXX is a quagmire that can only instill feelings of resentment, and it opens you up to argument, yelling matches, tears, and wringing of hands—*none* of these are constructive. Such a question personalizes the situation by setting up a power struggle between you and the employee. Remember, the struggle here is between the person and the rules or between the person and his or her performance. You are a neutral arbiter here. Behavior is a choice, and only the employee can do something about it. At this point, the best approach is a "you know the rules, you know the consequences" approach. Inform the employee that he or she has triggered the next step in the process and that your hands are tied. Note that the following example keeps *you* out of the picture.

   ■ *Example:* As you know, Billie, two warnings trigger the discipline we talked about earlier.

3. *Give the discipline.* Review the guidelines set up by your HR department and follow them carefully. If this is your first experience, you may want to talk to someone in your HR department before you proceed. He or she will be glad to help you. Discipline done poorly is cause for lawsuits.

4. *Get a commitment to change and develop a plan.* Try to get a commitment to change. If the employee refuses, make note of this in the critical incidents file and follow your organization's next procedure. If a plan was developed in the past, review it with the employee, discuss what changes might make the plan more useful, and ask the person to commit to it again. Develop a new plan, if necessary. Statements like "Your previous attempt didn't work; there must be a better way," are often helpful. With a personal problem, offer professional help again.

   ■ *Example:* Is there something you can think of that will help you remember to lift boxes the correct way?

5. *Summarize and state the follow-up.* Part of your follow-up is to document the discipline. If a written warning or suspension has been triggered, get the employee's signature.

PRODUCTIVITY

All of us would like to get paid more. However, if we earn more without producing more, the only way to maintain profits is to raise product prices to offset the increased wage cost.[30] Not only does this cause inflation, but increased prices damage an organization's competitiveness. Therefore, increasing productivity is the area organizations continually do battle in as they wage their war against loss of market share and inflation. Effective managers understand how to measure productivity, and they constantly look for ways to increase productivity. **THE RANCH** maintains productivity by keeping players to average game-completion times. Slow players/parties hold up players "in the pipeline" and can hurt customer satisfaction. The golf cars' GPS system tells the players if they are on schedule, and player assistants help players stay on schedule.

Long-term productivity trends show that efficiency appears to be improving.[31] The technological revolution we have witnessed in the past 30 years has been a central component of this trend. However, as this technological cycle winds to a close (there is a point beyond which faster, better computers can no longer create gains in productivity), about all that is left on the "productivity plate" is worker productivity. As we have noted throughout this text, managers affect employee performance in numerous and very important ways. Effective management of the workforce is therefore key to increasing productivity. Organizations are increasingly looking to counseling, job design, work teams, flexible schedules, telecommuting, and incentives to improve productivity.

Measuring Productivity

Productivity has been called a state of mind, because every manager worth his or her salt is constantly thinking of ways to increase it.[32] Measuring productivity can be complex, but it doesn't have to be.[33] In this section, we outline a simple, yet realistic, approach that you can use on the job to measure productivity on the micro level. The U.S. government measures productivity rates on a macro level for the entire economy as well as for various industries; these statistics give you standards against which you can measure your department and/or organization to see how you are doing.

Productivity measures performance by dividing outputs by inputs.[34] Let's say Exxon-Mobil wants to know the productivity of its new Formula One racing fuel. In this hypothetical test, the Formula One car traveled 1,000 miles and used 100 gallons of the new fuel. Its productivity was 10 miles to the gallon:

productivity
Measures performance by dividing outputs by inputs.

$$\text{Productivity} = \frac{\text{Output}}{\text{Input}} = \frac{1,000 \text{ miles traveled}}{100 \text{ gallons of fuel}} = 10 \text{ mpg}$$

Now let's say a sporting goods manufacturer wants to know the weekly productivity of its accounts payable department. We are going to simplify things here a bit, but this will give you an idea of how to get a realistic idea of your group's productivity rate.

1. Select a time period, such as an hour, a day, a week, a month, a quarter, or a year. In this example, the accounts payable manager decides to look at a week.

2. Determine how many bills (outputs) were sent out during that period. The manager checks the records and finds out that her three-person department sent out 800 bills last week.

3. Determine the "quick cost" of sending out the bills (inputs). Determining costs can be complicated if you determine total cost, which includes overhead, depreciation, and many other variables. In this instance, our manager uses only direct labor charges for the three employees, who are each paid $7 an hour. They all worked 40 hours during the week in question for a total of 120 hours. The total quick cost then is $7 an hour × 120 hours, or $840.

4. Dividing the number of outputs (bills sent out) by the inputs (direct labor charges) gives the productivity ratio—0.95 (800 / $840 = 0.95)—which of course can be expressed as a percentage (95 percent). It can also be stated as *labor cost per unit*. To determine labor cost per unit, simply reverse the process and divide inputs by outputs ($840 / 800). It thus costs $1.05 to send out each bill.

CALCULATING PRODUCTIVITY RATE CHANGES. Our manager now sets the 0.95 productivity rate as her base rate. In the next week, the accounting department again sends out 800 bills, but, due to computer problems, the three employees have to work overtime at an additional cost of $100. The productivity rate thus decreases to 0.85 (800 / $940). The labor cost per unit goes up to $1.175 ($940 / 800). To determine the percentage change, use the following formula:

Current productivity rate (85%) − Base productivity rate (95%) = Change (10%)

Change / base productivity rate (10 / 95) = 0.1053, or a 10.53 percent decrease in productivity

PRODUCTION VERSUS PRODUCTIVITY. It is important to think in terms of your productivity rate and not just in terms of increasing output, because productivity can decrease even though output increases. Suppose our hypothetical sporting goods company's accounts payable department sends out 850 bills, but doing so requires 10 hours of overtime (time-and-a-half at $10.50 an hour × 10 hours = $105)—productivity has *decreased* from 0.95 to 0.90 (850 / 945). In other words, if you measure only output and it increases, you can be fooled into thinking you are doing a better job, when in reality you are doing a worse job.

Increasing Productivity

10 LEARNING OUTCOME
State three ways to increase productivity.

There are three ways to increase productivity:

■ Increase output value and maintain input value ($\uparrow$ O $\leftrightarrow$ I).

■ Maintain output value and decrease input value ($\leftrightarrow$ O $\downarrow$ I).

■ Increase output value and decrease input value ($\uparrow$ O $\downarrow$ I).

Always compare your productivity during one period to previous periods, because productivity during any given period by itself is meaningless. What is important is whether it is changing for the better or worse, or whether it is stagnating. You can also set a certain productivity rate as your standard and make comparisons to the standard on an ongoing basis. This was done in the preceding Applying the Concept.

Measuring Functional-Area Productivity

Productivity measures are important for another reason—they indicate how well an organization is being managed. It therefore behooves organizations to look at functional-area

---

APPLYING
THE **CONCEPT**   *Measuring Productivity*

The standard monthly productivity rate in the golf club department is as follows:

   Productivity = Outputs / Inputs = 6,000 units / $9,000 cost = 0.67, or 67%

Calculate the current productivity rate for each month and show it as both a ratio and a percentage. Then calculate the percentage productivity change compared to the standard, stating if it was an increase or a decrease.

16. January: outputs = 5,900; inputs = $9,000   ratio: _____; percent: _____;
                                                  change: _____%

_____

17. February: outputs = 6,200; inputs = $9,000   ratio: _____; percent: _____;
                                                   change: _____%

_____

18. March: outputs = 6,000; inputs = $9,300   ratio: _____; percent: _____;
                                               change: _____%

_____

19. April: outputs = 6,300; inputs = $9,000   ratio: _____; percent: _____;
                                               change: _____%

_____

20. May: outputs = 6,300; inputs = $8,800   ratio: _____; percent: _____;
                                             change: _____%

_____

productivity. Exhibit 14–10 lists the various ratios that are used to measure functional areas. The numbers used to calculate the financial ratios are taken from the income statement and balance sheet (examples of which were shown in Exhibit 14–7). As indicated in Exhibit 14–10, these ratios are easy to calculate and understand, and they are used commonly as controls. In order to make meaningful year-to-year comparisons, three years of data are commonly analyzed.

MEASURING THE ORGANIZATION'S OVERALL PERFORMANCE. Note that the financial ratios indicate the organization's overall performance; they do not measure the performance of the finance area itself. Thus, the profitability ratios are based heavily on sales, which is a marketing function. However, the performance of the other functional areas is affected by how well finance does its job. Finance controls the budget, which helps (or hinders) the other functional areas. Marketing sells the products on credit, and finance (through its accounting function) collects the payments and pays for purchases made throughout the organization. Willowbend management uses a variety of financial ratios and percentages to measure performance at **THE RANCH.**

MEASURING PRODUCTIVITY IN MARKETING AND OPERATIONS. Marketing and operations in an organization can be likened to the heart and lungs in the body. The key to business success is for these two areas, with the aid of the other functional areas, to continually increase customer value. If marketing and operations do not work well and do not work well together, the organization may fail to thrive. Gross profit margin and net profit margin are also considered marketing ratios because they are based on sales.

Inventory turnover is primarily the responsibility of operations. However, operations depends on marketing's sales forecasts, which it uses to decide how much product to produce. If sales forecasts are too optimistic, operations will produce too much product, which will sit in inventory, which decreases the turnover rate.

Exhibit 14–10 Financial Ratios

FUNCTIONAL AREA	RATIO	CALCULATION	INFORMATION
Overall Organization			
Profitability	Gross profit margin	$\dfrac{\text{Sales} - \text{COGS*}}{\text{Sales}}$	Measures efficiency of operations and product pricing.
	Net profit margin	$\dfrac{\text{Net profit / Income}}{\text{Sales}}$	Measures product profitability.
	Return on investment	$\dfrac{\text{Net profit / Income}}{\text{Total assets}}$	Measures return on total capital expenditures or ability of assets to generate a profit.
Liquidity	Current ratio	$\dfrac{\text{Current assets}}{\text{Current liabilities}}$	Measures ability to pay short-term debt.
	Quick ratio	$\dfrac{\text{Current assets} - \text{Inventory}}{\text{Current liabilities}}$	This is a stronger measure of bill-paying ability, because inventory may be slow to sell for cash.
Leverage	Debt to equity	$\dfrac{\text{Total liabilities}}{\text{Owners' equity}}$	Shows proportion of the assets owned by the organization.
Operations	Inventory turnover	$\dfrac{\text{COGS}}{\text{Average inventory}}$	Shows how efficient the organization is in controlling its investment in inventory. The larger the number, the better, because this means that products are being sold faster.
Marketing	Market share	$\dfrac{\text{Company sales}}{\text{Total industry sales}}$	Measures the organization's competitive position. The larger, the better, because this means the organization is outselling its competitors.
	Sales to presentation	$\dfrac{\text{Sales completed}}{\text{Sales presentations made}}$	Shows how many presentations it takes to make a sale.
Human Resources	Absenteeism	$\dfrac{\text{Number of absent employees}}{\text{Total number of employees}}$	Shows the ratio of employees not at work for a given time period.
	Turnover	$\dfrac{\text{Number of employees leaving}}{\text{Total number of employees}}$	Shows the ratio of employees who must be replaced for a given period (usually one year).
	Workforce composition	$\dfrac{\text{Number of a specific group}}{\text{Total number of employees}}$	Shows the ratio of women, Hispanics, African Americans, and so on in the organization's workforce.

*COGS = cost of goods sold.

Balancing Financing in the Shadow of Bigger Sport Arenas, Skyrocketing Player Salaries, and Labor Problems

As we close this book, we would like to revisit problems facing professional sport management that are not likely to go away anytime soon. Not coincidentally, this discussion integrates many of the important issues we have discussed throughout the text. We use MLB as our example because, at this writing, management and players have managed to tiptoe past another strike, having just agreed on a new collective bargaining agreement (CBA). However, other leagues, such as the NBA and NHL, face similar problems when their CBAs expire.

STADIUMS—BIGGER, BETTER, MORE COSTLY, AND EMPTIER. As we noted in Chapter 2, the strong U.S. economy of the 1990s allowed the sport industry to grow in many ways.[35] Owners watched the long-term value of their teams increase even as the teams lost money on a yearly basis.[36] Many teams got cities to help them build new arenas and stadiums to provide skybox seating for corporate sponsors. These new stadiums and the expected new ticket revenues led to the increased franchise values.[37] Many cities took on serious debt to help teams build these facilities.[38] However, this high debt becomes hard to repay if the team doesn't win and attract large numbers of fans to its games.

PLAYER SALARIES—UP, UP, AND AWAY. At the same time, player salaries have entered the stratosphere. The average player salary in 1990 was $589,483. In 2000, it was $1,894,216.[39] Too many teams are finding that player salaries and new-stadium debt are outpacing revenues.

MEDIA MARKETS—THE BIG GUYS WIN; THE LITTLE GUYS LOSE. Meanwhile, it is becoming all too clear that big-market teams can generate huge profits from media contracts that are not available to small-market teams. New York media contracts are much more valuable than those for Kansas City or Cleveland. Teams in smaller markets are having to sell players for cash, trade high-paid stars for young, unproven players with smaller contracts, sell their teams outright, or move their team to another state.

MLB LABOR RELATIONS—NOT PRETTY. To make matters even worse, labor relations continue to haunt MLB. Even though MLB and the players agreed on a new CBA in 2002, many questions remain unanswered. For example, with regard to drug testing, the owners succeeded in getting players to agree for the first time to mandatory random testing. However, the players won a small victory by having the testing limited to only steroids. Hopefully, this testing will help answer the question of whether players in the last few years have had such huge offensive production due to the use of steroids.

The CBA calls for a competitive balance tax (called a *luxury tax*). The tax is based on team payroll. Teams with a payroll over the threshold amount—$117 million in 2003, $120 million in 2004, $128 million in 2005, and $136.5 million in 2006—will have to pay a tax of at least 17.5 percent for first-time offenders and up to 40 percent for repeat offenders.[40] The New York Yankees, Texas Rangers, and Los Angeles Dodgers would have to pay the tax based on 2002 salary levels.

The CBA also calls for an increase in revenue sharing from the 2001 level of $168 million shared by the lower-revenue clubs to an average of $258 million a year over the four years of the contract. This means local revenue sharing will jump from 20 percent to 34 percent. It will be interesting to see whether the luxury tax and increased revenue sharing will help the weaker baseball teams.

MAKING MAD FANS MADDER. Baseball Commissioner Bud Selig wanted to improve the profitability of teams by eliminating two financially weak teams. However, as part of the CBA, the contraction strategy was put on hold until 2006. Meanwhile, the weaker teams are still struggling. For example, Jeffrey Loria bought the Florida Marlins before the 2002 season. He has been forced to sell off star players, such as Cliff Floyd, to raise cash to pay for debt financing and reduce team payroll. Floyd was sent to the Montreal Expos even as the Marlins were in strong contention to win its division.[41] The situation spirals down from here—shrinking revenues cause star players to be sold, which causes fans to stay away, which causes revenues to shrink even further.

As a student of sport management and as a future manager, you must ask questions that we can only wonder whether people in the industry are asking themselves: What are the bad management decisions being made? What do these issues portend for the future of pro sports? What ripple effects might a severe recession in the pro sport team industry have on industries that depend on pro sport teams thriving? What strategies will bring back disgruntled fans and create new ones? The sport industry is an odd-duck industry—by its very nature, it will always have winning teams and losing teams. How can they all win at the biggest game of all—the bottom-line game?

THE FUTURE OF SPORT MANAGEMENT

The good news is that America's love affair with sports has lost none of its bloom. Look around you. There are fencing teams, dance studios, soccer teams, and figure skating clubs. The list is long, diverse, and inhabited by people from all walks of life who build their free time around these sports—doing them, watching them, teaching them, and traveling great distances to participate in them. The future of sport management is bigger, brighter, and more diverse than it has ever been. Whereas pro sport teams have some serious white water directly ahead that they badly need to find ways to negotiate, *sports* are thriving in America and around the world. Managers trained in sport management are in great demand. Opportunities abound in managing sporting goods stores; organizing athletic departments at educational institutions; shaping the future of sports in governing bodies such as FIFA, the NCAA, and the IOC; planning events; working in local community recreation centers and youth leagues; officiating; coaching; sport broadcasting; and numerous professional leagues. Maybe you took this course because you want to work for a professional team. However, we hope this book has helped you see just how many different sport organizations need great managers. (See Appendix A for an in-depth discussion of careers in sport management as the field enters the next decade.)

CHAPTER SUMMARY

1. Explain how controls function with the systems process.

The first stage of the systems process is inputs. Preliminary controls are designed to anticipate and prevent possible problems. The second stage is the transformation process. Concurrent controls are actions taken during the transformation to ensure that standards are met. The third stage is outputs. Rework controls are actions taken to fix an output. The fourth stage is customer/stakeholder satisfaction. Damage controls are actions taken to minimize negative impacts on customers due to faulty outputs. Feedback is used at each stage to improve the process to continually increase customer satisfaction.

2. Understand why feedback is a control.

Feedback is circulated through all the functional areas to improve organizational performance in the input, transformation, and output processes and to continually increase customer satisfaction.

3. Describe the control process.

The four steps in the control process are: (1) set objectives and standards; (2) measure performance; (3) compare performance to standards; and (4) correct or reinforce, with a feedback loop for continuous improvement.

4. List which control methods are used with which frequency.

Self-control, clan control, and standing plans are used constantly (continuously). Routine reports, budgets, and audits are used periodically. Observation, the exception principle, special reports, and project controls are used occasionally.

5. Differentiate between static and flexible budgets, and incremental and zero-based budgets.

A static budget has only one set of expenses, whereas a flexible budget has a series of expenses for a range of activities. With incremental budgeting, past funds are allocated with only new expenses being justified and approved. With zero-based budgeting, all funds must be justified each year.

6. Explain how capital budgets and operating budgets differ.

The capital expenditures budget includes all planned major asset investments. It consists of funds allocated for investments in major assets that will last, and be paid for, over several years. The expense budget contains funds allocated to pay for operating costs during the budgeting year. With expense budgets, the focus is on cost control. With capital expenditures, the focus is on the more important role of developing ways to bring in additional revenues through new and improved products and projects that will create customer value.

7. State what the three basic financial statements entail.

The income statement details revenue and expenses and the profit or loss for the stated time period. The balance sheet presents assets, liabilities, and owners' equity. The statement of cash flow presents the cash receipts and payments for the stated time period.

8. Use motivational feedback.

The objective of coaching is to improve performance. Positive feedback, such as giving praise, motivates employees to maintain and improve their performance.

9. Understand the role of EAP staff.

The manager's role in counseling is to recognize and refer. Recognize that an employee has a problem and refer him or her to the employee assistance program. EAP staff members then help employees get professional help to solve their problems.

10. State three ways to increase productivity.

Productivity is measured by dividing outputs by inputs. Productivity is increased by (1) increasing output value while maintaining input value; (2) maintaining output value while decreasing input value; and (3) increasing output value while decreasing input value.

11. Define the key terms discussed in the text.

Fill in the missing key terms from memory, or match the key terms from the list in the margin with their definitions below.

_____ is the process of establishing and implementing mechanisms to ensure that objectives are achieved.

_____ anticipate and prevent possible problems.

_____ are actions taken during transformation to ensure that standards are met.

_____ are actions taken to fix output.

_____ are actions taken to minimize negative impacts on customers due to faulty output.

_____ minimize negative impacts on customers due to faulty output by controlling quantity, quality, time, cost, and behavior.

Key Terms

budgets
capital budgets
coaching
concurrent controls
control frequencies
controlling
critical success factors (CSFs)
damage controls
discipline
employee assistance programs (EAPs)
financial statements
management audits
management by walking around (MBWA)
management counseling
operating budgets
preliminary controls
productivity
rework controls
standards

_____ are pivotal areas in which satisfactory results will ensure successful achievement of the objective/standard.

_____ are constant, periodic, and occasional.

_____ look at ways to improve the organization's planning, organizing, leading, and controlling functions.

_____ are plans for allocating resources to specific activities.

_____ use revenue forecasts to allocate funds to cover projected expenses.

_____ allocate funds for improvements.

The three _____ are the income statement, the balance sheet, and the statement of cash flows.

_____ gives motivational feedback to maintain and improve performance.

_____ is about listening, teaching, and facilitating.

_____ helps employees recognize that they have a problem, and then refers them to the employee assistance program.

_____ help employees get professional assistance in solving their problems.

_____ is corrective action to get employees to meet standards and to follow the rules.

_____ measures performance by dividing outputs by inputs.

REVIEW AND DISCUSSION

1. Why is damage control important?
2. Name five sport governing bodies.
3. Discuss the role of governing bodies in managing and controlling their sport.
4. Who are the primary customers/stakeholders for the outputs of operations, marketing, human resources, finance, and MIS departments?
5. Why do organizations measure performance?
6. What is shown in a performance report?
7. What is the role of reinforcement in the control process?
8. List the three constant-control methods, the three periodic-control methods, and the four occasional-control methods.
9. What are the three steps in the master budgeting process?
10. Why is the capital budget the most important budget?
11. State what the three financial statements show.

12. What is the objective of coaching?

13. How do managers commonly demotivate employees?

14. What is the performance equation and how is it used with coaching?

15. What are the three activities of management by walking around and what is the role of facilitating?

16. How do coaching, counseling, and disciplining differ?

17. Which of the eight discipline guidelines is most relevant to you personally? Explain.

18. Discuss the financial aspects of stadium costs, player salaries, and media rights.

19. Name the major ratio measures in finance, marketing, and human resources, and explain what they measure.

CASE

The Coaching Model

In this textbook, we have mentioned several famous coaches—Pat Summitt, Lou Holtz, Vince Lombardi, and Joe Torre. After much reflection, we believe that the best coaches all employ the coaching model described in this chapter. Somehow, they are able to use the four steps time and again with remarkable success. They are not afraid to take a player aside and describe his or her current performance. They move ahead and describe desired performance. They tell players exactly what the desired performance is in detail. They have honed their abilities to assess individual ability and motivation. Most importantly, they always get a commitment to the change. Their personal charisma makes players want to change. Lastly, they follow up and assess the individual's success or failure. If the player does not perform to expectations, he or she loses playing time, or is traded or released.

But is that everything? Great leaders also seem to find willing followers. Individuals change their behavior to help the team achieve success. Players and employees who have average abilities become very important as role players who support star performers. Success fosters more success because more individuals want to join the team.

The authors have also found that the coaching model is just as useful in office situations as it is on playing fields. Great managers are willing to sit down with employees and follow the four steps of the model. Likewise, poor managers shy away from discussing an employee's performance with him or her. Poor managers never get commitment from their employees. Poor managers never manage by walking around. They hunker down in their corner offices, shielded from the give and take, the small hurdles, and the large problems looming on the floor.

CASE QUESTIONS

Determine which step of the coaching model is being utilized in each situation. Support your answers by reviewing relevant material in previous chapters.

1. Athletic directors like Cheryl Condon (Chapter 1) are not afraid to take a player or employee aside and discuss his or her work.
   a. Describe current performance.
   b. Describe desired performance.
   c. Get a commitment to the change.
   d. Follow up.
   e. All of the above.

2. CEOs, such as Phil Knight of Nike (Chapter 1), set goals to motivate their employees.
   a. Describe current performance.
   b. Describe desired performance.
   c. Get a commitment to the change.
   d. Follow up.
   e. All of the above.

3. General managers, such as Pat Gillick of the Seattle Mariners (Chapter 2), tell players exactly what the expected performance is in detail.
   a. Describe current performance.
   b. Describe desired performance.
   c. Get a commitment to the change.
   d. Follow up.
   e. All of the above.

4. Presidents of governing bodies, such as Jacques Rogge of the International Olympic Committee (Chapter 2), assess individual ability and motivation accurately.
   a. Describe current performance.
   b. Describe desired performance.
   c. Get a commitment to the change.
   d. Follow up.
   e. All of the above.

5. Charisma, like that of Joe Torre of the New York Yankees (Chapter 7), makes players or employees want to change.
   a. Describe current performance.
   b. Describe desired performance.
   c. Get a commitment to the change.
   d. Follow up.
   e. All of the above.

6. Coaches, such as John Wooden (Chapter 9), summarize and assess the individual's success or failure.
   a. Describe current performance.
   b. Describe desired performance.
   c. Get a commitment to the change.
   d. Follow up.
   e. All of the above.

7. Coaches, such as John Amaral (Chapter 12), will talk to a player if the player did not perform up to expectations either on or off the playing field.
   a. Describe current performance.
   b. Describe desired performance.
   c. Get a commitment to the change.
   d. Follow up.
   e. All of the above.

8. Some coaches, such as Pat Summit of the University of Tennessee (Chapter 12), use autocratic methods such as yelling to successfully motivate their players. (Although this method works for Pat, it is not usually successful for most coaches.)
   a. Describe current performance.
   b. Describe desired performance.
   c. Get a commitment to the change.
   d. Follow up.
   e. All of the above.

9. The success of coaches like Vince Lombardi (Chapter 13) bred more success, because more individuals wanted to join the team.
   a. Describe current performance.
   b. Describe desired performance.
   c. Get a commitment to the change.
   d. Follow up.
   e. All of the above.

10. Pete Clark at The Ranch (this chapter) sets challenging goals for his employees.
    a. Describe current performance.
    b. Describe desired performance.
    c. Get a commitment to the change.
    d. Follow up.
    e. All of the above.

11. Overall, which step do you believe that these coaches emphasize most?

12. Did you ever play for a coach who inspired you to do truly great things?

13. Did you ever play for a coach or work for a manager who used the coaching model?

14. Have you ever been in a position to use coaching?

VIDEO CASE

Facility Security: New Safeguards at World Gym

Introduction

World Gym Showplace Square is located in San Francisco, California. At this location, World Gym services approximately 8,000 members and is open 19 hours a day, 7 days a week. World Gym Showplace Square offers a wide variety of services to meet a diverse clientele. Members range from professional bodybuilders to clients interested in weight loss. In the video segment that accompanies this chapter, World Gym's managers, reflecting a similar diversity, address security and privacy concerns at the Showplace Square location.

Focus Your Attention

To get the most out of viewing the World Gym video, think about the following issues: how World Gym employees with different functional expertise can learn from each other, how security decisions affect clients versus how these decisions affect employees, and how operational decisions can shape the future of the organization. Then answer the following questions after viewing the video:

1. What precautions has World Gym taken to discourage employee theft? What frequency and method of control is it using?

2. What departments implement functional-level operational strategies? Give examples of how World Gym might use these departments/strategies to improve its services for clients and its business performance.

3. How might World Gym plan and manage its operations to meet the diverse needs of its 8,000 members?

EXERCISES

Skill-Builder: Coaching

Objective:

- To develop your skill at improving performance through coaching.

Preparation:
Review the section on coaching.

In-Class Application

Complete the skill-building preparation noted above before class.

1. Role-playing (10–30 minutes): Break into groups of three and role-play the three situations, taking turns being the manager/coach and the employee. Remember that as the employee you are unwilling to follow the standing plan. The odd person out in each role-play is to observe and "coach the coach."

2. Comparison of student-written motivational feedback forms.

3. Informal, whole-class discussion of student experiences.

The Situations

1. Employee 1 is a clerical worker in the ticket office. The person uses files, as do the other ten employees in the department. The employees all know that they are

supposed to return the files when they are finished so that others can find them when they need them. Employees should have only one file out at a time. The supervisor notices that Employee 1 has five files on the desk, and another employee is looking for one of them. The supervisor thinks that Employee 1 will complain about the heavy workload as an excuse for having more than one file out at a time.

2. Employee 2 is a server in the concession area of the stadium. The employee knows that the tables should be cleaned up quickly after customers leave so that new customers don't have to sit at dirty tables. It's a busy night. The supervisor finds dirty dishes on two of this employee's occupied tables. Employee 2 is socializing with some friends at one of the tables. Employees are supposed to be friendly; Employee 2 will probably use this as an excuse for the dirty tables.

3. Employee 3 is an assistant fitness instructor in a fitness center. All employees at the fitness center where this person works know that they are supposed to clean a fitness machine if a member does not. When the fitness manager arrived at the fitness center, he noticed Employee 3 did not clean machines after members used them. Employee 3 normally does excellent work and will probably make reference to this fact when coached.

Make some notes on how you will coach Employees 1, 2, and 3.

1. Describe current performance.

_____

_____

2. Describe desired behavior.

_____

_____

3. Get a commitment to the change.

_____

_____

4. Follow up.

_____

_____

Observer Form
Observer, use the following form or use your coaching skills to develop a motivational feedback form. Feel free to research sayings of the great coaches and paraphrase them in your own coaching style.

1. How well did the manager describe current behavior?

_____

2. How well did the manager describe desired behavior? Did the employee state why the behavior is important?

_____

3. How successful was the manager at getting a commitment to the change? Do you think the employee would change?

_____

4. How well did the manager describe how he or she was going to follow up to ensure that the employee performed the desired behavior?

_____

Wrap-up:
Take a few minutes and write down your answers to the following questions:

■ What did I learn from this experience?

_____

_____

_____

■ How will I use this knowledge in the future?

_____

_____

_____

As a class, discuss student responses.

Skill-Builder: Disciplining

Objective:

■ To develop your ability to discipline an employee.

Preparation:
Review the section on disciplining.

In-Class Application

You will discipline, be disciplined, and observe a discipline session using Model 14–3. This is a follow-up exercise to the preceding Skill-Builder.

Procedure 1 (2–4 minutes):
Break into groups of three. Make some groups of two, if necessary. Each member selects one of the three situations from the preceding Skill-Builder. Decide who will discipline Employee 1, the clerical worker; Employee 2, the concession server; and Employee 3, the fitness instructor. Also select a different group member to play the employee being disciplined.

Procedure 2 (3–7 minutes):
Prepare for the discipline session. Write a basic outline of what you will say to Employee 1, 2, or 3; follow the steps in the discipline model.

1. Refer to past feedback. (Assume that you have discussed the situation before, using the coaching model.)

_____

_____

2. Ask why the undesired behavior was used. (The employee should make up an excuse for not changing.)

_____

_____

3. Give the discipline. (Assume that an oral warning is appropriate.)

_____

_____

4. Get a commitment to change and develop a plan.

_____

_____

5. Summarize and state the follow-up.

_____

_____

Procedure 3 (5–8 minutes):

A. *Role-play.* The manager of Employee 1, the clerical worker for a ticket office, disciplines him or her as planned. (Use the actual name of the person playing the employee.) Talk—do not read your written plan. Employee 1, put yourself in the worker's position. You work hard; there is a lot of pressure to work fast. It's easier when you have more than one file. Both the manager and employee will need to ad-lib.

The person not playing a role is the observer. He or she makes notes on the observer form below. For each of the following steps, try to make a statement about the positive aspects of the discipline and a statement about how the manager could have improved. Give alternative things the manager could have said to improve the discipline session. Remember, the objective is to change behavior.

Observer Form

1. How well did the manager refer to past feedback?

_____

_____

2. How well did the manager ask why the undesired behavior was used?

_____

_____

3. How well did the manager give the discipline?

_____

_____

4. Did the manager get a commitment to change? Do you think the employee will change his or her behavior?

_____

_____

5. How well did the manager summarize and state the follow-up? How effective will the follow-up be?

_____

_____

B. *Feedback.* The observer leads a discussion of how well the manager disciplined the employee. The employee should also give feedback on how he or she felt and what might have been more effective in getting him or her to change. Do not go on to the next interview until you are told to do so. If you finish early, wait until the others finish or the time is up.

Procedure 4 (5–8 minutes):

Same as procedure 3, but change roles so that Employee 2, the food server in a sports arena, is disciplined. Employee 2, put yourself in the worker's position. You enjoy talking to your friends, and you're supposed to be friendly to the customers.

Procedure 5 (5–8 minutes):

Same as procedure 3, but change roles so that Employee 3, the assistant fitness instructor, is disciplined. Employee 3, put yourself in the worker's position. You are an excellent fitness instructor. Sometimes you forget to clean the fitness machines after members use them.

Wrap-up:
Take a few minutes and write down your answers to the following questions:

■ What did I learn from this experience?

_____

_____

_____

_____

_____

■ How will I use this knowledge in the future?

_____

_____

_____

_____

_____

As a class, discuss student responses.

Internet Skills: Using Financial Ratios

Objective:
■ To use some of the common financial ratios to analyze a sport organization.

Preparation (50 minutes):
Go to http://www.hoovers.com and search for "Callaway Golf Company." Click on *Financials*. Then click on *Annual Financials* to find updated financial data for Exhibit 14–7. You can click the *Data Definitions* link at the bottom of the financial statements for help. Use Exhibit 14–10 to calculate the requested ratios.

1. Has Callaway's gross profit margin increased or decreased in the last three years? Explain your answer.

_____

_____

_____

2. Has Callaway's net profit margin increased or decreased in the last three years? Explain your answer.

_____

_____

_____

3. Calculate the company's current and quick ratios for the last three years. Have they improved?

_____

_____

_____

4. Calculate the company's debt-to-equity for the last three years. Is the company more or less in debt?

_____

_____

_____

5. Use the entire site at http://www.callawaygolf.com to evaluate the overall financial performance of Callaway Golf Company.

_____

_____

_____

Appendix A:
Careers in Sport Management

Career Search

A career search in the field of sport management is really no different than any other career search. A wise man who taught with us once said, "Nobody who completes a job search ends up without a job." The central idea is that any career management process requires a good understanding of yourself, your personal goals, your interests, your requirements for salary and benefits, and your desire to take a job that requires extensive travel. Any job in the field that interests you can and should lead to more responsible, higher-paying work later in your career. However, you typically have to start at the bottom and work your way up the organization.

Many career books are available to help you learn about conducting a job search. Our favorite career management book has been on the market for nearly 30 years—*What Color Is Your Parachute?* by Richard Nelson Bolles is an annual best-seller. Bolles asks two basic career questions: What do you want to do? Where do you want to do it?[1] The book helps you understand how to answer these questions.

Specific Fields in Sport Management

The field of sport management was covered in Chapter 1. You should review the different careers you can enter as outlined in Chapter 1. Remember that these careers include such areas as sport broadcasting, athletic administration, coaching, officiating, fitness center management, retail sport management, sporting goods manufacturing, and recreation and youth center management. In addition, every case in this book was intended to cover an area of sport in which a student might like to find a job and build a career.

Another handy reference is *Profiles of Sport Industry Professionals: The People Who Make the Games Happen* by Matthew J. Robinson, Mary A. Hums, R. Brian Crow, and Dennis R. Phillips. This is a new book that offers 48 profiles of successful sport managers. The book covers sport professionals in high school, the health and fitness industry, recreational sport, college athletics, international sport, professional sport, facility management, event management, media and public relations, sport communications, sporting goods and licensed products, sport commissions, sport marketing, and the academic world of sport management.[2]

Internships

Internships are a valuable method to gain experience in any career field. Internships will help you gain on-the-job experience that can lead to a full-time position. Although there is no guarantee that an internship will lead to a permanent position, it does often happen. So pick your internship wisely by selecting an organization you can see yourself with for a long time. If you like facility management or event planning, you should contact the arenas and stadiums in your area. If you like recreation management, you should contact the YMCAs or JCCs in your area. Retail sporting good stores are also good places to contact, because you will find this type of store in almost every area.

Some students are fortunate enough to land paid internship positions. However, most internships are unpaid and call for 120 to 150 hours to fulfill academic requirements. Most internships require students to write a paper or complete a journal of their experience.

Networking

Most students underestimate the power of networking. We take the word for granted, but think about the word *networking*. It is really two words—net and working. Is your net working? Do you know people in the sport field? Did you ever try to contact a sport administrator at your local sport arena? Fitness center? Recreation center? Television station? Newspaper? In today's electronic age, it is possible to e-mail these people and begin to build a relationship. Often, you can find their e-mail addresses at the end of an article in the newspaper or on their organization's web site. Be polite and make sure to tell the professional that you are a student looking for assistance in your quest to understand the field of sport management. You might be surprised to find out that these people are often very supportive of your efforts to learn about their business.

Keep a log of the people you meet in your networking endeavors. Make sure to add their e-mail addresses to your Internet address book. Send them quick notes on events you attended at their organization and how you enjoyed the experience. Building a good network is not about finding a job right away but about building a long-lasting relationship that is beneficial to both parties. Live the journey!

Web Sites for Sport Careers

The best way for us to help you find specific jobs in sports is to give you web sites that are geared toward this goal. These sites are excellent sources of information about jobs in sports. However, all sites are not created equal. Some sites provide more information than others. Some sites are more interested in having people sign up for their monthly service, while other sites provide job titles, short descriptions, and addresses to which to send a resume and cover letter. So use your judgment and decide which site is best for you. The Internet Skills exercises you completed in this textbook should have given you the research skills to determine the best links to use on each site.

- **http://www.allsports.com/network/content?site=1008&story=29153** Focuses on careers in sport writing.
- **http://www.wcupa.edu/_ACADEMICS/sch_cas.psy/Career_Paths/Sports/Career07.htm#employ** Includes a link on employment opportunities in sport psychology. Also includes information on associations one can join.
- **http://www.jobscircuit.co.uk/** Allows for job searches in the United Kingdom and Europe. JobsCircuit is the official recruitment service for the sport, leisure, and fitness industries and is operated by The Sports Industries Federation (http://www.sports-life.com/).
- **http://www.womensportsjobs.com/** Presents a list of hot jobs for the week. Don't let the name of the site fool you; this site is good for men as well as women. The site is also good for finding internships. For example, the current page as of this writing asks students to forward a resume and cover letter to the internship coordinator at the National Basketball Association. The internships last 13 to 18 weeks during the summer before the student's senior year. These internships even pay $200 a week.
- **http://www.sportscareers.com/** This site also lists hot jobs, such as tour management coordinator. The site is very well organized and easily displays recent job openings in sport management across the country.

Appendix B:
Sport Management and the Internet

Until the mid-1990s, it was hard to find information regarding a company that was being discussed in a case study. Today, there is a whole new science for conducting research to find company material. It is virtually impossible to go anywhere without hearing about the Internet. A major advantage of an online data search is that you dramatically increase the number of sources available to you. Also, home access to the Internet reduces the need to visit a physical library and enables you to conduct research in the comfort of your home or dormitory room.

Web Skepticism

Students do about 90 percent of their research online, yet few people question the accuracy of their sources.[1] You need to remember that anyone can set up a web site and write whatever he or she wants without anyone checking it to make sure the information is factually accurate. Therefore, you need to search reputable web sites. This textbook often referred to sport management sites such as http://www.nassm.com, http://www.sportsline.com, and http://www.espn.com as reputable sites with valid information.

The Internet

Assuming you have accessed the Internet, the next question is, How do I get information about the company discussed in the case study? You may go directly to the web site of the company if you have the address or enter key topics/words in a search engine (some popular search engines are discussed later in this appendix).

Company Web Sites

Company web sites are locations on the Internet that companies have set up to dispense information about themselves. Information ranging from financial reports to recent articles about the company can usually be found in the press-releases section of most large web sites.

At the end of the opening and closing case studies in each chapter of this book, you'll find the web addresses of the companies and organizations that were discussed. Simply type the web address into the Address field of your web browser to access the organization's information. For instance, Nike has an elaborate web site that can be accessed by typing http://www.nike.com. (Note: With most updated browsers, all you need to type is nike.com—the browser will automatically complete the address.) When you access the web site for Nike, click on the *About Nike* link to enter the area with information about the company and not just the area selling products to consumers. Learning how to navigate around a company web site is important if you want to find useful information.

Limitations of Web Sites/Need for Other Sources
A limitation of company web sites is that the company provides the information, so it may be biased and not indicative of what other sources are writing about the company. Also, researching only one journal/magazine/newspaper (no matter which one) is not enough to validate the findings of a company's web site. In other words, simply using a company web site is not enough; you need to use at least two—and preferably more—sources of information. Also, nothing can replace visiting a physical library. When you visit a library, you can work closely with the library personnel to find books, articles, and databases that will help you conduct your research. Of course, you could ask the library a question online, but it is often the interactive process of following a librarian around the library that leads to useful sources of information.

Finding Company Information on the Internet
Check with your college library to see if it has access to any specific sport databases. Two popular databases are http://sportdiscus.com and http://www.sbrnet.com. More general business research

can be found through your college library using InfoTrac College Edition SearchBank or EBSCOhost (Business Premier).

Other databases such as http://www.marketguide.com and http://www.hoovers.com are designed to give investors or researchers information about companies and are a secondary choice for sources. Additionally, you can access search engines such as http://www.google.com, http://www.nlsearch. com, http://www.altavista.com, http://www.excite.com, http://www.lycos.com, and http://www. yahoo.com to search for a desired topic.

Referencing Internet Material

Finding information on the Internet does not allow you to bypass proper bibliographic procedures. Referencing material found on the Internet is not quite as straightforward as citing books, journals, and magazines. Databases on the Internet can be found anywhere in cyberspace. Internet material is acceptable only if you can specifically document its origins as if you were writing a traditional reference. You must include:

- Author's name
- Title of the article
- Name of the publication/web site
- Date and page numbers

Your instructor will provide you with more details on his or her expectations of how to use and cite Internet material. Following is an example reference in APA (American Psychological Association) format taken from the Internet:

Alon, I. (2001). The use of franchising by U.S. based retailers. *Journal of Small Business Management,* 39(2), 111+. Retrieved January 18, 2003, from EBSCO database (Masterfile) on the World Wide Web: http://www.ebsco.com.

Options for Doing Internet Skills Exercises in Class

The instructor selects an option to be used in class for each specific Internet Skills exercise. Different options may be used with different exercises.

Option 1 (0–60 minutes with another option). Based on how the instructor will include the Internet Skills exercises as part of the grading process, students pass in their answers to the exercise questions as specified by the instructor. Passing in material may also be part of any of the other options below. With option 1:

(A) The instructor may not discuss the exercise at all in class; or
(B) The instructor may discuss only the questions that are not going to be graded, until after grading.

With option 1 (B), another option below is selected.

Option 2 (5–10 minutes). The instructor gives the answers to the exercise questions without discussion.

Option 3 (10–60 minutes). The instructor asks for volunteers and/or calls on students to give their exercise answers to the entire class. Student "professional" presentations may be scheduled. The instructor will determine if class members may respond to others' answers.

Option 4 (10–15 minutes). Students share their exercise answers in small groups of three to seven members. There is no class discussion, but the instructor may make concluding remarks and/or give answers to some or all of the questions from the exercise.

Option 5 (20–35 minutes: 10–15 minutes of group activity; 10–20 minutes of presentations). This is the same as option 4 with the following addition:

- The instructor assigns different questions to be answered by one or more groups based on the number of questions and groups. Each group selects a spokesperson to record the group's answers and present them to the class.

There is no class discussion following spokesperson presentations, but the instructor may ask questions or make comments following each presentation. The instructor may also make concluding remarks and/or give answers to some or all of the questions from the exercise.

Option 6 (45–60 minutes: 15–20 minutes of group activity; 30–40 minutes of presentations and discussion). This is the same as option 5, but class members may ask questions or make comments after each spokesperson's presentations, rather than just listen. The instructor may make concluding remarks and/or give answers to some or all of the questions from the exercise.

Internet Index

The following is a compendium of Internet sites referred to in this book.

SITE	ADDRESS	PAGE NO.
Adidas	http://www.adidas.com	53
AltaVista, search engine	http://www.altavista.com	415
Amateur Baseball Umpire home page	http://www.amateurumpire.com/mech/signs.htm	304
American Sports Partners Inc.	http://www.americansportspartners.com	143
Anaheim Angels	http://angels.mlb.com	104
Anaheim Mighty Ducks	http://www.mightyducks.com	104
Asheville, North Carolina, Civic Center	http://www.ci.asheville.nc.us/civic/main.htm	138
Ask the Commish.com	http://www.askthecommish.com	205
Augusta Chronicle, article on University of Georgia's Mark Richt	http://www.augustachronicle.com/stories/073102/uga_124-3210.shtml	146
Basketball Highway	http://www.bbhighway.com	54, 145, 237
Boys and Girls Clubs of America	http://www.bgca.org	275
Business Week	http://www.businessweek.com	78
Callaway Golf Company	http://www.callawaygolf.com	411
Canadian Professional Coaches Association, Coaching Code of Ethics	http://www.coach.ca/member/ethics_e.htm	26
Careers in Sports	http://www.allsports.com/network/content?site=1008&story=29153	413
Careers in Sports Psychology	http://www.wcupa.edu/_ACADEMICS/sch_cas.psy/Career_Paths/Sports/Career07.htm#employ	413
CBS SportsLine.com	http://www.sportsline.com	3, 168, 414
CNN/*Sports Illustrated,* Multimedia Central, "The Two Sides of Bobby Knight"	http://sportsillustrated.cnn.com/multimedia_central/news/2000/03/15/knight_mmc	232
Competitive Advantage Peak Performance Guides	http://www.competitivedge.com/peak.html	330
Competitive Analysis links	http://www.mapnp.org/library/mrktng/cmpetitr/cmpetitr.htm	82
Decision Sciences Institute	http://www.decisionsciences.org	54
Decision Support Systems Resources	http://DSSResources.com	54
Dick's Sporting Goods	http://www.dickssportinggoods.com	3
Disney	http://www.disney.com	104
Elms College men's soccer	http://www.elms.edu/campus/athletics/mensoc.htm#coach	348
ESPN	http://www.espn.com	3, 304, 414
ESPN Career Center	http://espn.monster.com	213
ESPN More Sports, "Almonte, Bronx Team Records Wiped Away"	http://espn.go.com/moresports/llws01/s/2001/0831/1246234.html	267
Excite, search engine	http://www.excite.com	415
Fast Company, Leadership Style Online Guide	http://www.fastcompany.com/online/resources/leadership.html	353

(continued)

SITE	ADDRESS	PAGE NO.
FennSports.com, Stress and Sports Center of America	http://www.fennsports.com	272
FIFA	http://www.fifa.com	81
Financial Times	http://www.ft.com	47
The Globalist	http://www.theglobalist.com	26
"Goal-Setting for Athletes"	http://www.geocities.com/Colosseum/Bench/6823/goals.html	330
Google, search engine	http://www.google.com	143, 415
Hawk, Tony, home page	http://www.tonyhawk.com	353
Heartland Institute, stadium-funding policy studies	http://www.heartland.org/studies/sports/sports-studies.htm	115
Hoover's Online	http://www.hoovers.com	112, 410, 415
HR.com	http://www4.hr.com/HRcom/index.cfm	206
Humanmetrics, Jung Typology Test	http://www.humanmetrics.com/cgi-win/JTypes2.asp	238
InfoSports.net, Youth Baseball Knowledge Base	http://infosports.net/baseball/arch/650.htm	304
Jewish Community Centers (JCCs)	http://www.jcca.org	275
JobsCircuit	http://www.jobscircuit.co.uk/	413
Leader X: Leadership Strategies	http://www.leaderx.com	300
Little League Baseball	http://www.littleleague.org	267
Lycos, search engine	http://www.lycos.com	415
Maccabi Games	http://www.jccmaccabi.org	115
Major League Baseball (MLB)	http://www.mlb.com	26, 178
Major League Baseball Players Association (MLBPA)	http://bigleaguers.yahoo.com	235, 325
Mind Tools, Sports Psychology	http://www.mindtools.com/spintro.html	82
MIT Athletics, strategic plan	http://web.mit.edu/athletics/www/plan/index.html	82
MIT Center for Sports Innovation, Project Gallery	http://web.mit.edu/aeroastro/www/labs/csi/gallery.html	175
MultexInvestor	http://www.marketguide.com	415
National Association for Sport & Physical Education (NASPE)	http://www.aahperd.org/naspe/template.cfm?template=domainsStandards.html	329
National Basketball Association (NBA)	http://www.nba.com	178
National Football League (NFL)	http://www.nfl.com	178, 205
NCAA	http://www.ncaa.org	237
New York Yankees	http://www.yankees.mlb.com	175
Nike	http://www.nike.com	19, 414
North American Society for Sport Management (NASSM)	http://www.nassm.com	3, 21, 250, 414
Northern Light, search engine	http://www.nlsearch.com	415
Occupational Outlook Handbook, "Athletes, Coaches, Umpires, and Related Workers"	http://www.bls.gov/oco/ocos251.htm	205
Ohio State University, 2001–2002 athletic department budget	http://senate.ohio-state.edu/AthleticBudget.pdf	376

(continued)

SITE	ADDRESS	PAGE NO.
Ohio State University, athletic department jobs	http://www.ohiostatebuckeyes.com/school-bio/osu-staff-directory.html	198
Oklahoma State University, Stress Management library	http://www.pp.okstate.edu/ehs/links/stress.htm	238
Positive Coaching Alliance	http://www.positivecoach.org/leaders/	275
Princeton University, Outdoor Action Guide to Group Dynamics & Leadership	http://www.princeton.edu/~oa/manual/sect9.html	353
Psyched—Athletic Performance Enhancement	http://www.psychedonline.org/Articles/Vol2Iss2/TeamBuilding.htm	275
The Ranch Golf Club	http://www.theranchgolfclub.com	376, 379
Salt Lake City 2002 Winter Olympics	http://www.ci.slc.ut.us	47
Speakers.com, Pat Riley	http://speakers.com/riley.html	350
SPORTDiscus	http://sportdiscus.com	414
Sporting News	http://www.sportingnews.com	26
Sports Business Research Network	http://www.sbrnet.com	414
Sports Careers	http://www.sportscareers.com/	413
Sports Links Central.com, sports radio links	http://www.sportslinkscentral.com/Sports_Media/sports_radio.htm	304
Sports Media Challenge	http://www.sportsmediachallenge.com	327
Sports News You Can Use	http://www.onlinesports.com/sportstrust/sportsnewslist.html	115, 175
Springfield, Massachusetts, Jewish Community Center	http://www.springfieldjcc.org	145
StadiaNet	http://www.stadianet.com	115
"Stadiums as an Economic Development Tool"	http://www-personal.umich.edu/~jeremyjm/stadiums/index.html	115
Staples Center	http://www.staplescenter.com	138
StarvingArtistsLaw.com, Sports Law page	http://www.starvingartistslaw.com/industries/sports.htm	205
Street & Smith's	http://www.streetandsmiths.com	3
Summitt, Pat, home page	http://www.coachsummitt.com	329, 342
Texas Tech Red Raiders	http://texastech.fansonly.com/sports/m-baskbl/text-m-baskbl-body.html	232
To the Next Level	http://www.tothenextlevel.org/docs/coach_development/delegate.html	145
Uniform Athletes Agents Act (UAAA) History	http://www1.ncaa.org/membership/enforcement/agents/uaaa/history.html	325
University of Idaho, Center for Ethics	http://www.ets.uidaho.edu/center_for_ethics	26
University of Illinois at Urbana-Champaign, Teamworks—the Virtual Team Assistant	http://www.vta.spcomm.uiuc.edu	54
University of Minnesota, Office of Institutional Research and Reporting	http://www.irr.umn.edu	173
University of Nebraska–Lincoln, A Toolkit for Volunteer Leaders	http://4h.unl.edu/volun/arlen/small.htm	276
University of Notre Dame, Mendelson Center for Sport, Character, and Culture	http://www.nd.edu/~cscc	26
U.S. Department of Labor, Bureau of Labor Statistics, "Salary Caps in Professional Team Sports"	http://www.bls.gov/opub/cwc/1998/Spring/art1full.pdf	205
U.S. Equal Employment Opportunity Commission	http://www.eeoc.gov	202

(continued)

SITE	ADDRESS	PAGE NO.
U.S. Office of Personnel Management, Employee Assistance Program page	http://www.opm.gov/ehs/eappage.asp	376
Washington Wizards	http://www.nba.com/wizards/	74
WFAN, sports radio	http://www.wfan.com	304
What You Need to Know About, Investing for Beginners	http://beginnersinvest.about.com/library/lessons/bl-introduction.htm	376
Wilson Sporting Goods	http://www.wilsonsports.com	369
WNBA	http://www.wnba.com	78
Women Sports Jobs	http://www.womensportsjobs.com/	413
Wooden, John, home page	http://www.coachwooden.com	373
World Stadiums	http://www.worldstadiums.com	50
Yahoo, search engine	http://www.yahoo.com	143, 415
YMCA	http://www.ymca.net	27, 275

Endnotes

CHAPTER 1

1. Information about Dick's Sporting Goods found at http://www.dickssportinggoods.com on July 15, 2001.

2. R. J. Hunter and A. M. Mayo. "The Business of Sport." *Mid-Atlantic Journal of Business* 35(2–3) (June–September 1999): 75–76.

3. A. D. Amar. "Sports Management: Budding Profession Needs Theoretical Foundation." *Mid-Atlantic Journal of Business* 35(2–3) (June–September 1999): 73–75.

4. L. Karlin. *The Guide to Careers in Sports.* New York: E. M. Guild, Inc., 1995, p. 190.

5. D. Mahony and D. Howard. "Sport Business in the Next Decade: A General Overview of Expected Trends." *Journal of Sport Management* 15(4) (2001): 275.

6. Ibid, 285.

7. Staff. *Wall Street Journal* (November 14, 1980): 33.

8. R. Katz. "Skills of an Effective Administrator." *Harvard Business Review* (September/October 1974): 90–102.

9. H. Lancaster. "Managing Your Career: What Do You Hate About Work? (Hint: It May Not Be Your Job)." *Wall Street Journal* (November 4, 1997): B1.

10. J. Guntner. "Staying Ahead of the Curve." *Risk Management* 45(4) (April 1998): 80–84.

11. S. Trussler. "The Rules of the Game." *Journal of Business Strategy* 19(1) (January/February 1998): 16–20.

12. E. Ghiselli. *Explorations in Management Talent.* Santa Monica, CA: Goodyear, 1971.

13. P. M. Buhler. "Managers: Out with the Old and In with the New Skills That Is." *Supervision* 59(6) (June 1998): 22–25.

14. Staff. "Limits of the New Corporation." *Business Week* (August 28, 2000): 180.

15. M. Shibinski. "Where to Look for Team Leadership." *Coach and Athletic Director* 70(12) (September 2000): 26.

16. P. Bissonette. *Newsletter.* Wayzata, MN: Learning Strategies Corporation, February 1995, p. 1.

17. L. Kurke and H. Aldrich. "Mintzberg Was Right! A Replication and Extension of the Nature of Managerial Work." *Management Science* 29 (1983): 975–984; C. Avert and A.

Al. "Managerial Work: The Influence of Hierarchical Level and Functional Specialty." *The Academy of Management Journal* 26 (1983): 170–177; C. Hales. "What Do Managers Do? A Critical Review of the Evidence." *Journal of Management Studies* 23 (1986): 88–115.

18. H. Mintzberg. *The Nature of Managerial Work.* New York: Harper & Row, 1973.

19. Staff. "Nike Quarterly Profit Up 28%; Co-Founder Knight Descending from Chair." *The Canadian Press* (June 27, 2002); link to "Bowerman" found at http://www.nike.com (July 15, 2002).

20. J. Pereira. "Apparel Makers Back New Labor Inspection Group." *Wall Street Journal* (April 10, 2001): B1.

CHAPTER 2

1. T. Kurkjian. "Put It in the Books." *ESPN The Magazine* (October 29, 2001): 68.

2. M. Hiebert. "Winners and Losers." *Far Eastern Economic Review* 164(29) (2001): 66–99.

3. K. Rosenthal. "His Two-Year Project Became the Miracle of the Mariners." *The Sporting News* (December 24, 2001): 56.

4. Ibid.

5. Staff. "Dr. W.E. Deming 1988/89 Winner of Dow Jones Award." *ESB* (Spring 1989): 3.

6. R. Ackoff. *Creating the Corporate Future.* New York: Wiley, 1981.

7. D. J. Collis and C. A. Montgomery. "Creating Corporate Advantage." *Harvard Business Review* 76(3) (May/June 1998): 71–84.

8. Collis and Montgomery, "Corporate Advantage," 71–84.

9. R. Telander. "Another Shot." *ESPN The Magazine* (October 15, 2001): 56.

10. D. McAbe and A. Wilkinson. "The Rise and Fall of TQM: The Vision, Meaning and Operation of Change." *Industrial Relations Journal* 29(1) (March 1998): 18–30.

11. V. O'Connell. "Corporate Focus Changing Tastes Dent Campbell's Canned-Soup Sales." *Wall Street Journal* (April 28, 1998): B1, B6.

12. Staff. "Team Canada's Captain, Mario Lemieux Teams Up with Campbell's Chunky Soup to Launch New Advertising Across Canada." *Canadian News Wire* (October 1, 2001). Found

at http://www.newswire.ca/releases/october2001/01/c2564.html.

13 B. K. Boyd and E. R. Elliott. "A Measurement Model of Strategic Planning." *Strategic Management Journal* 19(2) (February 1998): 181–200.

14 Collis and Montgomery, "Corporate Advantage," 71–84.

15 C. Reidy. "Reebok Rebounds with Deal to Provide NBA Uniforms and Sell Merchandise." *Boston Globe* (August 2, 2001). Found at http://www.cbc.ca/cgi-bin/templates/sportsview.cgi?/news/2001/08/01/sports/reebok010801.

16 P. D. Staudohar. "The Baseball Strike of 1994–1995." *Monthly Labor Review* 120(3) (March 1997): 21–28.

17 Staff. "Flying Away?" *Los Angeles Business Journal* 22(10) (March 6, 2000): 4.

18 D. C. Malloy and J. Agarwal. "Differential Association and Role-Set Configuration: The Impact of Significant Others upon the Perception of Ethical Climate in a Sports Organization." *Journal of Sport Management* 15(3) (2001): 195–218.

19 T. Raphael. "What a $252,000,000 Contract Means to You." *Workforce* 80(2) (February 2001): 112.

20 D. LaGesse and J. Perry. "Armchair Athletes." *U.S. News & World Report* 129(22) (December 4, 2000): 68.

21 L. Spencer. "Earnhardt's Bonds with Fans Will Never Be Duplicated." *The Sporting News* 225(10) (March 5, 2001): 44.

22 D. Mahony and D. Howard. "Sport Business in the Next Decade: A General Overview of Expected Trends." *Journal of Sport Management* 15(4) (2001): 275.

23 Information found at http://mariners.mlb.com/NASApp/mlb/sea/ballpark/sea_ballpark_history.jsp on July 29, 2002.

24 T. Peters. *Thriving on Chaos: Handbook for a Management Revolution.* New York: Knopf, 1987.

25 R. Ackoff. *Creating the Corporate Future.* New York: Wiley, 1981.

26 D. Parkhurst. "To Succeed in the Global Arena, Leadership Is a Must." *Nation's Cities Weekly* 2(21) (May 25, 1998): 6–7.

27 M. Hordes, J. A. Clancy, and J. Baddaley. "A Primer for Global Start-ups." *The Academy of Management Executive* 9(2) (May 1995): 7–11.

28 R. N. Lussier, R. Baeder, and J. Corman. "Measuring Global Practices: Global Strategic Planning Through Company Situational Analysis." *Business Horizons* 37(5) (October 1994): 56–63.

29 T. Kamm. "Continental Shift—Au Revoir, Malaise: Europe's Economies Are Back in Business." *Wall Street Journal* (April 9, 1998): A1.

30 W. Li and Y. Lu. "Sport Reform Over 20 Years: China as a Case." *Research Quarterly for Exercise and Sport* 72(1) (March 2001): A-93.

31 J. Birkinshaw, N. Hood, and S. Jonsson. "Building Firm-Specific Advantages in Multinational Corporations: The Role of Subsidiary Initiative." *Strategic Management Journal* 19(3) (March 1998): 221–242.

32 R. E. Washington and D. Karen. "Sport & Society." *Annual Review of Sociology* (Annual 2001): 187.

33 Ibid.

34 Staff. "Business Bulletin: A Special Background Report on Trends in Industry and Finance." *Wall Street Journal* (June 25, 1998): A1.

35 D. Pyke. "Strategies for Global Sourcing." *Financial Times* (February 20, 1998): FTS3-5.

36 Staff. "Yankee Doodle Dandy." Found at http://www.cnnsi.com (Feb. 7, 2001).

37 Information found at http://www.nfleurope.com/news/week18/15082000_histintro.html on July 31, 2002.

38 Staff. "Wallaby Players to Tackle Big Decision." *Queensland Australia* (October 11, 2001): 7.

39 Staff. "Vikings Tackle Stringer Dies from Heatstroke" (July 31, 2001). Found at http://espn.go.com/nfl/news/2001/0731/1233494.html on August 1, 2002.

40 Staff. "Infractions Appeals Committee Upholds Findings, Penalties of Former Head Women's Basketball Coach at Howard University." Found at http://www.ncaa.org on July 16, 2002.

41 E. M. Epstein. "Business Ethics and Corporate Social Policy: Reflections on an Intellectual Journey, 1964–1996, and Beyond." *Business and Society* 37(1) (March 1998): 7–40.

42 B. Ettore. "How's Your Report Card? Why Shouldn't 'No Guts, No Glory' Apply in the Corporate Suite?" *Management Review* 87(3) (March 1998): 1–2.

43 M. Barrier. "Doing the Right Thing." *Nation's Business* 86(3) (March 1998): 32–38.

44 R. B. Reich. "The New Meaning of Corporate Social Responsibility." *California Management Review* 40(2) (Winter 1998): 8–18.

45 H. Ulman. "Former 'Jimmy Fund' Poster Child Finally Throws Out First Pitch for Boston." *Associated Press* (May 22, 1998): 1–2.

46 Reich, "New Meaning," 8–18.

47 Information found at http://www.ncaa.org/releases/makepage.cgi/infractions/2002070202in.htm.

48 Staff. "NFL Players for Second Annual 'NFL & United Way Hometown Huddle,'" *BW Sportswire* (October 17, 2000): 1–5.

49 S. Foy. "Can Physical Educators Do More to Teach Ethical Behavior in Sports?" *Journal of Physical Education, Recreation & Dance* 72(5) (May 2000): 12.

50 Staff. "Nike, Inc. Announces Details of U.S. Job Reductions." *Press Release* (March 12, 1998). Found at http://www.nike.com on July 30, 2002.

51 M. Hammer and J. Champy. "Re-Engineering Authors Reconsider Re-Engineering." *Wall Street Journal* (January 17, 1995): B1.

52 Ibid.

53 M. Hammer and J. Champy. "Managers Beware: You're Not Ready for Tomorrow's Job." *Wall Street Journal* (January 24, 1995): B1.

54 D. Owen. "New Olympic Committee Chief Plans Reform Panel." Found at http://www.ft.com (July 17, 2001).

55 S. Keating. "Olympics-IOC Will Win War on Drugs, Samaranch Says," *Reuters* (July 2, 2001).

CHAPTER 3

1 K. O'Brien. "Adidas' Hoop Games: The Athletic Shoemaker Tries to Update Its Appeal to North American Teens." *National Post* (November 24, 2001): FP8.

2 Ibid.

3 Staff. "Adidas-Salomon Eyes Struggling U.S. Market Warily." *Financial Times* (March 9, 2001).

4 B. Herzog. "Adidas America President Discusses Plans for Company." *The Oregonian* (March 25, 2002).

5 Ibid.

6 R. Steiner. "Instinct Scores for Adidas Boss." *Sunday Times—London* (March 24, 2002): 20.

7 O'Brien, "Adidas' Hoop Games," FP8.

8 U. Harnischfeger. "Adidas Decides to Play It Cool to Boost Tired Image." *Financial Times* (June 10, 2001).

9 A. L. Sack and A. Nadim. "Strategic Choices in a Turbulent Economy: A Case Study of Starter Corporation." *Journal of Sport Management* 16(1) (January 2002): 36–53.

10 H. Einhorn and R. Hogarth. "Decision-Making: Going Forward in Reverse." *Harvard Business Review* (January/February 1987): 66.

11 Steiner, "Instinct," 20.

12 A. Muolo. "Decisions, Decisions." *Fast Company* 18 (October 1998): 93.

13 Herzog, "Adidas America President Discusses."

14 E. McFadzean and T. Nelson. "Facilitating Problem-Solving Groups: A Conceptual Model." *Leadership and Organization Development Journal* 19(1) (January/February 1998): 6–14.

15 Muolo, "Decisions, Decisions," 93.

16 Ibid.

17 Ibid.

18 J. P. Muczyk and R. P. Steel. "Leadership Style and the Turnaround Executive." *Business Horizons* 41(2) (March/April 1998): 39–47.

19 McFadzean and Nelson, "Facilitating," 6–14.

20 Ibid.

21 A. O'Leary-Kelly, J. Martocchio, and D. Frink. "The Art of Decision-Making." *The Academy of Management Journal* 37(5) (October 1994): 1285–1292.

22 Harnischfeger, "Adidas Decides."

23 H. Klean and J. Kim. "A Field Study of the Influence of Situational Constraints, Leader-Member Exchange, and Goal Commitment on Performance." *The Academy of Management Journal* 41(1) (February 1998): 88–96.

24 P. Miller. "Rappin' on the Door." *Sports Illustrated* 91(3) (July 19, 1999): 82.

25 G. S. Wood. "Making Meetings Productive and Fun: How to Transform Board Meetings into Creative, Energizing, Problem-Solving Sessions." *Association Management* 50(1) (January 1998): 48–52.

26 S. Greco. "Where Great Ideas Come From." *INC.* 20(5) (April 1998): 76–83.

27 R .L. Edgeman and J. Williams. "Select Leaders Using a Quality Management Process." *Quality Progress* 31(2) (February 1998): 78–83.

28 M. Wolfe. "A Theoretical Justification for Japanese Nemawashi/Ringi Group Decision-Making and an Implementation." *Decision Support Systems* 8(2) (April 1992): 125–140.

29 C. Heath and R. Gonzalez. "Interaction with Others Increases Decision Confidence but Not Decision Quality: Evidence against Information Collection Views of Interactive Decision-Making." *Organizational Behavior &*

Human Decision Processes 61(3) (March 1995): 305–327.

30 G. Levine. "Faces in the News." Found at http://www.forbes.com (July 15, 2002).

31 B. Wassener. "Adidas Boosted by World Cup Sales." Found at http://www.ft.com (August 7, 2002).

32 X. B. Costanza. "Reilly Sails the Seas for Growth." Found at http://cbs.marketwatch.com (August 9, 2001).

33 Staff. "Jordan Welcomes Brown to the NBA." Found at http://www.nba.com/draft2001/news/kwame_010628.html?nav=ArticleList (June 28, 2001).

CHAPTER 4

1 R. Grover and T. Lowry. "Smackdowns Are Taking Their Toll at the WWF: The Death of the XFL Is Just One of Its Many Bruises." *BusinessWeek Online* (September 3, 2001).

2 D. F. Mahony and D. R. Howard. "Sport Business in the Next Decade: A General Overview of Expected Trends." *Journal of Sport Management* 15 (2001): 293.

3 Staff. "Adidas-Salomon Profile." Found at http://www.hoovers.com (December 25, 2001).

4 Staff. "Salomon Acquires Canadian Outdoor Specialists." *Canadian Newswire* (December 4, 2001).

5 Mahony and Howard, "Sport Business," 283.

6 D. J. Collis and C. A. Montgomery. "Creating Corporate Advantage." *Harvard Business Review* 76(3) (May/June 1998): 71–84.

7 Ibid.

8 Ibid.

9 H. Weihrich. "The TOWS Matrix: A Tool for Situational Analysis." *Long Range Planning* 15(2) (April 1982): 61.

10 Mahony and Howard, "Sport Business," 283.

11 M. Boyle. "How Nike Got Its SWOOSH Back." *Fortune* (June 24, 2002).

12 L. Sanders. "Nike Stock Slips on Orders Outlook, but Q3 Profit Beats Expectations, Revenue Grows." Found at http://cbs.marketwatch.com (March 22, 2002).

13 Boyle, "How Nike Got Its SWOOSH Back."

14 A. Nucci. "The Demography of Business Closing." *Small Business Economics* 12(1): 25–29.

15 Information found at http://www.ballyfitness.com on December 25, 2001.

16 Staff. "Career Resolutions." *Wall Street Journal* (December 30, 1997): 1.

17 N. Deogun. "Pop Culture." *Wall Street Journal* (May 8, 1997): 1.

18 D. Bycura and P. W. Darst. "Motivating Middle School Students: A Health-Club Approach." *Journal of Physical Education, Recreation & Dance* 72(7) (September 2001): 24.

19 R. Rodgers and J. Hunter. "The Discard of Study Evidence by Literature Reviewers." *Journal of Applied Behavioral Science* 30(3) (September 1994): 329–346.

20 Information found at http://www.hoovers.com, capsule for Converse Inc.

21 D. Pyke. "Strategies for Global Sourcing." *Financial Times* (February 20, 1998): FTS3–5.

22 J. M. Gladden, R. L. Irwin, and W. A. Sutton. "Managing North American Major Professional Sport Teams in the New Millennium: A Focus on Building Brand Equity." *Journal of Sport Management* 15 (2001): 303–304.

23 Ibid.

24 T. Canavan. "Devils Agree to Sell to Affiliate of YankeeNets." *The Detroit News* (March 17, 2000).

25 Collis and Montgomery, "Creating Corporate Advantage," 71–84.

26 Staff. "Jordan Raises Endorser Bar, His Move Could Benefit Nike." *Footwear News* (April, 31, 2000).

27 Staff. "It's All About Marketing." *Wall Street Journal* (June 15, 2000): A1.

28 M. Sonfield and R. N. Lussier. "The Entrepreneurial Strategy Matrix: A Model for New and Ongoing Ventures." *Business Horizons* 40 (May/June 1997): 73–77.

29 M. Porter. *Competitive Strategy: Techniques for Analyzing Industries and Competitors.* New York: Free Press, 1980, p. 15.

30 Staff. "Roberto Goizueta in His Own Words." *Wall Street Journal* (October 20, 1997): B1.

31 S. Trussler. "The Rules of the Game." *Journal of Business Strategy* 19(1)(January/February 1998): 16–20.

32 V. Saran. "The Role of Life Cycles and Forecast Horizons in a Forecasting System: Reebok's Perspective." *Journal of Business Forecasting* 17(1) (Spring 1998): 23–25.

33 Information found at http://www.wnba.com on May 31, 2001.

34 Staff. "NBA All-Star Ratings Hit Low." Found at http://www.sportingnews.com (February 15, 2000).

35 Grover and Lowry, "Smackdowns."

36 L. M. Birou, S. E. Fawcett, and G. M. Magnan "The Product Life Cycle: A Tool for Functional Strategic Alignment." *International Journal of Purchasing and Materials Management* 34(2) (Spring 1998): 37–52.

37 A. Campbell and M. Alexander. "What's Wrong with Strategy?" *Harvard Business Review* 75(6) (November/December1997): 42–50.

38 Information found at http://www.mightyducks.com on August 16, 2002.

CHAPTER 5

1 Information about the Maccabi Games found at http://www.maccabiusa.com on January 12, 2002.

2 Personal interview with Claudia Fiks.

3 M. L. Walker and D. K. Stotlar. *Sport Facility Management.* Sudbury, Massachusetts: Jones & Bartlett, 1997, pp. 4–14.

4 L. P. Masteralexis, C. Barr, and M. Hums. *Principles and Practices of Sport Management.* Gaithersburg, Maryland: Aspen, 1998, p. 313.

5 Information about the Basketball Hall of Fame found at http://www.hoophall.com on March 29, 2002.

6 E. Spanberg. "Diplomacy Counts (Mike Crum Runs the Charlotte Auditorium-Coliseum-Convention Center Authority)." *Business Journal Serving Charlotte and the Metropolitan Area* 6(10) (August 10, 2001): 3.

7 L. Deckard. "When the Louisiana Superdome Turned Over Operations to a Privately Run Company Twenty Years Ago, Few Realized They Were Witnessing the Birth of a Whole New Industry." *Amusement Business* 109(29) (July 21, 1997): 15–18.

8 Staff. "SMG Pairs with Houston Firm." *Philadelphia Business Journal* 19(9) (April 7, 2000): 53.

9 B. Peters. "Event Planning 101: Fear of Dealing with a Caterer." *Birmingham Business Journal* 18(45) (November 9, 2001): 19.

10 D. Smart and R. A. Wolfe. "Examining Sustainable Competitive Advantage in Intercollegiate Athletics: A Resource-Based View." *Journal of Sport Management* 14(2) (April 2000): 133–153.

11 A. Rutigliano. "Cloudy with a Change of Leads." *Sales & Marketing Management* 146(8) (August 1994): 6.

12 Information about Red Sox ticket sales found at http://www.sportsline.com/u/baseball/mlb/teams/BOS/attendance.htm on February 6, 2002.

13 Information about Nike's market share found at http://www.snowboardnetwork.com/sports/athletic_footwear_market_share.htm on January 16, 2002.

14 D. Mahony and D. Howard. "Sport Business in the Next Decade: A General Overview of Expected Trends." *Journal of Sport Management* 15(4) (October 2001): 275–296.

15 A. Sack and A. Nadim. "Strategic Choices in a Turbulent Environment: A Case Study of Starter Corporation." *Journal of Sport Management* 16(1) (January 2002): 36–53.

16 R. Gordon. "A Role for the Forecasting Function." *Journal of Business Forecasting* 16(4) (Winter 1997): 3–8.

17 W. Keenan. "Number Racket: Are Your Salespeople Contributing to the Effort to Predict Tomorrow's Business Results?" *Sales & Marketing Management* 147(5) (May 1995): 64–71.

18 C. Li and Y. Wu. "Minimal Cost Project Networks: The Cut Set Parallel Difference Method." *Omega* 22(4) (July 1994): 401–408.

19 R. Laliberte. "Simplify Your Life." *Success* 45(4) (April 1998): 56–62.

20 K. Danylchuk and P. Chelladurai. "The Nature of Managerial Work in Canadian Intercollegiate Athletics." *Journal of Sport Management* 13(2) (1999): 148–166.

21 J. Laabs. "Executives on Hold." *Personnel Journal* 11(1) (January 1994): 18–20.

22 B. Lamons. "Just Do It: Managers Must Start Planning Ahead." *Marketing News* 32(2) (February 2, 1998): 10–11.

23 S. Covey. "First Things First." *Success* 41(3) (April 1994): 8A–8D.

24 Deckard, "Louisiana Superdome," 15–18.

CHAPTER 6

1 This case is based on an interview with Stuart Greene.

2 L. Gulick. "Notes on the Theory of Organization." *International Journal of Public Administration* 21(2–4) (February–April 1998): 445–90.

3 D. R. Dalton, C. M Daily, A. E. Ellstrand, and J. L. Johnson. "Meta-analytical Reviews of Board Composition, Leadership Structure, and Financial Performance." *Strategic Management Journal* 19(3) (March 1998): 269–291.

4 M. Farber. "Unlike in Other Leagues, a Captain in the NHL Not Only Wears His Rank on His Jersey but Also Can Wield as Much Influence over his Teammates as the Coach." *Sports Illustrated* 93(15) (October 16, 2000): 76–79.

5   A. Bernstein. "U.S. Olympic Committee on Notice with New CEO." *Washington Business Journal* 18(48) (March 31, 2000): 22.

6   Ibid.

7   P. Lawrence and J. Lorsch. *Organizations and Environment.* Burr Ridge, Illinois: Irwin, 1967.

8   S. Walter. "Big Events Call for Even Bigger Security: Security in a Changing World: What Cities Are Doing to Prepare." *Nation's Cities Weekly* 25(3) (January 21, 2002): 6.

9   Ibid.

10 M. Janofsky. "Safeguarding the Games Is Costly but Effective." *New York Times* (February 20, 2002, Late Edition—Final): D-6.

11 Bernstein, "U.S. Olympic Committee on Notice," 22.

12 D. Smart and R. Wolfe. "Examining Sustainable Competitive Advantage in Intercollegiate Athletics: A Resources-Based View." *Journal of Sport Management* 14(2) (April 2000): 133–153.

13 J. Mooney. "The Principles of Organization." *International Journal of Public Administration* 21(2–4) (1998): 535–545.

14 Regional information was updated using Nike's quarterly report ending February 28, 2002 (Form 10-Q).

15 M. West and M. Patterson. "Profitable Personnel." *People Management* 4(1) (January 1998): 28–32.

16 S. Field. "Does Team Spirit Make Economic Sense?" *OECD Observer* (Summer 2001): 55.

17 J. R. Rentsch and R. P. Steel. "Testing the Durability of Job Characteristics as Predictors of Absenteeism over a Six-year Period." *Personnel Psychology* 51(1) (Spring 1998):165–191.

18 R. Hackman and G. Oldham. *Work Redesign.* Reading, Massachusetts: Addison-Wesley, 1980.

19 C. Bartlett and S. Ghosal. "The Myth of the General Manager." *California Management Review* 40(1)(Fall 1997): 92–117.

20 J. Zoltak. "Making Sure Customers Get Satisfaction Discussed at Stadium Managers Seminar." *Amusement Business* 110(7) (February 16, 1998): 4–5.

21 G. Breivik. "Sport in High Modernity: Sport as a Carrier of Social Values." *Journal of the Philosophy of Sport* 25(1) (December 1998): 103–131.

22 L. E. Greiner, "Evolution and Revolution as Organizations Grow." *Harvard Business Review* 76(3) (May/June 1998): 55–64.

23 G. Gabriet. "Delegating Do's and Don'ts." *Working Women* 23(5) (May 1998): S15–16.

24 G. Adler. "When Your Star Performer Can't Manage." *Harvard Business Review* 75(4) (July/August 1997): 22–27.

CHAPTER 7

1   J. Torre with H. Dreher. *Joe Torre's Ground Rules for Winners.* New York: Hyperion, 1999.

2   Ibid.

3   Information found at http://www.yogi-berra.com/yogiisms.html on August 29, 2002.

4   M. Glendinning. "MasterCard's Global Stage: How Does the Company Plan to Make the Most from Its Sponsorship?" *SportBusiness International* 65 (January 2002): 43.

5   D. Hoch. "The Athletic Director and Change." *Coach & Athletic Director* 71(9) (April 2, 2002): 4–5.

6   Ibid.

7   Information found at http://www.ecybex.com/company/overview/timeline.html on April 3, 2002.

8   B. Streisand. "The Race for Speed: While the Athletes Train, Equipment Makers Work in Secret to Hone a Technological Edge." *U.S. News & World Report* 132(3) (January 28–February 4, 2002): 51–52.

9   An excellent site on the history of fencing can be found at http://www.ahfi.org.

10 Information found at http://www.ecybex.com/company/overview/timeline.html on April 3, 2002.

11 C. Conway. "Physical Education and the Use of ICT." *British Journal of Teaching Physical Education* 31(3) (Autumn 2000): 12–13.

12 Hoch, "The Athletic Director," 4–5.

13 L. Reynolds. "Understand Employees' Resistance to Change." *HR Focus* 71(6) (June 1994): 17.

14 Hoch, "The Athletic Director," 4–5.

15 Ibid.

16 Ibid.

17 J. Mariotti. "The Challenge of Change." *Industry Week* 247(7) (April 6, 1998): 140–141.

18 K. Hultman. *The Path of Least Resistance.* Austin, Texas: Learning Concepts, 1979.

19 Y. Liu and J. Wang. "Discussion on Sports Team Culture." *Journal of Capital College of Physical Education* 13(1) (2001): 28–33.

20 E. Schein. *Organizational Culture and Leadership.* San Francisco: Josey-Bass, 1985.

21 J. Macmullan. "Disappointed Yet Dedicated: O'Donnell Puts Joey Ahead of Himself." *Boston Globe* (March 28, 2002).

22 J. Chadiha and L. Munson. "Err Raid." *Sports Illustrated Online* (April 10, 2001).

23 J. Macmullan. "A Turn at Gates Is Just His Style." *Boston Globe* (April 4, 2002).

24 B. Moran. "Soft Walls Keep Indy Drivers Safe." Found at http://www.techtv.com/news/culture/story/0,24195,3386110,00.html (May 24, 2002).

25 G. Kelly. "Soft Walls' Debut a Smashing Success." Found at http://www.n-jcenter.com/2002/Aug/5/SPDWC3.htm (August 5, 2002).

26 Staff. "HR at the Forefront of Change Management at L.L. Bean." *International Journal of Retail & Distribution Management* 26(4–5) (April–May 1998): 192–195.

27 S. W. Pool. "The Learning Organization: Motivating Employees by Integrating TQM Philosophy in a Supportive Organizational Culture." *Leadership & Organization Development Journal* 21(8) (December 2000): 373.

28 D. Elmuti and T. AlDiab. "Improving Quality and Organizational Effectiveness Go Hand in Hand Through Deming's Management System." *Journal of Business Strategies* 12(1) (Spring 1995): 86–98.

29 D. McAbe and A. Wilkinson. "The Vision, Meaning and Operation of Change." *Industrial Relations Journal* 29(2) (March 1998): 18–30.

30 R. Zemke. "Systems Training: Excerpt from The Fifth Discipline: The Art and Practice of the Learning Organization." *Training* 38(2) (February 2001): 40.

31 Ibid.

32 D. Melilli. "Driving for Diversity: CART Program Out to Widen Participant Spectrum." *Crain's Cleveland Business* (June 21, 1999): G-8.

33 Ibid.

34 J. Inkrott. "Hot Wheels." *Sports Illustrated* (September 2, 2002): 38.

35 A. Doherty and P. Chelladurai. "Managing Cultural Diversity in Sport Organizations: A Theoretical Perspective." *Journal of Sport Management* 13(4) (1999): 280–297.

36 Staff. "The U.S. Foreign-Born Population Grew." *Wall Street Journal* (January 4, 2001): A1.

37 J. Schneider. "The Fairness Factor." *U.S. News & World Report* 132(8) (March 18, 2002): 63.

38 Ibid.

39 Ibid.

40 C. Hymowitz. "In Turbulent Climate, Pioneering Women Face Special Scrutiny." *Wall Street Journal* (March 31, 2001): B1.

41 M. C. Higgins. "Reconceptualizing Mentoring at Work: A Development Network Perspective." *The Academy of Management Review* 26(2) (2001): 264–288.

42 K. Tyler. "Mentoring Programs Link Employees and Experienced Execs." *HRMagazine* 43(5) (April 1998): 98–104.

43 J. C. Quick and J. H. Gavin. "The Next Frontier: Edgar Schein on Organizational Therapy." *The Academy of Management Executive* 14(1) (2000): 31–38.

44 K. Lewin. *Field Theory in Social Science.* New York: Harper & Row, 1951.

45 R. Blake and J. Mouton. *The Managerial Grid III: Key to Leadership Excellence.* Houston: Gulf Publishing, 1985.

46 Staff. "Sensitivity Training Makes a Comeback." *Work & Family Newsbrief* (December 2000): 5.

47 N. Merrick. "The Lions Share: Team-Building and Leadership Program for British Lions." *People Management* 3(12) (June 12, 1997): 34–37.

48 D. Crawford. "Corporate Driving School Accelerates Firm Team Building." *Business First—Columbus* 16(36) (April 28, 2000): 5.

49 H. Appenzeller. *Managing Sports.* Durham, North Carolina: Carolina Academic Press, 1993.

50 Ibid.

51 J. Glasser. "King of the Hill: In Big-Time College Sports, Athletic Directors Like Ohio State's Andy Geiger Rule." *U.S. News & World Report* 132(8) (March 18, 2002): 52–60.

52 Ibid.

CHAPTER 8

1 P. Keating. "Crunch Time: When the NFL Cap Comes Calling, No One, We Repeat, No One Is Safe." *ESPN The Magazine* 4(15) (July 23, 2001): 71–73.

2 M. Besack. "In This Ballpark, HR Is the Name of the Game." *Workforce* 76(9) (September 1997): 31–32.

3 J. E. Perry Smith and T. C. Blum. "Work-Family Human Resource Bundles and Perceived Organizational Performance." *The Academy of Management Journal* 43(6)(2000): 1107–1117.

4   Besack, "In This Ballpark," 31.

5   A. Colella and A. Varma. "The Impact of Subordinate Disability on Leader-Member Exchange Relationships." *The Academy of Management Journal* 44(2) (2001): 304–315.

6   A. McWilliams and D. Siegel. "Corporate Social Responsibility: A Theory of the Firm Perspective." *The Academy of Management Review* 26(1) (2001): 117–127.

7   B. J. Sharkey. *Fitness & Health,* 5th ed. Champaign, Illinois: Human Kinetics, 2002, pp. 399–408.

8   C. Pigeassou. "Improving Leadership of Human Resources in Fitness Centers: How Should Different Types of Management Maneuver Themselves?" *9th ASM Congress, Vitoria-Gasteiz* (September 19–23, 2001): 254–256.

9   A. Durity. "The HR Side of Pro Football." *Personnel* 68(9) (September 1991): 24.

10 J. Laabs. "Heading HR for the Olympics and the World Cup." *Personnel Journal* 73(10) (October 1994): 32–36.

11 J. Chadiha. "Saints Alive." *Sports Illustrated* (September 30, 2002): 63.

12 This job description was used with permission from Elms College.

13 R. D. Bretz, Jr., and T. A. Judge. "Realistic Job Previews: A Test of the Adverse Self-Selection Hypothesis." *Journal of Applied Psychology* 83(2) (April 1998): 330–338.

14 W. J. Weese. "Opportunities and Headaches: Dichotomous Perspectives on the Current and Future Hiring Realities in the Sport Management Academy." *Journal of Sport Management* 16(2) (January 2002): 1–17.

15 D. Goetzl. "ESPN and Monster Strike Deal; Alliance Will Create Web Site for Sports Jobs." *Advertising Age* 72 (June 11, 2001): 50.

16 K. D. Lyons. "Personal Investment as a Predictor of Camp Counselor Job Performance." *Journal of Park and Recreation Administration* 18(2) (Summer 2000): 21–36.

17 S. L. Rynes, A. M. Mullenix, and C. Q. Trank. "Do Behavioral Skills Increase the Employability of Business Students?" *Journal of Career Centers* (Summer 2001): 40–43.

18 Adapted from R. Lussier. "Selecting Qualified Candidates Through Effective Job Interviewing." *Clinical Laboratory Management Review* 9(4) (July/August 1995): 257–275.

19 T. Carbasho. "Welcome to the Family: Orientation Programs Help New Employees Get Up and Running." *Pittsburgh Business Time* 21(21) (December 14, 2001): 21.

20 Ibid.

21 Laabs. "Heading HR," 32–36.

22 S. Walker. "Baseball's Secret Boom." *Wall Street Journal* (March 1, 2002): W1.

23 J. Pfeffer and R. I. Sutton. *The Knowing-Doing Gap.* Cambridge, Massachusetts: Harvard Business School, 2000.

24 Staff. "Intel Cost-Cutting Spares a College Tour." *Wall Street Journal* (June 14, 2001): A1.

25 C. Hymowitz. "How to Tell Employees All the Things They Don't Want to Hear." *Management* (August 22, 2001): B1.

26 A. S. DeNisi and A. N. Kluger. "Feedback Effectiveness: Can 360-Degree Appraisals Be Improved?" *The Academy of Management Executive* 14(1) (2000): 129–139.

27 Staff. "Despite Dot-Com Hype." *Wall Street Journal* (October 31, 2000): A1.

28 E. C. Hollensbe and J. P. Guthrie. "Group Pay-Performance Plans: The Role of Spontaneous Goal Setting." *The Academy of Management Review* 25(4) (2001): 864–872.

29 Staff. "How Loyalty Comes by Degrees." *Wall Street Journal* (May 17, 2001): A1.

30 S. J. Lambert. "Added Benefits: The Link between Work-Life Benefits and Organizational Citizenship Behavior." *The Academy of Management Journal* 43(6) (2001): 1107–1117.

31 Staff. "A Few Insurers." *Wall Street Journal* (April 17, 2001): A1.

32 M. Roberts. "OSHA Investigates Stringer Death, Vikings Cooperate." Found at http://www.sportslawnews.com/archive/articles%202001/stringercontractosha.htm (August 7, 2001).

33 A. Schwarz. "Word for Word/Blast from the Past—Baseball in Crisis? Nah. It's Deja Vu All Over Again." *New York Times* (July 14, 2002): 7.

34 Information found at http://bigleaguers.yahoo.com/mlbpa/faq.html on July 5, 2002.

35 A. R. Hunt. "Major League Baseball: A Case Study in Mismanagement." *Wall Street Journal* (August 22, 2002): A13.

36 P. Weiler. *Leveling the Playing Field: How the Law Can Make Sports Better for the Fans.* Cambridge, Massachusetts: Harvard University Press, 2000, p. 121.

37 Schwarz, "Word for Word," 7.

38 Weiler, *Leveling the Playing Field,* 121.

39 Schwarz, "Word for Word," 7.

40   Ibid.

41   Weiler, *Leveling the Playing Field,* 129.

42   L. Koppett. *Koppett's Concise History of Major League Baseball.* Philadelphia: Temple University Press, 1998, p. 321.

43   Hunt, "Major League Baseball," A13.

44   Weiler, *Leveling the Playing Field,* 137.

45   Ibid, p. 138.

46   Ibid, p. 139.

47   A. Zimbalist. *Baseball and Billions.* New York: HarperCollins, 1992, p. 26.

48   Ibid, 25.

49   P. D. Staudohar. "The Baseball Strike of 1994–1995." *Monthly Labor Review* 120(3) (March 1997): 21–27.

50   S. Deitch. "Pennsylvania League Coaches Ink Collective-Bargaining Pact." *NCAA News* (July 8, 2002): 1.

51   J. Berger,. "One More Time." *ESPN The Magazine* (September 17, 2001): 112.

52   D. Ahlstrom, S. Si, and J. Kennelly. "Free-Agent Performance in Major League Baseball: Do Teams Get What They Expect?" *Journal of Sport Management* 13(3) (July 1999): 181–197.

53   Staff. "Rough Road Ahead for Nike: Company to Cut 1,600 Workers; Outlook Grim as Future Orders Fall." *CNNMoney* (March 18, 1998): 1.

54   Ibid.

CHAPTER 9

1   NCAA mission statement found at http://www.ncaa.org, the official web site of the NCAA.

2   A. Sack and E. Staurowsky. *College Athletes for Hire: The Evolution and Legacy of the NCAA's Amateur Myth.* Westport, Connecticut: Praeger Publishers, 1998, p. 35.

3   A. A. Fleisher III, B. L. Goff, and R. D. Tollison. *The National Collegiate Athletic Association: A Study in Cartel Behavior.* Chicago: The University of Chicago Press, 1992, pp. 158–159.

4   J. R. Gerdy. *The Successful College Athletic Program: The New Standard.* Phoenix, Arizona: American Council on Education and the Oryx Press, 1997, p. 112.

5   Staff. "NCAA Training Asks 'How to Avoid Cutting Teams?' 'How About Reforming Title IX,' Answers Independent Women's Forum." *PR Newswire* (May 9, 2002).

6   B. Wildavsky. "Graduation Blues." *U.S. News & World Report* (March 18, 2002): 70.

7   Ibid, 69.

8   D. Goetzl. "New Sport: Personality Contests; Shows Turn to Comedy to Lure Bigger Audience." *Advertising Age* 72 (November 12, 2001): 18.

9   Ibid.

10   S. McClellan. "ABC on the Hunt: Signs Madden for MNF, Chases Letterman for Late Night." *Broadcasting & Cable* 132(9)(March 4, 2002): 12.

11   J. L. Shulman and W. G. Bowen. *The Game of Life: College Sports and Educational Values.* Princeton, New Jersey: Princeton University Press, 2001, p. 16.

12   M. Manning. "Baseball Economics." *St. Louis Business Journal* 21(32) (April 13, 2001): 2.

13   A. Doherty and P. Chelladurai. "Managing Cultural Diversity in Sport Organizations: A Theoretical Perspective," *Journal of Sport Management* 13(4) (July 1999): 280–297.

14   M. A. Tietjen and R. M. Myers. "Motivation and Job Satisfaction." *Management Decision* 36(3–4) (May/June 1998): 226–232.

15   D. G. Gardner and J. L. Pierce. "Self-Esteem and Self Efficacy within the Organizational Context: An Empirical Examination." *Group and Organization Management* 23(1) (March 1998): 48–71.

16   A. Hill with J. Wooden. *Be Quick—But Don't Hurry: Learning Success from the Teachings of a Lifetime.* New York: Simon & Schuster, 2001. Visit http://www.coachwooden.com/ for an interactive tour of Wooden's Pyramid of Success.

17   C. Orts. "Relationships between Satisfaction, Attitudes, and Performance: An Organizational Analysis." *Journal of Applied Psychology* (December, 1992): 963–974.

18   R. Forrester. "Empowerment: Rejuvenating a Potent Idea." *The Academy of Management Executive* 14(3) (2000): 67–80.

19   W. L. Gardner and B. J. Avolio. "The Charismatic Relationships: A Dramaturgical Perspective." *The Academy of Management Review* 23(1) (January 1998): 32–59.

20   Staff. "Kentucky State University Placed on Probation for Two Years." *NCAA News Release* (April 10, 2002).

21   D. McClelland and D. H. Burnham. "Power Is the Great Motivator." *Harvard Business Review* (March/April 1978): 103.

22   Shulman and Bowen, *The Game of Life,* 120–121.

23 S. Robbins and D. DeCenzo. *Fundamentals of Management.* Englewood Cliffs, New Jersey: Prentice-Hall, 1995, pp. 10–11.

24 Doherty and Chelladurai, "Managing Cultural Diversity," 280–297.

25 C. M. Tamburrini. "Sports, Fascism, and the Market." *Journal of the Philosophy of Sport* 25(1) (1998).

26 J. Helyar. "Golfers to PGA: We're Playing Through." *Fortune* 143(6)(March 19): 32.

27 M. Rousseau. "Schema, Promise and Mutuality: The Building Blocks of the Psychological Contract." *Journal of Occupational and Organizational Psychology,* 74(4)(November 2001): 511–541.

28 Adapted from Always Improvement Training Materials, Bethesda, MD, June 2001.

29 Sack and Staurowsky, *College Athletes for Hire,* 95.

30 B. Parks. "Got a Conflict with a Colleague? Here's How to Resolve It Now!" *Instructor* 107(7) (April 1998): 74–75.

31 C. Hymowitz. " Managing Your Career: Managers Struggle to Let Someone Go." *Wall Street Journal* (July 28, 1998): B1.

32 Helyar, "Golfers," 32.

33 Parks, "Got a Conflict," 74–75.

34 Ibid.

35 K. O. Wilburn. "Employment Disputes: Solving Them Out of Court." *Management Review* 87(3) (March 1998): 17–22.

36 P. Lowe. "9 Secrets of Superstar Salespeople." *Success Yearbook.* Tampa, Florida: Peter Lowe International, 1998, pp. 38–39.

37 Ibid.

38 S. Lorge. "The Best Way to Negotiate." *Sales & Marketing Management* 150(3) (March 1998): 92–93.

39 Ibid.

40 Lowe, "9 Secrets," 38–39.

41 Ibid.

42 Wilburn, "Employment Disputes," 17–22.

43 Ibid.

44 Parks, "Got a Conflict," 74–75.

45 Ibid.

46 M. Barrier. "Putting a Lid on Conflicts." *Nation's Business* 86(4)(April 1998): 34–36.

47 Wilburn, "Employment Disputes,"17–22.

48 Ibid.

49 P. L. Perrewe, G. R. Ferris, D. D. Frink, and W. P. Anthony. "Political Skills: An Antidote for Workplace Stressors." *The Academy of Management Executive* 14(3) (2000): 115–123.

50 Staff. "The Memphis Grizzlies, the NBA Team, Has Announced the Hiring of Jerry West." *Arkansas Business* 19(18) (May 6, 2002): 13.

51 Staff. "Lousier Bosses." *Wall Street Journal* (April 4, 1995): 1.

52 M. E. Schweeitzer and J. L. Kerr. "Bargaining under the Influence: The Role of Alcohol in Negotiations." *The Academy of Management Executive* 14(2) (2000): 47.

53 Staff. "Survey: TV Sports Good for Stress Relief (After Terrorist Attacks)." *Mediaweek* 11(41)(November 5, 2001): 25.

54 C. P. Neck and K. H. Cooper. "The Fit Executive: Exercise and Diet Guidelines for Enhancing Performance." *The Academy of Management Executive* 14(2) (2000): 72.

55 Ibid.

56 R. Ross, I. Janssen, and A. Tremblay. "Exercise & Nutrition Update: Obesity Reduction through Lifestyle Modification." *Canadian Journal of Applied Physiology* 25(1) (2000).

57 S. E. Iso-Ahola and B. St. Clair. "Toward a Theory of Exercise Motivation. *Quest* 52(2) (2000).

58 Information found at http://www. littleleague.org on May 15, 2002.

59 Staff. "Almonte Bronx Team Records Wiped Away." *Associated Press* (August, 31, 2001). Information also found at http://espn. go.com/moresports/llws01/s/2001/0831/ 1246234.html.

60 Saul Steinberg, quoted in Harold Rosenberg. *Saul Steinberg.* New York: Knopf, 1978, p. 240.

CHAPTER 10

1 The mission for the Boys and Girls Clubs can be found at http://www.bgca.org/whoweare/.

2 M. J. Robinson, M. A. Hums, R. B. Crow, and D. R. Phillips. *Profiles of Sport Industry Professionals: The People Who Make the Games Happen.* Gaithersburg, Maryland: Aspen Publishers, 2001, p. 433.

3 G. Colvin. "Think You Can Bobsled? Ha! Managers May Talk a Good Game, but Few Have the Guts to Really Run Their Business Like a Great Sports Team." *Fortune* 145(6) (March 18, 2002): 50.

4. L. R. Offerman and R. K. Spiros. "The Science and Practice of Team Development: Improving the Link." *The Academy of Management Journal* 44(2) (2001): 376–392.

5. N. Knop, D. Tannehill, and M. O'Sullivan. "Making a Difference for Urban Youths." *Journal of Physical Education, Recreation & Dance* 72(7) (September 2001): 38.

6. G. L. Stewart. "Team Structure and Performance: Assessing the Mediating Role of Intrateam Process and the Moderating Role of Task Type." *The Academy of Management Journal* 43(2) (2000): 135–148.

7. Colvin, "Think You Can Bobsled," 50.

8. Staff. "Sports Franchise Values." Found at http://espn.go.com/sportsbusiness/s/forbes.html on June 27, 2002.

9. J. Gladden, R. Irwin, and W. Sutton. "Managing North American Major Professional Teams in the New Millennium: A Focus on Building Brand Equity." *Journal of Sport Management* 15(4) (October 2001): 298.

10. C. Gomez, B. L. Kirkman, and D. L. Shapiro. "The Impact of Collectivism and In-Group/Out-Group Membership on the Evaluation Generosity of Team Members." *The Academy of Management Journal* 43(2) (2000): 38–41.

11. Offermann and Spiros, "The Science and Practice," 376–392.

12. Stewart, "Team Structure and Performance," 135–148.

13. J. Diamond. "The Idea of Organization." *Wall Street Journal* (December 12, 2000): A26.

14. R. T. Barker, G. H. Gilbreath, and W. S. Stone. "The Interdisciplinary Needs of Organizations: Are New Employees Adequately Equipped?" *Journal of Management Development* 17(2–3) (February/March 1998): 214–233.

15. Colvin, "Think You Can Bobsled," 50.

16. G. Cuskelly, N. McIntyre, and A. Boag . "A Longitudinal Study of the Development of Organizational Commitment Amongst Volunteer Sport Administrators." *Journal of Sport Management* 12(3) (July 1998): 181–202.

17. P. C. Earley and E. Mosakowski. "Creating Hybrid Team Cultures: An Empirical Test of Transformational Team Function." *The Academy of Management Journal* 43(1) (2000): 26–49.

18. T. R. Zenger and C. R. Marshall. "Determinants of Incentive Intensity in Group-Based Rewards." *The Academy of Management Journal* 43(2) (2000): 149–163.

19. D. Ahlstrom, S. Si, and J. Kennelly. "Free-Agent Performance in Major League Baseball: Do Teams Get What They Expect?" *Journal of Sport Management* 13(3) (July 1999): 181–196.

20. Earley and Mosakowski, "Creating Hybrid Team Cultures," 26–49.

21. Colvin, "Think You Can Bobsled," 50.

22. Gomez, Kirkman, and Shapiro, "The Impact of Collectivism," 38–41.

23. D. Knight, C. C. Durham, and E. A. Locke. "The Relationship of Team Goals, Incentives, and Efficacy to Strategic Risk, Tactical Implementation, and Performance." *The Academy of Management Journal* 44(2) (2001): 326–338.

24. T. Pollock. "Mind Your Own Business." *Supervision* 62(2) (February 2001): 16.

25. Earley and Mosakowski, "Creating Hybrid Team Cultures," 26–49.

26. Knight, Durham, and Locke, "The Relationship of Team Goals," 326–338.

27. Gomez, Kirkman, and Shapiro. "The Impact of Collectivism," 38–41.

28. Earley and Mosakowski, "Creating Hybrid Team Cultures," 26–49.

29. K. Munroe, P. Estabrooks, P. Dennis, and A. Carron. "A Phenomenological Analysis of Group Norms in Sport Teams." *The Sport Psychologist* 13(2) (June 1999): 181.

30. Ibid.

31. Gomez, Kirkman, and Shapiro, "The Impact of Collectivism," 38–41.

32. R. B. Mitchell, T. Crosset, and C. A. Barr. "Encouraging Compliance without Real Power: Sport Associations Regulating Teams." *Journal of Sport Management* 13(3) (July 1999): 216.

33. B. Goff. "Effects of University Athletics on the University: A Review and Extension of Empirical Assessment." *Journal of Sport Management* 14(2) (April 2000): 85–104.

34. D. Gould, D. Guinan, C. Greenleaf, R. Medbery, and K. Peterson. "Factors Affecting Olympic Performance: Perceptions of Athletes and Coaches from More and Less Successful Teams." *The Sport Psychologist* 13(4) (2000).

35. K. L. Gammage, A. V. Carron, and P. A. Estabrooks. "Team Cohesion and Individual Productivity: The Influence of the Norm for Productivity and the Identifiability of Individual Effort." *Small Group Research* 32(1) (2001): 3–18.

36. Staff. "Chalk It Up to Teamwork." *Business Week* (3773) (March 11, 2002): 22.

37 Ibid.

38 D. Booth and J. Loy. "Sport, Status, and Style." *Sport History Review* 30(1) (May 1999): 1–26.

39 C. J. Auld and G. Godbey. "Influence in Canadian National Sport Organizations: Perceptions of Professionals and Volunteers." *Journal of Sport Management* 12(1) (January 1998): 20–38.

40 Knight, Durham, and Locke, "The Relationship of Team Goals," 326–338.

41 Auld and Godbey, "Influence in Canadian National Sport Organizations," 20–38.

42 Stewart, "Team Structure and Performance," 135–148.

43 Earley and Mosakowski, "Creating Hybrid Team Cultures," 26–49.

44 Stewart, "Team Structure and Performance," 135–148.

45 Knight, Durham, and Locke, "The Relationship of Team Goals," 326–338.

46 Offermann and Spiros, "The Science and Practice," 376–392.

47 Zenger and Marshall, "Determinants of Incentive Intensity," 149–163.

48 P. G. Clampitt, R. J. DeKoch, and T. Cashman. "A Strategy for Communicating about Uncertainty." *The Academy of Management Executive* 14(1) (2000): 41–60.

49 R. McGee and S. Pelletier. "Play Ball!: From Sports Marketing to Promotional Campaigns, These Strategies Will Help Boost Attendance—and Your Profile within Your Organization." *Association Meetings* 14(1) (February 2002): 36–38.

50 A. Wills. "Football Venues: Business Arenas—Football Clubs Are Extending Their Offer to the Meetings Market with Purpose-built Facilities in New Stadiums or by Expanding Existing Amenities." *Conference & Incentive Travel* (May 8, 2002): 47.

51 Staff. "Minor Memos." *Wall Street Journal* (February 2, 2001): 1.

52 Ibid.

CHAPTER 11

1 A. Eisenstock. *Sports Talk: A Journey Inside the World of Sports Talk Radio.* New York: Pocket Books, 2001, pp. 112–113.

2 Staff. "ABC, ESPN Agree to WNBA Pact." *Mediaweek* 12(24) (June 17, 2002): 40.

3 Staff. "WNBA." *San Antonio Business Journal* 15(24) (July 6, 2001): 21.

4 Information found at http://www.sportsmediachallenge.com/about/ on June 2, 2002.

5 C. Hymowitz. "In the Lead." *Wall Street Journal* (February 20, 2001): B1.

6 Ibid.

7 D. K. Lindo. "Are You Coaching the Bad News Bearers?" *Supervision* 59(6) (June 1998): 3–5.

8 N. B. Kurland and L. H. Pelled. "Passing the Word: Toward a Model of Gossip and Power in the Workplace." *The Academy of Management Review* 25(2)(2000): 428–438.

9 M. J. McDermott. "Listening with a Purpose." *Chief Executive (U.S.)* (February 2001): 35.

10 K. L. Armstrong. "African-American Students' Responses to Race as a Source Cue in Persuasive Sport Communications." *Journal of Sport Management* 14 (3) (July 2000): 208–227.

11 T. E. Weber. "E-World." *Wall Street Journal* (October 30, 2000): B1.

12 P. Lowe. "How to Boost Your Market Value." *Success Yearbook.* Tampa, Florida: Peter Lowe International, 1998, pp. 22–23.

13 Lindo, "Are You Coaching," 3.

14 A. S. DeNisi and A. N. Kluger. "Feedback Effectiveness: Can 360-Degree Appraisals Be Improved?" *The Academy of Management Executive* 14(1) (2000): 129–139

15 J. Ghorpade. "Managing Five Paradoxes of 360-Degree Feedback." *The Academy of Management Executive* 14(1) (2000): 140–150.

16 Hymowitz, "In the Lead," B1.

17 McDermott, "Listening with a Purpose," 35.

18 Kurland and Pelled, "Passing the Word," 428–438.

19 M. Messmer. "Improving Your Listening Skills." *Management Accounting (USA)* 25(2) (March 1998): 428–438.

20 S. L. Rynes, A. M. Mullenix, and C. Q. Trank. "Do Behavioral Skills Increase the Employability of Business Students?" *Journal of Career Centers* (Summer 2001): 40–43.

21 Hymowitz, "In the Lead," B1.

22 K. Davidoff. "The Sophomore Thinks." *Sporting News* (June 3, 2003): 26–28.

23 C. Hymowitz. "How to Tell Employees All the Things They Don't Want to Hear." *Wall Street Journal* (August 22, 2001): B1.

24 L. Karlin. *The Guide to Careers in Sport*. New York: Careers & Colleges Publications, 1995, pp. 100–129.

25 Ibid.

26 Ibid.

27 D. S. Mason and T. Slack. "Evaluating Monitoring Mechanisms as a Solution to Opportunism by Professional Hockey Agents." *Journal of Sport Management* 15(2) (April 2001): 107–134.

28 Information found at http://www1.ncaa.org/membership/enforcement/agents/uaaa/history.html on June 27, 2002.

29 Information found at http://bigleaguers.yahoo.com/mlbpa/faq.html on July 5, 2002.

30 B. Gordon. "Guest Editorial—Put Some National Bite in Sports-Agent Control." Found at http://www.ncaa.org/news/1997/970210/comment.html (February 10, 1997).

31 W. Friedman. "No Limit: Leland Hardy." *Advertising Age* (June 28, 1999): S24.

32 Staff. "Canada Sportsbreak." *Resource News International* (June 12, 2001).

CHAPTER 12

1 P. H. Summitt. *Reach for the Summitt: The Definitive Dozen System for Succeeding at Whatever You Do*. New York: Broadway Books, 1998, p. 100.

2 Summitt, *Reach for the Summitt*.

3 A. S. DeNisis and A. N. Kluger. "Feedback Effectiveness: Can 360-Degree Appraisals Be Improved?" *The Academy of Management Executive* 14(1) (2000): 129–139.

4 J. M. Farrell, M. E. Johnston, and G. D. Twynam. "Volunteer Motivation, Satisfaction, and Management at an Elite Sporting Competition." *Journal of Sport Management* 12(4) (October 1998): 288–300.

5 J. G. Clawson and M. E. Haskins. "Beating the Career Blues." *The Academy of Management Executive* 14(3) (2000): 91–102.

6 D. Markland. "Self-Determination Moderates the Effects of Perceived Competence on Intrinsic Motivation in an Exercise Setting." *Journal of Sport and Exercise Psychology* 21(4) (January 2000): 351–361.

7 A. Maslow. "A Theory of Human Motivation." *Psychological Review* 50 (1943): 370–396; and *Motivation and Personality*. New York: Harper & Row, 1954.

8 J. Brockman. "Living Legend; He's on Pace to Break the All-Time Home Run Record. Now,

He'll Have a Chance to Do It Where He Grew Up. With His Dad, the Hitting Coach. It's Almost Too Good to Be True." *Sarasota Herald Tribune* (March 3, 2000): 1W.

9 Clawson and Haskins, "Beating the Career Blues," 91–102.

10 C. Alderfer. "An Empirical Test of a New Theory of Human Needs." *Organizational Behavior and Human Performance* (April 1969): 142-175; and *Existence, Relatedness, and Growth*. New York: Free Press, 1972.

11 F. Herzberg. "One More Time: How Do You Motivate Employees?" *Harvard Business Review* (January/February 1968): 53–62.

12 Staff. "Work Week: A Special News Report about Life on the Job—and Trends Taking Shape There." *Wall Street Journal* (June 2, 1998): A1.

13 J. R. Rentsch and R. P. Steel. "Testing the Durability of Job Characteristics as Predictors of Absenteeism over a Six-Year Period." *Personnel Psychology* 51(1) (Spring 1998): 165–191.

14 D. J. Campbell. "The Proactive Employee: Managing Workplace Initiative." *The Academy of Management Executive* 14(3) (2000): 52–66.

15 Rentsch and Steel, "Testing the Durability," 165–191.

16 H. Murray. *Explorations in Personality*. New York: Oxford Press, 1938.

17 J. Atkinson. *An Introduction to Motivation*. New York: Van Nostrand Reinhold, 1964; D. McClelland. *The Achieving Society*. New York: Van Nostrand Reinhold, 1961; D. McClelland and D. H. Burnham. "Power Is the Great Motivator." *Harvard Business Review* (March/April 1978): 103.

18 J. S. Adams. "Toward an Understanding of Inequity." *Journal of Abnormal and Social Psychology* 67 (1963): 422–436.

19 P. Kuharsky. "Kearse Receives a Boost: Incentive Deal Might Aid Talks Later." *Tennessean.com* (June 27, 2002).

20 E. C. Hollensbe and J. P. Guthrie. "Group Pay-Performance Plans: The Role of Spontaneous Goal Setting." *The Academy of Management Review* 25(4) (2001): 864–872.

21 H. Klean and J. Kim. "A Field Study of the Influence of Situational Constraints, Leader-Member Exchange, and Goal Commitment on Performance." *The Academy of Management Journal* 41(1) (February 1998): 88–96.

22 D. Knight, C. C. Durham, and E. A. Locke. "The Relationship of Team Goals, Incentives,

and Efficacy to Strategic Risk, Tactical Implementation, and Performance." *The Academy of Management Journal* 44(2) (2001): 326–338.

23 C. Gomez, B. L. Kirkman, and D. L. Shapiro. "The Impact of Collectivism and In-Group/Out-Group Membership on the Evaluation Generosity of Team Members." *The Academy of Management Journal* 43(6) (2000): 1097–1106.

24 L. Holtz. "Setting a Higher Standard." *Success Yearbook*. Tampa, Florida: Peter Lowe International, 1998, p. 74.

25 V. Vroom. *Work and Motivation*. New York: Wiley, 1964.

26 M. J. McDermott. "Listening with a Purpose," *Chief Executive (U.S.)* (February 2001): 35.

27 B. F. Skinner. *Beyond Freedom and Dignity*. New York: Knopf, 1971.

28 P. G. Clampitt, R .J. DeKoch, and T. Cashman. "A Strategy for Communicating about Uncertainty." *The Academy of Management Executive* 14(1) (2000): 41–60.

29 A. J. Amorose and T. S. Horn. "Intrinsic Motivation: Relationships with Collegiate Athletes' Gender, Scholarship Status, and Perceptions of Their Coaches' Behavior." *Journal of Sport and Exercise Psychology* 22 (1) (February 2000): 63–84.

30 Kuharsky, "Kearse Receives a Boost."

31 J. Ghorpade. "Managing Five Paradoxes of 360-Degree Feedback." *The Academy of Management Executive* 14(1) (2000): 140–150.

32 Amorose and Horn, "Intrinsic Motivation," 63–84.

33 J. Curry. "Another Look in Texas." *New York Times* (February 28, 2002): D4.

34 Ibid.

35 McDermott, "Listening," 35.

36 F. Luthans and A. D. Stajkovic. "Reinforce for Performance: The Need to Go beyond Pay and Even Rewards." *The Academy of Management Executive* 13(1) (1999): 49.

37 This statement is based on R. Lussier's consulting practice.

38 This paragraph is based on R. Lussier's consulting practice.

39 Hollensbe and Guthrie, "Group Pay-Performance Plans," 864–872.

40 This case is based on an author interview with John Amaral on November 2, 2002.

CHAPTER 13

1 T. Layden. "What Is This 34-Year-Old Man Doing on a Skateboard? Making Millions." *Sports Illustrated* (June 10, 2002): 80-93.

2 M. Borden. "X-Treme Profits: The Economy Stinks. Tech's a Mess. Not Exactly Fun and Games Out There—Unless, Like Activision, You're Making Video Games." *Fortune* 145(5) (March 4, 2002): 149.

3 Staff. "What Is It about Leadership?" *Training & Development* 55(2) (March 2001): 21; B. Bass. *Stogdill's Handbook of Leadership,* 3rd ed. New York: Free Press, 1990.

4 D. A. Whetten and A. L. Delbecq. "Saraide's Chairman Hatim Tyabji on Creating and Sustaining a Values-Based Organizational Culture." *The Academy of Management Executive* 14(4) (2000): 32–33.

5 A. Kent, and P. Chelladurai. "Perceived Transformational Leadership, Organizational Commitment, and Citizenship Behavior: A Case Study in Intercollegiate Athletics." *Journal of Sport Management* 15(2) (April 2001): 139.

6 This comment was made in a discussion with Dr. Judith Neal on May 23, 2002.

7 J Quarterman. "An Assessment of the Perception of Management and Leadership Skills by Intercollegiate Athletics Conference Commissioners." *Journal of Sport Management* 12(2) (April 1998).

8 D. Foote. "Don't Kid Yourself: Leaders Are Made, Not Born." *Computerworld* (March 12, 2000): 32.

9 Bass, *Stogdill's Handbook*.

10 E. Ghiselli. *Explorations in Management Talent*. Santa Monica, CA: Goodyear, 1971.

11 For more information on Spirit at Work and its founder Dr. Judith Neal, visit http://www.spiritatwork.com.

12 N. Z. Dering. "Leadership in Quality Organizations." *Journal for Quality and Participation* 21(1) (January/February 1998): 32–36.

13 K. Lewin, R. Lippet, and R. K. White. "Patterns of Aggressive Behavior in Experimentally Created Social Climates." *Journal of Social Psychology* 10 (1939): 271–301.

14 R. Blake and J. Mouton. *The Leadership Grid III: Key to Leadership Excellence*. Houston: Gulf Publishing, 1985; R. Blake and A. A. McCanse. *Leadership Dilemmas—Grid Solutions*. Houston: Gulf Publishing, 1991.

15 D. McGregor. *The Human Side of Enterprise.* New York: McGraw-Hill, 1960.

16 P. Nystrom. "Managers and the Hi-Hi Leader Myth." *The Academy of Management Journal* 21(3) (June 1978): 325–331.

17 R. Trevelyan. "The Boundary of Leadership: Getting It Right and Having It All." *Business Strategy Review* 9(1) (Spring 1998): 37–45.

18 J. Torre with H. Dreher. *Joe Torre's Ground Rules for Winners.* New York: Hyperion, 1999, p. 81.

19 D. K. Scott. "Multiframe Perspective of Leadership and Organizational Climate in Intercollegiate Athletics." *Journal of Sport Management* 13(4) (July 1999).

20 Kent and Chelladurai, "Perceived Transformational Leadership," 139.

21 Ibid.

22 C. Gomez, B. L. Kirkman, and D. L. Shapiro. "The Impact of Collectivism and In-Group/Out-Group Membership on the Evaluation Generosity of Team Members." *The Academy of Management Journal* 43(6) (2000): 1097–1106; D. J. Campbell. "The Proactive Employee: Managing Workplace Initiative." *The Academy of Management Executive* 14(3) (2000): 52–66.

23 L. Varricchionne. "Session Examines Transformational Leadership Skills." *Nation's Cities Weekly* 24(11) (March 19, 2001): 13.

24 L. Tischler. "The Road to Recovery." *Fast Company* (July 2002): 82–83.

25 J. J. Sosik, B. J. Avolio, and S. S. Kahai. "Effects of Leadership Style and Anonymity on Group Potency and Effectiveness in a Group Decision Support System Environment." *Journal of Applied Psychology* 82(1) (February 1997): 89–104.

26 F. Fiedler. *A Theory of Leadership Effectiveness.* New York: McGraw-Hill, 1967.

27 Campbell, "The Proactive Employee," 52–66.

28 Tischler, "The Road to Recovery," 82–83.

29 J. R. Schermerhorn, Jr., Ohio University. "Situational Leadership: Conversations with Paul Hersey." *Mid-American Journal of Business* 12(2) (1998): 5–11.

30 R. Tannenbaum and W. Schmidt. "How to Choose a Leadership Pattern," *Harvard Business Review* (May/June 1973), 166.

31 Tannenbaum and Schmidt, "How to Choose a Leadership Pattern," 129.

32 R. House. "A Path Goal Theory of Leadership Effectiveness." *Administrative Science Quarterly* 16(2) (1971): 321–329.

33 Campbell, "The Proactive Employee," 52–66.

34 V. Vroom and P. Yetton. *Leadership and Decision Making.* Pittsburgh: University of Pittsburgh Press, 1978.

35 V. Vroom. "Can Leaders Learn to Lead?" *Organizational Dynamics* (Winter 1976): 17–28.

36 E. Fagenson-Eland. "The National Football League's Bill Parcells on Winning, Leading, and Turning Around Teams." *The Academy of Management Executive* 15(3) (2001): 48–55.

37 D. McEvoy. "Seeing the Game in a New Light." *Publishers Weekly* 248(16) (April 16, 2001): 40.

38 S. Kerr, J. Jermier, and R. Gordon. "Substitutes for Leadership: The Meaning and Measurement." *Organizational Behavior and Human Performance* 22(3) (1978): 375–403.

CHAPTER 14

1 Personal interview with Pete and Korby Clark on May 28, 2002.

2 Information found at http://www.theranchgolfclub.com.

3 P. White. "Back at The Ranch." *Commonwealth Golf III* (2002): 44–48.

4 A. Guttmann. *Olympics: A History of the Modern Games,* 2nd ed. Chicago: University of Illinois Press, 2002.

5 A. S. DeNisis and A. N. Kluger. "Feedback Effectiveness: Can 360-Degree Appraisals Be Improved?" *The Academy of Management Executive* 14(1) (2000): 129–139.

6 R. Zomke. "Systems Thinking." *Training* 38(2)(February 2001): 40.

7 C. Hymowitz. "How to Tell Employees All the Things They Don't Want to Hear." *Wall Street Journal* (August 22, 2001): B1.

8 DeNisis and Kluger, "Feedback Effectiveness," 129–139.

9 S. K. Majumdar and A. A. Marcus. "Rules Versus Discretion: The Productivity Consequences of Flexible Regulation." *The Academy of Management Journal* 44(1) (2001): 170–179.

10 Ibid.

11 B. Hohler. "Everett Hit with Fine after On Field Conduct." *Boston Globe* (August 18, 2001).

12 DeNisis and Kluger, "Feedback Effectiveness," 129–139.

13 Staff. "ABC, ESPN Agree to WNBA Pact." *Mediaweek* 12(23) (June 17, 2002): 40.

14 C. Gomez, B. L. Kirkman, and D. L. Shapiro. "The Impact of Collectivism and In-Group/Out-Group Membership on the Evaluation Generosity of Team Members." *The Academy of Management Journal* 43(6) (2000): 1097–1106; D. J. Campbell. "The Proactive Employee: Managing Workplace Initiative." *The Academy of Management Executive* 14(3) (2000): 52–66.

15 Staff. "Rigas Arrested in Conspiracy Charges." *Associated Press* (July 25, 2002).

16 H. K. Steensma, L. Marino, and K. M. Weaver. "Attitudes toward Cooperative Strategies: A Cross-Cultural Analysis of Entrepreneurs." *Journal of International Business Studies* 31(4) (Winter 2000): 591.

17 Ibid.

18 C. P. Stickney and R. L. Weil. *Financial Accounting: An Introduction to Concepts, Methods, and Uses,* 10th ed. Mason, Ohio: South-Western, 2003, p. 439.

19 Ibid, 279.

20 K. Blanchard and S. Bowles. "Get Gung Ho: To Create Boundless Enthusiasm, Catch Your Employees in the Act of Doing Something Right." *Success* 45(5) (May 1998): 30–32.

21 T. Pollock. "Attitudes That Can Help You Get Ahead: A Personal File of Stimulating Ideas, Little-Known Facts and Daily Problem Solvers." *Supervision* 59(2) (February 1998): 24–27.

22 J. White. "Don't Try to Coach Employees Like a Sports Team." *Business Courier Serving Cincinnati* 17(48) (March 9, 2001): 22; L. Holtz. "Setting a Higher Standard." *Success Yearbook.* Tampa, Florida: Peter Lowe International, 1998, p. 74.

23 D. Foote. "Don't Kid Yourself: Leaders Are Made, Not Born." *Computerworld* (March 12, 2000): 32; B. J. Tepper. "Consequences of Abusive Supervision." *The Academy of Management Journal* 43(2) (2000): 178–190.

24 T. Peters and N. Austin. *A Passion for Excellence.* New York: Random House, 1985, pp. 378–392.

25 K. R. Phillips. "The Achilles' Heel of Coaching." *Training & Development* 52(3) (March 1998): 41–46.

26 Staff. "Predicting Failure." *Wall Street Journal* (April 24, 2001): 1.

27 Staff. "Core Incompetency." *Wall Street Journal* (April 24, 2001): 1.

28 Information found at http://www.dpcgolf.com/managementservices.htm on November 30, 2002.

29 J. A. Lepine and L. V. Dyne. "Peer Response to Low Performers: An Attributional Model of Helping in the Context of Groups." *The Academy of Management Review* 26(1) (2001): 67–84.

30 D. Wessel. "Capital: The Magic Elixir of Productivity." *Wall Street Journal* (February 15, 2001): 1.

31 Ibid.

32 J. Shuman and J. Twombly. "Pearls by Peter." *The Rhythm of Business* (June 15, 2001).

33 S. K. Majumdar and A. A. Marcus. "Rules Versus Discretion: The Productivity Consequences of Flexible Regulation." *The Academy of Management Journal* 44(1) (2001): 170–179.

34 J. P. Guthrie. "High Involvement Work Practices, Turnover, and Productivity: Evidence from New Zealand." *The Academy of Management Journal* 44(1) (2001): 180–190.

35 D. Mahony and D. Howard. "Sport Business in the Next Decade: A General Overview of Expected Trends." *Journal of Sport Management* 15(4) (October 2001): 275–296.

36 J. Gladden, R. Irwin, and W. Sutton. "Managing North American Major Professional Teams in the New Millennium: A Focus on Building Brand Equity." *Journal of Sport Management* 15(4) (October 2001): 297–317.

37 Ibid.

38 M. Rosentraub and D. Swindell. "Negotiating Games: Cities, Sports and the Winner's Curse." *Journal of Sport Management* 16(1) (January 2002): 18–35.

39 Information found at http://bigleaguers.yahoo.com/mlbpa/faq.html on July 17, 2002.

40 B. M. Bloom. "Owners to Ratify CBA Pact on Thursday." Found at http://www.espn.com on September 30, 2002.

41 P. Gammons. "Marlins Ready to Scrap 2002." Found at http://www.espn.com on July 6, 2002.

APPENDIX A

1 R. N. Bolles. *What Color Is Your Parachute? 2003: A Practical Manual for Job-Hunters and Career-Changers.* Berkeley: Ten Speed Press, 2002.

2 M. J. Robinson, M. A. Hums, R. B. Crow, and
   D. R. Phillips. *Profiles of Sport Industry
   Professionals: The People Who Make the Games
   Happen.* Gaithersburg, Maryland: Aspen
   Publishers, 2001.

APPENDIX B

1 J. Pask. "It's on the Web, but Is It Right?"
   Wall Street Journal (November 4, 1999): 1.

Glossary of Key Terms

acquired needs theory
Proposes that employees are motivated by their need for achievement, power, and affiliation.

acquisition
Occurs when one business buys all or part of another business.

adaptive strategies
Prospecting, defending, and analyzing.

arbitrator
Neutral third party whose decisions are binding.

assessment centers
Places where job applicants undergo a series of tests, interviews, and simulated experiences to determine their managerial potential.

attitudes
Positive or negative evaluations of people, things, and situations.

attribution
The process of determining why people behave certain ways.

authority
The right to make decisions, issue orders, and use resources.

BCF statements
Statements that describe conflicts in terms of behavior, consequences, and feelings.

behavioral theorists
Look at the leadership style of effective leaders.

bona fide occupational qualification (BFOQ)
Allows discrimination where it is reasonably necessary to normal operation of a particular organization.

brainstorming
The process of suggesting many possible alternatives without evaluation.

budgets
Plans for allocating resources to specific activities.

business portfolio analysis
The corporate process of determining which lines of business the corporation will be in and how it will allocate resources among them.

business-level strategy
The plan for managing one line of business.

capital budgets
Allocate funds for improvements.

centralized authority
Important decisions are made by top managers.

charismatic leaders
Inspire loyalty, enthusiasm, and high levels of performance.

coaching
Gives motivational feedback to maintain and improve performance.

coalition
An alliance of people with similar objectives who together have a better chance of achieving their objectives.

collective bargaining
The negotiation process resulting in a contract that covers employment conditions at the organization.

command groups
Consist of managers and their staffs.

communication
The process of transmitting information and meaning.

communication process
The transmission of information, meaning, and intent.

communication skills
The ability to get your ideas across clearly and effectively.

comparable worth
Jobs that are distinctly different but that require similar levels of ability, responsibility, skills, working conditions, and so on are valued equally and paid equally.

compensation
The total cost of pay and benefits to employees.

competitive advantage
Specifies how the organization offers unique customer value.

components of culture
Behavior, values and beliefs, and assumptions.

conceptual skills
The ability to understand abstract ideas.

concurrent controls
Actions taken during transformation to ensure that standards are met.

conflict
Exists whenever disagreement becomes antagonistic.

consensus mapping
The process of developing group agreement on a solution to a problem.

consistent decision style
Taking time but not wasting time; knowing when more information is needed and when enough analysis has been done.

content-based motivation theories
Focus on identifying and understanding people's needs.

contingency leaders
Are task- or relationship-oriented, and their style should fit the situation.

contingency plans
Alternative plans that can be implemented if uncontrollable events occur.

continuum leaders
Choose their style based on boss-centered or employee-centered leadership.

control frequencies
Constant, periodic, and occasional.

controlling
The process of establishing and implementing mechanisms to ensure that objectives are achieved.

core values of TQM
A companywide focus on (1) delivering customer value and (2) continuously improving the system and its processes.

corporate growth strategies
Concentration, backward and forward integration, and related and unrelated diversification.

corporate-level strategy
The plan for managing multiple lines of businesses.

creative process
The three stages are (1) preparation, (2) incubation and illumination, and (3) evaluation.

creativity
A way of thinking that generates new ideas.

criteria
The standards that must be met to accomplish an objective.

critical path
The most time-consuming series of activities in a PERT network.

critical success factors (CSFs)
Pivotal areas in which satisfactory results will ensure successful achievement of the objective/standard.

customer value
The purchasing benefits used by customers to determine whether or not to buy a product.

damage controls
Actions taken to minimize negative impacts on customers due to faulty output.

decentralized authority
Important decisions are made by middle- and first-level managers.

decision making
The process of selecting an alternative course of action that will solve a problem.

decision-making conditions
Certainty, risk, and uncertainty.

decision-making skills
The ability to select alternatives to solve problems.

decoding the message
The receiver's process of translating the message into a meaningful form.

delegation
The process of assigning responsibility and authority for accomplishing objectives.

departmentalization
The grouping of related activities into work units.

development
Ongoing education that improves skills for present and future jobs.

devil's advocate
Group members defend the idea while others try to come up with reasons why the idea won't work.

direct investment
Occurs when a company builds or purchases operating facilities (subsidiaries) in a foreign country.

discipline
Corrective action to get employees to meet standards and to follow the rules.

downsizing
The process of cutting organizational resources to get more done with less as a means of increasing productivity.

dysfunctional conflict
Conflict that prevents groups from achieving their objectives.

empathy
The ability to understand and relate to someone else's situation and feelings.

employee assistance programs (EAPs)
Help employees get professional assistance in solving their problems.

encoding the message
The sender's process of putting the message into a form that the receiver will understand.

equity theory
Proposes that employees are motivated when their perceived inputs equal outputs.

ERG theory
Proposes that people are motivated by three needs: existence, relatedness, and growth.

ethics
Standards of right and wrong that influence behavior.

expectancy theory
Proposes that employees are motivated when they believe they can accomplish the task and the rewards for doing so are worth the effort.

external environment
The factors that affect an organization's performance from outside its boundaries.

feedback
The process of verifying messages.

financial statements
The income statement, the balance sheet, and the statement of cash flow.

forcefield analysis
Assesses current performance, then identifies the forces hindering change and those driving it.

free agent
A player who is free to negotiate a contract with any team.

functional conflict
Disagreement and opposition that help achieve a group's objectives.

functional-level strategy
The plan for managing one area of the business.

Gantt charts
Use bars to graphically illustrate progress on a project.

global sourcing
The use of worldwide resources for inputs and transformation.

goal-setting theory
Proposes that achievable but difficult goals motivate employees.

goals
General targets to be accomplished.

grand strategies
The corporate strategies for growth, stability, turnaround, and retrenchment, or a combination thereof.

grapevine
The flow of information through informal channels.

group
Two or more members with a clear leader who perform independent jobs with individual accountability, evaluation, and rewards.

group cohesiveness
The extent to which members stick together.

group composition
The mix of group members' skills and abilities.

group performance model
Group performance is a function of organizational context, group structure, group process, and group development stage.

group process
The patterns of interactions that emerge as group members work together.

group process dimensions
Include roles, norms, cohesiveness, status, decision making, and conflict resolution.

group roles
Expectations shared by the group of how members will fulfill the requirements of their various positions.

group structure dimensions
Include group type, size, composition, leadership, and objectives.

group types
Formal or informal, functional or cross-functional, and command or task.

hierarchy of needs theory
Proposes that people are motivated by the five levels of needs: physiological, safety, social, esteem, and self-actualization.

horizontal communication
Information shared between peers.

human resources management
Planning, attracting, developing, and retaining employees.

initiators
People who approach other parties to resolve conflicts.

innovation
The implementation of a new idea.

internal environment
Factors that affect an organization's performance from within its boundaries.

international business
A business primarily based in one country that transacts business in other countries.

job characteristics model
Comprises core job dimensions, critical psychological states, and employee growth-need strength to improve quality of working life for employees and productivity for the organization.

job description
Identifies the tasks and responsibilities of a position.

job design
The process of combining tasks that each employee is responsible for completing.

job enrichment
The process of building motivators into a job by making it more interesting and challenging.

job evaluation
The process of determining the worth of each job relative to other jobs in the organization.

job specifications
Qualifications needed to staff a position.

joint venture
Created when firms share ownership (partnership) of a new enterprise.

labor relations
Interactions between management and unionized employees.

leaders
Influence employees to work to achieve the organization's objectives.

Leadership Grid
Identifies the ideal leadership style as having a high concern for both production and people.

leadership style
The combination of traits, skills, and behaviors managers use to interact with employees.

leading
The process of influencing employees to work toward achieving objectives.

learning organization
An organization that learns, adapts, and changes as its environment changes to continuously increase customer value.

levels of authority
Inform, recommend, report, and full.

levels of management
Top, middle, and first-line.

line authority
The responsibility to make decisions and issue orders down the chain of command.

listening
The process of giving the speaker your undivided attention.

lockout
When management refuses to let employees in to work.

management audits
Look at ways to improve the organization's planning, organizing, leading, and controlling functions.

management by objectives (MBO)
The process by which managers and their teams jointly set objectives, periodically evaluate performance, and reward according to the results.

management by walking around (MBWA)
Is about listening, teaching, and facilitating.

management counseling
Helps employees recognize that they have a problem, and then refers them to the employee assistance program.

management functions
The activities all managers perform, such as planning, organizing, leading, and controlling.

management information systems (MISs)
Formal systems for collecting, processing, and disseminating information that aids managers in decision making.

management roles
The roles managers undertake to accomplish the management function, including interpersonal, informational, and decisional.

management skills
Management skills include (1) technical skills, (2) people skills, (3) communication skills, (4) conceptual skills, and (5) decision-making skills.

manager's resources
These include human, financial, physical, and informational resources.

market share
An organization's percentage of total industry sales.

mediator
Neutral third party who helps resolve conflict.

merger
Occurs when two companies form one corporation.

message-receiving process
Includes listening, analyzing, and checking understanding.

mission
An organization's purpose or reason for being.

motivation
The willingness to achieve organizational objectives.

motivation process
Process through which people go from need to motive to behavior to consequence and finally to either satisfaction or dissatisfaction.

multinational corporation (MNC)
A business with significant operations in more than one country.

networking
Developing relationships in order to gain social or business advantage.

nominal grouping
The process of generating and evaluating alternatives using a structured voting method.

nonprogrammed decisions
With significant and nonrecurring and nonroutine situations, the decision maker should use the decision-making model.

nonverbal communications
Messages sent without words.

normative leaders
Use one of five decision-making styles appropriate for the situation.

norms
The group's shared expectations of members' behavior.

objectives
State what is to be accomplished in specific and measurable terms by a certain target date.

OD interventions
Specific actions taken to implement specific changes.

operating budgets
Use revenue forecasts to allocate funds to cover projected expenses.

operational planning
The process of setting short-term objectives and determining in advance how they will be accomplished.

operational strategies
Strategies used by every functional-level department to achieve corporate- and business-level objectives.

organization chart
A graphic illustration of the organization's management hierarchy and departments and their working relationships.

organizational behavior
The study of actions that affect performance in the workplace.

organizational culture
The shared values, beliefs, and standards for acceptable behavior.

organizational development (OD)
The ongoing planned change process that organizations use to improve performance.

organizing
The process of delegating and coordinating tasks and resources to achieve objectives.

orientation
Introduces new employees to the organization, its culture, and their jobs.

paraphrasing
The process of having receivers restate the message in their own words.

path-goal leaders
Determine employee objectives and achieve them using one of four styles.

people skills
The ability to work well with people.

perception
The process through which we select, organize, and interpret information from the surrounding environment.

performance
A measure of how well managers achieve organizational objectives.

performance appraisal
The ongoing process of evaluating employee performance.

performance equation
Performance = Ability $\times$ Motivation $\times$ Resources

personality
The combination of traits that characterizes individuals.

PERT (Performance Evaluation and Review Technique) diagrams
These diagrams highlight the interdependence of activities by diagramming their network.

planning
The process of setting objectives and determining in advance exactly how the objectives will be met.

planning sheets
State an objective and list the sequence of activities, when each activity will begin and end, and who will complete each activity to meet the objective.

policies
General guidelines for decision making.

politics
The efforts of groups or individuals with competing interests to obtain power and positions of leadership.

power
The ability to influence the actions of others.

preliminary controls
Anticipate and prevent possible problems.

problem
Exists whenever objectives are not being met.

problem solving
The process of taking corrective action to meet objectives.

procedures
Sequences of actions to be followed in order to achieve an objective.

process consultation
An OD intervention designed to improve team dynamics.

process-based motivation theories
Focus on understanding how employees choose behavior to fulfill their needs.

productivity
Measures performance by dividing outputs by inputs.

programmed decisions
With recurring or routine situations, the decision maker should use decision rules or organizational policies and procedures to make the decision.

Pygmalion effect
Manager's attitudes and expectations of employees and how they treat them affect workers' performance.

qualitative forecasting techniques
Use subjective judgment, intuition, experience, and opinion to predict sales.

quality
Comparing actual use to requirements to determine value.

quantitative forecasting techniques
Use objective, mathematical techniques and past sales data to predict sales.

receiver
The person to whom the message is sent.

reciprocity
Using mutual dependence to accomplish objectives.

recruiting
The process of attracting qualified candidates to apply for job openings.

reengineering
The radical redesign of work to combine fragmented tasks into streamlined processes that save time and money.

reflecting
Paraphrasing the message and communicating understanding and acceptance to the sender.

reflective decision style
Taking plenty of time to decide, gathering considerable information, and analyzing numerous alternatives.

reflexive decision style
Making snap decisions without taking time to get all the information needed and without considering alternatives.

reinforcement theory
Proposes that consequences for behavior cause people to behave in predetermined ways.

reserve clause
Allowed teams to automatically re-sign their players at the end of the season.

responsibility
The obligation to achieve objectives by performing required activities.

rework controls
Actions taken to fix output.

rules
State exactly what should or should not be done.

salary caps
The maximum amount of money a team can spend on players.

sales forecast
Predicts the dollar amount of a product that will be sold during a specified period.

scheduling
The process of listing essential activities in sequence with the time needed to complete each activity.

selection
The process of choosing the most qualified applicant recruited for a job.

sender
Initiates communication by encoding and transmitting a message.

single-use plans
Programs and budgets developed for handling nonrepetitive situations.

situation analysis
Draws out those features in a company's environment that most directly frame its strategic window of options and opportunities.

situational favorableness
The degree to which a situation enables leaders to exert influence over followers.

social responsibility
The conscious effort to operate in a manner that creates a win-win situation for all stakeholders.

span of management
The number of employees reporting to a manager.

sport management
A multidisciplinary field that integrates the sport industry and management.

sport manager
The person responsible for achieving the sport organization's objectives through efficient and effective utilization of resources.

staff authority
The responsibility to advise and assist other personnel.

stages in the change process
Denial, resistance, exploration, and commitment.

stages of group development
Orientation, dissatisfaction, resolution, production, and termination.

stakeholders
People whose interests are affected by organizational behavior.

stakeholders' approach to ethics
Creating a win-win situation for all stakeholders so that everyone benefits from the decision.

standards
Minimize negative impacts on customers due to faulty output by controlling quantity, quality, time, cost, and behavior.

standing plans
Policies, procedures, and rules for handling situations that arise repeatedly.

status
The perceived ranking of one member relative to other members in the group.

strategic human resources planning
The process of staffing an organization to meet its objectives.

strategic planning
The process of developing a mission and long-term objectives and determining in advance how they will be accomplished.

strategic process
In this process, managers develop the mission, analyze the environment, set objectives, develop strategies, and implement and control the strategies.

strategy
A plan for pursuing the mission and achieving objectives.

stress
Our body's internal reaction to external stimuli coming from the environment.

stressors
Situations in which people feel overwhelmed by anxiety, tension, and pressure.

strike
When employees refuse to go to work.

structure
The way in which an organization groups its resources to accomplish its mission.

substitutes for leadership
Eliminate the need for a leader.

survey feedback
An OD technique that uses a questionnaire to gather data to use as the basis for change.

SWOT analysis
Used to assess strengths and weaknesses in the internal environment and opportunities and threats in the external environment.

symbolic leaders
Establish and maintain a strong organizational culture.

synectics
The process of generating novel alternatives through role playing and fantasizing.

systems process
The method used to transform inputs into outputs.

task groups
Consist of employees who work on a specific objective.

team
A group with shared leadership whose members perform interdependent jobs with both individual and group accountability, evaluation, and rewards.

team building
Helps work groups increase structural and team dynamics performance.

technical skills
The ability to use methods and techniques to perform a task.

three levels of strategies
Corporate, business, and functional.

time management
Techniques that enable people to get more done in less time with better results.

time management system
Planning each week, scheduling each week, and scheduling each day.

time series
Predicts future sales by extending the trend line of past sales into the future.

total quality management (TQM)
The process that involves everyone in the organization focusing on the customer to continually improve product value.

training
Acquiring the skills necessary to perform a job.

trait theorists
Look for characteristics that make leaders effective.

transactional leaders
Emphasize exchange.

transformational leaders
Emphasize change, innovation, and entrepreneurship as they continually take their organization through three acts.

transmitting the message
The process of using a form of communication to send a message.

two-dimensional leaders
Focus on job structure and employee considerations, which results in four possible leadership styles.

two-factor theory
Proposes that motivator factors, not maintenance factors, are what drive people to excel.

types of managers
General, functional, and project.

variables of change
Strategy, structure, technology, and people.

vertical communication
The downward and upward flow of information through an organization.

vestibule training
Develops skills in a simulated setting.

win-win situation
A situation in which both parties get what they want.

Name and Company Index

Subject Index